THE OLD BOYS

Also by Burton Hersh

THE MELLON FAMILY
THE EDUCATION OF EDWARD KENNEDY
THE SKI PEOPLE
GETTING THE MOST OUT OF GERMANY

THE OLD BOYS

THE AMERICAN ELITE AND THE ORIGINS OF THE CIA

Burton Hersh

CHARLES SCRIBNER'S SONS
New York

MAXWELL MACMILLAN CANADA
Toronto

MAXWELL MACMILLAN INTERNATIONAL
New York Oxford Singapore Sydney

Charles Scribner's Sons
Macmillan Publishing Company
866 Third Avenue
New York, NY 10022

Maxwell Macmillan Canada, Inc.
1200 Eglinton Avenue East, Suite 200
Don Mills, Ontario M3C 3N1

Macmillan Publishing Company is part of the
Maxwell Communication Group of Companies.

Library of Congress Cataloging-in-Publication Data

Hersh, Burton.
The old boys : the American elite and the origins of the CIA / Burton Hersh.
p. cm.
Includes bibliographical references and index.
ISBN 0-684-19348-5
1. United States. Central Intelligence Agency—History.
2. Intelligence officers—United States—Biography. I. Title.
JK468.I6H46 1992
327.1'2'06073—dc20 91-26890 CIP

10 9 8 7 6 5 4 3 2 1

Printed in the United States of America

For F.N.H.—
Forever in my corner.

CONTENTS

Introduction 1

BOOK I: THE FLOWERS OF VERSAILLES

1. The Roots of Versailles 11
2. Ahead of His Time, If on the Wrong Foot 31
3. A Proper Feeding Frenzy 45
4. The Last Gentleman Observer 58
5. The Cousins 77
6. Buried Blissfully in Switzerland 89
7. Unorthodox Diplomacy 105
8. The Bureaucrat of Death 119
9. A Reallocation of Target 136
10. Like a Prostitute in a Saloon 155

BOOK II: THE MAN WHO CARED TOO MUCH

11. To Stem the Tide 171
12. The Redeemer from the West 189
13. Across the Shifting Sands 215
14. The Mighty Wurlitzer 241
15. Help from Our Friends 261
16. To Rip Its Guts Out 282
17. The Scrambling Knights Templar 312
18. The Colossus of the North 328

19. The Doting Uncle 355
20. The Blood of Martyrs 377
21. The Last True Blow-off 405
22. Home from the Empire 434

Acknowledgments 455
Notes 459
Bibliography 514
Index 522

INTRODUCTION

In 1961 I was a kid attempting to break into magazine free-lancing. The Bay of Pigs debacle had barely overtaken the Kennedy administration, and through a well-intentioned friend I finagled an audience with the highly regarded progressive Carey McWilliams, long since the rock and senior brain around *The Nation* of that era. McWilliams's editorial office was small, I remember, with an ink-blotched, chipped-up desk that looked as if it had been dragged into an alley behind some principal's office somewhere and rescued by liberals from the Department of Sanitation. The plaster was grey, and crazed into cracks in a great many places, and smeared with a formless crescent behind where McWilliams tilted back his creaky oak chair and impatiently rubbed his scalp against the wall while hashing up story ideas.

Amidst all this atmosphere, McWilliams came right to the point. What with the end of the Eisenhower administration and the Cuban misadventure, the CIA was accessible for the first time. The moment was ripe to dig out a full-length exposé of the Agency, until recently seemingly untouchable. The Allen Dulles era was manifestly at an end. How about starting in for the magazine with that assignment? There could be no guarantee, but the magazine would probably pay expenses up to thirty dollars.

At that time of my life I had no experience of any kind with investigative journalism, a single friend with a couch in the entire

D.C. area, and a well-substantiated hunch that it was going to take at least thirty dollars to get to Washington. Worse, what little I knew about the CIA suggested that the place was a citadel, as impregnable as a carrier group out there in the oceanic Federal bureaucracy. I haven't—and did not have—much appetite for Kamikaze missions. I attempted a careful little smile and told McWilliams I'd have to think that over. That constituted my last visit to the offices of *The Nation*.

But no man can escape his destiny.

Twenty years passed. I wrote a great many magazine pieces, along with several books. One subject I poked away at regularly was politics, Washington. The vicissitudes of the Agency made more news every season.

In time I did manage a fairly extended article that traced one contretemps inside the intelligence community, and immediately there was publishing interest in a comprehensive workup of the history of the CIA. I began to read, peruse library sources, chat up a few retirees: the more I approached the subject, the more I suspected that what was going on in there would call for a lot more than a traditional reporting—even a thoroughgoing *investigative* reporting—scenario. I'd have to commit years.

The material I did come across began to provoke in me, beneath the action levels, a kind of intermittent reverie on America's unadvertised geopolitical intent. The pertinent questions surfaced: how did we choose to entrust our information gathering and assessment competencies—to say nothing of subversion and "action" programs—to a civilian (i.e., a commercially and politically rather than a militarily) driven system? Whom, in an open society, does a secret service serve? Just when did the meaning of the word "intelligence" pass beyond the accumulation and interpretation of strategically useful detail and begin to reference a thicker and thicker playbook of technologies for manipulating and strong-arming neighboring societies?

From these developed larger concerns. What kind of objectivity could any intelligence hierarchy claim which arrogated the right to bottle up information, then constructed its recommendations to accommodate its institutional purposes? How could one estimate the performance of a generation of intelligence professionals vain about its aptitude for disinformation and prepared without apology to repudiate even authentic accomplishments? Insiders breathed higher purposes. Like nations or tribes, the world's secret services appeared mutually antagonistic, yet all seemed obscurely and irresistibly in touch, their whispered exchanges often enough the last flutter before war broke out or obliteration threatened.

Should I be asking?

❑

Henry Luce decided publicly in 1941 that ours was the American Century. Perhaps Henry was accurate, give or take, although we started late and appear to be petering out any time these days. What Luce seems never to have mulled over particularly was what such a global mandate was going to *mean* to this unlikely crop of imperial Americans, let alone whether finding a century named after ourselves would turn out a particularly good thing.

The same year Henry Luce laid claim to the nineteen-hundreds, an extraordinarily nimble New York antitrust attorney named William J. ("Wild Bill") Donovan inveigled Franklin Roosevelt into underwriting the first encompassing intelligence instrumentality, the Office of the Coordinator of Information. Donovan's profession was relevant, and it is equally no accident that all three load-bearing protagonists throughout this work—Bill Donovan, Allen Dulles, Frank Wisner—achieved status in America by way of important Wall Street law partnerships. In many ways a trusted corporate attorney accomplishes substantially for his clients what today's one-stop national intelligence factory goes after for *its* patron: he puts the deals together, he damps down crises and flaps, he keeps the process as confidential as possible. He finds out everything he can and resorts to every means imaginable to shape the outcome. He proceeds by the case system, and preferably one emergency at a time.

Furthermore, an intelligence service concocted by lawyers—men accustomed not merely to spotting the problems but also to defining them to their clients and recommending appropriate action—is far more likely than a traditional military intelligence staff to reach in and condition policy. Attorneys have a seductive way of subordinating their clients, of insinuating their legerdemain until *they* become the movers. And thus it develops that in many strategic entanglements the lawyers have at least as much control over the outcome as elected officials.

❑

Although not just any attorney, of course, from anyplace at all. "Commonly authors assert," Robin Winks has written, "that CIA people tend to be from the Ivy League (to which the University of Virginia and West Point are sometimes admitted); or more specifically from Harvard, Yale, and Princeton." A Yale professor himself, Winks has discovered that more of Yale's graduates "go into intelligence work . . . than any other university." Winks's reprise of the careers in clandestinity of successive generations of Yalies, *Cloak and Gown,* points up New Haven's sturdy, regular contributions. Yet broadly—historically—there's lots of evidence that *Princeton* is likely to emerge as the forge of the Cold War, the caldron from which poured its true institutional leadership.

It's also quite likely that the intelligence community in the United States owes more than it acknowledges to the personality of Woodrow Wilson. As teacher and president of Princeton University, Wilson's horse-and-buggy high-mindedness coupled with a scholar's rigor shaped up successive generations of would-be global salvationists and implacable bond salesmen. A great deal lingered of the mission-school origins of the place. Behind those rosy stone-work facades both John Foster and Allen Dulles shed provincialisms, along with the ultimate doyen of *The New York Times*, Arthur Krock, such State Department groundbreakers as Dewitt Poole, and quite a proliferation of downtown investment prodigies like Ferdinand Eberstadt and James V. Forrestal.

Once he became President, the emerging leadership responded to Wilson's dry, prevailing Presbyterian heat. To define wartime intentions and sort out conflicting communiques, the President and his closest advisor Colonel Edward House secretly assembled at Columbia University a coven of academic intellectuals: The Inquiry. The Inquiry itself attracted a pair of the most independent-minded journalists around, Walter Lippmann and William Bullitt, who, along with the Dulleses, showed up in Paris to support the Peace Commission but deserted Wilson months before the ceremony at Versailles. That same year the unpredictable Columbia-trained lawyer and war hero Colonel William J. Donovan took on his first Presidential reconnoitering mission—to size up the Russian civil war in Siberia.

The world calmed down through most of the twenties; after 1933 the wind rose continually. With Franklin Roosevelt's election William Bullitt reappeared and provided his President, while ambassador to Moscow and Paris, a range of idiosyncratic political broadsides which corresponded, in their way, to the military assessments William Donovan had started to drag in via the back door of the White House.

By 1941 Donovan was in and out the front door regularly: Roosevelt set him up in charge of a broad-scale U.S. information-gathering and "unorthodox-warmaking" enterprise. The faction-ridden Coordinator of Information's office gave way in 1942 to the Office of Strategic Services (OSS). From then on a civilian-directed, operationally oriented spy service would top the wish list of America's emerging power elite.

In November 1942, under cover as special assistant to the U.S. Minister, Allen Dulles stole into Bern as Donovan's sounding board for occupied Europe. To OSS liberals, Allen and his classmates seemed far more intent on protecting the discredited "Versailles" regimes and contacting his prewar Nazi industrialist clients than bringing down Hitler.

Intelligence policy drifted for a couple of years after 1945. Inside Harry Truman's government Wall Street dragged on policy. Priority one was fending off Henry Morgenthau, Jr.'s proposals to deindustrialize Germany. The aging Stalin's opportunism helped. In 1947 the National Security Act specifically authorized the worldwide countercrusade. It included the newly enfranchised Central Intelligence Agency.

About a year later, in September of 1948, the State Department's Policy and Planning chief, George Kennan, set up an activist new entity, soon titled the Office of Policy Coordination (OPC), to stymie Soviet purposes by means of intensified covert methodology. To oversee this chamber of horrors in peacetime America, George Kennan annointed Frank G. Wisner.

Wisner wasn't quite forty. The stocky University of Virginia attorney was already a nonstop polemicist against the Soviets. Wisner staffed up quickly, parceling responsibility among a variety of veterans overseen by hyperactive little Carmel Offie. Allen Dulles, meanwhile, infiltrated the Committee for a Free Europe and worked his backstage skills on émigré politics. When Walter Bedell ("Beedle") Smith took over the Agency in 1950, Allen accepted a top position in the foundering bureaucracy.

Eisenhower's election as President carried John Foster Dulles into power as Secretary of State and, alongside him, as director of the CIA, Allen Dulles. A generation of fading Wilsonians awakened at Versailles and reprocessed by Wall Street now anticipated their last clean shot at history. Entertaining visions of "rollback" across the East, Allen and the overworked Wisner, currently operations chief inside CIA itself, programatically overloaded the books with paramilitary and political action projects, often at the expense of analysis or disinterested intelligence gathering.

Allen Dulles's deftness with publicity elicited among even influential Washingtonians a misperception of the Agency's results. Collapsed insurgencies in Albania and Poland and Indonesia never really made the news, while touchy, shortsighted triumphs like the intervention in Iran in 1953 and the 1954 Guatemala incursion mislead policymakers as to the practicality of covert. This delusion died hard—and embarrassingly—at the Bay of Pigs.

Undoubtedly the most durable legacy this fellowship of intelligence pioneers passed on was a profound belief in free-market mechanisms and the Wilsonian presumption that no modern society can forever remain content with oppression by outsiders. Decades after the fantasy of unleashing émigré brigades into the "captive nations" expired in Hungary in 1956, the bombardment of the East with broadcasts from Radio Free Europe and Radio Liberty maintained its slow destabilizing resonance. The flow of defectors broadened precious intelligence assets. Where threats failed, erosion registered. Those Ivy League spymasters who invented civilian intelligence went on to define—and delimit—the terms of the engagement.

❑

Before all else, I hope this plays for the reader as a group biography. Relying heavily on the *retour du personnage* techniques of contemporary fiction, I've attempted perhaps seven extended treatments of major personalities who, each in his way, opened up "special means." Most of the foreground of the text fills naturally with these insistent recurring figures—the Dulles brothers, William C. Bullitt, Wild Bill Donovan, Reinhard Gehlen, joined soon enough by Frank G. Wisner and the sinister and irrepressible Carmel Offie. But in and out as the expanding narrative dictates slip dozens of other strategic players, from the haunted, contradictory George Kennan to the high-hearted SS Obergruppenfuehrer Karl Wolff. Much of the expanded cast which mounted the Cold War here takes its belated turn, I hope in time to answer some questions for the reader as to how precisely we entangled ourselves so long in something which seems so arbitrary in retrospect.

Eight years of research and interviewing underlie the book which follows. I've counted well over a hundred *taped* interviews, not only with many of the surviving senior American intelligence figures but also with a number of their counterparts in England. Quite often I've been the first author permitted to talk to, let alone record, key sources. To supplement a thoroughgoing document search, which ran from Gestapo records to closed private collections and took in the papers of John Foster and Allen Dulles and the journals of David Bruce, I've had the chance to comb through what sometimes seemed miles of recently declassified State Department and OSS archives, Secret Intelligence Service debriefings, still-restricted notes on National Security Council deliberations, etc. I've dredged up thousands of pages of archival material from, among other federal offices, the Department of State, the FBI, and the CIA, by way of the Freedom of Information Act.

It's been my policy since I began writing to interview as fully—as shamelessly, perhaps—as I could manage. Then I have always turned down all requests to permit my subjects anywhere near the finished manuscript. Several have cajoled, and a few indeed threatened. But the editing process is conflicted enough, and so I've held fast. I've done that here, except where I went along with the clearing of a few specific quotes to satisfy the prearranged terms of an interview or the formal requirements of a literary bequest. This makes me especially grateful to everybody who helped me out. They deserve the credit; the errors and omissions, as the familiar disclaimer goes, are all mine.

BOOK I

THE FLOWERS OF VERSAILLES

Today of course I know the poor souls for what they were: members of that large, lost family of the British unprofessional classes that seems to wander by right between the secret services, the automobile clubs and the richer private charities. Not bad men by any means. Not dishonest men. Not stupid. But men who see the threat to their class as synonymous with the threat to England and never wandered far enough to know the difference.

John le Carré
A Perfect Spy

"This is a war," Leamas replied. "It's graphic and unpleasant because it's fought on a tiny scale, at close range; fought with a wastage of innocent life sometimes, I admit. But it's nothing, nothing at all beside other wars—the last or the next."

John le Carré
The Spy Who Came in From the Cold

1

THE ROOTS OF VERSAILLES

For over a week by then the tall man had been pressing toward the border while Panzer regiments mobilized. He'd suffered through *nightmares* with better organized timetables, Allen Dulles chuckled later, rehashing the frustrations over drinks with his wartime supremo, Major General William (Wild Bill) Donovan. To conceive of the fact that months after he'd cleared his reassignment as chief of espionage in Switzerland at Bern with the OSS's Washington Planning Group, and weeks and weeks after his application reached Foggy Bottom—as late as *October* of 1942 those knuckleheaded bureaucrats still bogged him down and kept him *praying* for his Spanish transit visa! That outraged Allen, it boiled him over each time he thought about it.

And with an invasion in the offing? Allen's was a forgiving temperament, but reminiscing to intimates years later and recalling the senselessness of it all, those crafty, importunate eyes would tend to narrow angrily behind Allen's rimless spectacles, he'd pluck the pipe from his mouth, his heavy jaw trembled.

The hop he snagged had barely left New York by November 2, 1942; that late substantial British Covering Elements were starting to jockey into formation inside the Mediterranean itself. By November 5, when Dulles finally touched down on European soil at Lisbon,

Nazi spotters above Algeciras were peppering Berlin with sightings of vessels from both Eastern Task Forces, already squeezing by Gibraltar to fall on French North Africa as specified by Operation Torch.

Allied intentions were obvious; exchanging pleasantries with strangers, Dulles felt his prospects tightening as kilometer by kilometer a succession of coal-burning *rapidos* crawled west across the Iberian Peninsula and started north into the Spanish mountains and up the coast toward Vichy France.

Without *any* invasion portending, Dulles would have congratulated himself for making it across the semi-occupied Vichy underbelly of the defunct Third Republic with which the Roosevelt government still nursed its tenuous diplomatic connection. What could he expect once Operation Torch struck? The Nazis were guaranteed to roll up Vichy.

Allen and his pickup traveling companions had already crossed into France, laying over between trains, when without warning a Swiss commercial traveler in his party burst through the restaurant door and delivered the inevitable shocker: " 'Have you heard the news? The Americans have landed in North Africa.' "[1]

And after that? German armor had already reached Lyons, Dulles told his wartime chief, and "it was a question whether I could get through"—Dulles took in pipesmoke: more reflective now, Mr. Chips in repose—"but I decided that having come this far I would proceed."

A display of negligent aplomb in the face of disaster recollected was long since Dulles's trademark. "We took the train to Cerbere," Allen continued to Donovan. "There was a terrific excitement among the French, who had the feeling that liberation was only minutes away since our troops had landed successfully in North Africa. I had a bottle of cognac with me and so we celebrated the occasion."

At every stopover throughout the long haul up the Rhone, Dulles slipped out of his wagon-lit until the locomotive fired up again. Nazi officials were likely to climb aboard and ransack the cars. His luck held beautifully until the customs station just short of Switzerland at Annemasse. "My Swiss friend went through the customs and told me there would be a Gestapo man there," Allen told Wild Bill. "The Gestapo man made only a cursory inspection of other passports but he fine-tooth combed my passport, noting down the numbers and other details and then handed it back. At that time a gendarme approached me and said that they had strict orders that no Americans were to pass the frontier. I took him in a corner and argued, pulling out all the stops—Lafayette and Washington, etc."

Except for a minimum of administrative documentation for the American legation in Bern, Dulles was saddled with "no papers," he assured Donovan, "no incriminating documents; also, no 'cover.' " He *had* to shoulder through these last maddening barriers. "I had several thousand dollars worth of Swiss and French currency in my pocket; at such a time, passing the border would have been worth whatever I had to pay—but the gendarme shook his head. He did not want any money.

"The gendarme said he would 'phone Marshal Petain at Vichy"; Dulles came back snappishly that he "had better not bother the Marshal." A face-off was pending, that much was evident; without warning the gendarme plucked away Dulles's passport, stated that he intended nevertheless to contact the doddering head of state, and vanished from the customs house. The hour approached noon. Perspiring into his tweeds, Allen sank into ever-deeper apprehension.

"With only fifteen minutes left until train time" Dulles hauled to his feet, abandoned the station himself, hobbled around the enclave until he had hunted the gendarme down, and demanded to be taken at once to any available Prefet of police. The gendarme marched the increasingly desperate lawyer along the cobblestones to the nearby constabulary. The Prefet was waiting. " 'Go ahead,' " the police chief greeted him. " 'You see our resistance is only symbolic.' "

"They had been stalling," Allen divulged to Donovan, "waiting until 12:30 when they knew the Gestapo went to lunch, so it would be safe to put me on the train!"

Allen delighted in entertaining people, and so the minutiae of his hairsbreadth insertion into Switzerland just as the frontier snapped closed was precisely the sort of anecdote on which he happily dined out. Every element was perfect: tremendous international stakes, himself as the shrewd, unflappable protagonist, a heartwarming and redemptive ending. Dulles selected his audiences. In another, somewhat expanded version of the border-crossing incident, he confided to less discriminating listeners his worries at the time that his valise might be searched, since it allegedly contained, along with two badly rumpled suits, a sheaf of extremely compromising documents, a certified U.S. check for a million dollars, and "certain of the more esoteric devices of espionage."[2] This may be accurate as well, but in his conversation with Wild Bill, Dulles never alluded to having lugged this security disaster across a well-patrolled Nazi satellite.

Like the cagey Donovan, Dulles was well aware of how a strategically applied exaggeration or two could bring the luster up on anybody's personal legend. One postwar rendition of Dulles's activities in Switzerland—which he himself edited—would tag him unabashedly as "the genius of the American spy group . . . grandson of one U.S. Secretary of State, General John W. Foster, and the nephew of another, Robert Lansing," whose "meteoric rise" within the Department of State had included "albeit extracurricularly and clandestinely" . . . "espionage networks into Austria" out of the American legation in Bern during World War I. "Thus it was that the OSS agreed with Dulles that Switzerland was the place from which he should operate."[3]

For somebody with Allen Dulles's lifelong aptitude for dissembling, the truth remained no better than another treatment of events to market as need arose. The fact was, the big, exhausted American who prowled the siding at Annemasse did not go back—*could* not go back—because his ego was battered enough by then so that the risks of pushing on seemed more acceptable than crawling home. Better internment and exile than another round of domestic captivity.

Bern! Gorgeous, the emotions it could arouse by 1942 in the depleted attorney. For all its crumbling patrician elegance, the Swiss capital retained its reputation as the bear pit of European espionage: the place his appetites woke up, Dulles had to admit to himself, where first he uncovered in 1918 his damned near *glandular* predisposition toward espionage tradecraft and quasidiplomatic subterfuge.

As life played out, he'd slogged through eight more years in the Foreign Service in hopes of again approaching such a rush. In 1926, after grinding out a night law degree at George Washington University, the middle-aged diplomat was able to prevail on his fast-rising elder brother Foster to take him in at Sullivan and Cromwell. He'd paid for respectability.

Self-respect came hard by 1940. Allen dabbled in politics, flirted with the internationalists around the New York Republican Party and the World Affairs Council, crept through the courts by day to salvage endangered properties for the firm's big, Nazified overseas clients.

So Allen had jumped in 1941 at William Donovan's spur-of-the-moment bid to help him pull together the Manhattan offices of the Coordinator of Information, precursor to the Office of Strategic Services. To skeptical New Dealers, Dulles looked like one more uneasy concession to crisis bipartisanship: at forty-nine a stagy, balding society lawyer whose haunted sideways glances called up the aging roué with ties to the armaments cartel.

Accordingly, Wild Bill proved more than understanding when Dulles himself proposed to finish out the war as OSS station chief in Bern.

He'd picked Manhattan clean, that Dulles himself realized, gimping along the tracks of Annemasse. Tension made his gout flare up. Discontent was eroding him; close as he was, the fountains and arcades of Bern had started his blood pounding.

His was a generation—Allen hoisted his grip into place—not lost so much as *preoccupied* much of the time. They'd enjoyed a false start, a premature breakthrough. How had they contracted it, this parasite of overexpectation? Why wasn't traditional success—respectable law practices, big money from investment banking—why wasn't anything satisfactory? What were they after in the end, these prodigies of a century that opened with the English hegemony, then confusingly turned American?

If one could identify the place the future broke through, undoubtedly it was Paris that first season after the guns went quiet. National attitudes tipped everything off, that Peace Conference spring of 1919. To astute Europeans, high civilization was over. For most of the United States contingent—a rabble numbering up to 1,300 when delegations overlapped, an infestation which took over wholesale the Hotel Crillon and popped in and out between commission meetings and twilight cocktails at the boîtes and receptions for the Maharajah of Bikaner, all relieved when time allowed by rest periods in delightfully specialized bordellos—that spring constituted America's geopolitical coming-out party. We had been bystanders since Columbus. Now we were participants.

So much began there. It was a fireworks of aspirant reputations colliding, as month after month they battered at The Treaty. Think of the names that emerged—the outrageous and irresistible Bill Bullitt, Christian Herter, Walter Lippmann, Jean Monnet, John Maynard Keynes, Dulles's implacable brother Foster. Who could imagine better?

Allen's train approached Geneva.

❑

In later years muckrakers tended to disparage the Dulles brothers by maintaining that neither of them would ever have made it to Versailles had not their mother's brother, Secretary of State Robert

Lansing, prodded their careers along. Contemporaries brush that off—the brothers were already on their way inside the conflicted wartime bureaucracies of the Wilson administration, Foster on the economic side and the inventive Allen manipulating away in Bern. The quickest way to the top was information from tested sources, interpreted quickly, then simplified, then conferred on grateful, overworked superiors. America was emerging unbelievably, an overnight world power, intelligence represented currency, and in fact there wasn't much mileage by 1919 to "Uncle Bertie's coattails," no matter how it looked.

More appropriately, credit Wilson. The U.S. President had set out originally for France in December 1918 to open the conference he insisted would end war forever. To millions on both sides, this juiceless Presbyterian academic epitomized what he himself had labeled a "peace without victory." Millions—too often the best—died, and with them order. Wilson understood their anguish. Here was a leader after all who traveled with a bible and a stomach pump, "like a Nonconformist minister," as Keynes noted, whose "thought and temperament were essentially theological not intellectual, with all the strength and weakness of that manner of thought, feeling and expression."[4]

Yet close up, this savor of Western Civilization revealed an unanticipated pettiness of character. "He takes every opportunity of sowing ill feeling between [his closest adviser Colonel Edward] House and Lansing," Stephen Bonsal noticed. "Why the President brought Mr. Lansing to Paris is an enigma, unless it was with the malicious purpose of heaping indignities upon him and seeing him squirm. He overlooks the slights, he ignores them, or, more probably he pretends to."[5]

Around Paris very often Lansing had been reduced to doodling wicked caricatures, to complaining sotto voce about the President's corrosive humorlessness. Insider sops and misinformation provided by British Admiralty agents helped Lansing move up from Department counselor to Secretary of State just after the sinking of the *Lusitania*. Subordinates pronounced Lansing sweet-tempered but lackluster, vain about his unconvincing British accent, and unreliable with details.[6] Before long the leverage in policy-making had shifted to Colonel Edward House.

House could fool you. A small, soft, ingratiating man with the forlorn proportions of a giant rodent, even House's rank—an honorific from the Texas legislature—deserved a corroboratory look. What the self-effacing Colonel was really masterful at was playing people off against one another, and early in the Wilson administration House understood that dominance depended on cornering the information flow.[7]

Lansing understood that too; a fitful fellow, the Secretary tried to raise up State as a clearinghouse for intelligence throughout the government. Then he lost interest, so that the day-to-day coordinator of intelligence around the Department became a pair of Groton-trained veterans, Department counselor Frank L. Polk and Gordon Auchincloss.[8] Reports and appraisals poured in: from the regional desks; from the reinvigorated Military Intelligence Division of Colonel Ralph H. Van Deman (who, coached by the bruising British intelligence consultant Lieutenant Colonel Claude Dansey, had perfected the attaché system and brought in Herbert Yardley to found the "Black Chamber" code-breaking section); from the Office of Naval Intelligence, the Secret Service, the Bureau of Investigation, the Treasury gumshoes, and increasingly from John Lord O'Brian's War Emergency Division, which struggled to reimpose civilian control on the vigilantes and counterintelligence fanatics the military authorities churned up.[9]

Gordon Auchincloss was Colonel House's son-in-law, but that didn't incline the Colonel to trust those timeservers around State. Furthermore, House quickly discovered, most nourishing to policymakers was what boiled into analysis. Accordingly, at Wilson's instigation, early in the autumn of 1917 House authorized the formation in New York of a clandestine, high-power study group comprised largely of academics and known as The Inquiry to research the combatants, define American war aims, and project a reconstituted Europe along Wilsonian principles. The Bolshevik takeover in November quickly gave The Inquiry scorching urgency. By October of the following year, 126 executives and research collaborators were pouring it on behind guarded doors at the American Geographical Society on Broadway. Under director Sidney Mezes—president of City College as well as Colonel House's brother-in-law—and executive officer Isaiah Bowman of the Geographical Society, the up-and-coming journalist Walter Lippmann took hold as Secretary of The Inquiry.[10]

Along with every other Wilsonian power center, The Inquiry was quick to attract the ubiquitous British Secret Service attaché, the all-seeing Sir William Wiseman. Colonel House went along and authorized for Wiseman a reciprocal connection between his Inquiry braintrust and the political intelligence specialists of the British Foreign Office.

The armistice had scarcely been agreed to when Wilson started staffing the upcoming Paris negotiations. Many of the aspirants who joined him on the USS *George Washington* served time on these overlapping intelligence instrumentalities. Lansing oversaw the State Department delegation, equally overbalanced with careerists hastily primed in counterespionage techniques: Joseph Grew, Leland Harrison, and Philip Pachin went along as Wilson's executive staff.[11] State included its Russian man, Frederick Dolbeare. Among Inquiry veterans no less than twenty-three analysts snagged berths on Wilson's overloaded "peace ship," broken down into regional desks almost like a portable State Department. Under General Marlborough Churchill's command, the hound-faced Ralph Van Deman and *his* military experts were especially conspicuous roaming the brocaded Louis XVI *fauteuils* in Sam Browne belts and tailored riding britches.

Like the disgruntled Keynes, most of the Inquiry academics winced as provisional drafts of position papers were picked up cold by French and British revenge seekers and locked in solid as terms to be imposed, a "final treaty," as Charles Mee has written, to be "thrust upon the Germans, and they would be forced to take it."[12] On March 13 Wilson returned to Paris to confront a document which flouted virtually every principle on which he staked his international reputation.

By then the State Department experts and Inquiry alumni had merged, pretty largely to Colonel House's advantage. Wilson made it plain, according to the colonel's diary, that it was not merely Lansing's heart problems or his incontrovertible stupidity but even more his *associations*—"mostly society folk and reactionaries"[13]—which made it advisable for House to deal with everything. House endorsed, as usual, his President's trenchant insights.

A number of the Colonel's slickest political moves he got from William Christian Bullitt, a compact, opinionated Philadelphia scion, still in his twenties, whose distinguished (if receding) hairline, lingering bedroom eyes, and gift for outrageous repartee in several important European languages made most other Peace Commission participants appear hayseeds by comparison. The cocksure, internationally connected Philadelphia patrician had survived a childhood of foreign governesses followed by four years at Yale. He listed as forebears an assortment of distinguished Americans from Pocahontas to the Jewish-Episcopalian dignitaries on his mother's side, the cultivated Horwitz faction. Bullitt endured a sniff of Harvard law school before the death of his father released him from *that* to ramble through the capitals of Europe as a war correspondent with his striking Society bride, Ernesta Drinker.

"Rising from the rich,"[14] as one co-worker commented, Bullitt began the war emergency as chief of the Washington bureau of *The Philadelphia Ledger*. There he cultivated House, who enticed this self-styled peace radical into the State Department and installed him as kingpin of its Bureau of Central European Information. As soon as Germany collapsed, Bullitt scavenged for backup personnel among contacts like his history instructor at Yale, Charles Seymour (already moiling away full time with The Inquiry at that point); thus, by the time the delegation set sail for Europe, Seymour was in charge of the critical Austro-Hungarian section.

It was to understudy Charles Seymour in Paris that the State Department came up with the twenty-six-year-old foreign service officer Allen Welch Dulles. Apart from his mother's relations, Allen's clergyman father was the nephew of John Welch, Hayes's envoy to England. Dulles had become conversant with Central European affairs through postings in Vienna, Seymour discovered from Department records, and the ebullient youngster had made himself felt in Bern soon after the United States joined the Allies. Seymour's own exalted position, as he wrote his wife at the time, "was due to a *coup de force* on the part of Wilson [read House]. Lansing was determined that we should all be pushed off to the side and had made all arrangements to have control put in the hands of his own men; Austria, for example, was to have been in the hands of Dulles, who is now to be my assistant." Dulles was "Lansing's nephew and of a diplomatic family," Seymour noted. "But he is, nevertheless, absolutely first-class—just as nice as he can be—young—very willing to work in any capacity, and very well acquainted with politics and persons in Austria."[15]

A group photograph survives of the U.S. Government's Current Diplomatic and Political Correspondence Staff—one of Allen Dulles's committees in Paris—and he is posed advantageously in the back row. The fledgling diplomat's long, prognathous lower face is mitigated by a moustache so deep and curling as to approach the villainous; his hair is close-trimmed, crinkly; his gaze casts demurely downward, as befits a very junior officer. There is the suggestion, even then, that Dulles had more in view than reissuing passports.[16]

In Paris the winter of 1919 House quickly appointed Bullitt his Chief of the Division of Current Intelligence Summaries, and charged the journalist each morning to brief the top-level Americans, Woodrow Wilson included. Seymour, Christian Herter, and Dulles served on the division's thirteen-man analytic staff, and pulled together filler for Bullitt's daily presentations. "Dulles is working out very well," Seymour wrote soon afterward. "I leave him to himself as he knows all about political intelligence and I know little. I like his point of view and the advice he gives out."[17]

Seymour too had started out regarding Robert Lansing as "stupid" and largely ignorant of conditions "over here." As for Lansing's nephew? Allen—along with his State Department colleague, Christian Herter—remained cordial and tolerant of the academicians, and there were dinners at La Rue's on Allen's tab as well as lunches at the Ritz during which Allen discreetly brought Vance McCormick and his Uncle Robert together with the ever-better-disposed Seymour. Seymour would soon confess himself lost when Dulles was absent briefly and there was no one with whom to discuss the crisis in Hungary or break down the cable traffic and compose a digest. When Dulles wasn't dictating to the two secretaries he imported from Bern, he tended to diplomatic niceties like rushing to the Gare de l'Est to hand the Paderewskis onto their Warsaw train.

As Seymour had divined, for all House's patronage, he remained the neophyte when it came to complexities out there. Dulles was the intelligence mandarin in their group. While stationed in Vienna, he had won over his superiors to back-channel approaches to dissident elements in Austria. From Paris Dulles monitored developments across the East, and installed a de-facto cable desk to keep himself up-to-the-minute. His military informant in Vienna, U.S. Army Captain Walter Davis, typically filled him in with detailed political appreciations salted lightly with gossip and gripes, from Polish maneuvering to grab Teschen from Austria to rumors that the British and French were draining off refugees for labor in their colonies.[18] Dulles kept himself detatched and agreeable when others exploded, solicitous of every backer, and adroit at evading unnecessary fuss or confrontation.

This aptitude for currying favor artfully was characteristic of the resourceful Allen. There is an album photo of four of the Dulles children rafting on Henderson Harbor. The surface is choppy; behind his sisters in their fanning Sunday dresses and black stockings, little Allen peers out unsteadily, round-faced and impressionable, a tot in knickers whose mouth looks pinched, overwhelmed. Poling the slippery timbers along—preternaturally grim, blank, almost scornful—

the eight-year-old John Foster Dulles stands above them all, in precise balance and totally in charge, the complete older brother.

In later years his sisters would remember the lanky Allen as moody and difficult to depend on much of the time, a self-serving adolescent who showed no compunction about exaggerating the touch of gout in his surgically corrected left club foot if that was what it took to raise a laugh or placate a discomfited elder.[19] The boy grew up in remote Watertown, New York, squirming under the eye of a watchful Presbyterian cleric of a father who was himself the offspring of a missionary and struggled against the impulse to interpret baby Allie's malformed foot as ominous and shameful.[20] The worried pastor brooded over the opportunistic streak in Allen, the hints of fleshiness behind his nonchalance, and although Allen traipsed into Princeton after the august Foster and showed up in classrooms often enough to graduate and even garner a quick M.A., the conviction was mounting around the family that where it really counted Allen was slack if not desultory, he rushed his school preparations, he postured before girls. Allen lacked grip.

Nor was the paster encouraged when Allen availed himself of a Princeton stipend and drifted around the Orient for a couple of years, indulging the White Man's Burden while distributing bibles and dabbling briefly at school-teaching at outposts of the British in India and China before he bobbed up in Watertown again in 1915, loose-jointed and detached as ever, running out of options. By then Robert ("Uncle Bertie") Lansing, the mobile, natty lawyer who married old John Watson Foster's other daughter, had reached the top at State. Lansing broached a diplomatic career. Very little else beckoned: Allen underwent what testing there was and took his modest place inside the venerable Department.

The training months passed; he served in Vienna; for Allen the revelation came just as that flat black Kiplingesque moustache of his came in as personal as a sneer across his long upper lip. By then America's involvement on the Allied side found Allen positioned happily along the buzzing margin of the war as Third Secretary of the U.S. diplomatic mission to Switzerland, in Bern.

Bern resonated with opportunity. Clandestine possibilities invaded Allen's imagination; accordingly, his pulses reportedly hammered the day the stiff First Secretary of the Legation in Bern, Hugh Wilson, summoned Allen and sloughed off on him the diffuse intelligence mission. "Keep your eyes open," Wilson instructed the stripling diplomat. "The place is swarming with spies."[21]

Several incidents became standbys. There is the tale of the pretty, good-natured Czech girl who helped out in the Legation's code room until British counterintelligence satisfied itself that she was blackmailed by the Austrians. Allen had been taking her out; by prearrangement one evening he bought her dinner. The two then ambled together in the direction of the Old Town, where Allen fed her to a couple of operatives from the Secret Intelligence Service lying low just outside the historic Nydegg Church.

Another anecdote Dulles loved to embroider involved his brush with Lenin. The Bolshevik was stranded in Bern for an afternoon and telephoned the Legation urgently in hopes of a few words with the resident Americans. Lenin's accent was glottal, uninflected, hard to make out; Dulles fluffed him off. Tomorrow perhaps. He had a tennis date. But the following morning Lenin undertook his one-way train ride courtesy of the German General Staff, headed toward the Finland station.

"Intelligence" bore, Dulles saw, on more than recirculated émigré gossip, on back-alley payoffs in return for a peek at documents or notes after pillow talk. Before the troops marched (and as often as otherwise before diplomatic appreciations made their interminable way from desk to desk) a kind of low-grade sounding-out process seemed to be going on incessantly. Accurate readings in advance could condition a nation's responses, even predispose major outcomes.

Dulles found himself alone at times before the possibilities espionage presented. Largely on his own he pasted together and ran nets of dissident Yugoslavs and Czechs in and out of Austria. Between his frock-coated political appointee of a U.S. ambassador, Alexander Stovall, and the indifferent Hugh Wilson, the enterprising young third secretary spotted openings nobody around really cared about. In January 1918 Dulles cabled his overseers at State complaining about the shortage of specialists in Bern to study "at first hand the problem of nationalities and to determine where justice lies in the various claims of the European races and nations, especially the Slavs."[22] Browsing Bern's reception circuit, Allen cultivated the hangers-on gravitating to the breakaway Czech intellectuals Thomas Masaryk and Eduard Benes, picked up the rush of devotion behind Ignace Paderewski, in perpetual transit for a resurgent Poland.

Statesmen vacillated; factions competed; anything—a touch of snideness in a misrouted telegram, a wink over dinner—could sink the wrong scale, permanently. Around The Inquiry itself, House's scholars were already resolved to throw their influence behind an independent Czechoslovakia and an independent Hungary. Lansing discerned little advantage in basting together the moth-eaten Dual

Monarchy; British Admiralty case officer Guy Gault was running the naturalized American Emmanuel Voska, who proceeded under State Department auspices to clap into place a Slav press bureau with 1,200 branches and 70,000 contributors in hopes of fomenting an uprising against the Hapsburgs.[23] Voska's contacts with Masaryk dragged United States policymakers in behind the Czech Legion, stranded in the Ukraine, a pretext for desultory Western intervention in the spreading Russian civil war.

One promoted one's opportunities. Allen Dulles had an uncanny way already of edging into important deliberations, an awareness nobody quite expected of this nonchalant Watertown High graduate, his bumpy plowboy's face enameled with restraint and cunning as he identified valuable contacts among the mélange of favor-seekers and would-be negotiating partners swarming through the Legation just then. According to middleman Dr. Heinrich Lammasch, it was the low-key but unremitting Third Secretary Dulles who tempted Holland's recent Minister of Justice, Dr. De Long van Beek en Donk, into sponsoring a series of undisclosed meetings at the villa of a Krupp director in a Bern suburb to look into the possibility of transforming the Dual Monarchy into some manner of United States of Austria.[24]

The Hapsburgs would desert Germany in return for an American commitment. Subsidized by the United States—which brought over to Europe the President's close adviser Professor George D. Herron to impart Wilson's vital imprimatur—this updated Hapsburg sovereignty must commit in advance to eradicating the Bolsheviks. A revitalized Austro-Hungarian buffer zone to fend off Soviet penetration of the Balkans turned into a lifelong chimera for Dulles, and spurred his devotion over the many years to some manner of "Danubian Federation." Better to reupholster authoritarians than risk something unmanageable.

Yet once the breakup became inevitable, Allen—characteristically—could not be bothered to look back. At Paris he fit right in as an influential member of the Czechoslovak boundary commission, and included the Sudetan highlands in the nation he tended to brush off afterward as having looked "something like a banana lying across the map there in Central Europe."[25] Voska was still agitating; Dulles opposed Allied sponsorship of the Germanophobe's insertion into Prague. Voska was inherently disruptive. Allen was quite active just then tossing off memoranda with titles like "Lithuania and Poland, the Last Barrier between Germany and the Bolsheviks,"[26] which agitated for military intervention against the Reds.

* * *

Allen's older, weightier brother had long since taken to heaving high his own picket against the presumptuous Bolsheviki. By 1919 the thirty-one-year-old John Foster Dulles bore very little similarity to the dreamy-lidded pubescent who wandered into Princeton at fifteen only to find himself a pariah around the eating clubs, a tongue-tied scholarship grind whose shaky Watertown education and flat, defensive mannerisms invited a career of weekends in the library.[27] Foster's grade average held up nicely, a performance to catch the eye of Princeton's exacting president Woodrow Wilson, who granted the prodigy his leave of absence in 1907 to serve on his grandfather's delegation to the Hague Conference in the guise of a translator of French.

During Foster's postgraduate year in Paris he first affected the umbrella and the bowler hat which convinced decades of bystanders that he was associated in some capacity with the English clergy. In 1911, just out of George Washington Law School, something about this clumsy youngster's presentation—big, tense, righteous, a world-class word-swallower and more than a little bit backwoods in his way of bearing down on problems—put off the interviewing partner at Sullivan and Cromwell. The interviewer rejected Foster. The aspirant lawyer thrashed inwardly before the insult, and called in his grandfather to plead with William Nelson Cromwell until the thankful if humiliated clerk went onto the rolls at fifty dollars a month.

Foster dug in immediately and shouldered the heavy traveling responsibilities it took to service the firm's important Latin American clientele—Sullivan and Cromwell conjured up the power play which created the Panama Canal—married his pretty, docile Watertown neighbor Janet Avery, and crunched toward reputation. There remained that country-relative aspect to Dulles, little came of itself, and so when Uncle Bert Lansing recruited him to poke around the Central American capitals early in 1917 to determine whether the Latinos were ready to cooperate in the event of war against Germany, Foster grabbed this opportunity to make the most of family connections and demonstrate how effectively he too could contribute when national interests summoned.

A prewar business trip to British Guiana brought on a case of malaria so acute that the extraordinary dosage of quinine it took to save his life afflicted an optic nerve, and left the forceful young litigator with severely weakened vision, a distracting tic, and a tendency to water from the left eye—"Foster's crocodile tears," as subsequent negotiating partners would refer to them.[28] The impairment ruled out front-line duty, but Dulles quickly wangled for himself a direct commission as a major and put in a year in Washington at the War Trade Board under Vance McCormick, the abrasive Harvester heir who supervised the Democratic National Committee.

Dulles looked after commercial relations with neutrals and directed a three-man committee McCormick founded to scrutinize the obstreperous oligarchy under Lenin, barely chivied into power. Dulles's committee rushed licenses through to expedite the shipment of weapons and supplies to the Czech brigades fighting alongside the anti-Soviet Russians; he served as secretary and treasurer of the U.S. Government–backed Russian Bureau, Incorporated, which dispensed $5 million worth of equipment after midsummer of 1918 in hopes of suffocating the revolutionaries.[29]

Fearful of nepotism charges, the increasingly out-of-favor Uncle Bertie turned down Foster's request to join the State Department contingent on the Commission to Negotiate the Peace in Paris. Foster quickly persuaded Bernie Baruch, the wartime head of the War Industries Board, to take him on as delegation counsel to the American side of the controversial Allied Reparations Commission. With this Dulles's real international career began. He brought Janet along to Paris to watch him weigh in. Foster traveled surprisingly; Arthur Krock would document the emergence of unexpected civilities in his big, owlish Princeton classmate once he was relieved of career stresses: unusually relaxed, on cordial personal terms with all the participants up to and including Wilson, overall "witty and merry and very, very companionable," and inclined to unpredictable surges of heavy-duty jocularity over the afternoon whiskey he preferred to stir with a ponderous forefinger.[30]

Contradictory reports needed reconciliation. The head of the newly formed Central Bureau of Planning and Statistics, Edwin Gay, deputized Foster to square the Inquiry papers with material from State and the military. Squabbles quickly broke out when Foster, as Wilson remarked with some pique, succeeded in entrenching himself as the "exclusive channel of statistical communication from Washington to the Peace Conference" as well as the principal intermediary between the American economic advisers and the intelligence faction.[31]

Foster Dulles had showed up initially in Washington little better than a glorified Manhattan errand boy with well-placed relatives. His months in Paris legitimized Foster to the emerging postwar power structure, kept him in daily working contact with leaders who appreciated that milling-machine intellect, his gift for breaking down and reconciling positions, his chilly, assured touch. He proceeded between meetings with an uncommon *mien* for somebody so young, his eyes set low and complacent behind his steel-rimmed spectacles, lips chiseled, aura censurious. Underlings who presumed on Foster could find him stolid as a carp.

As the negotiations proceeded Foster's dinner companions came to include the restive Keynes and Jean Monnet, the petit, inventive French armament negotiator. The three agreed quickly that what was emerging as Allied reparations policy toward Germany was tantamount, in Foster's words, to expecting "the policeman to receive his hire from the wrongdoer"[32]—an absurdity, a distortion, an invitation to chaos.

Europe was already fragile. That winter of 1919 there erupted like bedsores an outbreak of localized Communist takeovers in Central Europe, most sensationally the Spartakus revolt in Berlin and the Hungarian dictatorship of Bela Kun. Foster helped the Finance Commission frustrate Kun's attempts to liquidate Hungarian securities. He again seconded Vance McCormick, who directed the Western effort to blockade Russia, pressure neutrals to cut off trade with the Leninists, and attach Russian assets in the United States so they could be redirected to the anti-Bolshevik Whites in Siberia under Admiral Kolchak.[33]

You could trust Foster. He understood deportment; newly married, he remained emphatically uxorious, suffered for important clients, lived sternly by bromides it never really occurred to him to review as times changed. He preferred his vacations in the wilds, saltwater sailing and jigging for pike. Other U.S. comers around the conference, from Adolf Berle to Walter Lippmann, and Robert Taft and Arthur Krock and Edward Bernays and Samuel Eliot Morison and Henry Morgenthau, Sr. and Herbert Hoover, left impressed by Foster's somber force. Foster breathed precepts, yet even at that stage he discerned no inherent conflict between buying in and selling out.

People respected Foster, but people liked Allen—Allie—who luxuriated in the parties which permeated this season of victory, the elaborate teas and evenings in white tie and gala performances at the opera. Puccini was in town, along with Sarah Bernhardt and Ho Chi Minh.

Diplomatically, Paris crackled. As mandates passed around, opportunistic supplicants like Chaim Weizmann moved discreetly to cash in the Balfour Declaration on a Zionist state in Palestine both as a homeland for the Jews and a reliable fueling station, as Balfour himself foresaw, beside "the wasp waist of our empire, Suez."[34] A

Ukranian delegation lobbied for a new state independent of the Russians alongside the Dnieper. New nations seemed to be emerging hourly that giddy spring in Paris, an entire century loose for the taking.

For the apprehensive Germans the long-dreaded moment of capitulation arrived on June 23, 1919, in the barrel-vaulted Hall of Mirrors at Versailles where Bismarck had humbled the French in 1871. The youthful Allen Dulles, standing close enough in the jammed hall to observe the frightened, haggard leader of the Weimar delegation, saw how his knees were trembling, how unstrung he appeared. To ratify this, Count Brockdorff-Rantzau had insisted, meant signing "the death sentence of millions of German men, women, and children."[35] The weight of everything that had been heaped upon his country was more than the count could support just then, Allen told people afterward, and kept him crushed into his chair.

That spring in Paris, Allen Dulles missed very little. Years later General Walter Bedell Smith would reportedly maintain that Allen had lost his head over a gifted demimondaine who spread her wares at the infamous brothel The Sphynx. He set her up for himself in an apartment in Montparnasse.[36] Even then, Beedle Smith snorted, Allen was a great fellow for short-term infatuations. Smith was Allen's boss for a time at the CIA, and grew quite choleric over Allen's ineradicable offhandedness.

Foster wasn't pleased either, of course, but Allen was a mixer, and sociability opened doors. Before the year was out Foster arranged a business trip to visit his worldly younger brother at his next State Department post, Berlin, where Foster inaugurated his durable relationship with Hitler's financial wizard Hjalmar Schacht. Foster hung around, fascinated, to watch the right-extremist Kapp putsch break across the capital.

While the conferees debated into 1919, Lenin's seizure of power in Russia hardened into a second year. Especially to the Anglo-Saxons, the threat from Bolshevism was already eclipsing every postwar horizon.

Wilson himself remained philosophical. "My policy regarding Russia," Wilson informed William Wiseman, prodding for additional arms for the Allied landings, "is very similar to my Mexican policy. I believe in letting them work out their own salvation, even though they wallow in anarchy for a while."[37]

Nor did the uprising in Hungary and Berlin shake Wilson. History remained God's trash collector. "The only way I can explain the susceptibility of the people of Europe to the poisons of Bolshevism is that their governments have been run for the wrong purposes," he told Charles Seymour.[38]

Yet halfway into the conference there arose a panic, as Wilson confidant Stephen Bonsal wrote in his journal, that "The Reds are now in control in Budapest and in much of Russia, and they also seem to be sweeping all resistance before them in the Ukraine. . . ."[39]

Envoys rushed East. Under Jan Smuts a British fact-finding mission proceded to Budapest by rail. Harold Nicolson sniffed at Kun's "puffy white face and loose wet lips," along with his shaved head and shifty eyes: "the face of a sulky and uncertain criminal. He has with him a little oily Jew—fur coat rather moth-eaten—stringy green tie—dirty collar. He is their Foreign Secretary."[40] Kun lasted until August, when Admiral Horthy, who unleashed the White Terror, brought back the trappings of the traditional Hungarian monarchy.

Uprisings roiled Germany unceasingly those desperate postwar months—Kiel, Munich, Berlin, the Rhineland—and alongside the impulse to punish the Germans was the widening recognition that the loss of Germany as its economic flywheel could paralyze Europe. As early as February of 1919 Joseph Grew was lamenting to William Phillips that "there is hostility from all sides to our [State's] policy of relaxing the blockade and building up German industry."[41]

Some of this pressure could perhaps be eased if one way or another Lenin could be placated. Among Inquiry veterans the "general undercurrent of opinion" inclined toward overtures to the Reds.[42] It was against this possibility that William Bullitt undertook his pilgrimage to Moscow. Bill Bullitt was twenty-eight, but certainly he looked older—seemed older—what with his hair already going fast, so that the surviving forelock was plastered between his shining temples and conferred rather an ennobling if not a positively cherubic glow to the Philadelphia aristocrat's briskness, his brashness, the way his mobile features intensified with an almost simian inclination to mischief whenever something attracted his ever-ready appetite for ridicule. Bullitt loved to play the patrician iconoclast.[43]

Virtually from the outset, the Philadelphia enthusiast had regarded the Bolsheviks in Russia as full of possibilities, and disparaged the assortment of "gentleman investors now working on the President"[44] who received word of *any* popular outbreak with all the sanctimoniousness of fumigators scooping up rat droppings. As early as February 1918 Bullitt urged on House his notion that "it is obvious that no words could so effectively stamp the President's address with uncompromising liberalism as would the act of recognizing the

Bolsheviki."[45] Once Wilson returned for a time to Washington, Colonel House called Bullitt to his suite and informed him that the President and Lloyd George had resolved to dispatch a secret mission, behind Clemenceau's back, to seek out Lenin and ask after terms. With a small party which included the aging muckraker Lincoln Steffens, Bullitt found his way to Moscow. When Steffens challenged the unassuming Lenin as to his dependence on widespread terror and mass killlings to cow the populace, the revolutionary took brisk offense: "Do you mean to tell me that those men who have just generaled the slaughter of seventeen millions of men in a purposeless war are concerned over the few thousands who have been killed in a revolution with a conscious aim . . . ?"[46]

Astonishingly, the Bolsheviks were indeed prepared to strike a deal. If the Western nations would withdraw their forces, abandon the Whites, and end the blockade, Lenin promised to leave the anti-Soviet factions from Siberia to the Ukraine in charge of territory they already controlled and pay the Tsar's debts. Bullitt bounded back to Paris and laid out his triumph over breakfast with Lloyd George—Wilson had a headache that morning. By then the Northcliffe newspapers in England were bannering the Old Guard's determination that Lenin and his crowd must go, Churchhill was in full voice, and the ever-flexible Lloyd George stood up after coffee and disavowed the entire initiative, implying that the Bullitt mission was something of a surprise to him. Wilson remained quite miffed that *he* hadn't seen the peace bid first. Lenin's historic proposal collapsed, unconsidered.[47]

Having worshiped Wilson, Bullitt took his miscue hard. He pored over the treaty terms as soon as they were available, haughtily informed House that "This isn't a treaty of peace; I see at least eleven wars in it," and sailed for New York to elaborate on his disapproval before the Senate Foreign Relations Committee. His 139 pages of detailed testimony were instrumental in undermining Wilson's position, and in due course the Senate both refused to ratify the treaty and shunned the League of Nations. Democrats still with Wilson despised Bullitt, who withdrew from public life ranting about his idol who "ratted at Versailles."[48]

Policymakers in the West decided that negotiations had become extraneous. Rosa Luxemburg and Bela Kun were turning out to be as vulnerable as any other disturber of the established order to militia slugs and soldiers of fortune. Great Britain now concentrated its Secret Intelligence Service on mechanisms to spy on, discredit, and wherever possible subvert the ominous Soviet regime. France adopted the direct approach, and before the end of 1920 a boundary dispute between Poland and Russia had triggered an invasion by Polish troops—directed by a large French staff commanded by General Weygand—which pushed on most of the way to Moscow and enlarged Poland substantially. Wilson died. John Foster Dulles reembraced the law; William Bullitt divorced and remarried. The seeds of Versailles began striking their tangled roots.

2

AHEAD OF HIS TIME, IF ON THE WRONG FOOT

One comer who missed Versailles lost very little time in dealing himself a hand in the expanding Great Game. Two weeks after Lenin's negotiating deadline to the West expired, the newly promoted bird Colonel William J. ("Wild Bill") Donovan and what was left of his Sixty-Ninth Regiment, "The Fighting Harps," disembarked at Hoboken pier. Already a little full-faced, the self-contained thirty-six-year-old newspaper favorite sported across his dress tunic a chestful of decorations which ran from the Distinguished Service Cross through the Congressional Medal of Honor to the Legion d'Honneur and the Italian Croci di Guerra. He led his depleted "Micks" beneath vales of Fifth Avenue tickertape and into the peace between the wars.

It was still April of 1919. A few months later, ostensibly on a vacation with his wife to the Far East, Donovan inveigled the influential senior partner and Wilson intelligence pioneer in his Buffalo law office, John Lord O'Brian, into putting in a word for him with the Secretary of State so he might be included in a fact-finding mission about to canvass the action across Siberia. Bolshevik conscript armies were battling the holdover Tsarist regime of the mercurial Admiral Kolchak, while detachments of U.S. and British troops piled up around Vladivostok, awaiting orders to intervene. Rattling inland as far as Omsk by rail, Donovan recorded the devouring waves of refugees, the boxcar-loads of typhus victims too weak to drop out the doors and relieve themselves along the rails, the worm-ridden gangrenous limbs.[1] The "workers in Siberia," Donovan concluded, "are yearning for Bolshevism."

To salvage Admiral Kolchak, Donovan informed the State Department in October, would entail a U.S. donation of $94 million. He recommended the expenditure. Wilson mulled that over, and withdrew all Americans.[2]

It would be Donovan's lifelong fate to find himself well out ahead of his time, and on the wrong foot. The phenomenon who conjured up America's intelligence model was born, literally, across the tracks in Buffalo, New York. A reprinted snapshot reveals a round-headed tyke bestowing his mild if unyielding gaze somberly upon the cameraman, standing with brother Timmy in button-front priests' surplices, decked around the shoulders with blousy white lace. Will's father, gentle Timothy, had advanced from greaser on the locomotives to yardmaster of the Erie and Lackawanna terminal, a post of responsibility to lavish on a Catholic. Mischievous as most adolescents, Will impressed his brothers with something unbudgeable underlying his attitude. He had that remorseless quality—"this concept of himself, you see, and he was determined to live up to it," his priest brother Vincent remarked.[3]

One year before graduating from Catholic Niagara University Bill Donovan transferred to Columbia. There exists a group photograph of Columbia's varsity football team, Class of 1905. Slight for a ball player, more sinewy than muscular, with a pronounced wide nose and a big, smooth black-Irish sheaf of hair combed across his pasty temples, Donovan hasn't yet really begun to outgrow that punk look. He has been running cross-country, boxing and wrestling, managing his fraternity house, working in a baking-powder factory, rowing for the varsity, tutoring children in families whose connections looked promising. . . .

Processing into the Law School, Donovan's grades remained marginal, mediocre. After an extra year in the law school, Donovan graduated in 1908, went back to Buffalo, took on an associateship in a small area law firm and boosted himself to partner. He resigned almost immediately to start up a firm of his own with Bradley Goodyear, a scion of one of the city's ruling Protestant families. Within months he'd angled the merger of his offices with Buffalo's preeminent law shop, presided over by the Republican activist John Lord O'Brian.

In 1912, when organizers from the National Guard subscribed the First Cavalry troop, Donovan emerged as captain of the elite unit the newspapers soon dubbed the Silk Stocking Boys.[4] Thus class identity was not a problem on New Year's Eve of 1913–1914, at a black-tie dinner at the Buffalo Club, when Donovan met the daughter of the town's richest citizen, Dexter Rumsey. Ruth Rumsey was a girl of some bearing, a platinum blonde with searchingly blue eyes, rider to the Genesee Hunt. Ruth's mother reportedly resisted the union of her daughter and this Irishman from the Buffalo mud flats; a wedding photograph is said to have caught Wild Bill's mother-in-law hanging out an upstairs window of the Rumsey mansion in tears, dressed in summer mourning.[5]

On February 23, 1916, a telegram showed up in Donovan's legal chambers which quickened his adventurous heart, a signal from faster-moving galaxies. The carnage along Germany's Eastern Front had reduced Poland; would Donovan be interested, as an accredited representative of the John D. Rockefeller Foundation, in arranging for emergency supplies of food to relieve the famine?

Donovan crossed to Belgium and saw after the purchase of great quantities of milk powder and other supplies,[6] until a telegram overtook him. Woodrow Wilson had activated his National Guard troop for duty along the chaotic Mexican border.

In June of 1916, Donovan rushed down to McAllen, Texas, where the Silk Stocking Boys awaited their Tartar of a commander; following nine slow months the troop would return to Buffalo. After false starts, Donovan snagged a commission as a major and battalion commander in the infantry regiment known as the Fighting Sixty-Ninth. Ninety-five percent Irish-American, "The Fighting Harps" would be the first U.S. troops to reinforce the lines in France, the "touch of green" in Douglas MacArthur's Rainbow Division.

There is a fervor, an ecstasy at times, playing behind the Gary Cooper–genre newsreel which Donovan now conducted. "I don't expect to come back," he wrote his wife, already morbid with worry, "and I believe that if I am killed it will be a most wonderful heritage to my family."[7] What made this stocky, meticulously tailored major such a phenomenon among the green troops of the American Expeditionary Force was not only that he was prepared for day after day of mucking them through the squalor, the waist-deep mud, the chunks of torso and arms and legs and skulls broadcasting upward their brains as one of the shells lobbed by Ludendorff's big *Minenwerfers* cratered out a dugout or detonated a command post. Donovan expected to die; death came with leadership.[8]

In time Donovan lost 600 of his thousand enlisted men, the poet

Joyce Kilmer included. He finished his involvement with essentially a tactical conception of what mass warfare was all about. At his own insistence Donovan fought his war too far down the chain of command to grasp what stood behind many of the orders he received. At Bois de la Lyre, for example, against orders, Donovan's people held, taking very fierce losses and ruining an anticipated trap of German assault troops MacArthur had meticulously laid.

Perhaps this was lawyerly: Donovan's imagination proceeding by the case system. Yet over the years Donovan's administrative limits repeatedly compromised his gifts of imagination and nerve. Wild Bill's scale remained personal. Against history's larger purposes, heroics wouldn't seem relevant.

Barely returned from Siberia, Ruth Donovan was disheartened in February 1920 to hear that her husband had picked up yet another excuse to travel. He was quietly approached by representatives from the preeminent firm of J. P. Morgan and Sons. The country's most influential investment bankers were reconnoitering the market for a $2 billion package of securities around Central and Eastern Europe.

His valise padded out with State Department letters of introduction, the Buffalo attorney stole around Europe, interviewing in their turns pivotal personalities like Lloyd George and Secretary of State for War and Air Winston Churchill in Britain, Clemenceau of France, the leadership of the reconstituted Poland from Pilsudski down, Jan Masaryk in Czechoslovakia. A quick, absorptive reader, Donovan swelled his files with notes on his meetings with the Supervising Committee of the Polish Industrial Credit Corporation (naptha production in Galicia), a U.S. consulate report of politics in Silesia, the diary of a close female English friend of Leon Trotsky, a compilation of foreign loans issued in the United States in 1920.[9] This junket in and of itself amounted to a kind of one-man intelligence sweep, an effort to assimilate, interpret, and ultimately project as a finished report information on which both judgments and predictions might reasonably be based. Donovan's notes would amount to a rudimentary version of what later espionage services would title a national intelligence estimate.

Donovan banked his six-figure remuneration and set up a law firm entirely his own. The towering baronial doors the demobilized war hero ordered installed in his Buffalo warren of legal offices were barely in place before he again bumped everybody's plans out of the way. Under the new Harding administration there was an opening for U.S. Attorney for Western New York State.

One calamitous August evening in 1923 Donovan authorized a raid on Buffalo's elephantine Gothic-revival power center, the Saturn Club. While half the worthies of Buffalo scuttered up and down in panic among the potted palms and bulging leather Morris chairs, dozens of heavies from Donovan's flying squad hurtled through to arrest the bartender, herd all the whiskey-drinking members into a corner for interrogation, and sledge-hammer open the "lockers" in which they'd stashed their private liquor supplies.[10] The furor hadn't abated much when Warren Harding died; Coolidge appointed Donovan's teacher at Columbia Law, Harlan Stone, as Attorney General. Stone brought Donovan down, to run the criminal division of the Justice Department.

Donovan's notices were mixed. He presided over the transfer of power in Justice's Bureau of Investigation from the aging detective Williams Burns to twenty-nine-year-old John Edgar Hoover. When an alerted Donovan found out that the fresh-faced new Director was tapping politicians' telephones around town, he arranged for Hoover to be hauled before the moralistic Stone, severely dressed down, and very nearly fired. Hoover's unforgiving matinee-idol gaze settled permanently upon Donovan.[11]

After Coolidge foreswore renomination in 1928 Donovan attempted to attach himself to the front-runner Herbert Hoover, enticed by regular hints of his own claim on the attorney-generalship. As chairman of the Rio Grande Compact Commission, Donovan bounced in and out of town a lot. On each pass East, Hoover took him down a level. Not Attorney General now, but there was a slot in the cabinet as Secretary of War still open. Not Secretary of War, but the Governor Generalship of the Philippines was a historically glamorous appointment . . .

Donovan bit back anger and disappointment. The time was imminent, he told the new President, when there would be a shift in the public mood, "and you will need someone to stay here who can pull the sword for you."

"I don't think so, Bill," the phlegmatic President decided.[12]

❑

While Donovan retained legs—and gall—enough to clamber across each setback, the twenties looked tougher every season for other Versailles-era intelligence visionaries. For Bill Bullitt especially the wheel had been an eternity coming 'round. His break with Wilson had left him politically spent at twenty-eight, a well-heeled multilingual vagabond with a collapsing marriage. His elegant Main-Line wife was finding "Billy" talky and overstylized much of the time, and confusingly versatile. At Yale his specialty while director of the dramatic association had been in female roles—Mistress Page and Katherine from Shakespeare were favorites, along with Lady Gay Spanker in *London Assurance*.[13] Ernesta laughed with one Philadelphia friend about the evening Billy attempted to juice up their flagging sex life by elaborately stripping her and promising to plant a kiss on every-single-inch of her recumbent nudity.

"And did he follow through?" her confidante wondered.

"I haven't the faintest idea. I was asleep before he got to my left knee."[14]

In his subsequent roman à clef, *It's Not Done*, Bullitt portrays the Ernesta figure, Mildred Ashley, as a frigid socialite who brushes the protagonist off at every approach: "Do go into the next room, dear. . . . Only peasants sleep in the same bed."

The two bounced around between Europe and a farm in Ashfield, Massachusetts; that marriage was exhausted by 1921. Bullitt moved to Manhattan and accepted a position as managing editor for the Paramount-Famous-Lasky Corporation. Editing scripts, he encountered the handsome, free-thinking journalist Louise Bryant, John Reed's widow. In progressive Greenwich Village, where Bullitt pondered radicalism during his downtown hours, friends found him "emotionally caught up in a *posthumous* idealization of John Reed," whom Bullitt had dealt with extensively in 1918.[15] Reed was safely enshrined by then in the Kremlin Wall. "Bill seemed to make Reed *his* love mystique too," his contemporary George Biddle perceived.[16]

Louise and Bill were married in December of 1923. The daughter of a coal miner and roustabout labor agitator, Louise Bryant was already pregnant by then. This was an unlikely pairing, even for the experimental Bullitt. One biography of Bullitt[17] reproduces a painting of Ernesta Drinker Bullitt in a light satin gown at tea. A photograph of Louise Bryant presents her naked and raw, stretched out and propped up on her back, her slender arms veiled inside her unkempt anthracite mane. Her nipples are upturned, dark, and one long hollow thigh is inclined to receive the breezes off a Provincetown dune. While married to Reed, Louise had included Eugene O'Neill in her disheveled ménage.

Louise and Bill rented fashionably in Paris, they traveled, they took a mansion for a year in Istanbul overlooking the Bosporus, she drank too much and—Bullitt later charged—ran off to test her luck with a literary Englishwoman. He tried a fling with Eleanor (Cissy)

Patterson. The Bullitts' divorce was granted in 1930, and Bill got custody of six-year-old Anne.

After that he bobbed around Europe for several years, accosted the great, settled down in Vienna for some months to work with Sigmund Freud on a psychoanalytical study of Woodrow Wilson.

No contact went unexplored. Bullitt lamented to Walter Lippmann how entirely "Colonel House bamboozled us both. If I had known how much of Woodrow's work you were doing and if you had known how much I was doing, little Eddie would not have been able to convince us so entirely of the wisdom of his master."[18]

But opportunity closes wounds; as 1932 opened Bullitt was assiduously feeding high-level gossip to House from Europe, urging him to convince the leading Democratic contender that "I might not be altogether useless." Roosevelt knew Bullitt, slightly, and remembered being annoyed in 1919 by the political renegade's crust and swagger. Namedropping furiously, Bullitt bombarded House with reports from Europe's capitals as remote as Moscow, and back in the United States Bullitt pushed his way aboard the campaign train doubling as a speechwriter. Roosevelt liked his vivacity. Bullitt undertook a pair of semiofficial junkets around Europe on FDR's behalf, and early in May of 1933 he moved in for the new administration as a special assistant to the Secretary of State.

New Deal braintrusters expected problems. Raymond Moley could see how sharp and informed Bullitt was, but questioned his "strain of romanticism," which Moley diagnosed as "full of lights and shadows, plots and counterplots, villains and a few heroes. . . .[19] Those early months Bullitt's mentor was the courtly Virginian R. Walton Moore—"Judge" Moore—a congressman and crony of Secretary of State Cordell Hull as well as, fortuitously, a law school roommate of Bullitt's father. Moore served as Assistant Secretary of State.

To throw another anchor to windward at this point, Bullitt seems to have seduced Marguerite ("Missy") LeHand, the President's peaches-and-cream personal assistant. A refined woman of volcanic if subdued yearnings, she began her many years of total service to the President in 1920, shortly before the onset of his polio, and over time the tenderness and concern between the two was such that insiders referred to her as the President's "surrogate wife." James Roosevelt has referred to Missy's affair with Bullitt as "the one real romance of her life," and Eleanor was baffled, she wrote Lorena Hickock, as to "why F.D.R. has been so content to let Missy play with him!"[20]

This was by way of a royal indulgence, Eleanor concluded, since

Franklin intended to remove Bullitt shortly to Moscow. Perhaps there were other reasons. Bullitt was always subject to complex transferences of affection; his dedication to Roosevelt was such that many of his exchanges with the President concluded with verbal caresses he proffered directly—"I wish I were in the White House to give you a large kiss on your bald spot"[21]—or conveyed through Missy. Roosevelt welcomed the adoration.

After helping with preparations for the London Economic Conference, Bullitt had been directed to deal with the intricacies preliminary to diplomatic recognition of the Soviet regime. In November of 1933 the United States recognized Stalin's government, and William Bullitt was simultaneously appointed the administration's first ambassador to the Soviets. He grabbed the eager young Russian specialist George Kennan and rushed to Moscow to present his credentials—the first official U.S. representative since the outraged Dewitt Poole had cleared out fifteen years before.

Bullitt pronounced the Soviet dictator a small, ordinary-looking fellow wearing a common soldier's uniform, who smoked an "underslung pipe" all through the many courses of a typical Soviet marathon banquet. "His mustache covers his mouth, so that it is difficult to see just what it is like, but when he laughs his lips curl in a curiously canine manner."[22]

Bullitt had been charged in Washington with attempting to recover the outstanding U.S. loans to the Kerensky government, along with extracting assurances from the Soviets that the propaganda and subversive apparatus of the Comintern would not be brought to bear on the depression-ridden United States. Bullitt added a personal project. He wanted the Soviets to authorize the construction of a magnificent United States embassy building on a bluff inside the urban park which overlooked the Moscow river. The Soviets were worried at the moment about a Japanese attack on their Asian provinces; Stalin had approached Bullitt for 250,000 tons of steel locomotive track, new or used, to finish the railroad line to Vladivostok. Now—Bullitt wanted an embassy site? " 'You shall have it,' " Stalin proclaimed. "Thereupon, I held out my hand to shake hands with Stalin and, to my amazement, Stalin took my head in his hands and gave me a large kiss! I swallowed my astonishment and, when he turned up his face for a return kiss, I delivered it."[23]

So relations were moist initially, although they dried out. Debt negotiations went badly. Fear of the Japanese abated. The Third International affronted capitalists across the West. By spring of 1935 Bullitt reported that "The terror, always present, has risen to such a pitch that the least of the Moscovites, as well as the greatest, is in fear." Even "the three not-too-awful dentists of the town" were forced into exile for assisting foreigners, "leaving members of the American Embassy hanging on to temporary fillings."[24] Months earlier a concerned FDR had written his emissary that "Missy and I thought you sounded just a bit homesick,"[25] and Missy LeHand undertook an arduous trip to visit her lover in Moscow. She found Bullitt embarked on an affair with a ballet dancer, and readjusted her expectations.[26]

Observers since have commented on the concentration of talent Bullitt was able to lure to Moscow. His Counselor of Embassy was John Wiley, who, along with Loy Henderson, and Elbridge Durbrow, Ed Page, Charles ("Chip") Bohlen, and George Kennan, would reach ambassadorial levels. The naval attaché, Roscoe Hillenkoetter, headed up the CIA after it was authorized in 1947.

Loy Henderson was senior to the others as Secretary of Embassy, unbending but invariably conscientious about coping with the practical miseries involved in setting up properly in that bleak, jammed, overbureaucratized hardship assignment.[27] Charlie Thayer drifted in, their special projects man. He proselytized, for example, in behalf of polo matches with the Red Army. A lapsed West Pointer of good Philadelphia origins, he had the flair and background to stage-manage the celebrated ball Bullitt mounted for the rulers of Moscow, throughout which animals borrowed from the Moscow Zoo, ranging from zebra finches to mountain goats, mixed with the guests. A trained seal purportedly served champagne "from a glass balanced on its nose." The chief of the General Staff, Yegorov, ambled by and picked up a distressed bear cub which had slurped down an excess of Mumm's Cordon Rouge; before long it upchucked massively across the ribbons on his tunic.[28]

By no means as offhand as Thayer, although breezy and approachable enough, his roommate Charles Bohlen adapted with a characteristic professionalism to life in Moscow. Alongside George Kennan and Eric Kuniholm, Bohlen had been polished—or warped—by an ambitious area studies program recently fabricated by State's Eastern European chief, Robert Francis Kelley. Kelley screened carefully among upcoming Foreign Service youngsters for prospects with stuff enough to confront the "Boles." A Harvard product, Kelley's follow-up preparation at the Paris School of Oriental Languages and subsequent posting at Riga had exposed this working-class Boston-Irish bachelor to the mesmerizing charm and exquisitely cultivated awareness of loss which marked the Westernized Russian émigré. In

Washington Kelley battled to hold his peers to a policy he defined as "not merely a policy of nonrecognition of the Soviet government" but in fact "a policy of having nothing at all to do with that government."[29] George Kennan already reflected his mentor Kelley's attitudes: "Never—neither then nor at any later date—did I consider the Soviet Union a fit ally or associate, actual or potential, for this country.[30] Kelley expected his "boys" to emerge from their extended indoctrination thinking like "a well-educated Russian of the old, prerevolutionary school."[31]

George Kennan's extended matriculation in Kelley's academy alternated minor duties in Riga and Tallinn and immersion in the Russian Studies curriculum he opted for at the Oriental Seminary at the University of Berlin. He survived a severe appraisal by the local Consul General at the U.S. Embassy, the precocious anti-Bolshevik and snippy Old Princetonian Dewitt C. Poole. As ranking U.S. diplomat in Moscow during the Russian revolution, Poole had deserted Russia in 1919 aghast at the Leninist takeover and devoted himself to the intensely nationalistic and clericalist émigré groups already attempting to rally beyond the Soviet border. Bob Kelley would remain a dedicated worshiper in Dewitt Poole's parish. When Kennan wrote Kelley for permission to enroll in courses in Soviet finance and political structure, Kelley turned him down.

Kennan met his wife in Berlin—Annelise Soerensen, a Norwegian. Annelise was so impassive, George wrote his father, "that even I don't make her nervous."[32] Kennan's Delphic, self-deprecating asides about his own performances would become a constituent of his charm, and compensated to some extent for George's propensity to mix up reality with his overwhelming emotions toward whatever was at hand just then, his celebrated burning "intuitions." A self-admitted "oddball on campus"[33] at Princeton, Kennan began to experience in Berlin an expansion of sentiment which in effect bonded him to the German people, "feelings that took more thoughtfully into account the true complexity of their historical experience and recognized the existence within them of elements whose positive qualities, including courage and humanity, defied all efforts at negative generalization."[34] To the aspiring diplomat, Germany was achieved civilization, despite the Nazi overlay. On the other hand, Russia under the Soviets, Kennan wrote a friend in 1931, "is unalterably opposed to our traditional system," and unless "an economic cordon is put around one or the other of them . . . within twenty or thirty years either Russia will be capitalist or we shall be communist."[35]

George's State Department collaboration with Robert Kelley provided all concerned fair warning of Kennan's evolved beliefs, and once the grimness of the Soviet system and the programmatic deviousness of its leaders began to register, Bullitt's dramatic reversal began. "Bohlen and I were increasingly dismayed by the Soviet system," Kennan would later remark, "and we helped move Bullitt away from his optimistic views. It did not take too much work."[36] At first Bullitt attempted to chalk off his diplomatic setbacks to interference from "non-Russian" factions—he disliked particularly Litvinov's press aide, Konstantin Umansky, "an astonishingly loathsome Jew, capable of any baseness"[37]—but in the end he turned away utterly, without qualification or excuse, and became as inveterate an anti-Soviet polemicist as existed within the U.S. Government. He brooked no schismatics. When, in 1937, his senior military attaché in Moscow, Phillip Faymonville, whom Bullitt now found insufficiently dogmatic, applied for an extension, Bullitt in a letter to FDR lambasted Faymonville as "the greatest Bolshevik lover at large" who "constantly went behind the back of the Embassy to assure the Bolshies that they were loved by our Government. . . ."[38]

As Kennan would write, "We were in many respects a pioneer enterprise. . . . We were the first to cope seriously, for example, with the problems of security—of protection of codes and files and the privacy of intra-office discussion—in a hostile environment. For this purpose, Bullitt brought in a detachment of marine sergeants. . . . We endeavored to carry forward in our reporting work the same scholarly approach and standards that had previously been adopted in Riga."[39]

Third Secretary Kennan welcomed the ambassador's enlightenment. In photographs of Bullitt's grinning appearances around Moscow in swallowtail or greatcoat that inaugural December of 1933, George Kennan shows up almost always as a background figure: very much the aide-de-camp—stiff, his widow's peak starting to recede while on his closed, averted face the pinch of disapproval seems omnipresent. Whom were we solemnizing? Even within the American compound Kennan's astringency, his fitfulness, his susceptibility to an impressive spectrum of the minor illnesses from shingles to sinus attacks made him a challenge to befriend. He *was* bright. But he could also be insensitive and sententious almost to an excruciating degree, and afterward his companions would joke about pouring a few drinks into George at the dacha the delegation rented outside Moscow and then attempting to head him off when Kennan rounded suddenly and threatened to entertain the assembled with an interminable reading from Gibbon's *Decline and Fall of the Roman Empire.*[40]

All through the thirties the four-bedroom dacha served as a kind of clubhouse where the beleaguered Americans could relax and socialize, quite often with counterparts from the other uneasy Western delegations. Chip Bohlen struck up an acquaintance, for example, with the unpretentious nobleman Hans Herwarth von Bittenfeld, Second Secretary of the German staff, whom the Americans called Johnny and whom they permitted to buy a part interest in one of their battered brown riding horses.[41] Another widely appreciated colleague was Gustav Hilger, an expert on Soviet affairs and Germany's Counselor of Embassy. In December of 1934 the party leader in Leningrad, Sergei Kirov, was murdered, probably by the OGPU, and with that began the chain of events that produced the purges and show trials which electrified the rest of the decade in Russia. Police state regulations tightened, especially for diplomats, Moscow became even *more* claustral, and outsiders were thrown perforce into one another's company.

For anybody with Bullitt's constitutionally blithe and incandescent personality ("which he could turn on and off at will,"[42] as Bohlen would write), Moscow was becoming uninhabitable. His absences became extended. Perceptive as he obviously was, Bullitt began to find Kennan's tortured diatribes and burning glances and endless cables an increasing chore. "After half a year in Moscow, Bullitt had little use for George personally," Loy Henderson later said. "None of us took George's ideas as seriously as George did, but we knew that someday people would have to."[43]

As events worked out, the midpoint of 1934 coincided with the arrival in Moscow of Bullitt's new clerk, Carmel Offie. "Please send secretary who can stand Moscow and me,"[44] the ambassador wired Washington after a series of personal assistants had busted out or decamped. Offie at the time was twenty-four, a small, swart fellow with a feral Levantive physiognomy and the initial heavy fuzzing which became his trademark double-bar moustache—the sort of face that made people wonder even then whether he could *ever* have been young.

Carmel Offie had grown up in a big, poor Italian family in the coalfields around Sharon, Pennsylvania. Both parents were immigrants from the mountains outside Naples. Carmel's father was a railroad hand in Portage. At seventeen Carmel had made his way to Washington and picked up enough skills to work at the Interstate Commerce Commission as a typist and stenographer. After three years he returned home briefly to enroll in a one-year business course in Johnstown, Pennsylvania, then presented himself in 1931 for assignment to the State Department, where he was accepted at vice-consular level—in practice, a clerk.[45]

Offie's first assignment was to the mission at Tegucigalpa, Honduras, and it was there, at twenty-one, that he would first break out. Effectively managing the office was a woman of some cultivation, Miss Lucy Lentz. "And who should turn up?" observes a mutual friend, another State Department professional named Hector Prudhomme, "but this young squirt, who hardly knew how to speak English properly. Lucy nurtured him, and helped him with education and things—I don't know in what way she accomplished this exactly. But it was quite clear that this provided his start, the diving board from which Offie sprang. She taught him everything: how to serve, proper table manners, how to say hello. Because he was from a totally boorish background. I don't mean that in a bad way."[46] Already a quick study, Offie caught the attention of the mission chief, Lawrence Higgins, and his wife, Elizabeth, and they too appreciated his engaging personality and determination to please and did what they could to bring him along.

Accordingly, Offie reached Moscow at the end of June of 1934 with at least the rudiments of whatever Bullitt needed, both as a confidential secretary and a private amanuensis. "He never really looked very much like a gentleman," Prudhomme will concede. "He never would have gotten far with the Junior League in a place like Dallas." But diplomatic colonies even during the stratified thirties worked up their own pecking orders, like shipwreck encampments, and talent became paramount. Offie's natural industry, the ease with which he added German and Russian to the Latin languages he had already picked up, the positively demonic concentration he brought to clerical work (which he could rip through, assuming plenty of responsibility nobody else really wanted)—all this would register, quickly. Small, oily, susceptible (positively Chaplinesque), with quite a dark, delicious sense of humor much of the time and almost an uncontrollable eagerness to assist his betters, Offie started making friends.

It did him no harm that Bullitt delighted in his services. A dedicated sociological bottom-feeder, it tickled Bullitt's Pygmalion impulses to sponsor Offie's presentation. By October the two were bundled into a compartment on the Trans-Siberian Railroad so Bullitt could scout the Japanese threat as well as analyze the rise of Mao for Roosevelt. Bullitt arrived in Tokyo with a streptococcus infection, which Offie helped nurse.[47]

By 1935—Bullitt having no wife—important go-betweens like Louis Wehle were routinely including their "best to Offie." Carmel himself was tipping off Bullitt's patron Judge Moore that the ambassador was "not at all well, but as long as he gets plenty of rest he manages to go through his regular work." Still, Offie remained worried because his employer had started to resort to strychnine "to keep him going, but he hasn't taken any since April 25, which is somewhat encouraging."[48] A British Embassy informant sent Whitehall a report which elaborated on the travails of a "very decent clerk" whom Bullitt had promoted to "attaché": "This wretched young man puts up with being at his beck and call all day and all night, for if he has an idea during the night he calls for his attaché to take down a draft. He gets up in the morning at any hour between five and seven and takes the unfortunate fellow for a walk with him."[49]

Bullitt was soon pushing Washington to pay Offie more, since he was "more useful to this mission than any man here." Bullitt's efficiency report to the Department on Carmel reflects their augmenting relationship: Offie overworks, Bullitt must concede, and naturally "when Mr. Offie reached Moscow he lacked social polish and his eagerness and self-assurance often produced an appearance of 'freshness.' However, in the course of our trip around the world he acquired the social poise which he conspicuously lacked, and his 'freshness' is rapidly disappearing."[50] When the ambassador and his daughter relaxed in the sun that year in Odessa, Offie shuttled up and down with papers, on which they both worked "in a small rowboat," to guarantee security. The strep hung on; in September the pair vacationed in Sicily and Capri. From Capri Bullitt wrote Judge Moore that he and Carmel had "spent all our time in Ragusa taking sun baths, and I shall do the same . . . here. . . . Offie had proved himself just as good a doctor as he is a secretary. He has made me follow rigidly my doctor's orders and sees to it that I take my different medicines to the minute."[51]

Carmel Offie was entering history.

3

A PROPER FEEDING FRENZY

To relieve the drear of Moscow, Bullitt had a way of bouncing in and out of Berlin, where Franklin Roosevelt's unbending ambassador to Germany, William Dodd, brooked no apologists for the iniquities of the Hitler regime. Bullitt judged the University of Chicago history professor formal, and insensitive to the new Europe's political requirements.

In his turn, Dodd wrote, "Bullitt still impressed me as quite proud of himself, and rather more boyish than one would expect for a man of his years."[1] Dodd's peripatetic daughter Martha cut much deeper: While she was touring in Moscow, "Ambassador Bullitt called one day and asked me to lunch at his home. He was very lively and attractive superficially—a bald-headed, glistening face, with intense light eyes, a curious vitality in his vivacious speech and glances, a strong egotism under the brittleness and instability."[2]

Paradoxically, a number of prominent Nazis fell into the habit of drifting in and out of the embassy Dodd kept, obviously craving a breather. One regular was Hitler's "economic wizard," Hjalmar Horace Greeley Schacht. Obviously a divided man, Schacht's willingness to cosponsor the impudent Nazis had boosted him back into command at the all-important Reichsbank along with the Economics Ministry, now free at last to indulge his unique financial legerdemain. Frustrated by the unappeasable Goering, Schacht began to whimper to Dodd during down moments about expatriating to the United States, from where his parents had long before returned to Germany. "I wondered," Dodd muses to his diary, "what he was going to do with the Hitler statue in his parlor or with the painting of Goering which I saw in his house the last time I was there."[3]

Recurrent among the flow of visitors was Schacht's longtime confidant, the rising international corporate attorney John Foster Dulles, in town alongside Laird Bell of Chicago in behalf of the aggrieved American bondholders' association. They were out funds in excess of $1 billion, victims of an early Schacht reappraisal. Foster—who always preferred to preach to the converted, and picked his customers—regretted the momentary excesses, but told Dodd " 'My sister [Eleanor] lives here. She is an enthusiastic Hitlerite, and anxious to show me the German attitude for peace.' "[4]

In later years John Foster Dulles flinched at whispers that he had fluffed off Hitler as a "passing phenomenon," as Thomas Dewey quipped, to whom "the fat and happy should gracefully yield to avoid war."[5] The year Hitler arrived at power John Foster Dulles was forty-five. Even then, among Americans, many contemporaries still found him difficult to appreciate. A boating mishap eliminated the managing partner at Sullivan and Cromwell in 1926, and subsequently the elderly William Cromwell himself picked out the hardworking, self-aggrandizing Dulles to run the firm. There was a young-old aspect to Foster, what with his soot-black overcoats and walking stick and outdated English homburg. He remained for decades the last champion in America of the wing-tip collar.

Behind those heavy wire-rimmed spectacles his focus appeared to jump and frequently his eye watered; along with his fixed scowl and endemic halitosis this backed enthusiasts off. Foster loathed any displays of emotion in his presence, and responded with a coldness strangers interpreted as condescending. Subordinates found him suffocating.

What made Foster off-putting to Wall Streeters tended to impress foreigners. He was a voracious and precise legal craftsman, a Savonarola at litigation. Foster's months of service with the Reparations Commission imparted an insider's familiarity with many of the recherché financial corners of the Europe emerging from the Great War, and provided him the jump on his demobilizing generation. As early as 1920 he was already roaming the Continent "to make some investigations and carry on some negotiations on behalf of American bankers," as he wrote an acquaintance, "who desire to invest in

Germany, Poland and Czechoslovakia."[6] Foster's backers got together to form the Overseas Securities Corporation, with him as legal counsel. Simultaneously, Foster agreed to serve as counsel to the U.S. Government's War Finance Corporation, a device to underwrite American exports when routine channels failed.

Dulles's client list compounded until it was laden with corporations prospecting for overseas business. Latin America lay closest, and Dulles helped draft the legal empowerments which led to the internationalization of the utilities pyramid. He attended Central Europe, building up substantial institutional and private business in Hungary, Poland, Czechoslovakia; the key remained Germany, already reassuming its traditional role as economic springboard and colonizer of the East. By 1923 Foster was working on officials at the State Department for bureaucratic support when the Polish government expropriated the Possehl industrial works—in which the Overseas Securities Corporation had taken a substantial position—by arguing that German capital secretly controlled the operations. Challenged by State Department investigators to open Possehl's books, Dulles folded his inquiry.[7]

As the European appetite for dollars drove up the bond rates overseas, most of the aggressive Manhattan investment banking houses enlisted Foster to review the paper they fobbed off on investors. Dulles' client list included: Morgan; the National City Company; Kuhn, Loeb; Lee, Higginson; Dillon, Read; Brown Brothers, Harriman; the Chase National Bank. Any number of recovering German municipalities lined up for free money, along with banks and utilities and carriers like North German Lloyd. When 1929 hit, $1.2 billion in U.S. foreign securities—almost 13 percent of the nation's foreign lendings—depended on Germany's intent to repay.

Each time wayward State and Commerce department functionaries intervened to challenge the issuance of additional financial paper to entities already in default or functioning as flagrant cartel instruments, Foster brushed forward publicly, affronted by "the use of this power to carry out disputable and individual economic or political theories."[8] In *Foreign Affairs*, he emphasized the "prevailing conception in a large part of the world that the 'cartel system,' with government supervision of prices, is economically superior to our own principle of competition enforced by law."[9]

Mitteleuropa loosed a feeding frenzy each time the Reichsmark stabilized. Hucksters for the Wall Street investment houses hit the recumbent Germany like sucklings clambering aboard a sow. "During 1925 and 1926 not a week went by that a representation of a group of American banks did not come to see me for that purpose (making loans),"[10] the Prussian Minister of Finance marveled in 1931. "German authorities had been virtually flooded with loan offers by foreigners." Two underwriters quickly outdistanced all others in soliciting these high-risk bond issues, New York's National City Bank (whipped on by Henry Mann) and Dillon, Read and Company.

In 1926 Clarence Dillon took on a cocksure recent Princeton graduate and sent him across to drum up business. Acquaintances would describe Ferdinand Eberstadt as "neat, hard-boiled, and balding,"[11] and Eberstadt's journals and reports to Dillon suggest the push and aptitude for intrigue it took. The great opportunity that year was cornering financing for the Vereinigte Stahlwerke, the United Steel cartel Fritz Thyssen and the Stinnes interests were attempting to amalgamate under the direction of the brilliant Albert Voegler.

In Germany Eberstadt coordinated his sorties for Dillion, Read with those of a fast-moving influence peddler named Alexander Kreuter. Empires glimmered into view. Personages in the "London money market" may well regard his aggressive salesmanship as "threatening of the British industries,"[12] Eberstadt writes his chum from Princeton, James Forrestal, already a vice president and Clarence Dillon's right hand.

Treasury expert Parker Gilbert insisted publicly that Germany was "over-borrowed" by 1927, and in his capacity as American Agent General for Reparations in Germany announced that "I am constantly amazed at the recklessness of American bankers in offering to the public the securities of German States on the basis of purely German view."[13]

Statements like Gilbert's demanded refutation. Professor James Angell of Columbia would publish a treatise in 1929 entitled "The Recovery of Germany."[14] Angell lambasted the Versailles inequities. Trusts like United Steel adumbrated the industrial prodigies to come, Angell maintained, Germany led the Continent. Sponsors of this diatribe included Charles Mitchell of the City National Bank, the Dillon, Read partners, and Allen W. Dulles.

Foster advised the syndicates which funded the Dawes and Young plans, and funneled through $500 million in short-term private credits to Chancellor Bruening's government in 1931–1932. The era of write-downs and defaults was upon the Western democracies, the punishment of "debt conferences." Hitler consolidated the prostrate Reich, and six months later Hjalmar Schacht strode back and forth before Foster Dulles and other designated supplicants and advised them that debt questions might now most fruitfully be pursued "on the hypothesis that Germany would declare a virtually complete transfer moratorium." Deutschland expected to renig.

As Wall Streeters panicked, a man with Dulles's connections abroad looked like the only hope. In March of 1932 the Swedish "Match King," Ivar Kreuger, blew out his brains and left the international financial community to hose the plaster down. Dulles became the legal counsel for the Murphy Committee which investigated for the American victims. He insinuated his good friend Jean Monnet as liquidator for the Kreuger and Toll interests, attended closely by premier Swedish banker Jacob Wallenberg.[15] After years of negotiations and reorganization and desultory asset auctions, the shareholders got nowhere, although Dulles billed out his services at something in excess of $540,000.[16]

It seemed the weightier Foster got, the paltrier his own slow-moving career in diplomacy looked to his restless kid brother. Allen now seemed invariably in the wrong place at the wrong time. After Versailles broke up, Allen missed the boom of the Harding and Coolidge era while posted in Berlin and Istanbul with the State Department. His reputation as an observer solidified, and he returned to Washington to head up the Near East Division from 1922 to 1926. He analyzed Kemal Ataturk and masterminded U.S. bargaining moves at Lausanne, met most of the emerging Arab leaders, and fell into an acquaintanceship with the influential Zionist Chaim Weizmann which started him musing earlier than most Americans about the utility of a realized Jewish homeland.[17] Allen pushed the sluggish Department to invest in Arabic studies and cosponsored a program to develop linguists and policy analysts with the Sovietophobic Robert F. Kelly.[18]

Practical trade-offs became unbearable; Allen's negligible government salary was turning him into a charming Society freeloader, a perennial houseguest of wealthy and ambitious betters from Christian Herter to David Bruce, with now and then a golf or tennis match against Coolidge's relentless Assistant Attorney General, William J. Donovan. Allen would refer afterward to the twenties as "my Slough of Despond." Even then, serving time, he demonstrated his lifelong aptitude for beguiling the powerful, inviting contacts, leaving important doors ajar. One acquaintance was smitten enough to refer to Dulles as that rare temperament "with a rainbow in his soul."

Participation in international conferences on arms trafficking and disarmament boosted Allen into position to help formulate

Department policy apropos the politically sensitive munitions industry. Alarmed at a government-proposed embargo, a representative of the Du Pont Corporation dropped by and found Dulles "altruistic" toward the industry, full of easy assurances that any international agreement under study would not prove "burdensome to the legitimate manufacturers."

Asked at an industry conference whether any *particular* nations were to be excluded from the treaty, "Mr. Dulles stated that notwithstanding the fact that it was known that Germany was exporting arms and munitions, it was not possible from a diplomatic standpoint to mention Germany or any of the Central Powers in this connection since they were supposed to abide by the treaties which put an end to the World War."

The objection arose that "due to interlocking stock ownership of European arms plants" foreigners could easily circumvent American restrictions. He alternated between coy and facetious: "Mr. Dulles asked why should any European country be so ungrateful as to wish to hurt the United States after what the United States had done for them in the years 1914–1918. (Most of the gentlemen present smiled.)"[19]

If, increasingly, this maturing Chief of the Mideast Affairs Division fell into a tone which skirted the blasé, even cynical, he brought it off usually with a nice flair. In fact a life in striped pants for $8,000 a year was losing its justification, and Allen was phasing out. For four mid-twenties years he prepped evenings for his bar examinations at George Washington University; at Sullivan and Cromwell, Foster prevailed on the partners to give his debonair middle-aging brother a try. Allen's note of resignation to Secretary Kellogg blamed "financial burdens involved in the acceptance of a higher position,"[20]—there had been talk of an appointment to China—but to a friend he admitted that this professional shift was "hard to explain, even to my own satisfaction," since "my inclinations are all the other way." It felt like selling out, and Dulles was not sure at all of covering the loss he felt.

It wasn't his expectation to become a lawyer's lawyer. "Allen Dulles wound up the number five man in his law firm," Walter Pforzheimer says. "He was the business getter, he kept the old ladies happy on estate work."[21] Allen settled without dropping a beat into this downtown world of club lunches and charity balls and four o'clock squash matches, incomparably easier to meet than Foster if harder to pin down. His State Department credentials soon involved him in New York's prestigious Council on Foreign Relations, which alumni of the Wilsonian braintrust founded to keep their ideals in play; Allen became its secretary, and a dependable contributor to *Foreign Affairs.*

The downtown heavyweights relished Allen's cagey charm, brisk and urbane at moments and endearingly absentminded and open to suggestion whenever that might work. An excellent lifelong tennis player, Allen marshaled the restraint when useful to keep the outcome of a set undecided until the last few points, then dump it convincingly and leave a prospective client glowing. His demeanor of worldly ease and overflowing vigor made tantalizing by that little-boy-lost quality, he seemed to provoke in intense, cosmopolitan women with time on their hands a longing to cuddle Allen. Many volunteered their utmost.

These limpid tomcat moves of Allen's soon made his straitlaced family uncomfortable, starting with his wife, Clover. The two were married almost on a whim in 1920, he bursting with worldly experience—a great, impulsive diplomatic dandy (his deep moustaches rakishly uptwisted)—and she the fresh, rather ethereal Columbia professor's daughter with trust money coming down from her Baltimore forebears along with aspirations to redeem the needy. By the time they settled with their two small daughters into a four-story brownstone on East Sixty-First Street, even the babies were becoming aware that domesticity wasn't Allen's focus. A son was born in 1930, a worried-looking, rather precocious namesake who soon grasped that his father's amiable bluffness around the household served most often to fend off involvement.

Clover remained an imaginative, warm, frequently scattered mother who several times upset Allen by neglecting to pay the bills at a time when he was worried about his credit rating after an unnerving run of stock market losses. She rarely seemed to understand in any way his undiminished if transplanted ambitions, now focussed on Wall Street. One day she inadvertently caught a glimpse of Allen embarked on one of his dalliances on the grounds of his brother's estate at Cold Spring Harbor, possibly with the fetching White Russian émigré he introduced to friends that season as his regular "tennis partner."[22] Clover sneaked out afterward and bought herself an emerald drop at Cartier's on Allen's charge account. This precipitated a shattering row, which left Clover bewildered and depressed.

Allen's frustrations at that juncture centered on his replacement career. For several years Foster withheld from Allen meaningful cases of his own, and even after 1930, when he was accepted as a partner and his belated apprenticeship seemed thankfully at an end, his brother saw to it that associates better steeped in the law and forensics than Allen worked over the technical language. Allen's children would refer to parental jitters at the specter of their "imposing Uncle Foster, whose presence in the house" inspired "something like dread."[23]

Thus it became critical to Allen that he too round into an authentic force at Sullivan and Cromwell. What Allen made available to clients was an insider's deftness at circumventing government prohibitions, backed up by commitment and, when required, considerable doggedness. Du Pont officials, undoubtedly remembering his laissez-faire approach wherever munitions were involved, asked Allen in 1932–1933 to help find ways to bypass the export controls so they could ship the secretly rearming German Generals Staff propellants and explosives. Allen welcomed the opportunity they offered to acquire Du Pont securities at an insider price. He untangled a difficult lease problem for the United Fruit Company, then picked up at a timely moment a sizable block of stock in that embattled monopoly.[24] Foster cut him in on preregistration offerings by clients like International Nickel; once he felt comfortable about his practice, Allen took on a mortgage loan for a shore house not far from Foster's on Oyster Bay.[25] Parties along the cove remained vivacious and unpredictable.

To keep his diplomatic credits rolling, even as a private lawyer Allen served on various U.S. delegations to major international conferences. The disarmament talks of 1932 at Geneva not only helped him anticipate the outcome—he prejudged the chance of further arms reductions, correctly, as "problematical" at best—but paid off in introductions to national leaders from the embattled German Chancellor Bruening to Sir John Simon and Mussolini. In one tellingly deferential letter to Foster, he justifies these weeks away from the office with assurances that "of course I am doing a great deal in widening my acquaintanceship, and I am being given plenty of responsible work. . . ."[26] Later in the year he reassured his impatient older brother that he was drumming up lots of support for Foster's pet notion of "organizing the American creditor groups with a view to prompt and united action in collecting overseas debts."[27]

In May of 1932 Allen wrote Foster that "With the Prussian election it seems to me that the question of the participation of the Hitler element in the Prussian Government and then in the Reich Government will again be agitated. Personally, I hope that their participation will be worked out, as I feel that any Government in France would be very reluctant to enter into any far-reaching agreements with a German Government which was not in some way underwritten or approved by the Hitler element." He encloses an extra copy to pass on to Clover "with good advice not to let it get lost."[28]

This sense that Hitler was in the wings, that only his white-hot nationalism could cauterize Versailles, regularly overhung exchanges between the Dulles brothers. Foster viewed the rise of the European dictators as representing an inevitable redress by the downtrodden but "dynamic" younger powers of Europe against the "static" imperial hangers-on.[29] In an article in *Foreign Affairs* in October of 1933, Foster pleads Germany's case, citing Dr. Schacht's canard that it was the United States which profited from all those unrepaid lendings to Germany, which labored beneath " 'an import surplus throughout the period from 1924 to the middle of 1930,' " while the United States prospered. "Whatever one's individual views," Foster then concludes, "no one can shut his eyes to the fact that the volume of foreign financing we have already done strongly commits us to doing more."

The same month, in a letter to Hjalmar Schacht, Foster alludes rather gingerly to the possibility of "attachment of the ships" if at least some manner of token commitment is not forthcoming from North German Lloyd to shore up its $17 million in dollar bonds. The firm's German correspondent, Dr. Albert, will stay in touch. These negotiations remain "difficult . . . partly due to the fact that the leading bankers, Kuhn, Loeb & Co., are somewhat prejudiced in their attitude toward Germany."[30] By then the New York papers were playing up stories about SA flying squads clubbing Jews in the streets at random.

Allen reflected Foster's vision. "Granted that there was over-lending during the past few years," he will concede, "we nevertheless are perhaps inclined to exaggerate the bankers' share of responsibility." He too remains favorable to the formation of a foreign bondholders' association to pursue these debts. Such groups require backers: "Chiefly, however, the initial financing should be sought from those for whose benefit the association would be established, namely, the holders of foreign bonds. . . ."[31] Let the sheep petition.

In later years Allen would be queried from time to time as to the extent of his professional involvement with Germany under the Nazi regime. He often seemed bemused that anybody thought to ask. "You couldn't practice law there," he explained to one oral history interviewer. "People came to see you asking how to evade the law, not how to respect the law. When that happens you can't be much of a lawyer."[32]

Both brothers stayed close to German affairs as the crisis sharpened. Long after Hitler's ascendancy, Foster accepted a post as a director and representative of the American shareholders to the Consolidated Silesian Steel Company.[33] This amounted to a holding company through which the Nazi banker Kurt von Schroeder (who sponsored Hitler directly into power) boosted *his* arch patron Friedrich Flick (who directly controlled two-thirds of the stock) into dominance of Poland's biggest coal miner and largest industrial undertaking.

It continued to be Foster largely who basked in the important directorships, Foster who commanded financial headlines in celebrated litigation. Allen kept the secondary customers mollified, visited Paris from time to time, and looked in on the two small offices Sullivan and Cromwell maintained in Hamburg and off the Esplanade in Berlin. Allen had some German, of course, which Foster really didn't. Foster's children in their turn dismissed Uncle Allen as "light," "frivolous."[34]

❏

Brushed off by Hoover, Bill Donovan promptly applied a favorite personal adage—"Whenever we stumble, we always fall forward"—and relocated to Wall Street in March 1929 to start up the international law firm which survives as Donovan, Leisure, Newton, Lumbard and Irvine. Wild Bill would emerge in short order a tremendous Manhattan personage. His milky blue eyes, growing gradually more hooded now, gleamed above his quirky little smile as new clients were ushered before him into the big office at 2 Wall. Bill Donovan knew everybody, from Dwight Morrow to Bernie Gimbel, and both his Georgetown townhouse and his Manhattan duplex on Beekman Place became offstage watering spots for movie stars and diplomats, European financiers and U.S. labor leaders, and women of virtually every background. Donovan's troubled wife, Ruth, came in to stand at his side when he was entertaining in the grand style, but more and more she found herself relegated to weeks and months in isolated country homes.

Donovan's manners acquired unparalleled polish, more year by year. Difficult passages with Ruth now churned up financial matters. Astute as he remained, Donovan all his life shrugged off money shortfalls; he consumed his wife's large dowry; he drew down, little by little, advances from his law firm which ran finally to hundreds of thousands of dollars. For several mid-depression years he seems to have neglected to pay any federal income tax.[35] Then in 1932 Donovan jockeyed himself into nomination by the New York Republicans to run unsuccessfully against Herbert Lehman for governor.

Donovan's broad international practice now served as chum to attract his ever-widening interests. Wild Bill's contact salesmanship and the glamour of his reputation sustained his attraction as a business-getter; nevertheless, as one partner confessed afterward, "He devoted the minimum time to law practice, since he had no interest in accumulating a fortune, in making money for money itself. His interest was in world affairs."[36]

Those early fact-finding missions had left the agile, energetic attorney eager to track events. Months at a time—and normally without Ruth—would find him popping up abroad, frequently near some political trouble-spot. As early as 1923 he materialized in Berchtesgaden to share a beer in the *Gastzimmer* of a modest pension with Adolf Hitler. The clammy young rabble-rouser ranted to the sympathetic attorney that he, unlike the family dog, could not be beaten by his miserable father until he wet the carpet.[37] In 1931 Wild Bill appeared unannounced in Manchuria. In 1935 (having several times been fluffed off by the War and State Departments) Donovan exploited private contacts to hoodwink Il Duce personally into authorizing an extended tour of the Ethiopian battlefield conducted by Marshal Badoglio. Donovan returned with detailed notes on everything from the capabilities of a huge new Italian bomber to the posterns of the army mules. Even before he reached New York Donovan handed over his observations to experts from the British Foreign Office.

Back in the United States Donovan bounced by Pennsylvania Avenue to confide to the President his concern about Mussolini's revitalized legions. He played a deepening double role. In daily affairs he remained the Old-Guard antitrust specialist, directing squads of attorneys to frustrate the New Deal initiatives to break up the American Telephone and Telegraph Company or jail the executives of eighteen top oil corporations for Middle-Western price fixing.[38]

Among the business lunches, the bustle of cafe-society amusements, figures turned up regularly from within an informal network trading experience and gossip as Europe looked ever more ominous. There was the economist James Warburg, privy to the statistical workups on Germany coming out of his family's Hamburg bank. W. Somerset Maugham came by to compare readings, an eternal fund of rich innuendo from unexpected quarters. The wartime intelligence officer Noble Judah sufaced; Donovan arranged quiet dinners from time to time with Sir William Wiseman, currently advising Kuhn, Loeb.

In turn, as Anthony Cave Brown indicates in his study of its wartime chief Stewart Menzies, Wiseman served as interface for the Secret Intelligence Service with a group of New York Anglophiles "who believed that an Anglo-American understanding was fundamental to the containment and perhaps the liquidation of bolshevism" and met every month at 34 East Sixty-second Street in an apartment " 'with an unlisted telephone number and no apparent occupant.' " Privy to deliberations in "The Room" were Vincent Astor, Kermit Roosevelt, Nelson Doubleday, Winthrop Aldrich, and David Bruce. The Room apparently dovetailed into proceedings at the Walrus Club in New York, where Donovan was "certainly a member," as he "was probably also a member of The Room."[39]

Besides Donovan's social sources there were ambivalent contacts his practice opened up. As Nazi control solidified, alarmed spokesmen for Europe's established governing castes sought Donovan out. Descendents of the von Moltke family (related quite closely to the Hamburg von Schroeders), whose forebears virtually created the Prussian General Staff system, complained regularly in chambers to Donovan about the upstarts who seized Germany. Donovan attempted to intervene in behalf of the Rothschilds to recover their Czechoslovakian holdings. A close social friendship with the German Consul General in New York, Otto Kiep, alerted Donovan to the disgust with Hitler which pervaded the German diplomatic community. A contact Donovan developed within the German Reparations Commission, Paul Leverkuehn, evidently first set up lines of communication between Donovan himself and the newly designated Abwehr (military intelligence) commander Wilhelm Franz Canaris.[40] Hitler demagnetized everybody's compass.

In May of 1937—sneaking out on his alarmed partners, who fretted each time their rumpled top lawyer boned up on a major Supreme Court case he would be pleading within hours on the night flight home over the Atlantic—Donovan decamped to Germany to study the new German tank in maneuvers. A year after that he prowled the Sudentenland to arrive at his own conclusions about the toughness of the threatened Czech army. He continued his tour to work up contacts in the Balkans, stopped off to confer with Italian sources, accompanied the Fourth Spanish Army as an American observer along the Ebro River front, then switched sides again to accept a German General Staff invitation to watch Hitler's armored divisions rip through their paces at Nuremberg.

As Axis rearmament quickened, William Donovan shifted slowly from his role as a self-contained neutral dignitary on the reviewing stands and forward observation posts of Europe's gathering militias and adopted a viewpoint—almost week by week a measurably more *interventionist* viewpoint—based on his own perceptions of what precisely Hitler had in mind. He paid a visit to the U.S. Army's Chief of Staff and delivered a report on the amazingly lethal capabilities of the Germans' new 88-millimeter cannon.[41] Ordnance experts laughed him off, but within the White House the uneasy Franklin Roosevelt surveyed Donovan's notes as corroboration of his own dread that the unstable postwar order was breaking down terminally. By then the Right in America was solidifying into isolationism, with leaders like Burton Wheeler and Lindbergh and John Foster Dulles agitating against involvement. Donovan, along with Frank Knox and the seasoned Henry Stimson, quietly edged toward interventionism.

Between history and accident, it was as if the next twelve months precipitated every element of Wild Bill's life so far. Donovan's banged-up domestic life suffered recurrent jolts when (after years of quirky, depression-induced illnesses) Ruth underwent in September of 1939 a full-scale hysterectomy. His spirited daughter Pat, a student at Georgetown who lived in the Washington house, turned over a car coming around a curve washed slick with red Virginia mud and died of head injuries. Wild Bill almost couldn't bring himself to view the body.[42] His hair went white within a couple of weeks.

Even Donovan's desultory record-keeping contains evidence that, while he was taking on informal responsibilities as Franklin Roosevelt's "eyes and legs," he retained his habit of tipping off contacts in the British diplomatic and intelligence communities. During spring and summer of 1939 he managed three separate trips to Europe, the first alongside Franco's Fourth Army—during which he almost got blown to pieces by a Loyalist grenade—then more Nuremberg maneuvers, and finally a June–July tour which kept him scouring the Continent—Germany and France, Scandinavia, the Low Countries. He rounded off his trip with a tête-à-tête with R. A. Butler, the British Undersecretary of State for Foreign Affairs.[43] Given Donovan's unique sources, the news of Hitler's move on Poland amounted to an anticlimax.

4

THE LAST GENTLEMAN OBSERVER

If Donovan had successfully insinuated himself as the "eyes and legs" for the paralyzed Franklin Roosevelt, the resuscitated William Bullitt was keeping his jaded President amused with belle lettristic flashes of interpretation from across the summits of Europe. Nobody played the lightning bug like phosphorescent Billy Bullitt.

Before he abandoned Moscow, William Bullitt had represented the United States at the funeral of Marshal Pilsudski in Warsaw. Hitler's stand-in was Goering, whom Bullitt in an inspired letter to Roosevelt portrayed as sweeping into the Warsaw cathedral late, "as if he were a German tenor playing Siegfried. . . . He is at least a yard across the bottom as the crow flies," Bullitt observed, and insofar as "he is not even as tall as I am and encases himself in a glove-tight uniform, the effect is novel. . . ."[1]

That was in June 1935. Rolling back to Moscow with Litvinov, Bullitt dismissed the Soviet Foreign Minister's well-borne-out conjecture that under their new leader, Colonel Beck, the Poles were positioning themselves to "participate in a joint German-Hungarian-Polish demolition of Czechoslovakia."[2]

Bill Bullitt moved over to U.S. Ambassador to France in August of 1936; while he was there, several times his vantage point shifted.

A stopover in Berlin in November of 1937 resulted in a tête-à-tête with Goering. The Nazi Foreign Minister Konstantin von Neurath and Hjalmar Schacht both implored Bullitt to smooth the way to a German-French reconciliation. If war must come, Bullitt was already urging, why not between Germany and the East? "The chairs were so big that Goering looked rather less than the size of a normal man," Bullitt reported to Roosevelt, while "I must have looked like some sort of animated flea."[3]

The Nazi government wanted better relations with the United States, Goering stressed, but that was impossible while William Dodd remained the envoy, since he was "too filled with venomous hatred of Germany to have any relations with members of the Government."[4] Roosevelt moved to replace Dodd with the traditionalist Hugh Wilson. Bullitt returned to France, urging French officials to abandon their alliance with Russia and "admit that Germany, having lost the war, has won the final victory and will be henceforth the dominant factor in Europe, which would be, I believe, today regarded as the part of wisdom by the vast majority of the people of France who think about international affairs."[5] At all costs, the Russians must not be permitted out from "behind their swamps."

It was Bullitt's zenith. There was a period of some months when the jocund and overactive United States Ambassador to the Third Republic had plenty of grounds for regarding himself as FDR's viceroy for Europe. He became an intimate of Leon Blum—whose "quicksilver intelligence" he sketched out for Roosevelt, set off by "the little fluttery gestures of the hyper-intellectual queer ones."[6] In turn Edouard Deladier and Paul Renaud admitted Bullitt into their confidences. Embassy parties were spectacular.

So bald, so pink—Bullitt played the jackanapes, the nabob with impunity enough to carry it off. Whenever he was displeased or overjoyed a kind of deep spreading blush rose slowly to dominate his high, glistening temples, sometimes reflecting the scarlet of the blood-red carnations he affected in his hand-stitched buttonhole. These he discarded immediately once he detected wilting—like his many political enthusiasms, carpers around Roosevelt gibed.[7]

Another habit of Bullitt's which told on the protocol-minded was his propensity to talent-scout, poking around each duty station and overstimulating the mid-level help. His habit of using "consular and diplomatic officers interchangeably," Janet Flanner saw, turned the "upper bureaucracy" at State into his "severest critics."

Snide remarks passed; not long after Bullitt took over in Paris a buzz was audible whenever Bob Murphy's name came up. Murphy had been stagnating in Paris for six years, stuck on the consular side with passport recertifications and visa grants, birth records, and trade licenses. With William Bullitt's arrival, Murphy's prospects quickly enlarged. The Philadelphia charmer appreciated the resignation it must have taken this offspring of a hard-luck Milwaukee day laborer and his pockmarked and devout German wife to haul himself that far up the civil service ladder. To keep the intelligence flow surging, Bullitt "drove his associates in the embassy to maintain close and friendly relations with French statesmen and other leaders," Murphy would recall, from "Maurice Thorez . . . through Leon Blum" and a galaxy of others which included Camille Chautemps and Pierre Laval and Pierre-Etienne Flandin and along to the Fascist mainstays "Marcel Deat and Colonel de la Roque."[8] Another wire-puller Murphy nurtured was the astringent purchasing agent for the French steel trust, Pierre Pucheu, who remained in close touch with Kurt von Schroeder by way of the J. H. Stein partners and the smokestack baronage up and down the Ruhr. In prewar Europe too, whatever went around came around.

To Bullitt's reading, the Red Menace continued uppermost straight through the roundelay which led to Munich. Secondary interests remained secondary. "The Czech position is made somewhat more desperate by the fact that nobody in Europe likes Czechs, to say nothing of Czechesses, whose piano legs and aversion to soap are notorious from one end of the continent to the other," Bullitt divulged to FDR in 1936.[9] Benes he disliked especially. For his part, Eduard Benes would state that "the United States Ambassador in Paris, William Bullitt, did not at first express himself publicly in favor of appeasement like Joseph Kennedy, but he worked for it incessantly."[10]

Something of the shrillness behind Bullitt's ridicule owed to his realization that, back in Washington, the undertow of policy was powerfully reversing itself. Bob Kelley's long preeminence within the Eastern European division had ended, and without an echo. Both Roosevelt and Sumner Welles concluded that, given the Nazi threat, an area program which slanted its advisors "simply to give them a perspective on Russia which emphasized the negative cultural and social effects of bolshevism and taught them to interpret Soviet policy and behavior in ways appropriate to nonrecognition"[11] was now a decade behind the reflux of history. Bullitt's replacement in Moscow, Joe Davies, pronounced Bullitt alarmist and misguided. The Russians were rude, social life in Moscow was bleak, but there were wider considerations.

On June 15, 1937, Kelley's bailiwick passed into the far less doctrinaire European Division of Pierrepont Moffat, and the tall, self-contained crusader moved on, not happily, to Counselor of Embassy in Ankara, where a Commodities Credit Corporation scandal would squeeze him out of the Department in 1945. Chip Bohlen stepped in to salvage Kelley's irreplaceable archive of files and periodical runs on the Soviets[12] and found a satisfactory repository in the Library of Congress.

All this invited supping with the devil, in Bullitt's opinion. No spoon was long enough. By August of 1939, with rumors feeding back to the White House courtesy of German diplomat Johnny Herwarth of some sort of entente in the making between Hitler and Stalin, FDR decided to intervene. The Soviets had toyed with a joint British-French mission all summer in Moscow while dickering with Gustav Hilger and von Ribbentrop. Now Roosevelt sent over a top-secret letter in which he implored the President of the Soviet Praesidium directly to give the Western Powers a chance before recasting vital alignments. Douglas MacArthur II hand-carried the communication from Paris to U.S. Ambassador Steinhardt for top-level presentation. MacArthur stayed over a few days in Bohlen's apartment, and while he was there Bohlen took him along to a reception at the German Embassy. "Getting off in a corner, and drinking, and pretending to carouse, as diplomats do," MacArthur recollects, "Chip, out of the corner of his mouth, told von Herwarth that I had arrived with this letter. And Johnny von Herwarth said, 'You've come too late. We initialed the non-aggression agreement last evening.' "[13]

The Russians were like that, Bullitt contended furiously. Devious, and backstabbing. So why raise hopes, or worry about niceties? When Jacob Beam reached Paris from what was left of the U.S. Embassy in Berlin at the end of August with a tip from Alexander Kirk that Germany would march on Poland on August 26, Bullitt rushed to the nearest telephone in the chateau he rented at Chantilly to pass this along immediately to the French premier, Deladier. Beam was beside himself: "Hold on a minute, for Christ's sake," he exclaimed to Bullitt, "This is so secret it can't be put in writing." Bullitt waved him off.[14] Secrets were for capitalizing on. Increasingly, what struck people about this cosmopolitan envoy with the lapidary French and the expression of a mischievous Humpty-Dumpty was the astonishingly *unguarded* character of everything he said. Open—tactless, "one of the President's risks," Department stalwarts felt, "the soul of indiscretion."[15]

In 1937 Sumner Welles moved up to Undersecretary of State, a move personally resented by Bullitt's mentor, Assistant Secretary of

State Judge Moore, who found himself sloughed off to one side into the newly created post of Counselor of the Department.

Early in 1940 FDR authorized, in the face of resistance from both his cabinet and all his principal representatives in Europe, a capital-to-capital junket by Welles which diplomatic establishments everywhere he went took as a repudiation of the United States ambassadorial corps. This wounded Bullitt especially, who felt, Robert Murphy later wrote, that "he had an understanding with President Roosevelt which made him the principal White House advisor on European affairs."[16] It happened that Welles reached Paris while Bullitt was himself in Washington, an overnight interventionist now fervently lobbying congressmen and attempting to expedite airplane deliveries with his great friend Jean Monnet.

Welles intended to mount one final peace initiative; he appeared suddenly in the major capitals toting a briefcase loaded with eleventh-hour disarmament proposals: in effect a "deathtrap," as Robert Vansittart commented, with Hitler at countdown.[17] The hot-tempered, unforgiving Philadelphian determined that Sumner Welles had dealt France the rejection which crippled hope. The gauntlet was now down, and neither statesman would survive politically.

His years as Bullitt's amanuensis in Paris left Carmel Offie, if not a butterfly precisely, an astonishingly evolved moth. Now commissioned a foreign service officer, Bullitt brought Carmel along with care. When disturbances broke out shortly after the two arrived, Bullitt wrote FDR, "Offie pretends that it is unsafe to walk on the Champs-Elysees; but he hasn't learned yet how sweetly and gently Frenchmen can riot." The same day the ambassador chortled to Judge Moore: "You will be pleased to learn that last night Offie was the guest of honor at Maxim's at a dinner given by the Marquis and Marquise de Polignac, who are the greatest snobs in France. . . . I think you will agree with me that our child is already going fast and far. The Marquise herself drove him home at midnight!"[18]

Offie was Bullitt's pet, his performing spaniel, whose moist-eyed deferential efficiency while scampering through his protocol niceties left international Society clapping. There exists an archival photograph of Bullitt escorting Sigmund Freud—whom he has pulled strings to extract from post-Anschluss Vienna—along the sooty platform of the Gare Saint-Lazare. Hanging on Freud's arm is the floppy Princess Mathilde Bonaparte, once a patient. Bullitt himself lopes along, carnation and cigarette in place, his expression impassive beneath his pale diplomatic homburg. Offie leads the parade—pinched, musing, hands in his trouser pockets, eyes casting modestly downward. His big nose is conspicuously shiny.[19]

So Bullitt launched Offie, and appreciated his increasingly knowing performance. By the end of 1937, the ambassador writes the President: "You will be glad to know" that the Duchess of Windsor's "favorite bridge partner is Offie."[20] British officials had been concerned for a time at rumors of a love interest between Bullitt and Wally Simpson—"I had an invitation from a charming Maryland lady," Bullitt had in fact informed Roosevelt early in 1936, "but I had to move on to Moscow before the date fixed."[21]

Bullitt loved to play with the notion of pert, lumpy little Offie as fascinating to the great. On June 6, 1940, at the apex of the "phony war," while French arms failed and nobody in the West quite dared to breathe, Bullitt dispatched a long, chatty letter to Roosevelt devoted mostly to the antics of the mistress of the French premier, Countess Helene de Portes. A bucktoothed, dumpy little manipulatrix with collaborationist impulses whose hold over Premier Paul Renaud helped compound the travesty, the Comtesse had never scrupled to call on political influence to supplement her boudoir requirements. "Needless to say," Bullitt informed his Chief Executive, "Offie enjoys the most intimate relations with the Comtesse de Portes, as with everyone else. She summons him for intimate conversations to her 'love nest' almost daily, and he keeps her within reasonable bounds. I have less patience than he with lack of character so that more than ever, Offie is the power behind the throne. . . . A few days ago, the Comtesse de Portes said to him that if the American Embassy had any difficulty with any department of the French Embassy or the French Army, he had only to let her know and the matter would be settled to our satisfaction at once. He tried it once and it worked!"[22]

This projection of Offie as already by way of a force in his own right wasn't entirely Bullitt's whimsy. Offie remained a presence during the complex negotiations with Polish Ambassador to France Juliusz Lukasiewicz, which helped push France, then England, to commit to Poland's defense.[23] Offie was already lining up on the Old Guard around Eastern Europe.

The summer of 1938, Joseph P. Kennedy, Jr., and John F. Kennedy, the sons of the U.S. ambassador to the Court of Saint James, Joseph P. Kennedy, arrived in Paris and stayed over first with Bullitt for a week on the Avenue d'Iena, then moved into Carmel Offie's digs on the Rue de Rivoli. "I remember Jack sitting in my office and listening to telegrams being read or even reading various things which actually were none of his business but since he was who he was we didn't throw him out," Offie reminisced long afterward.[24] Later, Bullitt arranged a stopover for the Kennedy boys in Warsaw with Ambassador Tony Biddle, and Offie personally put in a word with diplomat Franklin Gunther in Hungary. A year afterward, just as the initial confirmations of the Molotov-von Ribbentrop treaty were starting to bubble to the surface in Moscow, Chip Bohlen would recount walking into a German embassy ball in Moscow with Joe Kennedy, Jr., along with—Carmel Offie.[25]

Some months before that, according to a State Department report Bullitt himself turned in, Joseph Kennedy, Sr., was making it a "habit to call Offie on the telephone and ask for his advice whenever he considers a question of sufficient importance for Offie to decide. . . . Kennedy followed Offie's advice, and sometimes called Offie on the phone as many as four times a day." Ultimately, "Ambassador Kennedy had made large financial offers to Offie in order to obtain Offie's full-time services. . . . Offie could make $50,000 a year by becoming Kennedy's personal employee."

" 'I wish you could add the salary of the Counselor of Embassy in London to Offie's,' " Bullitt himself was quoted. "For the past year, Ambassador Kennedy has used Offie as Acting Counselor of Embassy in London," Bullitt wrote Howland Shaw at State directly. If "the Embassy in London has not made more messes than it has made, the thanks are due to Offie." As often as Kennedy calls, "if the calls were more numerous, the actions of London would be wiser."[26] Bullitt had already finagled a direct appointment to the professional foreign service for his multitalented prodigy, who ranked now as a Third Secretary.

Carmel sweated to preserve his standing with Bullitt as primus inter pares. With Embassy Counselor Edwin Wilson and First Secretary for Treasury Affairs H. Merle Cochran out of town that June 1937, "the other boys . . . are so useless," Bullitt groused, "that the Paris staff consists in reality of Offie and myself. We keep going about eighteen hours a day, and I do not know how long I can hold the pace."[27] By 1939 Bob Murphy had got himself promoted, Roscoe Hillenkoetter was called in as assistant naval attaché, and two of the Department's ablest young professionals, Douglas MacArthur II and H. Freeman ("Doc") Matthews filled out the working staff.

Bullitt still couldn't really leave anything important alone. The storm was up; history battered the windows; too overstimulated to sleep, both at the Paris residence and at the "little chateau" at St. Fermin he arranged to lease and restore in the Park of Chantilly, Bullitt routinely summoned Offie at three in the morning to smoke, play chess, listen to the radio, and get an early start on the day's dictation.

Himself a young, impressionable career foreign service officer in 1938 when he was assigned to the Paris embassy, Douglas MacArthur II remembers how staggered he was as bit by bit he came to understand the range of responsibilities Bullitt heaped on Carmel. Offie's working day began very often at four in the morning. Since he was charged with running the residence, he and the cook would show up at the Paris produce market, Les Halles, to pick over the meats and vegetables for upcoming entertainments. By eight Offie was back at his desk in the ambassador's outer office, "going over all the telegrams," MacArthur would see, "sorting out the junk and making sure everything important got onto the ambassador's desk, the stuff from the sections coming in and so forth." As time went by, matters of any but the highest importance and diplomats from secondary missions tended to get shunted along to Offie. "And then of course he did dine out a lot," MacArthur emphasizes. "He had a *vibrant* personality. We used to joke about Offie and say that each of us are born with a set of glands and had to operate accordingly on a twenty-four-hour shift. But he had three sets, and just shifted over every eight hours so he could keep going indefinitely.

"He had a mind, you know, almost like a tape recorder. And he was very interested in everything that was going on, whether it was with the staff or internationally." Paris was the center of a pan-European system of courier runs; as the diplomatic pouches came off the boat-train the people on Bullitt's staff would alternate picking up this secure correspondence and distributing it to all the missions and legations around the Continent, from Ankara to Moscow to Stockholm and down again through Berlin. In each capital the minister or ambassador and his staff would present Bullitt's envoy as complete a wrap-up of the local situation as possible, and when the courier got back to Paris "you made a complete written report about all the salient things that were of interest," MacArthur says, "that tied them to the rise of Hitler and the threat he represented." In that the embassy at that stage had no intelligence officer as such, "Offie coordinated all these observations, and appreciations, and judgements, and worked them up for Bullitt as everything came in. Of course, by then, he had many service friends and acquaintances around Europe. Tony Biddle, for example, had arranged for Offie to come to Warsaw to help him pull the embassy together when he went in there. And naturally Offie was involved in preparing Bullitt's private correspondence with Joseph Kennedy. . . ."[28]

Ubiquitous as he'd become, Carmel inched toward recognition at *every* level. "Tell Offie I count on him to prevent you from spending more than ninety percent of your capital in the next few years,"[29] FDR wrote Bullitt as early as 1937. Offie provided a foil, the inspired churl who kept the action proceeding smoothly while sustaining the important actors. On his own initiative Carmel worked up a confidential exchange with Missy LeHand, to whom he dispatched little trinkets when he got the chance which ranged from perfume to foie gras. One communication is accompanied by Offie's insistence that she "*please* sweep every document off the Great White Father's desk and place this one before him at once."[30] Bullitt was "completely run down and should have a vacation," Offie warned her at another point, urging her to inform the Boss. "He is extremly popular here and is doing a swell job," but to "live up to his reputation he is kept constantly on the go from fourteen to eighteen hours a day, and it's too much."[31]

To Roosevelt himself Offie sent along stamps from time to time. "I do hope you are enjoying Paris," the President himself ended one note of thanks. "From all reports you must be."[32]

Once Paris came under siege in 1940 Bullitt persevered until the end, and beyond. His efforts to arrogate certain *strategic* decisions to himself ultimately exasperated Roosevelt to the extent of responding to his ambassador's demands that the "Atlantic fleet" move into the Mediterranean to intimidate Mussolini with the unusually dismissive comment that the President "cannot of course give you a list of the disposition of our ships but if you knew it you would not continue fantasies."[33] Roosevelt was wearing down; at a small dinner in the White House in February the President had collapsed of a "very slight heart attack" in Bullitt's presence. Missy LeHand too was deeply fatigued; Bullitt's cavalier handling of his affair with her reportedly troubled the patrician Roosevelt; when, unexpectedly, a stroke felled this relatively young woman in 1941 the President suffered afterthoughts. As matters would develop, 1940 wasn't over before Bullitt was reduced to letting Offie telephone Harold Ickes in hopes that something important was around for the ambassador once he was back in Washington. Ickes put a word in, and Roosevelt told him frankly that Bullitt wanted to be Secretary of State—"and I can't do that"—he talked too much, and overall seemed "too quick on the trigger."[34]

As hourly the Wehrmacht moved closer to Paris and authority closed down, another delusion which started to afflict Bullitt grew out of tales that Communists were sabotaging France's defenses and intended to seize Paris before the Germans moved in. Along with his instinct to protect the city, these fears appear to have compelled

Bullitt to ignore his instructions from the State Department to follow the retreating French government and in effect appoint himself the provisional mayor of Paris. Department regulars charged grandstanding. From June 12, 1940, until the end of the month Bullitt and his picked entourage appointed themselves monitors of the occupation, intervening where they could and roving the paralyzed precincts to satisfy themselves that Nazi depredations throughout the open city remained at a minimum.

Newspaper accounts singled Offie out for having "rendered vital service to hordes of Americans desperately seeking passage home," as well as a "master at slicing through diplomatic red tape," so that, "if humanly possible, they made their ships."[35] Bullitt's cables to Roosevelt were replete with grateful good-byes and we-die-at-dawn assurances that "since the age of four I have never run away from anything."[36] On June 30 a five-car caravan directed by military attaché Roscoe Hillenkoetter finally started south. It included Robert Murphy, Offie, and Mr. and Mrs. Dudley Gilroy. Mrs. Gilroy was a childhood friend of the ambassador, and she and her British husband were entered in the documents as Bullitt's butler and maid. "She is not a maid," a Spanish frontier official charged, judging by Mrs. Gilroy's fashionable ensemble.

"Of course not," Offie piped up, never at a loss. "Don't you understand that the ambassador has a mistress?" The group crossed over.[37] Carmel Offie remained inimitable.

Bullitt insisted on abandoning the rump government at Vichy and pressing toward Washington in the face of State Department—and Roosevelt's—conviction that he could be of the most use close to Petain. Just then, as Ambassador MacArthur recalls, "Mr. Bullitt expected to be named either Secretary of War or Secretary of the Navy. Mr. Bullitt really did not, I think, want to get caught up in that kind of a thing—in which he couldn't get disengaged if it [the government in Vichy] went on in North Africa. After that the opportunity—or the possibility—of filling one of those two jobs would be gone.

"The ironic business was, while he was locked up in Paris, both posts were filled—the one by Frank Knox, and the other by Stimson."[38] Bullitt's most respected contacts—Leon Blum, Reynaud, Peladier, Guy La Chambre—meanwhile disappeared into Fascist penitentiaries.

Once Bullitt finally wangled papers from the Germans he "took off swiftly for Lisbon," MacArthur saw, "without communicating his intention to the President. When he arrived in Portugal he sent FDR a telegram to tell him that he was already in Lisbon. The President wired back that, whatever he was doing in Portugal, he should turn around and stay with the French government."

He took the Dixie Clipper to New York instead. Once back in Washington, Bill Bullitt talked very fast to explain to FDR and others that somehow he missed Roosevelt's urgent communication. But it was quickly ascertained, MacArthur remembers, "that he got the telegram the day he left."

From then on, Roosevelt remained as sociable as was appropriate whenever Bullitt stopped by. But in the President's mind, consideration of Bullitt for anything of policy-making stature had now been effectively foreclosed. Once Bullitt repatriated himself, the President reluctantly closed down his system of ambassadorial listening posts and relied to an ever-increasing extent on his compounding professional intelligence services. The era of the amateur observer in America was over for good.

❑

Even more than Bullitt, the storm of war already gathering over Europe in 1938 caught many prominent Americans eagerly trolling still in murky Fascist waters. The Dulles brothers drew their share of unwelcome attention. Afterward, buffeted from the Left, the aspiring Republican statesman John Foster Dulles would assert that "I have never had anything to do with, or even met, Baron Kurt von Schroeder," the Cologne banker who intervened personally to broker Hitler into power. Nor was he attorney for the Franco regime, not to Pierre Laval's son-in-law the Count de Chambrun, and ". . . neither I nor my firm had ever represented in any way I. G. Farben. . . ."[39] This last in particular calls for a breathtaking aptitude for technical gerrymandering, although it is conceivable that Dulles hadn't dealt directly with the doctrinaire Rhineland baron.

While admittedly never the Farben cartel's primary counsel in America, Foster had been selling his advice and influence to the eventual managers of the world-girdling chemical and explosives monopoly long before its reorganization in 1926. He'd attempted unsuccessfully to intervene as early as his U.S. War Trade Board days in 1917 in behalf of Metallgesellschaft,[40] one future Farben constituent, and advised another, Badische Anilin (BASF), in 1920 to declare bankruptcy to escape the Alien Property Custodian.[41] In the sensational aftermath, payoffs from BASF evidently reached as high as Harding's crooked Attorney General, Harry Daugherty. Midway through a trial in 1926, Daugherty's flamboyant attorney, Max Steuer, accused the shaken Dulles of having strutted about the Peace Conference promoting himself as "Lansing's nephew" while "carrying a bag"—looking for a bribe—misdirecting his client, and comporting himself overall as a "scoundrel who should be disbarred."[42]

Foster shook the whole thing off. The Farben combine did business everywhere once the cartel solidified. It promised all along to emerge a tremendous market force, potentially a superclient. Its aggressive components synthesized everything from aspirin to poison gas. There were a myriad of subsidiaries, many cloaked. As both a director and a member of the executive committee of the International Nickel Company of Canada (INCO), Dulles was a party to the 1934 market-sharing agreements between INCO and its French affiliates and the Farben concerns. Sullivan and Cromwell drafted the elaborate cartelization and joint venture agreements which divided markets among Solvay & Cie of Belgium, the British giant Imperial Chemical Industries, and Farben. Dulles led the team which brokered Allied Chemical into the cartel.[43] As Kilgore Committee witnesses complained a few years afterward, one-sided patent provisions such giants as Standard Oil signed with Farben stymied progress in the United States in vital materials from Buna rubber to synthetic gasoline, and crippled our belated rearmament. After John D. Rockefeller, Jr., Farben owned the major outside chunk of Standard Oil stock.

The Second World War overtook Foster still intervening to protect Farben's U.S. assets. As late as 1942 lawyers under Foster's direction were conspiring to block the seizure by the Alien Property Custodian of 4,725 shares of General Dyestuff Corporation, which did business palpably under the control of Farben agents.[44] Another action that invited publicity was Sullivan and Cromwell's last-ditch litigation to protect the General Aniline and Film Corporation (né American I.G.), the stepchild (91 percent owned) of I. G. Chemie, the cartel's impregnable Swiss umbrella corporation. At the insistence of Secretary Henry Morgenthau, Jr., Treasury agents seized the Farben branches, whose thousands of dye salesmen and blueprint and film processors worked closely with the U.S. Army, potentially an inestimable resource to German intelligence.[45]

The braintrust at Farben was concerned enough over the prospect of losing General Aniline to dispatch Marcus Wallenberg, Jacob's brother and co-manager of Stockholm's Enskilda Bank, to the United

States to assume title (along with the Robert Bosch branch in America) until the war ended. Working through its Wall Street friends—James Forrestal was registered as a vice president of General Aniline—the Farben management kept after the U.S. Government to permit either Walter Teagle of Standard Oil or Sosthenes Behn of ITT to function as proxies throughout the emergency.[46]

The Alien Property Custodian, Leo Crowley, was on the payroll of the New York J. Henry Schroder bank, General Aniline's depository, where Foster and Allen Dulles both sat as board members. Foster arranged an appointment for himself as special legal counsel for the Alien Property Custodian while simultaneously representing General Dyestuff's Ernest Halbach *against* the Custodian after the General Dyestuff seizure.[47] After several bewildering months (during which the unemployed William Bullitt caught a temporary commission from FDR as titular Chairman at GAF) a shuffle in place left Crowley as administrative director of General Aniline. He reciprocated by designating Farben spear-carrier Ernest Halbach chairman at GAF. Simultaneously, Dulles pressed his suit for the impounded General Dyestuff properties, and reportedly secured Halbach $696,544,000, plus interest.[48]

Foster's other public disavowals of fascist sympathies stand up no better. While never Franco's attorney, Dulles represented the Bank of Spain toward the end of 1938 when it was undeniably Franco's creature. By the later thirties Dulles was self-consciously retailoring his persona to accommodate the Christian Statesman mantle. Much of his private correspondence runs down to mealymouthed dilations, hints to annoyed apologists for Fascism that they can count on him once matters have solidified a bit. The reparations provisions he worked on himself, he feels as early as 1932, permitted "unordered plundering. . . ."[49] Solicited for the "America First Committee," during the late thirties he confesses to "a mental quandary. I am very much opposed to our getting into wars; on the other hand I am not an isolationist." He blames the "present troubles" on "the inevitable breakdown of a world order based on supernationalism."[50] He can't send money, but his wife does. While "one may disagree, as I do, with many of Hitler's policies and methods," he feels duty-bound to acknowledge "One who from humble beginnings, and despite the handicap of alien nationality, had attained the unquestioned leadership of a great nation. . . ."[51]

As early as 1935, Foster's stance transcended reality. He scorned "the time-honored expedient of postulating a 'personal devil.' Hitler,

Mussolini, and Japanese war lords in turn become the object of our suspicion, or we visualize an international ring of munitions makers plotting war for their personal profit." Held down too long, "Germany had become increasingly restless and had begun, in fact, to rearm. The time had come to release her from the treaty limitations. This was not done, with the result that Germany, by unilateral action, has now taken back her freedom of action." Dulles applauded the flexibility of Germany's neighbors in conceding what she extorted as having "immeasurably increased the possibility of continuing peace. . . ." But this was offset by their outmoded insistence that "the disarmament provisions of the Versailles Treaty continue binding upon Germany."[52]

In 1939, launched into a strange philosophical monograph called "War, Peace, and Change," Dulles disparaged the rising interventionism in the United States as merely "that form of patriotism which personifies the nation as a living being endowed with heroic qualities, who lives bravely and dangerously in a world of inferior, and even villainous, other-nation personalities."[53]

One must accommodate Hitler, who incorporates the inevitable. Dulles truckles, overexplains himself, wrings his hands tirelessly before the German Consul, before Lindbergh, before every impatient race-baiting crypto-Fascist who tracked down his office address.

Contemporaries who despaired of Foster anticipated better from Allen. Somehow nobody seemed that sure of anything. There was an amphibious quality about Allen much of the time, and even his regular collaborators couldn't tell whether he was committed to principle, or swam more naturally among stock commercial predators.

The adaptable Allen managed particularly well with the partnership in Germany between the wars which served as Sullivan and Cromwell's corresponding counsel, headed up by Drs. Heinrich Albert and Gerhard Westrick. The two energetic Germans had built a practice out of foreign corporations; Albert represented the Ford holdings in Germany while Westrick presided over the International Telephone and Telegraph properties all over Central Europe for Sosthenes Behn.

Both lawyers adapted nicely to the resurgent New Order. On assignment for the Kaiser in New York during the Great War, Heinrich Albert had doubled up as privy counselor to the German Embassy while working out of offices at the Hamburg-American Line headquarters. He directed a nationwide espionage and sabotage ring for Germany's top military attaché, the inimitable Capt. Franz von

Papen. Albert's mission ended abruptly one afternoon when a U.S. Secret Service agent light-fingered a briefcase loaded with incriminating papers while Heinrich nodded off in the New York subway.[54] Dr. Albert and Papen would remain in touch after their simultaneous expulsion from the United States, and Albert gave government work another whirl between the wars as a conservative Minister during the Cuno chancellorship.

Westrick joined Albert's office just after the armistice, a blocky, earnest workaholic normally in a perspiration from the effort of lugging around the complicated aluminum apparatus which replaced the leg he lost to a British shell. Foreigners smiled at Westrick's frenzy to satisfy every identifiable superior; Dr. Albert would dismiss Westrick as "always in the good graces of the government," any government.[55]

Even the Nazified Freiherr Kurt von Schroeder, who promoted his own nomination as director of ITT in Centraleuropa, was reportedly quite stumped at how this self-made amputee cornered so much influence. Westrick seems to have prevailed on the American ownership in no way to repatriate what cash reserves were piling up in Germany, but let the ITT profits run to fuel the Third Reich's accelerating armaments economy. When one ITT subsidiary, Lorenz, an ascendant munitions maker, demanded overnight expansion, Westrick doubled the capitalization by turning over shareholder control to Goering's Economics Ministry. Shortly before the war, Lorenz absorbed 25 percent of Focke Wulf, the major fighter-bomber fabricator.

Allen Dulles worked closely with the accommodating Gerhard Westrick; Allen's private correspondence abounds with expressions of gratitude for informative lunches at the notorious Herrenklub in Berlin or rounds of family golf together at Oberdorf. As late as June of 1939 Allen fondly assured Westrick that if he did manage to get abroad that summer he'd let the bustling German know. By then the crisis over Danzig was sizzling.

Neither Dulles brother precisely welcomed Hitler, whose mildewed origins quickly affected even the best-aired drawing room. Soon after Hitler's accession to the chancellorship Allen alluded to a "sinister impression" around Berlin. By 1934 Hitler's boycott of Jews was clearly underway, while "alien"-looking citizens were banged around routinely in public forums. Valued clients of ancient standing such as the Warburgs of Hamburg were unnerved, and murmured in their palaces of pervasive Gestapo listening devices.

Once Nazism took hold, both brothers grew cautious about speaking for the record. Hitler's medicine was virulent at times—undoubtedly repulsive toward Jews of importance—but what would it take to purge the abuses of Versailles? Allen subsequently grew fond of casting himself in the liberal's role at the celebrated partners' meeting at Sullivan and Cromwell late in the summer of 1935. Two of the senior partners were of Jewish descent, and several of the younger people were incensed that the firm still maintained formal offices in Berlin. Group resignations were bruited about, while Foster protested with uncharacteristic vehemence that the loss of even the reduced business emerging from Germany might endanger the cash flow. Blue-ribbon customers like Remington, Standard Oil, and General Motors wanted German representation. The meeting got raucous, Allen allegedly threw in with the insurgents, and once the vote went onesidedly in favor of closing down Berlin, Foster was said to have stalked off in open tears.[56]

Like many of Allen's anecdotes, this tale is pointed up by what it omits. One mammoth client Allen himself lured into the shop, Du Pont, was badgering him badly about the Nazi tyranny.[57] Another partner who ostensibly sat in on the controversial meeting maintains that once the vote was tallied Foster "fully acquiesced."[58] Allen later went so far as to deplore the U.S. arms embargo against the Spanish Republic "while its antagonists were kept supplied by certain European governments."[59] On the other hand, he refused to name these Fascist governments publicly. Meanwhile, according to his obituary in *The New York Times*, Allen had been working on both the Farben and Vereinigte Stahlwerke accounts.[60]

The brothers would remain available to clients of every conviction, anywhere in Central Europe. According to his business records, Foster visited Germany every year but one until war broke out. It told a great deal that Allen had no apparent compunctions not only about signing on as a director of the New York branch of J. Henry Schroder, but subsequently assuming the much increased work load—and banking the augmented salary—which went with the post of Schroder's General Counsel. The influential Schroder investment banking houses in New York and London remained affiliated, through blood and commercial ties, with descendants of "die Gebruder Schroeder." They included—emphatically—Baron Kurt von Schroeder, Heinrich Himmler's special angel.

An analysis by R. Harris Smith specifies that "half of Dulles' legal case load was linked to New York Schroeder [sic] investments by the late 1930s. . . ." As Smith himself suggests, the bulk was routine legal paperwork which pertained to Schroder financing from Chilean manganese to Oklahoma gas. But much concerned Germany, directly and indirectly; when, year by year, war became more probable, the Schroder bankers responded to Schacht's intensifying requests for strategic materials. Along with the fast-moving venture capitalist Henry Mann at National City Bank, Schroder evaded the U.S. Treasury strictures on Germany by engineering sophisticated dollars-for-Reichsmarks swaps to help stockpile copper and cotton.[61]

Even a superficial perusal of Allen's case sheets for the late thirties and into the forties brings up an ever-heavier incidence of suggestive items like SCHRODER TRUST: United Steel Read. Plan or SCHRODER: Swiss Agreements.[62] A Kilgore Committee inquiry pinpointed the formulation inside Schroder at Nazi behest of the "New York Overseas Corporation" to deal with foreign exchange hassles. James Stewart Martin testified that the "Chase National Bank of the City of New York, and J. Henry Schroeder [sic] Banking Corporation of New York refined and enlarged the procedure in conjunction with the German Economic Ministry . . . to effect sales of the so-called Rueckwanderer marks in the United States." Much of this foreign exchange was channeled through a cloaking entity, Intermares, (all presumably with General Counsel Allen Dulles's involvement) to underwrite German trade in South America and arrange the purchase of strategic materials which could be transshipped around the British blockade to German producers.[63]

Another of Allen's regulars, the Schroder Rockefeller investment banking combination, effected a bridging role. Partners in this 1936 hybrid were Avery Rockefeller (John D's nephew, a 42 percent participant) and the cousins Bruno (founder of the London branch) and Kurt von Schroeder (47 percent combined). Both Dulleses cleared out legal obstructions.[64] Disclaimers appeared each time the liberal press sighted in, and spokesmen repeatedly emphasized that the New York Schroder branches functioned independently of the London house, let alone the Gebruder Schroeder in Hamburg or J. H. Stein in Cologne. It remained a fact that the dominating shareholder in both J. Henry Schroder offices continued to be the majestic Baron Bruno in London, on whom his first cousin Baron Kurt still depended periodically to underwrite flagging Rhineland suppliers.

With Hitler progressing steadily, Bruno and the Baroness were actively proselytizing among the English ruling classes to broaden understanding for the new Germany. They introduced Joachim von Ribbentrop to society when he became Hitler's ambassador to Britain.

As General Counsel of the Manhattan Schroder's, it behooved Allen to examine Baron Bruno's resplendent orchid collection at his estate near Cliveden, to attend the Baron's lament over the inequities perpetrated against "my poor old country."[65] Schroeder's recriminations seemed reasoned enough compared with the fevered anti-Bolshevism of other Dulles contacts like Sir Henry Deterding of Royal Dutch Shell, now vociferously worshiping Hitler.

Bent now on proving himself, especially to the captious Foster, Allen upgraded his practice; he reserved for close friends a touch of liverishness at times. To many around Manhattan he'd become a difficult fellow to peg—tallish, inveterately chipper, a high-priced tousled party-goer whose real feelings he dissembled effortlessly.

Allen labored on undisturbed, it would appear, after two friends who worked for the British Schroeders, the State Department's former Russian specialist, Fred Dolbeare, and Rebecca West's husband, Henry Andrews, threw up their positions in the aftermath of a row over the Hitler outrages. America had no place in fights over "oppressed races and lost causes,"[66] Allen announced, but he and Foster quietly helped out with expropriated Jewish bankers and the occasional businessmen passed along for resettlement in New York. Meanwhile, Lehman Brothers had become an important client for Allen.

Expedience couldn't cover everything. Like FDR, Allen had an unnerving way of taking on the political complexion of the last forceful person he'd had a drink with. When his ex-colleague Hugh Wilson served briefly as ambassador to Germany and observed that while one may "deplore the brutality" of the maneuvering which produced the Anschluss, one "must admire its efficiency," Allen hadn't appeared perturbed. Even Foster was stunned for a moment by Hitler's invasion of Czechoslovakia, but Allen passed it off, in that paralyzingly blasé manner he favored when everybody else was raving, by observing that "Hitler's batting average in taking over states is a good one."[67] He had just run for—and lost—the Republican nomination for New York's Sixteenth District, lambasted as an internationalist. Already, setbacks brought to the fore a strain of negligent brutality in Allen's complicated makeup.

Through him, many spoke. There was that approachability and egalitarianism about Allen: he'd utilize almost anybody. He remained close personally to Hamilton Fish Armstrong, the liberal interventionist who edited *Foreign Affairs*, and ventured rather guardedly as war closed in that, while "concessions" to the rising Axis powers were overdue, if they were made "under duress" they would be "interpreted as a confession of weakness" and overstimulate "the appetites of competitive Powers . . . ," presumably the dreaded Soviets. Yet over the same months Allen maintained a close, an admiring and supportive relationship with Colonel Truman Smith,[68] the longtime U.S. military attaché in Berlin who returned so impressed by the dedication and efficiency of the German military establishment that he established a kind of peace-at-any-price coven of like-minded officers such as Albert Wedemeyer, and supplied assorted America-First spear carriers like Charles Lindbergh and Senator Burton Wheeler whatever facts and figures they needed.[69]

The Dulleses remained inexorably hostage to the past. When, in June of 1940, the German Foreign Office and the Texas Company combined forces to sponsor the United States tour of the eternally bumptious Dr. Gerhard Westrick—an opportunity to fraternize with his many American clients, and perhaps thaw out the impounded $25 billion in Axis currency and notes locked away in behalf of victims of Nazism—several reporters cornered Foster and charged him with serving as Westrick's "legal counsel."[70] Foster denied having had anything much of a professional character to do with Westrick for perhaps a decade. They'd shaken hands, certainly, but only for old time's sake.

Much of the American industrial leadership thronged to a gala hosted by Westrick at the Waldorf Astoria that season. Westrick and his soignée "secretary," the Baroness Ingrid von Wallenheim, pitched vigorously the many advantages of enhanced business arrangements with the emerging New Order. As things developed, Foster claimed "another engagement" the night of this "dinner for the German Red Cross." He personally would be "very much surprised" if Westrick was "doing anything in this country which was illegal or dishonorable." Foster sent along a copy of his responses to Allen.[71] Shortly, the FBI arranged to expel Westrick, whose activities Hoover's special agents decided were calculated to reconnoiter sites for prospective industrial espionage.

Neither Foster nor Allen could resist the needs of any imaginable client.

5

THE COUSINS

The Dulleses might waver; by 1940 William Donovan was sure what lay ahead—war!—and where his sympathies lay—with England—and he was scrambling hard behind the scenes to guarantee himself a substantial role. He lobbied, without success, for a generalship in the marines. He turned down Frank Knox's offer of Undersecretary of the Navy. Something better was coming, that he could tell, and he was less than surprised on June 21, 1940, when the British/Canadian industrialist William Stephenson sailed into Manhattan and telephoned Donovan before his luggage was off the *Britannic*.[1]

Like Donovan, Stephenson broke through to national celebrity as a war hero out of the cultural hinterlands, in Stephenson's case in service with the Royal Flying Corps, for which he purportedly shot out of the sky twenty German fighter pilots including one of the von Richtofen brothers. Rarely photographed, the wiry, pinch-faced little Sopworth Camel ace from Winnipeg had returned to England on the suggestion of Donovan's intimate, the Naval Intelligence pioneer Blinker Hall. Blinker was already worried that England was dropping behind Germany in telecommunications.

Stephenson emerged a principal in two emerging British giants, General Radio and Cox-Cavendish. A millionaire at thirty, Stephenson helped found the BBC, developed radio-telegraphy, and became a sponsor of research into a broad range of defense-related specialties which led to early British advances in atomic and laser technology, radar, the guided missile, and the turbojet aircraft. He took his place quite naturally within a clique of alert, self-made freethinkers around the disquieted Winston Churchill.

As the emergency sharpened, Stephenson placed his skills and contacts at the disposal of a new kind of intelligence entity, the Z-net, under development just then by Edward ("Uncle Claude") Majoribanks Dansey, a foul-tempered half-blind old-timer in the Secret Intelligence Service (SIS) who had been surviving one life-threatening errand or another for the King since hunting down on horseback rebellious Matabele warriors with the African Territorial Police in 1896.[2] Dansey had no patience with the chinless scions and silk-underwear Foreign Office transfers who constituted the mid-level SIS. The service's focus remained single-mindedly the Red Threat. By 1935 fully a dozen of the nineteen regular outstations of England's Secret Intelligence Service (MI6), its well-known "Passport Control Offices," were strung out like pickets along the perimeter of Bolshevism—from Tallinn and Riga on the Baltic through Warsaw and Sophia and Istanbul.[31]

As Hitler raised blood pressures, activists like Robert Vansittart, the Permanent Undersecretary around the Foreign Office, convinced the reigning Secret Service chief, "C," Admiral Sir Hugh Sinclair, that it might be just as well to rig something up to supplement the long-blown "Passport Control Office" system, something to confront Germany. Dansey concocted the Z network. There wasn't much enthusiasm among Tory ideologues for mucking Berlin over at public expense to benefit a lot of Slavs and Jews, so "Uncle Claude" solicited business backers—many of them Jewish and apprehensive—from the Oppenheimers of DeBeers and the heirs of Barney Barnato to Lord Duveen of the transatlantic galleries and the London Films monolith headed by Alexander Korda.

As informants, Dansey reached out for freewheelers with nets of their own, including the politically ambidextrous James Mooney,[4] president of the General Motors Overseas Corporation, Nubar Gulbenkian and Basil Zaharoff of Vickers, senior coordinators of French military intelligence, and Frederick ("Fanny") vanden Heuvel, British director of Eno's Fruit Salts whose status as a papal count afforded Dansey a unique entrée to Vatican archives.

Referred to by insiders as the Albany Trust,[5] the Z-network combed Germany itself and picked up Social Democrats, a smattering of aircraft officials, a cross-section of first-round resistance personalities including Carl Goerdeler and Robert Bosch, the high-handed rightist politician Gottfried Treviranus, and inevitably a scattering of German diplomatic corps career men along with a General Staff major who amounted to a back channel to Admiral Canaris himself.

Industrialist William Stephenson too started out a resource for the Dansey group. As one of the principals of the Pressed Steel Company, Stephenson provided backbencher Winston Churchill the details behind the Nazi arms resurgence he needed to take on the slack Tory leadership. In May of 1940 Churchill became Prime Minister. One preliminary executive decision had been to call Stephenson in and persuade him to pack his bags and book a passage for Manhattan. He would be supervising, indefinitely, all aspects of England's "unconventional warfare" programs throughout the Western Hemisphere. It would be Stephenson's mission to combine in his Manhattan offices both intelligence and counterintelligence functions, along with a more recent outgrowth of MI6 authorized in 1938 "to investigate every possibility of attacking potential enemies by means other than operations of military force." By genuinely unorthodox methods, what evolved into "covert warfare."

William Stephenson had very little idea precisely how much leeway the Americans would permit an alien under passport control officer cover. He'd require advice, immediately. He began his June 1940 mission with a telephone call to William J. Donovan.

Surviving annals record the avidity with which the gadabout Wall Street attorney was courted for the next few weeks by the diminutive Canadian industrialist, whose depthless slotted eyes and impassive demeanor made him the unlikeliest of suitors. Never an unalloyed Anglophile, nor immune from his generation's revulsion at out-and-out colonialism, Donovan understood that Hitler was fully capable of razing civilization to assuage his megalomania. It took a hard nut—and Winston Churchill personally was believed to have code-named William Stephenson *Intrepid*—to arrive at the end of a month which began with Dunkirk and convince strategically placed Americans that, far from beaten, the English maintained a secret edge over Germany with a whole new generation of weaponry and war-making techniques. All they really needed, even now, was a shipment of overage American destroyers, a bomber or two, and rifles for the Home Guard.

The role Stephenson envisaged for Donovan was as a sort of expert witness for FDR, a go-between through whom the British might argue that they justified a few additional political risks. "I am your biggest secret agent,"[6] Roosevelt informed Stephenson: The secrecy was crucial for a President up for reelection. At U.S. Government expense Donovan left New York by Pan American Clipper on July 14. The next two weeks, alternately spellbound and horrified, Donovan underwent his Cook's Tour of tomorrow's warfare.

Outgunned, outmanned, the English were bent on bypassing Hitler's methods. The key was information: knowing first, misdirecting the enemy, discrediting the other side's propaganda and substituting and projecting a perversion of reality best calculated to weaken and confuse. The aggressor becomes unmanned, according to Churchill's own prescription, by "an element of legerdemain, an original and sinister touch, which leaves the enemy puzzled as well as beaten. . . ."[7]

Two breakthroughs looked promising. The first was radar; the other was ULTRA. Ultra entailed a methodology for second-guessing the critical German code-keying systems, a technique to translate, through electronic means, the barrage of messages with which the constantly shifting electrical circuits and rotating drums of Germany's Enigma encryption machinery were filling the military frequencies. The British were finding themselves, as their computers evolved, in position, in effect, to read the minds of the Nazi high command. Clustered around their celebrated stolen Enigma encrypting apparatus, British mathematicians were struggling to break out patterns after each periodic key change. They worked under guard in Nissen huts scattered across the parkland below the vast, remote Victorian brick pile of a receiving compound at Bletchley Hall.

As a communications specialist, Stephenson was well aware that the United States led the democracies both in the development of encrypting equipment and in the cracking of codes. He now lobbied Roosevelt for the loan by the United States of such advanced technicians as William Friedman, whose U.S. Army team was at the point of breaking the similarly phased Japanese military cyphers (MAGIC). To insure an effective and timely exchange of strategic information between the U.S. President and the activists around Churchill, Intrepid would coordinate with—and use—the U.S. Federal Bureau of Investigation.

One tip-off to Donovan's importance was the extent to which his July reconnoitering trip to England was papered-over by layer upon layer of public, then quasi-official, finally top-level insider explanations. Donovan's true intention, obviously, would be to counter the defeatist interviews Joe Kennedy was granting by 1940 and pull together a better balanced predictive estimate. Roundly briefed in Washington, the President's ruddy envoy bounced off the plane from Lisbon on July 17 and checked into Claridge's in time for a heavy Luftwaffe attack. The next several weeks the attorney would make the rounds of officialdom up and down the island, asking questions and taking in enough every minute to tax even his bottomless gluttony for military details and recherché tidbits.

Donovan definitely had clearance. ". . . I urge you," William Stephenson had himself written King George VI preparatory to Donovan's visit, "to bare your breast to him." When Wild Bill appeared before the monarch the King himself handed over a paper the Ultra team had come up with which contained a communiqué from Hitler to his field commanders of a few days earlier informing them that he had "decided to prepare a landing operation against England" as soon as the British Air Force had been "so reduced morally and physically that it is unable to deliver any significant attack against the German crossing."[8]

The next two weeks Donovan scrambled about England. What impressed him first was the backs-up intractability of the citizenry. What couldn't be hidden were the gruesome shortfalls in standard British armaments, the handful of field guns and the 259 surviving tanks and a Royal Navy "like a fleet of old bathtubs riddled with holes,"[9] as Donovan wrote Stephenson in the midst of his tour of the military installations, with which the English must confront the forty well-equipped divisions of the Wehrmacht poised across the Channel. The pool of adequately trained fliers was depleting fast. Churchill found the English gold reserves expended. He was already gambling—and losing—much of the fleet and armor to protect the approaches to Suez.

The urgent question remained: Could the Air Force hold? Despite the "meat-grinding air attacks" of the Luftwaffe, Goering's pilots had not been able to destroy the patched-up Spitfire squadrons or knock out the widely dispersed support bases. Aprowl in his siren suit like a cigar-smoking infant, Churchill presided over his badly lit labyrinth of administrative dungeons beneath Whitehall. His reinforcements were gusto, belief in the Empire, plans, entire battalions of card catalogues, the perfection of an insidious strategy his brandy-soaked bones assured him was about to "set Europe ablaze." While Donovan was making his rounds that July of 1940, most of the functions and personnel associated with covert-warfare-oriented Section D were already moving over into yet another instrumentality, the Special Operations Executive (SOE), just authorized by cabinet directive, responsible directly to the Minister of Economic Warfare, the elephantine Laborite Dr. Hugh Dalton. The war breaking round them would obviously be played in another key.

* * *

Convinced when he left that the English would stave the Luftwaffe off, Donovan boarded his flying boat still clutching the wish list his hosts wanted pursued with Roosevelt. Wild Bill tore Washington apart making his first-hand case for England. One of Donovan's associates ransacked the Library of Congress to find a statute carried in the books since the Barbary Pirate Wars (1804–1815) to permit the President to bypass the isolationists in Congress and transfer the fifty American destroyers Churchill hankered after. Lend-Lease was presently underway.[10]

As 1941 opened, the English again picked Donovan up. Wild Bill was treated to a two-month state visit of most of the major surviving outposts of the British Empire between Baghdad and Madrid. In Belgrade, where at that moment the regent, Prince Paul, was hours from opening the borders to the Wehrmacht to spare the Yugoslavs a slaughter like Poland's, Donovan informed the monarch that it was the policy of the Roosevelt administration to assist all nations with resolve enough to fight for independence. Donovan hunted down the restive Yugoslavian Air Force Commander General Dusan Simovic and handed him a secret telegram from FDR personally, which emphasized that "the United States is looking forward not merely to the present but to the future, and any nation which tamely submits on the grounds of being quickly overrun would receive less sympathy from the world than the nation which resists, even if this resistance can be continued only a few weeks."[11]

Nevertheless, Paul joined the Axis; just after the Nazis invaded Greece to rescue the Italians, Commander Simovic brought off a coup in Belgrade with the help of the subversion specialists of the SOE and infuriated Hitler into tying up main-force Nazi air and armored units. The Yugoslavs were crushed—17,000 died in Belgrade alone—and hope of assistance from the West wafted away in the havoc. By egging the Yugoslavs into engaging the Wehrmacht, Churchill and the SOE jarred Hitler's timetable, compelling the outraged Fuehrer to delay his assault on Russia from May 14 to June 22. Winter overtook the Germans stalled in summer uniforms before the blizzards of Moscow. To contrive this stalemate in the East the back of Yugoslavia was broken, and unanticipated armies of partisans came ominously to life. "You big nations are hard," Prince Paul later breathed, "You talk of our honor, but you are far away.[12]

The SOE turned stomachs across the regular establishment. This tramp's dinner of hoodlums and radicals built into a force in excess of 1,500 in thirty-three schools, with air and naval capacity. The spring of 1942, punctuated by the gruesome commando losses at Dieppe and the German success in "turning" key members of the

Dutch resistance (Operation North Pole), ushered in a government-wide disenchantment with "unconventional warfare." Invasion fears were passing, and Churchill had replaced the impetuous Dalton with the more plodding Lord Selborne. Lord Selborne reoriented the SOE toward tactical services in support of the vast armies now training in the West.

Once he launched Donovan, the limber little Stephenson bore down in the United States. America provided a fall-back base, a "junction box" from which to protect shipments as Cash-and-Carry formalized into Lend-Lease, direct the advanced training of Special Operations Executive specialists, screen transatlantic communications, and—should it come to that—help prepare a haven to which the government might repair and the Royal Navy sail in case the British Isles went.

A forty-four-year-old workaholic whose cold, absorptive manner turned sprightly when the occasion required, William Stephenson moved in quickly. He helped call down the barrage of press attention on Gerhard Westrick which ended the bluff lawyer's stateside promotional tour. Stephenson turned up once to view the cramped, dingy side room of the British Passport Control Office in Exchange Place and never went back. Intrepid was an uptown operator. The self-styled British Security Coordinator went on to spacious quarters high in the International Building at Rockefeller Center, the legendary Room 3603.

Secure on the premises of an old farm, at Oshawa near Toronto, Stephenson organized a crash course in covert warfare methodology. He arranged for raid-hardened SOE Baker Street Irregulars from the London headquarters to demonstrate to more than 500 trainees, U.S. and Imperial, how much copper wire was necessary for slipping off a sentry's head. Young female volunteers even of adventurous spirit looked thoughtful while Scotland Yard smuggling specialists graphed out which recesses of the vagina might best conceal a pod of microfilm throughout a body search. The latest in paramilitary gear—pens which squirted cyanide, booby traps indistinguishable from camel dung until somebody drove over one or attempted to kick it away—got handed around during classroom breaks. Toronto alumni bobbed up throughout the worldwide combat zones.[13]

Broke as England was, even clandestine war involved brutally mounting costs. Why not stir into existence some kind of civilian intelligence organization within the United States Government? This they might big-brother, borrow from, lean on, patronize.

Virtually since he disembarked he had been "attempting to maneuver Donovan into accepting the job of coordinating all U.S. intelligence," Intrepid cabled "C,"[14] Stewart Menzies. Convincing FDR how urgent was the need for some kind of American clearinghouse came next, Stephenson would remember, and "I enlisted the help of several avenues of influence at the White House. [Newly appointed U.S. Ambassador to Great Britain John] Winant and [Robert] Sherwood were the most persistent and effective, I think."[15]

Not that Wild Bill much needed goading. Through most of the war the proliferation of would-be intelligence agencies around the capital provided the captivated Roosevelt his intrabureaucratic tank of sharks. Along with the venerable and well-fortified G-2 section of the U.S. Army and the Office of Naval Intelligence, the FBI had taken up responsibility for subversion prevention throughout the Western Hemisphere while young Nelson Rockefeller grabbed status as Coordinator of Inter-American Affairs. Elements of various Departments, from the Library of Congress to the regional desks at State to the Secret Service and the Treasury's IRS and Alcohol, Tobacco, and Firearms sections—all felt instantaneously endangered; every bureaucrat simmered at the very suggestion of this umbrella agency the President presented Donovan on 11 July, 1941. The Office of the Coordinator of Information! Whose information, *their* information?

The Office of the Coordinator of Information (COI) lasted eleven chaotic months. Congregating throughout the middle floors of the decrepit National Institute of Health building on Twenty-fifth and E (through which surged odors from the ongoing animal experiments above, concentrated along the stairwells), the hard-bargaining corporation lawyers and insurance brokers and random academics from every part of the haute-bourgeois forest soon overenergized the headquarters, in the words of a regular army intelligence officer who innocently dropped by, into something which "closely resembled a cat house in Laredo on a Saturday night, with rivalries, jealousies, mad schemes, and everyone trying to get the ear of the director." Radio Berlin quickly termed the effort "fifty professors, twenty monkeys, ten goats, twelve guinea pigs, and a staff of Jewish scribblers. . . ."[16]

Donovan liked it that way. We now must "play a bush league game, stealing the ball and killing the umpire,"[17] he urged Roosevelt, leading into his plan to combine psychological warfare, sabotage, special intelligence, and guerrilla operations under one command. He had in mind, clearly, Intrepid's arrangement in America, free of backstairs rivalries and sustained in large part by Stephenson's off-camera relationship with Churchill. But Roosevelt wasn't prepared yet to risk his intelligence credibility beneath the menagerie on E

Street, and hedged his commitment by authorizing yet another—a much better hushed-up—information-gathering system presided over by the American journalist John Franklin Carter and funded by Stephenson's—and Donovan's—unremitting nemesis at State, Assistant Secretary Adolph Berle.[18] When a journal full of classified data about U.S. defense industries turned up in British hands, and produced British bellyaching about the sharing of armaments, the President was quick to guess the source, and lopped off COI access to word of upcoming production programs.[19]

After four disillusioning decades, even the very fondest among Wild Bill's protégés concede that, as in administrator, he tended to be . . . uneven, at the very least. Much like the checker-playing dog, the wonder wasn't really how erratically he played, but that he managed at all. For all the mature Donovan's plump, puckish ways—a manner one acquaintance would characterize as "bland of eye, butter soft in voice, and composed of equal parts of fire, iron, and pink leather"[20]—Donovan's gifts were tactical, and he was mousetrapped easily.

One early aide, Atherton Richards, compared "Bill Donovan's method of running an organization" with "pouring molasses from a barrel onto the table. It will ooze in every direction, but eventually he'll make it into some sort of pattern."[21] Well before it expired, half of the COI had landed on the floor. Soon after starting up, Donovan recruited the towering, emotional playwright Robert Sherwood to lead the overseas broadcasting wing of COI, the Foreign Information Service. A speechwriter for FDR and White House habitué, Sherwood's back went up at the suggestion that misleading material—lies—might now be strategically planted in Voice of America broadcasts to confuse the enemy. With that Sherwood began conspiring with Archibald MacLeish of the Office of Facts and Figures and a wide assortment of other well-positioned flacks and lyric poets.

Whatever Donovan's bureaucratic disabilities, he had the wit to install in Washington several of the partners in his Wall Street firm to carry on business while he kept scrambling. Otto Doering moved down and ran things day to day, smoothing the internal waters and fending off the ever-marauding interservice coordinating committees. James Murphy, summoned unceremoniously to drop everything and "keep the knives out of my back," built up the counterintelligence side into perhaps the first truly professional element inside the uneven "clandestine services," a mechanism to watch and appraise all others.[22] Ned Buxton proved dependable as Donovan's regular deputy.

Novices; transplants; yet even their earliest scrawled-over schematics show virtually every part in place, the prototype from which American intelligence would never really deviate, each segment of the espionage and operations continuum which would develop before the decade ended into the CIA. Most advanced right away was the Research and Analysis Division, Donovan's "College of Cardinals," directed by the touchy, stentorian Harvard history professor William Langer. Valuable to the Joint Chiefs for coming up overnight with landing beach overlays and Axis rail-center buildups, Langer's people "continued to suffer from a sense of being second-class citizens," Bradley Smith would note, and "were usually the last to find out what was going on in O.S.S. and invariably received small allocations of money and personnel."[23] Rank, too, came slower than elsewhere. This prejudice stemmed partly from the traditional condescension to academic woolgatherers by men of affairs.

Donovan's accessibility to any recommendation startled traditionalists throughout the government. The idea was field-tested of dropping tremendous numbers of bats on Japan—based on the mistaken belief that the Japanese were morbidly terrified of bats and would disintegrate psychologically. Only the unexpected discovery that the creatures froze almost instantly upon being released into the stratosphere and shattered across the desert like so many refrigerated wine glasses ended that inquiry. Similarly, unwillingness by Air Force brass to risk valuable fliers scotched one proposal to shower Berchtesgaden with pornographic leaflets studiously devised to overload der Fuehrer's suggestive nervous system, and render him insane.

Wild Bill's worried coevals saw no practical limits. As late as June of 1943 Donovan's most dogged counterpart, the U.S. Army's adamant G-2, General George Strong (who authorized his own durable espionage and covert backup, "The Pond," under Col. John V. ["Frenchy"] Gromback), lit into one attempt by Donovan to define his organization's role by way of a "Field Manual." This "hydra-headed" thing, Strong stormed, was "constantly at war with other Government agencies," and repeatedly had made the effort to reduce the military intelligence units "to the status of reporting agencies and research bureaus for the O.S.S." It ignored clear restrictions, defining its mandate in language "devoid of reference to moral considerations or standards," and claimed the wartime right to assume "the ethical color of its enemies in all particulars." The manual in itself, Strong sniffed, was another wily "lawyer's paper," concealing purposes with words.[24] Revised virtually to a pamphlet, Donovan's truncated manual appeared briefly in 1943.

* * *

Slowest to gain momentum would be the operations people. Those weeks of trooping the lines in Britain left even the indefatigable Donovan with, at best, little beyond an inkling of what Anthony Cave Brown would term "the paraphernalia of secret service—the hidden bank accounts, the meaning and importance of cover, the importance of security, the need for rapid telecommunications, loading a silenced pistol or setting a tire burster, or the difference between codes and ciphers." From how to rent a safe house to legalities behind setting up dummy corporations in neutral capitals as conduits for agent payoffs, from selecting a cutout to fusing a road mine—the expertise looked daunting.

Donovan depended on impulse. His initial pick as Secret Intelligence—espionage—manager was a balding Sorbonne-educated hunchback named Wallace Banta Phillips, a businessman with commercial informants from France to the Balkans. In 1939, Phillips doubled as a special assistant to the director of U.S. naval intelligence, from where he volunteered his "K Organization" to Donovan in August 1941. The scraps of gossip Phillips remitted from London were expensive but irrelevant; worse, Donovan's English backers found Phillips too secretive, too much of a "loner" to abide in such a sensitive role, and Donovan eased him out and replaced him with the penetrating though conciliatory David K. E. Bruce.[25]

This gratified the British: They'd educated Bruce themselves. Just as the COI was tottering to its feet, William Stephenson lent Washington his personal aide, Lt. Comdr. Ian Fleming. In turn Fleming's replacement was the SIS careerist Col. Charles H. ("Dick") Ellis, a sturdy, genial Australian-born survivor of the intelligence wars from Paris to the Soviet border "without whose assistance," David Bruce remarked afterward, "American intelligence could not have gotten off the ground in World War II." Largely on Ellis's recommendation, Donovan retained Ellis's "old friend," the hard-liner Polish Lt. Col. Robert M. Solborg, to build up his operations side.[26]

Solborg was pushed forward by Ellis as the ideal prospect to set up an SOE-style subversive-operations capability for the COI. After a long autumn boning up in the SOE, Solborg concluded that he would be dramatically out of place even attempting, as he grumbled subsequently, to "reconcile" himself to the "haphazard ways and stuntlike propensities of Donovan's procedures."[27] Donovan promptly replaced Solborg with the more manageable Hearst publisher Col. M. Preston Goodfellow. Solborg himself Donovan restationed in February of 1942 as the COI representative in Lisbon.

By winter of 1942 the COI was struggling for its life. Donovan had been sidelined in the New York St. Regis after a taxi accident threatened that a long-contained embolism in his war-torn knee might break loose and travel toward his heart. With Wild Bill down, his opponents at State, along with Nelson Rockefeller and J. Edgar Hoover, kept at the President in hopes of convincing him to cannibalize the COI and crimp Donovan's ambitions—early. Simultaneously, the "Welles-Rockefeller-Hoover Axis" within the government (backed up by Budget Director Harold Smith and Attorney General Biddle) kept drumming away in memos to Roosevelt about the ninety unauthorized agents Donovan was alleged to be running in Mexico—in reality, a handful Wallace Phillips carried over, largely as a favor to the Office of Naval Intelligence.

This bright red herring—joked up in Washington as "The Case of the Famous Ninety Humpty-Dumpties"[28]—was typical of the bureaucratic produce heaping fast in Donovan's vestibule. He lacked the protection of either a political or an administrative cover. Bureaucrats everywhere labeled Donovan a kind of universal "thorn in the side" (at least) who "knew no bounds of jurisdiction," and was attempting to override policy by training up his personal "private army."

His own aides found him anything but Machiavellian. "He is so honest," wrote James Grafton Rogers, Donovan's Planning Group chairman, "so aggressive, so scattered, so provocative. Day by day I see him getting near elimination because he excites anger."[29] Never one to ignore the politics pressing in around himself, FDR set down his signature on Executive Order and Military Order of June 13, 1942, which severely root-pruned Donovan's proliferating COI. The "white" (open) propaganda staff, more than 800 of 1,600 employees, now became the independent Office of War Information under the liberal newscaster Elmer Davis.[30] Wild Bill was hard put to justify his more than $10 million budget from the President's secret $100 million emergency fund. His astute military rivals had boxed Donovan into a niche of his own on the flow charts as a well-watched subsidiary of the Joint Chiefs of Staff. The espionage and covert warfare remnant the executive order rechristened the Office of Strategic Services and Wild Bill Donovan, promoted to Brigadier General, was quite fortunate to survive as Director. Roosevelt's thunderbolt had struck while Donovan was in London. It provided a "perfect example of the bureaucrat's classic fear of being reorganized while out of town,"[31] notes the CIA historian, Thomas Troy. Wild Bill had earned his star the hard way.

6

BURIED BLISSFULLY IN SWITZERLAND

One find of Donovan's who regularly brought hackles up around the District was his New York branch manager, Allen Dulles. Eleanor Roosevelt would complain in a memo to FDR that Allen, a recurring personage in "Bill Donovan's outfit," was "closely tied up with the Schroeder [sic] Bank, that is likely to be representative of the underground Nazi interests after the war," one of "a great many people who are pretty close to the business side."[1] State Department professionals were alarmed to find Dulles engaged almost overnight in quasi-diplomatic maneuverings "practically unlimited in concept or financial scope,"[2] especially in the Balkans, while subject to dubious advice from a string of discredited German political figures and far-right hotheads he himself eagerly legitimized.

Signing on with the COI had seemed to promise the uneasy attorney a fresh start. The Allen Dulles Donovan originally coaxed into the Coordinator of Intelligence appeared a man divided. Wild Bill had known the Dulles brothers much of his life. Their background was similar, in a way. They all reached Manhattan from upstate New York families of no immediate distinction. If once his betters tended to write Donovan off as a bumptious self-promoting Mick, the Dulles boys arrived exuding a whiff of the parsonage. Both eked through

Princeton, then moiled for degrees from declassé law schools. Donovan expected the amiable if notoriously flightly Allen to muddle along indefinitely subject to the pompous Foster.

Both lawyers were delegates from New York to the Republican convention of 1940, where Foster's patron, Thomas Dewey, lost out to the upstart Willkie. Allen must have slumped as he dragged out afterward, because halfway through the throng in the lobby of their Philadelphia hotel a hand suddenly banged Dulles hearteningly on the back while beside his ear Donovan's soft, beguiling tenor recommended that the two might perhaps adjourn to the bar to hash things over a bit.[3]

Donovan had barely returned after the first of his red-carpet tours of the British Empire at War; what with the welcome he got from FDR personally and plaudits from Stimson and his people for rigging the "destroyer deal," Wild Bill was high on himself. Allen Dulles was not. Apart from domestic strains, he squeezed along day by day between his misgivings about Hitler and duties as an officer of J. Henry Schroder. There was a price in self-respect to pay after mornings spent scrounging around in Schacht's behalf, followed by a board meeting at the Council on Foreign Relations given over to bemoaning an era, as he and Hamilton Fish Armstrong wrote in 1939, in which "Americans count the preservation of liberty here and the survival of human liberties in other countries as of only trifling importance in a world given over to Machtpolitik."[4]

Stress showed. Foster could be patronizing, glaring at this supple kid brother who barely glanced through some associates' drudgery before slipping out early to pursue an assignation or a tennis match. Foster's briefcase went home overloaded every evening. Beneath his surviving forelock Allen's tall face looked wary and cornered now a lot of the time: There was a fixed, unresponsive cast to his lidless eyes lately which bordered on the sinister.

He understood an uncomfortable amount. Foster continued to crayfish; Allen, as William Bundy notes, "was a strong interventionist by then, but I think he had the feeling that Foster and the German clients of the firm had pulled his coattails."[5]

One way to escape these contradictions might be a crisis-justified leave of absence. War certainly appeared inevitable. Wild Bill recurred flatteringly to Dulles's performance in Switzerland during the first war. Why not come in at the New York end and help him assemble a coherent intelligence outpost? Dulles joined the Office of the Coordinator of Information in October of 1941, took over the Manhattan division, and evicted a diamond merchant and a guild of organists from the twenty-fifth floor of 30 Rockefeller Plaza to set up working areas. Spencer Phenix came aboard, along with Murray Gurfein and Arthur Goldberg. Available one floor below, William Stephenson and his British imports quickly demonstrated to Dulles that there was more to the intelligence game than flat-footed information gathering. "He had much to teach me," Allen later conceded, "and I picked his brains." The British, among themselves, referred to the Dulles enlistees as "Rough Diamonds, Ltd."[6]

Even then Allen Dulles seemed incomparably less parochial than most transplanted Wall Streeters. There was a wised-up, donnish quality about this middle-aged lawyer, a willingness to cock his head and fiddle with his well-worn Doctor Grabow and avoid final judgments. Nobody was too bizarre to imagine for *some* role. Donald Downes, the pudgy, iconoclastic prep school instructor who had come into the COI from British intelligence, exonerates Dulles while castigating "the nervous supervision of certain ex-diplomats and scaredycats who infested OSS in its early days."[7] Under Dick Ellis's tutelage, David Bruce was coordinating worldwide with "other companies in our behalf."[8]

Dulles began with Germany. He ordered an encyclopedic shakeout of who was who across the Nazi hierarchy under the direction of the escaped diplomat Baron Wolfgang von und zu Putlitz, surviving on his uppers in New York after a trying decade throughout which his aristocratic patent and guise of rustic simplicity had kept him alive on diplomatic assignments while he filtered secrets from Ribbentrop's classified traffic to Jacob Beam at the U.S. embassy along with the SIS.[9] Labor lawyer Arthur Goldberg (already in regular touch with survivors from transport-worker unions throughout Europe, and abetted by contacts in the Jewish Labor Committee) pieced out an anti-Hitler émigré group to cover resistance operations. Goldberg's original nominee to chair the committee had been the Socialist psychologist Dr. Karl Frank, a Popular Front booster and enthusiast of Eleanor Roosevelt's.

On Dulles's strong recommendation, the chairmanship was slated to go to Dr. Heinrich Bruening, in exile at Harvard. The bemused-looking Catholic-Party "Hunger Chancellor" who preceded Hitler was a familiar of both Dulles brothers.[10] This opened the way to import from Canada a controversial Bruening cabinet minister from the old days, Gottfried Treviranus, once Minister of Occupied Territories. The ultranationalist Treviranus had rattled around for years between the low-lying outlaw "Black Reichswehr" and quite a medley of terrorist Freikorps bands.

Treviranus had stayed in touch with a selection of grudge-nursing reactionaries still active in the Nazi government and fulminating over the 1934 Night of Long Knives. His list was headed up by the Gestapo's well-placed Arthur Nebe and Hans von Dohnanyi, a close and conscientious staff director in the Wehrmacht's military intelligence section, the anxiety-ridden Abwehr, now packed with closet dissidents under its ambivalent chief, Admiral Wilhelm Canaris. Treviranus insisted that his contacts awaited no more than a signal from him to exterminate the Nazi leadership. Treviranus had a way of pressing his signet ring on staffers around the Rockefeller Center suite, assuring everybody who heard him out that merely at the sight of his revered family seal the peasants of Prussia would erupt en masse.[11]

There was a simultaneous flirtation with the defunctive Black Front of Nazi renegade Otto Strasser. In time—just in time, evidently—rumors of these antics reached State Department observers, already persuaded that COI was coordinated, in Lord Halifax's telling aside, like "a disorderly day's rabbit shooting." Senior State Department officials brought pressure to dump these "dangerous Communists" and "hopelessly reactionary generals and Junkers."[12] Even the risk-loving Donovan concluded that Dulles was much too impressionable for high-level administrative decision making. Ready as his sympathies appeared, he lacked political resonance. His was a laugh, as the British intelligence chief Sir Kenneth Strong later remarked, which "always seemed to enter a room with him," yet "Even when I came to know him better in later years I was seldom able to penetrate beyond his laugh, or to conduct any serious professional conversation with him for more than a few sentences."[13]

As 1942 proceeded Allen saw well enough that he was wading among discredited projects, arguing for unfunded proposals. Clover was scratchy again, quarrelsome and then frantic at moments at confronting the realization that, as Allen's sister put it, "There were at least a hundred women in love with Allen at one time or another, and some of them didn't even get to close quarters with him."[14] After years of splurging on a piece of expensive jewelry each time she discovered Allen straying, Clover confided to a friend, she "had to stop because I was running through the family fortune."[15] In this matter too the convivial attorney was increasingly divided against himself, and tension triggered gout attacks.

He'd request overseas duty. Donovan had compounding doubts now about turning over anything with too much autonomy to Dulles, and pressed him earnestly to take on the West European Secret Intelligence desk, already established in London under David Bruce.

That did seem flattering, Dulles would allow, but he'd already reconciled himself to a "less glamorous post, but one where I felt my past experience would serve me in good stead." Frankly, he would not work any longer "with a lot of generals looking over my shoulder."[16] Through Spencer Phenix, Dulles was prospecting by August for a "trading position" which might allow "for the assignment to Berne of some additional American personnel."[17]

Against State Department grumbles, Dulles wangled a slot as "Special Assistant to the United States Minister" at the Swiss capital, Bern. Thus it had developed that the landings in Africa overtook Allen one quick hop ahead of the converging Wehrmacht; in Bern, Dulles prayed, his life would ignite again.

The war howled in; for two years Allen Dulles remained "buried," as he put it, "in Switzerland." Blissfully unaffected by Donovan, nosy OSS accountants, his judgmental older brother, even Clover's pained remonstrances, Dulles found himself a palatial flat in the neighborhood of the cathedral along the ancient cobblestoned Herrengasse. Most of the staid fifteenth-century mansion was leased to the Belgian Legation. Dulles's street entrance was inconspicuous along a commercial arcade. Unofficial visitors could find the servants' entrance, accessible after a circuitous climb among grape arbors overhanging the river Aare, which rimmed the foothills of the Bernese Alps.

Too late by then, Dulles acknowledged, to push into Germany "foreigners or exiles from the Third Reich with forged papers who could make contacts of value and then get out with their stories. . . ."[18] Let malcontents find him. He was barely installed before a notice appeared in the *Journal de Geneve* identifying him inaccurately if tantalizingly as "a personal representative of President Roosevelt" attached to the U.S. Legation to look after "special duties."[19] Dulles ordered a brass plaque engraved with his name and mounted beside his door at 23 Herrengasse.

Allen Dulles popped up, one British professional reported, "like a man with a big bell, who rang it to attract attention, saying 'I've got plenty of money and I'm willing to buy information.' "[20] He pursued the obvious leads. The Bolshevik-loathing head of Sullivan and Cromwell's Paris offices, Max Shoop, had parlayed his aristocratic acquaintanceship into informants from the French military's underground Deuxième Bureau. Shoop relocated to Geneva, where Dulles soon had him watering his parched Parisian contacts with dollars in return for fifty pages a week of sophisticated political feedback.[21]

The Vienna correspondent of Sullivan and Cromwell, Kurt Grimm, was waiting in Bern when Dulles's train pulled in. Along with an introduction to his tailor, the portly bourgeois had compiled a list of sympathetic financiers and industrialists throughout the Nazi hegemony. Grimm was already servicing the SIS. As quid pro quo to reassure his friends in German military intelligence, Grimm indicated to Allen, he'd like something tradable bearing on U.S. aircraft production figures. Dulles handed over projections guaranteed to terrify the Luftwaffe.[22]

Grimm was in touch with notables up to the ousted Chancellor Kurt Schuschnigg, languishing in a Nazi dungeon. Schuschnigg vouched for the American to principals of the "Committee of Fourteen," a vital subgroup in the Southeast European "Dogwood" chain. This ring of Viennese anti-Nazis included the concert pianist Barbara Issikides and the director-general of the Semperit Rubber empire, Franz Josef Messner ("Cassia"). Under Dulles's cautious control, Messner slipped through targeting information—pinpointing Semperit competitors, OSS cynics noticed—which ranged from "shadow factories" to plans and photographs of launch sites for V-rockets at Peenemuende. Before long the acid Colonel Dansey found out that prime sources were drawn to—and outbid by—this cosmopolitan American; he admonished his head of station in Bern, Frederick "Fanny" vanden Heuvel, to chat Dulles up if he liked but "above all keep his nose away from our files."[23]

A glib Viennese Feldwebel, Fritz Molden, picked up whatever messages Grimm's contacts could provide from time to time and carried them to Dulles jammed into the bottom of his rucksack across the snowfields of the central Alps. A Vienna journalist's son who barely escaped a Nazi punishment battalion before piecing together resistance nets out of far-flung family connections across Italy and into the Balkans, the big, spirited boy turned up without warning and very often laid over a day or two with Dulles in his sumptuous hideaway on the Herrengasse.

Dulles welcomed Molden's coltishness. Just short of fifty, Allen was now fighting the temptation to cast himself once and definitively as another Society lawyer. His persona was identifiable enough: the greying hair, closely cut, grizzled and quite thin at the crown; his extended barrister's face, dignified by a well-clipped flat triangle of a boardroom moustache. After years of high-priced hand holding, people remarked the shallowness of Allen's attention at moments, that "hollow mirthless laugh"[24] when news wasn't welcome.

In Switzerland Dulles's decompression was very quickly palpable. He took a small boy's delight in the routines of the conspiratorial. In his baroque study, behind the massive red draperies while a log fire leapt hypnotically, Dulles loved to prod and invite confidences from even the most innocent of arrivals. After an excellent meal, over brandy, his bad foot elevated—nothing escaped Allen's curiosity. His visitors carried away the echo of Dulles's gusty, infectious chuckle. Even truly malignant informers succumbed to promptings and cajoleries by this ebullient American. It seemed to matter very little in the end that Dulles's Swiss cook was reporting to Ribbentrop's local lackeys,[25] that even his rheumy little valet and butler, Pierre of the bristling moustaches, kept current a log of arrivals and departures for Fanny vanden Heuvel.[26]

Dulles's eyes, many would report, had a way of twinkling whenever the gossip descended. He relished his confessor's role, especially to the younger men. Always a productive partygiver, Dulles put the Legation's cellar to use by stewing together such anomalies as Junker resistance personality Adam von Trott zu Solz and the parlor pink Noel Field, turning loose the overemotional Gestapo attorney Hans Gisevius upon his late-war assistant Tracy Barnes, whose remorseless naiveté could absorb anybody's suspicions. Another stalwart of Allen's midwar salon was Emmy Rado, the perky wife of a local psychiatrist who sold him her World Council of Churches intermediaries as one avenue for stirring up Christian Socialist discontent around the Reich.

Emmy's shrewdness tickled Dulles. Women continued to relax Allen, who foraged for diversion whenever his overbooked timetable permitted. The underemployed Mary Bancroft would one day base her memoirs on Dulles's hit-and-run performances. He took up, for a seaon, with Toscanini's daughter, Wally Castel-Banco.[27] The wholehearted appetite for life his years on Wall Street left constrained, conflicted, now broke out stronger than ever before. A continuous current of risk and trust and affection was revitalizing the stagnant lawyer. They came, to him, from every imaginable faction. He now touched history unfolding here, minute by minute. Across the blockaded ocean, Foster was growing dimmer by the month.

At best an absentminded father, Allen found in himself a knack for arousing the devotion of subordinates which left him reborn by 1945 into "The Great White Case Officer." The entrancement of covert would remain only too powerful, Dulles confessed to Robert Murphy in 1951, and "Once one gets a taste for it it's hard to drop."[28]

Allen Dulles's splashiest espionage production was ultimately a walk-in. This find, Dr. Fritz Kolbe, awaited a skeptical Dulles a few minutes after an August midnight in 1943 in the spare bachelor apartment of Gerald Mayer, an American Office of War Information propagandist and erstwhile Sullivan and Cromwell client. Mayer took Kolbe seriously after the local British military attaché, Col. Henry Cartwright, shooed away the diffident German civil servant.[29]

Dulles respected the intensity with which this stumpy, tonsured Beamter, straining from his chair, proclaimed that the only hope of redemption for him as a believing Catholic now lay in betraying what he knew, turning over a culling from the incessant cable traffic that crossed his Foreign Ministry desk. He prayed the 186 carbons in the swollen, pleated briefcase on his lap would serve as testimony to his dedication.

Until the war ended Kolbe bounced between Berlin and Bern, his diplomatic pouch crammed with strategic documents which brought to light everything from Economic Ministry difficulties in bootlegging tungsten from Spain in orange crates to Himmler's coup preparations to depose Hungarian Premier Nicholas Kalay. In time Dulles presented his number-one agent in place a microfilming camera which Kolbe set up in the storeroom of the clinic of the illustrious Dr. Sauerbruch, one of Hitler's physicians. Sauerbruch's nurse was Kolbe's girlfriend. Most of Kolbe's choicest items could never be trusted to the scrambled radio-telephone broadcasts which went out nightly over Swiss commercial lines. As Kolbe's product approached 1,600 messages, the encryption problems overwhelmed Dulles. Allen invited vanden Heuvel's staffers in.

The stuff piled up. Kolbe was branching out, extending his little cell of the Schwartze Kapelle in the Aussenministerium to prelates and military acquaintances, comrades from his Wandervoegel days, businessmen, ultimately twenty-two trustworthy members of the "inner circle" who fed the doughty agent, loaded him with mail drops, warned him of raids by the SS's deadly Sicherheitsdienst (SD). Kolbe covered his unremitting requests for courier duty with tales of a romantic conquest in Switzerland. . . .

In London, of course, all this looked set up. Dansey—whom even the large-spirited David Bruce denounced as "a crusty old curmudgeon who could not stand interference or rivalry from the Americans—indeed, we could hardly do anything right in old Claude's eyes"—sneered at the windfull as "clearly a plant."[30] It aroused his contempt that "Dulles had fallen for it like a ton of bricks."[31] Dansey worried that such a success would tempt the bumptious OSS arrivals to "run riot all over Switzerland, fouling up the whole intelligence field."[32]

Washington wasn't much happier. Military specialists with blades out wrote off the entire submission as disinformation, a stunt by von Ribbentrop, a scattering of chicken feed. Kim Philby was seconding Dulles's efforts at the London end while experts collated this "Boston Series" against the Enigma/ISOS gleanings. A great deal matched, precisely, and filled in blanks enough at times to permit the cryptographers to break down the German diplomatic codes far faster than normally. But suspicion was keen, and Donovan lumped in these "George Wood" messages, as Kolbe's telegrams were code-named, with Dulles offerings altogether when he took his Bern chief down a peg by speculating that some sort of Axis countercampaign in the intelligence area was perhaps to blame for the "degeneration of your information which is now given a lower rating than any other source." This came six months after Kolbe initiated deliveries.

Subtler analysts, reviewing this tremendous file, suspected broader, thematic possibilities. ". . . Could this [sic] data have been planted with a viewpoint which could influence operations in such a way as to affect [Germany] vitally?" queried Ferdinand Belin, Dulles's Washington case officer. He had in mind Kolbe's tendency to load up the cable selections with forebodings about Red Army breakthroughs into Eastern and Central Europe. To induce among intelligence consumers, as Anthony Cave Brown specified, ". . . the impression that the only power capable of stemming the Soviet onrush was Germany, that if the Western powers destroyed Nazi Germany, no power would be left to resist the Russians, and that unless the Russian advances were checked, there would be enormous problems in the future."[33]

Had all this material been edited to awaken spectres in the receptive Dulles mind? Belin alluded rather gingerly to "gambles . . . for the purposes of attaining some greater advantage. . . ." Dulles sloughed this off. Kolbe's motives were "persuasive"; the faction of the Schwartze Kapelle with which he associated included "Leobe, previously president of the Reichstag," Dulles informed Belin, as well as "Dr. Walter Bauer, who was previously the German manager of the Prague-Petchek interests."[34] He could himself testify to the solidity of Bauer: Allen and his brother Foster handled legal matters for the Petchek family of Prague for some years. Equally compelling: it took all the persuasiveness Dulles could muster to convince Kolbe to keep his distance from the Underground, which Dulles had reason to believe was penetrated by the SD.

Yet Kolbe was by no means the naif he presented himself as. One of Dewitt Poole's questions to Kolbe in September 1945 elicited the news that as early as 1943 Kolbe had journeyed to France to tip off an SIS source in Alsace that somebody "close to Churchill" was leaking to Berlin by way of Stockholm. This disclosure upgraded Kolbe's reputation in England, and enhanced his overall credibility. Kolbe (and his backers) hankered after a wider audience.

Waiting up for Dulles's arrival in Bern was Gero von Schulze Gaevernitz. Gaevernitz represented a hybrid, the son of a liberal Quaker Reichstag politician whom Dulles met as early as 1916 and a sophisticated Jewish mother. The preceeding generation's refinement came through in Gaevernitz's distinctive widow's peak, his ready, deferential smile. Gero's sister married Edmund Stinnes, older son of the precocious Hitler backer and megacapitalist Hugo Stinnes; Edmund had been excluded from the Stinnes iron and coal combine and bided his time with academics on the Haverford faculty.

As the twenties proceeded Gaevernitz jumped back and forth between the Ruhr and Wall Street. He acquired an economics doctorate and styled himself an "investment counselor." Reinforced by his conciliatory manners, contacts from the Warburg bank in Hamburg to the vaults of Basel, and impressive bilingualism, Gaevernitz landed a job in Manhattan as an associate of the Equity Corporation. One of his fellows there was Ellery Huntington, a confidant of Donovan's; Gaevernitz maintained a close transatlantic association with the German financial expert Edward von Waetjen, whose mother was American, and himself married into a branch of the Rockefeller family. In 1936 Gaevernitz took out U.S. citizenship papers.[35]

In 1939 Gaevernitz's parents resettled in Switzerland; Gero, still in and out a great deal, now made his base in Bern, from where he watched over his brother-in-law's property near Ascona. When Allen Dulles appeared with a letter of introduction from Huntington, the gently spoken, beautifully brushed Gero, a bit past forty, impressed Dulles as ideally suited to function as his surrogate throughout the German-speaking émigré community.

It is certainly conceivable that Dulles wasn't up to speed on Gaevernitz's checkered involvements. Gero was a finagler by instinct, a high-style commission peddler. As late as October of 1941, Gaevernitz listed his occupation in Switzerland as agent for Schildge Rumohr, Inc., a New York dummy corporation known subsequently as Transmares (the financing for which Dulles himself had expedited through J. Henry Schroder), and identified by the Department of Justice as a front for circumventing the British blockade with strategic materials for embattled Germany. Gero pocketed a 30,000-franc payoff from Maritime Suisse for inducing North German Lloyd to permit the cross-registration of a vessel from Finnish to

Swiss flag, then sanitized the money in Lisbon through the notorious E. V. D. Wight. He continued to oversee Stinnes holdings in Germany and Switzerland.[36]

These involvements were obligatory, Gaevernitz would explain to Dulles, "as additional cover for my trips to Germany and for my contacts with Germans."[37] He required commercial bona fides to mask his services to British intelligence; then, after war broke out, he rummaged widely at the behest of Brigadier General Barnwell Legge, the U.S. Military Attaché in Bern. Gaevernitz had indeed rendered, Legge later wrote, "most valuable service by gaining contact with prominent German industrialists and business men who visited Switzerland."[38]

Whose agent *was* Gero? A confidential postwar memo refers to an interrogation of Dr. Wolfgang Krauel, until the Reich collapsed the German Consul at Geneva. Krauel had unhesitatingly ticked off the roster of "former Canaris men" in Switzerland—Hans Bernd Gisevius, Max von Engelbrechten, Graf Auersperg, von der Muehle—and specified that "Canaris sent these men here to make contact with the Americans; they were ordered by Canaris to work through von Gaevernitz. C. took this step because he *early* became pessimistic about war's outcome."[39] Eddie Waetjen and Theodor Strunck too joined the Canaris delegation in Switzerland. Years later, congratulating Dulles on his appointment as CIA director, an intimate of Canaris wrote Allen: ". . . I have known since 1942 how highly Canaris esteemed you. Even at that time Canaris ordered me to align myself with Dulles as soon as possible. I was also in touch with one of your most capable co-workers through a very clever banker. I was able to obtain from your staff, without any difficulty, some information very important for us. I would prefer to say nothing more about this now."[40]

Messengers from the subtle, lisping little admiral who presided over German military intelligence, they came as envoys, confident of their welcome. Dulles's abiding link with what he subsequently dubbed the German Underground was the chronically malcontented Hans Bernd Gisevius, that vast, floppy, walleyed Prussian handed along from rightest security expert Rudolf Diels to Hjalmar Schacht to the elusive Admiral Canaris himself. A confirmed Stahlhelm reactionary with financial ties to the Lutheran Synod, "the fanaticism of Gisevius" proved instrumental, Bruening had warned Dulles, in subverting a decisive faction of the Nationalist Party between 1931 and 1933.[41] Gisevius had hung on as a Gestapo lawyer before Canaris parked him as a vice-consul in Zurich.

There, Canaris appointed Gisevius his representative to Madame

Halina Szymanska, the widowed Polish cutout through whom his military intelligence apparatus selectively leaked political insights to vanden Heuvel and the SIS.[42] Dulles was soon sneaking the immense, baby-faced German into the drawingroom at 23 Herrengasse. They arrived at an understanding to keep the agile American up to date on the succession of plots on Hitler's life. Hopefully, through his purported access as "President Roosevelt's personal representative," Dulles might benefit both their nations by conveying to Washington's ruling circles the settlement the insurgents were preparing to tender to the West.

They'd reviewed Dulles's portfolio: as representation for the Enskilda Bank of Stockholm, Allen and his brother had argued for the Wallenbergs as late as 1940, when Marcus Wallenberg appeared in New York and attempted to immunize the American-held certificates of the Robert Bosch Company. Later on Allen pleaded with Marcus to publicize at least a selective reference to ". . . your contacts and to my contacts with the [Resistance] group prior to the July 20 putsch. Unless there are some local reasons at your end of which I cannot judge here, it might be well to get this out in the open a little more. . . ."[43]

Like the ambivalent Wallenbergs, magneto king Robert Bosch—whose nephew was a principal inside the I. G. Farben leadership—covered quickly once prospects darkened. "I had official information then," Dulles would divulge to a correspondent, "which I subsequently confirmed, that the Robert Bosch Company was used by Goerdeler as a cover for many of his activities in connection with the organization of the German plots against Hilter."[44] On official Reich passes one heir to the vast Good Hope industrial empire, Alfred Haniel, importuned Dulles in Bern repeatedly.[45] Dulles's work at J. Henry Schroder was appreciated, as was his closeness to Thomas McKittrick, long Allen's legal client, currently president of the Bank for International Settlements. The BIS was originally a creature of German interests which Hjalmar Schacht set up to offload reparations responsibilities, and through the war years an invaluable clearinghouse for Third Reich prizes across Europe and abroad.

Following a leisurely meal, Dulles had conducted the giant Gisevius into his study where—alternately poking at the log fire and fussing with his indispensable pipe—he found this emissary from Canaris every bit as pedantic, quirky, hidebound, and self-absorbed as mutual friends insisted. Gisevius—whose defective vision now forced him at times to keep craning forward, sometimes all but falling across the relaxed American—announced at the onset that he would not "demean myself by being a common thief, stealing trivia from office filing cabinets."[46] Dulles interpreted the big Prussian's awkwardness as emblematic of his authenticity.

Gisevius remained Dulles's primary link to the plotters; as early as February of 1943 Gisevius appeared to vindicate himself with word from Berlin that several of the Legation ciphers and one of Dulles's private codes had recently been cracked by Nazi cipher teams.[47] A year later—interestingly enough, just as Admiral Canaris lost control of the Abwehr—Gisevius tipped Dulles off that Vice President Henry Wallace had been confiding since 1942 in his brother-in-law, the Swiss Minister in Washington, Charles Bruggmann.[48] These gleanings had reached the Abwehr promptly, for many months, although Gisevius never mentioned this scandal while Canaris was in place and benefiting.

Once Gisevius seemed endangered, Eddie Waetjen started working the Berlin–Bern circuit; when he fell under suspicion Theodor Strunck couriered messages. Strunck died after July 20, 1944, in the SS mop-up. Dulles kept a rein on Gisevius by arranging for his occasional mistress, the forthright Mary Bancroft, to drag out the translating of the Prussian's interminable memoirs. Meanwhile, Dulles hoped to interpret for himself the diplomatic subscript which underlay Gisevius's mission.

Both Washington and London continued to discount the "Christian-West" approach Allen warmed to, which emphasized a coup against Hitler, his replacement by a government of nationalists free of the Nazis's hallucinated racism and counterproductive ethnic slaughter, military collaboration with the "Anglo-Americans," and the "continued holding of the Eastern (Russian) front," as this matter was touched on delicately in Dulles's careful editing of the official treatment of his sojourn in Bern. "His superiors in Washington," the treatment stressed, "advised him that it was unlikely a group of this size and character could exist clandestinely in Germany."[49]

The truth was, the plotters around Goerdeler (code-named *Breakers* by Dulles) and important figures in the Nazi government (and particularly the SS) were edging toward pretty much the same gloomy anticipations. Goerdeler and his bumblers were permitted their antics precisely because important Nazi functionaries dismissed them as ineffectual, yet speculated that something helpful could yet emerge from their ill-disguised flounderings. Historians have regularly traced parallel peace initiatives by Abwehr activists and pessimistic SS officers. Often there were distinctions emphasized which turned on very limited differences.

Hans Gisevius, for example, had retained his rank as a *Sonderfuehrer* in the SS. When the hesitant Himmler's liberal conduit to the bourgeois resistance, the lawyer Carl Langbehn, began to bruit about the possibility of an early, compromise peace throughout the neutral capitals, the sympathizer he usually dug out on his Swiss stops was Gero von Gaevernitz.[50] As early as the spring of 1939 Langbehn was visiting London regularly, he told his expatriated ex-law professor Fritz Pringsheim, "because he belonged to a strong wing in the [Nazi] party which recommended an agreement with England."[51]

Most of Langbehn's faction couldn't quarrel with Nazi priorities at that stage—rearmament; repudiation of reparations claims; incorporation of the Saarland and Austria and Czechoslovakia as well as Hitler's intention to recover by bluff or invasion the Eastmark; pruning back the Jews, especially on the bench and throughout the academic professions. It awaited the Blitzkrieg accompanied by unadorned broad-scale butchery to arouse the drawingroom theologians whose voices reached Dulles now. Only atrocities enough—and on a grand enough scale—could swamp the traditionalist agenda.

Langbehn's approaches to Gaevernitz interested Walter Schellenberg especially. Within the SS the SD (Sicherheitsdienst) looked after more sensitive matters, like doctrine and subversion. As the SD's Amt VI (International Affairs) chief, Schellenberg amounted to Foreign Minister for the SS. He coveted the Abwehr's stagnating apparatus. How long could Canaris last? Schellenberg's bow lips and dark, insinuating glances had already won over the susceptible Economics Minister, Funk. Schellenberg honeycombed Funk's bureaucracy with commercial informers.[52]

As early as winter of 1942 Schellenberg hinted to the uneasy Himmler that he now intended to launch discreet soundings. These ranged from Abram Stevens Hewitt in Stockholm to Theodore Morde, a *Reader's Digest* correspondent in Ankara. Inevitably, Schellenberg discovered a go-between with lines to Allen Dulles, and early in 1943 a series of discussions ensued.

Thus opened the contested exchanges between "Mr. Bull" (Dulles) and "Mr. Pauls" (Prince Max Egon zu Hohenlohe-Langenburg).[53] Max Hohenlohe had long been an international-set acquaintance of Dulles, a bustling, polished socialite from the Sudetenland whose status as a minor royal drew customers for munitions from the Skoda works, a concession Schellenberg helped him snag. Hohenlohe already bestowed over vast landed properties in Spain after marrying into the Hapsburg family; he was currently hedging his political future by traveling on a Liechtensteinian passport.

A Canaris familiar, Prince Hohenlohe caught Schellenberg's attention early in 1942 by sending the rising SD official his own jaundiced appraisal of prospects in Europe. With the all-seeing SD Commander Reinhard Heydrich assassinated at the end of May, possibilities had obviously widened for the opportunistic Schellenberg. Barely thirty, scarcely beyond his baby fat, the Amt VI chieftain resembled an SS doll decked out in death's-head campaign hat and tailored parade uniform.

With Schellenberg's cautious sponsorship Max Hohenlohe trotted out a line of provisional peace proposals, first with the British Ambassador Sir Samuel Hoare—always a soft touch—and the sympathetic American Counselor of Embassy William Walton Butterworth (an intimate of George Kennan's since Princeton), with Vatican sympathizers, with Fritz Klein (a friend of both the Dulles brothers), and—evidently at the recommendation of American negotiators in Lisbon, where Kennan and Colonel Solborg were stationed—with Allen Dulles himself toward the middle of February 1943.

Exactly what was agreed upon has become a matter of dispute, largely because the SS summations of the exchanges appear to have passed through Russian hands on their way to the archives, after which the USSR News Services waited until 1948 and the upheavals of the Cold War to put them out as dispatches. Nevertheless, much of their thrust is borne out by related RSHA paperwork, private journals, and intelligence files from a variety of sources.

What seemed most scandalous at the time was Dulles's reported pique with "outdated politicians, émigrés, and prejudiced Jews." The hope in America was that these malcontents could be resettled, perhaps in "Africa." As one in close touch with Vatican circles, Dulles maintained, he strongly urged the "German bishops" to "plead Germany's cause" in America, keeping in mind that "it had been the American Catholics who forced the Jewish-America papers to stop their baiting of Franco Spain."[54]

This has the look of crumbs spread upon the water. Pronouncements alternated with rich meals in a Liechtenstein chateau; Hohenlohe bit by bit exposed his quasi-official status as a spokesman for SS elements within the German government who now looked beyond the "wild men" in control.

What casts a longer shadow is the outline of Allen's geopolitical ideas. The peace he has in mind, Dulles indicates, must avoid the excesses of Versailles and permit the expanded German polity to survive, Austria included and possibly at least a section of Czechoslovakia, while excluding all thought of "victors and vanquished . . . as a factor of order and progress." Within this decentralized nation the importance of Prussia must be reduced, to ward off for the future—Dulles is quoted directly here—the " 'inwardly unbalanced, inferiority-complex-ridden Prussian militarism.' "

The resultant "Greater Germany" would backstop the "formation of a cordon sanitaire against Bolshevism and pan-Slavism through the eastward enlargement of Poland and the preservation of a strong Hungary." This "Federal Greater Germany (similiar to the United States), with an associated Danube Confederation, would be the best guarantee of order and progress in Central and Eastern Europe."[55]

Schellenberg wasted Hohenlohe's expense money. The Unconditional Surrender pronouncement at Casablanca a month before was ringing still: not even a memo pertaining to Dulles's post-Wilsonian conceits seems ever to have reached the Joint Chiefs of Staff. Dulles did pass along appeals from the diplomat Adam von Trott zu Solz to heed recent "Breaker" signals.[56] An Abwehr officer, F. Justus von Einem, later claimed to have sat in on a carefully prepared meeting at Santander in Spain in the summer of 1943 during which both Menzies and Donovan agreed to Christian Wester terms as recapitulated by Canaris personally.[57] If this exchanged occurred, Donovan kept it quiet.

Such exploratory talks pointed well beyond the uproar of the moment. "I have known Max Hohenlohe since the days of the war," Dulles assured a lawyer at Sullivan and Cromwell in 1965, apropos a legal favor requested by the aging prince, "when he worked with me on some rather difficult and delicate problems."[58] The exchanges in Liechtenstein amounted to a reconnoitering.

7

UNORTHODOX DIPLOMACY

To naysayers around Roosevelt, exploratory exchanges with scoundrels like Hohenlohe epitomized the sort of back-channel mischief making Wild Bill routinely sponsored. Donovan prized his own thick skin, and even he was bridling as flaps multipled throughout 1943. The expansions of wartime meant more administrative responsibilities and fewer battlefield diversions for the overworked Director. The Coordinator of Information had presided over hundreds; by summer of 1943 the OSS numbered 4,500, headed fast toward the perhaps 14,000 employees with which it finished the war.[1] Donovan's imported legal cronies—Atherton Richards, James Murphy, Otto Doering, Ned Buxton, Edwin Putzell—still ran the office machinery. But more and more, military professionals like General John Magruder and Admiral William Standley took control at planning levels.

An in-house memo prepared for Otto Doering in August of 1943 states baldly that "no one in the organization, with the exception of those who are very close to the General, can put his finger on anything concrete that the organization has accomplished."[2] That same year one of Donovan's more hardheaded aides, James Grafton Rogers, defined the OSS as " 'the bargain basement' of the military services . . . full of remnants and novelties, all underground."[3]

At heart still very much a small unit commander, Donovan ignored channels and continued to encourage his men in the field to sell him directly, feel his enthusiasm. There was a meeting of the OSS executive committee the autumn of 1943, which produced a memorandum proposing that the organization slough off its catchall character and "confine its future activities to those of intelligence, special and morale operations, and counterespionage," in hopes of concentrating its recources. More pointedly, the "tendency to accentuate the para-military (if not military) activities of the OSS is detrimental to its primary mission of intelligence."[4] Even Roosevelt was restive. He confided to Adolf Berle he'd thought recently about assigning Donovan to "some nice, quiet, isolated island where he could have a scrap with some Japs every morning before breakfast . . . and would be out of trouble and entirely happy."[5]

Donovan fired back. An agency for the conduct of unorthodox warfare is "not a bank and should not be run as a bank . . . ," he instructed Magruder. "It must be made up of a diversity of units and while certain fundamental principles must be kept in mind the whole organization must be a flexible one to meet any particular ends. . . ." With coevals from J. Edgar Hoover to Harold Smith at Budget waiting for this fighting beetle to stop skittering long enough to squash, internal insurgencies were no help.

Donovan scratched around widely. Despite a Presidential prohibition on "black chamber" activities, OSS installed its own codebreaking subsection. Donovan and David Bruce worked up independent exchanges with several of the exile governments in London—Polish, Czech, Norwegian, Dutch—and talked officials at the British Ministry of Economic Warfare out of data Roosevelt was denying Donovan in Washington.

Then, following through on an early 1943 executive order which authorized a full, energetic internal security capability, Donovan talked his way into an unprecedentedly close working relationship between James Murphy's young counterintelligence unit and both MI5, British counterintelligence, and the counterintelligence staff of MI6. Already scraping, the British were apprehensive about the vast counterespionage responsibilities the upcoming invasion promised. In return for OSS men and materials, the British now proposed to throw open their legendary ISOS London archives, that worldwide register of suspects, those precious card catalogues. Furthermore, OSS counterintelligence specialists were authorized to "study and summarize British decodes of any [Axis] intelligence message," including raw Abwehr decryts.[6]

With this single breakthrough the OSS was made. One declassified OSS after-action study states: "Here was a field in which OSS would have otherwise been unable to participate effectively at all. The British provided files, sources for information, operating techniques, trained assistance and facilities which proved indispensable. It would have taken OSS perhaps decades to gain by itself the experience reached in only two years of British tutelage, and to build up the extensive files it was able to copy from British sources."[7]

What made this possible, apart from Stephenson's way with Churchill, was the luxurious operating budget Donovan retained from FDR. Still pipelining on "emergency money"—i.e., Congressionally unmonitored discretionary funds, already up by 1943 from $10 million to $35 million annually, and ballooning fast—the OSS was viewed by drudges throughout the bureaucracy as, in Buxton's language, "a mysterious Midas who exudes as entertainment rare viands, priceless vintages, steam yachts, beautiful women, and collects earth shaking secrets."[8]

Bill Donovan had turned a flank on almost the entire U.S. military community. The secretary to the Joint Chiefs, General John Deane, conceded that Donovan's zoo was "more apt" to access important intelligence materials than "either the ONI [Office of Naval Intelligence] or the MIS [Military Intelligence Section]."[9]

Donovan now demanded operational parity. In many sectors the British, with apologies, withheld access to their airfields and facilities on grounds that, lacking coordination and advance liaison, everybody risked wasting resources and blowing agents. Donovan soon carried his case directly to the Joint Chiefs.

The underlying British proposal, Donovan pleaded in his brief, ". . . suggests 'coordination' and 'agreement,' but as employed here the word 'coordination' means 'control' and 'agreement' means 'dependence.'

"Physical circumstances permit the British to exercise complete control over United States intelligence. . . . The habit of control has grown up with them . . . through their relations with refugee Governments and refugee intelligence services. . . . We are not a refugee government."[10]

American counterintelligence was the immediate beneficiary. By June of 1943 those low-profile, meticulously trained young security specialists under James Murphy were emerging as a genuinely professionalized elite. That June they forsook Secret Intelligence (SI) and became a branch in their own right, the dreaded X-2. Whenever somebody trusted the wrong friend, or blurted out too much in an unfamiliar bed, or lost a shipment of bullion, it was the X-2 team which squeezed the truth to the surface. X-2 made arrangements of its own with the refugees and worked up a liaison with the suspicious French the disapproving British couldn't match. When Allen Dulles in Bern persisted in dealing through a source X-2 suspected, insists one authority, arrangements were reportedly made through MI5 assets to have him "terminated with prejudice"—iced.[11]

It was a unique schooling, and even during those break-in months notice was being taken of a tall, young, blackly tailored ex-law student, Captain J. J. Angleton, already difficult and authoritative, whose stoop-shouldered, cigarette-bedizened funk was redolent of the class grind in a very good boarding school. The fellow had talent, along with larger appreciations, and already "earned my respect," notes the omnipresent Kim Philby, "by openly rejecting the Anglomania that disfigured the young face"[12] of the American services.

Puzzled at the time, it may have been Kim Philby himself who sensed most truly what motivated his superiors to embrace these disheveled Americans. A lot is implicit in Donovan's dismissal of English midwar restraints as "short-sighted and dangerous to the ultimate interest of both countries." Philby fleshes this out: "Stephenson, like many others, saw that the creation of such a service was, in the long run, inevitable. . . . What is beyond doubt is that the decision in favor of cooperation doomed the British services, in the long run, to junior status."[13]

❑

Military balances were shifting; for Dulles in Bern, peace proposals, like secrets, pooled up in any direction he set a foot. Allen maintained a formal office well down the Herrengasse from his flat, close to the Legation, where he and his assistants could direct the continuing flow of refugees and volunteers. The clientele turned over daily, from paper-mill impresarios to the inspired Pole, Stanislaw Appenzeller. The head of Swiss intelligence with the Axis services,[14] Colonel Roger Masson, kept Dulles abreast of Schellenberg's fitful soundings, his attempts to gauge whether his resident agent Wilhelm Eggen's rather downbeat reports about Dulles's receptivity might possibly be overdrawn.[15] Allen got together regularly with Captain Hausemann, chief of the shadowy Buero Ha, and cultivated Major Waibel, in charge of Swiss lines to the Western powers. Before long the German

Ambassador to Switzerland, Theodor Kordt, turned up in Allen's wide pockets.[16]

In due course Dulles happened on Halina Szymanska, and left her to Gisevius and the SIS. He built up his own sources around the Polish Legation, who kept him in contact with the underground spreading fast in Poland.[17]

Allen turned his charm on anybody with threads to pull. It happened that the son of a gentle American Quaker biologist he'd enlisted as an informant in 1918, Dr. Henry Haviland Field, hightailed over the border within hours of Dulles. This second-generation agent, Noel Field, headed up the Swiss-based relief operations of the Unitarian Church. A towering, messianic administrator, Field had been out to redeem the world since graduating from Harvard in 1926. Soviet intelligence recruiters once worked on Field while he was still plugging along in the State Department. Field preached of Communism, but he was quirky and headstrong—his flat a welter of neglected cat boxes around which he stumbled proclaiming his devotion to bucolic nudity and free love to the point of deranging his phlegmatic wife, Herta. Noel bullheadedly turned away the invaluable German desk assignment the GPU was plaguing him to grab while pushing through a transfer into the League of Nations Secretariat so he could jump in on the Republican side of the Spanish Civil War. By then Moscow Center seems to have despaired of making anything subterranean out of the feckless Quaker. But Noel kept bobbing up, and over the years Field helped the Russian apparatus out with a broad selection of incidental favors.

During the Vichy phase Field directed a sizable Unitarian relief center in Marseilles, where astute Communist functionaries like Paul Merker were quick to seize on Field's ingenuousness to shunt the shipments of food he received from America to comrades in Petain's internment camps. His staff soon filled in overwhelmingly with Party members. Field oversaw an underground railway in and out of Switzerland; another Unitarian Service Committee employee, Dr. Robert Dexter (secretly affiliated with the OSS), directed Field to Allen. Before long Communists as high in the Party as Leo Bauer were tapping the submerged membership in Germany for details of factory production and the extent of bomb damage and even—as in Bauer's case—concealing their illegal involvement with the American after the Swiss police rounded them up. Dulles handed out $10,000 to Communist paymasters through Field, and afterward insisted privately that he got back more than his money's worth.

At one stage Field introduced a pair of pro-Tito Yugoslavs to Dulles, whom Dulles would later credit with having helped initiate the shift of Allied resupply away from the royalist Mihailovic. After Field had extracted the top Hungarian apparatchnik Laszlo Rajk from an internment camp at Vernet, Dulles helped recycle him and several friends back to Budapest by way of Yugoslavia.

When, shortly after the Stalingrad surrender, the Russians soldered together the Free Germany Committee, a loose-jointed, heavily propagandized Popular-Front-style exile movement spearheaded by captured German General von Seydlitz and Field Marshal von Paulus and calibrated to provoke defections among the Eastern Wehrmacht, Noel scurried around Switzerland canvassing for presentable liberals for Moscow. Anybody he came up with who also seemed both willing and informed enough to extend Dulles's feelers he provided without obligation to the OSS.[18]

Word of this Free Germany Committee was guaranteed to chill the entrails of Dulles's more familiar clientele. It suggested how completely the Soviets were preparing to remachine the traditional order. Senior Nazis panicked; one midwar Dulles report spoke of a deal pending between the Gestapo and the German Communist Party.[19]

The conspirators must *do* something, change something, present the West an unblinkable demonstration of intent. The attempt on Hitler's life now swelled in importance. Gisevius kept Dulles abreast of the plotting, and he informed Washington as "The Breakers" progressed. Dulles entered into a pattern of stratagems intended to pick loose the secondary Axis allies—elements of his envisioned Danube Confederation—ahead of the advancing Red Army.

Most vulnerable was Hungary. For all the zest with which Admiral Horthy and his entourage had wolfed down scraps of Poland and Czechoslovakia along with stretches of the Carpatho-Ukraine, something in the very single-mindedness with which the Nazi commanders went about the enslavement of the East put off the peppery, horse-loving Magyars. Contacts with the SIS remained unbroken. The Reds annihilated the First Hungarian Army at the battle of the Don, after which grumbling spread. Feelers to the Allies from Budapest commenced in the spring of 1943.[20]

Just before the end of 1943 the Hungarian military attaché in Turkey, Lieutenant Colonel Otto von Hatz, indicated to the chief figure in the OSS net which covered the Balkans, the controversial Czech "Dogwood," that major personalities among the General Staff in Budapest wanted to switch sides. Donovan, always enthusiastic, consulted Dulles, who advised that "fence-sitting is an art highly developed by the Hungarians," and sent along word that Kolbe's cables suggested leakage. Slow down, Dulles urged.[21]

The OSS's Istanbul station chief, Lanning McFarland, continued nevertheless to waltz Hatz around in hopes of trading off Axis military secrets in return for vague political assurances. Then Dulles reversed himself. His ministerial contact in Bern, Count Bessenyey, by now a trusted asset who freed up gasoline for the U.S. mission, had hinted that the Horthy regime was ready to chance a break with Hitler if the United States would commit to keeping the Red Army out. Donovan's pending scheme to drop three OSS officers into Hungary to prenegotiate with the chief of Hungarian intelligence, General Ujszaszy, had now became practicable, Dulles wired on March 3, ". . . under circumstances which, to my mind, curtail the risks attendant on any project of this nature. . . ."[22]

Donovan delegated Arthur Goldberg to come up with the team to insert. Goldberg recruited Guy Nunn, just then a radio operator but normally the research director of the United Auto Workers, Al Suarez, and as chief liaison officer Colonel Florimond du Sossoit Duke, a Time, Inc., executive. Code-named "Sparrow," Duke had superintended an earlier attempt to schedule an exchange of views with Admiral Canaris. After a layover in Algiers the three stood by at Brindisi, and at approximately 2:30 on the morning of March 19, 1944, an RAF Halifax dumped the trio into Hungary just over the Croatian frontier. A representative of Hungarian military intelligence collected them by noon and drove them at once to Budapest, where they were lodged comfortably in open cells in preparation for their interview with General Ujszaszy.[23]

Not only the Hungarians were keeping their eye on Operation Sparrow. Schellenberg's Amt VI coordinator for southeastern Europe, SS Sturmbannfuehrer Wilhelm Hoettl, knew well in advance that Duke and the other Americans were on their way. Apart from the Dogwood leak, Hoettl had been monitoring the wireless negotiations between Bern and Washington. Cryptographers for the Hungarian military had broken a number of OSS cyphers.

Like his mentor Schellenberg, the gossipy, rather epicene Herr Doktor felt small compunction about giving history a shove whenever nobody was looking. He personally, Hoettl later divulged by way of a stage aside, regarded the arrival of Duke and his team as "tremendously important news. I strongly hoped that through this man we would be able to establish the link between my pro-Western friends in the Hungarian service and the West. Of course, we first had to capture him, get him out of the clutches of whoever might have him, and then turn him back to the West." Duke might then return "with important messages not only from the Hungarians but also from those among my German contacts who were yearning for a chance to realize their own political conceptions in the South East."[24]

Radio intercepts by the Hungarians had already alerted Hoettl to "the existence of a man by the name of Dulles who sat in Berne and the kind of reports he sent to Washington. Not all of them, mind you. But enough. We all admired Dulles. . . . I admit that I soon made it my prime personal task to make contact with Mr. Dulles." Hoettl finagled this initially through an Austro-Italian industrialist named Westen and then himself visited Switzerland a number of times, employing as a go-between the German air attaché and Abwehr designee, Prince Auersperg. "My service to the Dulles office," Hoettl added, "consisted in delivering intelligence information, not about Germany, as I surely want to make clear, but about what we had found out about the Russians."

Long convinced that Hungary had remained a hotbed of decadent aristocrats and their degenerate Jewish advisers, on receiving word of the Sparrow team der Fuehrer unleashed Operation Margarete I—the occupation of Hungary. Hoettl rushed to a senior Foreign Office official named Hewel, Ribbentrop's liaison with Hitler's command post on the Obersalzberg, and through him slowed down the pathological Fuehrer for fear of igniting a minor Balkan war behind the Eastern Front.[25]

According to Arthur Goldberg, the Gestapo liquidation specialist who had mashed up Czechoslovakia after the Heydrich assassination, Dr. Otto Geschke, agitated for the chance to work over the Sparrow mission. The terrified General Ujszaszy fled to the Regent's protection. Meanwhile, Hoettl moved the Americans to Berlin for extended—time-buying—interrogation, after which they passed into Red Cross jurisdiction and sweated out the final year of the war at Colditz castle near Leipzig.

In years to come, Duke himself attempted to determine whether it was his mission alone which precipitated the subsequent Hungarian landslide. His troops in place, Hitler unleashed Otto Skorzeny to extract the Regent from Budapest in October; the beefed-up German administrative presence quickly scheduled the extermination of Hungary's several hundred thousand Jews. Allen Dulles seemed fuzzy about the episode afterward, although he did emphasize to Duke that "no missions of this nature were mounted by me or my

Berne office without full clearance and coordination with Washington headquarters and under their instructions."[26]

The OSS was out there rampaging on its own. Lawrence Houston, who wound up General Counsel of the CIA during its start-up decades, later searched government archives, and concluded that "There is no indication that the Department of State, the Joint Chiefs, or the White House were involved in the planning and execution of this mission." Apart from the procurement of undefined "military intelligence," Houston observed, the optimum goal here was "to test the bona fides of some Hungarian government officials who had made contact with the Office of Strategic Services in Switzerland."[27]

Were the Soviets informed? "Well," Arthur Goldberg recalls, "we relied upon Allen Dulles, as with the Italians, for instance, to communicate to the Russians what was going on." Whether he actually did, Goldberg didn't know. In any case, the whole thing was still in the "embryonic stage. Had the Germans permitted them to surrender, I'm sure we would have had to advise the Russians. . . ."

After 1941 Yugoslavia remained a favorite target, Churchill's ever-tempting "soft underbelly" of southeastern Europe. Soft-underbelly extrapolations suffered as the war played through from the ever-expanding control by Josip Broz—Tito—of much of the Serbo-Croatian hinterlands. Whatever the P.M.'s pipedreams, the strapping ex-Comintern revolutionary had no intention of permitting an imperialist expeditionary force to coopt the Balkans. According to Hoettl's memoirs, by early 1943 the Partisan leader believed—with justice—that it was London's intention to reimpose the monarchy. Stalin informed the Partisans that the Western Allies envisaged landings along the Adriatic coast, and urged Tito to hedge his situation through secret discussions with the German High Command. A courier from the Partisan chief turned up at the headquarters of the Consul General in Zagreb, the Austrian General Glore von Horstenau, Hitler's plenipotentiary to the fanatically reactionary Croatian state the Nazis installed. Horstenau ruled through close collaboration with the well-informed Superior General of the Jesuits, Count Wlodzimierz von Ledochowsky.[28] Information was reaching Dulles that Horstenau was accessible, that he intended to survive defeat.

Mopping up after Stalingrad, the Soviet ruler concluded that the Western Allies were prepared to allow the Germans and the Red Army to trash one another indefinitely. He sponsored the Free

Germany Committee to open up the possibility of a second wartime reconciliation between Moscow and Berlin; he initiated a regular channel of negotiation with the Germans in Stockholm—the Peter Kleist exchanges. All this was probably to prod the Allies, although Allen Dulles certainly took the whole thing seriously and made it a regular subject of his long, prosy reports to Donovan.

Donovan joined Allen in leaning toward proposals which promised to hive off Hitler's Eastern allies in time to forestall Stalin. In an August 20, 1943, memo to Brigadier General John Deane, Secretary to the Joint Chiefs, Donovan reported that "The anticipated collapse of Italy intensifies the fears of the Balkan ruling classes that the Axis will be defeated and that Soviet Russia will dominate Eastern Europe." Donovan proposed to "capitalize on those fears" and exert "certain subversive pressures" on Bulgaria, Rumania, and Hungary which "may induce these countries to withdraw from the war, or at least to cause difficulties for the Axis."

Donovan urged the establishment of OSS missions in volatile Balkan countries above and beyond "such S.O.E. organizations as exist." While "the governments in power are composed of Nazi collaborators . . . feeling among the Slavic peoples is strongly pro-Russian but not Communist," and "the hope of Anglo-American sympathy is lively." In each nation, the "official class . . . manipulate for their own advantage whatever popular or democratic forms of government may exist." Since the "more intelligent and far-sighted individuals, if not whole governments, now realize that the war will be lost by the Germans, and won, in Eastern Europe at least, by the Russians," the "first step to be taken is to establish contact secretly with Hungary, Rumania and Bulgaria with influential members of the ruling classes who are not regarded as wholeheartedly in sympathy with the Nazis." By "openly joining the United Nations" these societies may expect "better treatment . . . at the peace conference," "lend-lease" benefits, and potential markets for commodities. Along with many tactical advantages, the withdrawal of Bulgaria, Rumania, and Hungary would "establish the basis for a Balkan peace settlement along rational lines and without social revolutions, leaving the local nationalities in a position to work out their own future."

As usual the stinger is in the tail: "Consultation with the Russian Government should precede any steps in connection with this plan. But detailed discussion with them should wait until we have already carried out preliminary negotiations with Balkan leaders. It is to be hoped that the Kremlin will see so much to be gained by the execution of the plan that it will give its support without hesitation. . . ."[29]

Best a fait accompli. Intentions were clear enough, and years afterward the FBI would surface indications that Donovan's assistant, Major Duncan Lee, was passing to the Soviets details of "peace maneuverings going on between the satellite Axis nations through the medium of OSS representatives in Sweden and Switzerland."[30]

As matters stood, a subordinate of Dulles's while he was still in New York, Murray Gurfein, had long courted the Bulgarian banker Angel Kouyoumdjisky ("Kiss"), who claimed to be in touch with personages in the court of Czar Boris III interested in overthrowing the pro-Nazi government. Dulles okayed the project before he started for Switzerland. The whole thing guttered over the question of the dandified Kouyoumdjisky's ultimate purposes—he was a Macedonian separatist—and evidence that the Istanbul-based operation leaked.[31]

Donovan had sounded Dulles out shortly after he arrived in Bern about another set of possibilities coming off the bottom in the Balkans. Most of the armaments industry in Rumania still belonged to the Ausnit brothers, Edgar and Max, a pair of hard-headed Jews fighting to keep control of what OSS Balkan specialist Bernard Yarrow termed their "former dominant financial position in Rumania." The two hung on by virtue of their closeness to the Fascist Prime Minister Ion Antonescu.

In January of 1943 Edgar—who reached New York—got to the OSS with the message that if a guarantee of Rumanian independence could be procured from Russia and backed by the United States, "then Marshal Antonescu [sic] will be ready to join the United Nations."

In February Donovan asked for Allen Dulles's opinion; Dulles got right back with quotes from a letter which "one of his sources" happened just to have received from Max Ausnit himself. Antonescu wanted the pre-1940 frontiers, traditional constitutional protections, and some sort of "Confederation of southwestern and central Europe. . . ." oriented toward "cooperation with democratic governments of the west. . . ." This last sounds suspiciously like the "Danubian federation" Prince Hohenlohe was pitching to Dulles that same eventful week.

Dulles's timing was way off. As soon as the New Deal's whiz kid at State, Adolf Berle, who despised Donovan's quasi-diplomatic adventuring, discovered what was up he stormed in threatening to drag the whole thing before Franklin Roosevelt personally. That ended that. The matter, Dulles was advised, was "temporarily suspended." ". . . Of course," Donovan indicated, in a follow-up to Allen, "we are Russia's loyal allies, and without that in mind we could do nothing."[32]

* * *

Until the Normandy landings, Dulles cleared his important moves with Donovan. Yet he was increasingly mindful, as he wrote later, that if a man "tells too much or asks too often for instructions, he is likely to get some he doesn't relish, and what is worse, he may find headquarters trying to take over the whole conduct of the operation."[33] The prospect of a Soviet breakthrough or suspicion that the Reds might again work out their own deal with Hitler had started to haunt Allen. He'd surveyed the field, identified likely allies, individuals who shared his worries, from functionaries in the Vatican to farsighted commanders scattered among the Allied headquarters and foreign service sympathizers. Donovan had already sat down with Nazi diplomat Ernst von Weizsacker under the auspices of the Pope: peace in the West was America's for the asking, so long as the crusade against Bolshevism got driven to its appropriate culmination.[34]

The time had come for Dulles to initiate tentative—and deniable—approaches of his own.

By September of 1944, with Red Army elements massing along the northern frontier of Yugoslavia and main-force units of the partisans threatening Belgrade, the OSS Balkan expert attached to Mihailovic's Chetniks, Lieutenant Colonel Robert McDowell, got word from the German command in Belgrade that its officers would prefer to surrender to either the Chetniks or Americans. Two meetings were concluded before Allied headquarters got back with sharp orders to break these discussions off.[35]

This seemed to trigger another, undisclosed, approach. The leader of the OSS detachment at Tito's headquarters near Istyria was the twenty-nine-year-old guerrilla specialist Frank Lindsay. "Sometime—I would say, about September of '44—I was sent a radio message," Lindsay remembers. "Quite a cryptic message, which didn't disclose much at all. But the idea was, I was to go to Zagreb and make a contact with an unknown. There was an exchange of messages back and forth. . . . There was an agent in contact with von Horstenau, who had indicated that he would like to surrender to the British or the Americans but did not want to surrender to the Partisans or to the Russians. My recollection is, I told them I could not operate as an individual, that was something impossible to do without the knowledge of the Partisans and essentially their cooperation. And then I guess I pointed out that there was not a replacement for me." Lindsay had served both as an intelligence officer and helped with operations—receiving air drops, cutting rail lines, etc.

"I was told that that would be taken over by British officers, who would be dropped to me. That was delayed. It took me about a month to get outside of Zagreb. . . . I sent a courier into Zagreb to find out, a sort of initial reconnaissance, and he reported back that von Horstenau had been arrested, I think it was two weeks before. It was only after the war that I learned that the contact was an Allen Dulles contact. My recollection is, it was a businessman in Zagreb who had business reasons to go back and forth to Switzerland. Then I ran into two memoranda by people in Caserta. Very cryptic memoranda, they were very conspiratorial, proposing that I come out, be briefed, then be dropped back in. . . . They were very loathe to give me any information, I had to sort of pull it out. . . ."[36] This game had many blinds on every level: Willi Hoettl, Horstenau's sponsor, kept agents in Tito's camp and read the Partisan cyphers. Hoettl made sure Allen Dulles got everything he needed to prod him into making it easy for Horstenau to link up with sympathetic Western representatives.

Freshly declassified message records out of the Bari–Caserta–Bern loop fully document this scheme to detach Yugoslavia. Dulles's go-between, "K-6," was back in Switzerland by September 27 "bearing a personal message from Glore [von Horstenau]." He now stood ready to cooperate. While he had been relieved of his main role as liaison between the Wehrmacht and the Croatian government, he expected to be reassigned to the Zagreb area to exert his influence on the native military. The Germans had already cleared the Croatian coast and were under orders to vacate Trieste and Monfalcone "in the event of an Allied landing. . . ." Von Horstenau's friends "are also ready to collaborate with us," including the Austrian, Demarest, "in command of Croatia and the whole area between the Danube and the Adriatic."

Details, bribes, and elaborate agent contacts lace the exchanges. "According to K-6, the military strength of Glore lies in the fact that he believes that he can convince two each White Guard and Croatian, German, Divisions to surrender to the Allies. (However not to Tito)." While "K-6 had been in touch with the Partisan Kommissar, Sunjarevic, for some time," and recommends the use of Partisan radios to contact Zagreb, the implication is plain enough that Tito and his people must not be brought in.[37] The attempt to forestall Soviet ambitions by seizing the Balkans, which even Winston Churchill had forsaken, Allen Dulles now conspired to bring off largely on his own, relying on black diplomacy and subversion.

One made one's way with a maximum of circumspection against established Allied policy. Lindsay's desk officer (the man who also broke in his predecessor in Tito's camp, Charlie Thayer) was the head of Balkan SI at Bari, Robert Joyce, a U.S. Foreign Service loaner to the OSS and one of the younger men most closely attuned to the thinking of Robert Murphy, by then Eisenhower's principal diplomatic adviser. After the "Darlan deal" and his frontal role in brokering Marshal Badoglio into power in Italy, Murphy was keeping his head down as Political Advisor in Caserta, where Carmel Offie had attached himself to the late-war military and now proceeded to exert his astonishing psychic energies on every operational level.

Once Dulles moved out of Bern for Germany, Robert Joyce would replace *him*. By 1944 the next round of problems were plain enough—Tito's lieutenants were unruly, and the future of Trieste could turn into the Danzig of upcoming East-West confrontation. Just below command levels, a network of apprehensive younger Sovietophobes were already identifying one another.

8

THE BUREAUCRAT OF DEATH

All through the war's last year, few measures struck Allen as farfetched in the wake of Count von Stauffenberg's botched attempt to blow up Hitler. After July 20, 1944, the walls of jailyards across the Reich were pocked from the extermination of personalities Dulles had been depending on "to rid Germany of Hitler and his gang and establish a decent regime."[1]

A photograph has come down of the civilian ringleader of the conspiracy, Leipzig's ex-mayor Carl Goerdeler, braced before the People's Court. Despite the pallor of confinement there is a composed, even expectant expression on Goerdeler's open face, the assurance that even in extremis he remains a member, as Graham Greene phrased it, of the "untorturable classes."[2]

As Dulles would soon point out in his 1947 publication "Germany's Underground," Goerdeler was an optimist, a self-appointed political revivalist who dreamed of illuminating the Nazis. What Dulles never highlighted was the buildup of evidence that, given Goerdeler's values, the regime's true mistakes were primarily of means, not ends. Goerdeler personally welcomed the Nazi takeover as the mayor of Leipzig, he presided as the price-setting chief of Germany as late as 1936, and until the outbreak of war he visited his worldwide following of businessmen and conservative intellectuals under the patronage of Hermann Goering.

As late as 1941, deeply into conspiracy, the peace platform Goerdeler endeavored to peddle to sympathizers abroad required that the Allies go along with the German annexation of Austria, the Sudetenland and Memel and a return to the 1914 frontiers—i.e., hang onto Alsace-Lorraine and most of Poland. He wanted Germany's colonies back.[3] A Wilhelminian public servant to the gallows, Carl Goerdeler would never rubber-stamp the continuing travesty of Versailles. "It took a Hitler," as Dulles remarks, "to make such a man a revolutionary."[4]

The other top official among the Breakers, Johannes Popitz, the unstable Minister of Finance of Prussia, verified his nationalist credentials by maintaining that "in Jewish questions I, as a competent expert on the conditions during the time of the System [i.e., the Weimar Republic] was absolutely of the opinion that the Jews must disappear from economic and political life."[5] The conspiracy's Gestapo contact, Arthur Nebe, who ran the Criminal Police Department, was turned against the Party, according to Dulles, by "the practice of issuing *blank* 'murder orders' for the convenience of the Gestapo."[6] Dulles omits to mention that, when Holocaust technocrat Reinhard Heydrich challenged each of his Heads of Division to prove themselves "real men" by assuming command of a liquidation unit in the East, it was the conscientious Nebe who jumped out first. His Einsatzgruppe reported 45,000 Jews murdered.[7] The equivalent performance by Nebe's fellow Division Head Otto Ohlendorf ultimately got him strung up at Nuremberg.

Others weren't much prettier. Count Ernst Helldorf, the chief of police in Berlin and thus a lynchpin for the plot, originated, like so many other effective traitors to Hitler, in that sewer of the SA the Nazis never drained completely after the Roehm putsch. Konrad Heiden, himself a fallen-away Nazi well qualified to know, characterizes Helldorf as another of Captain Roehm's "homosexual creatures," an "adventurer and military profiteer of the worst sort."[8]

More than the outraged pastors and tea-table intellects of the Kreisau Circle or the Wednesday Group, it was these calcified, heedless Nazi functionaries reporting from their command posts who gave the conspiracy whatever prospects it had. Yet even their celebrated point man checked out as something other than the sunlit democrat Dulles banked on to encourage Washington. There was a dynamism about Klaus Philip Schenk, Count von Stauffenberg. Atrocities on the Russian front had horrified the saturnine, war-mutilated Wuerttemberg aristocrat, and begun the germination of a mystical Pan-Slavism which led him to believe "liberalism to be decadent," as

Dulles wrote, "and the adjective 'Western' a synonym for 'bourgeois.' . . . Gisevius told me Stauffenberg toyed with the idea of trying for a revolution of workers, peasants and soldiers. He hoped the Red Army would support a Communist Germany organized along Russian lines."[9]

The bomb went off; that day Stauffenberg died, followed quickly by hundreds more. Dulles looked on stoically, raddled with complicated feelings. Suppose Plan Valkyrie had succeeded? Where might the fracture lines have carried them all? "Germany has now had its Badoglio coup d'etat," he radioed Washington, "and it has failed." Allen discouraged any thought of backing another insurgency, since "it would probably mean the slaughter of further elements in Germany who might possibly be of use in the future. In fact, I do not think we should encourage the organization in Germany of an anti-Nazi government with whom we could negotiate an armistice, as it is probably preferable that an armistice and other preliminary provisions regulating Germany should be unilaterally imposed. . . ."[10]

The resistance was played out, Dulles recognized: there remained in place only the SS. Weeks after the putsch collapsed the most persistent of Schellenberg's footpads, Wilhelm Eggen, again approached the Dulles offices in the hope of reopening communication.[11] But Allen wasn't receptive, and when, soon after that, a delegation of erstwhile business cronies of the Dulles brothers—Gerhard Westrick, Karl Lindemann, Alexander Kraeuter—dropped by in Berlin to propose to Schellenberg that *they* might possibly get somewhere with their openhearted American colleague of so many years' association, Schellenberg let it go.[12]

That winter of 1944–1945 matters deteriorated from worrisome to desperate for anybody who intended to outlive the Third Reich. Most of the Waffen-SS divisions—six—lurked behind the heavily fortified Siegfried line to protect the West Wall, while elderly reservists and children and remnants of the Wehrmacht and scrapings from the POW camps got shoveled pell-mell into the path of the relentless Red Army onslaught. On August 10, 1944, selected managers from the major German industrialists had met in Strasbourg to ponder alternative proposals for recovering from the inescapable defeat. Information was made available to pinpoint the likeliest sources of foreign capital and identify such welcoming depositories for Nazi assets as the Basler Handelsbank and the Schweizerische Kreditanstalt of Zurich.[13]

It now become priority number one that as much of Western

Europe as possible fall to the capitalist West, and as intact as possible. To this end, Schellenberg seems to have concocted an extremely subtle disinformation campaign, designed largely to convince one man. On February 4, 1945, Allen Dulles wired the State Department that "Colonel MASSON head of Swiss SI who, as previously reported, has had close contact with his German opposite number SCHELLENBERG advised that envoy from Schellenberg was here and hinted he wanted to see me. Envoy apparently tried to create impression that stiff resistance on West Front and maintenance Italian Front as contrasted with rapid withdrawal East Front was part of plan to open all of Germany to Russia but that possibly if Anglo-Saxons disposed to modify unconditional surrender contact with Western Powers might be useful. Envoy also hinted at some understanding between Germany and Russia to open door to latter.

"Believing that this might be trap to cause trouble between Russians and ourselves particularly at this junction I expressed *NO* interest in seeing envoy."[14]

By the time he reached the Allied Command in Paris a week later, Dulles had apparently reconsidered. In an extended report dated February 11 from Robert Murphy to European Affairs Division Chief Matthews at State, Murphy alludes to the SS approach and summarizes Dulles's estimate: "Allen said that all indications currently received from Germany indicate a definite trend toward the idea that Germany's only salvation lies to the East. The conviction seems to be growing that while the Russians may be hard and brutal, even cruel, and that they will punish the principal National Socialist offenders, they still offer an affirmative economic and industrial future which will protect the Germans against starvation and poverty. They believe that the Russians will be dependent on German industrial products which means that German plants will continue to work at full capacity and that the unemployment problem will thus be solved.

"On the other hand, looking at the West, the Anglo-Americans offer nothing of an affirmative nature and the principal publicity is to the effect that the American intention is to reduce Germany to an agricultural basis with no provision for the millions employed in industry." To overcome the much-publicized Morgenthau plan proposals, "Dulles urged very vigorously that something of an affirmative nature be communicated in one form or another to the German people and also that some explanation of what we have in mind under the policy of unconditional surrender be given. He expressed the conviction that chaos will reign in Germany after the collapse." Since the day he arrived in Bern, Allen had been insisting that only the fear of Communism inhibited the German resistance. Dulles now pushed for the exploitation of captured German officers to sway the population in the Reich, since "Russian military successes in the East are due not alone to military prowess but to treachery behind the lines, a good part of which has been inspired by the German generals now in Russian hands."

"You may know," Murphy concludes, with a hint of jaundice, "that the OSS is now in the process of parachuting into Germany a certain number of German nationals for intelligence purposes." Others were already on hand to guide and advise the occupation. "Most of these people apparently are Social Democrats. I discussed this with Hugh Wilson"—the starchy foreign service careerist who served with Dulles in Bern in 1918, filled in for some months in 1938 as ambassador to Nazi Germany, got seconded into the OSS, and soon proved himself so rigid and vociferous as to be written off as a "monumental pain in the ass" even by Dulles's aides.[15] Wilson "promises to keep me informed of developments," Murphy assured Matthews. "He also states that these individuals will not be used for political action and that our State Department representatives will be kept advised of the results of their work. I had made it quite clear to Hugh and Allen that while we were not interested in many of the details of such an operation, that we must be kept informed of any of its political aspects." Classified Top Secret, the letter was typed up by Carmel Offie.[16]

By insinuating that Germany might *prefer* the Bolsheviks, the SD intellectuals were angling unceasingly for negotiating leverage. They fed Dulles rumors that Hitler was ill and broken, and prepared to step back and play the Hindenburg role while Himmler settled accounts. Another inspired late hoax that Schellenberg and his braintrust seem to have foisted on Dulles was the apparition of the Redoubt. "The information we get here locally seems to tend more and more to the theory of a final Nazi withdrawal into the Austrian and Bavarian Alps," one of Dulles's newsy, speculative January dispatches to Donovan asserts, "with the idea of making a last stand there."[17] By February the cable traffic pertaining to the Redoubt was frantic, with brewery cellars purportedly requisitioned for ammo dumps, escape tunnels under construction from the basements of the castles into adjoining valleys, and even a hunting pavillion set aside for Himmler's personal use. The April wire identifies 300,000 soldiers already manning the Redoubt—thirty divisions were scheduled—3 million refugees, and 600,000 wounded soldiers. Food was on hand to sustain 10 million holdouts for two years, poison gas had already been spotted in canisters, and there were plans to construct similar pockets of Nazism in Norway and Schleswig-Holstein.[18]

Allied tacticians took note, and troops stood by. Only at the end did U.S. intelligence analysts catch on that the Redoubt was chimerical. Throughout that chaotic spring, Willi Hoettl insists, "I was in close and daily contact with Allen Dulles in Berne."[19] The Tyrolese Gauleiter, Franz Hofer, had dreamed up a memorandum in which he proposed that a vast contingent of die-hard Nazis repair to the reaches of the Alps and entrench themselves for years. Even "Hitler at first ridiculed Hofer's fantastic plan," Hoettl maintains, but "the German secret service recognized in it an opportunity to mislead the Allies. Phony blueprints were drawn up and intelligence was leaked to the Americans, who seemed to be most prepared to believe such a romantic military plot. . . . I discovered that he [Dulles] was most interested in intelligence about the Redoubt. A plan was worked out to gain as much genuine information as possible and then to win over to our side those who were slated to command Hitler's desperate last stand."[20]

As in Hungary and Yugoslavia, Allen Dulles seems to have entered into a pas de deux with the Sicherheitsdienst to neutralize critical territory in the envisaged Danubian Confederation ahead of the devouring Russians. Even the slow-thinking Ernst Kaltenbrunner, Reinhard Heydrich's replacement as chief of the security services, stepped in to add a certain upper echelon cachet to the preliminaries. Hoettl would later indicate that he, Horstenau, Kaltenbrunner, and others in the "Austrian faction" had determined to save "the common homeland" by playing it into Western hands in return for a token occupation of Austria.[21] The Redoubt would fall undefended before the Anglo-Saxons before it could be manned and equipped. On March 25 and April 15 Hoettl turned up in Bern to set up the deal. But that late Dulles and his top aides were already distracted by competing negotiations with SS Obergruppenfuehrer Karl Wolff for the German Army in Italy.[22]

Not that Dulles neglected to push for Austria. His dispatch of January 20, 1945, emphasizes that, given the lassitude of the Austrians, they were about to find themselves "faced with the alternative of becoming a second Hungary and Vienna a second Budapest or making it so uncomfortable for the Nazis that they will decide to draw their defense lines in the Austrian Alps to the West of the capital." Dulles urges that the major Allies operate as "joint trustees" to "constitute an independent Austria. . . ."[23]

Afterward, when historians inquired, Dulles tended to deal with any mention of the Redoubt in that airy, mock-forgetful, oh-yes-I-remember-*some*thing-about-that-I-think mode of address he reserved for reviewing any remote and distasteful turn of events. Like the oppositional subterfuges he presented de Gaulle by supporting the Vichy-lining Paul Dungler, or his ambivalence toward Mihailovic, Dulles's concern over the Redoubt reversed itself in retrospect. "We did receive in Switzerland in those days a great many reports about the alleged Redoubt," he wrote one author, "but I trust I am correct in my recollection that in Switzerland we did not take them very seriously although we did not exclude the possibility that Hitler—in view of his characteristics and his sentimental attachment to the Berchtesgaden philosophy—might seek a spectacular end in the mountains."[24]

Sir Kenneth Strong, the plain-spoken British military professional who ran the Combined Intelligence Staff for Eisenhower, recalled circumstances differently. In line with his obligation to filter out bad intelligence headed toward the tactical branches, he never would forget ". . . a period when Allen Dulles was responsible for passing a good deal of information directly to the Americans under Eisenhower—especially information concerned with the so-called 'National Redoubt' in Germany; if I had not taken steps to counter some less reliable information about this 'Redoubt' it could have had a considerable effect on Eisenhower's strategy."[25]

❑

One of the talking points behind Operation Sunrise, the overnight surrender of the German forces in Italy Dulles trucked into place toward the very end, was the possibility that it would trap the million or so Nazi soldiers stationed along the Po before they could populate their mountain fortress. The negotiations are interesting, in that they surfaced a functionary at the very top of the SS, Obergruppenfuehrer Karl Wolff, as Dulles's regular negotiating partner. By then the orchidaceous Schellenberg was very busy scrounging for a patron like Count Bernadotte to help him through, while struggling to demonstrate humanitarian bona fides by utilizing Wilhelm Eggen to stage a January White Sale of almost starved Jews.

Wolff is worth noting among the Nazi leadership in that this big, susceptible-looking, pink, distinctly phlegmatic personality undoubtedly got as far as he did precisely because he lacked the hellpot mentality, the broiling fanaticism, common to the founders. Wolff relaxed people. For many years Himmler depended on his "Wolfie" (*Woelfchen*) to salve the hotspots throughout his normally frenzied day, and it was only when Karl Wolff insisted on ditching a wife of whom Himmler approved and wheedling permission from the Fuehrer to marry a divorced Countess, the Grafin von Bernstorff, that the painfully prim Reichsfuehrer SS felt obliged to banish this favorite to command of the SS complex in Italy.[26]

Unlike a number of the senior Nazis, Wolff's background was solidly top-drawer bourgeois—a rural solicitor's son, Wolff had held a Life Guard commission with the Grand Duke of Hesse before managing an advertising agency—and accordingly he tended to make his way largely through his powers of conciliation and charm, abetted by organizational follow-through.[27] Himmler trusted him enough to give him unique access to Konto S—the account in the Dresdner Bank into which the industrialists of the Freundekreis Heinrich Himmler deposited their annual tribute. Wolff saw to liaison with the I. G. Farben potentates and set the RM 3 daily rate to the SS for inmates at I. G. Auschwitz (1½ for children); he related to the Reichsfuehrer SS very much as Bormann did to Hitler.[28] Deeply divided and close to panic as Himmler so often was, the timid, crampy Reichsfuehrer SS tended to look to Wolff, the perennial head of his personal staff, for direction when he hesitated, some way to mollify the sharp, seething elements. Wolff also interceded as Himmler's liaison to der Fuehrer himself.

Karl Wolff was rarely inclined to wrap himself up too conspicuously in many of the dimestore Valhalla aspects of the Nazi creed, and long before Hitler began to play *Liebestod* records to himself in the evening and dream of turning the ancient capitals of Europe into his funeral pyre, Wolff had started peeking around corners in hopes of identifying the exit. By summer of 1942 Wolff, along with Schellenberg and Rudolf Brandt and Felix Kersten, was central to the SS clique most eager to talk to understanding foreigners like Carl Burckhardt in re some compromise solution. A year later, when Langbehn showed up in Bern to inquire as to how Gero von Gaevernitz and his American patron might feel about a reordering of the top jobs in Germany preparatory to a settlement with the West, the "senior SS leader on Himmler's staff" on whose authority Carl Langbehn presented his ideas was the reasonable-seeming Obergruppenfuehrer Wolff.[29]

All this meant no more in philosophical terms than that Wolff was unfailingly practical. He kept the true believers happy by making sure the boxcars ran on time. Even after the war, fraternizing with Allied officers, he offhandedly referred to Poles as "Slavonic mongrels."[30] When Schellenberg agitated in favor of tossing the irreconcilable von Ribbentrop to the Allies as a political hors d'oeuvre, Wolff ended these petty machinations with an appeal for loyalty to "the Order."[31] Schellenberg mousetrapped the venal Martin Luther instead.

Nevertheless, Wolff remained a man you could have a drink with. As 1945 opened bleakly for the Third Reich, Wolff was increasingly apprehensive that the ragbag of renegade "Italians, Russians, Serbs, Croats, et al."[32] which comprised the Waffen-SS contingent in Italy might soon find the well-armed partisan militia which surrounded it much like their counterparts in Greece and Yugoslavia—both ready and able to settle six years of scores in blood with the Nazi remnant. By November 1944 a range of Vatican and industrial visitors from Italy were hinting to Dulles that SS functionaries in Italy were uneasy about the situation. According to his later statement, the approach originated with his prewar contact, with industrial scion Baron Guenter von Haniel, a disillusioned young SS officer whose family was close to Kurt von Schroeder. In September of 1944 Haniel had swum across Lake Constance; soon afterward, in "December 1944 I was asked by Mr. Allen Dulles, OSS Mission to Switzerland, to contact the Swiss secret service and find out if they were willing to cooperate with OSS."[33] Haniel claimed to have brought in Major Waibel and Captain von Baldegg of the Swiss secret service.

Then, on February 25, 1945, the Swiss intelligence professional Max Waibel reached Dulles with news that two dignitaries of his acquaintance, the Swiss professor and boys' school prefect Max Husmann and his ex-student Baron Luigi Parilli, had something of importance to relate to the American special envoy.[34]

The baron was a widely connected Italian industrialist and Knight of Malta whose fears that the Germans might obey their Fuehrer and conduct a scorched-earth operation throughout the Northern Italian industrial plain were matched by his misgivings that the partisans might nail down control and grab his property. There were other considerations—most of the electrical grid across the region was owned by a multinational called "Italian Superpower," one director of which was the father of James Russell Forgan, the incoming OSS commander in Europe.[35] It was in nobody's interests—certainly not the Swiss—to let the walls cave now.

Parilli had contacted a busybody SS acquaintance of his, Guido Zimmer, who carried his concerns up the ladder to the urbane SS

Colonel Eugen Dollmann. Obergruppenfuehrer Wolff was supposedly aware of the overture and sympathetic. Skeptical, Dulles delegated the follow-up to a member of his staff, Paul Blum.

Dulles told Blum to inform the SS negotiators that if Wolff were genuinely involved, and serious, he would welcome as proof the release from German captivity, into Switzerland, of two top resistance leaders the OSS had supported: Ferruccio Parri and Antonio Usmiani. Parri was a leading Socialist. Dumfoundingly enough, on March 8 Waibel informed Dulles that both partisan leaders had arrived in Switzerland along with an SS delegation conducted by Wolff himself.[36]

Thus the chase began. Dulles met Wolff that evening when the Obergruppenfuehrer was led to him at a safe house the OSS maintained in Zuerich. Dulles had already ignited the logs in the library fireplace to insure the "subtle influence in a wood fire which makes people feel at ease and less inhibited in their conversation."[37] Settling in with a round of Scotches, Dulles jockeyed to establish the true drift of his large, ruddy visitor. Paperwork Wolff sent ahead made much of his efforts to protect the treasures of the Uffizi and the King of Italy's coin collection, his intervention to prevent the dynamiting of Rome and settle a general strike and arrange an amnesty with the partisans across the North which warded off mass conscription into Mussolini's militias or German labor battalions. The Cardinals of Milan and Venice had invariably found Wolff easy to collaborate with; as character references Wolff listed Rudolf Hess (Herr Dulles might himself be something of a Buchmanite, perhaps?), Father Pankratius Pfeiffer, Superior of the Salvatorian Order in Rome, and Pope Pius XII. Wolff had already initiated the scrupulous process of reinsuring himself by pledging his personal cooperation during an unheralded audience with the pontiff.[38]

A regular fellow, overall. Gaevernitz reflected both his and Dulles's first impression of the SS general in a letter to the 12th Army Group G-2, Ed Sibert: Wolff seemed "determined, energetic, with a quaint mixture, so typical of certain Germans, of romanticism and cold realism. For several years I had known through friends that he represented the moderate wing of the S.S., and that he disapproved of the Gestapo terror."[39]

As historians later toted up the occupational side effects, units under Wolff's command had "tortured hostages, slaughtered whole villages, such as Marzabatto, and carried out the Fosse Ardentine massacre." Wolff himself would pass these incidents off as "a few little lapses," and characterized his performance overall in the field as "soldierly."[40] He was now prepared to barter a couple of hundred interned Jews and guarantee the safety of British and American prisoners. Dulles found him handsome, a bit vain, and possibly a little headlong in his confidence that "his stock with Himmler, or possibly Hitler, was so high he could do no wrong."[41] In his turn, Wolff obviously agreed with the standing SS assessment of Allen Dulles as very much the "sporting type," with "good teeth and a lively, unaffected and gracious manner."[42] Poking at the embers, taking in Wolff's explanations—looking up to punctuate the exchanges from time to time with his rich, round, appreciative chuckle—the American was soon able to convince the Obergruppenfuehrer that he was negotiating with a lodge brother.

As soon as the Combined Chiefs discovered that such an exchange was in the air they wasted no time in informing Moscow, and rushed two top military officers to Switzerland before these OSS socialites and their friends could destroy the Alliance. By March 19 Lt. General Lyman Lemnitzer and his British opposite number, Terrence Airey, backed up by two colonels brandishing impressively large machine pistols, had made their way to the Stinnes compound at Ascona which Gaevernitz looked after, where Dulles had already set himself up to cater an extended seminar.[43] After several hours of conversation, both generals had concluded that there was much less here to proceed on than they had been given to believe. Wolff provided enough tactical tidbits to keep things interesting, but he was obviously a long way from qualified to speak either for the recently arrived Wehrmacht commander in the North of Italy, the stiff, unimaginative General Heinrich von Vietinghoff, or Field Marshal Albert Kesselring, whom Hitler had weeks before pulled out of Italy and shoved into the unenviable post of chief of the German armies now retreating behind the Rhine. Airey, who had to be cornered physically before he would shake Wolff's hand, pronounced the Obergruppenfuehrer crafty-looking and nervous, and was distinctly put off by the way Wolff's sleek jowls rounded into a trio of chins as well as his coquette's habit of overloading his fat fingers with diamond rings.[44]

By then the real breakthrough would be some intervention with Kesselring himself to generate a surrender up and down the Western Front. Wolff promised to visit Kesselring—with whom, he claimed, he'd shared many confidences in Italy, and who he could assure the gentlemen entertained thoughts like his own. He would be back within the week. Lemnitzer and Airey settled in at Ascona. Dulles, meanwhile, arranged with Henry Hyde to borrow his top radio operator, "Little Wally"—a Dachau alumnus—and sneaked him through to Milan to pass messages directly between Wolff's headquarters at Bolzano and Bern.

After several anxious weeks, Wolff got word back that Kesselring—by that time frantically juggling field telephones—had nothing against Vietinghoff's working something out as events might dictate with the Anglo-Americans. But he was busy. Meanwhile, Himmler had found out about the Zurich meeting betweeen Wolff and Dulles and "taken the liberty" of placing Wolff's blonde countess of a wife and his children "under my protection."[45] Wolff was jerked back to Berlin and informed that peace initiatives were better left in the hands of Schellenberg and the more Jesuitical specialists in Amt VI. Wolff had "uselessly utilized," Schellenberg would bellyache later to the English, "and without effect, one of my most important contacts, whom I had been watching over and nursing ever since 1942. . . ."[46]

Such abrupt exposure cooled even Wolff's ardor for conspiracy for the time being. It was Wolff's thought, Schellenberg told the SIS interrogator who debriefed him, to offer the "maintenance of order" in "this particular industrial area . . . of importance to the Western Powers" in view of the threat from "Communists and Partisans." The trade-off he expected was for ". . . the German troops to retain their weapons, and thereby become a type of commissioned Police Force of the Western Powers." They might subsequently undertake a withdrawal "with military honor," and perhaps fulfill "law and order" commitments inside Germany.[47]

The Soviets reacted badly to word of Dulles's brainstorming sessions, and cooperation stopped. It was soon apparent to the U.S. military attaché in Moscow, General Deane, that "this was the festering sore." Stalin wrote Churchill and Roosevelt, curious as to what could be motivating the Germans to "surrender without any resistance" in Italy while sacrificing their men against the Red Army for "some unknown junction . . . which they need as much as a dead man needs poultices."[48]

Dulles made every attempt to keep the Italian partisans, the "Garibaldini," ignorant of his dealings with Wolff and the SS. Nevertheless, word leaked and Parri, who in early March had broken into tears of gratitude at the sight of Dulles, was lamenting to his comrades that the Anglo-Saxons seemed far more interested in heading off a revolution from the left than permitting the overdue Italian underground to "rise for the kill."[49]

Stalin remained profoundly aroused. While armies of partisans prepared to storm Bologna and Turin and Milan and Genoa, Molotov inveighed against "separate peace" arrangements "behind the back of the Soviet government, which had been carrying on the main burden of the war against Germany." President Roosevelt—who had indeed gone along with the recommendation by Averell Harriman to exclude Soviet delegates from the sensitive exchanges—protested such "vile misrepresentations of my actions. . . ." But even Winston Chruchill recognized privately that Stalin had a point.[50]

Still endeavoring to quiet Russian apprehensions over the incident, FDR had abruptly died. On April 13 Wolff received another summons from Himmler to return to Berlin immediately. Karl Wolff appeared in the bunker on April 17 with Kaltenbrunner nipping at his heels. It took a double helping of the disarming sincerity of manner on which Wolff built his success to convince the shaky, drooling Fuehrer that he had been undertaking these probes to open up possibilities for the Reich, while protecting the authority of the dictator by taking the responsibility on himself. Flabby and bewildered, Hitler declared his intention to wait for the imminent break between the Anglo-Americans and the Soviets, and "join the party which approaches me first. It makes no difference."[51]

While Wolff was sweating out this ominous second recall to Berlin, Baron Parrilli and Doctor Husmann looked in on Dulles at Bern and found him, Waibel wrote, "tired and initially somewhat apathetic." It happened that several days earlier a person who introduced himself as General Consul Gysling brushed in on one of the subordinates in Dulles' office and announced that "he wished to help bring the surrender to its completion, and for that reason would like to speak with Mr. Dulles, to present him with an important message from General Wolff."[52]

Gysling, it developed, was a protégé of Kaltenbrunner. Some Kaltenbrunner flunky a month before had offered to remove Bormann and the other " 'warmongers' in the Fuehrer's entourage." Wolff shrugged the latest incident off by admitting that Gysling and his Herr Kollege Schwendt, the celebrated SS counterfeiter, had guessed what was going on and then had indeed tried to cut themselves in on the benefits to come by threatening Wolff with disclosure to Kaltenbrunner unless they too might climb aboard in time.[53]

Perking up, Dulles started to bombard the Joint Chiefs with cables, vouching for Wolff's efficacy, urging continuance of the talks "to spare the lives of our troops and bring us into the heart of the German Reduit," and stressing that a surrender even this close to the end insured that "our forces [in] Italy would probably be the first to occupy Trieste," which "now constitutes an even more important objective for Russians than Berlin."[54] It did no good. On April 21 an order of the Combined Chiefs came through: break off the Sunrise contact.

By then the Gothic Line across Northern Italy was crumbling. At a nod from Vietinghoff, Wolff grabbed his supporters and bolted for Lucerne. Dulles rushed to Lucerne too, but refused to parlay. At the Hotel Scheizerhof, Waibel noted in his long-suppressed monograph *Kapitulation in Norditalien,* Dulles stayed in bed in "serious pain, and his physical condition was not a favorable omen for the discussion." Furthermore, ". . . under the influence of his attack of gout [Dulles] had become even more distrustful of Wolff."[55]

None of this totally blotted out Dulles's anxiety that his own credibility was seriously in danger—especially after the Redoubt fiasco—if nothing now emerged. His cables openly pleaded with Caserta to let him clear the way to triumph. The deputy of Vietinghoff, Colonel von Schweinitz, who had accompanied Wolff to Lucerne, Dulles protested, was a secret anti-Nazi as well as a "descendent of Chief Justice Jay." The list of bargaining counters the Germans were known to carry was "more or less eyewash."[56] But Washington's orders remained in force.

Wolff languished in Lucerne for two jittery days, while much of the American Fifth Army poured across the bridgeheads along the Po and turned the main German lines. Panic-stricken, Wolff recrossed into Italy, where detachments of partisans cut off the roads all around him at Villa Locatelli near Como.

Orders or not, Dulles averted his eyes and sent forth Gaevernitz and Waibel to constitute a rescue party which included the OSS agent Donald Jones, who had been helping supply the partisans and so could talk his way around their proliferating road blocks. The motorcade pushed through, extracted the flabbergasted Wolff in the middle of the night, and smuggled him back over the Swiss border before slipping him around into Italy and safer country near his Bolzano headquarters.[57]

Dulles later told Donovan that he had kept Wolff in touch by sending the Czech radio operator Wally to Bolzano, where Wally called down selective air strikes. Shortly—when negotiations guttered—Allen pulled Wally back, since "If the deal were called off the Germans would certainly have slit his throat."[58]

It required Stalin himself to reclaim the despairing Dulles's masterpiece of gamesmanship. The Combined Chiefs proposed to the Soviets an exchange of representatives at each other's military headquarters in the event of a major surrender. This cleared the air somewhat. "Shortly after I arrived at my office on the morning of April 27th," Dulles later wrote, "three signals came in, all marked TRIPLE PRIORITY." The surrender of the Axis forces had already been scheduled in Caserta. "There were to be no conferences or discussions in Switzerland."[59]

Gaevernitz bunked at Caserta with the Nazi contingent. The papers were all but signed before the Germans stopped wriggling in hopes of attaching a few face-saving conditions to their unconditional surrender status.[60] It was too late for that. While the plenipotentiaries argued, Hitler shot himself. On May 2, the day the Italian surrender was announced, Berlin fell. A week later the caretaker Nazi government of Admiral Doenitz had capitulated to both the West and the Soviets.

What had they produced, these weeks of house-partying with this hodgepodge of opportunistic Nazis? The political situation in Italy did stabilize for the moment, and the vulnerable power stations continued to hum. With the capitulation of Vietinghoff's Army Group C there was a race between the Allies and Tito for Venezia Giulia, the region surrounding Trieste. This produced a kind of simultaneous land grab, and poisoned relations between Yugoslavia and the West for several years.

Perhaps they established Dulles, fortifying his intelligence legend. Even that involved costs: in times of tension he tended to ignore his gout pills, and sometimes his foot throbbed almost to the knee and kept him bordering on savage. The Caserta surrender announcement very nearly exposed him in the act of deliberately flouting a direct order to leave Wolff and Company alone. "According to report from Waibel," Dulles telegraphed Caserta slyly while he was exfiltrating the SS general, "Wolff succeeded in working his way back to Switzerland from Como and when your message received he was on his way to Feldkirch frontier."[61] Caserta never inquired further.

And why not attempt a dance or two with the ingratiating Obergruppenfuehrer, whose crinkling blue eyes and broad face and high strawberry-blond forehead had watched a lot of Central-European history go down, much of it screaming? Dulles obviously didn't mind, although others in the OSS—whose men had died under torture on the general's orders—were incensed.[62] But how can you resist a man who snags the Pope as a credit reference? Wolff awakened some resonance, obviously, because when Kaltenbrunner sent somebody around, Pacelli made it plain that his good offices were spoken for so far as the SS went.

It's hard to establish how valuable the papal imprimatur was afterward. Once indictments started coming down, both Dulles and Gaevernitz pushed hard in Wolff's behalf. He skinned through the initial round of Nuremberg indictments, and cheerfully offered testimony as a prosecution witness. In 1946, apparently in the grip of a delusion that even his Sunrise colleagues had betrayed him and that Jewish demons were after him everywhere, he spent a season in a mental sanitarium.[63] He remained in easy confinement at Gmunden, where the occupying authorities put him to use as an alternately beguiling and hard-hitting interrogator of other POWs in return for a pleasant life with his family, plenty of PX cigarettes, and even a cruise on his own yacht whenever the time came to refresh his spirit.[64]

Between his mental state and his American boosters, nobody was quite sure how to proceed against this captivating senior sharper whom even his keepers now referred to as the "white sheep" of the defunct SS. He played his aces with no small skill. On August 11, 1947, the ubiquitous Robert Murphy, by this time the Political Adviser to the head of the U.S. Military Government in Germany, General Lucius Clay, sent off a top-secret telegram to Washington which concerned this unexploded mine Allen Dulles left everybody: "SS General Karl Wolff claims that in connection with Operation Sunrise leading to surrender German forces in Italy certain oral promises were furnished him by von Gaevernitz of OSS, as well as Dulles, regarding personal immunity for Wolff and his assistants, in particular Dollmann and Wenner. Wolff alleges Major Waibel Swiss general staff was witness and guarantor to these promises. Sworn interrogatory between Wolff and Swiss national Max Husmann on 5 July 1947 indicates that this may have been the case. Some U.S. intelligence authorities in Germany are of definite opinion that military honor requires pardon and immunity for Wolff and his adjutants who are at present in automatic arrest category. It appears that General Vandenberg was informed of role played by Wolff group."[65]

Six months after that James Riddleberger of the U.S. Office of Military Government was staving Gaevernitz off when Gero pursued an inquiry into Wolff's well-being, alarmed by the report that after the British War Crimes section finished with Wolff "it will give some consideration to extraditing him to Czechoslovakia or some other country which has requested his extradition as a possible war criminal."[66]

With time, with friends, Wolff beat every charge. Lemnitzer, Airey, and Dulles wrote affidavits when finally the British rather unenthusiastically put the ex-Obergruppenfuehrer on trial in

Hamburg in 1949, and Gaevernitz appeared as a defense witness. Wolff won an acquittal. He was the highest ranking officer in the SS to remain at large.[67]

Twenty years after Sunrise Allen Dulles and Gero von Gaevernitz hosted a reunion for the participants at Ascona. Many of the participants appeared, although Karl Wolff, contrary to reports, wasn't able to make it.[68] Details from the Eichmann trial in Jerusalem happened to reinforce evidence from an Ulm mass-murder proceeding which generated fresh testimony. Statements taken at Nuremburg indicated that Himmler and his Wolfie were fond of stealing away to the Luftwaffe experimental station at Dachau, where they could watch inmates subjected to high-altitude conditions inside a pressure chamber. The subjects would routinely go mad, and tear open their heads and faces and "pull out their hair in an effort to relieve the pressure," an assistant remembered.[69] Dulles's good-natured co-negotiator seems to have had a scientific side. Research must go on, after all, and the New Order forbade vivisection.

As time passed, fresh curiosity as to Wolff's role during the Hitler days built up—some of it conceivably among the SS colleagues Wolfie helped the U.S. authorities incriminate. Collaborating with Otto Skorzeny, Hjalmar Schacht, and other hardy Third-Reich carryovers, Wolff had developed into an important international arms merchant. A West German court brought down a war-crimes indictment in 1964. The single piece of documentary evidence against Wolff, Allen Dulles later wrote, was a 1942 paper he signed which "requested additional freight cars from the Ministry of Transport for use in Poland. It seemed that there was evidence that the cars were for transporting Jews to the extermination camps. Wolff claimed at his trial that he did not know they were for that purpose."[70]

But Allen didn't quote from the document, which expressed to the State Secretary in the Transportation Ministry Wolff's "special joy that now five thousand members of the Chosen People are going to Treblinka every day."[71] The West German prosecutor was to demonstrate that between July and September of 1942 alone Wolff arranged for the boxcars which transferred 300,000 Jews from the Warsaw ghetto to Auschwitz. "He was continuously engaged and was deeply entangled in guilt," the presiding judge concluded, sentencing Karl Wolff to fifteen years. "Himmler found in him his bureaucrat of death."[72]

9

A REALLOCATION OF TARGET

Much of the urgency behind Dulles's "Secret Surrender" initiative stemmed from his recognition that the war was ending, and with it—unless there were more to show, soon—undoubtedly the OSS. Dulles reflected Donovan's heat. In September of 1944 Wild Bill picked Dulles up in a resistance hideout in France, and subsequently the two flew back to Washington for a breather, playing bad bridge interminably.[1]

Dulles's widely advertised coups made even Wild Bill wonder. Had Allen actually wormed those informers of his into place to unearth this stuff? Or was he functioning as an outlet for certain of the shrewder Nazis?[2] Were many of the quasi-diplomatic initiatives he pumped for truly calculated to abridge the combat phase in any meaningful way? Or were they stratagems to deliver from Red Army control entire cultures in the East economically colonized by Sullivan and Cromwell's clients?

With Germany under siege, Donovan was casting about for methods to infiltrate the Reich directly. During those final months the OSS did indeed manage to crank something like two hundred agents in across the chaotic Nazi dominion. The British looked on, tongue in cheek.

Perhaps it was Donovan's example which accounts for Dulles's contradictory maneuvers. For two years Dulles had been saturating Washington with communiqués and radiograms warning that unless the West toned down its unconditional surrender demands, even sympathizers in the Axis nations would give up and countenance "a series of internal revolutions" such that their societies "would turn communist."[3] By summer of 1944 Dulles was conjecturing that after so many years throughout which Goebbels flogged the United States and England as "reactionary, plutocratic countries dominated by the power of money," few effective moderates survived in case "A breakdown in Germany will bring back the demobilized soldiers and put on the streets millions of war workers. It will open the gates to the prison camps and free the foreign laborers. All will be in a revolutionary spirit. So far, the people of these classes are inclined to look to Russia." His industrialist friends ostensibly were pushing Himmler to cut some arrangement with Stalin; Dulles recommended the establishment of a ". . . confidential consultive committee of Germans of trusted anti-Nazi sympathies, who would act solely as an advisory body, particularly with regard to the selection of personnel. . . . I believe it is important to be thinking along these lines now, since otherwise we will be faced with German government made in Russia with which it is proposed that we deal."[4]

The view of France from Bern was equally alarmist. A report on resistance periodicals quotes spokesmen as "united together not only in the fight for our country, but in the will to remake it." These insurgents represented "a force which must be reckoned with," one January 1944 Dulles radiophone summary concludes. "It is fanatically Gaullist in character, and in spirit closer to Russia than to the Western powers."[5]

That month the OSS's Henry Hyde in Algiers had arranged to drop the Petainist Alsatian Paul Dungler into France behind the backs of de Gaulle's leadership; Dungler sought out surviving Abwehr elements. Dulles was clearly party to this, and de Gaulle himself would allude to a last-ditch "scheme that inclined to silence or set [him] aside" by smoothing things over between the Allies and Pierre Laval through the mediation of a M. Enfiere, "who was in touch with Mr. Allen Dulles' services in Berne. . . ."[6] Dulles would later deny any involvement "categorically," and insisted that he "consistently advised Washington that de Gaulle was the only leader for whom the French underground had any real enthusiasm."[7]

These almost daily radio dispatches from Dulles achieved surprising intragovernmental distribution. Not only were old-school ideologues inside the OSS like James Grafton Rogers, Dewitt Poole—now chief of the influential Foreign Nationalities Branch—and John Wiley assiduously stuffing their files, but OSS liberals kept Henry Morgenthau and his progressive cohorts well attuned to Dulles's musings.[8]

This makes it harder to pin down what tempted Allen to abet a number of the most single-minded and resourceful Communist Party operatives afloat in Western Europe just then, awaiting orders from Moscow before machining Dulles's worst fears into postwar reality. Possibly it was ambition: Donovan himself couldn't resist such opportunities to cover bets across the political spectrum. Around Christmas of 1943 the OSS chief bounced in and out of the Soviet capital to rig a system of information exchanges with General P. N. Fitin, a senior NKVD security honcho.[9] The arrangement broke down the summer of 1945; by then William Donovan was primed to his epaulettes for full-scale Cold War, and before the fighting slackened he had taken such precautions as infiltrating a squad under Pittsburgh banker Adolph Schmidt to bury ten shortwave radios behind Russian lines.[10]

Donovan seemed to crave a few late feathers to spruce up the OSS's moulting war bonnet. Prodded by Wild Bill, his London Secret Intelligence manager, William Casey, sought out the recommendations of the devoutly Stalinist Free Germany Committee to drum up likely paramilitaries. A handful came forward—craftsmen largely, leathery, competent, highly motivated working-class Communists who picked the codes right up and bailed out into the ruins of Germany to document the war's last weeks.[11]

It reflects the fast-results-over-judgment biases of the late-war OSS that Casey's go-between, Joe Gould, permitted the hard-core Stalinist economist who recruited Klaus Fuchs, Juergen Kusczynski, to provide his agents. Dulles passed through London briefly while these missions were making up. Possibly his juices stirred: was this what Donovan expected? The two were chatting over drinks at the Hotel Savoy bar; David Bruce had already asked for another assignment. This left the senior OSS slot for Europe open. "There are lots of guys shooting for the job," Donovan assured Dulles, whom he was well aware *spoiled* for the promotion, ". . . good guys with marvelous records. . . ." But—Donovan was invariably cute—"just because they're brilliant station chiefs doesn't mean they can handle London—all that administration. Nearly all of them are lousy administrators." So Bruce stayed put—for the moment.[12]

If it was Communists Donovan had in mind, what about the Field network? Once Paris was on its own a branch of the Free Germany Committee popped up, the Comité de l'Allemagne Libre Pour l'Ouest, known by its acronym, CALPO. Dulles in his radiograms had plugged the growing number of disillusioned German officers around the POW compounds. Some could supply propaganda voices; others might provide background to the occupation personnel. In December 1944 Field sought out Dulles to argue that Germans he was closest to were perfect for airdrops into the collapsing Reich.

Dulles bucked Field along to OSS headquarters in Paris, where eventually he turned up before the brisk twenty-seven-year-old desk sergeant who tended the political analysis section of the combined SI/Research Branch, Arthur Schlesinger, Jr. Never an easy sell, Schlesinger judged Field at minimum a born gull, indestructibly simple-minded regarding worldly matters and smug and self-righteous enough to make him dangerous in the end.[13]

Schlesinger's judgment paralleled Arthur Goldberg's. Goldberg's aides were beginning to pinpoint important younger Social Democrats around the proliferating POW camps, many directly out of Hitler's punishment battalions. These Goldberg brought forward—with Allen Dulles's quiet backing, despite the discomfiture of State Department rightists like Hugh Wilson and Robert Murphy—to consult with occupation authorities.

But Goldberg remained chary about vociferous self-propagandizers such as the legendary apostate Jay Lovestone. "They provided some contact with ex-Communists like themselves," Goldberg would later concede. "We stayed away by and large from the Communist underground. Other sections of the OSS tried to collaborate with them but I did not, because I early came to the conclusion that their allegiance was to Moscow, and that they were not, for our purposes, trustworthy. And they were not.

"Irving Brown and Lovestone were helpful up to a point. But I had developed pretty much our own lines of communication. They did provide names, people who could be helpful in occupied Europe. . . ."[14]

So Field's recommendations were quashed in Paris but—versions vary here—Dulles appears to have cottoned to a number of Field's people, rounded up American uniforms for several, and scattered them ahead of the troops or infiltrated them not merely in Germany but also in Yugoslavia, Hungary, and Czechoslovakia. The OSS helped Leo Bauer back into the American Zone, from where, quite quickly, he entered the Soviet quadrant and held down a senior propaganda post until a Stalinist shake-up found him recrossing to the West, whence he would later emerge a key adviser to Willi Brandt. During the immediate postwar months, Dulles seconded Field by backing a left-wing underground tabloid called *Neues Deutschland,* which shortly evolved into the official newspaper of the East German Communist Party.[15] Until the last bullet flew, Dulles seems to have adhered in his way to Donovan's edict to support every anti-Nazi—monarchist or left-winger, Gaullist or disillusioned Vichyite—even as his dread deepened incident by incident.

Political turnabouts were unpredictable. Just as the war was ending Dulles's protégé Fritz Molden, barely twenty, agitated at SHAEF headquarters for treatment of Austria as a liberated rather than a hostile power. Molden's attachment to Allen was such that for a period just after the war he attempted a marriage to Dulles's daughter, Joan. Nevertheless, British intelligence resented his influence, and MI6 seems to have convinced the X-2 representatives of OSS that Molden was quite likely a German plant.[16] Dulles sent Gerald van Arkel to Paris to put in a word for Fritz.

Allen's determination to keep working *something* into the political lacunae produced one long-haul ally. In November 1944 the facile von Gaevernitz met Brigadier General Edwin Sibert, the inexperienced G-2 for Omar Bradley's twelfth U.S. Army Group. Silbert bought Dulles's contention that many of the Wehrmacht commanders behind the West Wall were vulnerable to propaganda from colleagues the Allies had interned. Senior American brass from Admiral Leahy down concurred with the aseptic Major General George V. Strong: Whenever an idea savored even faintly of OSS connivance, it deserved the heave-ho.

Sibert didn't go along. A deliberative, straightforward artillery officer with attaché experience to reinforce his distrust of the Soviets, Ed Sibert welcomed Gaevernitz's advisory dispatches, and lost one bid for War Department permission to constitute a propaganda board led by Luftwaffe Major General Gerhard Bassenge. Then, on December 16, "slight penetrations" of the Allied lines just short of the Rhine were noted. Within hours the Wehrmacht's thrust through the Ardennes, "the Battle of the Bulge," was breaching the Allies' rolling offensive; Sibert's "nose" for intelligence was judged a disaster area.[17] Dulles kept in touch.

The hostilities in Europe ended formally on May 9, 1945, and it was almost as if, with that, for Dulles, the spell was broken. While Allen was on and off the trains between Bern and Paris the winter before, Donovan had quietly eased Russell Forgan into David Bruce's post as chief of OSS–Europe. When Forgan himself resigned Donovan evaded Dulles's hungry eyes, and explained that each of the European stations would function on its own, subject only to Washington. He'd done it that way, Donovan told insiders, because Dulles "is such a damned poor administrator."[18] Allen spent the remainder of 1945 as chief of the OSS country mission in Germany.

Dulles now found himself attempting to direct an OSS detachment at Biebrich, a suburb of Wiesbaden, abetted shortly by a subsidiary station out of the State Department compound in Berlin. He padded out his German venture with co-workers from Switzerland—Emmy Rado, the faithful von Gaevernitz. But romance travels poorly, and it remained a comedown to forsake the patrician ambiance of Bern for the occupation army's welter of disheveled barracks and hectic summer orderly rooms. At that stage the OSS was one among many intelligence detachments scrambling to justify its mission in the Central-European chaos.

By then, of course, something epochal was gathering. Charles Mee has noted that "four days after Germany surrendered Truman cancelled Lend-Lease aid to Russia without advance warning; ships that had been loaded were unloaded; ships that were steaming toward Russia were called back."[19] Later—ruefully, yet obviously a touch vainglorious over all this unanticipated influence—George Kennan would concede that back in Moscow he had "plagued Averell," and deserved especial criticism for "inspiring and encouraging Washington into stiffness,"[20] starting with the "cancellation of Lend-Lease. . . ." Berlin had been gerrymandered; when the Russians cut off the power to the American sector the commander of the Potsdam garrison, General Wedemeyer, got permission to dig up and block the sewer pipes which relieved the adjacent Soviet compound.

God knows the Soviets continued to rouse Kennan's enmity, yet toward the Germans his feelings remained difficult to resolve. In 1938 and 1939 George Kennan spent a year in Prague, officially attending the final takeover. The day Nazi troopers marched into the capital "I found that I myself had a refugee," Kennan recorded, "a Jewish acquaintance who had worked many years for American interests." Kennan denied him asylum, but permitted him to remain briefly "as long as he was not demanded by the authorities." "For twenty-four hours he haunted the house, a pitiful figure of horror and despair, moving uneasily around the drawingroom, smoking one cigarette after another, too unstrung to eat or think of anything but his plight. His brother and sister-in-law had committed suicide together after Munich, and he had a strong inclination to follow suit. Annelise pleaded with him at intervals throughout the coming hours not to choose this way out, not because she or I had any great optimism with respect to his chances for future happiness but partly on general Anglo-Saxon principles and partly to preserve our home from this sort of unpleasantness."[21] "As to the situation here," George advised his superiors in the Department soon afterward, "I should like to say that I think the press has been a little inclined to exaggerate the horrors of those first two weeks of the German occupation."[22]

Once war broke out the antiseptic Kennan moved on to Berlin; George served out much of the hostilities in Lisbon, where he turned away a Donovan proposal to destabilize Salazar. The diplomat was assigned to London near the end of 1943 as a planner with the European Advisory Commission; he drafted his own objections to recommended denazification procedures: "Whether we like it or not, nine-tenths of what is strong, able, and respected in Germany has been poured into those very categories which we have in mind [i.e., Nazis and Nazi sympathizers]."[23]

Nor would Kennan reconsider. In the summer of 1944 he found himself standing on a Moscow curb and "watching the passage of some fifty thousand German prisoners in process of being marched several miles across town from one railroad station to another." The Nazis had done worse, Kennan supposed, but "still, I came away from the sight shaken, saddened, and unsatisfied. . . . Five years ago, when the war began, they had been mere boys."[24]

Where were the Poles in Kennan's long, artful apostrophe, or the Jews, or the Yugoslavs or the French or the Danes or the Norwegians—on whom these mere boys brought down their hetacomb. Hitler lay pretty heavy on the stomach, Kennan conceded in 1940, but even with him around the Soviets constituted the primary threat to Europe, and in his way the Fuehrer was "acting in the best traditions of German nationalism."[25] Out of his gloomy boyhood in Milwaukee, with *its* envenomed ethnicities, the alienated young thinker drags forth his profoundly saturated prejudices. Races deserve their destinies. From Moscow, in 1945, influencing U.S. Ambassador Averell Harriman, George Kennan's shadow grew longer every week across U.S. policy.

Perusing all his cables from Moscow, the one-time haberdasher from Missouri was miffed that Stalin seemed to be ignoring the intent of the Yalta agreements and imposing whatever governments he chose upon his conquests in Eastern Europe. Until they were "reorganized," Truman informed Stalin at Potsdam, none of the $10 billion worth of reparations the Russians had bargained for from Germany was available in the Western sectors. A pragmatic soul, Uncle Joe hung out his wry smirk and confirmed the only settlement possible: "Let me put it more specifically: the German investments in Rumania, Bulgaria, Hungary and Finland go to us, and all the rest to you."[26] The Iron Curtain descended.

By then for some months such farsighted planners as Assistant Secretaries of War John McCloy and Robert Lovett, the highly regarded "Heavenly Twins," had deputized any number of steamed-up Manhattan financial specialists to prowl the debris of Europe in collapse. Capitalism also requires commissars. J. Henry Schroder vice president Lada Mocarski was transferred from his adviser's post in the War Department to Bern in time to take over as U.S. Consul. In late March 1945, Hjalmar Schacht's harried protégé and Walter Funk's preceptor, the Reichsbank's troubleshooter Emil Puhl, hurried over to Bern after stopping by the offices of The Bank for International Settlements and briefing a conference of German industrialists in Basel on which of their technicians had better be tucked away for the time being in selected neutral countries. Puhl arrived to reassure Mocarski that nobody at the Reichsbank had anything to do with all the widely reported Nazi gold looting. "Frau Puhl should not talk to MUSEUM," Morcarski wired his OSS contact a month later, "tell her to do nothing until she hears from us."[27]

Mocarski sent Puhl up the street to Dulles. Finishing out in Switzerland, Allen asked for a list of "the responsible Germans who were not Nazis at heart, and with whom the U.S. Occupation authorities could do business. . . ." Dulles's cable to Washington emphasized that key "Nazis had made careful plans to go underground, that every essential figure had his designated place . . . that Nazism was like a religion not merely a political regime." Puhl had fended off the proposal that he personally assume ". . . responsibility under occupying forces if asked to do so" as too dangerous "both physically and politically" still, since "men who collaborated too soon would be sacrificing their subsequent utility and that useful men should wait until the public they seek to influence is prepared to accept loyal collaboration with the democracies."[28]

Through Per Jacobsson and others at The Bank for International Settlements, Allen Dulles had remained abreast of many of the activities of the BIS, and with his lawyer's instinct to try for a settlement soon nudged his erstwhile client Thomas McKittrick to surrender at least a portion of the remelted gold which once constituted the Belgian national reserve. This would look generous; besides, Belgium was Foster's client.

Another name from the past in Dulles's mail as Germany went down was of that beefy perennial Gerhard Westrick. Struggling with his mandate to babysit the ITT subsidiaries, Westrick overflowed with gratitude that Allen was decent enough to pass along his reports to ITT Chairman Sosthenes Behn in New York.[29]

By spring of 1947 Allen Dulles in New York had filed away unanswered several rending appeals from Irmtrud and Gerhard Westrick. Westrick had been in and out of confinement and interrogation for years, his health wasn't good, and both were desperate. An intermediary on duty in Germany got word to Dulles via von Gaevernitz that Westrick was currently in jail at Nuremberg, where he had been "closely interrogated . . . about his relations with Alan [sic] and John Foster Dulles." The pressure was considerable, and one well-disposed German national close to the process "doesn't think Westrick can resist continued interrogation for very long."[30] Dulles covered his back by disavowing to Secretary of War Robert Patterson any current relations with Westrick.[31] Nevertheless, by July the prosecutors at Nuremberg had decided to cut Westrick loose.

Closer to the bone that transitional summer of 1945 were disclosures which touched on von Gaevernitz personally.[22] A U.S. Treasury Department—Safe Haven—inquiry into the activities of the omnivorous influence peddler E. V. D. Wight produced indications that Gero and Wight had conspired in a number of instances to exploit von Gaevernitz's quasi-official position with the U.S. Legation to turn a questionable profit or ease some prospective deal onto the rails. Wight worked as European representative for Henry Mann—until 1940 the dealmaker around the Third Reich for Brown Brothers, Harriman and National City Bank, and now seeking major action for himself at 63 Wall.

Among the revelations the Treasury's bloodhounds in Bern had dug up by fall were evidence that the urbane Gaevernitz had leaned on the Swiss representative of North-German Lloyd to okay the transfer of a Finnish vessel, the SS *Ergo*, into Swiss hands. For this Gaevernitz cut up a substantial commission with his "old Berlin associate" Wight as soon as the cash got laundered through Lisbon. A long-standing association with UFA movie producer Gunther Stapenhorst seemed to have led to talk of a Swiss film-distributing company, for which Gaevernitz reportedly offered to help unblock $50,000. There were subsequent discussions of making a film in Germany with assets locked up in Switzerland. Gaevernitz offered Stapenhorst a position with the American authorities in Germany.

Beyond everything else, Gero had purportedly advised German citizens in Switzerland that the American Legation in Bern had "no ojections to their proposals to dispose of German assets including patents here"—a particularly gaudy flouting of Safe Haven guidelines. An airgram—A-1052—covering this and more left Bern on September 15, 1945. The U.S. Minister of Switzerland, Leland Harrison, had signed it, and designated as recipients the Secretary of State, the London Embassy, and Robert Murphy. "In view of recent press reports of arrest of Hugo Stinnes, Jr., in Germany," the top-secret airgram ended, "Department may wish to consider, with other interested agencies, advisability of having former Stinnes associate employed by American Government agency to advise military as to German nationals helpful in building democratic Germany."

The thing obviously blindsided Dulles. He composed an extended, indignant letter in Gaevernitz's defense to Harrison and demanded the withdrawal of the airgram. In what turned into an extremely nasty contretemps between Dulles and the principal Treasury watchdogs Harry Conover and Karl Hapke, Dulles explained away whatever Gaevernitz was up to as part of his double game of drawing in and flattering Nazi businessmen, whom Gaevernitz on Dulles's instruction had euchred "into believing that through him they might reestablish, upon the termination of the war, contacts with Allied business firms." From such exchanges, useful information flowed.

To justify Gero's current employment in Germany, Dulles maintained that ". . . von Gaevernitz in particular was to report on developments in the German zones occupied by our Allies." He stated that Gaevernitz had "many contacts in the Russian occupied zone, including contacts with Communists from whom he had obtained very valuable information, particularly with respect to the Russian seizure of machinery located there."

Nowhere in his rambling defense of von Gaevernitz did Dulles touch on the inexpungeable fact that his principal assistant had listed himself in his 1941 passport application as an agent for Schildge Rumohr, Inc., better known as Transmares. So far as he knew, Gaevernitz now shrugged, Transmares was merely another New York–based trading company "engaged in the import and export business," the officers of which had retained him to prospect for customers while he resettled in Switzerland. In actuality, Transmares had been set up by the Nazi economic ministry as a corporative blind by means of which American steel products might reach the Latin American subsidiaries of German companies as well as a cover for Nazi agents in Chile and a Farben intermediary. Transmares made sure cotton and rubber cargoes were directed into the hands of Axis agents and circumvented the British blockade en route to German ports. Gaevernitz had no idea, he indicated with some concern, any more than he seemed to be aware that, during the months he claimed to be keeping an eye out for business for the company, Allen Dulles himself was winding up his service as General Counsel for J. Henry Schroder. According to a postwar study, "the relationship between the Schroeder interests in the United States and Transmares was close."[33]

Harrison's telegram looked calculated to raise an unholy stink just as other reservations about Dulles were spreading. Allen had been particularly worked up to discover that the contents of the top-secret cable were "known all over Germany." The Treasury attachés reversed that by observing "that it was difficult to avoid construing Mr. Dulles' remarks other than to constitute an indictment of Mr. Murphy." Suspicion coated every exchange.

The Treasury investigators wondered about another of the financially hyperactive E. V. D. Wight's enterprises.[34] Implicated from the outset in shenanigans which ranged from purchasing Finnish machine guns for the Nazis to brokering a buyout of the Ausnit position in Metalunit for the Reichswerke Hermann Goering, Wight claimed intelligence credentials and convinced both the hapless U.S. military attaché to the Legation, General B. R. Legge, and Dulles that he could be trusted to put deals together with companies "blacklisted" by the U.S. Treasury. As the war sputtered to an end Dulles seems to have promoted the idea that Wight buy into the proscribed Takvorian tobacco company, with an eye to developing espionage nets across the wayward Balkans. Wight also got behind an oil pipeline from Genoa to the Swiss border, "which he had been endeavoring to arrange in behalf of Allen Dulles," Hapke's rundown specified.

By then a group of desperate Hungarian businessmen fronted by Count Szechenyi were hoping to unload their industrial properties on Americans, who just might reason that the Soviets would recompense their wartime allies in the event of expropriation. As usual, Wight was out front. For years both the Hungarian Minister in Bern, Baron George Bessenyey, and Barcza, the Minister to London currently relocated in Lausanne, had maintained close ties to Dulles, who underwrote their anti-Nazi Committee of Hungarian Ministers after the 1944 German invasion of Hungary. According to a Safe Haven report, Wight and his middleman Antoine Heinrich (for years a spokesman for the Manfred Weiss interests) involved Dulles in putting his own connections to work in disposing of the shares of the beleaguered Hungarians at advantageous prices to Henry Mann and his backers. Both Allen and the OSS representative in Zurich, van Ness, were reportedly affirmative about the deal. "Reports indicate," the U.S. Minister, Harrison, emphasized in his wire to State, "that certain OSS officials have given them encouragement." Mann was simultaneously maneuvering to pick up the Farben remnants in the British Empire. Dulles denied any conversation with Heinrich and "was quite certain he had never discussed said proposals with Wight."

Officers around the Legation also bristled at rumors that it had been Allen Dulles whom agents of the Nazi-era Hungarian Credit Bank approached to receive the Hungarian gold reserve—something on the order of 30 million francs—in return for protection for the bank's 450 employees. Allen informed his U.S. military government cohorts, who accepted the hoard and bivouacked the refugees at Spital am Pyhren in Austria. But there are interdepartmental uneasiness at how these potentially touchy manipulations of Allen's were laid to rest.

Altogether, it put off as straitlaced a career man as Leland Harrison to assume even *cover* responsibility for anybody like Dulles, whom he had watched darting in and out since Paris in 1919. Harrison ignored Robert Joyce's bellyaching to Magruder about the lack of "efficiency, discretion, and security of the office of the Commercial Counselor . . . in connection with an endeavor to attack a member of Allen Dulles' staff. . . ."[35] There was a boyishness at times which verged on scatterbrained about Allen, a born rogue's receptivity predicated on a confidence that he could explain away anything. Espionage, he liked to confide between pulls at the pipe, was not a business for Archbishops. One anticipated breakage.

Certain of Dulles's informants grew odious in time, like rats dying inside history's walls. Consider Willi Hoettl. Hoettl intended to trade his nets in Hungary and Rumania for favors in the West; to head him off, Donovan tipped off General Fitin to the NKVD, and deputized Allen to push the collaboration through. But Fitin remained wary, and demanded a workup of *other* Yankee contacts. The Joint Chiefs reconsidered. Bartering was already underway between representatives of the Chiefs and Wehrmacht intelligence wizard Reinhard Gehlen, whose Fremde Heere Ost files brimmed with niceties about the Russians.[36]

Brooding in the lockup at Nuremberg, Hoettl alluded pointedly to the innumerable courtesies he'd distributed among the OSS in Switzerland and Italy. The impudent little Balkan specialist evidentally pinked the right nerve, because he was out in less than a month.[37] Ultimately—to Dulles's horror—Willi discovered his pen. His self-glorifying books and magazine articles rarely scanted his close, reciprocal liaison with Allen Dulles in Bern. At one point Allen was reduced to signing a deposition to the effect that he was *never* in personal contact with the gregarious ex-Sturmbannfuehrer. In one 1953 CIA memorandum, an aide who has just reviewed Hoettl's latest nervously assures the CIA Director that "on close inspection I find that he nowhere claims to have actually seen you, although the implication is there."[38]

Finally, decent employment behind him, Hoettl founded a boarding school.

Allen Dulles's slow summer and fall in Germany played as an entr'acte. It was temporary duty. Switzerland retained its allure. Soon after the Swiss–French frontier opened Clover had made her way to Bern. Allen was obviously devoted in his way to Clover, even then a comely woman with an assurance in matters of civilization her preoccupied husband tended to brush off. Once Clover caught up with Allen in Bern he kept her at arm's length, especially where intelligence duties beckoned.

On several occasions she "didn't know what had become of him," she later told one companion. "Whether he was alive or dead. Once, they'd gone to a sidewalk cafe in the morning, to have a cup of coffee, and a couple, a man and a woman, came by. And they sat down at the table with no introduction, and there were a few desultory comments, and then Allen and this man got up without any explanation and walked off. And she was left sitting with this stranger, whom she had never seen before, and after trying to make conversation they decided to part. She went home, and she never saw him for three days. She said he was constantly disappearing that way. The agony of worrying about him—was he alive, or dead, or kidnapped?—was a great strain."[39]

Dulles intended to spare his wife, Mary Bancroft concluded, "a certain moral queasiness at various activities in which we were forced to engage."[40] In time Allen fobbed Clover off on Mary in Zurich, and soon the well-bred American women became close. Her husband's raw, inexplicable ambition continued to tell on Clover. "Someone once said," she confided to Mary, " 'The Dulles brothers are like sharks.' And I do think they are."[41] Mary Bancroft introduced

Clover to the intricacies of Jungian psychoanalysis. When Allen pushed on to Germany Clover stayed behind in Zurich with Mary.

❑

Although Dulles's importance decelerated the moment he crossed into defeated Germany, the careers of other contemporaries were speeding up. One emphatic success story by then was that of Robert Murphy, who emerged in 1945 as the pivot man around General Lucius Clay's U.S. Military Government in Germany, OMGUS. As political advisor to OMGUS, one of Murphy's duties was to collect every tidbit of information he could, on everything from political affairs to agricultural projections.

Murphy was soon grateful for the input of Clay's Economics Division head, Brigadier General William H. Draper, Jr. Draper was a dentist's son from New York City who had hung onto his First World War reserve commission while forging a career in the investment banking business. In 1927 he joined the go-getters around Dillon, Read, and by the end of the thirties he'd reached senior management along with James V. Forrestal and Paul Nitze. A slim, well-met, stately looking smoothie with commanding black brows and a crooked smile, Draper was expected to administer the controversial directives in Joint Chiefs of Staff 1067, which bore on decartelization, restitution of assets to Germany's recent victims, and reparations deliveries.

It would have been hard to uncover many candidates for the slot whose backgrounds predisposed them less. An outspoken free-enterpriser, Draper showed very little interest in mincing up such conglomerates as Fritz Thyssen's Vereinigte Stahlwerke, the German steel cartel he and his fellow promoters at Dillon, Read underwrote late in the twenties.

Draper and his successors shouldered into the fray like top-drawer legal talent imported fast to shut up an array of temporarily deranged senior shareholders, in this instance several batches of would-be social engineers from the Justice and Treasury Departments. Advising Draper was Laird Bell, the outspoken Chicago barrister with prewar conditioning in Germany as Foster Dulles's traveling companion throughout their junkets in behalf of defrauded American bondholders.

The group drew heavily on assessments by Captain Norbert A. Bogdan, an ingratiating financial man on loan to the War

Department from his vice-presidential post at J. Henry Schroder. Bogdan had landed in Algiers with Eisenhower to back Murphy up on the financial side, then relocated to Caserta. After France was liberated Bogdan appeared frequently in Bern to update Allen Dulles and Lada Mocarski.[42] As Germany went under, Bogdan first attempted to head off a U.S. Army Finance Division investigation of the J. H. Stein bank, Baron von Schroeder's stronghold, by dismissing it as "small potatoes," then agitated for travel orders to Cologne even before the city had fallen to bottle up the Schroeder records.[43]

One unmistakable little figure arrived at Murphy's elbow: his special assistant Carmel Offie. Since 1940 Murphy had been maneuvering with persistence and ingenuity to add Bullitt's squat, magnetic sidekick to his own staff. His moment came halfway through the war, when Roosevelt's uneasiness about Bullitt's kid-glove insubordination after Paris fell blew up into real resentment over the Welles affair.

Bullitt had overreached, catastrophically. Still agitated over Sumner Welles's European tour in 1940, Bullitt's vanity was "wounded," Murphy saw, and Bullitt easily attributed his downfall to Welles when Roosevelt slipped Bullitt's ambassadorship out from under him days after the 1940 elections and leaked word of Admiral Leahy's appointment while Bullitt was assuring newsmen he intended to soldier on in the post.

It became an obsession of Bullitt's to take Welles down alongside himself. Welles presented many paradoxes. A kind of personal protégé of Franklin Roosevelt's since his Groton days, Welles indulged a variety of aristocratic predilections. He drank quite heavily—compulsively, from time to time—and as he blacked out he longed for sexual favors from younger men, the coarser and swarthier they came the more to his liking. Then, in September of 1940, Welles overdid the whiskey on the Presidential train returning from the funeral of House Speaker William Bankhead and seems to have summoned a couple of bewildered black Pullman porters to his compartment; there he demanded services not routinely on order to passengers on the Pennsylvania Railroad.[44] One commentator would maintain that the two were pushed on the statesman for entrapment purposes by J. Edgar Hoover.[45] Whatever their original motivation, the porters saw fit to file a complaint about Welles's solicitation with officials of the carrier, and it was this document which subsequently reached Bullitt and provided him the evidence he longed for.

For some months Bullitt propagated stories in Washington which not only embroidered on the incident but suggested that Welles's heiress wife, Mathilde Townsend, was carnally involved with a Russian agent who compelled Sumner to turn over bushels of Department of State secrets. In April 1941 Bullitt hand-carried to FDR an affidavit from the railroad which detailed Welles's indiscretion. He'd brought this in, Bullitt confided to FDR, in fulfillment of a deathbed promise he'd made to the recently deceased Judge Moore. The President glumly conceded the validity of the charge, and told Bullitt that he was now having Welles watched by a "guardian."

The interview upset Roosevelt. After that he threw Bullitt a sop from time to time—a mission to Cairo, the chairmanship in passing of General Aniline—but connived to keep his mischievous ex-confidant well away from anything substantive.

For anybody as morbidly sensitive as Bullitt to fluctuations in the political barometer, these put-downs became unbearable. When Hitler invaded Russia, Bullitt belabored the President with reminders that, whatever the commonness of the cause, the "Communists in the United States are just as dangerous enemies as ever, and should not be allowed to crawl into our productive mechanism in order later to wreck it when they get new orders from somewhere abroad."[46] He espoused de Gaulle. Swallowing hard, Bullitt moved sourly into a Special Assistant office in the Navy Department the president stuck him in and assured Roosevelt in June 1942 that "I am most happy to have found a spot—however minor—in which I can render real war service."[47]

Of course, he wasn't. It happened that Carmel Offie was in and out of Washington regularly during those months, detailed to the Navy briefly (where the head of the OSS Planning Group James Grafton Rogers quickly dubbed him "Bullitt's slave").[48] He sat in routinely at the weekly "Russian lunch" John Wiley then sponsored at Hall's, along with Elbridge Durbrow, Fred Reinhardt, and newcomers to the Slavic specialities like Robert Joyce. In company with several of his luncheon mates Offie felt the heat by then from his increasingly attentive draft board, stirred up by Cissy Patterson's *Times-Herald* broadsides at cookie-pushers in the Foreign Service "who do not choose to fight."

It was on one of these descents into Washington that Bullitt handed Carmel a pile of incriminating railroad documents and directed him to distribute these handbills around Capitol Hill. Then Bullitt pushed in on Roosevelt and told the aghast FDR that he "could not ignore the scandal any longer, because now every Congressman, every Senator knows." By April of 1943 Maine Senator Owen Brewster was leading the pack, privately threatening to dump the entire matter squarely onto the agenda of the Truman Committee.[49] Roosevelt gave it up and accepted Welles's resignation.

The President was irate. Bill Bullitt was finished. He joined the Fighting French as an aide to General de Lattre de Tassigny and landed in the South of France in 1944. A jeep accident crippled him, and although he survived the war and remained a force in Society for some years, after that his effervescence and puckishness went flat for good.

In March of 1943 Carmel Offie got assigned to Bob Murphy's staff on the U.S. Advisory Council for Italy, and for the next five years *Murphy* functioned as Offie's guarantor. Murphy brought Carmel with him to Frankfurt and Berlin when he himself moved up as Lucius Clay's political adviser. Offie was unique.

Donald Heath was serving at the time as Murphy's deputy, observes the State Department's Jacob Beam. While Offie didn't have much to do with policy, Beam says, "he became Bob Murphy's sort of batman, increasingly. He knew all the people [in the U.S. missions] in Moscow and Poland and he was useful to us in that respect," Beam notes. "If you wanted a job done—an undercover job, getting around regulations—he was very good at it. It was no trouble. . . . He had some contacts, particularly the French . . . he was into all sorts of things. You had to keep a pretty close eye on him, which Murphy did. He was very fond of him. He was *very* useful. He was very close to the military. They ran all the planes."[50]

Under normal circumstances this short, rather clownlike figure with the bulging eyes and the slicked-back patent-leather hair and the overpowering stream of insider references probably couldn't have propelled himself to heights like these while still in his middle thirties. What made him competed for, fought over by senior officials was the handle he seemed to have on specifics around Europe, minutiae, his world of contacts so dense that he became a genie to well-wishers. One rub accomplished anything.

To this Offie added the availability of cast-iron bureaucratic balls. He retained an aptitude for darting between the cracks in the government, for sensing when better-groomed, more pretentious superiors were leery about something and moving in at his own initiative, risking reprimand or disaster to get the damned thing behind them. He liked to chuckle over the weekend in Caserta just at the tailing-out stage of the war when there was nobody around the headquarters, and one day a directive came down from Washington to discourage Tito and his people, who were making noises about consolidating their grip on Trieste. Carmel did not hesitate. He grabbed a secure telephone and ordered on his own authority that a major segment of the U.S. Fifteenth Air Force—hundreds, thousands of combat aircraft—take off from their bases and overfly Trieste at as low a level as possible "to give the Jugs an idea of what they were trifling with," an associate of Offie's remembers. "He spoke of it afterwards with great glee."[51]

Yet it was Offie's social nerve that astonished people. A functionary in the Budapest Legation recalls receiving an urgent message from Frankfurt: Contact Carmel Offie! He called Germany immediately. Offie wasted no time. There was a certain variety of petit-point handbag only the Hungarian embroiderers made. He wanted one immediately—if necessary, by the diplomatic pouch—as a special present for Mrs. Clay.[52]

"In these days Bob Murphy was mostly in Berlin," General Richard Stilwell says, "and Carmel was running the show in Frankfurt. He accomplished a lot with his magnificent ability to reciprocate favors. He had the best cuisine in Frankfurt, he brought back delicacies, his chef was superb. A dinner at Offie's was a treat, much sought by senior personalities. I remember that he considered that one general and his wife were fourflushers to the nth degree. So he invited them to a dinner party, and told his chef to empty their snail shells, and restuff the shells with hamburger.

"When everybody rose from the table later on, Carmel made it his business to leave with the general's wife. He asked her how she liked her snails. 'They were the best I ever tasted,' she told him. That amused Offie. It substantiated his judgement."[53]

On one of his briefing runs to Washington, Clay stumbled onto the fact that a plethora of vital detail about Germany was getting back to the State Department concerning which he himself was completely in the dark. "That was where Ambassador Murphy ran into trouble with General Clay," Hector Prudhomme recalls. Prudhomme was a neophyte State Department desk officer in Frankfurt at the time. "General Clay being a fearfully positive sort of person," Prudhomme says, "it was not of course agreeable to General Clay that because of Ambassador Murphy's reporting system the Department usually knew more about what was going on in Germany than General Clay and his crowd. So he issued an order that nothing was to go out of Germany except over his signature."[54]

It was to circumvent that directive that Prudhomme subsequently found himself in Frankfurt serving as a kind of State-Department cutout for whatever intelligence product Murphy intended to deny

Clay; Prudhomme was to relay it to Jack Hickerson at Foggy Bottom. Carmel Offie brought it over on regular shuttle runs.

This was when Prudhomme and his wife met Offie. "I don't know by what magic Offie drew people to him," Prudhomme admits, "and made it possible for him to do all the things we all wish we could do and never can. But he did." Offie promoted himself onto a first-name basis with all the generals, Prudhomme remembers. He picked up Walter Gieseking, the brilliant virtuoso pianist just beginning to emerge from under a cloud for having entertained Hitler. "Offie would have soirees, and all the important people in military government would come to Offie's house to enjoy hearing Gieseking play."[55] Pressing favors on the important figures he knew, accumulating chits, Carmel built up an aura that excited expectation and gratitude wherever he went. He would catch a hop to Italy on an errand, Prudhomme remembers, and the next morning an eighteen-inch Gorgonzola cheese would appear at the Prudhommes' door.

"Offie would come sweeping in here," Prudhomme says, "and before you knew it we'd all be at a much higher level of endearment, of communication and interest. And then before you knew it he'd dash out, and go do it somewhere else." But still, for all the whitecaps of gratitude forever foaming in Carmel Offie's wake, even the inexperienced Prudhomme recognized that "one had the feeling, without wishing to probe, that he was involved in a whole lot of things that he would never wish to tell us about. . . . Who was it that said about Offie that either he was going to be Secretary of State some day or his body was going to be found floating down the Potomac River?"

10

LIKE A PROSTITUTE IN A SALOON

Another conjurer who very quickly made himself felt across the uneasy Military Government was Donovan's surrogate Allen Dulles. Already crowded by Murphy, Lucius Clay didn't welcome another pretentious and unruly civilian attempting to call up *his* agenda. He brushed Allen off. The New Yorker's clubby, raffish style could lead to trouble, Clay sensed: Dulles had a way of manipulating things, calling on his friends to bypass the chain of command.[1] As recently as July, tipped off by Per Jacobsson of the Bank for International Settlements that the Japanese were looking for a back channel to initiate an orderly surrender, Dulles rushed to Jack McCloy. McCloy arranged for a sweltering interview with Secretary of War Stimson the same week the Big Three were parlaying at Potsdam. It amounted to one last Dulles gesture to exclude the Soviets. Stimson heard Dulles out, and let the matter drop.[2] The "fat men" were all but loaded into the bellies of their superfortresses, and Truman's inner council had decided on an alternative approach to sobering up Stalin.

Dulles's weakness for old-boy grandstanding, OSS-style, made him a questionable player to many of the institutional nut-cutters. They recognized a quirk in his makeup which kept him quite ruthless, quite irresponsible when dealing with forces out there, on paper.

But close in, Allen's gregariousness, the pleasure he took in placating his followers, loaded him with attachments which threw his judgment off.

His mind worked anecdotally: He liked to get things started, then let fly. One bunch Dulles fought for now was his Crown Jewels, the handful of putative "Good Germans" who survived the attempt on Hitler's life. They swarmed now for special consideration. American investigators arrived at the farm of the Good Hope industrialist Alfred Haniel outside Düsseldorf to find a contingent of U.S. troops "especially assigned to protect him—no one seemed to know by whose order." His passport indicated a dozen trips to Switzerland, as recently as September 1944, where "his contact . . . had been with Mr. Allen W. Dulles. . . ."[3]

Another Haniel family member who'd gotten to Dulles that month was Guenther, Baron von Heimhausen. The thirty-six-year-old scion had sought Dulles out soon after he fled Germany on September 13, 1944, terrified that he had been implicated in the July 20 plot. Haniel swam Lake Constance loaded down with heirloom jewels worth 450,000 Swiss frances.[4] Dulles recruited Haniel for clandestine missions to Germany, from which he returned with details of Gestapo and SD activities, and "helpful information regarding industrial combines, intercorporate relationships and industrial personnel."

In 1948 Haniel was still litigating to recover his impounded jewelry—Guenther's Jewish stepmother, Mrs. Kent von Branca, had filed a counterclaim—and Haniel retained Dulles to represent him before the Allied Commission. Its British and French representatives were "reluctant" to return the assets in view of their findings that Guenther had been an enthusiastic Nazi virtually from the takeover. In 1934 the Baron had moved over from the SA to the SS, in which he reached the rank of Oberscharfuehrer in 1938. ". . . It was not unlikely," the commissioners had concluded, "that his later services to the OSS were motivated more by opportunistic factors than by a desire to serve the Allies and to crush Nazism in Germany."[5]

Even more awkwardly, Dulles repeatedly pulled strings around the American Military Government for barefaced Nazi sympathizers like his aged correspondent attorney in Berlin, Heinrich Albert. Albert's was a name that showed up first on U.S. secret service watch lists as early as 1914, as paymaster for the ring of dynamiters who set off the Black Tom explosions. Characterized then by Senate investigators as "the mildest mannered man who ever scuttled a ship or cut a throat,"[6] Albert was expelled from the United States. A devout National Socialist, Albert kept an eye on the Ford Company's huge Cologne plant throughout the Second World War. Allen Dulles lost little time in insinuating Heinrich onto a government payroll as supervisor of U.S. and British properties around Berlin. Cognac from the Dulles brothers arrived every Christmas. Albert's thank-you notes tended to be circumspect, noting that ". . . there are obvious reasons to be rather vague."[7]

A slew of cables from and to Dulles between August and October 1945 project as clearly as pins on a tactical map his personal concerns. His support people needed special attention: Fritz Kolbe certainly deserved some time in Switzerland "for rest and recuperation," while Erika Glaser was welcome "as secretary for a trial period." Dulles fussed a little to release "certain payments . . . for completion war diary work" to Gisevius, and relayed the wishes of "Dr. Albert," then "anxious to get in touch with his daughter Mrs. Elizabeth Berger. . . ." Concerning Prof. Dr. Sauerbruch, Hitler's physician—so accommodating to Kolbe, and willing, Dulles later divulged to Donovan, to risk his own neck by carrying a sheaf of diplomatic intercepts over the frontier to the OSS in Bern—Dulles cautioned Wiesbaden that "From investigation here convinced SHAEF card listing him as SS STBF [Sturmbannfuehrer] is erroneous and due to typing or other error."[8]

Allen forgave and forgot, with perspicacity and discrimination. One cable is devoted to making sure of ground transportation and appropriate introductions in Germany for the BIS's Thomas McKittrick. Another requests that "Tiny [Gisevius] endeavor ascertain Blessing's address Frankfurt." Carl Blessing had been a senior Nazi banker and reliable celebrant at Freundekreis Heinrich Himmler festivities until deep into the war, but disaffected enough the last year so that his name bobbed up in 1944 on resistance-government lists; ultimately, Blessing would become the Bundesrepublik President who engineered the rescue of Krupp.[9] Another dignitary in Dulles's sights was Dr. Hans Globke, "considered for Interior" on the slate he submitted for vetting. Globke was the bureaucratic phenomenon who wrote the operative commentary on the anti-Semitic Nuremberg Laws in 1935, reappeared as Adenauer's primary i-dotter, and solidified his Richelieu-like control of postwar Bonn by making sure the Chancellor provided consistent—furtive—backup to Reinhard Gehlen's intelligence complex, his "Org."[10] Meanwhile, von Gaevernitz was pestering the Allied Command in Rome to pressure U.S. Army counterintelligence in Austria into turning over to SS General Karl Wolff's impatient family their requisitioned St. Wolfgang estate.

Having designed his own war, Allen anticipated no difficulties with organizing the peace.

* * *

After Admiral Doenitz surrendered, it was quickly apparent that there would be no Redoubt, no block-by-block infantry mop-up, few last-ditch adolescent Werewolves still pressing to breast the machine gun fire of armored personnel carriers to revenge the cremated Fuehrer. Germany was instantaneously supine, limp before the conquerors. Dulles and his OSS holdovers had rolled into a political vacuum. By then Allen's mind tended to wander among attachments, and around OSS installations in both Berlin and Wiesbaden a catch-as-catch-can mood was up. Individuals groped for priorities, and nobody seemed interested.

At Wiesbaden, for example, Arthur Goldberg's old sidekick Gerhard van Arkel had set up his Labor Desk after a few months in Bern to try and reinvigorate trade unionism, while his secretary-interpreter, Noel Field's foster daughter Erika Glaser, ferreted out Communist functionaries around the district and pressed on them documents filched from her employers.[11] Emmy Rado followed up her World Council of Churches contacts to push into local governments moderates such as the Socialist Erich Ollenhauer instead of Moscow-directed Communist professionals. "She was a really shrewd cookie about what was going on in Germany," her new boss, Frank Wisner, reflected later. And "long before everyone else got off their white horse."[12]

Frank Wisner showed up heavily touted around Washington to look after Secret Intelligence at the Wiesbaden station after five celebrated months in Rumania in 1944 just as the Red Army arrived. Wisner garnered his first burst of acclaim by negotiating the release of 1,800 downed Allied airman in camps around the Balkans; a spring of sparring with the commissars had abraded something once and for all in Frank. There was a coiled, expectant quality about the articulate thirty-four-year old Wall Street attorney, something few could miss which drove him exceedingly hard. Wisner was boiling over with an anti-Soviet sense of mission which was already beginning to take people aback.

It happened that Arthur Schlesinger, Jr. wound up his months of service in Europe at Wiesbaden. The main building in the OSS compound was a requisitioned Champagne factory, and Schlesinger still recalls with something of a gleam the practice of doling the bubbly out after hours at ten cents a glass. For Wisner just then, such amenities meant very little. "He was already mobilizing for the cold war," Schlesinger says. "Very eager to get all possible intelligence about the Russians, and using the Germans for the purpose. I was not aware then of the extent to which we were extracting those people from the denazification process and sending them around the world."

Schlesinger remembers his commanding officer as a "high-strung, demanding sort of fellow without really being pompous or standing on rank." Of average height, the impatient Lieutenant Commander Wisner seemed sometimes to brace himself when speaking, as if even then what he had discovered about the Soviets hammered in the air. His wide, canted eyes gave him almost a Hungarian look, and tended to narrow once he was launched into his opinions (his jaw thrust forward, lips flared to expose the gap between his powerful incisors), so that at times it could be quite a project to drag him off his subject. "I myself was no great admirer of the Soviet Union," Schlesinger says, "and I certainly had no expectation of harmonious relations after the war. But Frank was a little excessive. Even for me."[13]

Between trips to Switzerland, Allen Dulles kept busy that summer. Von Gaevernitz was constantly sifting the POW cages for veterans with experience behind Soviet lines; the mobs of displaced Ukranians and Balts and Poles stewing in their camps attracted many services. One team the OSS sent out to retrieve a German general was ambushed with its prisoner, its marshals clubbed senseless with Red Army rifle butts while their quarry disappeared.[14] A first-hand look at the sort of broad-scale collectivistic brutality Stalin applied to border revisions, his slipshod reshuffling of entire populations, now stirred in Dulles a visceral repugnance. Wisner had the picture right.

Overhanging the OSS all year had been a 54-page study pieced together by Colonel Richard Park, who ran the White House Map Room through much of the war. Something of a protégé of George Strong—who turned over Army G-2 a few months before to the like-minded Major General Clayton Bissell—Park had been authorized by Franklin Roosevelt personally to attempt an "informal investigation of the Office of Strategic Services," and report back. He isolated more than 120 items detailing "incompetence, insecurity, corruption, 'orgies,' nepotism and black-marketeering." Park pointed up what amounted to an abject dependency on the British intelligence community.[15]

This reflected on Dulles in particular: by autumn of 1945 the story was around the command of a handful of OSS officers operating out of Dulles's station in Berlin who organized a black marketeering free-for-all which transcended the endemic petty trafficking in watches and spun off a range of commodities ranging from U.S. visas to herds of cattle and museum-quality art treasures. Tipped off by concerned aides that the mover behind the operation, an OSS major, had taken over the soignée wife of an absent Berlin banker along with his butler in livery—and now was servicing his customers out of the missing plutocrat's mansion—Dulles couldn't get that exercised, really. "No evidence," he reportedly decided aloud. "You can't condemn a man without evidence."[16]

Lucius Clay wasn't surprised. "How the hell can you expect those guys to catch spies," he is said to have erupted when he heard of it, "when they can't smell the stink under their own noses?"[17]

When Clay wanted intelligence work, he relied on the G-2 crowd, or counterintelligence, or the archivists setting up the Document Center in Berlin. Between his hanky-panky in Switzerland and all those carbuncular reactionaries Allen liked to romanticize, who knew what dead cats the OSS might bedeck them with?

This atmosphere of letdown to the verge of anarchy bemused the trim, sleek, rather noncommittal-seeming naval officer to whom Dulles left the administration end of his Berlin section. Lt. Richard Helms started out in New York plotting German submarine routes in the North Atlantic in 1943; he turned down one chance to transfer into the OSS, then found himself requisitioned onto Donovan's payroll because of the French and German he'd soaked up in Continental boarding schools and as a United Press reporter based out of Berlin. Helms was carefully bred—he'd proved a comer at Williams; his grandfather, Gates McGarrah, had been the first president of The Bank for International Settlements—but he was not rich. A flyer in advertising as well as his exposure to shoeleather journalism convinced Helms he would be best advised to select some organization, and gamble on diligence and alertness and loyalty. By 1945 he had a lot of time invested in intelligence.[18]

As irregularities piled up, Helms eased to one side; he surveyed the corruption with a characteristically surprised air, as if he alone was taking in the fine print. Peter Sichel, who replaced Helms as commanding officer at the Berlin outstation, flew in on October 1, 1945. Helms met his plane. On the drive back Helms remarked to Sichel in either French or German that the man driving the limousine was already worth a couple of hundred thousand dollars from black market profits. "And that's the problem you're going to have here," Helms told Sichel, "you're going to have to get rid of all these people, because otherwise you are never going to be able to run an intelligence unit."[19]

Along with chasing Nazis and identifying scientists, Helms was already being pushed by Wisner and Dulles to "find out what the Russians were up to." Alongside the romantic if lackadaisical Dulles and the sometimes overwrought Frank Wisner, Helms provided a sustaining presence, their branch-office manager. While Dulles attended receptions, Helms looked after housekeeping requirements. "Before CD completely liquidated," he wired out of Berlin as October ran out, "have sent here Russian typewriter and small stocks of basic German blanks such as Kennkarte, Reisepass, Fremden Pass also selected rubber stamps of German police authorities." Carryover obligations kicked up.[20] "We warned Allen Dulles that a number of his friends were on the Black List,"[21] Sichel recollects. As late as November of 1945 a Helms cable recurs to a "phone conversation between Bessermann and Wight, and requests proper authorization to transport certain designated Germans."[22]

Once 1945 ended, and Wisner and Dulles returned to corporate law, Helms himself signed on as Whitney Shepardson's SI assistant in the War Department's intelligence remnant. On trips to Washington Dick Helms was somebody to lunch with to remain abreast of developments around "The Business."

❑

Germany was a shambles. At Belsen British troopers who could bear the stench stood watch with bayonets fixed over SS noncoms while two by two they heaved the stripped, knobby remains of corpses onto open lorries for immediate burial in mass graves. Entire families squatted camped in urban debris, with sometimes a flowered sofa or what was recognizable from a tea service with which to resume civilities.

Intelligence detachments seemed equally disoriented. Escapees from POW holding pens traded tips with black marketeers still redolent of DP delousing baths. Decades afterward, in retrospect, it seems the real prize would be the clutch of Soviet experts and the fifty-two steel cases of microfilmed records a subdued ex-Wehrmacht general by the name of Reinhard Gehlen pulled out of the pastures above Elendsalm in the Bavarian Alps. Gehlen and his confederates had buried their hoard days before the shooting stopped.

Former Major General Reinhard Gehlen was forty-three at the time, a puny, flap-eared intelligence prodigy cold-blooded enough to have submitted a situation report which stirred his goggle-eyed Fuehrer to brush Gehlen's papers and maps to the floor and shriek that the analyst belonged in a lunatic asylum.[23] But inside two weeks that autumn of 1944 the Soviet First Byelorussian Army had borne Gehlen out by grinding across two-thirds of the sandy East Prussian backlands and panicking Berlin. Gehlen survived into spring.

Gehlen personally was trapped between his devotion as a Nazi and his technician's compulsion to assign data and derive conclusions. The dedicated little Junker represented four generations of duty-ridden Prussian staff officers from Breslau. He'd built his first reputation as Field Marshal Erich von Manstein's sharpest operations specialist, an important hand in the detailing of virtually every Wehrmacht campaign in the East beginning with the walk-through of Austria.

Once war came, general officers up and down the army were competing for the services of this ruminative little major with the mousy thinning hair—indeed, there was a rodentlike scurry and quickness to everything Gehlen attempted, accentuated by his crimped, sharp features and all-seeing impersonality. Gehlen's break arrived in April of 1942. The Army's troubled Chief of Staff Franz Halder had conceded that behind the Red Army's show of strength before the gates of Moscow were guns and men unanticipated by his high command. Everything pointed to an intelligence shortfall. The intelligence subdivision responsible, Fremde Heere Ost (FHO), needed closer direction. Halder installed the tiny lieutenant colonel. Gehlen had very little intelligence training, but he had been fixated on the Soviets much of his life, and quickly pulled together a series of order-of-battle studies and prisoner interrogation workups which provided the fighting commanders their first coherent presentation of Soviet troop dispersal and reserve industrial capacities.

Gehlen ignored Nazi prejudices: one preliminary study dismisses the "debatable notion" that the average Russian was some manner of inferior creature as "indubitably an error of the first order.[24] Ignoring purists, Gehlen instructed his disaffected Desk IIk chief, a Baltic baron named Alexis Freiherr von Roenne, to proselytize for sincere Eastern defectors; Roenne stamped into being the controversial anti-Soviet army of renegade Lieutenant-General Andrei Vlassov. To cover himself politically, Gehlen put in for a consultant from the Foreign Office, Soviet specialist Gustav Hilger, George Kennan's long-standing counterpart as Counselor of Legation in Moscow. Should anything go awry, Hilger's credentials might distract the eternally vindictive von Ribbentrop.[25]

Gehlen was soon pillaging Admiral Canaris's divided Abwehr. Much of Gehlen's raw data originated with the far-flung Walli groups playing back and forth across Soviet lines under the direction of the Abwehr's fluttery, Odessa-born Major Hermann Baun.

The test for Gehlen arrived that last, pitched year of the war. Throughout the bitter campaigns, Gehlen had done what he could to keep his field personnel unmuddied by the sensational atrocities perpetrated under SS auspices by Stefan Bandera's OUN and UPA, those *Nachtigall* and *Roland* regiments of the Ukrainian Freedom Legion which butchered compatriots wholesale along with whatever Jews and Poles turned up. But Gehlen had understood all along precisely when and what to compromise after years of intimate collaboration with Himmler's notorious battle units.[26]

It was the *tonalities* of the SS which bled into everybody's sensibilities. Gehlen's Abwehr stepchild, Hermann Baun, flavored up his reports on Russian morale with references to the "strong Jewification of the rear echelon" and the "generic affinity of Jewry and the Bolshevist system."[27] Years before he died following an ambush in Prague in 1942, Reinhard Heydrich, the scorching, brilliant impresario of the SS counterintelligence service, the Sicherheitsdienst, started pushing to extend the SD's tenuous paramilitary franchise. He authorized Operation Zeppelin, a program to pick over Russian POWs for legitimate anti-Communists to infiltrate as saboteurs and sappers behind the Soviet lines. Others would be trained in signal techniques to radio out Red Army formations and resupply bottlenecks. Reinhard Gehlen and Heydrich sat down at Vinnitza the spring of 1941 to divide up operational requirements between the FHO and these projected Zeppelin Sonderkommandos.[28]

Gehlen caught Himmler's eye when briefly the Reichsfuehrer SS assumed command of Army Group Vistula: before long Gehlen and the swashbuckling Sturmbannfuehrer Otto Skorzeny accepted supply responsibilities for the "Werewolves," that deathbed hiccup of children and defectives with which the Party intended to harass the rear areas.[29] By now a general officer, Reinhard Gehlen proved himself a stubborn, reliable patriot to the very end.

Nevertheless, he determined as early as 1942 that military victory wasn't likely. On April 9, 1945, infuriated by one last report from "crazy General Gehlen," der Fuehrer had attempted to relieve this nagging little fury of his unwelcome command. Gehlen was too busy to worry about his own dismissal. He kept his staff at work reproducing their cross-indexed card file, the product of a lifetime of pondering the Soviet menace. Days ahead of Patton's spearheads, Gehlen oversaw the burial of the fifty-two steel cases with which he intended to bankroll a postwar career. After that he lay low and awaited his opportunity.

Gehlen anticipated an honor guard, but there were many generals wobbling out of the woods just then. It would require weeks of being bumped around from one Seventh Army POW transit cage to the next before Gehlen stood before Twelfth Army G-2 Brigadier General Ed Sibert, who made him describe on paper his wartime activities at Fremde Heere Ost. The 129-page resume he came up with turned into his job application.[30]

Sibert tipped off Beedle Smith, Eisenhower's Chief of Staff; the two avoided informing the Supreme Commander, since Ike still treated the antifraternization decrees with surprising respect. So Smith approached sympathizers in the War Department. Shortly before August ended, Gehlen and a half dozen FHO staff veterans were spirited out of Germany on Beedle Smith's assigned aircraft and relocated under heavy guard at Fort Hunt, Virginia.

Gehlen made his presentation before an intimidating cross-section of the emerging Cold-War establishment. William Leahy, Harry Truman's chief of staff, came out for the initial conference, along with the G-2 specialists Generals George Strong and Alex Bolling. Out of the OSS leadership Major General John Magruder sat in, flanked by senior analysts Loftus Becker and Sherman Kent. In town for the exchanges, according to several reports, was Allen Dulles.[31]

Dulles appears to have been excluded from Gehlen's summer-long debriefing in Germany, but he'd been aware of the acquisition. As early as April Fritz Kolbe tipped Dulles off to the availability of this Wehrmacht concentration of Soviet specialists, which Kolbe had reason to believe was prepared to exchange its matchless archives for unspecified advantages.[32] Dulles purportedly deputized Frank Wisner to look in on Gehlen shortly after his capture.[33] Nothing came of that; Ed Sibert kept Allen informed, but only at the meeting in Washington was Dulles invited officially to contribute his opinions.

By then the terms of the deal were already hardening. The United States government would fund for Gehlen's group an autonomous intelligence apparatus zeroed in on Russia and the Eastern bloc. Liaison with the Americans was closely held by U.S. army officers "whose selection Gehlen would approve." This unit would undertake nothing contrary to "German interests." When Germany was sovereign again, Gehlen and his "Org" would revert to it.

The Americans wanted everything on the microfilm exhaustively translated and analyzed, which meant it ate up close to a year before Gehlen and his team got back to Germany. This wasn't the best bargain imaginable, and certainly the Americans realized that. While Gehlen was negotiating, Sibert retained the sloe-eyed ex-Lieutenant Colonel Hermann Baun to activate his "Flamingo" team in Moscow and insurgent bands in the Ukraine and Poland out of the "Blue House" at Taunus.[34]

Simultaneously, Sibert's own G-2 along with the U.S. Army's Counter Intelligence Corps (CIC) were up and competitive along with the British and French services. Gehlen saw right away he'd have to claw to survive.

The Americans were depending on the fact that they were dealing with clients, not equals. Germany survived largely as a staging area from which to confront the Soviets. Throughout the pacification phases, the Alsos mission of Boris Pash was searching out German atomic scientists, while under the authority of U.S. Operation Paperclip, rocket experts from Peenemuende trekked onto White Sands Proving Grounds. The American suzerainty commenced.

❑

Once Hitler's Europe crumpled, Donovan detailed a number of his most trenchant officers—John O'Gara, John C. Hughes, William Maddox, Francis Miller, William Casey, Ray Cline—to project a peacetime utilization of OSS capacities. In September 1944, Eisenhower's chief of staff, Beedle Smith, asked after the most expeditious way to integrate the OSS permanently into the military establishment. Donovan proposed a Fourth, or "Strategic Service" Arm—this at a time when senior professionals were praying that their reserve commissions would survive inside a catastrophically reduced military. Donovan's proposal was instantly buried.[35]

Budget Director Harold Smith was already circulating a directive from the President which sought recommendations and approaches "necessary to convert from a war to a peace basis or to liquidate as the case may be."

For two months Donovan haunted the President with documents outlining "The Basis for a Permanent U.S. Foreign Intelligence Service." To make things easy, the optimistic OSS Director had included in his November 18 version a draft directive all ready for signature. Donovan's plan looked simple. There was to be established, now that the military emergency was passing, an independent central intelligence service which operated directly out of the office of the President. It would be advised by an open-ended board, with representatives from War, Navy, and State. The intelligence service's functions derived from its mandate to "coordinate, collect, and produce intelligence," including all aspects of espionage and counterespionage, conduct "subversive operations abroad," and perform "such other functions and duties relating to intelligence" as the President might direct. The service would control its own personnel budget, call on the other services for backup people, and revert to the control of—or, Donovan hinted wistfully, perhaps only coordinate with—the Joint Chiefs of Staff in the event of a national emergency. The service undertook no law-enforcement functions nor should it infringe on the rights of the regular services to "collect, evaluate, synthesize, and disseminate departmental operating intelligence."

As JCS 1181, this brave document began its rounds through offices the occupants of which despised everything they saw. Donovan's hardened adversary, ex-G-2 Strong, characterized Wild Bill's belated brainchild as unnecessary, "new and somewhat cumbersome and possibly dangerous." At one point in January, an insider told Donovan, "such harsh things were said, apparently about you by [FBI representative Edward A.] Tamm, that it was decided that no one outside the meeting should have" the minutes.[36]

What blew the lid off was the publication, the first on February 9, 1945, of three sensational articles heavily bannered across the front pages of McCormick-Patterson newspapers from the Washington *Times-Herald* to the New York *Daily News* and the Chicago *Tribune*. Over Walter Trohan's byline, tremendous headings announced "New Deal Plans to Spy on World and Home Folks, and Super Gestapo Agency Is Under Consideration." Having jarred the liberals, Trohan pandered to his sizable audience of Father Coughlin followers by divulging that the purported unit was already alluded to as "Frankfurter's Gestapo," since the insidious Supreme Court Justice's sister, one Miss Estelle (Stella) Frankfurter—in fact, an early recruiter for Donovan's office—"held a confidential personnel post in OSS," and might be expected to "pick key personnel . . . at the suggestion of her brother." Trohan followed up by printing virtually the entire highly classified document.[37]

Political dust a mile thick settled over Donovan's plan. What prospects Donovan had ended, abruptly, when FDR died in Warm Springs, Georgia, on April 12, 1945. To one with Harry Truman's sere, prairie-toughened personality, the odds ran sharply against any kind of extended collaboration with a Black Republican leprechaun like Wild Bill, whose combination of Wall Street lubricity and low-key directive mannerisms put Truman off instantly. Donovan finally broke through into the Presidential suite on May 14. The incoming Chief Executive congratulated the intelligence pioneer, but weighed in immediately with the opinion that "the OSS belongs to a nation at war." Truman met Donovan's pitch with the unwelcome announcement that "I am completely opposed to international spying on the part of the United States. It is un-American." Truman's entry in his appointment book for the date notes: "William Donovan came in to 'tell how important the Secret Service is and how much he could do to run the government on an even basis.' "[38]

Just after this interview Donovan ran into Douglas Dodds-Parker, Colin Gubbins's understudy at the Special Operations Executive and something of a friend. "I explained to the President, 'Here's what I think you should do about postwar intelligence,' " Donovan reported to Dodds-Parker. He'd handed Harry Truman an envelope which contained a neatly typed copy of his proposal. " 'Of course, I won't be involved personally, I've got to return to private life to look after my own interests, etc., etc.' "

The President had looked at Donovan a moment. " 'Thank you very much, General, for all you've done for your country,' " Truman said to Donovan. "And then he took the envelope," Donovan told Dodds-Parker, "and tore it in half, and handed the two halves back to me." Donovan showed the Englishman both halves of the document.[39]

It looked bad. By summer the Joint Chiefs, prodded by George Marshall, were withdrawing key personnel. Donovan opened another front, a tremendous public relations campaign to leak self-glorifying versions of successful OSS endeavors to well-disposed media organs. Allen Dulles supplied *The Saturday Evening Post* with his interpretation of Operation Sunrise. Journalists on Donovan's staff were nauseated by what one of them, Wallace Deuel, now regarded as a shameless and dishonest self-promotional splurge by a desperate pack of "Wall Street corporation lawyers, aspirin salesmen, advertising executives, and teachers in boy's private prep schools. . . ."[40]

This approach was badly advised vis-à-vis Harry S. Truman. By September 5, 1945, the President told Harold Smith to reduce excessive intelligence capacity, and within the week the President's Committee on Agency Liquidation determined to "dispose of OSS by a transfer of its research staff to State and its clandestine activities and administrative facilities to the War Department." Washington still owned Wall Street. Donovan lost his temper, and issued a series of self-aggrandizing press releases through the United States Information Service. But Truman didn't waver, and on September 20 he signed the dissolution order.

It came too suddenly, almost, to amount to news. The Office of Strategic Services had been croaked, as one historian put it, citing Heine, "like a prostitute in a saloon." American intelligence would remain a fatigue duty for the military.[41]

BOOK II

THE MAN WHO CARED TOO MUCH

For some time now I have thought it possible to believe that America was going insane. In her own way. And why not? . . .

. . . America had had her neuroses before, like when she tried giving up drink, like when she started finding enemies within, like when she thought she could rule the world; but she had always gotten better again. But now she was going insane, and that was the necessary condition.

In a way she was never like anywhere else. Most places just are something, but America had to mean something too, hence her vulnerability—to make-believe, to false memory, false destiny. And finally it looked as though the riveting struggle with illusion was over, and America had lost.

Martin Amis
London Fields

11

TO STEM THE TIDE

Demobilized as 1945 ended, the handful of corporation lawyers integral to the OSS—Donovan himself, Allen Dulles, and down the pecking order to younger anointed like Frank G. Wisner—folded away their reserve uniforms and reappeared behind desks along Wall Street. Many endured the tensions of historicus interruptus. From Warsaw to Le Havre the Continent was ravaged. Inflation boosted the Hungarian pengo to 11,000 trillion to the dollar.[1] Shell cratering had depleted an astonishing percentage of Europe's ancient topsoil. The Soviets were jackhammering Bulgaria and Rumania and Poland into political submission, while statesmen in the West already rolled their eyes whenever Molotov brought up the $10 billion worth of machine tools the Soviets anticipated from the Ruhr.

Priorities were still confused. Joyce and Gabriel Kolko would adduce a United States "strategy of controlling Lend Lease so that the British would emerge from the conflict neither rich enough to stand aloof from American economic pressures nor so weak as to be forced to impose an autarchic program of trade and currency restrictions." It was the French who resented the Anglo-Saxons the most at first, and even by October 1946 Stalin divulged while chatting with American journalists his hopes for a loan from the United States along with a widening of commercial relations.[2]

So public sentiment foundered. With demobilization underway, why support an enlarged intelligence capacity? Whom should we spy on? Penetrate which governments?

Support levels plummeted accordingly. At Undersecretary Dean Acheson's behest 1,362 OSS analytic people reappeared as the Interim Research and Intelligence Service at State, where regional desk-holders resented this "sudden dumping" of purported experts into "the poor old Department." Congress was reducing overall the funds available for intelligence; the colonel in charge of integrating the new people, a Wall Street litigator named Alfred McCormack, was suspect for "collectivist" sympathies by the Department's cast-iron traditionalists.[3]

Many of the analysts with a taste for government work gravitated to the larger of the OSS remnants, the Strategic Services Unit. Responsibility for the SSU devolved on that workhorse of the War Department, Assistant Secretary John McCloy, who passed it along to Donovan's SI chief, Brigadier General John Magruder. Magruder made what he could of the couple of thousand veterans out of an OSS recruitment five times that size still clinging to the payroll.

The wind was shifting. Commissioned by Secretary of the Navy James V. Forrestal, the New York investment banker—and Princeton and Dillon, Read stablemate of Forrestal's—Ferdinand Eberstadt pulled together in June of 1945 a study which proposed a "National Security Council," subordinate to which a "Central Intelligence Agency" be established to oversee "clandestine intelligence operations abroad in peacetime.[4] Their prime target was already passing before the range finder. Forrestal had been steeping as the war ended in Averell Harriman's telegrams from Moscow, which pitched to a wider realization "that the Soviet program is the establishment of totalitarianism, ending personal liberty and democracy as we know and respect it." Harriman now mentioned that, even permitted "The creation of a unilateral security ring through domination of their border states," Moscow intended "The penetration of other countries through exploitation of democratic processes on the part of Communist controlled parties with strong Soviet backing to create political atmosphere favorable to Soviet policies."

It now dawned on Harriman that, however ambiguously, we ourselves signed off on the Kremlin's plan to take "unilateral action in the domination of their bordering states. It may well be that during and since the Moscow Conference they feel they have made this quite plain to us. You will recall that at the Moscow Conference Molotov indicated that although he would inform us of Soviet action in Eastern Europe he declined to be bound by consultation with us. It may be difficult for us to believe, but it still may be true that Stalin and Molotov considered at Yalta that by our willingness to accept a general wording of the declarations on Poland and liberated Europe, by our recognition of the need of the Red Army for security behind its lines, and of the predominant interest of Russia in Poland as a friendly neighbor and as a corridor to Germany, we understood and were ready to accept Soviet policies already known to us."[5]

Projections of his own kept Stalin up nights. With Eastern Europe decimated, what was to hold out American capital? Why wouldn't it "penetrate unhindered" these feeble, ravaged ex-colonies? Molotov challenged his bargaining partners. Wouldn't " 'equal opportunity' . . . in practice mean the veritable economic enslavement of the small states and their subjugation to the rule and arbitrary will of strong and entrenched foreign firms, banks and industrial companies?"[6]

Washington turned the arguments around. They'd come full circle, and it was 1919 again. Germany was in convulsion, the Bolsheviki threatened, and this time the United States held important trump. What combination of policies could protect the West, compensate for Franklin Roosevelt's optimism, retrieve—roll back—these costly, tragic lapses?

❑

Caged in once more with Foster at 48 Wall, a lot of Allen Dulles's frustrations went into a one-man campaign to reeducate postwar public opinion. He began with his book-length tribute to the "German Underground," those holdouts from the "other Germany" who rescued the integrity of the nation by mounting their belated resistance to Hitler. Vital for the moment, Allen felt, was opposing those bitter-enders still bent on extirpating a culture they misunderstood. But where to begin? It seemed "an appalling thing," he confessed to John Kenneth Galbraith, "to come back, after heading a spy network, to handling corporate indentures,"[7] and Allen's eye wandered. By February of 1946 he'd identified sympathizers in and out of government.

Dulles's talent for networking drew irreconcilables like DeWitt Clinton Poole, another devout Princeton graduate and State Department retiree whose tenure as director of the OSS's Foreign Nationalities Branch had kept his hand in around Eastern Europe. From 1918 on, when he had shut down the U.S. Embassy in Russia out of disgust at the "cynicism and cruelty" of the new Leninist masters, the podgy-seeming but fiercely opinionated educator had fretted over Soviet expansionism.[8] During the autumn of 1945 the State Department shipped Poole to Wiesbaden to interrogate important Nazis; once both got back the newly elected President of the New York chapter of the Foreign Policy Association, Allen Dulles, invited Poole to Manhattan to speak at the association's monthly luncheon. Poole startled his auditors by urging what amounted to the permanent division of Germany. The "more Christian western German type" could enter into a confederation with France, while the "more pagan trans-Elbian type" might work out nicely as part of a "central European federation" along the Danube, to include the less important Slavic and Magyar groups and provide the West its buffer against Stalin.[9]

Dulles and Poole talked, and two weeks afterward Poole forwarded to Dulles a long, handwritten letter in which he summarized the answers he got while canvassing the Department to explain the continuing "barbarous" conditions imposed on Germany. Relying in large part, it would appear, on confidences from the chief of State's Central European Division, James Riddleberger, Poole established that there had indeed been a coherent "middle-of-the-road program" prepared by State and approved by FDR on March 10, until "Morgenthau broke loose" and "1067 and all that" effectively stampeded the bureaucracy. Eisenhower refused to "come to grips with things," while the War Department "was motivated by a wish to preserve Eisenhower as a symbol and influence toward the attainment of ends, such as military training, which it deemed more important than Germany. . . . Apparently PM's headlines are cabled to Berlin ahead of everything else."

Just then most alarming was the mismanagement of "the economic part." Department specialist Charles Kindleberger "is all right as far as he goes, but he doesn't appear to control the raft of young Jew boys under him. In the fulfillment of the Potsdam program they put ahead of everything the dismantling of German plants and shipment of machinery to Russia." There had been some "headway with details": "Of the 100,000 Nazis now arrested, 20,000 are soon to be turned loose. The British have vigorously protested the low ceiling put on German steel production."

Since "the Harry White boys continue on the job" at Treasury, some "change must be engineered at the highest levels"; the time has come to convince the President, or at least Secretary of State Jimmy Byrnes, that to "continue to ruin Germany by indiscriminate de-Nazification and unrelenting deindustrialization can only confirm Europe as a liability." Through all this, "It is not impossible" that the Russians "are not only applauding but abetting our ineptitude."[10]

After warning all recipients to rip this thing up upon absorbing its contents, Allen circulated Poole's memorandum to like-minded old Germany hands like Laird Bell of Chicago; the Chicago banker and president of the local Council on Foreign Relations was already "engaged in a one-man crusade against 1067." Bell had been stalking the Foggy Bottom corridors himself in hopes of leaning on sophisticated officials. He too found Riddleberger and Company "quite allergic to what they believe to be public opinion," he wrote Dulles on February 9, 1946, and fearful of "the residual power of the Morgenthau group. If this is right, it is apparently going to be necessary to whip up a more discriminating public interest through the usual channels—a rather depressing project." He discovered Dean Acheson "rather discouraging about any change of direction of policy, but admitted that he was getting very tired."[11]

A week later, Bell responded to the copy of Poole's letter and alluded to a contact he was developing with a group centered around Notre Dame University and "headed up by some of the Catholic hierarchy" who had formed a "Save Europe Now Committee" and were promoting a "congress." "I dread the prospect," Bell confessed to Dulles, "but apparently something will have to be done to create public opinion." He hoped to "do something through the Chicago Daily News."[12]

"I am a little apprehensive about the sponsorship of the 'congress' to which you refer," Dulles responded, "but undoubtedly such a group would swing votes and this has its influence."[13]

Dulles had been thinking about Poole's readiness to capitalize on the accident that "Germany is now parted at the Elbe and that the fissure deepens." This accorded with Allen's own thought that Germany be "de-Bismarckized and de-Prussianized,"[14] a longstanding remedy. In a May 11, 1946, sketch for *Colliers* he proposed that the bomb-gutted ruins of Berlin be in effect abandoned as a capital, a symbol which at its best "gloried in some of the ugliest architecture the world has ever seen," and now would best serve peace as a "dead city," unrestored, "a perpetual memorial to the Nazis and to Prussia."[15]

Like many Dulles answers, this Faustian proposal that the West cast loose the demonic precincts of the Reich to protect his "Good Germans" betrayed Dulles's self-serving romanticism, his propensity to subordinate realities in favor of private attachments. The fact was, Catholic Bavaria along with many of the Rhenish industrialists Allen cherished had programatically nourished the Brownshirts, while by and large the acerbic Berliners laughed Hitler off.

That war was over, Allen stressed: it was the Soviets who constituted the problem. Characteristically, one of the last to admit the threat was Foster, whose reflex it remained to apologize for despots. As late as February of 1944 John Foster Dulles was rationalizing Soviet intentions around Eastern Europe with a remainder that "'Aggression' is a subtle thing," which we ourselves rarely scrupled to practice: "And does it include political interference in another country which brings about revolutionary change of government from which a foreign nation is a beneficiary, as, for example, Texas, Panama and, perhaps now, Poland?" He pointed out that Russia was "perhaps more directly engaged" than the U.S. when the Moscow underwritten Groza government was unloaded upon Rumania, and urged on Secretary of State Byrnes a "non-provocative" stance.[16]

Foster's eyes remained averted. Early in 1946—by then the Gouzenko affair had broken and Soviet troops were dug in across northern Iran—Foster composed a foreign-policy essay for *Life*. Foster still anticipated "some satisfactory accommodation" between Stalin and the West. "I doubt this," Allen reportedly contested his brother, "since liberties anywhere in the world" constituted a "menace to their system." Russia must be "insulated" while the West waited out a "modification of the communist system. . . .[17]

Events overtook the debate. Stalin's maneuvers to blackmail the Shah led to a formidable American task force steaming into the Eastern Mediterranean. Intervention in Greece followed. We had begun to operate on the premise that anything which displeased us anywhere in the world we could afford to remedy.

❑

Intelligence needed another look. That modest, shrunken vestige of the OSS, the Strategic Services Unit, survived in the War Department. Even there it unsettled traditionalist watchdogs like columnist Joseph Alsop, who ascribed governmental efforts to "hold down the whole German economy to a level of drab, unrelieved, unbearable misery" not only to Morgenthau agents like Bernard Bernstein, but even more directly—more insidiously—to the "uncontested . . . fact . . . that a considerable number of American Communists found posts in the economic division, the information-control division and even the counter-intelligence branch of the military government."[18] Suspicion now centered on the seven extant SSU stations abroad, largely in the hands of OSS hangers-on.

To guarantee the Army some undercover instrument independent of Donovan's grandstanders, Major General George Strong and his deputy Brigadier General Hayes Kroner had long since deputized Colonel John V. ("Frenchy") Grombach to develop in Europe a covert force of his own. Well covered, referred to by senior Army brass as "The Pond," its operatives built nets, exfiltrated sources, executed elaborate deception schemes, fed raw information back to the Pentagon so that Army planners could prepare estimates independent of State or the Office of Naval Intelligence. The Pond survived demobilization, a back-alley anomaly overseen in a general way by the State-War-Navy Coordinating Committee which materialized for several years as a forerunner of the National Security Council.[19] Security for The Pond was so tight that its very existence first broke the surface on May 18, 1947, when *The New York Times* announced that the Secret Intelligence Division of the War Department would shortly be merged into the upcoming Central Intelligence Agency.

Colonel John V. Grombach was known as a "born conspirator"; nothing graveled him worse than the unappetizing prospect that he himself and his patriots might wind up subject to the descendants of the slippery, self-aggrandizing civilian lawyers and bankers who rigged the OSS. That such a thing was contemplated Grombach attributed to the bureaucratic inevitability that "the people who had these coordinating agencies started to build an empire," and resolved to bring the whole thing down, soon. Grombach was particularly riled when Allen W. Dulles, whom senior military *never* trusted, prevailed during classified hearings and convinced the Congressional subcommittee which drafted the National Security Act of 1947 to permit an undefined *operational* capacity to the projected intelligence clearinghouse.[20]

Leaks to trustworthy newspapermen helped humble the SSU. Early in 1946 the arthritis-riddled first director of the SSU, Brigadier General John Magruder, turned over the depleted command to his executive officer, Lieutenant Colonel William Quinn. After that Donovan's heritage was largely in the hands of a lieutenant colonel, a young, bluff, canny officer who picked up his intelligence wherewithal as the G-2 of the Seventh Army under General Patch which came ashore in the South of France—Operation Anvil.

Charged by Assistant Secretary of War Peterson to "preserve the assets of the OSS and eliminate its liabilities," Quinn supervised the whittling-down of the outfit from 12,000 to less than 2,000 "in about a year." He turned back real estate, from the Congressional Country Club—its fairways and manicured greens churned open and trenched and heaved up into mountains of sod by waves of training exercises—to dozens of demonstration safe houses all over the country.

Donovan's organization chart, Quinn discovered, resembled the Japanese flag: "You picture the sun in the center, and the rays going out. Donovan is in the middle. . . . In cities around the world SI had its own facility, X-2 had its own facility, morale operations had its own, and they were all reporting individually back to Donovan. Consequently, SI and X-2 in many instances in certain world capitals were spending as much time trying to penetrate each other as they did whatever the opposition was.[21]

"Being a military unit, and having a so-called stupid military mind, I went about changing the organization. . . . I said, there is one guy in one country who is going to be the commander of that unit, the chief of station and *he* reports to *me*. Then I appointed a personnel officer who ran the personnel. Then I ordered a logistics directorate which took care of logistics for *everybody*."

The lieutenant colonel had reordered his shrunken empire in a way which profoundly affected postwar intelligence: autonomy to the stations. Heir to a charge of cash budgeted for his much larger predecessor—$8 million in unvouchered leftover OSS funds he took delivery of largely on his signature—Quinn allocated payments freely to the station chiefs on a pro-rata basis, no questions normally asked unless some project got overly rich, over $100,000 perhaps. These semifeudal arrangements gave rise to that generation's intelligence barons, its mysterious, mission-oriented professionals who held themselves accountable to nobody, unconcerned with constitutional limitations, in important capitals frequently more powerful than the ambassador.

❑

Among these most destiny-marked was James Jesus Angleton. "I made Jim Angleton station chief for Italy," Quinn remembers, but he discovered soon that "Jim had what you might call tentacles which reached out far beyond Rome to the different areas—Austria, Germany, Spain, even the islands, Malta, Switzerland. . . ." The hostilities had ended, but Angleton's furtive reach grew longer every month. There is an archive photograph of the prodigy which dates to 1946. Posed against one massive travertine pillar just before the steps of the Vatican, General Donovan stands plump and four-square in banked medals and soft campaign cap; from a full head above him the cavernous twenty-eight-year-old Captain J. J. Angleton looks lost in his meditation, his arms woven limply before his severe black overcoat and at least the aura of his deadly all-seeing calm reflected in his precocious stoop.[22]

Angleton had been a great help in taking the edge off one of the OSS's late-war humiliations. Even during his COI days Donovan had cultivated close relations with Pope Pius XII, and capitalized on these by plugging into the political roundups of the anti-Comintern (and for a time anti-Nazi) operation known as Pro Deo, the so-called Black Reports.[23] The way was open, accordingly, when the OSS SI chief in Rome, Vincent Scamporini, picked up a startlingly productive agent, "Source Vessel," with access to the diplomatic traffic at the top of the Vatican.

Under Angleton's practiced needle "Source Vessel" was winkled out, and in the light turned into a chubby, prolific little journalist named Virgilio Scattolini, whose previous accomplishments included an underground masterpiece of pornography entitled *Amazons of the Bidet.*[24]

Word spread. Well before his Wiesbaden summer, Paul Blum and others had regaled Dulles with anecdotes about this austere and painfully self-possessed stripling with an outdated generation's preference for funereal haberdashery and a disquieting habit of turning almost any question against its originator. In October 1945 Dulles made his way via Switzerland—where he detached Clover, not overjoyed to go, from her redemptive regimen of psychoananlysis—to a stopover in Rome. Angleton was already ensconced. Like Dulles, Angleton had no problem with the Vatican's hypothesis that Nazism got nasty every once in a while, but communism was a threat forever. In the Dulles' comfortable suite at the Hotel Hassler the dusky, fine-boned Angleton felt much at home; the two were quick to compare, as William Smith has written, "Their common perception of the Red challenge, and of the drastic sub-rosa measures required to meet it—including the recruitment of influential Italian agents, without overscrupulous concern for past Fascist affiliations. . . ." Allen shared Angleton's optimism about tapping the arterial Jewish Agency, a pipeline for people and information all through the chaotic, congealing East.[25] Dulles's Sunrise beneficiary Ferruccio Parri was premier of Italy for the moment, but Dulles expected his unstable coalition to collapse at any time.

Dulles appreciated right away the reflexes he saw at work: the gaunt youngster's passionate meticulousness, the instinct to chew something twice and taste it three times. At Yale just before the war Angleton edited a quarterly of avant-garde poetry, and this helped reaffirm his born aesthete's suspicion that everything he encountered could ultimately be interpreted in a variety of ways, few innocent.

Called up out of Harvard Law, young Angleton had appeared in

London out of a collection of OSS classrooms and training farms, just after the dead noon of the momentarily stalled war. Archibald MacLeish had already failed to snag Angleton a berth in the United States Information Service; young Jim was recruited into the X-2 branch of the OSS by his Yale professor John Holmes Pearson.[26] He appeared open-minded, assuming, as he later remarked, that "because they have been in the world a long time, the British brought a quality, a personality, a talent to counterintelligence work" that "only wartime" would ever induce them to share with the newcomers.[27] Malcolm Muggeridge later characterized the crop as "arriving like *jeunes filles en fleur* straight from a finishing school, all fresh and innocent, to start work in our frowsty old intelligence brothel."[28]

Angleton picked up the game fast—Kim Philby later faint-praised the gangling American as the one trainee in the lot prescient enough to shrug off his crowd's prevailing "Anglomania." X-2 founder James Murphy would term Angleton "a natural for counterespionage. In the early days he steeped himself in its intricacies, mastering the use of counterespionage files, and while in England slept on a cot in the office in order not to waste time coming and going from his billet."[29] To judge for himself the importance of records MI5 held back, Angleton allegedly seduced the appropriate file clerk and availed himself of case reports.[30]

Before 1944 was out Jim Angleton slipped unnoticed into the political dissolution of central Italy, threatened as the Germans collapsed by widespread civil war between devotees of senile Victor Emmanuel and Communist-directed partisan armies. Angleton pursued old leads—his father, the peripatetic J. H. (Hugh) Angleton, bought out the National Cash Register dealership for Italy when James was sixteen, and wound up president of the American Chamber of Commerce. His tall son in effect commuted from Milan to Malvern College in England and Yale and Harvard Law. Staying on in Rome as head of the postwar SSU caretaker regiment in Italy, the unearthly young espionage novice did business out of a fusty, piled-up little office on the Via Archimede, never in the best of health but more than competent to summon up one final devastating implication, imaginative to the point of fantasy, temperamentally suppressed yet daring.

Hugh Angleton had also bobbled up in Rome near the end of the fighting, a major in the OSS who resuscitated his connections throughout Italian industry to promote as Mussolini's successor the ultramontane Marshal Badoglio, conquerer of Addis Ababa. By then his ambitious son was systematically bribing all the key officers in the national carabiniere "as they were being put back together." Angleton arranged a jail-break for George Sessler, the Nazi counterintelligence chief for Northern Italy, and tucked him away behind a second identity in the south of France. He tipped its code clerk $100 a week for extra copies of the Vatican's worldwide intelligence reports.[31]

Those early, brutal postwar years Angleton kept bumping into nervy, dedicated Zionists from the resuscitated Jewish underground, pipelining the leftovers of the camps through Italy into Palestine. Should Israel be established, Angleton foresaw, there would be the potential for an invaluable slag of information and documents as Soviet Jews poured in from Russia. The young spy nurtured these associations, locking up the future "Israeli account."

Although 1946 found Angleton in Rome as Bill Quinn's station head, his unit itself—in military nomenclature a DAD, a Department of the Army Detachment—remained insignificant among regular Army missions around the War Department. One U.S. Army counterintelligence career man posted to Milan just then remembers how astutely Angleton and his subordinates were able to take in hand and put to use any like-minded among the regulars. "There was that feeling left over from the war that the Russians had been our allies," the veteran notes now, "and a lot of our people didn't believe that there was any kind of a threat."

Before long he and others in his Milan unit were moonlighting for Angleton's well-heeled detachment, "doing favors on the quiet, so to speak, sometimes out of reasons that were not so altruistic." Nobody knew quite yet which way the Yugoslavs were likely to jump, and CIC units in Milan and Vienna were particularly active in attempting to open up Eastern Europe. "I did some of the support work for operations in Yugoslavia," the officer admits, "sending people in, setting up escape routes, exfiltrating people." Soon enough the CIC renegades were "helping set up routes for Angleton's agents to come over, establishing friendly contacts, that sort of thing."

Angleton became his counterpart commander. "Jim was a very odd fellow," he acknowledges freely enough. "The first time I entered his office, whether it was to impress me or not, he drew the shades down. He sat behind his desk, I sat opposite, he sort of whispered to me half the time. Maybe it was his way of impressing me with the seriousness of the occasion."

Even then, the CIC officer saw, "You could never figure out which way Jim was going. He sort of ran things out of his vest pocket, with only the senior man knowing what he was engaged in. He used to, right or wrong, bypass established channels on a number of things he was doing.

"I would set things up," he recalls, "and then I would pass the information along to Angleton's man in Milan, an ex-X-2 guy named Paul Paterni. He would pick it up from there."[32]

Documents squeezed only recently out of the Army Intelligence annals hint at one-time FBI-man Paterni's contacts. For decades by then British and French intelligence had been collaborating with the Vatican to reconstitute some form of Allen Dulles's political panacea, an anti-Communist league along the Danube. Projected "under direct leadership of the Pope," according to one CIC summation, this "proposed Pan-Danubian Federation" was "planned to include in that union all the countries formerly under the Austro-Hungarian monarchy and even parts of Italy and Bavaria."[33]

This essentially Balkan construct would anchor an even more engirdling buttress system against Bolshevism, the Intermarium nations. The Intermarium directorate soon came to include a broad spectrum of sawtoothed reactionaries and ambitious malcontents from Balkan and Slavic refugee encampments. Many were regular go-betweens for British and Abwehr agent-handlers, veterans of the Prometheus nets the British rigged between the wars.[34] The American control officers now joined the universal hunt for "assets."

In Italy in 1946 the displaced Croatian community looked especially promising for covert initiatives. Their stockades were replete with smouldering, violent men eager to invade their homeland for a day's tobacco, wards of the UNRRA bureaucrats and international distribution agencies. Many considered themselves Ustase, a sect of followers of a heavyset and unsmiling terrorist named Dr. Ante Pavelic, who had conspired for decades to break Croatia out of the Yugoslav confederation.[35]

After Germany marched into the Balkans Hitler had presented these revolutionary Croatians a kingdom of their own. The summer of 1941 Pavelic's Roman-Catholic Ustase devoted were loosed to murder Serbs and Jews and Gypsies in cartloads, and once reportedly presented to their leader a wicker basket overflowing with forty pounds of human eyes.[36]

Nineteen-forty-five produced a panic-stricken exodus of Ustase families, with thousands winding up in internment camps in Austria and Italy. These refugees tugged continually at Pope Pius XII's heartstrings; he interceded repeatedly with the United States occupation authorities in behalf of the "many hundred Croatian families" in camps in Italy. . . ."[37] Yugoslav refugee organizations stirred up the West with reports of a rebellion brewing among opponents of Tito who "escaped into the forests," backed up by "growing discontent of the workers." An Ustase-based anti-Communist movement, the Krizari (Crusaders), claimed widespread sabotage successes—including a "Military Technical Institute"!—along with arms and supplies straight out of "the Vatican, where the center of the Command is currently located."[38]

A CIC Special Agent who specialized in tracking down Fascists, William Gowen, located the fugitive Ante Pavelic himself—by one account browsing inside the papal library. "Pavelic's contacts are so high and his present position is so compromising to the Vatican," Gowen's status report admits, "that any extradition of Subject would deal a staggering blow to the Roman Catholic Church."[39]

By 1945, Jim Angleton would concede, he was coordinating many matters with the Vatican's sophisticated intelligence apparatus. They shared the confidences of the Secretary of the Croatian Cofraternity of Saint Jerome in Rome, Dr. Krunoslav Draganovic. CIC agents in Italy had tagged Draganovic as an unreconstructed Ustase and the "Croat representative to 'Intermarium' in a quasi-official capacity."[40] Draganovic facilitated the American services in Italy (a $1,400 payoff was standard) by providing safe houses across his syndicate of Rat Lines. Along Draganovic's underground railway the Jewish Agency regularly smuggled its coordinators in and out of Soviet "denied areas." Both SPINNE (Otto Skorzeny's pervasive exfiltration network for SS officers on the run) and the CIC in Vienna depended on the swarthy Croatian prelate to bribe off harbor officials before shipping through some terrified ex-Nazi—Klaus Barbie, among many—to Paraguay or Buenos Aires.

Angleton never drifted far from what was boiling in the camps. "Following from J.J. reference leaders Trieste indicates increased activity among émigrés in organizing and planning anti-Tito uprising in spring," one SSU wrap-up specified. "Dr. Eugen Laxo Macek emmissary to Croats in Italy" was negotiating toward an agreement among all anti-Tito segments, especially "Ustashi Crusaders with Ustashi most important."[41]

❑

In Washington that first year activities in the field made much less difference than skirmishes at home. "I took a hellova beating," Bill

Quinn will concede in his sly, folksy way. "There were a lot of resignations, and some I asked to leave.

"G-2 was hostile, and the FBI and the ONI did not want a central intelligence agency. They kept pounding about breaking the SSU up, and give the assets to the navy and so forth, to a point where certain columnists got active. The Alsop brothers and Mr. Ickes, who was Secretary of the Interior and then became a columnist. The theme was, Quinn was clean, but he harbored Communists. And that the OSS suffered because of the looseness of its nature, it even had criminals, and lock pickers, and counterfeiters. Which we did."[42]

Worse yet, "we had this general exodus, and an awful lot of principals were deserting their agents. We were trying to stem the tide of this disintegration of intelligence collection."

Prejudiced officials were impossible to placate. The day the SSU procured the plans, including armament details, for the Soviet Baltic fleet, Quinn rushed his roundup over to the chief at ONI. He got a chilly reception. " 'Quinn, I've looked you up,' the admiral responded, 'and so far as I'm concerned you're just a GI doing your job. Did you know that you are riddled with Communists? I wouldn't touch this with a ten-foot pole, because it's probably deceptive.' "

Quinn left, he recalls, feeling "like a whipped dog." Soon afterward, the SSU managed to insert an agent into the code room of another nation's embassy. The SSU chief hurried to the director of the Army's cryptologic section, and suffered through more of the same: "Quinn, what kind of a sonofabitch are you? . . ."

The baffled lieutenant colonel decided to breast the thing head on. He applied for an audience with J. Edgar Hoover, and found himself ushered into the FBI sanctorum to confront the icon himself. "Mr. Hoover," he confessed, "I need your help. You know what everybody in town is saying about my unit. I would like you to vet every one of my 2,500 principals—both criminally and subversively."

Hoover wove his hands behind his head and let himself back into his chair. "Colonel, all this is unbelieveably refreshing to me," he told the downcast intelligence officer. "You know, I fought that Donovan in South America primarily, and wherever in the world. A hard-headed Irishman. And to have you as his successor come to me for help is just taking all the steam out of my hatred." Inside of five weeks—fast, as if he'd expected this—Hoover got back. "Colonel Quinn," he told the SSU chief, "I have some good news and maybe a little bad. You're not riddled with Commies, that's the good news. You do have a girl working in logistics who has been dating what we call a fellow traveler who is a very close friend of one of the diplomats in the Soviet embassy."

The aging Colonel House shares a back-porch confidence with Governor Franklin D. Roosevelt. *Bettmann Archive*

America's Anglophile Secretary of State Robert Lansing. *Library of Congress*

A diplomat with ideas of his own—Allen Dulles in 1920. *Library of Congress*

Boarding the *Aquitania*—international lawyer John Foster Dulles in 1923. *AP/Wide World Photos*

Dr. Hjalmer Schacht *(left)* and future OSS (and ABWEHR) agent Otto Kiep *(right)* visit the White House—1930. *Library of Congress*

Between heroics—Assistant Attorney General William (Wild Bill) Donovan in 1930. *Library of Congress*

U.S. Ambassador to the U.S.S.R. William Bullitt *(left)* and his personal assistant Carmel Offie at sport in Moscow—1936. *Bettmann Archive*

Ambassador Bullitt *(right),* Sigmund Freud and Princess Mathilde Bonaparte *(left),* all preceded by the omnipresent Carmel Offie—1938. *National Archives*

Offie *(left)* and Bullitt deplane in Baltimore—1940. *AP/Wide World Photos*

Before the Fall—Ambassador Bullitt confers with Undersecretary Sumner Welles. *National Archives*

Buried with diplomatic honors. *Author photograph*

The girl was let go. The next day Quinn picked up his suitcase and hustled over to square matters with the Office of Naval Intelligence.

While Quinn struggled along, the Percherons at the top of the government hauled off in opposing directions, and clods of bureaucracy were pelting the onlookers. It hadn't taken many weeks before the President himself—not to mention the light-sleeping Bess Truman—got sick of answering the telephone at 3 A.M. to deal with international flaps. That autumn of 1945 he pushed his cabinet people to insulate him from this confusion. Robert Lovett ran studies for the War Department, while Colonel Alfred McCormack staked out the intelligence franchise for State.[43]

The bitterly resented compromise, which Truman promulgated on January 22, 1946, ladled up a very heavy serving of fresh alphabet soup. To coordinate intelligence activities a supervisory board came into being with representatives of the Army, Navy, State Department and a fourth delegate selected by the President personally, the National Intelligence Authority (NIA). To oversee day-to-day undertakings the President mandated the Central Intelligence Group (the CIG). As its lead administrator Truman appointed a reserve rear admiral on active duty, Sidney Souers, whose priority it remained to get the hell back to the insurance game in Saint Louis at the earliest opportunity.[44] Souers chafed for five months as the initial Director of Central Intelligence (DCI). Much of what supervisory work got done fell to the persuasive international investment banker Souers recruited as Deputy Director, Kingman Douglass, normally a managing partner at Dillon, Read. Douglass had broad World War II experience in Air Force intelligence.

Truman's reorganization gained momentum after June of 1946, when the ambitious, boyish-looking Lieutenant General Hoyt Vandenberg took over as DCI and occupied himself while awaiting his fourth star along with his appointment as Air Force Chief of Staff with force-feeding his infant bureaucracy. Under Vandenberg's regime of colonels the CIG alone swelled from an authorized strength of 165 toward a projected 3,000. McCormack's carryovers stayed on, technically, at State, but now attended primarily to needs of the CIG directorate as the renamed Office of Research and Evaluation (ORE). Vandenberg intended to assume day-to-day control of "all clandestine foreign intelligence activities" and scooped up the SSU—rechristened now the OSO, the Office of Special Operations—the Foreign Broadcast Information Service, Frenchy Grombach's Pond, and even the FBI's South American Special Intelligence Service, in which J.

Edgar Hoover personally had long taken an ominous amount of pride.[45]

General Vandenberg's success in reassembling Humpty-Dumpty owed partly to his dash and reputation as a hot-shot Air-Force administrator, and every bit as much to the consideration that he was the favorite nephew of Michigan Senator Arthur Vandenberg, the plump, touchy ex-isolationist Chairman of the Senate Foreign Relations Committee on whose good offices—especially after the Democrats had lost control of Congress in 1946—early Cold War bell-ringers like Acheson and Forrestal depended. Truman's NIA directive had been intended as a stopgap, an attempt to coordinate for the moment the feuding and contradictory claimants until proposals were drafted to bring into being a permanent peacetime intelligence service. Yet what this makeshift arrangement did in effect was cut in deeper the Donovan-engendered habit of permitting the intelligence instrumentalities—while directed, if loosely, by some central clearinghouse authority—to proceed under the vaguest of auspices while defending their mandates as subsidiaries (if only for rations and office space and funding purposes) of established outside bureaucracies like War and State. This left questionable activities much harder to pin down, and ultimately produced hybrids like G. Gordon Liddy and Oliver North.

Scrambling for his career at middle levels of the War Department, William Quinn still sweated over his embattled assignment. He promoted Richard Helms, convinced the scholarly Harry Rositzke to set up a Russian Section, and cut himself in on Reinhard Gehlen's priceless data base—Soviet order-of-battle, subject file, all fifty-odd cannisters-worth—along with shared access to whatever raw information Gehlen's "Org" turned up as soon as the denatured little master spy bobbed back into Sibert's command in the summer of 1946.[46] One of Gehlen's Danish agents had located the Soviet Baltic Command data, while another—a charwoman trained in cryptography—swabbed out the Red Army headquarters in East Berlin every evening. Between bursts of mopping she directed her Minox at whatever caught her fancy inside the unlocked desk drawers.[47]

Such penetrations helped Quinn hang onto enough prospective funding from Congress to keep the OSO intact through 1947. Simultaneously, Hoover's cohort in the State Department, Assistant Secretary of State for Latin American Affairs Spruille Braden, kept after a congressional committee to deny funds to "these swarms of people . . . mostly collectivists and 'do-gooders' and what-nots."[48] G-2 and ONI obstructed the CIG liaison efforts, which made the "CIG's primary mission an exercise in futility," one Senate report admitted.[49] Experienced agent handlers like Henry Hyde, who oversaw operations briefly for the CIG, passed out of the unhappy bureaucracy, he later noted, "like shit through a goose."[50]

Hoover, a fatalist about bureaucratic progressions, soon recognized that Vandenberg's power grab was impossible to reverse. Whatever Hoover couldn't pick off outright he intended to penetrate and influence. According to William Corson, even before the advent of the Vandenberg reshuffle, transfers from the FBI had been signing on in suspicious numbers around the SSU, almost always where the unit was receptive, at the operational levels. Quinn soon became dependent on ex-Bureau personnel William Thorn and William Doyle and Raymond Leddy while he was still executive officer to Magruder, and with the West Pointers forever agitating to get out of this dead-end intelligence backwater, Hoover seems to have directed a regular stream of purported FBI malcontents into the OSO.[51]

Of these the weightiest catch was William King Harvey. Harvey remained a bona-fide Bureau product: a doleful, hard-bitten street investigator who preferred his Jack Daniels out of a flat pint bottle and so gained several pounds of fast-moving flab annually. A lifetime thyroid condition made his pale, hooded eyes goggle—"stand out on stems, practically," one colleague maintains: as the weight went on, he acquired his office sobriquet, "The Pear." A gun and knife collector, Harvey liked to maintain an emergency revolver, tucked underneath the sweatband at the back of his trousers and enveloped by the cleavage of his formidable hindquarters. At work Harvey indulged a penchant for diddling with one of his many pistols at his desk while chewing the rag with visitors in his hoarse, whiskey-raddled patois (spiked when anything struck Harvey wrong with bursts of petrifying obscenity) and sometimes was known to level a .45 at a companion's forehead while good-humoredly clicking off the safety. Such mannerisms put off the more genteel OSS alumni around the OSO, who chuckled over Harvey's free-swinging personal habits. The big man detested publicity, and made it his business to keep whatever he was up to out of the paper flow.[52]

Not far into 1947 Harvey joined the OSO. The story was spread that Harvey overdid it one evening at a party, and collapsed in his car in Rock Creek Park. Hoover threatened a transfer, and Harvey resigned.[53] The spring he left the Bureau, the bumptious young security specialist was running the sweeping headquarters operation against the senior Communist case officer Gerhart Eisler. The Pear was simultaneously sorting out the dozens of touchy leads supplied

Hoover's people by Elizabeth Bentley—a political minefield, replete with numerous recollections by Nathan and Helen Silvermaster intended to implicate New-Deal–era assistants Laughlin Currie and Harry Dexter White as well as—glancingly—Alger Hiss.

Based on Bentley's charges, as ex-Special Agent Robert Lamphere has written, "there were many firings and enforced resignations in the State Department, the OSS, the Office of War Information and the Foreign Economic Administration," despite the fact that little emerged precise enough to stand up in a court of law.[54] Politics drove the priorities. The obstructionism of officials like Laughlin Currie and Harry Dexter White on important questions such as rebuilding Germany needed to be bulldozed aside.

When James J. Angleton gave up his Rome station in 1947 and signed on to work for the OSO in Washington, he found William Harvey propped up and directing a miniscule counterintelligence offshoot called Staff C. Angleton took his place as Assistant to the Assistant Director for Special Operations (ADSO),[55] and one of the legendary Laurel and Hardy acts anywhere in the chronicles of government opened to mixed reviews.

Along with the pop-eyed Harvey's impatience with so many Ivy League featherweights to fluff all day, the strain of protecting his Bureau connections contributed to Harvey's drinking. Of these the most important involved access to the well-protected Venona material. By postwar counterintelligence standards the Venona decrypts were comparable with the Ultra breakthrough. The acquisition of a charred Russian codebook on a Finnish battlefield had opened the way for Army Security Agency cryptanalysts—torturously, little by little, over at least a decade—to collate against wartime file copies intercepted Soviet cable transmissions. Out of those dry aging encryptions came code names, agent reports, monitored exchanges between the Allied leaders.[56] Fragments of the traffic between New York and Moscow ultimately led to the investigation of Klaus Fuchs, Donald Maclean, and (once Guy Burgess skipped) the ineffable Kim Philby.[57] Bill Harvey's encyclopedic memory missed nothing, spared nobody. It would be Harvey who risked his rejuvenated career on hints that Philby was unreliable.

High times were coming up fast.

12

THE REDEEMER FROM THE WEST

Another zealot the rejuvenated CIG kept after was Frank G. Wisner. In August of 1946 Wisner's SI boss in Cairo, the Arabist Dr. Stephen Penrose, slipped up to New York expressly to romance Frank firsthand at his law offices at Carter, Ledyard and Milburn. Young Wisner was known to be "closely associated with" ex-Carter Ledyard partner Bill Jackson, Omar Bradley's wartime G-2 and currently the dynamic managing partner of J. H. Whitney and Company. Like the disgruntled Allen Dulles, William Jackson was much in demand as one of Wall Street's advisory eminences to Washington's shaky intelligence restructuring. Wisner turned out "not at all unwilling to join provided he could be sufficiently persuaded of the permanence and freedom of the operation of CIG," Penrose reported.[1] But evidently the rank Wisner demanded, at Deputy Assistant level, wasn't available. Expectations on both sides eased for the moment.

What kept Frank's dossier jumping out of the files just then was enthusiasm all up and down the late-war power elite about Frank's performance in Rumania in 1944, his compelling display of "forcefulness, tact and a high intelligence," as his Caserta control officer Robert Joyce summed it up.[2] It clearly took moxie and finesse to maneuver among the occupation elements in Bucharest while NKVD button men replaced the Sicherheitsdienst. On political levels, Frank remained ever-solicitous of senior personalities, and backed this up with a stunning capacity to get the paperwork out. Reliably tight-lipped when discretion was indicated, the boyish Mississippi-born lawyer turned animated and even boisterous when it was time to relax, or lapsed quite unselfconsciously into the elegaic courtliness of the cultivated, well-placed Southerner.

His descendants would compare Frank with the hard-bitten originator of the Wisner fortune, his father, Frank *George* Wisner, who started out as little more than the offspring of a drifter who deserted his birthplace in the East and skirmished as a foot soldier at Shiloh before wandering into Clinton, Iowa, to keep a store briefly until he died. Frank George was raised by his schoolteacher mother above the family storefront. A burly, deliberate kid, Frank George gave up on education to knock around the cornfields, sawing ice out of the winter Mississippi or joining an occasional railroad shape-up. In time he fell in with a partnership of ambitious lumberjacks who over the years clear-cut a swath along the timber harvest which ended at the crossroads of Laurel, Mississippi. Laurel really wasn't much: an opening in the Southern yellow pine just off the Tallahala, a yarding area to strip logs and start them downriver direct to the Gulf.

There were several Gardiners among the incorporators of the timber business, descendants of the Gardiners who settled Gardiners Island, and Frank George attracted one, Mary, a sweet, fey, generous-hearted woman who came up with the stake which permitted Frank George to become a principal in the Eastman-Gardiner Company. Eastman-Gardiner was already taking its place in logging throughout the region, with ties to Weyerhaeuser and the George Mason who developed masonite.[3]

Capital accumulated. A casual Christmas snapshot taken just below a power line right-of-way in 1920 shows twenty-one assorted Gardiner and Wisner and Green and Eastman and Rogers forebears, the women milling around in their unbrushed furs over watered silk, and men with vests and dark, ambassadorial fedoras. By that point Mary and Frank George were raising two children: Elizabeth, who was already senior enough to merit a stole of her own among the sedate adults, and "brother," Frank *Gardiner* Wisner, eleven, on whom the doting Elizabeth keeps half an eye while he crouches glowering in front with three other youngsters from the clan. At eleven young Frank's big head is clippered to a burr, and now he glances up not unsuspiciously while clutching the neck fold of a woebegone German shepherd.

Frank George in middle age gave off the rugged self-sufficiency of a gentrified Francis X. Bushman, a big, swart, deaconlike industrialist who devoted himself largely to tending the banking requirements of the expanding lumber combine. His descendants would characterize their grandfather as a "dour, hard man, very religious." He and the other partners ultimately raised their mansions in a row down Laurel's Fifth Avenue, great shadowy Greek-Revival structures which left no visitor in doubt as to who owned everything worthwhile along *that* bend in the river.

The men remained Democrats, if of the Southern persuasion, and it was up to the women at first to see after the library and parade their civic-mindedness. Young Frank's musical sister, Elizabeth, recognized that even at six the black cook's daughter had promise, and subsidized into Juilliard the soprano who developed into Leontyne Price. Frank George in later years espoused land grant colleges around the state and contributed heavily to Negro education. He led the community into underwriting a black YMCA; ultimately, townspeople named a technical high school after their rough-hewn benefactor.

The Klan lashed back at do-gooders who encouraged the colored of the period; night crosses were burned on the lawn in front of the Wisner mansion. Frank George was not to be intimidated. Young Frank grew up in awe of the flinty paternal standards yet uncomfortable with the churchiness that stiffened family exchanges. Out on his own he sidestepped religion. It was his indirect, adoring mother he looked to, and close friends maintain that her death in the middle fifties helped eat into Wisner's waning psychological reserves.

The honors which descended on Frank George included a stint on the War Industries Board in 1918 and, capping everything, a term as president of the National Lumber Manufacturers Association, a lobby which headquartered in Washington. Elizabeth attended the Cathedral School; when young Frank—Frank *Gardiner* Wisner—finished high school in Laurel with slapdash grades and quite a reputation in town for "whoopin' and jumpin' around," his displeased father agreed to ship him off to Woodberry Forrest School in Orange, Virginia. Woodberry Forrest catered unabashedly to hard cases from comfortable Southern families, its masters well practiced at shaking the rakehell out before the boys tried higher education. Yet even as a preppie young Wisner's academics remained slipshod, although his ever-welling animal enthusiasm and prowess as a track athlete had started a number of senior faculty watching. Nevertheless, it took family pull to get him enrolled at the University of Virginia, class of 1931.

College made the difference. The vitality carried over, Frank's aptitude for games and badinage and challenges and absurdities and well-wrought imaginative fun; what showed up month by month at UVA was a singular capacity to get down to business *immediately* when the need arose. In classes he concentrated on philosophy and psychology, "with a potential English major,"[4] as he would specify afterward. Something he wanted now was out there, waiting for Frank.

Around the UVA campus Wisner was an eye-catcher—compact at five-ten, with narrow-eyed, chiseled looks, a strong set of good-old-boy teeth gapped extravagantly for whistling and spitting purposes. Something about the go-to-hell arch of his back, his benevolent lingering glance, wilted Wisner's admiring classmates. He was well recognized around UVA as a potential world-class sprinter and long jumper, a sure bet for Phi Beta Kappa. For all his snap Frank carried himself with a responsiveness, a deference before authority rare in a back-hills undergraduate. Still, "Frank was no back-slapper; he had a calmness, a poise which was remarkable and which appealed to older people," one classmate remembers; he was already being singled out for "leadership qualities."[5] He made the top club, The Ravens, along with The Sevens, a fiercely secret order of anticipated luminaries. Frank had enough confidence to ditch the bloods around the DKE house to chat up a grateful professor emeritus, or patronize the odd duck who admired his quick, devastating cartoons. Wisner was already capitalizing on the fact that bright, lonely outsiders would exhaust themselves for crumbs of recognition.

Frank moved on directly into three years of law school at Virginia, made top grades, and held himself to Jeffersonian ethical standards. At this juncture Wisner's promise as a track athlete peaked; he'd placed quite high in shakedown meets around the Southeast Conference, and so was invited onto the U.S. squad in training for the Berlin Olympics in 1936.

The country was foundering; in Laurel the family remained asset heavy ("in-the-South-rich," as the saying went), but sales were way off. Frank George saw no percentage in fooling away a summer with time trials, and directed his only son to forget collegiate sidelines and get into something. The disappointed young athlete looked hard for work in New Orleans, got no bids, and trooped along to Wall Street, where Woodberry Forrest classmates helped snag him a trainee berth at Carter, Ledyard and Milburn, attorney to the Stock Exchange, where Franklin Roosevelt practiced.

Manhattan is a grindstone. In afteryears his widow would concede that while Frank was extremely intelligent he was in important ways unsophisticated, that he remained acutely aware of where people came from since "as a Southerner he felt slightly at a loss living in the North." Frank's apprenticeship on Wall Street soon brought up a measure of touchiness over the fact that he had not prepped at Groton or St. Paul's, Virginia wasn't Yale, and he might never again approximate the kind of easy, bursting celebrity which came without effort throughout his schoolboy days.

In many ways the painstaking, imagination-killing requirements of litigation helped sort Wisner out. Frank looked just then not unlike the fledgling Marlon Brando; his hairline had inaugurated its retreat above his bulging temples, while something of Brando's rapt, faintly sardonic gleam, the pressure of unspoken opinions, complicated his play of lips. He already seemed precocious for his restraint with demanding clients: he alone got through seven years of litigating in behalf of the engineers at Bechtel.

He liked things perking along, every minute; one friend still recalls a trip to Charlottesville in the midst of those early years when the entertainment flagged, and Frank bet every other man in the group that he could jump lower, squat higher, and win a race against any of them using only one leg. "Of course he picked a short enough distance so he could win it," the friend laughs: Wisner lived to stir people up, but he was never a pushover.

Elizabeth Graham, who knew Frank well by then, insists that even at that stage "he had sort of an inner push, a drive, that kept him reaching out in whatever he was doing." She and her husband once took a vacation to Jamaica with the Wisners, and even as the young couples sat around the beach "his sand castles were more castley," the female forms he patted together seemed expressive, complete females. When others were resting or playing golf he'd set off on his own, "exploring the villages, the people, whatever was around." Once, teasing both their moods, he presented her with an elaborate cartoon in which two fantasms confronted each other, which he titled "When a Blue Funk meets a Pretty Howd' Ye Do."[6]

In 1936 Frank married Mary—Polly—Knowles, the daughter of a Greenwich, Connecticut, businessman, John Ellis Knowles, a polished amateur golfer who made several fortunes in the undependable shipping business. Polly was a plain-spoken, high-geared, doggedly loyal, endlessly curious graduate of fashionable St. Timothy's boarding school in Maryland. Her ambitions and appetite for company matched Frank's own; the pair fell quickly into an easy, bantering, live-and-let-live relationship that got them through. She chided his naiveté; when her natural spontaneity tempted Polly into exaggerating, he dubbed her his personal "Mass of Misinformation." "I really don't think either of them could have been married to anybody else," remarks one friend who knew them over the years. Four children came along at rational intervals, starting with another Frank in 1938, then Ellis, and rounding out with a girl, Elizabeth—Wendy—and ultimately the baby, Graham.

One law school classmate remembers Frank as unsettled in Manhattan. "The big-shot law firms survived, but they were struggling. Before long Frank was getting in on big cases all right, but since he was not of the New York elite, the Harvard and Yale aristocracy, in time he found fairly stifling the business of apple polishing, of seeing the right people all the time. He needed to express himself, he wanted to work with people his own age."[7]

Weekends too became formalized; endorsed by his in-laws he joined the Apawamis Club in Rye, and once the war looked likely he relocated his family from West 57th Street to Greenwich. By 1940 Wisner was angling for a reserve commission in the navy. He went on active duty as a Lieutenant (JG) in July of 1941; after November of that year Wisner went in as Liaison Officer and Assistant Head of the Information Department of Cable and Radio Censorship.[8]

His office at 90 Church Street was warm, safe, and accessible by subway, and Wisner detested it. While technically part of the Office of Naval Intelligence, Frank griped to one friend, he found himself "assigned to some kind of goddamned public affairs office downtown, cutting out clippings. 'Jesus,' he couldn't help complaining, 'when the war's over I don't want my kids to remember me as in command of a *cutter*! . . .' "[9]

Donovan had barely inaugurated the Coordinator of Information offices before Wisner started buttering up Wall Street acquaintances in hopes of transferring in. Through Turner McBaine he kept the reminders flowing to David Bruce. When that wasn't productive he walked McBaine through the Cable Censor's office, dwelling on his regular exchanges with OSS, "principally through Mr. Gurfein," and observing, as McBaine noted, that he and his fellows saw traffic "which obviously concerned the OSS and seemed to them indiscreet. He mentioned one concerning 'Allen' whom he recognized to be Allen Dulles."[10] Once McBaine got stationed in Cairo in 1942 Wisner rushed word to him that "so far as his present chiefs are concerned, a transfer could be arranged now."[11] It still took until July of 1943 before Wisner's assignment got changed. At one of the X-2 training courses near Washington Frank specialized in "foreign intelligence techniques, including codes and ciphers, guerrilla warfare, sabotage and positive and counter intelligence activities."[12] He landed in Eygpt with his musette bag and .38 on Christmas eve of 1943.

Wisner had meanwhile moved over into Secret Intelligence (SI) and came into the big Cairo base as Reports Officer. According to his own account Wisner made "intensive studies" of British SIS methods, briefed agents, tightened up reporting and cut back "housekeeping" expenditures, and overall "assumed a position of considerable importance in the shaping of intelligence aims and overall policy of the Cairo office."[13]

This projection of himself as briskly—even punishingly—efficient snagged Wisner a transfer he really didn't appreciate. Just before the middle of June 1944, "The undersigned went unwillingly and under protest to Istanbul where he found an even worse state of affairs than he had expected," Frank's after-action write-up specifies. Outside China, there wasn't another OSS mission anywhere spilling sawdust like Turkey. Donovan had been touting Istanbul to the Joint Chiefs as a crossroads of raw data "so plentiful that the basic difficulty is in providing sufficient trained personnel to screen it."[14] In February a couple of third-rank employees of Paul Leverkuehn's Abwehr station in Istanbul, Erich Vermehren and his wife, Countess Elizabeth von Plattenberg, defected to the pol and banker from Winnetka who managed the station, Lanning ("Packy") MacFarland. Lieutenant Colonel MacFarland shipped the Vermehrens off to Cairo, where they made plain to interrogators that Dogwood, the OSS's principal contact and manager of the fifty-three subagents of the illustrious "Cereus" chain, had all along been subject to unstinting German control.[15]

"Frank was an absolutely marvelous raconteur," recalls his deputy in later years, Frank Lindsay, "and as he told it there was 'real concern that Packy was totally out of control and going wild,' and Wisner was sent from Cairo essentially to relieve him. Frank went by train across Palestine and Turkey," Lindsay says, "and his cover was that of an American clerk going to the consulate. He began to wonder about how he should behave as a clerk—would it be too ostentatious to take a taxi? Well, he was sort of worrying about this when the train pulled into the Haidar Pasha station, people pulled down the window, there was Packy MacFarland on the station platform. He spotted Wisner, and as Wisner told it he had a brass band with him, some sort of welcoming committee, and immediately announced to Wisner through the window: 'Wisner's my pal, and anything he wants he gets.' They went to where the ferries were, to go across the Bosphorus, and instead of a ferry Packy had a navy crash boat there, in which they churned across at twenty knots. . . .

"Packy dropped Wisner off at his billet, telling him that they would meet again at such-and-such an address at two o'clock. Still attempting to recover from shock, Wisner walked to the address, found it, and it was a night club. Again wondering what to do he walked to the darkest corner of the ballroom bar and waited. After a half hour or so the orchestra stopped, a spotlight went on Packy standing at the steps leading down to a dance floor, while the orchestra broke into 'Boop, boop, baby, I'm a spy!' "[16]

Allen Dulles had warned Washington that Istanbul was quicksand. That summer MacFarland left, the Nazis moved in and prepared to behead Dulles's Cereus contact, the industrialist Franz Josef Messner, and Dogwood dropped from sight, permanently.[17] Wisner patched up relations with the OWI, Office of War Information, British intelligence, and the Turkish secret police (who slipped in their own agent as Frank's chauffeur).[18] He junked the Cereus agents wholesale, fleshed out the Rose chain, revised operational methods, and touted on "the few officers who were willing and able to do sound work."[19]

Wisner was already promoting "the preparations for the next important phase of operations against the enemy, i.e., the forward movement into the Balkans." By then Frank was undoubtedly party to the Donovan-Dulles cabal to preempt the Soviets in the East; "while I was there" the CIA's eventual attorney Larry Houston would recall, "Donovan had sent us in Cairo an oral directive to change our targets to Russian intelligence targets in the Balkans."[20]

Even during his months in counterespionage school, Wisner highlighted for Fred Dolbeare scraps of information he came across pertaining to the Free Germany Committee.[21] When, early in August of 1944, emissaries of the floundering Rumanian dictator Marshal Antonescu showed up in Turkey and "informed us that they had been sent to Istanbul for the express purpose of negotiating peace terms with the Anglo-Americans," Wisner emphasized in his cable to Washington that "One interesting aspect of their approach was the fact that they strongly indicated, without actually saying so, that they hoped to reach an agreement with the British and American authorities, as well as the Russians, if not independently of the latter."[22]

By August 26 the newly promoted Lieutenant Commander Wisner was importuning Colonel John Toulmin in Cairo for permission to scramble over to Bucharest. By August 23 the Antonescu regime had succumbed to a coup, Rumania switched sides, and "in all humility" Wisner rushed down his lawyerly (if urgent) proposal to inaugurate "forward operations in Rumania and Bulgaria." Wisner raked up Donovan's recent cable "to the effect that the General is desirous of having as complete a penetration as possible of the Balkans with or without the prior consent of the Russians," and cited Whitney Shepardson's finding that "we should proceed with our activities independently and without asking permission of our Allies" in view of the "recent unannounced and unexpected landing of a Soviet Mission in Greece and by other incidents." Wisner's crew was "ready and waiting" and "probably in as good a position to get to Bucharest as are the boys in Italy." The "more pro-Allied" Rumanians were offering visas, the British were on the move, and now the Wisner plan "awaits only your order to become operative."[23]

Toulmin's okay came through; on September 1 Wisner packed his suitcase radio and code book and caught a hop to Bucharest on the return flight of a fighter-bomber coopted by escaping British agents. The next day Wisner convinced the Rumanian Foreign Minister to turn the plane around to pick up his subordinates and equipment. Frank's arrival was providential—spotters claimed to have identified a division of Waffen-SS armor lurking in the woods outside Bucharest, Nazi pilots were mounting three days of vindictive sorties over the capital, the Red Army hadn't yet arrived, and who besides Frank had rank enough to take things over as "chief of the permanent OSS intelligence mission in Rumania"? For two supercharged months Wisner amounted to a major Western intermediary in the central Balkans, cutting deals with power centers from King Michael to the regional commander of the Russian secret intelligence service and in the process annealing Rumania's future to his own.

Across OSS desks the outpouring of reports from Wisner's Bucharest City Team—Operation Bughouse—by way of Bari and Caserta provided the fall's most engrossing gloss on Soviet strategic intentions. Part of the enjoyment was ferreting out the real-world identity of Wisner's agents and sources, code-named in most cases after virulent diseases. Wisner himself was Typhoid. He personally composed most of the dozens and dozens of dispatches pouring through from Bucharest, and promotors of Cold War around the government would maintain that it was Frank's excruciating rendition of the mechanics of the Russian takeover which convinced them that FDR's hopes for "tripartite consultation and joint action" in the Balkans were delusionary.[24] The Bear had arrived, to devour.

Yet mulled through day by day, this welter of dispatches gives back a reflection of their author—improvisor, elbow-rubber, the sharp young advocate abroad—stomping around the vacuum behind the collapsed Antonescu regime. So far as the Russians knew officially, Wisner and his unit reached Bucharest entirely to fly out downed airmen and work on targeting studies. The evacuation of the fliers turned into an easy, well-publicized success. Before September was over 1,888 airmen, many in from Bulgaria and Yugoslavia with Tito's help, got back to Western support areas, ferried over by the B-17s of the Fifteenth Air Force and Air Rescue Crew. Bomb damage assessments of Ploesti refineries went in, along with logistical detail from both the Rumanian General Staffs and spokesmen for the Russian Second Ukranian Army.[25]

Wisner and his team had barely dumped off their gear around the Ambassador Hotel in Bucharest before Rumanian police officials and General Staff consultants revealed cabinet after cabinet of abandoned Nazi documents. After rapid screening, Wisner's analysis man, Russell Dorr, notes, "approximately one ton of documents were removed to Italy, a considerable portion of which contained new items of intelligence."

At first the emphasis fell on evidence of a Folke Wulfe assembly plants here, or there a vulnerable refinery cooling system. But soon the mother lode emerged from the desks and vaults of Landesgruppenleiter Kohlhammer, the upper-level Nazi party and SD official who managed Schenker and Company, the German transfer agent for oil shipments to the Reich from Rumania in return for munitions to the Rumanian forces.

Kohlhammer functioned, Rumanian securities tipsters insisted, as "the center of German espionage activities." "Schenker's material," Dorr noted, "containing valuable lists of Nazi party, agents, offices, etc., was turned over to the X-2 Branch of OSS and arrangements were made for further cooperation with the Romanian police in handling counterespionage matters. This material is believed to represent an unusually good set of leads on Nazi party organization and the espionage system."

". . . Because of the reluctance of some officials to talk freely," Dorr remarks, it became "necessary to have the police close the office temporarily to permit examination, and to encourage the employees to talk freely." Dorr doesn't mention how. His operatives were working fast. Shortly after their arrival the Russians turned the Bucharest Gestapo headquarters over to the local Communist Party, and "When the OSS group wished to examine these buildings for captured documents it became apparent that the Romanian police did not care to make any issue with the Communists over entry into the buildings."[26]

Even then "with numerous setbacks and disappointments, according to a subsequent award citation he himself helped compose, "Lieutenant Commander Wisner effected a liaison between his command and the Rumanian representatives of the Russian secret intelligence service (NKVD), an agency notoriously secret and aloof in its dealings with others." This "unique" success afforded Wisner the chance to interrogate "German military and political prisoners possessing strategic information and held by the Russians" and exchange tips "with respect to enemy agents and suspects in Roumania and adjacent countries." The commendation cited Wisner's "unusual judgment and discretion in order to avoid giving offense to the Russian Command."[27]

Much of this phraseology replicated Frank Wisner's own voluminous after-action report of March 27, 1945, part of his drumbeat of intimations to his superiors to look to him as nut-cutter and shirt-sleeve diplomatist extraordinaire. U.S. Fifteenth Air Force technicians rotated supplies and personnel and got out secure "pouch material." "They relied upon us for a variety of services," Wisner would observe, "and we in turn profitted by the ready made Air Force cover thus afforded for our non-military operations."

It remained these "non-military operations" of Wisner's which preoccupied officialdom. Frank and his American Military Unit now found themselves attempting to tiptoe into power in a kind of political seraglio in which nothing must be interpreted in too final a way. Wisner's mission hit Bucharest a week after the Rumanian king, Michael, presided over his August 23 coup, which ejected the entrenched military dictator, Marshal Ion Antonescu, and installed the apolitical General Constantin Sanatescu to head a coalition government. The king pronounced his troops cobelligerent with the oncoming Red Army; twenty-one of Hitler's divisions were mousetrapped and decimated.

Rumania's is a history which teems with reversals. It remains a daydream of the Rumanians that they are the descendants of the Romans. But in the intervening millennia virtually every bypassing horde, from the Mongols to the Goths, has given its genes a romp in this oil-rich granary off the Black Sea between the Carpathians and the Danube.

Rumania entered this century a lead player in the unending game of trans-Balkan grabass, with lots of political murders and bayonet-point boundary revisions. When Hitler invaded Russia, thirty Rumanian divisions bulked out the Wehrmacht's southern flank. After reannexing Bessarabia, they ripped across the Ukraine, proclaimed the territory between the Bug and the Dniester the new Rumanian province of "Transnistria," beseiged Odessa (where Rumanian troops massacred perhaps 15,000 Jews), and fought alongside the German forces as far as Stalingrad. Setbacks awaited them there. By 1943 envoys from the palace were starting to intimate to the Allies that Rumania was guttering. In March of 1944, Prince Barbu Stirbey in Cairo explicitly offered to produce the Rumanian forces as "cobelligerents" to the Allied side in return for guarantees of postwar independence and protection from Hungary and Bulgaria.[28]

Rumania was inherently unstable, its internal alignments crazed in the aftermath of Antonescu's savagery in putting down the Iron Guard in January of 1941. This bloodthirsty anti-Semite "Legion of the Archangel Michael" had once boasted top Guardist Horia Sima as deputy premier in the Antonescu regime.

But Guardist spokesmen resisted initiatives by the German Ministry of Economics to sop up for the ever-ravenous German banks and the Hermann Goering Werke the Malaxa and Ausnit holdings and expropriate the French, British, and Belgian oil interests.[29] Civil war broke out by January 20, 1941, and Legionary insurrectionists occupied most of official Bucharest. On Hitler's advice, Antonescu rolled in his armored personnel carriers against mobs of Legionaries preoccupied with sideshows like butchering Jews and hanging their severed remains on hooks tagged "kosher meat."[30]

Under cover of his patent as head of the Mineral Oil Subdivision of the German Ministry, a knockabout SD stringer and Mideast expert named Otto Baron von Bolschwing had coordinated with Sima and his followers. Von Bolschwing laid out an infiltration route for the desperate Legionaries. The baron stuffed Sima, the Guardist Minister for Economics Papanace, the rabid student leader of the Legionaries Viorel Trifa, and ten more management-level social terrorists into a German ambulance and shipped them out pell-mell to take their chances in the Reich.[31]

At least the overspray of all this political bloodletting spattered the ton of onionskins Wisner shipped to Caserta that September of 1944. Except for sporadic bombing, Bucharest took her leave of war with her vaunted Frenchified ambiance intact, her delicate, cloying *douce decadence.* The Americans had now appeared, and forthwith the nobility and the propertied classes descended from their villas in the Transylvanian Alps to pursue the season's amusements. In April, fishing for a coup, Molotov himself had publicly disclaimed all Soviet intention "of conquering any part of Rumanian territory or of changing the existing social order in Rumania."[32]

The vigorous young Hohenzollern monarch, King Michael, welcomed Wisner and his men at the Ambassador Hotel. Hours after his radios were functional, the first of the eager lieutenant commander's transmissions reached Washington, charged up with appreciations of the tycoon Nicky Caranfil and Marshal of the Palace, the Baron Stircea, "a nice-looking, highly-cultured man of about 37 or 38 years of age" who "is ambitious."[33] Stircea interceded for the King in dealings with Rica Georgescu, the influential Undersecretary of Commerce who doubled as representative of the Standard Oil Corporation (Standard's vast Astra-Romana/Romano-Americana installation at Ploesti represented 14 percent of the nation's capacity). Georgescu's independent-mindedness had landed him in prison throughout the ecstatic phases of Antonescu's flirtation with Hitler. Wisner arrived with introductions to the urbane Georgescu, rumored to have maintained regular telephone contact with the British Secret Service before and after incarceration.

So Wisner had landed at the very top of Rumania's palace-oriented social system, a square-set, highly charged redeemer from the West, tricked out in British battle dress. Frank jumped at the offer to resettle his crew into the mansion of Mitu Bragadiru on the Alea Modrogan.[34] Bragadiru was a beer magnate; his wife, the vivacious dark Tanda—née Princess Caragea—would function as den mother and chatelaine.

Under Tanda's expert guidance the Champagne glasses brimmed continuously, and there were plenty of couturier gowns and flirtations and tureens of whipped cream and salvers of caviar behind the tall windows shadowed by the graven stone balustrades which overhung the boulevard. Outside, Rumanian army sentries in leftover Wehrmacht battle helmets patrolled the brickwork. Locked inside the dooryard behind the mansion were jammed something more than 150 Mercedes limousines and Hispania Suizas, "donated" by the Bucharest leadership to the Americans for safekeeping until the Soviets stopped impounding whatever moved.[35]

By mid-September the flurry of dispatches from Wisner reflected the forebodings of his hostess. The Russians had barely secured the capital before a Red Army goon squad "smashed the seals on the door to the Nazi Legation in Bucharest," allegedly out after furniture, and requisitioned ambulances. "Persons connected with the government and industrial leaders are of the opinion that Great Britain and America violated their promises and left Rumania to her fate," and furthermore a "dependable industrial source" reveals that "the Soviet Union is attempting to subvert the position of the government and the King," initially by refusing to meet them and ignoring all offers of "cooperation in the struggle against Hungary and Germany." The Soviets were confiscating radios.[36]

On September 12 an armistice went into effect between Bucharest and Moscow: along with the twelve infantry divisions and $300 million in reparations, the Rumanians would shoulder the costs of the occupation and give back Bessarabia. The supervisory Allied Control Commission was subject to the Allied (Soviet) high command.[37] Wisner's hosts had anticipated that "armistice conditions would be more generous."

Donovan provided the Russians more than 1,500 pages from Wisner's purge of Nazi records. He also made sure that skeptics throughout the government—the White House, Harriman, Forrestal—got breakdowns of Wisner's dispatches.[38]

It became a water torture. King Michael promulgated a decree to "purify" the administration of fascists; the Soviets barely yawned, and rounded up trucks and tractors. Stircea protested to Wisner that the Communists were recruiting Iron Guard thugs and corrupt intellectuals, organizing soup kitchens and worker syndicates, burning country homes and retracking the railroads to Russian gauges.

While conceding in one report that "the Old Guard has succeeded to date . . . and few important removals from office and arrests of important persons have taken place,"[39] Frank's bias was unmistakable: As October opened Donovan himself was cautioning Wisner "against speech or action" which might be construed as "supporting any group of Rumanians" or evidencing "antagonism to Russia." He expected reports "carefully, accurately, and systematically to cover in turn every important phase of the economic, political, sociological, and military."[40]

Donovan was not alone in diagnosing prefabricated political attitudes. Soon after the war had ended a member of Wisner's Bucharest team, the whimsical but trenchant *National Geographic* editor Beverlie Bowie, published an arch, semi-farcical roman à clef derived from their exercise in Rumania.[41]

In Bowie's 1947 *Operation Bughouse* the Wisner prototype became "Commander Drowne," a hair-triggered psy-war enthusiast whose fighter-bomber had no sooner landed before he unhesitatingly agreed to "set up headquarters in the mansion of Madame Nitti," the regent's mistress, "a large white building which resembled a rather expensive funeral home." Bucharest was in fact quiet, but Drowne's opening telegram maintained that the government had already been seized by "coalition worst elements including communists, other riff-raff, after days and nights looting, rioting, encouraged by Red Army. . . . Startling rise in number rapes already, while harvests halted by requisition all livestock. Responsible elements urge me plead with you for dispatch twenty American divisions here and immediate declaration of war on USSR. . . ."

Drowne's bellicose inventiveness regularly counterpoints the narrative: "Morning sunlight fell impartially on Commander Drowne's bald spot, the golden curls of his new White Russian secretary, the dark locks of his Carpathian barber. . . ." The hot towel has barely cleared the pompous commander's jowls before he hops on word that a Russian soldier has inadvertantly nicked another member of the U.S. delegation. Exhilarated, the monomaniacal commander demands "All the details: how many Reds jumped him; how many he shot before he died; names; times; places—" Facts roll off unattended. " 'You know what this means don't you?' " Drowne challenges the underling who brought the news.

" 'Not exactly, sir.' "

" 'War.' The Commander gave his belt a final tug. 'Well, I've got to run. Important meeting.' "

Crosscurrents were plucking Donovan; men close to the President's ear remained preoccupied with Stalin's intentions. On October 3 a dispatch via Robert Joyce at Caserta reached Wild Bill's desk. The London Poles wanted U.S. help in evacuating a number of Polish intelligence agents "in grave danger capture Soviet NKVD. . . ." These men had been collaborating with British SI in Bucharest under Colonel Gibson, but the British "in order not to offend the Russians have withdrawn previous assent to evacuate them." Just then, "this matter being handled on a very high AFHQ level with [Carmel] Offie and American group in favor of our assisting in the evacuation. . . . As matters now stand, Wisner should be told that the policy has not been decided upon in the upper strata. . . ."[42] The game as Caserta saw it was already changing, fast, and Carmel Offie sat closer every day to the probable next dealer.

In Bucharest the monarch dithered. Moldavia was sinking. The Russians closed down the leading newspaper, *Universal,* and cancelled a National Peasant Party rally on grounds that "Fascist elements" were heard to abuse the Red Army while lauding Horia Sima.[43] From Moscow George Kennan sent through a warning that only the Communist militia in Rumania was scheduled to retain arms.[44]

While political Rumania tottered, intercourse picked up remarkably on the personal level. Wisner himself was wounded at Donovan's implication that he was loading his communiqués: "We have at all times exercised utmost care to avoid giving any impression whatever that we sympathize with or take the part of Rumanians as against Russians. Our relation with staff of 2nd Ukrainian Army and Commandant of Bucharest are most cordial as evidenced by fact that Generals Vorobiev and Burenine are attending tonight a dinner at our headquarters and bringing with them some 6 officers of their staffs. . . . as requested by 109 we will continue to give broad coverage to all phases intelligence situation here."[45]

There has come down a montage of photographs of several of these entertainments, culminating in a high-spirited New Year's Eve party at the unsinkable Max Ausnit's.[46] Until November the after-hours haven for the Americans remained the sprawling Bragadiru residence, where the animated Princess Tanda could direct her corps of well-trained servants in their immaculate smocks as wine glasses needed refilling or spell the City Team's senior translator, Capt. George Bookbinder. A tawny, soignée woman, always perfectly coifed, the princess's effervescence and welcoming, hands-on quality comes through in picture after picture, and this is especially true whenever Frank Wisner gets trapped by the camera, all brass and sleeve braid in his well-cut naval officer's uniform. Tanda's graceful fingertips have a way of draping fondly over a shoulder or poking around an elbow. These were special circumstances. Later on a member of Wisner's group would record that "After about two months, the American Military Unit decided to move away from the Bragadiru residence in Alea Modrogan. Eating, working, sleeping, drinking and loving other men's wives all under one roof while husbands and enlisted men were around was just a bit too much for some of us."[47]

Wisner and his Bucharest City Team then moved into the opulent town house of Professor Mihai Antonescu, the deputy and namesake—but no relative—of the deposed *Conductor,* where $12 million worth of napoleons, Swiss francs, and gold bars came out of sand poured along the roof stringers.[48] Wisner's dispatches now rang with yelps from the Rumanian power elite. "On Saturday October 28," one urgent summary opens, "Russian Officers began loading large amounts of refinery equipment and accessories at Romana Americana and Astra Romana factories for shipment to Russia. According to Nescu over 200,000 kilograms of equipment were loaded Saturday and a larger load Sunday."[49]

By now the Soviets were squeezing the ruling coalition, demanding jurisdictional control of the police, forcing in the head of the Communist-staffed Ploughmen's Front, Petru Groza, as Vice-President of the Council of Ministers.[50] According to Air Force G-2 an estimated 1,200 English-speaking NKVD agents already infested Bucharest, tapping every telephone line. Somebody penetrated the American mission and stole a diplomatic pouch.[51]

What hope the Rumanians had rested with the American delegation awaited by the Armistice Control Commission. Just after the third week in November the tall, exceedingly businesslike Brigadier General Courtland van Rensselaer Schuyler finally presented himself, preceded by a warning to Wisner from SI chief William Maddox in Caserta that "you would be instructed to show all reports to him and inform him your activities." Schuyler intended to reduce the OSS presence in Bucharest, and Wisner's prospects "would depend largely on extent to which you maintained cordial relations with Russians since he would not allow his work to be embarrassed or jeopardized." Schuyler included in his party a ministerial-rank State Department representative, Burton Berry, lately the Consul General in Istanbul.[52]

As cold showers will, this brought considerable blood to the surface. Schuyler waded in gamely to register a protest to the Russians at their expropriation of the Standard Oil refinery equipment; Soviet commander Vinogradov retorted (as an extended Wisner brief marked Secret-Control had anticipated) that the Romano-Americano apparatus had German markings and had been largely stockpiled for use by Nazi technicians once they overran the Russian oil fields. Accordingly, they were legitimate Soviet plunder.[53]

Reporting varied. A memorandum from OSS Acting Director Buxton for FDR emphasizes the comparative moderation of Soviet forces in the Rumanian countryside, slowed down largely by the "lack of cooperation from the Ministry of the Interior in Bucharest, and only unimportant members of the Fascist Iron Guard have been arrested."[54] Max Ausnit went along with this appraisal.[55]

Before long a turf scuffle erupted. When Berry was unable to compel Wisner to restrict all communications to Control Commission channels, he insisted on the State Department's monopoly on dealings with the local powers, particularly the royals and Romano-Americano.[56] Donovan wired Buxton that "Wisner at Bucharest reports that State Department representative Berry stated to American A.C.C. representative, General Schuyler, that he did not believe it necessary for O.S.S. in Rumania to continue independent reporting of intelligence," into which Wisner turned the knife by attributing it to "attitude State Department in Washington toward O.S.S. activities in general." At Donovan's urging, "Joyce discussed foregoing matter frankly with Offie, Kirk's deputy as American Political Advisor, AFHQ," who "acknowledges excellence of O.S.S. political intelligence from Balkans and particularly from Rumania. I am advising Wisner of this reaction and instructing him to continue his intelligence activities, keeping Berry constantly advised. . . ."[57]

By then Wisner was shoving back to neutralize the internal security sharpshooters of the X-2 inspection teams, warding off these "vexing problems" through "complaints . . . to the appropriate officers and authorities in Caserta and Washington,"[58] especially "Colonel Glavin through the intervention of Mr. Joyce."[59] Joyce protected Wisner's flank, with Offie in the sidecar.

Offie was after chits. His phenomenal cultural range and the incisiveness of his opinions, especially about Eastern Europe, were breathtaking, intimidating, especially to provincial military. By March of 1945 Frank Wisner had departed the Balkans, but one of his SI team, Henry Roberts, circulated a Research and Analysis report General Schuyler ordered suppressed "on grounds it did not represent situation as viewed by Schuyler," Joyce wired General Magruder. "I informed Offie of Schuyler's action and discussed Roberts' report with former. Offie considers report in general as excellent study." The report received circulation.

It was his final, January weeks in Bucharest which seem to have incited in Wisner that heightened, superengrossing vision of barbarism grinding closer, the anticipation of sellout precipitating a death-agony in the West. All through the holidays he maintained his characteristic high-spirited, hard-grinning, flesh-pressing Captain-of-Cadets demeanor: snapshots from the family album represent a man in his off hours indulging in the lark of a lifetime. In one, his dark naval-issue overcoat slung across his back like a cape, he stands with a rifle pointed backward on his right shoulder, grimacing with concentration into a makeup mirror with which he is sighting a target behind himself among the winter chesnut trees. At thirty-five a softening of his jawline and the retreat of hair beside a vestige of wet-combed strands already imparted to his warm, eager responses the authority of somebody much older, riper, better seasoned. In another picture he stands in riding boots and plus-fours showing off a fine day's bag of pheasants. Cigarette in hand, he is a constant circulating presence at the Ausnit Christmas celebration, the man on familiar terms with all the digniaries to guarantee the top uniforms like Generals Schuyler and Vinogradov have something to talk about between flashbulb explosions.

Outside in the neighborhoods, history slaughtered the undefended. The defection of Rumania a month after Stauffenberg's briefcase bomb exploded provoked the half-mad Fuehrer to unleash a Vienna-based Rumanian National Government, headed up by Horia Sima along with the rightest General Averamescu and Prince Sturdza. They were to lead their encampment of Guardists into action against the Soviet occupiers.[60]

Given Stalin's paranoias, this made it past time to deal with suspect elements inside Rumania. On January 6, 1945, the tyrant promulgated through General Vinogradov one of those shotgun-blast edicts through which he would effect the deportation, expulsion, forcible relocation, and often as not the deaths of an estimated 30 million souls. Between the tenth and the twentieth of the month all men seventeen to forty-five and all women eighteen to thirty except nursing mothers who could be determined to be "of German ethnic origin, regardless of citizenship" were to be "mobilized for work." In ravaged Mother Russia. Communist-directed review boards made up of two Rumanians and one Russian went into action overnight, and Rumanian police were dragooned into cooperating.

There would be no distinction between descendants of the Transylvanians whose forebears settled into the foothills of the Carpathians in the thirteenth century and detested Hitler and floating local SS cadre assembled by Andreas Schmidt. They were all Volksdeutsche: barricades sealed off neighborhoods, house-to-house searches combed flat after flat at the direction of functionaries with revised lists. By afternoon prepositioned fleets of trucks and automobiles began off-loading an estimated 80,000 Rumanians into the long lines of boxcars on parallel sidings at the Mogoshoaia freight station for shipment north to Soviet camps and mines. It continued for days, while terrified teenage girls and old men in nightshirts shuffled onto trains "steaming through the snow-covered fields," one witness wrote afterward, "loaded full of human freight—thirty to a box car—carrying them to slavery and death."[61]

For Frank Wisner himself, his widow insists, this was reality descending after all the toasts in vodka and promises of global solidarity, the handclasps before photographers and badinage with curly-haired little Vinogradov with all his medals flopping across his tunic. "My husband was brutally, brutally shocked," Polly says. "It was what probably affected his life more than any other single thing. The herding-up of those people and putting them in open boxcars to die on their way as they were going into concentration camps. While they were being hauled off as laborers by the carload in the middle of winter."[62]

After this performance, how must one evaluate Stalin's readiness at Yalta to confirm "the right of all peoples to choose the form of government under which they will live"?[63] Wisner was particularly aghast. He and his X-2, Major Robert Bishop, had read for months the traffic from the Kremlin circulating through the headquarters of the Rumanian Communist Party, unequivocal in its marching orders: Communize Eastern Europe. The Rumanian Security and Counterespionage Service, the fabled Sigurantza, sought Bishop out and bootlegged to the West their achives on Russia since the Leninist takeover, a windfall to which Bishop attributed "Eighty-eight percent of the information contained in the War Department's first staff study on the Russian Intelligence Service."[64] As 1944 ended, Bishop was radioing out to X-2 chief James Murphy a wealth of instrumental detail as Red Army commanders began to impose the "broad democratic basis" Stalin had in mind. At one juncture, Wisner discovered, the Russians permitted two trapped Nazi divisions to escape to step up the pressure on American units cut off at the Ardennes.[65]

Allied solidarity kept blinking out. For all his earlier claims to some kind of pipeline into the NKVD, Wisner wound up stymied by Soviet stonewalling. So week by week Wisner's mission shifted from even the pretense of coordination with the Soviets to billboarding for Washington the enormities of the occupation. They came through day after day, his rendition of exactly how the Red apparatus was pulping this seductive, bibulous society of merchants and industrialists, of chamberlains to the monarchy and richly paid managers for the Western interests. Before winter ended Wisner planted a subsource in the headquarters of Marshal Malinovsky, Stalin's commander along the entire southwestern military district. Through agent Tonsillitis—the Rumanian General Staff veteran Theodore Mannicatide—Wisner pushed through to Caserta endless order-of-battle details along the fourth Ukrainian front. Tonsillitis was "thoroughly pro-American in his sentiments," Wisner assured Donovan, from "a respectable upper class family" and "has an unblemished reputation for honesty, integrity and loyalty, traits very rare among Roumanians as a whole."[66]

Honor bright, stealing secrets. OSS reports from other capitals offered a second interpretation. One informant attributed the political upheaval in Bucharest to the extent to which "the American and British Intelligence Services had encouraged the National Liberal and Peasant Parties in their fight against the leftists. . . ."[67]

Matters came to a head toward the end of February; Moscow was reinserting hard-core provocateurs to stir up street demonstrations and heckle the government. Ana Pauker in particular had become a kind of Grendel's mother to the frightened conservatives. On February 27 the plane of Soviet Deputy Foreign Minister Andrei Vyshinsky set down in Bucharest. Vyshinsky told King Michael that he was to form a new government under fellow-traveler Petru Groza. He pounded on the table each time the king attempted to demur, and when he finally walked out on the royal presence he slammed the door so hard plaster cracked.[68] The evening of March 1 the Soviets took control of the newspapers, sent troops to ransack the Rumanian Ministry of the Interior, secret police headquarters, the prefecture, the War Ministry, Peasant Party headquarters, and any other potential center of resistance they thought of, including the palace itself.[69]

Donovan, eternally walking his political wire, reported to FDR that his informant "thinks the Russians were forced to interfere because the Left had committed so many errors and because the Anglo-Americans continued to support Maniu and the historical parties. The latter threatened Russian prestige vis-à-vis the Anglo-Americans. . . ."[70] By then the civil war had broken out widely in Greece, and elements of the British Army were fighting the left-oriented EAM/ELAS revolutionaries. When FDR protested the imposition of the Groza regime, Churchill read him a screed on Great-Power etiquette: "We have been hampered in our protest against these developments by the fact that, in order to have the freedom to save Greece, Eden and I at Moscow in October recognized that Russia should have a largely preponderant voice in Rumania and Bulgaria, while we took the lead in Greece. Stalin adhered very strictly to this understanding during the thirty days fighting against the Communists and ELAS in the city of Athens, in spite of the fact that all this was most disagreeable to him and to those around him."[71]

❑

Wisner was relieved of his chief of mission duties in Bucharest on January 27, 1945, and made it back to the United States by February 8. He arrived to find himself treated as something of a minor prophet by a small but extremely well-positioned circle across the government who relished his conclusions. Frank Wisner was not the type to let his moment expire, and he had more in mind. "Feels his greatest contribution would be in liaison work with Russians in European Theater," the lieutenant who debriefed him noted.[72]

By February 11 Lieutenant Colonel Maddox followed up on Wisner's preference that he be "earmarked for Czechoslovakia," and in successive cables proposed that the lieutenant commander go into Prague as "over-all man. Avoid large city team and work under cover State or M.A." Late in the month Washington shot that down, charging Caserta with "devising plan without unity, overlooking our previous reference to Wisner's full responsibility," and furthermore rejecting the "whole idea of cover which they had previously approved."[73]

In Washington Wisner continued to press in hopes of duplicating his Bucharest triumph. As he presented it to Assistant Secretary of State Julius Holmes, Wisner would go in as a "Special Assistant" to the designated U.S. Ambassador to the anticipated Benes government "in advance of the Ambassador to evacuate imprisoned Americans, check out the embassy premises, install a secure code and radio room, etc." As before, "it is not believed that there will be any necessity for obtaining the prior approval of the Russians." Priority would go to "the establishment of liaison with the Czech military intelligence agencies (with which our organization has heretofore had very favorable relations in London and the Middle-East) for the purpose of obtaining positive and counterintelligence regarding strategic objectives in Germany and German agents," along with "documents and background information about Czechoslovakia, including the activities of persons in opposition. . . ."

When better to effect "the establishment of liaison with Czech secret intelligence agencies and the Czech 'underground' for the purpose of obtaining secret military and political information regarding Germany and German activities in Czechoslovkia, including the organization and composition of the German 'stay behind' organizations"? He intended to encourage "the possible recruitment and use of undercover agents and secret means of our own for the same purposes and for the further purposes of obtaining military and political information concerning the situation and developments in Czechoslovakia."[74]

All this sounds plausible enough, until the dateline surfaces. Although German troops were bottled up in Prague for the moment, on the day in mid-March 1945 that this memorandum was submitted to Magruder and Shepardson, British and American divisions were well across the Rhine, while Marshal Zhukov's tank battalions lay massed along the banks of the Oder thirty miles outside Berlin. Very few were worrying about "strategic objectives in Germany." What Frank was plainly after was a crack at the German archives in Prague before the NKVD could organize its sweep, his chance to nail down an espionage center in the embassy while locking up underground assets friendly to the West. The commissars would soon enough begin their inexorable sorting-out.

While this went around, Wisner ignited a diplomatic sparkler entirely on his own. He had approached Franklin Roosevelt earlier by sending the President an assortment of Rumanian stamps. Wisner followed this up by submitting through channels a personal letter from King Michael to which he himself attached a detailed palace memorandum warning of the kingdom's prospects under Soviet occupation. Donovan rather gingerly put through these enclosures to the exhausted President, adding that the "officer in question" who had been entrusted with these royal communications "holds views of underlying causes for and the significance of recent developments in Rumania which are considerably at variance with reports which have been released to the world press from other sources, and for this reason it is believed that it might prove of interest to one of your assistants to discuss these matters with him."[75]

Wisner was ahead of himself. His proposal to run a city team into Prague seems to have expired along the paperwork trail, and there is no evidence that any of the Presidential aides solicited his opinion about Rumania. What seems to have carried the day was a recommendation to Whitney Shepardson by a low-key naval lieutenant who hadn't yet met Wisner, Richard Helms, that insofar as Wisner had done an "excellent, workmanlike job in Roumania . . . he be considered for the position of Chief, SI, or some other top SI job in occupied Germany."[76] That soon got backing, and on April 19, 1945, cleared for Top Secret and sporting the Legion of Merit, Frank Wisner climbed onto a flight headed back toward Europe to go to work as Allen Dulles's assistant in the German country mission of the OSS.

It was as chief of Dulles's Secret Intelligence Branch headquarters, run out of the Haenkeltrocken Champagne warehouse at Biebrich, that the acute, even peppery young Sergeant Arthur Schlesinger, Jr. first ran into Frank G. Wisner and found him bright and approachable enough if inclined to trumpet forth at times as concerned the menace of Communism. Wisner laid over three weeks in Paris to pick his staff and contemplate blueprints for a centralized secret intelligence system intended to blanket Germany, Poland, and Czechoslovakia. It speaks to the level of *output* the lieutenant commander had in mind that eight weeks after he and his staff pulled out their typewriters there were ten "field production units" scattered around out there throughout Germany and Czechoslovakia, which had already provided 278 reports on military, political, social, and economic developments. By October 1, 814 reports were in, and by December 1 the total was 1,203.[77]

This was particularly notable in view of the epic decompression many other mid-grade reservists were evidencing. Most were devoted primarily to raising a satisfactory amount of hell between swings through the orderly room to pester the company clerks about demobilization orders.

One who was not in a hurry was Peter Sichel, the wry, cosmopolitan twenty-two-year-old Alsatian-born captain who took over Helms's slot as chief of base in Berlin after qualifying with Dulles toward the end in Switzerland. Sichel remembers his summer and fall of 1945 as unambiguous by Cold War standards, a matter of tracking down prospective war criminals and identifying people who might be of interest to Paperclip and tossing out the black marketeering ring he inherited with his so-called Peter Unit. He built up an effective range of intelligence sources in East Germany through selective recruiting among the Russian and Polish defectors while "staying away from all the walk-ins the Russians sent us from Ukrainian resistance groups and the like. Along with professional paper mills, of which there were many."[78]

Survivors agree that Allen Dulles was *presiding* more than he was running things out of Wiesbaden. "Allen was a hellova nice guy who would have made a very good headmaster in a boy's school," Sichel notes. "He was impressive to look at, a boy scout, a dreamer who had a wonderful patrician way. But he was not particularly sophisticated." Most of the hard-core management originated just then with Wisner, whose "long experience and dominating personality were essential to the task of creating overnight a large working organization and then refining it," as a draft of Wisner's Oak Leaf Cluster citation elaborates.[79]

Even here, Sichel saw, Dulles jollied the heavyweights along, but it was Wisner who kept the steam up. "We had a whole collection of Southern gentlemen in the OSS," Sichel observes. "Lawyers, advertising people. . . . And in a way Frank was one of them, but in a way he was slightly different. He wasn't from the Eastern Seaboard establishment, but he had worked in the North. Socially, he was one of the most charming men I have ever met. Yet he was a very, very complex man, his emotions really drove him. He was very accessible, he would listen to people and he was rather sophisticated, he was interested in history and background motivation, which made him different from the other guys in that way. . . ."

This knack for projection, the ability to imagine in his guts what entire populations were experiencing, imparted to Wisner an authenticity—at times, even then, almost a grating strenuousness—few people up the ladder and fewer yet under his immediate command ever found the wherewithal to dismiss completely. His Oak Leaf Cluster citation refers to his "close personal liaison with the Theater G-2, the Director of Intelligence OMGUS and the Political Adviser's Office," while a surviving fact sheet emphasizes the extent to which he "himself took charge of the planning of operations for the procurement of intelligence regarded as indispensable to General Sibert and Clay and by Ambassador Robert Murphy."[80]

Like the cosmopolite Gaevernitz, Wisner provided Allen Dulles something well beyond one more accommodating junior dogsbody: the sharp youngish officer with just a touch of the luxuriance of the South about his dense dark lashes, that hardworking shirtsleeves look (although retaining his dress-uniform necktie on even the most frantic of afternoons). Frank's long classic oval of an American face, the emerging thinker's temples, set off his constitutional vibrato: one found oneself responding to the almost excessive fitness which rang from the hollows and sinews of Wisner's powerful wrists, his well-kept sprinter's calves. That compelling first impression was gratifying to a man with Allen Dulles's eye for polish in women and underlings. Dulles appreciated Wisner's talent for the deft, eviscerating aside, his way of galvanizing subordinates when need be with a commanding display of impatience.

As August ended, and Wisner compiled points enough for demobilization, the two looked into various ways to keep Frank on in Germany without taking on an extended hitch. When Harry Truman folded up the OSS on September 20, 1945, and junked it like a leaky umbrella, Frank Wisner immediately "returned to Washington," as the draft of his Legion of Merit citation pointed out, and "acquainted himself first-hand with the plans for a continuing intelligence service. He then returned to Germany, revisited the principal branch units and succeeded in consolidating the organization's hold on its key personnel."[81] There were studied inquiries both ways as to the feasibility of Frank's making a career in peacetime intelligence; then, overreacting to a routine War Department turndown of his request for a consignment of bicycles on which his agents might prowl the Soviet Zone, Wisner blew up unexpectedly one day and turned in his application for discharge.[82] Idealism would remain idealism. But peace threatened, and bureaucracy was again bureaucracy.

13

ACROSS THE SHIFTING SANDS

Like Allen Dulles himself, Frank Wisner did not intend to bury his *own* career in the "shifting sands," as Allen phrased it, of postwar intelligence policy.[1] It speaks to Wisner's footwork that the impression he left with War Department brass was gratitude at his willingness to extend his service in Germany while he was arranging to break it off. The summer of 1945 he made full commander; upon his reappearance around Carter, Ledyard the firm was quick to offer him a partnership; he and his family resettled without ado in a substantial Manhattan apartment with an appropriate Park Avenue address, 1050. Whatever his global anxieties, Frank Wisner hadn't lost his head when it came to moving up.

With seniority at Carter, Ledyard he could expect top money. He was already received almost as a peer by personages around Wall Street. After Frank George died a marketable pool of oil had come to light under timberland around Laurel over which the family hung onto mineral rights. Sizable royalty checks arrived. God knows the elements of a rewarding, top-drawer future were converging virtually of themselves. Yet Frank was extremely, *exceedingly* restless.

"I saw Frank down on Wall Street," Peter Sichel says. "Whenever I came back. I came back in '46 to become a civilian, and Allen and Frank and I had lunch down there. I was a very *junior* Old Boy but they were very anxious for news, to keep in touch. It was like belonging to an old school, you know. . . . By then Frank and Allen were close, very close. . . ."[2] It was at this juncture that Stephen Penrose endeavored to recruit a receptive Wisner into the CIG. General Magruder kept calling, Polly remembers; each overture left Frank "moaning and groaning," clearly divided against himself. Ambassador to the Soviet Union Averell Harriman summoned Wisner to Washington for a briefing before the Moscow Conference, then raked him over for anti-Soviet vehemence.[3]

Staffers at the SSU were also suspicious of Frank's intentions. According to William Corson, the "West Point colonels and others who were determined to eliminate the Donovan influence on post-war intelligence" had turned away an earlier Wisner feeler; people regarded the hard-hitting Mississippian as "another Donovan who'll run away with the ball."[4]

Blocked by these regular-army "whiskey colonels," as many of the OSS hotshots sometimes dubbed their torpid military counterparts, Wisner contrived another avenue. The general on temporary duty at the State Department to interface as Assistant Secretary for Occupied Areas, John Hilldring, stepped down the summer of 1947. The job was passed along to financier Charles Saltzman. Through much of the thirties Saltzman had been an officer of the New York Stock Exchange, where there was lots of involvement with Carter, Ledyard, and then and after the war he'd bumped into Wisner often enough. Frank was quite junior still by Wall Street measurements, but he had consistently struck Saltzman as a young man of "very good judgement," of "strong, honest, dependable character," and when his carryover deputy moved on, Saltzman approached Frank Wisner to take his place.[5]

Other forces prodded. "I thought you might be interested to hear the outcome of the matter which I discussed with you shortly prior to your departure for Europe and in the inception of which there appears to have been a trace of that fine Dulles touch," Wisner wrote Allen Dulles on October 1. Frank had become an active member of the Council on Foreign Relations, where Allen was president. Dulles's "interest in this matter" and "very helpful advice and information about the position" were much appreciated, and Wisner "should like to feel free to call upon you for your advice in connection with aspects of my new work as to which I am certain I would be greatly assisted by your views."[6]

The post Frank Wisner accepted carried a lot more clout than outsiders might imagine. Its official job description delegated to the Deputy

Assistant Secretary, subject to "general executive direction," power over "any phase of policy coordination" which related to the Occupied Areas—Germany, Austria, Korea, Japan, and Trieste.[7] Wisner was quickly functioning as Saltzman's alter ego on interdepartmental committees and turning up abroad at major conferences. He doubled as the alternate for Saltzman as chairman of the State-Army-Navy-Air Force Coordinating Committee (SANACC) on "matters of U.S. political-military policy of interest to the four Departments." As the updated successor to the State-War-Navy Coordinating Committee founded late in the war to provide "more centralized decisionmaking"[8] about psychological (and, increasingly, a wide range of quasi-covert) activities, its membership was already concentrating on methods of confronting and countering Soviet incursions worldwide. Most of the regularly scheduled meetings of SANACC took place in Wisner's conference room;[9] he would fight doggedly within the committee to reserve for State—himself—the opportunity "to set up an entirely new propaganda agency within this Government. . . ."[10]

Wisner started breaking in just as the Coordinating Committee gave way to the newly constituted National Security Council (NSC). With Germany on line by then as the principal staging area for the upcoming Cold War, Frank took on "the responsibility for the coordination of Occupied Areas policy between the Department of State and the Department of the Army."[11]

This left him stepping around as only Wisner could among the archons of Congress, his superiors at State—he was soon involved on a day-to-day basis with Undersecretary Robert Lovett—and the irascible U.S. Military Governor for Germany, General Lucius Clay. Clay nurtured a reputation for pistol-whipping State Department flunkies, a practice which sometimes left him "so riled that he almost habitually announced his imminent resignation."[12]

With New Deal holdovers dropping off the stern, fewer every month stayed on to press the Military Government about JCS 1067, especially its embattled decartelization and de-Nazification provisos. In August 1947 the dapper Dillon, Read veteran William Draper was promoted over Clay's head to Undersecretary of War. It was this same appointments list which featured the designation of Rear Admiral Roscoe H. Hillenkoetter as the initial director of the Central Intelligence Agency. It, along with the newly amalgamated Defense Department and the National Security Advisor and his staff, broke through like molars to facilitate the National Security Act. The Executive required bite enough to meet his Cold War responsibilities.

The primary Occupied Area by then was indisputably Germany,

especially to the Eurocentric assemblage of lawyers and bankers who stage-managed the Truman administration. By 1947 the dreamers around Roosevelt were gone; most of their successors were idealogues of the Acheson variety (who hoped to restrain the Soviets through economic counterpressures) or activists like James V. Forrestal (who spoke by 1945 of "showdowns" with this sinister, monolithic menace whose "interest lies in a collapse of . . . a world in which a capitalistic-democratic method can continue. . . ."). [13] Both groups could concur that the sooner Germany was back on its feet and paying its own way the better, and to hell with Yalta.

Germany's backers put feelers out. In the April 1947 issue of *Foreign Affairs*, Allen Dulles expressed his fear that "Reparations from current production of heavy industry [i.e., the machine tools and equipment the Soviets were still expecting] might tend to stimulate German heavy industry artificially to an undesirable point." He anticipated that "The political separation of the Ruhr from Germany would have unwelcome political consequences." He espoused currency reformation and warned that "Drastic financial reforms which go to the heart of the structure of property ownership cannot be carried out, even on a restricted scale, without affecting all property relationships." Leave the cartels alone.

In September and October of 1947 Allen Dulles signed on as legal consultant to the Select Committee on Foreign Aid of the House of Representatives. Generally known as the Herter Subcommittee on Germany and advised by Carl Friedrich of Harvard, who regularly provided economic advice to Clay and Draper, its report pressed Congress to collaborate in reviving Germany. Meanwhile, in February 1947 a strenuously coached if doddering Herbert Hoover was conducted through the Ruhr to exact his judgment that "concessions must be made to the old-line financiers and industrialists. . . ." [14]

Inquiries by the Ferguson Committee carried out in 1948 on Harry Truman's request revealed that "The U.S. occupation officials have failed to smash a single one of Germany's giant monopolies under a crackdown now two years old." [15] As early as 1946 Undersecretary of War Robert Patterson was arguing against exposing German industrialists to trial in Russia "in view of the many connections between the German and American economies before the War. . . ." The Fourth Reich glimmered. They'd left their armbands in drawers, but on the commercial level the leadership of Germany under Adenauer was all but indistinguishable from that of Hitler's crackling economy. [16]

❑

Frank Wisner grabbed up his oar at State without recorded demurrers. Conferences with the Soviets originating with the Paris exchanges in spring of 1946 had yielded little more than further evidence that the Soviets were expansion-minded. The confrontational 1947 meeting in Moscow of the Council of Foreign Ministers hardened everybody's attitude. George Marshall gave up on the politically vacillating Czechs, and agreed to a policy of heavy-handed economic blackmail which contributed to the panic which finished off Benes.[17] A lot of State Department energies went into lawyerly devices for excluding the Russians from support programs for the West while sidestepping anything "the Soviets might construe . . . as an invitation to reassemble the quadripartite machine"—that is, promote reunification of Germany.[18]

The terminal rending came the spring of 1948, when Washington danced around serious proposals to shore up the hopelessly inflated currency the Grand Allies originally mandated for the Germans. Frank Wisner protested suggestions to solidify the currency under Four Power auspices as less than "desirable from the U.S. standpoint, since quadripartite currency reform might enable the Soviets to frustrate further the economic recovery of western Germany." Acknowledging that harder money limited to the Western Zones would "represent a very definite move toward recognition of the East-West partition of Germany," he urged it nevertheless as "an important move toward much-needed economic stability in Germany."[19]

The Western governments announced on June 23 that they would trilaterally circulate new marks in their sectors, in effect recasting Trizonia into a separate political entity. The next day the Soviets closed the land routes between the West and Berlin. A train of events was picking up speed which produced in short order the Air Lift, the imposition of a Stalinist government on Hungary and the faceoff in Korea, and decades of unambiguous Cold War.

By then Frank Wisner was established within the administration as an inveterate hard-liner. He caught the earliest available plane to London to speak for State in crisis meetings in Berlin with Draper and another Dillon, Read loaner, Lawrence Wilkinson, along with the U.S. commander of the Berlin garrison, Albert Wedemeyer.[20] "I remember when Truman unexpectedly was reelected and appointed Dean Acheson Secretary of State," Charles Saltzman says. "Wisner was very distressed by that. He was like Kenneth Royall, the Secretary of the Army, he had no use for Truman and he thought Acheson was too liberal.

"One thing bothered Frank that bothered me very much. When the Russians put the Berlin blockade on in the spring of 1948, I thought and he thought and I think a great many people thought that that was the time when we should have acted very emphatically by organizing a task force—which we did, it was in command of a friend of mine, General Arthur Trudeau—a self-contained task force with its own engineers and its own artillery and its own communications and everything—and gone to Berlin, fighting our way in if necessary. The Russians did not have the atomic bomb then. Had we done that, I've always felt it might have obviated the rest of the Cold War. We both felt that, very strongly."[21]

It was undeniably exhilarating, this awareness that decades to come were soft still, barely out of the egg. Each decision affected millions. Yet even at that stage, Wisner's dreams were brushed by obscure moral premonitions. One withheld grain credits in Czechslovakia to help the "anti-Communist forces in the government," and that played through as Masaryk sailing out a window. One protected the Ruhr, Wisner told one friend at the time, because if the Reds got that, "the rest of Europe is gone." If this meant babying certain defunctive Nazi arms profiteers, power required a knack for discriminating the greater good. Enhanced production was important.

Not that one relished the *implications* much. " 'Look, I'm not going to stay in this town,' Wisner assured one fellow he'd known since law school. " 'I'm not going to get Potomac fever.' " Frank blurted this out with a rare, almost plaintive note of uncertainty in his voice. "He already saw," his erstwhile classmate realized, "that where events were taking him it was deadly."

Which made it more to be appreciated that another role was looking for Frank Wisner, a position with so much glamour and potential that there was really no turning it down. When Secretary of State George Marshall got back from the Foreign Ministers' conference in Moscow in the spring of 1947 "he was disappointed," Paul Nitze recalls, "in the *quality* of the preparation which he'd been given before he went off on that trip. He needed a group of people who were looking at the overall problem, in all its aspects. Not just from day to day. The longer-range possibilities, with objectives and strategic questions in mind as well. . . . So he asked Dean Acheson to create such a group, and Dean asked George Kennan to head it up."[22] Kennan founded the State Department's germinal Policy and Planning Staff.

Marshall installed Kennan in a suite of offices which adjoined his own, and lent his own enveloping prestige to the ruminations of this brilliant, mavericky, neurasthenic cheese-parer whom Forrestal called back from Moscow to contribute to deliberations at the War College.

It was Kennan's mandate, Paul Nitze remembers, to deal as broadly as possible with events, from economic tendencies and population rates to dangers in South America and Africa. Broadly, but in a Cold-War context. Kennan concentrated on experts on Soviet potentialities. Many, starting with Kennan's Moscow stablemate Chip Bohlen, were State Department products: executive secretary Carleton Savage; China specialist John Davies; Wisner's nemesis in Bucharest, Burton Berry; George McGhee, lately with Will Clayton's trade advisorial staff. Columbia professor James Angell, exponent of the German cartel arrangements, went in, along with economist Jacques Reinstein and Joseph Johnson and Col. Charles Bonesteel III, a Marshall Plan consultant, to contend with Clay as the European Recovery Program heaved onto its feet.[23]

One man Kennan asked for but did not get was Paul Nitze. The wiry little investment banker and protégé of Forrestal at Dillon, Read had made himself essential to the implementation of the Marshall Plan. Nitze bore down effectively as Deputy Assistant Secretary of State for Economic Affairs, a post which kept him in touch with Wisner while Nitze directed the preparation of the "brown books" which assimilated the capital positions, needs, and requirements of nations awaiting their dollar infusions. When Kennan's requisition came through, Nitze says, "Acheson thought I was not the sort of intellectual planner he had in mind, that I was more of an operator. So he blackballed George's selection."

While Policy and Planning staffers wrote voluminous reports, the Russians continued consolidating. Nitze himself brings up a conversation he got into in 1946 in London with a member of an AFL delegation to a World Federation of Trade Unions conference. The delegate was stunned just then by a timetable one of the Communist participants trotted out anticipating Communist takeovers across the West. There were already deadlines—a few months for Italy, less than a year for France, then on to Germany, and perhaps four years at the outside in England's case. This perception of a Communist master plan accorded nicely with the establishment of the Cominform in 1947. By then, Nitze says, "the question had arisen as to whether or not we shouldn't compete with the Soviet Union in some of the things that they were doing. Such as the enormous effort that they were putting into trying to capture the intellectual and cultural world. Shouldn't we be making some comparable effort to assist the Western intellectuals to resist this attempt on the part of the Soviets to set up front organizations of one kind or the other to capture innocent and not very knowledgeable people. . . . And then there was another very dramatic incident, in which it was clear that the Soviet Union—the KGB, really—was interfering in elections, bribing these people, and those people, and others, and it was clear that this arm of the Soviet activities was a very important arm of their conduct of policy.

"It was quite contrary to our past traditions for the U.S. government to engage in such activities. But what were you going to do? Were you going to let the Soviets freely subvert all the rest of the world and bring the whole foundation of Western culture into ruins? Or were you going to try to do what you could to combat that?"[24]

Groping for the fire bell was routine in Washington, and worst-case scenarios were ideal to jump-start Congress. Pressure from the United States just after the war ended—the possibility was bruited about of withholding UNRRA stocks—helped fracture the Parri government in Italy and brought in conservative leadership. In January of 1947, fortified with a $10 million loan from Washington, Christian Democrat Alcide de Gasperi reentered Rome and maneuvered the surviving Communist ministers out of his shaky coalition.[25] The Reds went quietly, but money from the Kremlin started pouring into the hands of Communist chief Togliatti's organizers. As 1947 wore on, local Communists did better and better in by-elections for municipal offices.

His hair on end, the newly appointed initial Secretary of Defense James Forrestal arranged for the transfer of arms stocks from U.S. storehouses in Germany to reliable Italian supporters, many hardcore Mussolini veterans. An alarmed George Kennan—evidently unnerved by Lucius Clay's March 1948 telegram to Washington warning of a Soviet military move which "may come with dramatic suddenness"—recommended that the Italian government outlaw the Communist Party "and take strong action against it before elections. Communists would presumably reply with civil war, which would give us grounds for reoccupation Foggia fields or any other facilities we might wish. This would admittedly result in much violence and probably a military division of Italy; but we are getting close to the deadline and I think it might well be preferable to a bloodless election victory, unopposed by ourselves, which would give the Communists the entire peninsula at one coup and send waves of panic to all surrounding areas."[26]

So much for democracy and its rites. That the reflective Kennan panicked speaks to that moment in Cold-War history. The next instrument Forrestal grabbed was the unsteady new Central Intelligence Agency, and at the first formal meeting of the National Security

Council on December 19, 1947, he rammed through an unpublished annex to policy directive NSC 4, which required the Secretary of State to coordinate anti-Communist propaganda. The annex, NSC 4A, instructed the Director of Central Intelligence to take on covert psychological warfare. With Presidential and Congressional backing, NC 4A emerged as the legal basis for the establishment within the Office of Special Operations section of the CIA of a so-called Special Procedures Group, a covert action instrumentality DCI Hillenkoetter charged immediately to *do something* about the national Italian elections looming on April 18.[27] Solicited for his opinion, CIA General Counsel Larry Houston ventured that meddling in politics overseas was outside the Agency's mandate.[28]

James Angleton had returned from Italy in November, purportedly to string together an index of documents on the Soviet Union. He'd returned in time to influence the Special Procedures Group. Collaborating with Vatican go-betweens, OSO veterans fell back on political techniques from home and abroad, including, as Professor Robin Winks of Yale writes tellingly, something between $10 and $30 million a year "to influence elections at the local level, for campaign expenses, the financing of splinter groups that might divide the Communists, straightforward bribes, and anti-Communist propaganda."[29] Most of these cash transfers went through from Exchange Stabilization Fund accounts, frozen assets the Safe Haven administrators had confiscated from Nazi sources, much of it looted originally from Europe's helpless Jews.[30]

American foodstufs flooded in, along with threats to politicians that there would be no aid to any future government that included Communist ministers. "Italian-Americans were organized to write anguished (and sometimes subsidized) letters to friends and relatives in Italy, telling them how they should vote." Hollywood stars recorded radio messages for their worshipers in the villages.[31] Meanwhile, "new weapons and supplies were hurried to the Italian army with the obvious hint that, should the Communists achieve a government, a military coup was called for." Angleton contributed to a court case against the luckless pornographer and document fabricator Virgilio Scattonini, the Vessel source, to showcase a verdict which glorified the Vatican and discredited the encroaching Left.[32]

Angleton called the election—the electorate went centrist by 58 percent. Washington was universally overjoyed to discover that democracy remained permissible, and adrenalized by the cut-rate possibilities covert seemed to provide.

* * *

Paradoxically, now that the OSO had demonstrated effectiveness, Forrestal, Marshall, and their lieutenants decided to withdraw this function largely from the newly enfranchised CIA—where everything that went on risked review by the National Security Council—and create a new, less visible instrumentality. Something handier to the movers around the government yet outside the normal oversight loop. Until Italy went critical George Kennan had tended to describe the underlying Soviet strategy as accretive, cautious, a matter of testing and probing and pulling back where anything might nip Moscow's paws. That spring of 1948 panic was in the air, and Kennan had decided that since the Russians seemed to "prefer to do the job politically with stooge forces" it was now urgent for the United States to bring into being "small, compact, alert forces" of our own, "capable of delivering at short notice effective blows in limited theaters of operation far from our own shores."[33] Make special operations permanent, and match the Soviet programs. Kennan retained an inkling, at least, of how such things were managed after sitting in as Hoyt Vandenberg's Soviet consultant in 1946.

Where policy was headed that spring is evident from paperwork thrown off by the State, Army, Navy and Air Force Coordinating Committee study group looking into the "Utilization of Refugees from U.S.S.R. in U.S. National Interest (SANACC 395)." As many as 700,000 fugitives and émigrés from Russia were understood to be adrift under a variety of auspices in Western Europe, a mélange which ran from played-out Menshevik irreconcilables to staff officers from the Vlasov regiments who slid by the postwar Soviet roundup along with Byelorussian triggermen from the SS Einsatzgruppen extermination teams. Many were established repeaters on Allied CROWCASS lists as bona fide war criminals. Soviet specialists at State understood that few of the turncoats they thought they could use were likely to survive even the most cursory examination by Immigration and Naturalization. What they were after for openers was some manner of blanket authorization to bring in up to 250 people annually, no clearances required: something like the Paperclip proviso which had permitted the War Department to tuck away its slew of Nazi rocket scientists. Charlie Thayer at the Voice of America hankered after technical advice, and George Kennan kept talking about a think tank devoted to Eastern problems, already emerging in the position papers as the Eurasian Institute.[34]

Much more was obviously coming up. Years later George Kennan would ridicule proposals to install "a nice pro-American government made up of 'democratic elements' in Russia," while "escapees and immigrants, mostly recent ones, from the non-Russian portions of the postwar Soviet Unions, as well as from some of the Eastern European satellite states" were "passionately and sometimes ruthlessly attached" to the idea that "the United States should, for their benefit, fight a war against the Russian people to achieve the final breakup of the traditional Russian state and the establishment of themselves as the regimes of various 'liberated' territories." Several—the Byelorussians, the Ukrainians, the Moldavians, and extremist factions among the Albanians and the Croats—still savored the blood of power they'd relished briefly under the Nazi suzerainty. It was their "expectation," Kennan observes, "that they would be permitted and encouraged by us to line their recent political adversaries up against the wall . . . after which they would continue to rule, with our help, by their own brand of dictatorship."[35]

This appeared in 1972. In 1948 Kennan's ideological triggerpoints were still largely where they might cater to career purposes. ". . . There are a number of interesting and powerful Russian political groupings among the Russian exiles," Kennan wrote in NSC 20 during the summer of 1948, "any one of which would probably be preferable to the Soviet Government, from our standpoint, as rulers of Russia." Should the Soviet government happen to collapse, let everybody go back, and we should "see to it . . . that they are all given roughly equal opportunity to establish their bids for power."[36]

Let 10 million pistols bloom. But how to destabilize the area to open the way? One started with intelligence. "The Soviet satellite areas like the USSR are tending to be come a terra incognita," a March 4, 1948, Policy and Planning Staff study maintained, and apart from analysis the staff was counting or identifying "political figures among the refugees" for utilization as "the potential nucleus of possible Freedom Committees encouraging resistance movements in the Soviet World" while "providing contacts with an underground."[37] As early as September of 1947 Frank Lindsay and Charlie Thayer had trumped up memos for a "guerrilla warfare corps."

By May of 1948 an ideologically more explicit SANACC workup was making the rounds, advocating a major program in behalf of "native anti-communist elements . . . which have shown extreme fortitude in the face of Communist menace," along with " 'know-how' to counter communist propaganda and in techniques to obtain control of mass movements. These elements include, for example, Socialist, trade union, intellectual, moderate right-wing groups and others." To mobilize these "natural antidotes to Communism" the working paper called for $5 million laundered immediately into some likely military component, then bootlegged through State for "secret disbursement." Some "private American organization" was called for to "dovetail with this plan generally," with payments taken care of by compliant labor unions or bank branches abroad. There must be backup provisions "for the evacuation to safe countries of key foreigners involved in these activities if the internal situation in these countries jeopardizes their security."[38]

Allocated the codeword Bloodstone, this undertaking was manifestly dicey, fraught with political flaps.[39] Even the declassified paperwork leaves no doubt that most of the grease behind these subversion proposals originated with the clutch of born-again Sovietologists swarming in and out of State at the moment—Llewellyn Thompson, Kennan, Gohlen, John Davies, Charlie Thayer—each with some favorite of his own to juice up their anti-Bolshevik brain trust. As Acting Member for State on SANACC, Frank Wisner was racing around all spring scrambling up unified support for Kennan's paper counteroffensive. Copies of the formulating memoranda poured through the selected senior officials—Bill Draper and Albert Wedemeyer, "Sec. Forrestal (Mr. Blum)," CIA Director Hillenkoetter. The working committee itself was stacked with hard-core Sovietophobes—Robert Murphy, Colonel Robert McDowell, Boris Pash, John Earman of the CIA.[40] By June 25, 1948, Frank Wisner was already penciled in to meet with Clay and Murphy in Berlin to discuss "remittances to Europe, Inc. payroll deductions," their unmistakable business cover.[41]

By that point it had become clear all around that they would need something with lots more clout than a subcommittee to enliven the Eastern programs. With George Marshall's consent a half-defined new administrative entity popped out of the bureaucracy on June 18, 1948, when NSC 10/2 superceded NSC 4A and authorized the Office of Special Projects, soon changed to the blander and less revealing Office of Policy Coordination (OPC). It would be constituted to counter the "vicious covert activities of the USSR, its satellite countries and Communist groups to discredit the aims and activities of the US and other Western powers." Its efforts were to be "so planned and conducted" that were they to break the surface the U.S. Government could "plausibly disclaim any responsibility. . . ." Covert operations themselves included "propaganda, economic warfare; preventive direct action, including sabotage, antisabotage, demolition and evacuation measures; subversion against hostile states, including assistance to underground resistance groups, and support of indigenous anti-Communist elements in threatened countries of the free world." Administrative teeth were bared, but 10/2 remained defensive essentially, a punctilio for counterpunchers.[42]

People in surrounding offices weren't sure whether George Marshall tailored the job to Wisner's reputation or whether Frank Wisner himself convinced State that he was their man. Part of the confusion perhaps stemmed from the fact that within one year, at forty, Wisner had built himself into far more than an upper-middle-level bond lawyer on leave of absence from Wall Street to the State Department. He gave and took already on level terms with all but the most powerful. When Rumania's King Michael visited Washington, Wisner sponsored his royal claims and had him over for dinner. The personal history statement Frank submitted on assuming control of the OPC would present as character references Lovett, Saltzman, Assistant Secretary of the Treasury John Graham and Gordon Grey, while among his social familiars he listed William Draper, Wild Bill Donovan, and Brig. Gen. C. V. R. Schuyler. As permanent address he typed in Locust Hill Farm, Galena, Maryland, a big working spread on the Eastern Shore he picked up primarily for summers and weekends. The farm was three hours north of miasmal D.C., perfectly sited for bird shooting.

What continued to impress as tough a critic as Marshall was the extent to which Wisner clearly *had* a visceral position in the face of this threat from the Soviets. For all his inborn congeniality, his skill at promoting friendships helpful to his career, his ornate wit, the man was anything but a bullshitter: if Wisner didn't know something he'd bear down fast and check it out. Among jargon-gabbling bureaucrats Frank roused regular astonishment at the way his intensity fueled articulateness; while he and Polly stood making their goodbyes after a Georgetown dinner party, as often as not he could not resist a final glittering-eyed burst of thoughts and insights into this crisis or that aspect of world conditions until he too little by little ran down and the couple pushed along, quite frequently the last. Wisner cared so enormously, he brought such *physical* energy to everything he did. Who else was around with glands enough to organize the crusade?

Commentators are always struck by the unique administrative hookup through which at the outset the Office of Policy Coordination was wired into the corpus of the fast-changing government. While attached for bookkeeping purposes—rations and quarters—to Hillenkoetter's CIA, the OPC director would remain an appointee of the Secretary of State and pursue a proliferating array of projects under the immediate supervision of State's Policy and Planning Staff, with input from representatives of the Department of Defense. The OPC thus functioned as a covert political action arm to promote unpublicized aspects of State Department policy, a "support function," in Kennan's words, of American diplomacy. Both Marshall and Acheson, who resurfaced as Secretary of State in Truman's new administration, regretted the way Jimmy Byrnes had let intelligence slip away from State, and hoped to take back what control they could. The OPC could depend on a tremendous slug of unvouchered money all apart from routine CIA budgeting, and from the outset Wisner rarely bothered with staff meetings Hillenkoetter might announce. More important projects were underway in his dingy, bustling office suite in the dilapidated war-surplus L Building just off the Reflecting Pool into which he settled his high-energy staff after an autumn in the old Naval Hospital's S Building. S had been handy—perhaps too handy—for interlopers from State.

The cry from every quarter was: get this thing flying, right away, and let the peasants scatter. John Ranleagh has astutely observed that the "OPC also had a well-defined mission (although this was never spelled out in writing), arising out of postwar conditions and the Italian elections: it was to develop German democracy and support resistance groups in Eastern Europe in preparation for a 'hot' war which was generally thought to be coming."[43] Any minute.

Years later John Bross would shake his head over Wisner's stubborn effort to stamp out of his collection of mouldering OSS files and intragovernmental personnel records, contacts on university campuses and random Manhattan acquaintanceship something novel to Washington, to "put these lawyers and bankers and guerrilla fighters and kids just out of college together and give them some structure."[44] In *texture* the OPC has often been compared with the OSS, what with its top-heavy admixture of grey-flannel administrators and social-register paper-shufflers. The journalist Stewart Alsop, whose connections to Wisner and his shop were close—perhaps fatally close—in time came up with the catchword "Bold Easterners" to distinguish Wisner's charges. To convince the people he was after to throw in with the OPC despite its shadowy authorization and uncertain prospects, Frank prevailed on General Marshall to allow a number of promising government employees to transfer in at GS ratings often two and three rungs higher than their prevailing rank. Formidable outsiders frequently began at pay and promotion levels well above their counterparts in the OSO, the CIA's clandestine side.[45] Even at the time, the OSO careerists Alsop dubbed the "Prudent Professionals" couldn't help being rankled.[46]

Men of the sort Wisner wanted were almost always cut to the politically enlightened Ivy-League pattern, with perhaps more emphasis on humor and a well-tutored social touch than job descriptions required. Democrats predominated—Wisner himself, after all, remained a nominal Democrat—or, at the worst, Rockefeller Republicans. Almost all were liberals, or imagined they were, although (unlike the OSS) nobody took it upon himself to kick the tires of capitalism before buying in. This thing was life or death, and dogma must not intrude.

❏

The times had shifted; Donovan's damn-the-torpedos mentality was out of date, and he, as ever, would be the last to know. Demobilized, Wild Bill was recurring unhappily to his prewar role as self-deputized beekeeper of the world's buzzing intelligence outback. "I just want to seem to be an aging little fat man," he told people, ducking photographers, and hung the emphasis on *seem*.[47] To many who attempted to follow his postwar career he had it just about right. A decade of financial mismanagement had saddled Donovan with hundreds of thousands of dollars worth of tax delinquencies, and he would never really recover his prewar life-style. Ostensibly to promote recovery he, William Stephenson, and Edward Stettinius, along with members of the London Hambro family and quite a delegation of other at-large bigshots, had started up the World Commerce Corporation, a Panama-registered entity which seemed to fall somewhere between an import-export combine and a commercially oriented espionage network. Primary among its functions would seem to have been the reequipping and upgrading of the German industrial plant.[48]

Typical of the deals Donovan attempted to throw together was one which involved the removal of a $17 million Czech steel mill to Western Germany, payment by way of Switzerland in unblocked funds, and the release of an incarcerated Western spy by the Czechs to round matters off. State Department functionaries trembled each time Wild Bill showed up to pitch his latest.[49]

Nothing squared quite right for the bumptious and ever more irritable Donovan. After preliminary discussions, he flounced out as an Associate Justice of the Nuremberg tribunal when Chief Justice Jackson insisted on basing the prosecution of the top Nazis on documents, not testimony. He pestered the Command and Staff school for "a chair on irregular warfare." Donovan's participation on the Lippmann Committee investigating the murder in Greece of newsman George Polk went badly: staff members were irate when Donovan underwrote official concern that "if the extreme right committed this murder and were discovered, that this may upset our aid program to Greece," and he was subsequently accused of blocking investigation leads which might have implicated the corrupt Greek government.[50]

There developed something close to an intimidating undertone in his many approaches to officials: in a letter to Forrestal dealing with Communist tactics in France during the summer of 1947 he lectured the uneasy Secretary of Defense about what precisely "Our French friends there" would need to continue "making a fight," and alluded to "the possibility of dealing with this matter independent of government action. . . ." Donovan pronounced himself "sure you would think it unwise to let this pass beyond your control."[51] Dulles and his friends were already remarking privately about what a load old Bill was turning himself into.

Of course, they needed his reputation still. His abiding interest in refugee problems made Donovan the perfect director for the International Rescue Committee, and after that he presided as a figurehead over the American Committee on a United Europe. But he required watching. Bill lost no time in reviling the hard-won NIA where once the United States possessed "the makings of a real intelligence service, but chose to disband it and dissipate its assets."[52] His court preparations deteriorated, as did his share of his law partnership. In 1946, already foraging for wide-ranging support as he attempted to stake out the Republican nomination for the U.S. Senate, Donovan took a call from Thomas Dewey, the Republican presidential nominee in 1944, who offered to get behind Donovan in return for Bill's support in 1948. "I don't think you're qualified for president now," Donovan snapped at the front runner, "and you won't be qualified then." So much for political ambitions.[53]

Both Dulles brothers had *attached* themselves to Dewey at that stage. Donovan's hubris looked suicidal.

❑

Allen Dulles was especially restive, bored with his clients and ambling in his negligent, purposeful way toward something he could call his own. Where *could* one stand now that the estimable Foster was such a pillar-at-large? As Tom Dewey's prime international-affairs wheelhorse in 1944 and 1948, Foster worked on Arthur Vandenberg to include him as a delegate at all the major conferences, a kind of duenna for the Republican Right. At times he radiated disapprobation, but Foster was far too habituated to power realities to buck the emerging status quo. Over "private luncheons" with Soviet diplomatic officials he pointed up the disillusion slowly overtaking the West, but afterward he had no problems with allotting Stalin's minions "their own sphere of influence" in Eastern Europe. At Sullivan and Cromwell he pressed litigation successfully in behalf of clients like the Petcheks of Czechoslovkia: With an assist from confederates in the State Department he salvaged for the Petcheks an $8 million settlement in the face of Prague's nationalization edicts.

Like his durable friend Jean Monnet, Foster was already championing the notion that the Western Allies could solve a great many problems at once through the "Europeanization" of the Ruhr: "The basin of the Rhine, with its coal and industrious manpower, constitutes the natural economic heart of western Europe." The East was gone.[54]

Then Dewey lost unexpectedly to Truman in 1948; this ran the timetables of both Dulleses straight off the rails. Allen Dulles had traveled with Dewey as his brother's spokesman, standing by to press on the candidate the freshly decoded obiter dicta from Foster by way of a Republican message center in the Hotel Roosevelt. When news of Truman's victory reached Foster in Paris he abandoned his copyrighted lusterless demeanor to groan that History was about to tag him the "former future Secretary of State."[55]

Allen too felt heartsick. Circumspectly, never overtly pushing anybody, Allen had been lobbying in his own way: over sumptuous Manhattan lunches, alternately boisterous and appreciative; regaling a roomful of Palm Beach dinner guests with anecdote after anecdote about the back-alley "secret war" the government was mounting in Europe. Candidly—even indiscreetly at moments, it seemed, until one realized afterward how little he divulged.

Meanwhile, Allen pitched in. With Europe apparently crumbling, short-tempered policymakers in the Truman administration from Harriman to Acheson (who almost to the man detested Foster's Council-of-Churches sanctimoniousness) relished Allen's more intimate uptake. When Jim Angleton got word out that Communists in Italy were buying up all the newsprint in the country toward the end of 1947, and Forrestal panicked because there seemed no loose cash anywhere around the government with which to blanket radio time or bribe the traditional middlemen, Allen pitched in without a qualm. A collection plate circulated among the Morris chairs of the Links and Brook clubs, and within days one of Angleton's Special Procedures people in Rome was turning over millions of lire in a satchel to a well-dressed intermediary inside the Hotel Hassler.[56] On election eve in Italy—with a U.S. convoy at anchor off Naples to evacuate Americans in case an overnight Red Republic blew out of this thing, and asylum laid on in Spain or Ireland for the Pope—Allen spent the long night of counting votes holed up in Forrestal's Washington mansion, handing intelligence decrypts back and forth to the edgy Defense Secretary as they came off the teleprinter from the Rome station.[57]

Dulles had known Forrestal over many years in a variety of capacities. The pair were contemporaries at Princeton, which Forrestal quit early to battle his way to fortune at Dillon, Read. Fatigued as he was, the Defense Secretary was vulnerable to charges from the left that he and other one-time Wall Street in-and-outers were rigging the European Recovery Program to plump up their ex-Nazi business counterparts. The attack was incessant just then, with many of the most telling hits coming in from *PM* and George Seldes's mordant little *In Fact*, a culling of Congressional broadsides and small-press sniper fire. By 1947 the Dulles brothers were also regularly featured as targets. A muckraking church publication Paul Tillich helped sponsor, *The Protestant*, kept after Foster especially out of annoyance with his ever more grandiose public posturings as a self-appointed vicar of contemporary Christianity.

Many of the most damaging fusillades came out of the Madison Avenue offices of an organization which called itself The Society for the Prevention of World War III, Inc. Its pamphlet-sized bulletin, *Prevent World War III*, etched out in deeply researched, repetitive detail the relationships between the New York bond houses and the German cartels, between Sullivan and Cromwell and the ubiquitous Schroeders. It was Allen Dulles's habit to fend off criticism with a jovial chuckle, a word or two of disavowal and perhaps a wave of his pipe. But this peppering hurt. Nettled, he seems to have retained a safecracker from the OSS rolls to burgle the Society's uptown offices. Dulles's footpad crept back to confide that his perusal of the advisory and sponsor list yielded refugees of "extremely liberal views." The sophisticated Dulles already know from the masthead of its bulletin that the Society was advised by a roster of intellectuals and clergy which ran over many years from William L. Shirer to Clifton

Fadiman and Lewis Mumford and Allen Nevins and Louis Nizer and Mark Van Doren and Mary Ellen Chase and Christopher La Farge—culture heroes every one—and backed off. The attacks continued; fellow warriors like Forrestal would have to understand that Allen had done what he dared.[58]

In February of 1948 Forrestal had summoned Allen to his bleak Pentagon office and commissioned him to direct Bill Jackson and another New York attorney, Matthias Correa, in roughing out a set of proposals for restructuring the floundering CIA, a project he hoped would dovetail with the expected Eberstadt Task Force recommendations on defense policy. The three lawyers conferred for close to a year in one of the board rooms at J. H. Whitney, and early in 1949 presented Forrestal a 193-page survey and report which assessed the damages and recommended a full-scale shake-up and reorganization.[59]

It was now obvious around Washington that Marshall, Forrestal and Company were navigating blind, increasingly schizoid to discover that even Lucius Clay's famous cable was politically inspired, the military governor's response to the Joint Chiefs' request for something to galvanize Congress, "propaganda for the Hill."[60]

We'd conspired to terrify ourselves; nobody really knew anything. One roving operative from the Army's own deep-cover unit, "The Pool," still despairs over the finesse with which the NKVD was rolling up assets up and down the Balkans. Working alongside the British—"You could smell what they were up to"—he remembers his colleagues' desperation one day in the autumn of 1947 when 102 agents disappeared from the streets in Hungary, forever, leaving MI6 bankrupted. The carriage-trade informers on whom the Z-net had relied since the thirties, many sophisticated Jewish businessmen, lost touch after collectivization.[61]

Unlike the hobnailed Gestapo, the NKVD cleaned house with a frustrating aptitude. A U.S. Office of Naval Intelligence sharpshooter, a certain Captain Carp, was quietly attempting to convince a low-lying Abwehr veteran, one Scharenbroit, with whom he shared a mistress, to turn over the remnant of his chain in Rumania and the USSR when somehow the captain fell off a train to his death between Salzburg and Innsbruck. "At about the same time we lost our naval attaché in Poland, his jeep drove off a non-existent bridge. In the fog. . . ."[62] It was already clear that there would be very little coming back from any of those radio drops in the Soviet Union, from the Flamingo net to the Smolensk group both Gehlen and Baun once promoted to the expectant Sibert.

At that point Marshall was heard to observe sadly that all he really wanted was twenty-four hours notice in case the Russians invaded.[63] The blockade of Berlin came as a total surprise. What little slipped through got dredged out of deserters and refugees, hungry domestics, sailors who jumped ship, and even this detritis was so adulterated with disinformation the Soviets sloshed across and junk from forgers that nobody trusted anybody. One half-baked 1947 effort by the OSO to infiltrate several gung-ho OSS veterans and cause some political disruption in Rumania got dragged into a People's Court, and supplied the Communists under Groza a pretext to clamp down harder.[64]

Dulles in his wrap-up set forth the outlines of all of this. The Agency needed control of the intelligence efforts overall, organization, clear lines of demarcation to spare everybody another rewrite of State Department analyses, and far fewer "Whiskey Colonels." At least a rudimentary scientific intelligence unit might be a good idea. The Dulles report proposed the clean-cut separation of the research and analysis people from the clandestine section—the control officers who ran agents, counterespionage, any political dirty tricks. So far as "covert" undertakings were concerned, Dulles tended to insist that even as promising a chap as Wisner should be doing business from inside the Agency. It remained Allen's preference that irregular warfare be directed by an experienced civilian. Not that he recommended anybody. Just yet.[65]

It made little difference. Harry Truman was back for four years, he "would have none of" Dulles (whose hints of availability as Ambassador to France the President also ignored).[66] Now, week to week, Dulles's sponsor, Jim Forrestal, was faltering: close to distraught at moments, leaking cables to Arthur Krock of the *Times*, unable to keep from ranting his disgust with Truman's policies over lunch with other Cabinet members.[67] The CIA plodded on under Admiral Hillenkoetter, and for the time being Wisner would have his chance.

❑

It might be relevant that Frank Wisner was phasing in as James Forrestal was phasing out. Halfway through the war the high-strung, messianic Forrestal had materialized inside the Roosevelt administration as Wall Street's apostle to the deviant New Dealers, alive with apocalyptic visions of Stalinism rampant, the anti-Christ rolling

Westward. As 1948 ended Forrestal was manifestly burned out. Over decades of investment banking and round-the-clock government service the bantam boy wonder had immolated himself in public view: where once were lips there survived a scraggly, broken line, and even Forrestal's well-brushed scalp was torn at the crown into scabs he scratched desultorily as he penciled away at documents. Mentally, his wife had deteriorated. With a sigh of relief from both sides he turned his Defense portfolio over to Harry Truman on March 2, 1949, and collapsed into the depression which put him almost immediately into a sixteenth-floor Bethesda hospital room, out of which he leapt to his death the night of May 21/22.

By then the load-bearing responsibility for contending with the Soviets had shifted. Much was already settling onto Frank Wisner's shoulders.

It was Wisner's fortune, just as he found himself wheeling and scrounging most energetically to get something underway, that the administrators of the Marshall Plan were laying out their far-flung distributive infrastructure. Wisner had immediately resolved that he did not want his officers tangled up with the routine OSO espionage undertakings; he exploited his State Department backing to affix the OPC as a "virtual appendage to the Marshall Plan organization," Richard Smith has observed, and commandeered its resources of "men, foreign currency, and official cover to OPC in its covert campaign to compete with the Russians at every 'unofficial' level of European life."[68]

This overlap between United States aid programs and opportunities for political warfare specialists turned into a Cold-War commonplace. With largesse went control, and OPC toted hardware. By far the heftiest slice of Marshall plan money was headed to Germany—28 percent the first fiscal year.[69] One wrinkle Congress accepted in the European Recovery Program legislation turned out to be quite invaluable to Wisner as he phased into the OPC. To assure happy political outcomes, the Marshall Plan insisted that each beneficiary nation match in its own currency the amount it received from the United States. Like our dollar expenditures, these "counterpart funds" would go 95 percent for projects the United States sanctioned. The remaining 5 percent was reserved in the local currencies for the United States to use for its own purposes.[70] Over four years the Marshall Plan allocations amounted to something over $13 billion. Five percent of this approached $200 million a year, kicking around in a budgetary limbo few knew about and fewer still were entitled to scrutinize. The economic vizier who devised these arcane dispensations was an extraordinarily long-legged one-time Yale economics instructor named Richard Bissell, who brought to the process, according to his coeval Harland Cleveland, a prescient recognition that "the important thing was not the volume of our aid, but the effects in Europe and our influence in Europe upon national economic and financial policies."[71]

Wartime introduced Dick Bissell to the divertissements of Washington, and by the later forties the storklike economist's fussy, explosive gestures were familiar around the conference rooms. Congenitally explaining, conveying, holding forth on options while irresistibly enforcing his own opinion, Bissell couldn't help squeezing the maximum out of everything he did.

Dick Bissell's clipped, unwavering delivery and computerlike command of statistics flattened entire congressional committees, and William Bundy later identified him as "the real mental center and engine room of the Marshall Plan."[72] For Frank Wisner, as fast as he was starting to expand, a footnote like counterpart funds seemed more than a godsend. "I suspect that for a couple of years it was a principal source of funding for the OPC," Bissell will now concede. "How this was handled administratively, and in terms of accounting at the Treasury, I don't know. . . . Frank Wisner was very reticent with me about what he was doing, and properly so. He said he couldn't tell me about it, he told me Averell Harriman had pretty complete knowledge of it, and Averell concurred in that. I had the impression of a pretty competent operator going about his business, of which at the moment I knew absolutely nothing."[73]

Along with a truckload of money nobody intended to account for, Bissell bequeathed the OPC perhaps his most promising assistant, Frank Lindsay. A deliberative management expert whose slow smile and jug-handle ears hinted of Eisenhower-like shrewdness, Lindsay had come home after his many months as an OSS operations coordinator on assignment with Tito and signed onto Bernie Baruch's delegation to the United Nations to deal with atomic energy questions. Lindsay put in time alongside Allen Dulles as a consultant to the Herter Committee on Foreign Aid. Dulles and Wisner met often while Wisner was mapping out the OPC, and Dulles was enthusiastic when Averell Harriman released Frank Lindsay from his responsibilities on the executive committee of the Organization for European Economic Cooperation and shooed him over to Wisner's ramshackle headquarters at 21st and Virginia. When he looked in initially in

October of 1948, Lindsay would remember, no more than two or three people were actively at work. This seemed a very limited army with which to order back Stalinism.

Accordingly, Lindsay saw, OPC opened up "almost on a war footing." Finding themselves "overwhelmed by people who wanted us to do absolutely everything," Wisner's proliferating employees launched into "lots of things that were not terribly secure, we took risks we certainly should not have taken." Anticipating a massive Red Army advance, the Pentagon demanded the formation of stay-behind groups from Norway to Italy. Curtis Lemay was clamoring for escape lines for SAC bomber crews, safe areas into which his people could parachute with well-established courier systems to help them elude capture.[74]

As Wisner's operations chief and second in command throughout the start-up months of the OPC, Lindsay tilted for balance, jostled from one side by OSO careerists like the acerbic Lyman Kirkpatrick (who viewed this explosion of covert-action amateurs as guaranteed to disrupt and compromise serious intelligence collection) and from the other by direct-intervention hot dogs like Army Colonel Robert McDowell (who pressed for the formation of commando teams to be dropped raw into Eastern Europe, where they would tear up Communism catch-as-catch-can). Wisner staffed out feverishly, grabbing people he hoped were qualified from every available direction. From 302 employees in 1949 the OPC listed 2,812 in 1952, plus 3,142 overseas. Half operated in Europe, almost all—1,200—from bases in Germany. These same years the regular budget jumped from \$4.7 million to \$82 million, while the number of foreign stations went up from seven to forty-seven.[75] The Establishment was investing in covert, and demanded tremendous dividends.

One commodity covert eats up fast is cohorts in need, expendable allies, disgruntled outsiders in bunches who can be bought cheap and written off afterward with few public recriminations. On anything approaching scale, covert operations bounce along according to the immemorial rules of "Let's You and Him Fight," and by the subtlety with which he sets up these free-for-alls between strangers the best covert action professional quickly distinguishes himself.

For somebody with Wisner's allegiances, two groups seemed immediately at hand: refugees, and the labor movement. Historically, several of the foremost labor groups had long been programmatically committed to slugging it out with Marxists at home and abroad, well aware that Moscow had been training organizers even before the start-up of the Comintern to infiltrate and control the locals. Just then the handiest chair to break over the heads of the Communists was unmistakably the AFL. True to the anti-Socialist commandments of Samuel Gompers, leaders of the American Federation of Labor had resisted the dominance of successive far-left Internationals since the 1920s, when officials pitched in at the request of the Military Intelligence Division of the U.S. Army to help suppress "class conscious organizations" in South America.[76] AFL honchos squirmed all through the Second World War at the apparition of Communism coming up as Nazism went down, and at a 1944 convention the union appropriated its first million dollars to fund the Free Trade Union Committee to combat "the growth of Communism as a world force" intent on bringing "a new and alien element into the international labor movement."[77]

Their wartime effectiveness in Italy and France helped confer plurality status on the Communist Parties in both countries, and after the liberation their leaderships at first preached moderation to the rank and file. But within a year the pitch of Communist militancy was deafening the electorate. Grain off the Marshall Plan cargo ships was reviled as an instrument of American "political enslavement" of the Continent.[78]

The electrified Forrestal convened a top-secret meeting in his offices at the Pentagon which included Admiral Hillenkoetter, FBI Director Hoover, and a resilient immigrant from the Pale of Lithuania named Jay Lovestone, who served as the executive secretary of the AFL's Free Trade Union Committee.[79]

Not out of his forties yet, Jay Lovestone kicked off his long and controversial career as a dedicated Marxist, emerged during the early twenties as the General Secretary of the Communist Party of the United States, and infuriated Stalin in 1929 by siding openly with Nikolai Bukharin before fleeing the despot to organize his own noisy American-based assembly of splinter Marxists, the Lovestoneites. Simultaneously, Lovestone came forward to advise the AFL on how to purge the Stalinists in its ranks. After backing one losing faction at the AFL, Lovestone found the sponsor he needed in David Dubinsky, the redoubtable little strongman of the immense International Ladies Garment Workers Union. In 1944 Dubinsky, William Green, and George Meany authorized the Free Trade Union Committee (FTUC), and with that Lovestone arrived at real legitimacy.[80]

With Lovestone went Irving Brown. An ally from skirmishes inside the AFL, Brown already had ties to the U.S. government as the director in passing of the Labor and Manpower Division of the Foreign

Economic Administration. Brown now moved over and became the roving European representative for the FTUC, a kind of one-man demolition squad whose function it became, mostly in France, Germany, and Greece, to detonate any ominous-looking combinations on the left.[81]

In November of 1947 James Angleton got back from Italy to work on his Soviet register and back up William Quinn's replacement, Colonel Donald Galloway. Angleton lost no time in establishing a close and mutually beneficial association with Jay Lovestone, whom he would finally characterize as "one of the only really great men of the labor movement,"[82] a discerning student of international politics, and custodian over "the finest archives that ever existed on the Communist Party." Jim Angleton had recognized in Lovestone a peer in clandestinity, a fellow adept of "many covers, many passports," perfectly positioned to expedite liaison between the CIA and George Meany over at the AFL.[83]

In many ways these nervy, strong-willed little Jews in the trade union movement paralleled the Haganah functionaries Angleton cottoned to earlier. While promoting trade unionism in Germany to the annoyance of General Clay, Brown discredited where he could the old-fashioned left-leaning CIO liberals still cluttering up the Military Government and plugging for consideration of Russia.[84] With Berlin under siege, Lovestone conducted a delegation of German trade unionists into the offices of the Secretary of the U.S. Army in October 1948 to offer a contingent of "former German war pilots" to work the airlift.[85]

All was developing nicely, Angleton felt, and then their world slid over on itself. "One day we had the whole responsibility" on the operational side, Angleton would later recount, and then, "on a given day," he and the others discovered that the creation of the Office of Policy Coordination had "eviscerated the director of the OSO. We didn't necessarily know what was going on, OPC had its own people abroad who were not in our channel of command. . . . They had their own charter, their own chain of command which ran up through their would-be director to the Secretary of State." Galloway protested at once that "you couldn't have two covert chiefs, that either he or Wisner would have to take things over, and Hillenkoetter took the decision to Truman, who backed the idea of the OPC." Galloway left.

By Angleton's lights the OPC had taken on "sort of an impossible task. It covered the waterfront. It had left the classic lines of one chief, with a defined function according to a charter, and of course there was great confusion as to how the remainder of the OSO was to be cut up." Already obsessed with security, Angleton was especially dismayed to contemplate the explosive expansion of Wisner's anthill by the Reflecting Pool, the way he seemed to be pulling acquaintances and acquaintances of acquaintances in from every direction with barely a pretense at vetting anybody. There simply was not, Angleton realized, "any counterintelligence function at OPC."[86]

What perhaps hurt most around the OSO was finding themselves cut off from resources already ripening. Money told the story, as is the custom with clandestinity: after 1948 those critical subventions to Italian politicians, the payments which Tom Brady would cheerfully confess quickly mounted to $2 million annually by way of Brown and Lovestone to keep their labor friends in Europe in line—the gentry from Wisner's shop would look after details like that.[87] The irregular refugee armies and vast unjammable propaganda transmitters and wherewithal to penetrate and before long to pull the wires behind international conferences in every captial—the genuinely *active* measures—these became the OPC's monopoly. Political action rang the cash registers, as they say. This left Hillenkoetter's CIA ferreting out its tips here and there around the world and musing over what it had, "a bunch of old washerwomen," as Wisner himself dismissed them, "exchanging gossip while they rinse through the dirty linen."[88] Wisner had something in mind more appropriate to the emerging champion of the solidifying Free World.

14

THE MIGHTY WURLITZER

Wisner's heyday at OPC was hectic and comparatively short. Frank backstopped his independence by convincing George Kennan to repatriate from Trieste that suave State Department regular Robert Joyce—an ally of Wisner's since the Rumanian exchanges, and no less dogmatic as to the Soviet threat—as intermediary between the Policy and Planning Staff and the subversion gamesters flooding into the OPC. Kennan had recently filled out his Policy and Planning roster with G. Frederick Reinhardt, whose months of collaboration with Clay's staff on German problems had kept him in close sync with moves around that Cold-War cockpit[1].

Frank Wisner was already adept at playing the power centers off one against the others. Whenever the Defense Department bristled at Wisner's "hot button" approach to political mischief making he inferred that disruption was uppermost to the leadership at State. When State feared diplomatic blow-backs Wisner embroidered on the military situation, already tense after the Berlin blockade and explosive once North Korea moved in June of 1950. The OPC budget rocketed. Planners from the Joint Chiefs were suspicious that Korea amounted to a Soviet diversion, and Europe was next. Wisner and his mob could amount to their best shot at destabilizing the Commies.

It was the zenith of the "Chicken Little" era in Harry Truman's Washington, the sky was falling, and 1949 and 1950 were Frank's best years.

As OPC operations proliferated, it seemed to CIA that Wisner had concocted a kind of clandestine warfare subcontracting syndicate, through which his uptown friends could lean on—and pay off—whatever interests looked promising. They'd coopted, grumbled OSO veterans, the "easy thing," nothing dangerous or involving or requiring a scintilla of tradecraft like running agents or analyzing conflicting data. To Hillenkoetter's cadre, Wisner's principal function appeared the constant writing of tremendous untraceable checks.

It was as if Wisner *hunted down* people who knew virtually nothing about the nitty-gritty of information gathering, whose credentials—beyond gentility—included a predisposition to splash back and forth together through endless, irrational brainstorms. To keep his hand on everything at once, Frank organized his proliferating stations under regional "division" chiefs, backed up by political action and psychological warfare staffs and special units to deal with economic measures, escape and evasion behind the lines, cover and deception, and sabotage and countersabotage.[2] This resulted in enough overlaps so Wisner could assign subordinates from different units to the same operation (often without their realizing it at first), and crank the pressure up.

With hundreds of newcomers signing on by early 1949, Frank Lindsay moved over to administer the all-important Eastern European division, the vital "denied areas," while Merritt Ruddock went on as Wisner's immediate deputy. Ray Cline worked closely with Ruddock through much of the war, and sizes up the agreeable young ex-corporal as a "personal manipulator of ideas and people, somebody who would have been a great salesman. The kind of guy who was always trying to persuade people that what he wanted to do was a great idea for them."

A bottle of good booze forever at hand in his capacious desk drawer, Cline saw now, Ruddock pushed his ideas by "doing a favor for people, show 'em you're a good guy, get 'em on your side, then tell them what you're worried about."[3] Most of the cosmic projections Ruddock left to Wisner, already stockier than a few years earlier and inclined to indulge among subordinates a markedly loftier—and murkier—tone.

Many throughout the OPC were high-hearted carryovers from Wisner's military days, brought in and spotted around the offices. For some months the head of administration was Ed Green, an amiable enough veteran who "wandered in and out of places," one fellow recruit remembers. He'd been the base chief at Bari for the Navy, so Frank "just kind of had him around." In Bari Green was the man, Frank Lindsay reflects, you'd radio "when you were running out of gasoline, or somebody needed to send in an airplane."[4] His associates joshed Ed, calling him "the praying coach of old Sy-wash," and he was invariably good for a comeback.

Bob Mandelstam hung in as Wisner's private secretary. Gil Greenway helped out with administration, and over the upcoming years a seconded foreign service officer, a big stooped West Pointer named Charlie Hulick, came to identify his own future with Wisner's, winding up as Frank's executive assistant, his "Colonel House," one OSO skeptic gibed. Another persistent voice around the offices belonged to minute, peppery Arthur Jacobs, an outspoken government attorney who had adored Wisner since the pair were class leaders at the University of Virginia Law School. Wisner had retained Jacobs to review a number of the documents which authorized the OPC. In 1951 he came on full time; his terrierlike devotion soon earned him the sobriquet "the Ozzard of Wiz." "I'm here as the conscience of Mr. Wisner," he told one startled staffer in San Francisco when he arrived to pick apart the nutcake enterprises under development by the Free Asia Committee.[5]

Army Colonel Boris Pash signed on to honcho what was referred to as Program Branch 7, a catchall special-operations category intended to deal with defectors and exfiltrations and put together kidnappings and even assassinations. These extreme measures were no more than "a matter of keeping up with the Joneses," Wisner observed in a memo, since "Every other power practiced assassination if need be."[6] But beyond the planning stage assassination proposals had a way of expiring, partly out of fear of leakage and partly because even the greenest personnel could see that "wet affairs" was no category in which to go up against the experienced KGB.

Administratively, the place was mushy from the outset; even fervent Wisner acolytes don't bother to deny that. The wish was overwhelmingly father to the plan, a mind-set heightened by boot-camp intellectualizers like James Burnham, the pioneer rollback theoretician. Entire teams either muddled along for month after month planning operations they knew their superiors would never condone, like assassinations, or never really coalesced, like economic warfare, or tangled up in intersecting layers of administrative authority, like political warfare, where dogfights kept erupting over who was genuinely in charge.

There remains some confusion as to whether Gerry Miller or the Vanderbilt economist Joseph Frank bore the overall responsibility for political initiatives in Europe, or whether final control rested with the division chiefs and/or operational managers.[7] James McCargar, who honchoed early U.S. contributions to the Anglo-American program to subvert Albania, remembers well being summoned to a meeting one day by Joe Frank. "He outlined the Albanian operation, which I was running, to this roomful of people," McCargar says, "of which I was one. He had this big table-of-organization chart on the wall, and he said, we need somebody here, and we need somebody there. And then he said, 'To do this, we'll require 437 bodies.' Meaning bodies, no brains. I said, 'If that is what you want, that is what you'll get.' I didn't understand what the hell the man was doing in my back yard to begin with. And, you know, he never spoke to me again about the operation so I still don't know what the hell his function was. But obviously Frank Wisner had him in there doing something. Wisner was a very clever divide-and-rule man, which may account for some of the confusion."[8]

Like his sponsor Dulles, Wisner had already learned to avoid troublesome operational details—where mistakes glared, and the blame accrued—and identified his own role with strategic vision, with elevated phraseology. He'd learned from Saltzman and others the niceties of projecting power, the enforced Brahmin composure, which kept him at an appropriate distance from subordinates yet elicited both admiration and loyalty and reinforced his leadership.

Beautifully tailored, well-manicured at all times, Wisner kept himself somehow an attractive physical type despite the premature baldness, his increasingly sallow skin, the onset of girth. He nourished a Southerner's pleasure in his ability to stay longer, drink more, than anybody at a party and still be first to bustle into the office a few hours later. Appointments tended to open with a delectable joke or two, since Wisner took justified pride in his gift for storytelling, and he was careful to draw his employees out before he ventured his personal recommendations, which frequently weren't anything like what underlings expected or hoped for.

Coordinating officials from rival staffs usually found him more than competent, if overall a "cold, ruthless kind of guy, and very purposeful," as Colonel John R. Deane, sitting in an organizational meetings for the Department of the Army staff, would later allege.[9] Annoyed or let down he could be contemptuous, even cutting (though usually in a low-keyed way those early, scrambling years), but once a project was solidly onto the rails he stayed in close contact and supported his operators in the field. Wisner calculated his chances, and then he backed his people.

Perhaps this was most evident in the dispatch with which he hauled the storm-tossed Carmel Offie aboard. Beneath the bureaucratic surfaces Offie's career was churning, the tide of rumors was up, and Frank Wisner personally had to ask for Carmel on waivers to bring him in at all. Not that the paperwork betrayed even a ripple of anything so problematical: by May of 1948 the cable traffic between Frankfurt and the State Department was cluttered with commendation statements and regrets and encomiums from a range of dignitaries extending from European Command Chief of Staff Lieutenant General Huebner ("His friendly, gregarious personality and his companionable ways have endeared him not only to his work associates. . . .")[10] to George F. Kennan at State ("Much distressed to learn of your resignation. Hope you will keep me informed of your plans and let me have chance to see you as soon as you get home.")[11] Robert Murphy felt particularly bereft. He alluded in covering letters to Offie's "determination to engage in the practice of the law," while he himself would "continue to hope that he may return to the Foreign Service sooner or later."[12]

Behind this shower of kudos, Offie had been in effect booted out. A routine pouch check in 1947 in Paris by the Department's chief inspector, Merle Cochran (a big bald-headed Irishman who took his standards from George C. Marshall personally) turned up an unauthorized $4,000 bundle of bills from Offie in Frankfurt forwarded by one-time ambassador Anthony Drexel Biddle to his ex-wife, Margaret, at the Hotel Meurice. Currency transfers violated occupation regulations. Offie had worked closely with Biddle in Vichy immediately after the German invasion, and after that went in as Third Secretary "near the exiled governments of Poland, Belgium, Norway, Netherlands, Czechoslovakia, Yugoslavia and Greece" once they were established in London.[13]

Offie's appetite for paperwork along with his dexterity with the fractious émigré communities soon endeared the gifted little courtier to Biddle. Like Bullitt, Biddle discovered a multiplicity of errands for Carmel. Payoffs via the diplomatic pouch put Merle Cochran off, however—Cochran's investigation divulged unauthorized traffic by Offie in diamonds, black-market rubles, and even 300 lobsters flown into Frankfurt on random military aircraft—and Offie was promptly informed that his name had now been removed from the list of middle-level officers eligible for promotion. "I am fully aware," Cochran wrote in his report, "that Offie has many supporters in the Department and in the field who would resent any move that would clip Offie's wings or limit him as an 'operator.' I am aware, on the other hand, of a considerable element in the Foreign Service who feel that Offie should never have been a member of that Service. I share that feeling."

With this, Offie decided to resign.

Offie left the Foreign Service straining to maintain dignity, like somebody spotted pantsless emerging from a brush fire. There was a crackle of innuendo and disclosure around the Department licking up at Offie's reputation. Chatter had gone back and forth for years implicating Offie and Bullitt, including hints that during the panic after the French military collapse in June of 1940, when both hung on in Paris for several weeks in violation of State Department orders, Bullitt commissioned his protégé to buy up houses and flats at collapsed occupation prices. Well after the war Offie appeared to control an astonishing variety of real estate throughout the French capital, which now and then he grandiosely made available to acquaintances of promise.

Colleagues were still chuckling over Offie's prewar notoriety as the boudoir darling of the collaborationist demimondaine; Robert Murphy felt obliged to reassure Doc Matthews in April of 1945 while Murphy was bucking for Offie's services as administrative officer at POLAD, which directed the U.S. presence in Germany: "I promise you that he [Offie] will stay out of French politics."[14] Where Carmel was concerned one arranged things with a certain delicatesse. Visitors alluded to glimpses of Bullitt and Offie walking together near the ambassador's retreat at the Great Chateau at Chantilly, ostensibly hand in hand.

It wasn't solely Bullitt's assets, but Tony Biddle's too, that Bob Murphy assimilated once he picked Offie up. In Italy, as in France, Carmel Offie had networked like a dervish. His Moscow experience backed up his foragings among the exile missions on London; as, warily, many of the émigrés returned to their Eastern European capitals, he kept his files current. Once he hit Frankfurt Offie's desk was manifestly the clearinghouse for bids from malcontents and conspirators from the East, for suppliant ex-Nazis and spokesmen for irredentist factions which blazed with plots to liberate their homelands.

Offie's renown as a troubleshooter around the Bloc seems to have preceded the occupation. Still closing down Caserta, Carmel oversaw impromptu plans for Austria; by August 1945 Carmel had "already visited Tirana and Belgrade," ambassador to Italy Alexander Kirk reported in a telegram to Washington, "with mutually beneficial results to offices there and AFHQ." As Deputy U.S. Political Adviser–Caserta, Offie "really carried the entire burden of that Office," Kirk wired Julius Holmes, and "if it had not been for his ability, judgement, indefatigable energy," Kirk's own "position there . . . would have been untenable. Not only has he carried on personally the mass of administrative work in the office including all information activities, as well as the establishment and supervision of recently opened missions in the Balkans," but Offie was priceless at conferences and properly earned tremendous respect "at the highest level."[15]

Diplomats and senior brass alike responded to the aplomb, the sureness of touch, with which this impudent, hyperaccommodating, superconcentrated little midlevel dandy moved into their offices and dealt with absolutely everything. At post after post a kind of frenzy broke out each time it appeared that Offie was up for transfer. Offie basked in his own worth. He gloried in assignments like membership in the U.S. delegations which advised the Council of Foreign Ministers on Germany and related hot-spots in 1947. "Imagine our astonishment," Cy Sulzberger later wrote of a visit with Robert Murphy to the headquarters of the sacrosanct Russian fur trust in March 1947, "when we were finally conducted into a large store room and there, amid a pile of furs, only his head showing, the grinning Carmel Offie, an American diplomat, heaving pelts around and saying: 'I'll take this, not that, not that, this. . . .' What an operator. I still don't know how he got there."[16]

As some appropriate recompense, Murphy secured Offie the Medal of Freedom in 1946. His bosses sometimes had to admit he talked too freely. "Well, it's set for November," Offie had rolled out of the London embassy and blared to onlookers not long before Operation Torch; a clutch of U.S. Army counterintelligence watchdogs dropped on him instantly, and it had taken both Bullitt and Jacob Beam to break him out of a detention cell.[17] But wasn't he effective? He seemed to sense just when and how to introduce an option, capitalize on a panic, nudge for a policy change so subtly his superiors remained hard pressed to identify his input.

As early as July of 1946 Offie was cautioning "all responsible United States personnel" to report "fully and regularly" on dealings with the Soviets. It already seemed "reasonable to expect that broadcasts in Russian will be made to the Soviet Union in the near future from the United States Zone in Germany."[18] He endorsed over to General

Huebner the views of one professor Dr. Kurt Hesse, exculpating prominent Nazis. Offie was coordinating closely with Edwin Sibert. The two were collaborating on labor developments, Jewish affairs, reports on the movement of German scientists from the American Zone into France, individuals who had eluded Paperclip.

By early 1948 Offie's East-bloc connections were tugging them all toward associations unimaginable a few seasons before. The Policy and Planning Staff groped for responses to the Soviets. Clandestine armies were patently required. But how? Involving whom?

In September of 1947 a delegation of thirty-nine members of the "Bandera group" crossed into the U.S. Zone to end their trek from the Ukraine. "Frankfurt" immediately wired Murphy, having already advised General Huebner to "hold these men in internment, interrogate them, and then make up our minds as to what disposition is to be made of them." Huebner had "asked me whether we should not send them back! I feel, of course, very strongly against any such idea and would appreciate your views."

A workup for Llewellyn Thompson from Offie in April 1948 dropped broader hints. Offie had been visited by three of the leaders of the Bandera organization, who presented proposals "which may be of interest to you and may tie in with an idea which, I believe, is being worked on at home at the present time." The OUN representatives wanted to contact U.S. officials "empowered to deal with them and tell them how they may help in the event of an emergency." They claimed their nationalist groups were "ready to revolt" and suggested a dynamic Voice of America program in "White Ruthenian (Byelorussian), Georgian, Ukrainian, Armenian and the Baltic languages." They agitated for publicity for the "Ukrainian Partisan Army (UPA) which is somewhat of a striking arm for the Supreme Liberation Council (UHWR) in the Ukraine," and "is engaged in armed conflict with the Soviet troops in the Ukraine at present." They wanted "a Federation or a United States of Europe, or at least of Eastern Europe."

"If," Offie nudged "as I understand, there is some planning going on with regard to how such groups as referred to above might be best used in our interests, it might be useful to follow up this matter. In any event, the Bandera boys are here in our Zone and are available at any time. I should be grateful for any information which you feel you can give me on this general subject."[19]

State backed off. While "Some active work has been undertaken on setting up procedures and organizations for dealing with émigrés of all kinds," Thompson replied, ". . . the thinking here appears to be that we have to be very careful not to give much encouragement to Ukrainian Nationalists because of the effect this might have on racial Russians. . . ."[20] Offie dug in, venturing "to inform you that I have received a request from the various Ukrainian groups in the United Zone of Germany, who are now united, that the Ukrainian language be added to the Voice of America programs . . . at the direct instance of Ukrainians in the Ukraine, with whom they are in constant touch. . . ."[21]

But Washington still hesitated. Bandera and his people had long histories of alien control—they had been subsidized by the SIS until the midthirties, then after the war again; while Hitler dominated the East they kowtowed to the Abwehr and the Sicherheitsdienst; currently—Lord knows the OSO professionals were alerted to this—the Ukrainians were assumed to be penetrated, probably by the KGB. Their enthusiasm as utility meatcutters for the SS was revoltingly well documented: overt recognition risked geysers of outrage in the liberal press, followed up by Congressional inquiries.

Futhermore, Harry Rositzke's Soviet Union Division of the OSO was in fact already attempting by then to support the established 30,000 authentic Ukrainian ZPUHVR rebels in the Carpathians with airdrops of medical staff, cash, and wireless transmitters to radio out order-of-battle specifics. "The overall purpose of our operations was to provide an early warning system, to tip us off if there were indications of mobilization in the area," Rositzke says. "That's what the Pentagon wanted. It was perfectly clear they would not survive."[22]

As he cleaned up his desk at POLAD the spring of 1948, talent of every description flooded in on Offie. In April seven Hungarians showed up, routed out of Budapest by Cardinal Mindszenty with some kind of half-baked assurance of support from the U.S. military attaché. They were to "establish an information service abroad to furnish the Hungarian émigrés there true report conditions in émigré circles in the West." The leader of the delegation, Dr. Jozsef Skoverffy, would be "transported to Frankfurt and interviewed at earliest opportunity by Mr. Carmel Offie, USPOLAD, Frankfurt, who would direct him to top military men exempting him from interrogation by low echelons Intelligence Service."[23]

But Washington shrank back. "We have talked to people around Washington who would normally be interested in this type of thing," Walworth Barbour at State wrote Offie, "but they have shown no interest, apparently because they believe Skoverffy and his people are 'blown.' " Around State the leadership was "reluctant to give such assistance as might well be construed as supporting a Catholic underground."[24] Offie was manifestly disappointed: he had already jumped in and alerted local ambassadors as to the names of Hungarians who would be turning up soon.[25]

One of Offie's functions at POLAD had been to rake through the flotsam churned up by the postwar disorder—the defunctive Nazi exluminaries and cutthroat émigré politicians and papermill impresarios of promise—and help the CIC and others plug legitimate experts in around the emerging Cold-War bureaucracies. Nazi apostate Otto Strasser was agitating to return to the American Zone, while the exhausted Communist parliamentarian Ernst Torgler aspired to relocation in the United States.[26] Offie recommended against Torgler: who knew what baggage Torgler brought with him after battering among the factions for so many decades? . . .[27]

Others Offie pushed. After thanking Offie for intervening to pay the passage of a couple of servants in April 1948, George Kennan subscribes in a note to Carmel's proposal to find something in Washington for Gustav Hilger, the adroit German career diplomat they both valued highly as a colleague in Moscow late in the thirties. Hilger represented the Ribbentrop foreign office as counselor of legation. The stolid Russian specialist was vital throughout the drafting of the Molotov–von Ribbentrop pact; after 1941 he provided the diplomatic cover to exploit the Slavic malcontents so precious to Gehlen in the FHO while dredging up respectable Nazi sponsors for the Vlasov army. Hilger bestowed over the restive Eastern puppet governments-in-exile. "Collaborators," John Loftus has observed, "were Hilger's specialty."[28]

Carmel Offie was among the earliest to identify Hilger as indispensable for the Policy and Planning draftsmen, perfect for the "institute"; Kennan promised to "look into it as soon as I get back: and we'll see what we can do. Hilger would certainly be a natural for it."[29]

Offie had resurfaced Hilger as early as 1946, when Gehlen quietly negotiated a place for him in G-2's Technical Intelligence Branch (Operation Rusty). Hilger arrived in Washington with a plethora of references, a compendium of tips to help his new masters select among émigré warlords still festering in detainment centers and backstreet enclaves.

Both Robert Murphy and George Kennan helped arrange for the visas and military travel orders "under assumed names" it took to sneak Hilger into the United States. Before long Hilger carried measurable weight inside the American foreign policy apparatus—arguing down the British while persuading the U.S. policymakers that Adenauer was the fellow to support, sitting in on strategy sessions with Kennan and Bohlen once Korea erupted.[30]

Other wandering friends surfaced. In 1945 a nonplussed Charlie Thayer spotted "Johnny" Herwarth von Bittenfield in an Austrian POW cage. Herwarth and ex-General Ernst Koestring, the Hitler government's prewar military attaché in Moscow and Herwarth's superior in the East, fed through to Policy and Planning the names and qualifications of other purported experts.[31] With Bloodstone gathering momentum the search picked up.

Carmel Offie was rounding off his career in Frankfurt at that point, doubling as a kind of booking agent for many of the "refugee scholars" Kennan's staff was after. In March of 1948 John Davies wired Offie to get hold of "Nikolai N. Poppe," an "outstanding Russian authority on Mongolian and Turki areas," believed an "underground DP" and "contemplating suicide."[32] The CIC brought Poppe in from the British Zone, Offie wrote in May, chaperoned by a British intelligence agent. "Poppe looks like a walking skeleton," Offie reported back. "His head, which is long and narrow, is shaped like that of Orson Nielson except that he has hair on it."[33]

Poppe was, in fact, a veteran anti-Soviet Quisling who scouted for the Nazi regiments which overran Mikoyan-Shakhar. Offie was clearly interested in what he heard from Poppe, because he followed up his longer letter to Davies with a May 19 warning that "if we do not act quickly in Poppe's case we may lose him to the British.[34] The same week U.S. CIC reports specified that Poppe's "presence in the British Zone is a source of embarrassment to British Military Government, as the Soviet authorities are continually asking for his return as a war criminal"; the British had appealed to their American cousins to "take him off their hands and see that he is sent to the U.S. where he can be 'lost.' "[35]

Thus Offie was bustling to the end at Frankfurt—cutting corners, running errands, gossiping deliciously, bestowing breathtaking remembrances everywhere—the insider's insider whose talent for gnawing away to purposes of his own he masked with other, more prestigious goals, with visionary intentions. He inquired into the intraceable opinions of a mysterious Soviet defector who alleged that the Soviet Union was "attempting to plant Tito within the ranks of the Democratic countries as an informer," to draw "economic aid for Yugoslavia thus putting an extra burden on the Marshall Plan."[36]

To Murphy he passed along French General Bethouart's query as to "whether you had heard anything further from Washington with regard to his plan for building up resistance elements throughout Europe."[37]

By then Offie realized his Foreign Service career was stymied; Frankfurt felt increasingly remote. In March of 1948 Carmel wrote Kennan: "I have definitely decided that I want to do law and I submitted my resignation over a month ago. I shall therefore look forward to seeing all of you sometime this summer during which I shall take my first holiday in eighteen years, prior to going to school."[38]

Given Kennan's delicate stomach, it's clear that his feelings were mixed as Offie prepared his return. In his report on Offie's performance at the National War College the fall of 1946, while praising Carmel's energy and sociable nature, Kennan couldn't really help but sniff at "the lack of a well-rounded educational background and a certain lack of measure and discretion in his speech. In his work at the College, Offie suffered from an unfortunate inability to ask questions of the visiting lecturers without giving the impression that the questions contained broad and somewhat unfriendly innuendos."[39]

❑

Kennan was surely aware that Offie wasn't headed toward law school. He reentered a Washington transfigured by the Berlin blockade, gearing up for apocalypse. Chip Bohlen, friends agree, brought Offie to Wisner as somebody who understood the East, but months before that, by March of 1948, Charles Saltzman was after Offie and detailed Charles Hulick, who knew him, to bring Carmel over. All along, from Frankfurt, Offie had been firing back memos underlining his own continuing interest in the Soviet Bloc to Department specialists like Bohlen and Llewellyn Thompson and Charlie Thayer and John Davies.

Already talking up rollback, Wisner really couldn't afford to reject this prodigious little Italian-American whose pretensions made everybody in Washington blink. Robert Joyce, Wisner's interface with State, remained a potent Offie booster. Furthermore, the OPC was designed, realistically, to deal in dirty, subtle tricks, and even his greatest boosters recognized that there was a raw, off-putting, at times a damned-near-*sinister* evasiveness about some of Carmel's moves, for all his elaborate learned manners. Offie could prove invaluable for operations in the shadows.

In fact Frank Wisner had encountered Offie, briefly, as early as 1936. "It happened that Frank and I went to Europe on our honeymoon," his widow Polly remembers, "on the George Washington. And on the boat there was Bullitt. With his entourage, led by Offie. It was like a court. He would come down, and you might be sitting around a table before lunch, say, and Offie would come up and he would selectively ask certain people to come and have cocktails with Ambassador Bullitt. It was the United States Line, and so all of the diplomats were on it, people who had something to do with the Government. Frank and I were never asked, but, you know, there wasn't any reason. We were not of any interest to him. To us, Offie himself was extraordinary, almost like the Secretary to the Queen."[40]

The prancing in place by somebody of his own age struck Wisner in 1936 as repellent, effete. By 1948 his appreciation for the variety of humanity it required to maintain a civilization had broadened. From Wiesbaden in 1945, and on his State Department hops later, Wisner could evaluate for himself the grease Carmel Offie provided Murphy's wide-ranging advisory setup to keep it smooth-running and crisis-free. When Offie came available, Wisner pulled him in as a kind of trouble-shooting special deputy, with immediate responsibility for refugee affairs.

For two largely hell-for-leather break-in years the Office of Policy Coordination functioned in a power warp, largely outside the allotted bureaucratic constrictions of close operational oversight and line accountability. After decades of sucking up to people—available always (and betraying at times a sort of brusque concern in dealings with the desperate and unprotected), irreverent enough to amuse but never to threaten superiors, insinuating his own ideas as opportunity and situations allowed—the sheer unanticipated *release* Offie now underwent almost put his personality through the bends. One co-worker remembers his way of breaking wind suddenly, resoundingly, with a kingly disregard. Another—well up in the military by then—was taken aback on several occasions by Carmel's habit of looking him in the eye while pinching his own nipples unceasingly throughout their meandering conversations. Everybody in that office brings up Offie's practice of stamping in early every morning to place a round of calls to OPC stations in London, Paris, Rome, Frankfurt. Fortified, he'd summon his staff and pass assignments out with both hands. Discussion was not encouraged. "He just swept everybody aside," an operations manager sums up, "with his big-dealer act."

"Carmel Offie had these people a hostage," another officer of the period weighs in. "Jim Angelton was independent, he wouldn't let anybody meddle with his shop. But Offie was arrogant, contemptuous, totally. He thrived on dismissing or demeaning those he didn't need. The fact that subordinates found him distasteful or were suspicious of him or knew what he was up to was of no interest to him. His constituency was a very few senior people, whom he could manipulate. He was a consummate opportunist. Worse, he was a charlatan, who had no real commitment at all to the purposes or ideals of any organization."[41]

Offie's untouchable status outraged the carryovers putting together the CIA. The personnel security specialist Lloyd George Wiggins checked Offie's work area regularly and found his desk piled up with "material classified top secret. He was guilty of very flagrant security violations, to where anybody who happened to walk in could look at it." Wiggins passed this along to Agency Security Chief Colonel Sheffield Edwards, who had already determined that on security grounds Offie was "about the worst of the OPC employees being blanketed in, some of whose backgrounds were horrible." Edwards attempted to remedy the situation, but quickly found, Wiggins saw, that "Offie was being looked after by somebody very high in the State Department or the OPC. . . ."[42]

His years of scrambling in behalf of Bullitt and others as a royal dwarf afflicted Offie as he approached forty with an impatient air of permanent fatigue. His features were enlarging: a colleague describes him as "one of the ugliest men I've ever known, short and knobbly, with a long, swollen-looking face and a head made up mostly of lumps." Under heavy brows a kind of uncertain glare was wont to shine for an instant in Carmel's sticky Mediterranean eyes: his ardent, transitory please-love-me look. One sensed him contending with the very expression on his face at times: the way his teeth thrust forward each time he parted those extraordinarily fleshy lips, which Offie had attempted to relieve by cultivating a trim, inky-looking chevron of a grenadier's moustache. A five-o'clock shadow never deserted his pugnacious chin, his long demanding jaw. Offie's wire-like hair was starting to thin; time was already limited; this was his breakthrough moment.

Which made it that much more remarkable how effortlessly he seemed to propel even worldly visitors out into richer, steeper air. "He had an instant—I wouldn't say charisma," one associate remembers. "He was so intelligent that you could feel the intelligence coming out of Offie in waves. His intelligence was in breadth rather than in depth. He was a consummate operator."

Until Carmel Offie came home most of the planning sessions around the government which dealt with stopping the Soviets, rolling Eastern Europe back, amounted to that entirely—talk. He supplied the spark plug: with Offie on board suddenly the politically unthinkable became inevitable, what once seemed remote turned into the shortest distance between two policy objectives. Both John Bross and Larry Houston allude to Offie as the go-between who prenegotiated the blank-check arrangements between the powerful Free Labor Committee of Lovestone and Brown and the resource-hungry OPC.[43] Red tape disappeared fast once Offie decided to exert his time-tested versatility at boondoggling the military. Ethical limits fell away. Trading on Frank Wisner's indulgence, Carmel Offie moved in to reorder the assumptions according to which Americans did business in the world, forever.

❑

With Frank Wisner staffing up at such a prodigious rate, grabbing talent, emerging in less than a year as one of the lever-pullers around the District, there was an inevitable shift which affected his relationship with Allen. Soon after his initiation at State Wisner responded to Dulles's request for a draft of the proposed European Recovery Program bill with the accustomed deference, his cover letter replete with the usual "at the possible risk of expressing a view with which you may not be entire sympathy"s and eager expectations of receiving "the benefit of your views in this connection."[44] Within a couple of months Wisner's responses were crisper. As to the Department's willingness to encourage the "contemplated activities" of one of the groups currently closest to Allen's heart, the "American Committee to Aid Survivors of the German Resistance," Wisner demanded "more specific information concerning the criteria of eligibility for assistance which the Committee intends to establish."[45] Wisner remembered from Biebrich his old chief's embarrassing susceptibility to disillusioned Nazis.

Allen remained a joiner. After Dewey's startling defeat, Foster had removed himself from the diplomatic picture momentarily by accepting an appointment to fill out Bob Wagner's unexpired term in the U.S. Senate. This put an additional burden on Allen around Sullivan and Cromwell. But Allen was miserable without a hand in *somewhere* while Cold War policy was malleable still.

One opportunity came right along. Count Richard Coudenhove-

Kalergi, the president and founder of a movement devoted to a United States of Europe, the Pan-European Union, attempted to revamp its American branch. At the crucial meeting in April 1948 Senator Fulbright went in as president and William C. Bullitt as vice president of the group, after which, Coudenhove-Kalergi lamented, "The Committee decided to ask its Member, Allen Dulles, to assure its immatriculation."

Restructuring as he reregistered, Dulles gutted the board. The Count later charged him with changing the name of the organization, drumming in William Donovan as chairman of the reconstituted assembly, dumping out the surviving elected officers "while new persons joined the Board. My name disappeared from the letterheads, in spite of the protests of many Members of our Committee." According to Coudenhove-Kalergi's information, "This Committee is working for some kind of European Commonwealth of Nations. It is violently opposed to our *Paneuropean Movement. . . .*"[46] The Count was furious, although he continued to welcome financial contributions.

This gave him a little leverage on the international front, Allen hoped, but now he craved something immediate, something structural, a way of involving himself inextricably with the emerging covert community. The broad intelligence anyalysis that he and Bill Jackson labored over was incorporated into NSC-50, and Hillenkoetter was expected to put it to effective use. But without a top-tier sponsor it effectively landed in a drawer once Truman bounced Forrestal out in 1949 and installed the unsympathetic Dean Acheson at State.

Then something turned up. What he could use, Wisner confided to Dulles, was recourse to the hundreds, perhaps thousands, of dispossessed Eastern European notables fidgeting throughout the West, swept out by Stalin likes rats before a flood. NSC-50 had pushed for "relationships with anti-Soviet resistance groups";[47] the State Department quailed at the thought of involving itself directly—background checks were useless, impossible in many cases, and who wanted public responsibility for that unwieldy mob of bloodthirsty refugee clergymen and squabbling culturati and overheated backbenchers from defunct parliaments? The British had already served notice in Washington that *they* had no intentions of again backing into the government-in-exile business.

Refugees were Allen's meat. On an inspired hunch, Dulles conducted Wisner to General Dwight Eisenhower—just then marking time as President of Columbia—and sold this livest of Republican hopefuls on assuming a lead position in what the OPC soon designated the "Free Europe Committee," a front group of prominent Americans dedicated to assisting where they could this diaspora of "political and intellectual leaders who fled Communist tryanny in Eastern Europe." Eisenhower would lend his name to the money-raising arm of the projected committee, its Crusade for Freedom.[48]

Behind Eisenhower's prestige, Dulles picked up backers from everywhere in the Establishment. Contributors included senior executives across the Dow Jones spectrum along with like-minded Sullivan and Cromwell clients, while onto the letterhead went power-structure standbys from Jim Farley and Laird Bell and Adolf Berle to Henry Luce and William Green. Dulles settled in as chairman of the executive committee of what was registered by the spring of 1949 as The National Committee for Free Europe, Inc. The OPC braintrust was obviously of two minds about the energetic Dulles. ". . . You will recall the plan for the so-called Committee for Free Europe which was first presented to you by Mr. Wisner and myself several weeks ago," Kennan wrote the new Secretary of State, Dean Acheson, in April of 1949. Its State Department sponsors had already determined "not to urge Mr. Dulles to become a co-chairman," and were looking further.[49] As treasurer Dulles recommended his understudy at the World Affairs Council and personal financial adviser, Lazard Freres banker Frank Altschul. Frederick Dolbeare became secretary and operating manager. Ambassador Joseph C. Grew, as spruce and vapid as ever, took on the chairmanship. After thirty restive years, many of the celebrants at Versailles were regrouping for one terminal blow-off.

For people whose motivations remained in the end clandestine, the Free Europe Committee set up with extraordinary fanfare. In an extended release Grew proposed to support and champion these escapees "temporarily bedeviled by the frustration of exile, but free and politically dynamic." To promote "peaceful efforts to prepare the way toward the restoration in Eastern Europe of the social, political and religious liberties," the committee staff intended to underwrite "suitable employment" for these "exiled leaders" while promoting contact with other 'outstanding exiles" from the "Yalta countries." Tyler Royall went out to found an exile university at Strasbourg. Changes in the legal systems would come under scrutiny; in company with the Carnegie Endowment there was a study projected to determine "the future of the Danube Valley."

One plank stuck out: "A principle aim of the National Committee for Free Europe is to enable exiled leaders to speak by radio to their fellow-citizens in Europe—to those in DP camps, those scattered here and there this side of the Iron Curtain, and above all, to the millions enduring Communist oppression in the homelands." Since the Voice of America "works necessarily under numerous restrictions," the committee backers concluded that "In the contest of ideas there is much that private initiative can accomplish best, and it is our American habit not to leave everything to governement."[50]

What Dulles was conjuring up here out of the crypto-diplomatic deep far exceeded any foundation-underwritten research proposal. Allen Dulles and Charles Saltzman at the Occupied Areas desk at State worked over the legal documentation.[51] The 135,000-watt medium-wave transmitter which went on the air as Radio Free Europe out of a row of prefabs in Munich's Englischer Garten early in 1951 was intended as a leading-edge communications center for the reconquest of the East. Allen cocked an eyebrow at demands from purists like Hamilton Fish Armstrong that he must screen out reactionaries with "dubious past records and unpredictable future," and went on recruiting the "tough, slugging" propagandists who pressed for the "democratic remaking" of the satellites according to the "principles of Christian civilization."[52] Ever since the twenties, from the Ustase leadership to the Archangels of the Iron Guard, such rhetoric came marinated in genocide and fascism.

Grew assured the press that backing to underwrite the Free Europe Committee could easily be provided "entirely by private contributions." There would be *no* government support. Such claims were never, even remotely, true. Everybody knew all along that an elaborated governments-in-exile program and its unceasing propaganda blitz would be substantial, expensive, beyond charity. From $10 million a year at first the bills reached $30 million and more. An estimated 90 percent came out of undisclosed government accounts, laundered for accounting's sake through major foundations (Carnegie, Ford, Rockefeller) as well as accommodating charities.[53] Into these went an estimated $2 million of impounded Nazi money from the Exchange Stabilization Fund.[54] "In 1971," admits Cord Meyer, who ran the International Organizations side of the Agency for many years, "the widely held belief that these two radios received most of their funds from the CIA was officially confirmed by Republican Senator Clifford Case, of New Jersey."[55] By that time, needless to say, the hayride was ending.

Not that the Free Europe Committee construed of itself as a creature of the OPC. Exploiting the greedy, faction-ridden, feud-oriented newcomers was like trying to harness the energy of an exploded anthill. Intermediaries negotiated ad nauseum with these opinionated ex-personages, and whatever anybody agreed on had then to be cleared through Dewitt Poole, who handled political considerations. Poole, "otherwise known in the OPC as 'Little Napoleon,' " one of the negotiators recollects, "typified a problem that has existed to this day, he was bound and determined he was not going to be a patsy to these guys in Washington. He was going to run his own organization. And in this he had the protection of his board. These were prominent people who had lent their names, and they weren't going to be mere tools of the funding organization." Soon there were protocols drawn up; it took the direct intervention of the Secretary of State to override the committee executives. Wisner confronted the possibility that Allen Dulles and his friends were quite capable of slickering his OPC novices out of any hope of utilizing fully the all-important exile encampments.

The teeth and claws of the committee grew out of Radio Free Europe. Frank Altschul was first to push for emphasis on the Radios, endorsed heartily by C. D. Jackson of Time, Inc., a big armchair psychological warrior. But mandating these facilities didn't bring them into existence, and here, as across the board, Carmel Offie gave Wisner his chance to control the makeup of the thing. Offie scrounged up the first of Radio Free Europe's transmitters, a mobile unit borrowed from the Army, and initiated the Czech broadcasts. Then, calling on his many contacts throughout the occupation command, he secured "a decent status for the Radios in Munich," one participant remembers. "The East Europeans on the staffs were obviously in danger from the services of their original countries, as time showed—those places were bombed enough times—so Carmel got Gehlen to supply security to the Radios. Offie had gotten to the Gehlen thing very early, before OPC existed."[56]

The Political Advisor of Radio Free Europe, Prof. William E. Griffith of MIT and Tufts, began to consult with Gehlen's Eastern European experts and soon amounted to a secondary channel between OPC and the maestro at the Org. On George Kennan's inspiration a Free Europe offshoot called the American Committee for Liberation from Bolshevism was authorized to sort out the major Russian fugitives. To cover its purposes AMCOMLIB founded research institutes—its Brooklyn and Munich centers were run by the most flagrant of the Slavonic Nazis—and soon beamed broadcasts of its own at the Soviet Union as Radio Liberty.[57] Kennan was pushing Wisner. After examining the OPC project list for 1949–1950, he termed the proposal "the minimum of what is required. . . . There may be one or two instances in which we will have to ask you to add to the list. . . ."[58] Kennan's mentor since the 1920s, the Sovietophobic Robert Kelley, finished out his career seconded to Radio Liberty.[59]

The Radios were pacesetters among any number of organizations validated only by whatever worked for the moment. There were innumerable committees—the Free Asia Committee and the American Committee for the Liberation of Russia headed a growing list—along with councils—the Council Against Communist Aggression—and funds and foundations and congresses; most illustrious, certainly, was the Congress for Cultural Freedom, which jousted for intellectuals against the Soviets' own clanking apparatus. There would be magazines and labor unions and student associations, some founded by Wisner and his operatives, others bought into judiciously. A carefully conceived story planted abroad could easily be picked up and propagandized at home or in some target country either through the media or one of the government's information megaliths. Collectively, Wisner liked to josh, these produced the organ tones which blotted out Soviet efforts, they provided his "Mighty Wurlitzer."

The Radios remained favorites: in time they broadcast 11 1/2 hours daily in tongues from Bulgarian to the Ural-Altaic dialects of Mongolia, twenty-nine stations round the clock.[60] They alternated among "forbidden" music and provocative answers to questions smuggled out, with close attention to denunciation of police informants around the satellites.[61] The Free World Press directed by Samuel Walker sprayed out not only a galaxy of books and magazines but leaflets by the hundreds of thousands sent up in flotillas of balloons to stipple the sunsets over Poland and Czechoslovakia and Hungary, to litter the countrysides with propaganda for months. At the University of Indiana gathered the émigré scholars of the Mid-European Study Center under Robert Byrne.

Perhaps it told something when the Free Europe Committee established four secondary divisions: Communist Bloc Operations, Free World Operations, West Europe Operations, and Exile Political Operations.[62] To intelligence professionals *operations* is a weighty term, generally primed with dynamite and aimed at somebody. All this was out there now, at another remove, the way the OPC floated just outside the CIA, and the CIA itself seemed of and yet at times not really central at all to the National Security Establishment. At some level, industrial America and its advisorial wowsers seemed to be pulling themselves together to dominate the play directly, since certainly the *government* was continuing to flounder. Who knew even then where this might carry them all?

15

HELP FROM OUR FRIENDS

The OPC was barely on the flo-charts, just rolling into winter, when real action burst upon them all. As 1948 was ending a clutch of aroused British civil servants—Foreign Office primarily, with representatives of the defense branches closeted in alongside the SIS—constituted itself the Russia Committee. It pledged its best brains to dishevel and wherever possible peel back the encroaching Soviet margin.

Just then the ELAS/EAM partisans were amok again in the back country of Greece. The Albanians were perceived as a main source of supply and something of a haven to the stubborn Greek insurgents, and latter-day Britannia buffs remained chagrined at the insolence with which the Albanians shelled a couple of Her Majesty's best cruisers in 1946. London newspapers lambasted the Stalinist government of Enver Hoxha as heartless and repressive. Seventy-six percent of the population, reports asserted, were victims of tuberculosis.

It might be feasible, Chairman Gladwyn Jebb and his supporters on the Russia Committee concluded, to bring Hoxha down. To foment civil war. Jebb himself had cofounded the SOE, and understood special action.[1] Unfortunately, subversion could get pricy, the Exchequer was tapped out, and "Church mice," as one Foreign Office toff volunteered, "do not start wars."[2] So inquiries went out. Before very long,

Dean Acheson noted confidentially, British Foreign Minister Ernest Bevin "asked me if we would basically agree to bring down the Hoxha (Communist) government. . . . I said yes. . . ."[3]

So we were in, at least our money was. In March 1949 a delegation of Britishers led by Gladwyn Jebb and the British Embassy's Balkan expert Lord Jellicoe reached Washington for a three-day conference with Robert Joyce and Wisner, during which the excited Americans pledged to help "detach Albania from the orbit."

Consequent to the dissolution of the Special Operations Executive in 1946, whatever convert ambitions the English aspired to fell back on the SIS, which inaugurated its Special Operations Branch and Political Action Group.[4] To the eager Americans, here was their moment to participate (at minimal risk, flies on the wall) while Secret Service operatives crafted one of those back-alley miracles which generated the Empire. Furthermore, the order to tailgate the Brits originated at the State Department. As Frank Lindsay remembers, "The Communists were supplying their guerrillas in Greece out of their bases in Macedonia, Bulgaria, and Albania. The requirement came essentially out of State: we have to do something to relieve the pressure on Greece by stirring up a little trouble in their own back yard."[5]

We'd remain at arm's length, naturally, with no British nationals and a maximum of deniability. Inevitably the *participants* in this scheme would have to be Albanians, refugees. Three groups looked promising. Followers of the Kryeziu brothers from Kossovo, Said and Gani, chafed in Italian exile. There was a contingent of hangers-on around the court of the dethroned King Zog, a towering, operatic autocrat whose retinue had withdrawn to Cairo. His supporters now constituted themselves the Legaliteti, subject to a palace guard of venturesome, dedicated monarchists, headed by the fiery tribesman Abas Kupi.

Also available for recruitment—many in DP camps in Italy—was what was left of the National Front group, the Balli Kombetar, a "progressive" faction directed by the bookish ex-diplomat Midhat Frasheri. Frasheri's lieutenants were tarred in many of their countrymen's eyes for having colluded with the Italian and, later in the war, the remorseless German occupiers. As early as 1947 Frasheri began to pester the U.S. embassy in Rome in hope of visas for fifty of his followers; Midhat promoted them as eager now to resettle in the United States and deal with the pro-Communist "intrigues" in the immigrant Albanian communities. Heading up Frasheri's list was Hasan Dosti, Albania's Minister of Justice throughout the Italian occupation. State checked its biographical register and turned Frasheri down on grounds that the "political backgrounds of many of the Albanian exiles in Italy are somewhat checkered and . . . might sooner or later occasion embarrassment. . . ."[6]

On April 14, 1949, Wisner bobbed up in London for a lunch at Buck's Club with Albanian Hand Neil ("Billy") McLean. The Old Firm was effectively launched into the logistics of the undertaking. A small private schooner, the *Stormie Seas*, had already been chartered and its crew was training to put ashore insurgents. A well-disposed arms dealer put in a word with the Greek forces, whose backup was indispensable since many of the influential Balli leaders worked out of Athens. Recruiters quickly weeded out the thirty or so young warriors the British intended to train up in Malta from the excited throngs of volunteers in holding camps outside Naples. By early July the chairmanship of the Free Albania Committee had devolved on Frasheri.

In Cairo, Zog pouted over promiscuous talk of governments in exile he himself didn't dominate; a pair of fluent British diplomats hurried down to assure the king that after the takeover a simple referendum would permit Zog's subjects to reactivate his throne. The king agreed somberly to involve his followers.

Ten weeks of training now ensued on the parade fields of an unused castle on Malta. Their patient British instructors did what they could with the Naples recruits, "these untidy little men," as several openly characterized their charges. Morale fluctuated; on Albanian National Day several of the bravos got fried on ouzo and awakened the countryside by pitching grenades into the moat. During one hilarious episode the cook came off the drawbridge in a heavy truck and missed a turn and tore loose an embankment.

Personalities became an issue. The OPC's own observer at the fort, John Papajani—a fat, wild, charming, and completely unpredictable buddy from Frank Wisner's Cairo days—grated on the British. The monarchist delegate Gaqi Gogo was already dismissing this pickup army of would-be liberals as "men with narrow chests and necks like chickens," while instructors became despondent over the conditioning and resilience of these tempestuous little tosspots, and labeled them "pixies."

On October 2, 1949, the first squad of nine men waded ashore off Albania's Karaburun Peninsula, where goat tracks wove across the mountains and into the interior. Several succumbed to ambushes at once: the Albanian military waited. Slipping through security cordons, a handful of the guerrillas crept into their home town, Nivica. They handed out reading matter and exhorted their incredulous relatives to form into resistance groups, after which the United States and Britain would smuggle in gold and radios. But nobody promised anything; after several embittering weeks four of the nine were lucky to pick their way across the northern Greek border and report to the British on Corfu.

Theirs was the fortunate expedition. Successive parties crawled ashore; tribesmen—even relatives—remained so inscrutable the infiltrators were terrified of spending their nights in the villages. Few made it back. By British calculations such losses were acceptable—information was coming out, and it was Albanians who confronted the security police before they died. It took a long time before analysts began to link the betrayal of the Albanians with the September 1949 briefing Kim Philby received, just before he sailed to take up his new post as liaison with the American services.

Philby's true role vis-à-vis Albania remains a subject of heated disagreement. The self-possessed Englishman's ripe, teasing manner and his eternal readiness to banter through another drink made him a social prize around Cold-War Washington. With the Albania project reaching operational phases, a Special Policy Committee was constituted to track the venture. Alongside Joyce for State and Lindsay for the OPC sat Jellicoe and Philby. Philby collaborated on the detailing with James McCargar, whose years of field work in the Balkans with The Pond made him the OPC's senior coordinator. McCargar's ingenuity at covert impressed even the Brits. "I believe I'll give this back," Gladwyn Jebb had proclaimed after perusing one list of recommendations McCargar handed over. He held it aloft between two manicured fingertips, McCargar noted, "like a dirty dog's ear."[7]

Later Philby would characterize his fellows on the Special Policy Committee as "convivial," by which he seemed to imply approachable and humorous, green, and more than cold-blooded enough to keep their distance emotionally from all those poor doomed devils scrambling over Albania's scrubby beaches. For Frank Lindsay personally this effort to unseat Hoxha stirred complicated apprehensions. Lindsay nurtured wartime ties with Tito, and through his OPC position arranged for five shiploads of U.S. weapons to reach the Yugoslavs quietly enough to avoid giving Stalin a pretext for marching on Belgrade.[8]

Lindsay understood Tito's dilemma whenever it came to Albania. Having midwifed the Albanian Communist Party personally out of a melange of anti-Zog intellectuals in 1941, Tito cherished his repute among Marxists as Enver Hoxha's "elder brother." Nevertheless, once the war ended, Tito grabbed back the Kossovo district with its 500,000 ethnic Albanians. Tito quietly authorized regular cross-border sallies of his own to keep Hoxha's manners on the deferential side. But collude with capitalists? How could anybody guess what political miscarriage the Western powers might foist on his rocky little southern neighbor? The Greeks too aspired to important chunks of Albania.

Washington was already auditioning. On September 11 Midhat Frasheri and his counterpart among Zog's supporters, Abas Kupi, hero of the Legaliteti, flew into New York. As spokesman for the projected government-in-exile the British preferred Kupi, a bewhiskered old rascal with a smashing reputation as a mountain raider. During one slow interlude Kupi spotted a snake at a BBC lawn party for the revolutionaries, plucked it up, and chased the doddering Frasheri in and out of the foliage.

In the United States Allen Dulles's newly formed National Committee for Free Europe was resolved to entertain openly these "lost, abandoned people," as one of the second-string Albanians was quick to characterize their assemblage. Llewelyn Thompson at State heard out the representatives. It was already evident that Kupi wouldn't do—most Albanians couldn't fathom his dialect—and so the OPC managers now settled on Frasheri to speak for the fragile exile government. Frasheri and an aide were installed in Manhattan at the Lexington Hotel. Very early on October 3—within hours after the first nine "pixies" staggered ashore into Albania—the New York police contacted the project's field director, Robert Low, with word that there was a dead, elderly gentleman in the Lexington with Bob Low's name and telephone number on a slip of paper in his jacket pocket. An inquest ensued, and amid many whispers Frasheri's demise was attributed to natural causes.

It was becoming plain that the Attlee government had now grown queasy about this undertaking. Spokesmen for the Greek services remained ambiguous, while SIS hotheads at Broadway were convinced the "pixies" were skulking in caves instead of sowing useful discord or patriotically blowing the country up.

Before 1949 ended their OPC understudies had started to dog the British preceptors, edge toward the controls. Skirmishes over the summer had pretty largely eliminated whatever partisans hung on in Greece. By now a preliminary wave of McCarthyism was breaking across the United States, American papers carried frightening rumors that Valona Bay on the Albanian coast was fast becoming an important Soviet submarine base, with rockets already jamming its caves so Russia could overwhelm the Adriatic. James McCargar went out and rustled up the freewheeling Michael Burke, a self-dramatizing one-time football star with a bona fide Hollywood presence and an OSS reputation for juggling unstable resistance groups. Under cover as the Rome representative of "Imperial Films," Burke got in touch with the émigré encampments throughout Italy and attempted to piece together an *American*-directed strike force.[9]

At the Washington end, Kim Philby couldn't imagine that Hoxha had a lot to worry about. Philby judged Frank Wisner rather "a youngish man for so responsible a job, balding and running self-importantly to fat. He favored an orotund style of conversation which was disconcerting."[10] America shouldn't cause problems.

❑

As Albania turned American, the activist who kept everything percolating was high-powered little Offie. To proportion this properly, American-style, the OPC logistics specialists decided that we'd have to bring to bear *substantial* numbers of fighters, hundreds. The place to prepare our incursion was manifestly southern Germany, where we as the primary occupying power could mask the intent of forces under training. The OPC "special advisor" to the newly appointed High Commissioner to West Germany, John McCloy, was currently the savvy Lawrence de Neufville, who arranged for Albanians brought in from Italy to be passed off as "labor battalion" workers attached to the U.S. Army. Guard units from DP camps were already a commonplace around Trizonia.

Offie cobbled it together. Tom Powers has tagged Offie as "always the last man to see a piece of paper before it went to Wisner," and characterizes him as "gifted with a sort of split brain. He was ambidextrous, but to such an extreme degree that he could write a chatty personal letter with his right hand while drafting a government document with his left," or hold a telephone conversation while proofreading somebody's proposal, penciling in rough changes between sardonic asides.[11] With Germany their staging area, Carmel was particularly indispensable.

The move on Albania provided Offie precisely the break he was looking for to justify an inspired display of intrabureaucratic claim-jumping. The summer of 1949 the OSO side of the CIA had taken over control of the Gehlen organization. By then the moody, proper little Junker had survived several generations of U.S. Army commanders, originally Lt. Col. John R. Deane, then G-2's Colonel Liebel—whose blowhard mannerisms and heavy-handed attempts to cut back Gehlen's operational range infuriated the master. Gehlen disposed of Liebel through third-party rumors circulated among his OMGUS supporters in Frankfurt.[12]

As early as 1946 Offie had contrived to penetrate the original Gehlen encampment near Oberursel. He prevailed on Deane to let him pop in once in a while to cheer up Gustav Hilger, whose sinecure at Fort Hunt's P.O. 1142 Personnel and Material Branch led to an appointment within the Org as an economic evaluator before Kennan resurrected him. Hilger earned Gehlen's gratitude by trumping up an excuse for the general to plow under Hermann Baun, whom Ed Sibert had foisted onto Gehlen as chief of collections.[13]

Once he had Baun and Colonel Liebel out of the way, Gehlen persuaded his primary Army chaperon, Captain Eric Waldman, to recommend as base commander the easygoing, premissive ex-commandant at Oberursel, Colonel William R. ("Rusty") Philp. By then the real managerial powerhouse around the U.S. intelligence complex in Frankfurt, Colonel Robert Schow, was detailed to Washington to look after OSO collection.

Gehlen was already poking into émigré politics. Waldman personally deflected one overture by the Bandera activists. Gehlen supported regional insurrections in the Baltic countries and opened courier channels via Austria and Switzerland through Hungary to the Balkans, swapping accommodations with White Russian relics in Paris and Armenian separatists like the grandstanding Drastamat Kanajian (General Dro). Around Christmas of 1947 Gehlen resettled his evaluators into a redoubt of their own, the deteriorated walled compound at Pullach (until 1945 the twenty-building Martin Bormann enclave) seven miles from Munich along the meandering Isar. By then the tong war among intelligence detachments around the Zone was cresting, with CIC units bumping one *another* around and raiding and discrediting everybody else's sources.

Gehlen abhorred such chaos; the CIA had scarcely been authorized before feelers from the Org reached Washington. An appraiser from the Agency, Sam Brossard, showed up and "rattled around with Rusty Philp," James Critchfield recalls, and concluded that Gehlen's more pretentious undertakings had very little to recommend themselves. "They pretended they were looking beyond the DDR," Critchfield says, "but it was mostly DDR."[14]

The Army wanted out. "In the opinion of the Pentagon,"

Critchfield could see, "the United States public was not ready to salvage a significant part of the German General Staff." Fear of a recrudescent Junker militarism was an abiding bugaboo; *any* political action spooked the Joint Chiefs.

James Critchfield was already on hand around Munich to manage the OSO operational base near the English Gardens, so Richard Helms, who looked after German collection around the OSO, sent word to Critchfield to attempt a five-week inventory of Gehlen's projects at hand. A low-key, battle-hardened North Dakota country doctor's son who won his eagles at twenty-seven with Lucian Truscott's armored infantry, Critchfield had bumped through a "very steep learning curve" while managing a CIC intelligence annex in quadripartite Vienna. In 1948 Colonel Galloway had inveigled Critchfield into the patchwork OSO, remarking that he was a "damn fool to come aboard, but we're glad to have you."

At Pullach Critchfield concluded right away that Gehlen had reconstituted his Felde Heere Ost technical staff; the Org was an "accomplished fact," with thousands of professionals under contract and outstations across Germany and Austria. After word got out that Hillenkoetter had consented to take in the Gehlen crowd, "there was a great deal of footwork among all kinds of Agency people to avoid that assignment at any cost," Critchfield says, and midway into 1949 he himself moved down full time. "I arrived there in an old beat-up black Chevrolet, with a typewriter in the front seat and an OSS-type secretary in the back. I really was not briefed. It was very curious. One would have thought there were files. Nobody really had funds for it. The Army never really had budgeted for it, and it was running off the black market more than anything else. The Army was functioning primarily by offering administrative support and attempting to buffer the hundreds of flaps that kept breaking out between the organization and elements of the occupation." Critchfield dug himself in less than 100 feet from General Gehlen's desk, and dealt with Gehlen hourly for the next eight years.

What we were really after was tactical information. How many MIG-17s set down in Dresden that week, with how many pilots, flying how many training hours? Critchfield affixed from time to time some political or economic commentary; Henry Pleasants spruced these up—Henry was a Europeanized music critic under diplomatic cover in Bonn.[15]

Critchfield understood that Gehlen was nurturing certain . . . certain long-term projects. Elements of the Org were tasked with the Balkans as well as problem areas in the Soviet Union. There was the Professorengruppe, a panal of experts, many steeped in Eastern developments; after 1950, with Eric Waldman gone, ever more trotted out their sheepskins from the lamented Sicherheitsdienst.

Refugees preoccupied the meditative little general, and through his compatriot Colonel Heinz Danko Herre—a Vlasov Army attaché—Gehlen endeavored to godfather these anti-Soviet irredendists.[16] Which left, as Critchfield sums it up, "the weird and wonderful politics of the NTS."

"As far as I know," Critchfield maintains, "Frank Wisner and Gehlen never met." But where the refugee groups intersected the situation was "all mixed up. Everybody knew everybody, and nobody was under much discipline. I have no doubt that a large number of personalities in touch with Gehlen's East European Section were also in touch with and worked for Radio Free Europe." As history-flecked native speakers in large numbers began to congregate inside RFE, Offie exerted his influence around Pullach to lay on counterterrorist support for William Griffith's charges. Angleton too ran "lines of his own into the Gehlen organization," Critichfield will concede. "They traced back to Jay Lovestone.[17] His contacts, and mine, and those of Allen Dulles personally very often overlapped."

❑

Once Michael Burke reached Rome, and Operation Valuable, by now the code name for the Albanian incursion, moved into its training phases, Jim McCargar's authority began eroding. In effect, McCargar realizes now, "the connection between OPC and Germany was entirely Offie." To get things started "Offie brought in Clay to see Wisner. From 1946 on Carmel was witting on the whole Gehlen affair, at least none of the rest of us in Washington were in on it."[18] Ed Sibert was seconded into the Agency directly as an assistant to the director; Sibert's durable working relationship with Schow—who was already extricating himself from this civilian intelligence quagmire to serve as G-2 at Eisenhower's NATO headquarters—opened up further channels to the Org.[19]

The counterrevolution the OPC intended would need a sophisticated steering committee. Wisner bootlegged through Congress the classified One-Hundred-a-Year CIA Act, which opened the door for Offie to bring in unmonitored a hundred refugees each year whose dossiers wouldn't survive a peek by Immigration and Naturalization.[20] This provided the enticement the OPC had lobbied for to convince a number of harder-bitten aliens—men frequently on watch lists throughout the West as Nazi-lining war criminals—to lash their followers toward the anticipated holy wars. However the Indians fared, the chiefs could dream about secure Stateside retirement.

"Insofar as OPC imported those Nazis," McCargar now says, "it was Offie who was doing the arranging. When the time came and we needed army facilities in Germany, Offie set up the labor battalions on the Albanian thing." For James McCargar personally the crisis of conscience started sharpening when Midhat Fascheri kicked off under suspicious circumstances at the Lexington Hotel. By then the preponderance of the Albanian-American community, including editorialists for the leading newspapers and the respected Greek-Orthodox prelate in America, Marko Lipa, were publicly in opposition to the prominence on the Free Albania Committee of known Fascist functionaries. "By then the big problem was," McCargar pulls a face, "with Fascheri gone, who's going to be the successor chairman of the Committee? And then Offie comes forward very forcefully with the suggestion of Hassan Dosti. Now, Dosti had been the Minister of Justice in Albania during the Italian occupation, a lead figure in their puppet government. I and several others screamed bloody murder on this. I said, you can't use somebody with that background, it's a blot on everybody's escutcheon.[21] But Offie won the battle, he had no qualms about using these people, about associating with them."

In April 1950 McCargar passed over his duties as coordinator of Operation Valuable to Colonel Gratian Yatsevich, a tough, suave, Balkan-wise intelligence officer of resilient political intestine. Before long another churchman, Bishop Fan Noli, came ashore in America to contest Lipa for control of the Armenian-American Orthodox Episcopy.[22] A bevy of Hitler-era stooges appeared. Perhaps the most controversial remained Xhafer Deva, the Minister of the Interior in Tirana who reportedly conscripted the dreaded Skenderbeg Division for the SS out of his flunkies in Kossovo, and supervised a Gestapo massacre of Albanian partisans in Tirana on Feb. 4, 1944.[23]

Philby himself sighed afterward that his OPC counterparts kept excluding the English, and "stole a march on us by railroading a handful of Albanian refugees in New York into forming a National Committee, and electing as its head a certain Hassan Dosti. . . . Despite repeated requests, I never came face to face with Dosti."[24]

Such caviling is something of a departure from the bemusement with which Philby recapitulates his year among the Brobdingnagians. Offie himself escapes mention. That Offie would leave Philby out of his Liberation Committee staffing project suggests . . . wariness, perhaps. Perhaps Washington's most unembarrassed social climber by 1950, Offie seems to have made it a point *never* to appear in public with Philby, just then the intelligence crowd's greatest lion. Juxtaposition could invite sparkouts.

Back "on the ground," as the phrase goes, the "insertions" into Albania continued sporadically through 1950. The volunteers were culled from the pool of hot-eyed, restless volunteers in Company 4000 guarding ammunition dumps at Hohenbrunn and Waechterhof in the Munich sector, brushed up near Heidelberg in airborne techniques and infiltration and radio procedures. Once target areas were cleared with the Albanian executive in Rome, the OPC training cadre accompanied their men to jump-off points, normally Athens. There the Americans sprang for a meal or two along with drachmas enough for one of the local women. To allay the jitters. Intimations of the project's mortality rate had started to filter back to Company 4000, and there were unattractive failures of nerve.

A crew of daredevil Polish airmen under British contract waited at a military field near Athens to haul these would-be guerrillas up over the mountains and put them out onto designated drop zones. To skim in under radar surveillance the pilots were forced to hug the terrain, normally brushing the treetops at fifty feet; they pulled up no higher than 500 feet before dumping their terrified little tribesmen off static-line into the Albanian darkness. Canopies sometimes opened; several hit the ground so hard various limbs snapped. Whoever got down whole now concentrated on eluding the dragnets of security police who seemed to be checking them one by one off lists. Most relatives remained far too terrified to take them in. Hoxha's Sigurimi was ostentatious about shooting during public shows most of the commandos they caught, along with identifiable family members.

Frank Wisner was professional enough to concede privately the limited success of these OPC-directed air drops without sacrificing his perspective. Albania was, after all, he told Bob Joyce, "a clinical experiment to see whether larger rollback operations would be feasible elsewhere."[25] In hopes of improving results he pushed his people. A Radio Free Albania went on the air temporarily, but there was very little electricity in the region (let alone radio receivers), and definitely no batteries. The Polish pilots endeavoring to fly out over the mountains by fixing on the villages concluded that there were perhaps three working light bulbs in this entire godforsaken rockpile. When Research and Analysis asked for a Tirana telephone directory, a case officer bucked the request along to the Italian Legation in the Albanian capital. The answer came back that there really wasn't any telephone book. There were in fact only five telephones in Tirana, and everybody already knew those numbers.[26]

While hope was possible Wisner sent his Psychological Warfare head, Joe Bryan, to London to draft an announcement of the formation of the Free Albania Committee in case the OPC insurgents carved out their foothold.[27] It seemed to Bryan, later on, a waste of airplane tickets and space at the Ritz. "We had a few small triumphs," Bryan says now, "but I never disabused myself of the feeling that we were a bunch of amateurs."[28]

The OSO side agreed with *that*. There is a tendency in the literature to portray the initial Director of the CIA, Rear Admiral Roscoe Hillenkoetter, as rather an unimaginative old sea dog whose aptitude for clandestine management was limited. The fact was, Hillenkoetter was fluent in four languages, with experience as a naval attaché going back to Moscow in 1934. He became an expert on the Marxists. Inside Vichy he specialized in escape routes, and finished the war as Nimitz's chief of intelligence for the Pacific area.[29]

Hillenkoetter remained a problem for activists in both the OPC and OSO, in that the tall, brush-cut sailor continued to subscribe to what he took as the original concept of the CIA as a clearing house for, a redistributor of, information provided by other branches. The involvement of even a nominal subsidiary of the Agency in covert undertakings—sabotage, paramilitary exploits, black propaganda—remained obnoxious to the straitlaced rear admiral. As early as October 1945 Hillenkoetter had himself conceded that some manner of "psychological operations" was "vitally needed" to counter the Soviets, according to the Church Committee Report, but "believed that such activities were military rather than intelligence functions and therefore belonged in an organization responsible to the JCS."

By 1950 Hillenkoetter "resented the fact that he had no management authority over OPC, although its budget and personnel were being allocated through the CIA. Hillenkoetter's clashes with the State and Defense Department as well as with Wisner . . . were frequent."[30] Even Wisner's most tolerant operatives would concede that Hillenkoetter was "a pretty good guy," one recalls, "but he didn't have the wits or the wickedness to deal in that post-war situation."

Just then, Philby noted, the "driving force" around the OSO was Angleton, generally believed to hanker after wider operational duties. Yet he too argued against throwing people away over Albania, thereby risking the handful of OSO agents-in-place.[31] Wisner inevitably found himself, Dick Stilwell recalls, mostly "trying to get the CIA to avoid withholding support."[32] Part of the justification for mounting such a sideshow was to relieve Tito. But Angleton—and Joyce as well—remained skeptical of Tito's intentions, and went along with Lindsay's shipments of weapons to the Yugoslavs in hopes that, estranged from the Russians, Tito's regime might collapse and usher King Peter back onto his throne.[33]

The day the *Stormie Seas* put out of port early in October 1949, a "flurry of telegrams" reached Angleton in Washington from supporters throughout the Italian services. In "great glee" Angleton summoned McCargar to his office and spread before the project director the array of operational details to which *he* was privy already. What must the Communists know? "His motive was ostensibly to warn me as a colleague," McCargar was quoted afterward, "but I imagine that he was also anxious to show off his own omniscience to us OPC newcomers."[34]

In Athens, OSO professionals watched these benighted Albanian forays. "That was an OPC show," remembers one. "It was a joke. There they were, with all that rank, and unlimited money, and it looked to us as if Wisner, who was a pretty forceful guy, was hiring just about anybody who came around the corner. They wanted to show that you could change a regime at limited cost."

Alfred Ulmer took over as OPC station chief for Greece at about the point the British withdrew; after 1951, Ulmer and his staff filled in with planes and pilots and continued to sprinkle in pixies. "We had planes in those days," Ulmer will concede now, "and we were dropping people. We realized after a while that we were dropping them into a controlled situation. The usual warning signals came up, not only on the communications thing, because the guys did try to slip through their danger signal, but also the repeated requests for arms and things, for drops, where they would shoot at the planes, try to get the planes. So I was for stopping it. It was very hard for our case officers to believe they were under control." Of course the case officers "were under some pressure from Washington. Frank was interested—very interested—in the Albanian operation, and I don't know who else. But they also had some clowns involved in it too—that guy in Rome . . . he was a public relations man who had no business in intelligence. . . ."[35]

Ulmer meant Joseph Lieb. An irrepressible bon vivant, Lieb reveled in celebrity around the nightclubs and casinos of Rome. Anybody he ran into was treated to his calling card, imprinted with his purchased papal title.

Richard Helms, attempting to follow the Albanian project from his angle as chief of Foreign Division M (Germany, Switzerland, and Austria) liked little he saw. "I viewed some of these operations OPC was taking on as being overly ambitious, too big to be really secure," Helms says now. "These operations involving émigré groups in Europe: they were natural targets for penetration, it would be very difficult to get enough of them together to do a useful job. I was sort of a naysayer. . . . I was sort of raised in the Agency and in the OSS on the secret intelligence side of operations. When one is immersed in that, one soon realizes that it is very difficult to get a successful operation, particularly when you have many people involved. The controls break down, the motivation turns to mush in some cases. It's usually a strong fella and a bunch of followers, who may or may not be loyal. I guess it became my conviction over the years that when any operation got over a certain size—and the size was determined by what you were intending to accomplish—that then you were probably *doomed* to failure."[36]

❑

Like many around Washington, Helms begins with Philby in explaining the breakdowns of Albania. Philby proved most valuable to the KGB as an agent provocateur. He seems to have devoted his year in America to introducing as many tainted assets as could be broken loose into inexperienced American hands. Especially productive were Fascists on the run, handy either to embarrass the capitalists afterward or turn when required, since many were susceptible to payoffs and blackmail.

In June of 1982 a persevering trial attorney named John Loftus put out a small volume, *The Belarus Secret*, which startled and depressed more intelligence veterans than even the Church Committee Reports. Loftus had slogged through a couple of years with the Office of Special Investigations of the Criminal Division of the Justice Department, a subdivision created to ferret out and bring to trial Nazi war criminals living in the United States. Few, Loftus quickly discovered, had falsified their backgrounds, or stolen across a border. They came by invitation. Their sponsor was Frank G. Wisner.[37]

According to Loftus's reading, Wisner saw his opening as early as 1948, when he had appeared in Berlin to appraise the blockade for himself.[38] Well briefed by Hilger and others, Wisner coveted the sprawling DP empire of uprooted Slavs who fled for their lives once the Eastern Front turned. An estimated 40,000 boasted military preparation, generally by the SS.[39] This could get ticklish, politically, since many of these retirees had pitched in not long before with major genocide assignments from the Nazis. To protect such fugitives, Clay's intelligence staff (still subject to Offie's input) issued updated directives for the U.S. command: Expected Elements of Information. The thrust was: Inform yourselves, but do not interfere.[40]

As September ran out in 1948 Undersecretary of State Robert Lovet got off an action cable to Murphy and Riddleberger. "Department anxious undertake soon as possible careful study documents and publications of Vlasov movement,"[41] the telegram opened. It was followed in two weeks by a Riddleberger note to Murphy which passed along a file on the "proposed Ukrainian National Guard organization," and concerned the "rapid expansion of this unlicensed and illegally organized military movement . . . which will form a large reserve potential in case of an armed conflict between the United States and the Soviet Union." One of its membership had contacted James Forrestal directly to offer the services of this admittedly unauthorized but potentially enormous low-lying army of more than 100,000 Ukrainians in the Western Zones; the Guard boasted more than 10,000 officers and noncoms, many "of the Bandera Party." As for "making use of dissident elements in combating Communism," Riddleberger tipped Murphy, his information now indicated "that it had been decided in Washington to turn the entire question over to CIA, but that it would be handled in some special manner under Frank Wisner."[42]

We'd require knowledgeable guidance; American intermediaries approached Gehlen. The pallid, self-effacing general consulted Dr. Michael Achmeteli, who ran an Ost-Institut for Hitler. Achmeteli recommended Dr. Franz Six, at war's end provost of the Wannsee Institut, unfortunately earmarked for prison until the McCloy amnesties arrived. In 1940 the youthful political scientist had presided over the SD study group devoted to "Ideological Combatting of Opposition," the subjects of which were Freemasonry and Jewish Political History. Inside the revamped security administration, the RSHA, Six inherited Amt II.[43]

Under Six's wartime authority the Byelorussian separatist Radislaw Ostrowsky and his military chieftain, Franz Kushel, rounded up a 20,000-man militia and extinguished an estimated 42,000 Jews in company with whatever commissars or intelligentsia fell into their clutches. Their methods were noteworthy, even by SD standards: well plied with vodka, Kushel's deputies raped girls they expected to shoot and smashed in the heads of whatever infants they didn't flip alive into mass graves to suffocate beneath parental corpses.[44]

Kushel's 20,000 mujik terrorists fled West ahead of the Soviet battle tanks, and during the war's last year fought on in a variety of SS units. With Germany collapsing, Ostrowsky evaded Gustav Hilger's invitation to join his broad-based Slavonic Committee for the Liberation of the Peoples of Russia. He founded the Belarus Brigade.

The Belarus troopers marked time around the French Zone, many on United Nations payrolls, in hopes of repackaging themselves as Poles. At that point Gehlen—who hadn't forgotten the energetic Ostrowsky from combined operations in the Smolensk area—offered support in return for convincing data to feed to the intelligence-ravenous Americans. Wisner was already working on a network of "Special Forces" bases spotted throughout the south of Germany from Bad Wiessee to Kaufbeuren, location centers for shock troops prior to the anticipated rollback. In DP camps around the American Zone at Backnang, Michelsdorf, Osterhofen, and Aschaffenburg, the Byelorussians formed up and administrated their indigenous communities. Kushel and the brutal Stanislaw Stankievich went in as commandants.[45]

It had been Philby's job all through the postwar months as Chief of Section 9, the Soviet intelligence branch of the SIS, to revive British control over anti-Bolshevik malcontents, and he was quickly in touch with Bandera and his Ukrainians along with the Abramtchik schismatics. Before long the cost of subsidizing these émigré encampments was breaking the English. Unloading "the Communist-infiltrated Abramtchik organization upon the all-too-eager Wisner," Loftus writes, would stand as "Philby's biggest coup." "Philby also threw in the entire NTS network to serve as the foundation for a Pan-Slavic anticommunist bloc in exchange for access to the intelligence produced."[46]

The NTS (Narodnyi Trudovoy Soyoz, literally, National Labor Council) had evolved since its founding in the twenties by disgruntled Socialists and Mensheviks into a kind of catchall for Greater Russian defectors lying low throughout Europe. It sharpened up its industrial-grade propaganda mix with a dose of reactionary cant and the familiar mustards of Tsarist-era anti-Semitism. Once war broke out the NTS membership jumped in against Stalin, until finally the undisguised anti-Slavic ferocity of Himmler's Jagdkommandos put off the NTS leadership. The U.S. Military Government picked up the option on this far-flung community of perhaps 100,000 unreconciled authoritarians, and underwrote its incendiary printings as well as its "secret operations committee," the wellspring of repeated attempts at subversion inside the motherland along with Radio Free Russia and an academy for saboteurs just outside Bad Homburg.[47]

These fast-decaying assets occasioned a fair amount of bickering in Washington, Philby divulges, "many skirmishes over the various Russian émigré organizations. . . ." For some months Lindsay and others faulted Bandera's "extreme nationalism, with its Fascist overtones," his "roots in the old emigration," and the fact that he was "accused flatly of being anti-American."[48] But before long Bandera too crawled into the fold. Radical times invite extreme remedies.

Meanwhile, both English and U.S. agencies continued to sow agents into the Soviet hinterlands, picking targets as knowledgeably as possible once "parachute-dropping season" opened. Little of note came back. "I do not know what happened to the parties concerned," Philby conceded in one case with a transcendental wink. "But I can make an informed guess."[49]

Sibert remained Gehlen's champion, and referred to the Org around Washington as "my baby."[50] This made it less of a risk every month for SS dignitaries to declare themselves. Who didn't find work? One SD alumnus never far from notoriety was Baron Otto Albrecht Alfred von Bolschwing, the pogrom enthusiast and SS envoy to Rumania so frequently in evidence throughout Wisner's *Bughouse* documents. Von Bolschwing was out of favor in Berlin and dormant in the Tyrol in January 1945 when, he testified subsequently, "I was contacted directly by Allied authorities."[51] From then on he labored in one capacity or another for U.S. military intelligence until 1954.[52] When the CIA assumed liaison responsibility for Gehlen, the U.S. military off-loaded von Bolschwing onto Pullach.

The Baron transferred hard. Ex-comrades remembered sourly von Bolschwing's eagerness to rat out Hitler. "In a number of conferences," he told an investigator later on, "I met individuals whom I had known from the past and who had been members of the [Hitler era] political intelligence groups," and found himself assailed by "the uneasy feeling that we, namely U.S. Intelligence, were being misused for German nationalistic purposes." He bristled at the prevalence of "General Staff and political intelligence and military intelligence" officers, many with wartime colleagues in the employ of Russia. Von Bolschwing "feared that we were being penetrated by the East, rather than were penetrating them." The Baron's patrons in U.S. intelligence stepped in to help him emigrate to the United States, where ultimately he put together a third career as a consultant with the Cabot Corporation.

Von Bolschwing was not alone in brooding about Gehlen. The Americans couldn't help but acknowledge their dependency on Gehlen's Org, and over the decade shoveled through an estimated $200 million, a lot from unacknowledged U.S. and Bundesrepublik business coffers.[53] U.S. and SHAPE (Allied) military committees ultimately looked to the general for an estimated 70 percent of its order-of-battle detailing of the East. Gehlen manned the battlements. Visitors found him accommodating, patriotic, impassive—his skinned-looking features rarely gave anything away, although a true shocker could start those protuberant faceted ears waggling like a bat's.

Never that picky politically, the general preferred operatives "suitable," as he would write, "to undermine the East German State Security Service, which was largely manned by ex-SS men." He recruited competitively, promiscuously. Eric Waldman was back in academia after 1949, which liberated the headhunters around Pullach from the outdated ethical prejudices of this Viennese-born Catholic.[54] Once military government gave way to the High Commissioner's office, most of the slapdash, semiautonomous CIC detachments around the Zone either dried up or relinquished accountability for the refugee encampments. The notorious 7970 CIC Company, for example, shucked Klaus Barbie for rat-line disposal while releasing into the intelligence pool the notorious Eichmann adviser Dr. (SS Colonel) Emil Augsburg. Gehlen snapped Augsburg up to fortify his Professorengruppe.[55]

Gehlen appointed as head of personnel the unreconstructed Nazi Hans Schroeder. *His* deputy was one of Schellenberg's RSHA section chiefs, Heydrich's sidekick SS-Oberfuehrer Willi Krichbaum. In September 1951 Krichbaum optioned Heinz Felfe, another SD floater, with credentials as a Russian specialist on the counterintelligence side. Unfortunately, the Soviets had already struck their arrangement with Felfe. The KGB built Felfe by alloting him a circuit of informers in Moscow. Heinz's promotions came rapidly, and before long Felfe took over counterintelligence for the Org while doubling as Gehlen's designee to brief—and debrief—his counterparts around NATO.[56]

❑

Nothing pointed up the vulnerability of the West more starkly than our two-year dalliance with WIN. WIN stood for Wolnose i Niepodlenose, Freedom and Independence. Our opportunity burst upon us in 1949, when a Pole with impeccable resistance credentials, S. Sienko, turned up in London to electrify several members of Wladtslaw Anders's staff with tiding that remnants of the Polish Home Army, of which the last major unit was reportedly extirpated in 1947, had now been reconstituted and only required support in documents, trained men, guns, radio equipment, and "financial aid" "to carry out in Poland espionage, subversive activities and sabotage."[57] Anders himself presided over 110,000 men under arms in the United Kingdom, marking time against the imminent Communist collapse at home.[58] According to Sienko the "WIN Home Organization," as it called itself, numbered 500 active opponents, along with 20,000 sympathizers and 100,000 inclined to take up arms, a force-in-being ideally constituted to ambush and retard that long-feared Soviet rollover across the West.[59]

In November 1950 an agreement was struck between an OPC Colonel, Sapieha, and Colonel Aciolek and Edward Kulikowski of "WIN Center Abroad" in London. In return for training, money, personnel, and air drops, the London Poles would "conduct espionage and subversive work for the American secret service." Walpole ("Tad") Davis moved in as control officer, with John Evalovsky backing him up.[60] Throughout the next two years the SIS and—overwhelmingly—the Americans came up with well over $1 million worth of gold sovereigns with which to bribe wavering officials, obtain pistols with silencers, order overflights on request, remunerate demolition specialists. Even WIN Center control officers were denied so much as the cover names of the individuals they nurtured long distance for battle with the underground. The Poles were adamant about protecting their heroes inside the unhappy motherland.

Most of the financing originated in those free-flowing OPC accounts. The program got serious in the pandemonium which surrounded the Korean War. Much of the pressure to take a chance on WIN was exerted by Joint Chiefs of Staff adviser Colonel Robert McDowell, that last-ditch Mihailovitch admirer and SANACC and Policy and Planning visionary.[61]

Once equipment went in, tactical information seeped out; the totals looked better with every message decoded. OSO spoilsports cocked eyebrows at something as friction-free as this while officers from counterintelligence examined dossiers on WIN Center Abroad. But hopes kept compounding.

On December 27, 1952, it all tumbled down. "Security authorities in Poland" proclaimed on international radio frequencies that as early as 1948 the commanders of the WIN Home Organization, J. J. Kowalski and his deputy S. Sienko, sought out the Communist authorities in Warsaw, heartsick with the realization that what was intended initially as a "continuation of our activity during the Nazi occupation" had degenerated into "criminal, anti-Polish activity." Responsible support dried up, the ones "who stayed were killers," while "the agents who were sent to us from abroad were also adventurers, cynical hirelings indifferent to the lot of the nation. . . ." Meanwhile, Poland was being recreated. "Our correspondents abroad . . . were desperately clinging to the most bellicose American groups," while "talks held in the Vatican with Father Turowski, General of the Pallotine Order," concerned "the prospects of an early war."[62]

Another specter was rising: "Harriman, the American coal and steel magnate . . . undoubtedly dreams of returning to our Silesia, to his former mines and steelworks." Having disbanded for all but disinformation purposes, the WIN Home Organization announced, "We could not reveal to anybody the structure of our sections, such as the 'T' section—military—or 'Notec'—intelligence—at headquarters, for the simple reason that they did not exist. . . . The only thing which we sent them after repeated and insistent requests (besides the fictitious and invented information) was the menu from one of the Warsaw restaurants. . . ."

Negotiations reaching as deep inside the U.S. government as Chief of Staff Omar Bradley and Wisner patron Secretary of the Army Kenneth Royal had tempted the Anglo-Saxons to divulge to the WIN spokesmen their "Volcano Plan." Once war erupted, the United States intended to hold Europe three months, long enough to destroy the industry of Germany, France, Italy, etc. The strategists wanted detailed information on bombing targets—rail junctions, freight-handling centers—their planes could decimate while stay-behind commandos produced "an armed subversion" and retarded the Soviet onslaught. "In other words," the broadcast emphasized, "the Americans and their émigré hirelings demanded that we help them in bombing and destroying the largest centres of our country." Otherwise, the WIN organization would "undergo a change which will find its expression in a cut or even a withdrawal of financial and material assistance. . . . Anders' General Staff, after petty bargaining and amendments, advised us to accept such a plan. . . ."

This proposal shamelessly demonstrated "the boundless bellicose arrogance of the Ridgeways, . . . the profound contempt of the

Dulleses for all human values which can neither be estimated nor bought for dollars," and now "These documents require us to make a final end of even the fictitious activity of WIN" to thwart the " 'Prussian King,' the Harrimans . . . the Adenauers, who are greedily stretching out their paws for our Western territories."

Much of the florid, indignant tone of the broadcast reflected the East-Bloc compulsion to vilify and hobgoblinize. One of his stool pigeons inside the U.S. intelligence community had passed along a transcript to the disgruntled Bill Donovan, conceding in a cover note that "Most of the broadcast is correct, except that these people did not surrender. They were arrested sometime in 1947–49 and the whole operation was doubled on us and to a lesser degree the British."

"This is considered one of the worst operations ever run by CIA," Donovan's informant notes. "It appears that from the time CIA accepted this project it was already under enemy control and run back as a provocation operation."

However heavy its touch, this final, paralyzing transmission from the WIN Home Organization resonated with object lessons which would continue to escape our covert warfare professionals. Know your ultimate recipient. Abiding loyalty isn't purchasable. Effective clandestine intervention works only in genuine conjunction with the authentic political purposes of even the most reduced of subject groups. Anything else has no better prospect than intimidation and chicanery.

16

TO RIP ITS GUTS OUT

Bill Donovan wasn't surprised that Warsaw so easily took in a politicized service subject to a "committee of secretaries," as Wild Bill dismissed postwar intelligence. This timid, makeshift compromise, concocted for the military along with "a striped-pants State Department dandy or two."[1]

By 1950 Harry Truman was doubtful as well. The Agency under Admiral Hillenkoetter was lumbered for missing every call so far, from the collapse in Prague to the communization of China, along with the Israeli rollover in Palestine and the anti-American riots in Bogotá. Hillenkoetter dredged up estimates to demonstrate that his people *had* seen these significant turns coming. But Truman wasn't convinced. The North Korean onslaught in June of 1950 in effect blindsided the administration; Hillenkoetter's tenure as DCI was finished.[2]

To guarantee the results he wanted, Truman brought in an administrator more likely to play a blowtorch across the divided Agency, Lieutenant General Walter Bedell ("Beedle") Smith. Later on Beedle too would grouse that what the leadership community demanded from the CIA was not to be had: "They expect you to be able to say that a war will start next Tuesday at 5:32 P.M."[3]

What Beedle *could* contribute was something approaching forty years of taking the heat and giving the heat, of cold-blooded analysis and brutal decision making. A fussiness about details and the capacity to hang on, jaws closing, when he was tasked with problems had pushed Smith along by 1942 to become Secretary to the Combined Chiefs, after which he crowned his military career as Chief of Staff for Eisenhower throughout the battle for Europe. Whenever something seemed more than routinely problematical to Ike, or diplomatically distasteful, or threatened to splash back on Eisenhower's own reputation, Smith caught the assignment.

He'd become, in Churchill's phrase, "America's bulldog," and appeared the ideal foil to deal with Stalin as U.S. ambassador to Moscow between 1946 and 1949. He'd evolved beyond recognition from the alert Indianapolis schoolboy who won his battlefield commission in 1918, skipped West Point, and now could silence a room by stepping through the door and perusing the company. "He prided himself on ruthlessness, on being Machiavellian," one Wisner aide notes. "And he knew Machiavelli, this National Guardsman from Indiana."[5]

Smith had deplaned in 1946 as U.S. ambassador to Moscow, he wrote afterward, in hopes that "my previous association with them might be helpful in breaking through the hard crust. . . ." He returned home convinced that Stalin remained intent on hearing the "funeral dirge . . . sung over . . . world capitalism."[6] His years on history's whetstone were wearing Smith thin, and once he had returned to the United States in 1949 and settled in as commander of the U.S. Second Army headquartered at Governor's Island, he underwent an ulcer operation which cost the uneasy general the bulk of his stomach.

One midsummer day in 1950, after Smith was back on his feet, the CIA's principal attorney, Larry Houston, was chatting with the Agency's current Executive Director, Ted Shannon, when there was a call from General Smith's aide at Governor's Island. The general was interested in having a look, at once, at all valid personnel charts for the CIA. Material was hurried together, and very soon thereafter Houston ambled into Smith's offices.[7]

The general was fifty-five, down fully fifty pounds from his weight as Eisenhower's Chief of Staff, and swimming in his uniform. He retained the careful neat part, the overclippered country-boy haircut of his prairie upbringing, which set forth a pair of outstretched, bracketing ears of a sort Midwestern kids are called on frequently to defend at recess. Everything else he'd worked on, starting with his long, mealy mouth (normally pinched with judgment), the prominent honky cheekbones, and especially those wide-set bearinglike eyes: level, never missing an evasive maneuver, lit as occasion arose by a respect for true capability or a grim twinkle of amused contempt.

Here was the staff officer, after all, who engineered the demise of Patton.

Smith made one early convert in an unexpected quarter. He accepted the responsibility for rebuilding the CIA while Kim Philby was rounding out his tour in Washington. Later on Philby wrote Leonard Mosley that "It was fortunate for the CIA that it was Smith, not Dulles, who presided (1950–1953) over the post-war raggle-taggle that followed Truman's disbandment of the OSS. I fear that Dulles would have confounded confusion. But Smith was no chairman. He was the boss, and a boss of outstanding intellect and character. Many times I saw him read a long memorandum, toss it aside and, without pause for thought, paragraph by numbered paragraph, rip its guts out—real virtuoso stuff. . . ."[8]

Immediately, Houston remembers, "General Smith struck you as somebody you'd listen to." The CIA personnel chart was no sooner propped up at Governor's Island before the interrogation started. I know that fellow, what does he do? What are your real programs? Why wasn't there some group working on overall, periodic national estimates in the problem areas? And above all, approached from various angles: what was all this about the special, outside accountability of the OPC compared with the OSO? How could you have a CIA director without authority over his most controversial, fastest-growing unit?

General Smith sent Houston back to Washington to draw up a paper for him.

Smith moved into his new headquarters in October 1950. He'd barely been in town a week when he called in Houston along with Frank Wisner and promulgated a direct order. The OPC, he informed them both, was about to be incorporated without reservation, meat and hair, into the CIA.

Houston wondered whether the general was interested in looking over legal papers to accomplish this.

"I'm not interested in seeing anything," Smith said. "Just do it."

So Wisner and Houston got together to pore over the empowering documents. As least at that stage, so far as Houston could tell, Frank wasn't especially perturbed.

❑

Bringing in a shit-stirrer like Beedle reflected the Truman administration's decision to militarize U.S. policy. Not only the Korean invasion, but also irrefutable evidence that the Soviets had detonated an atomic bomb, changed in one season the scale and stakes of commitment. The pressure was truly on, Joe McCarthy was brandishing his list of 205 known "Communist spies" in the State Department,[9] the whitewash rolled thicker every month across the dossiers of Nazis (in Bonn U.S. High Commissioner John McCloy was abridging prison sentences and returning confiscated industrial properties eight-to-the-bar), and Treasury money was earmarked for the French to salvage Indochina. Everything we didn't like was clearly the outcome of subtle Soviet machinations.

The document which incarnated this hard-edged Weltanschauung was NSC-68, which Paul Nitze crafted under Dean Acheson's eye. Based as it was on "institutionalized crimes," the paper opened, the Kremlin simply intended to maintain the "total subjective submission of the peoples now under its control," reducing them to "concentration-camp"-like circumstances in which the individual "participates affirmatively in his own destruction." Worse, "It is quite clear from Soviet theory and practice that the Kremlin seeks to bring the free world under its domination by the methods of the cold war." To stave this off, NSC-68 proposed a greatly expanded limited war capacity to supplement the strategic bombing umbrella, major ground defenses in Europe—within which a reconstituted West German army was clearly unavoidable—and vigorous, well-funded clandestine initiatives across the entire covert range, from propagandistic to paramilitary.[10] It projected 1954 as the "crisis year" unless forces were steadily stepped up, perhaps to the $50 billion annual level.[11]

"The conclusion of the paper was to reaffirm the conclusions of the preceding paper which had been written by George Kennan," Nitze says now. "But it went into much fuller analysis of world trends—what made the USSR tick, except that George Kennan's preceding piece had been pretty damn good on that. . . . But George later changed his opinion. He denies it, but it's the truth." Nitze's musings are deliberative, considered; every now and again an observation passes back through something, like a fine wire garrote. "George has remained a close friend of mine," Nitze offers. "Over all these years we've had no disagreements. Except on substance."[12]

By 1950, manifestly, George Kennan was badly torn. The exhaustive, bruising debate at policy levels over whether to authorize the development of the hydrogen bomb had convinced the gentle neurotic that pursuing an approach which invited the end of civilization was misguided, criminal ultimately. He now perceived more ominous threats than the outcreep of Stalinism. He reiterated that Communism was not monolithic, that Stalin would remain conservative, adventitious, concerned largely with Russia, not expanding Socialism. He opposed the European Defense Community. Kennan found himself outvoted on central issues by activists on his own Policy and Planning staff, and regularly heard "all he wanted to" before disappearing until further notice into a hideaway he reserved deep in the Library of Congress.[13]

One factor upsetting Kennan was his recognition that the Germany now emerging from the debarking machinery of U.S. policy-making would resemble in very few particulars the "historical experience" which Kennan so venerated. He'd understood at once that driving through the 1948 currency reform was likely to perpetuate the German division, and actively opposed the formation of the European Defense Community along with related economic efforts to bond the Germans of the West to France and the Benelux countries.[14] The administration's frantic backwatering in September of 1951, when DDR Prime Minister Otto Grotewohl came up with his no-strings-attached offer of free elections preliminary to merging the two Germanies, demonstrated absolutely that both in Washington and Bonn reunification was a subject for propaganda, not a priority of statecraft.[15]

The Bloc nations ultimately needed to be conquered, not validated by peer negotiation. By 1951 the planning chief at the Defense Department, Rear Admiral J. C. Stevens, was jibbing Wisner directly to step up his participation in "Joint Campaign Plan Europe" by creating "supporting forces" to destabilize the "Iron Curtain countries."[16] The Military Security Act of 1951 set aside $100 million "to help form residents or émigrés from Russia or the satellite countries into elements of the military forces sustaining NATO or used 'for other purposes.' "[17]

George Kennan was aghast. To trade the possibility of a reconstituted German nation for *this*, some kind of paramilitary puppet show decked out with squabbling Slavic exiles—how could that benefit anybody? Under John Foster Dulles "The militarization of policy toward the Soviet Union was no smaller, but also not much greater, than it had been in the final two or three years of Mr. Truman's presidency," Kennan would conclude sadly.[18]

A shift of orientation this profound left Kennan something less than the ideal choice to target a meat-eating young bureaucracy like the Office of Policy Coordination. In January of 1950 Paul Nitze took over as director of the Policy and Planning Staff, and ran the team that drafted NSC-68 as a kind of paperwork monument to Nitze's long-time mentor at Dillon, Read and throughout his government career, James Forrestal. Kennan, more surely every season, decided that there were methods, however effective, that we as a society must renounce: "Earlier in this century the great secular despotisms headed by Hitler and Stalin introduced into the pattern of their interaction with other governments clandestine methods of operation that can only be described as ones of unbridled cynicism, audacity and brutality." After the Second World War "our government felt itself justified in setting up facilities for clandestine defensive operations of its own. . . . As one of those who, at the time, favored the decision to set up such facilities, I regret today [1985], in light of the experience of the intervening years, that the decision was taken. Operations of this nature are not in character for this country."[19]

❑

Simultaneous with the CIA's announcement on August 18, 1950, that General Walter Bedell Smith would assume control, word came that another veteran, ex-Colonel William Harding Jackson, would leave Manhattan concurrently to serve as deputy director. Smith had been acquainted with Jackson in passing as Omar Bradley's wartime deputy chief of intelligence, but it was primarily as the coauthor of the Corea-Dulles-Jackson report on prospects for upgrading the CIA that Jackson had drawn Smith's interest.

Jackson arrived in Washington with perhaps more readiness than fitness for the post. The Nashville-born lawyer was made a partner at Carter, Ledyard just as Frank Wisner signed into the training program, and worked with his fellow Southerner until both took military commissions. Jackson had returned briefly, then joined his good friend Jock Whitney as managing director of Whitney's venture capital house. This was rarified company—never lost on Wisner—and when Jackson got down to Washington Frank welcomed him with gusto and looked to him to smooth the Beedle Smith reorganization. And beyond this, Wisner's widow, Polly Fritchey, maintains, Jackson's reappearance helped resolidify inside the government the old Carter, Ledyard crowd, with all the swashbuckling, down-home possibilities that implied.

Jackson was a man's man. Throughout their Manhattan youth, "Bill Jackson had this extremely loyal sort of coterie around him," Polly says, "who admired him enormously. Tracy Barnes and Gordon Gray were in that, and Archibald Alexander, the Undersecretary of the Army, and Frank. . . . They all just doted on Bill. But Bill was very, very difficult, he didn't like women around him, and naturally all the wives couldn't bear Bill Jackson—not that he couldn't be attractive when he wanted to be. But he became more and more difficult as time went on. And then the booze got him. . . ."[20]

Smith seems to have realized soon enough that the frequently closed, contained Jackson lacked background in many aspects of subversive technique as well as the sort of broad administrative feel Beedle needed to fine-tune the broad-scale restructuring he had in prospect. He contacted the other primary author of the intelligence study, Allen Dulles, and invited him to consult with the CIA on a regular basis.[21] At this point Bill Jackson remarried abruptly and departed for an extended honeymoon. Before Jackson left he recommended to Smith as a possible executive assistant one of the tall young OSO division heads he'd already run into during his headquarters days in France with Bradley, Lyman Kirkpatrick.

Smith called Kirkpatrick in, sparred with him conversationally in the manner he tended to—a mixture of sharp, unpredictable questions and heavy-handed allusions to his own accomplishments, which left only the smaller bones fractured—and settled on Lyman. Kirkpatrick's background in reporting and tactical analysis, abetted by something of a wintry makeup, struck Smith as perfect for the task at hand. It was now urgent to chill the lush, tropical optimism endemic to the OPC, to impose a dose of reality on Wisner and his Ivy-league pranksters. Kirkpatrick became Smith's acolyte, his legatee, the bearer of his torch.[22]

As Philby points up, early in his tenure Smith all-but-single-handedly reordered the contemporary CIA. It remained his first imperative to uncover the tangle of wires that jacked in everywhere and nowhere around the bureaucracy, clip back and simplify, coordinate intention and result. As trunk-line instrumentalities, Smith originated the three central directorates: Administration, Intelligence, and Plans. The Deputy Director for Administration (DDA) looked after mundane requirements like finance, security, and transportation. (Smith would keep training, personnel, and communication under his own control.) The Deputy Director for Intelligence (DDI), the lineal descendant of the old Research and Analysis chief at OSS, oversaw the collation and interpretation of information gleaned worldwide, mostly from overt sources like technical publications and expert testimony. In Agency parlance the acronyms (DDA, DDI, DDP) would refer at the same time to the office and the individual who led the directorate at the time.

To channel this inexorably rising tide of data Smith authorized the extra-Agency twelve-man Board of National Estimates, all people of genuine reputation backed up by a permanent staff of specialists. They were to prepare definitive studies from time to time on matters of national concern. William Langer came back to chair the initial Board, seconded by Sherman Kent of Yale. In addition Smith created the Current Intelligence Office, intended to boil out of the welter of detail coming in from everywhere a daily intelligence summary which he as director could present the President every morning, a few pregnant pages which suggested the patterns and movements of events and pinpointed the hot-spots. Kingman Douglass of Dillon, Read returned to get the current intelligence office underway.

Smith's greatest—riskiest—invention he dubbed, with a characteristic mordant blandness, the Directorate of Plans. Plans incorporated the clandestine services. And into this administrative tiger cage Smith escorted both the staid, rather alarmed OSO veterans and Wisner's hipshooters in the OPC. "How did they get along?" Jack Blake mused years later, recalling the hubbub. "They got along like—like a couple of porcupines attempting to make love. Whatever they did together they did very, very cautiously, each watching the other."[23]

To bring this off, Kirkpatrick notes, Smith simply "wrote letters to the Secretaries of State and Defense and advised them that as of that date he was taking over the direction and control" of the OPC. He welcomed "advice or guidance." "His methods amazed all," Lyman notes, "annoyed some, delighted others. And though there were those who attempted to mobilize opposition against him, no one could stop him."[24]

From Frank Wisner's vantage point, the Smith reorganization amounted to a severe double demotion. Obviously, from then on, he couldn't really play Defense and State off one against the other while accommodating his own purposes. Beedle would be monitoring. Furthermore, as matters had developed he would be losing his effective sovereignty, and survived as head of one subsection in one of the newly formed directorates. His boss for the moment, signed in as of January 1951 as head of Plans, was Allen W. Dulles.

"I never heard Frank complain, I know he felt he could live with Beedle Smith's iron-fisted way of doing things," one Wisner flunky insists. "Smith didn't know fuck-all about intelligence, but he knew organizations." For two brutal years Smith subjected Wisner to training in the subject. Wisner's efforts to force the growth of the OPC, the general soon determined, had produced an unwieldy entity more fungoid than organic. Institutional loyalty ranked everything, and Wisner had proved very adroit at buffering off his people by drawing "on the web of New York law firm connections that existed in postwar Washington," as the Church Committee probers concluded, "as well as on his State Department ties to gain support" for his main mission, which remained, to the end, political redress in Eastern Europe. The OPC responded to demands on it from the Departments by devising a "project system," according to which an officer gained prestige proportionate to the "importance and number of projects he initiated and managed."[25]

Guidelines were calculatedly fuzzed. Although Wisner met once a week or so with "designated representatives of State and Defense," the projects were now at least as likely to originate in the OPC, since Wisner had assured himself of dealing with totally like-minded counterparts, Bob Joyce and General Joseph McNarney, the Sovietophobic recent commander of U.S. Forces in Europe.[26] Big programs got thrashed over among the regional heads before presentation to what Richard Stilwell characterizes as "a kind of a validating board which met in Wisner's office. . . . It really consisted on the one hand of Paul Nitze, and Brigadier General John Magruder representing the Secretary of Defense. We had progress reports and we had new initiatives." The group would meet "at least quarterly, and on call for an important project. When you went up to the Smith-Dulles level you had then to reflect the concurrence or dissent of the two major Departments."[27]

Magruder was a tested ally, while the entrepreneurial Nitze's seething distaste for anything that suggested the imprint of Moscow made him a natural sell. Paul Nitze remembers still the arguments which led to the utilization of SS experts and Ukrainian irreconcilables: "The CIA was interested and the Pentagon was interested," Nitze says, "and my recollection is that Frank Wisner was interested in working on that program." Wisner "thought well of Gehlen."[28]

Most exchanges were instrumental—could something be done, how do you support people? Nitze alludes to interminable discussions as to the feasibility of backing the Montagnards in Laos "against the various factions." Nothing seemed farfetched. When Communist China moved on Tibet the OPC leadership decided that something must be mounted to preserve the ancient Himalayan civilization. A delegation of Tibetans arrived in Washington to barter for weapons. Conducted to Nitze's offices, their spokesman proposed in trade an important regional product. He offered, chuckles Nitze, "yaks' tails," which he recommended as "very good Santa Claus beards." With this began years of fiddling with the supporters of the Dalai Lama, especially his Khamba cavalry. Paramilitary irregulars underwent training at Camp Hale, Colorado; for over a decade Agency contract mercenaries fed them back into Tibet over the mountain passes from India to die in fruitless raids and senseless harassment forays against the Peking-imposed regime.[29]

"Policy direction," the Church Committee experts concluded, "took the form of condoning and fostering activity without providing scrutiny and control" or "establishing firm guidelines for approval."[30] Wisner built his covert-action factory around procedures analogous to those which prevailed in the important law firms, where high-powered business getters easily cornered the lucrative partnerships, brought in preferred clients, raked off contingency fees and skirted the more controversial details when delineating touchy cases in front of staid senior figures. The key was breadth, internal velocity, compounding billable hours. The impact on society, like the ethics of the client, appeared beside the point.

"It did not work out at all the way I conceived it," George Kennan would confess, dumfounded at this frenzy he'd unleashed—by 1952 a matter of close to 5,000 operatives in Washington and scattered around the forty-seven foreign stations, many in military uniform or scurrying in and out of the Marshall Plan suboffices around Europe. "We had thought," mused Kennan, "that this would be a facility which could be used when and if an occasion arose when it might be needed."[31] Instead, there soon were *thousands* of covert action projects at various stages at any one time, forty by somebody's count in one small East-European country alone. Representatives in the field evaded the control of Washington, while staff officers and activists in the divisions within the OPC itself emerged as competitors, fought over jurisdiction, finagled to cross-purposes.

Clandestine collection veterans atop the OSO now found their flesh crawling as Wisner's bouncy trainees started to pop up in many of the punkier corners of Europe like chiggers at a barbecue. Many faces they recognized: cheerful drinking buddies from bachelor officers' quarters of a decade earlier, back on Frank's payroll and cruising for a sample of Cold-War romance. They definitely were action-oriented. Harry Rositske brings up one early request from the enterprising Frank Lindsay as to the feasibility of doubling up a man Rositske with great difficulty had managed to insert into a major Soviet atomic facility. Was there any chance Rositske's plant could get in close enough to jam the uranium turbine?[32] Alerted to the existence of

Lieutenant Colonel Pyotr Popov, the GRU agent in place whose seven years of tactical details smuggled to his OSO handlers unquestionably made him the first really productive supplier the American service was able to develop inside Russia, a suggestion came over from OPC that during his home leaves the already unraveling Soviet spy might profitably be put to use organizing some kind of Moscow sabotage ring. Among Wisner's confreres, any secret sounded humdrum compared with the gratifying paaa-ROOOOOM of plastique going off.

It worked both ways, of course. Tipped off that a substantial bribe was en route by way of an OPC officer in Rome to an important Italian politician, Jim Angleton slunk in to inquire as to whether several of his people might not be positioned within camera range to record the cash transfer. A photograph or two could nail down cooperation: sometimes individuals suffered afterthoughts, or seizures of conscience, and attempted to renig.

❑

The wrangles over Italy pointed up the toe tromping that ensued when there were too many spies in the room. Italy came on live consequent to the electoral crisis of 1947–1948. "We couldn't have Eddie Page just hanging out the window of the U.S. Embassy and passing out money to the Christian Democrats," Jim McCargar says.[33] McCargar had just returned from Italy after a tour for The Pond and wrote the 20-page working paper on where and how to affect the Italians as requested by the Policy and Planning Staff. Once Wisner got cranked, the millions pushed through soon "constituted the largest sum of money the Agency ever pumped into a political-action operation,"[34] Bill Colby commented afterward.

"Relations between OSO and OPC were, well, difficult for a period," recalls W. Mark Wyatt, an OSO careerist who worked the territory for many years. "There were certain rather stuffy types that came out to Italy for OPC, and they were kind of a different breed from those of us that were involved in collecting intelligence, recruiting assets, running positive intelligence operations against hard targets like the Soviet Embassy. They disdained the idea of mucking with liaison. . . . It was very compartmented, and the black bags were given directly to the senior politicians. It really was a very splendid operation.

"The OPC had splendid direct contact with high officials of the three or four parties of the center that we dealt with for covert action purposes."[35] Perhaps the heaviest indemnities reached officials of the pervasive and influential Actione Catholic movement, a tightly organized lobbying operation with 30–40,000 activist members unceasing in its efforts to "organize opinions," slather up the anti-Communist posters, and get out votes enough to frustrate the Reds at the polls. While the energetic Luigi Gedda actually ran the organization, there wasn't any doubt that Catholic Action prospered beneath the "guardianship" of Giovanni Montini, long the driving personality in the papal secretariat of state and subsequently Pope Paul VI.

Inside the Agency itself, Montini was reputed to be "close to Jim Angleton," and Angleton stayed in touch. One mid-level functionary for the OSO in Italy admits that Angleton was on the telephone with him in the early evening every week or ten days, and "Angleton never gave me a bad lead." When Montini was archbishop in Milan the prelate needed only to hint that Catholic Action could benefit from a squadron of sound trucks, and they were all but loaded on the next eastbound freighter.

Following Angleton's contacts in, OSO operatives were able to infiltrate and ultimately pretty much coopt the Italian security services. "This was an Angleton-Rocca thing," a participant observes. "We had officers working right in with every branch of Italian intelligence—naval, air force—and the relationships were extremely close. . . . Then on the sensitive side you went further. You were able to get very senior officers in the service to focus on what *we* wanted done unbeknownst to their bosses." Of course, "You have to see that they're happy. Their motivation is high, they want to work with you, deep down, but at the same time you want to have an element of control. . . . You're not only offering gifts but you're saying, Geez, you're trying to put that son of yours through college, and it's a little rough, and we'd be delighted to assist you. . . . I don't think that's venality, I think that's good common intelligence sense."

Money into sympathetic channels permitted Washington to re-etch local intelligence circuits from the inside out. Most vital were "important liaison services that we could guide and direct and have influence on," one professional emphasizes, "to see that they worked on the *Soviet* target, dammit, and didn't get involved in a lot of their routine crap, you know, even though their bosses might not necessarily agree. . . . To duplicate it, we would have had to have a station of a couple of hundred people. . . . The Communist Party was a huge thing in Italy, and there was a lot of sensitivity about working against a legal party in that country."

With so much accessible, operators in the field tended to forget public-relations amenities. Mark Wyatt remembers briefing CIA director John McCone in the back of a limousine shortly before McCone attended an audience with His Holiness Paul VI. It might be productive, Wyatt suggested, to remind Montini of the many services the CIA had provided over the years, starting with those sound trucks.

An extremely strict Catholic, McCone was aghast. "Are you proposing," he asked Wyatt, "that I go in there and attempt to recruit the Pope?"[36]

Political action breakthroughs in Italy made the Italian desk something of a favorite inside the Agency. Like Iran later, and Cuba and Guatemala and Nicaragua, its level of penetration in Italy gave Washington a secure feeling. Italian consulates were invaluable throughout the East Bloc countries, from where strategic bits and pieces came out of satellite rail junctions and backwoods parade grounds whenever Italian businessmen got debriefed as part of the Legal Traveler program. At first British Intelligence nursed assets in Italy as well, mostly in the Ministry of the Interior along with a few in the security service itself, SIFA, but "we were gradually able to move them out of both," a CIA operative acknowledges, and of course "we used to screw the French all the time." General Gehlen was careful to remain "very close to the chief of the Italian service." Italian contractors were building a great deal of the utility infrastructure throughout Egypt and the Middle East—while Gehlen's SS retirees were plumbing in the intelligence services—and inevitably both Gehlen and his American backers "wanted to tie into their operations."[37]

In Italy the money was so major, so decisive, so successfully applied, that everybody wanted credit. When he turned up as political operations chief in Italy in 1953 William Colby found a well-articulated system of "outside officers"—genteel cutouts—to pass along those stuffed black bags to luminaries with clout. Angleton semi-independent "singletons" had coopted a number of the "outside officers," and yearned for a restoration of the House of Savoy while resisting Washington's proposals to cater to Pietro Nenni's Socialists. Colby savors one evening on which he was "authorized to fill the back seat of my Fiat with millions of lira and pass them on through my outside agent, an ostensible student. . . ."[38]

❑

This maelstrom of loose currency swirling across the capitals sucked many straight down. One hotshot whose service record soon caught

Beedle Smith's quick eye was Carmel Offie. Not only the State Department and the FBI, but even the D.C. metropolitan precinct stations were fattening their active files on Offie-related tidbits. There had been wartime arrests, reportedly for the solicitation of youthful male vagrants in the stalls of the gentlemen's lavatory at Lafayette Park, and initiates on the OSO side were starting to wonder just how a verified copy of the police blotter might play in the newspapers during the era of Tail Gunner Joe. "Even now it's hard for me to understand why Wisner would risk keeping at his right hand one of the most notorious homosexuals in the United States at the time," Lyman Kirkpatrick says.[39] Offie's own view, typically cavalier, was that if he was so well known it would be purposeless for anybody to try and blackmail him on security grounds. But Smith wasn't buying that, and once he settled in he summoned Wisner and told him to get rid of Carmel Offie.

Wisner did, and didn't. "Frank kept Carmel on contract status and turned him into a conduit with the Free Trade Union Committee, which was a big front through which Jay Lovestone and Irving Brown ran those unvouchered subsidies of theirs to free-world unions," one contemporary divulges. With or without Smith, the knives were out for Carmel around the Agency. His scathing one-liners left underlings especially "spattered with blood," Jim McCargar remembers, and he recalls one break before a staff meeting when Lyle Munson, a hard-right conservative who ultimately helped railroad John Davies out of the State Department, started on the latest apropos the "Awful Offie," as many now referred to the little man. In Munson's version of the durable chestnut, some newly damned soul finds himself treading water next to Dean Acheson in a vast lake of dissolving ordure. The unhappy spirit turns to Acheson and exclaims, "This is *hell!*"

"If you think this is hell," observes the imperturbable Acheson, "wait until Carmel Offie comes by in his speedboat."

"Jesus," McCargar relates, "the room absolutely fell apart. At this moment Offie comes in and asks what all the laughter is about, but of course nobody could tell him. . . . I think that was the only time I ever saw Offie really uneasy."[40] Meanwhile, according to another source, Offie's detractors within the OPC were compiling—evidently with Wisner's approval—a thorough investigative job on Carmel, about whom everybody recognized that there was "much to investigate," and there were plans afoot to leak the essentials to contacts at *The Saturday Evening Post.* The threat of that should dislodge Offie without the predictable acid geyser of recriminations and threats and uncontrolled vindictive overspray nobody wanted to contemplate.

Carmel Offie had planted himself—his little legs dangling, one malicious assistant noticed, "almost to the floor"—astride a primary Agency artery.[41] As both a conduit for funds and a general advisor to Jay Lovestone and Irving Brown," reminisces Tom Braden (who had entered the OPC to pull together the International Organization Division of the CIA), Offie became the last government employee to touch almost $2 million annually before it disappeared. "The CIA was handing over enormous sums of money to Lovestone and Brown for their network abroad, and it was always a sore point that we never got any accounting from them. Lovestone and Brown successfully managed to say, well, we spent that in Marseilles, or that in Paris, or there's a Communist dock strike and we broke it up." Word drifted back from Paris that Brown in particular seemed to enjoy a very lavish life-style, "like a capitalist."[42] Agency legend still treats the labor operations of the period as perhaps the most effective of the undertakings, but Braden himself later wrote that after a couple of years the CIA unilaterally "cut the subsidy down, and with the money saved . . . set up new networks in other international labor organizations." If anything, that improved matters.[43]

Dropped in by air to Poland or left on deposit at Dupont Circle, money remained a commodity the OPC seemed determined to look away from. Safer to operate blind. By 1951, when Braden was digging in, some premonition of the damages the OPC was doing to its reputation by rolling along the Albanian operation was starting to get to Wisner and his intimates. "People talked of nothing else," Braden says. "It was a tragedy, a searing defeat, a perfectly terrible thing. It governed much of the suspicion around the real security problems of the Agency. For years."[44]

Even Wisner would acknowledge that management was far too casual. He attracted into the OPC two urbane operations men with solid, well-deserved reputations tempered during the Second World War, Alfred Ulmer and Col. Frank Holcomb. For some months, he kept them circling both Lindsay and each other in hopes that they somehow might rescue this woebegone and compromised "sharp" project. Then he sent both off to clean things up in the field, Ulmer at the Athens jump-off and Holcomb in Rome.

Colonel Holbomb was and is a warm, acute, rather fine-boned man with a game leg, well traveled and extremely fastidious in the way of somebody who habitually trusts his intuitions with his life. He was just settling into Rome when one afternoon Irving Brown called up—"I knew Irving pretty well," Holcomb says, "and I liked him, and I definitely was going to go to great lengths to keep him away from our labor operations"—and said he wanted to have a chat. "I asked him to come out to my house," Holcomb says, "and lo and behold he had Carmel Offie with him." The two visitors informed Holcomb that their committee would be taking over his labor activities in Italy—which Holcomb concedes freely were "big, big, big, and involved money"—and Offie spoke up then to put things in perspective.

"Now, what we've got to do at this point," he told Holcomb, "is to let you know: Don't get in the way. Just get out of the way, and swim around for a while, and we'll take over. And then we'll get something for you afterward."

Holcomb reacted viscerally, but said nothing. Once they were gone he headed into town to the embassy and composed a five-page cable to Washington with all the detail he could summon up. Afterward, the head of OPC for Western Europe, Gerry Miller, remarked to Holcomb that his cable was "the best thing that ever happened because, using it," the Agency was "able to put an end to these people's games."

Offie's future in government now threatened to collapse on itself. Soon after that, Holcomb caught a glimpse of Carmel pumping across the tarmac at the airport outside Rome, and "under each arm he had a big silver candelabra. That sort of summed up Offie for me. He'd got something someplace, and he was bringing it back."[45]

❑

So throughout Beedle's tenure the mice thrived. Worse, Wisner's construct was supported by power brokers all up and down the Truman administration. Smith nevertheless intended to drag this swarming administrative nightmare into parade formation.

He had a lifetime of manuevers to draw on.[46] Now, in response to Harry Truman's complaint that nothing effective was being done on the interagency level to orchestrate "psychological warfare" against the Communist threat, Smith and William Jackson visited Chapel Hill to offer the chairmanship of the newly concocted Psychological Strategy Board to Gordon Gray.

Gray was a North Carolinian of reputation, heir to an R. J. Reynolds fortune, and a one-time Secretary of the Army. He'd been an acquaintance of Wisner's since summer camp and Woodberry Forest days, and arranged Wisner's introductions around Carter, Ledyard. The mission of the Psychological Strategy Board would be to coordinate the various psychological-warfare programs already budding at State, throughout the military, and—overwhelmingly—at OPC, where Wisner's "Mighty Wurlitzer" was chugging and blasting from Central Europe to the fringes of Asia. Smith intended that Wisner's admiration for the soft-spoken but penetrating Gordon Gray would help accustom Frank to outside direction and control.

But Wisner was dexterous at squirting out from under. Just as with Hillenkoetter, Wisner rilled excuses to duck out on PSB staff meetings. Gray couldn't really curtail anything nobody told him about.[47]

A much more imposing stricture Smith contrived to tighten on Wisner was the Senior Representative arrangement he devised in 1952 to oversee the five overseas action sectors. OSO and OPC field officers continued to compete viciously for agents, fouling each other's lines, tripping over one another, not infrequently at cross-purposes. Smith simply echeloned-in his Senior Representative as a kind of referee and viceroy to each area. These primarily military designees would now approve substantial initiatives in the field before *anybody* went ahead.

To Germany, for example, Smith shipped across Lieutenant General Lucian Truscott. Howard Roman, the local OSO branch chief, remembers a typical encounter requested by the veteran agent-runner Charles Katek, who had been winkling what particulars he could out of what survived of good society in Prague while helping with the twenty or so case officers running secondary agents out of Jugenheim for the wily Frantisek Moravec, the chief of prewar Czech intelligence. Katek—"Mr. Czecho"—was a practiced enough intelligence pro, Roman acknowledges, but like many others among Wisner's OSS favorites he was "a bit of a snow-job expert sometimes"; that day he was pushing what seemed to Roman a highly dubious proposal, "blowing up the whole thing to make it sound very good. But after a few minutes Truscott could clearly see that this was a bit of a snow job, that there were holes in Katek's presentation." So the proposal died.[48]

What didn't get squelched Wisner had to account for personally in Washington. Shortly after taking over, Smith found that Wisner had interposed his own man to monitor communications between OPC headquarters and its field stations, holding back whatever items might disturb the DCI. "The operators are not going to decide what secret information I will see or not see!" Beedle exploded, and after that everything that came or went passed through his personal cable secretariat.[49]

Beedle Smith's entire career was based on translating highflown directives into something effective, into nitty-gritty; as a voracious *user* of intelligence he had his own ideas as to what worked and what didn't. Many of the individuals he found himself saddled with riled Beedle's ulcers. When one recent employee who demonstrated a weakness for farm animals got shipped off to Saint Elizabeth's (in which the Agency already maintained its own closed ward), Smith sent for his personnel man, Trubee Davison, seconded in from Standard Oil. "For Christ's sake," the general erupted, "can't I get people who don't hire people who bugger cows?"[50]

"Kindly do not bring in here any more of those goddamned *balloon* projects of yours," he instructed one petrified supplicant.[51] Smith's testiness reached overload levels at staff meetings, where he was "brutal, brutal," Larry Houston recalls, lifting an image from Wisner: "Every staff meeting was a squash court, and you never knew who was going to get hit next. He used to say that every officer has a right to one mistake—and you've just had yours."[52]

The outbreak of war in Korea put overwhelming pressure on the OPC to destabilize the Chinese, an undertaking made no easier in view of the fact that Douglas MacArthur persistently resisted the CIA. Richard Stilwell oversaw Asia for Wisner. Stilwell had collaborated closely with Lindsay and Allen Dulles on the Herter Committee, and entered into the OPC initially in 1949 as Lindsay's deputy. Stilwell's West-Point fundamentals, augmented by a wealth of experience in the field, made him their logistics ace. Stilwell found Wisner overenergized by his very eagerness to "save the world. . . . He was at that period fighting some very substantial bureaucratic battles in Washington. Not only that, he was briefing people as to what we were all about while doing his best to make sure that the CIA, of which we were not an organic part, provided support or at least avoided the withholding of support."

Outsiders weren't proving dependable. "Without your own substantial support infrastructure," Stilwell could see, "the sum of the means which you control, you cannot run effectively—let alone covertly—an operation of any size and visibility." Stilwell was soon dickering with Tommy (the Cork) Corcoran over the purchase price of Claire Chennault's Flying Tiger airline. It became the first of the unnumbered CIA "proprietaries," its clandestine empire of weapons dumps and banks and harbor facilities and foundation accounts and refugee armies under training which accorded the Agency its controversial mobility, its capacity to project power and mislead opponents foreign and domestic.

In retrospect, Stilwell won't deny, "It is a *general* criticism of OPC . . . that we started more operations than we should have, we did less detailed evaluation of gain/loss/cost calculus, and as a result we had a number of totally counterproductive operations." Operations money flooded Taiwan to such an extent that insiders were afraid it would overinflate the currency. Stilwell summons up with a puckish gravity "my efforts to create a Third Force on the China Sea. There were a lot of non-Communist assets who wanted no part of Mao or Chiang, who had no real political leadership themselves and really no place to go." Stilwell set up perhaps a thousand of these free-lancing Chinese leaders with training and logistic bases in the Trust Territories, Saipan largely. "That proved to be a costly operation," he will now concede. "You couldn't keep something like that totally . . . submerged. Made Chiang Kai-Shek suspicious of our motives, and we were never able to operationalize 'em. Because even assuming you could politicize them, putting their flagstaff in the U.S. Trust Territories isn't very credible." But just then the Far East seemed to be going up in flames, Stilwell remembers, and "I had a hellova budget."

Once Smith took command Stilwell felt his weather eye. "I remember Beedle Smith's disparaging description of the Koumintang element we were supporting in Northern Burma, the forces of Li Ni. The object was to get him into Yunnan to raise trouble for the Chinese Communist regime. In my report I said he was not quite inside Yunnan but almost there. Then when he did report elements in we usually found corroborating evidence that they were not in.

"So Smith said—Beedle Smith, God bless him—said, 'All that guy does is skate up and down the wrong side of the border.' "[53] Li Ni and his brigands never amounted to much of a problem for Mao, and before long they settled in permanently on the side of the border they liked best, terrorized the peasants, and brought to market "almost a third of the world's illicit opium supply." Like many Agency offshoots, these rowdy precocious wards of the OPC developed over time into an important commercial asset for the CIA.[54]

Beedle Smith liked Stilwell, and after a number of months of pulling and hauling okayed his return to the regular military once he had recruited and broken in Desmond Fitzgerald to be his deputy for Asian affairs. "I'm approving this thing," he told Stilwell, who was in line to go to Korea as a regimental commander. "Just don't get your ass shot off." In Beedle's repertoire, this was a violin cadenza.[55]

Frank Wisner fared differently. John Bross was a polished senior OSS veteran and a lawyer who had come into the OPC in 1951 directly from a post as John McCloy's Assistant General Counsel in Germany. "The fact was," Bross says, "Frank got treated very badly. It was as much in Smith's manner as in what he said or wanted to do. Wisner had created this new and rather shiny organization to operate in conjunction with the high policy people in the government, so Smith gave him the treatment, which was Smith's idea of disciplining the troops. Beedle Smith was well regarded, but he was a *very* authoritarian fellow, like his Prussian grandfather, whom he strongly resembled. He saw Wisner as a target: here was a fellow who had been operating on his own, so he let loose on Wisner just to cut him down to size."[56]

Wisner hadn't gotten that far losing his composure before superiors, and so he held himself in and waded through Beedle's tantrums. Gratian Yatsevich surmises that Wisner must have appeared to quail at times before the autocratic Smith, and "if you did that he browbeat you mercilessly."[57]

Smith made his opinion of Wisner and his cronies plain within a month or so of assuming office, when he dispatched an underling to tour the Washington party circuit, where he was well aware a number of the operations people Frank lured to town were accustomed to congregate off-hours. Many had, after all, the senior management posts around the OPC because, as Polly Fritchey doesn't mind pointing out, "They had enough money of their own to be able to come down."[58] By Smith's lights, this made them "dubious security risks and dilettantes." "I don't care whether they were blabbing secrets or not," Smith allegedly declared. "Just give me the names of the people at Georgetown cocktail parties."[59] Approximately fifty left, probably the most inclusive slaughter of the operators until Admiral Turner struck. Wisner resisted wherever possible, sometimes countermanding an order Smith gave and covering the outcome by fudging the cable traffic.[60]

In 1952 Robert Amory replaced Loftus Becker as Deputy Director—Intelligence, and so sat in on meeting after meeting lit by one after the next of Smith's ulcer-triggered, Jovian flashes. He calls up one situation when Smith was venting his disgust at scientists like Vannevar Bush and James Conant, who shirked their military duty in laboratories and testing facilities. Amory had had enough. "As far as I'm concerned our scientists did as much as anybody in uniform to win the war," he blurted at Smith, who grabbed up a heavy glass ashtray and cocked his arm. Beside him, Amory saw, Wisner "shrank back in his chair."[61]

" 'Well,' " Amory remembers Smith relenting, " 'That's the spirit I like to see.' "

As if to drive one final excruciating nail into the kidney of Frank Wisner's pride, Smith authorized the establishment of a Project Review Committee. Its members—two, Stuart Hedden and Kenneth Giniger—were empowered to boil down the calculatedly overlong, prolix, and often enough deliberately misleading project proposals passed along from Wisner by way of the newly selected DDP, Allen Dulles. Smith now expected no more than a page or two.

Giniger was a mild-mannered, religiously oriented editor and publisher for whom Smith had conceived a lot of respect during the late war, and whom he expected to "cast a sort of businessman's, outsider's eye" on what was going on. "There was a lot of fairly harebrained stuff coming up," he observes now, including "a scheme to assassinate Stalin." This got by the DDP and reached the Project Review Committee in good part because "Wisner and Dulles were basically very sympathetic to any type of operational scheme, and they would tend to let things go to the Review Committee rather than turn them down themselves because these were their boys proposing these things."[62]

Giniger was also uneasy in 1952 about a month or so of controversial theatrical performances and lectures being underwritten by the CIA as part of a big blowout mounted by the Congress for Cultural Freedom in Paris. The Congress was organized in June 1950 by Melvin Lasky, founder of the German literary magazine *Der Monat*, and funded by the CIA through money Lovestone passed.[63] This was a particular favorite of Wisner's, who liked to hobnob with artists and intellectuals, and brought in avant-garde luminaries like the Nabokov brothers and Stephen Spender, the editor of *Encounter*, as spokesmen for the West. Giniger also went after "a lot of commercial front operations that were enriching people and that were basically purposeless, especially in book publishing."[64] Giniger was increasingly put off at the ease with which operators could walk into the local stations and emerge with "pockets full of counterpart money." Lovestone made him dolorous.

Wisner himself maintained an intense interest in phrasing and shaping the propaganda originating in the Agency—often laboring over releases personally for hours, to the despair of colleagues fighting for a moment of his overscheduled time—and soon became resentful of Giniger's unceasing quibbles and intrusions. No man is a hero to his editor. "Wisner disliked me actively," Giniger notes, with resignation. "I was an obstacle man."

The summer of 1951 the guard changed. "Basically," Lyman Kirkpatrick says, "Jackson was a better intelligence officer than Dulles, but the two didn't get along terribly damn well together," so Bill Jackson slipped out and returned briefly to Wall Street. ("You perfidious little bastard!" a bystander overheard Smith greet Jackson soon after he got the news.)[65] Allen Dulles went up to Deputy Director. Wisner ascended to DDP. By then Beedle had decided that penning the OPC and the OSO up together only led to more opportunities for the "constant feuding and bickering between the two offices" Kirkpatrick in particular decried, and OSO professionals were especially maddened by the extent to which their OPC colleagues clogged up the information flow with expensive dreck pawned off by émigré papermills.[66] They could not coexist; they must be merged, completely. As the OSO's Assistant Director for Special Operations, Lyman Kirkpatrick sat down with his opposite number on the OPC side, Colonel Kilburn (Pat) Johnson (the son of Ironpants Johnson) and worked out precisely how the counterpart units would now be integrated. For the next year Kirkpatrick jumped around the world combining the stations in the field and the divisions in Washington. Desk chiefs were selected alternately from the competing organizations, and a lot of the OPC volunteers abroad came home, so that, one veteran noticed, "the OPC largely dried up in the field."[67]

In Washington, at the senior levels, Wisner's appointees predominated. Gerry Miller continued to run Western Europe, Kermit Roosevelt looked after the Near East, Desmond Fitzgerald oversaw the Far East, and Frank Lindsay remained responsible for the Soviet Bloc. A carryover from FBI days, J. C. King, managed Latin America. While he was willing to move Frank Wisner up to DDP without argument, Smith intended to install the nitpicking Kirkpatrick as overall operations chief to function as a governor on the precipitous attorney. Before the appointment could go into effect Lyman contracted poliomyelitis—apparently on a junket to Bangkok to try and calm down a tiff between the OSO and OPC chieftains—and while he endured his long, painful, limited recovery the promotion itself went to Richard Helms.

Helms too was intended to lay down a cold spray of realism across the planning process.[68] He too harbored doubts about the efficacy—the use—of big subversive action takeouts, especially the paramilitary extravaganzas. Overall, Helms still believes, "Most of us who had known Frank felt he was a good choice to be head of the DDP. He knew the various movers and shakers around the State Department of those days, and this would definitely be an asset." Helms welcomed

Wisner as a "sensible fellow, a good leader, and certainly a very hard worker." In many areas Wisner had developed into "a careful planner. He wanted to work over every detail, particularly everything that was going to be published, clandestinely or otherwise. One of his great phrases was: 'Let's see if we can't find some language to cover this.' "[69]

To the incessant pressure, the breakouts, the regular flaring-up of something approaching emergency-room semihysteria around the DDP Richard Helms contributed balance, the assurance of continuity. "Wisner like most lawyers was more interested in ideas and themes than in administration, or budgets, so he was prepared to leave these things to me," Helms says now. Helms found it wiser—and safer—to cool inspirations down more often than he approved anything.

Colleagues remember him prowling the offices after their occupants had checked out for the night, shuffling together and locking up the strew of classified documents more imaginative leaders like Wisner and Dick Bissell left around the desks and conference tables. At forty Richard Helms had matured into an agile professional with something of the mien of a transplanted British civil servant, what with his vests and sedate garters and the steadily deepening widow's peak where began the sleek hair curling up shaggy at the nape. Helms had a way of planting his elbows on his desk and regarding each visitor, his scant lips blocked off by bladed palms, his narrow eyes smouldering reflectiveness. Helms intended to survive.

❏

Perhaps it cost Wisner more than anybody realized to weather the long Smith restructuring. "Beedle Smith I just don't think *liked* Frank," Wisner's widow says. "Smith was very very intelligent, very tough, and quite a mean man," and she recurs to Norie Smith, "a nice woman, but forever cowering in the background."[70] During the early months Wisner repeatedly considered resigning, but Chip Bohlen, by then an intimate and a regular lodger at Wisner's Georgetown house in summer, applied his notable persuasiveness and talked Wisner out of the idea. He could expect support. As Smith drafted reforms, and Kirkpatrick worked on Smith to scrap the OPC and incorporate the culls in an expanded OSO, Wisner appealed to Dulles, who carried the case to Smith convincingly enough to protect Wisner's autonomy for the moment. Tom Powers mentions one appeal by Wisner through Richard Bissell to Averell Harriman to keep the OSO from scuttling a project.[71] The undertaking continued, but this was not a technique to rely on a second time. In Washington personal chits tended to wilt fast, and reputations which depended on favors got bushwacked in the cloakrooms.

Subordinates felt this turbulence at the top secondhand. Once Albania started souring James McCargar would find it all but impossible to arrange a conference with Wisner. "After three days of ducking me he told me I could walk with him to his car," McCargar recalls. "I was furious. That wasn't the usual Wisner. The usual Wisner, you walked into his office and you got an impression of power. You recognized it and you deferred to it."[72]

As pressure built up Wisner's support people began to notice, as one remarks, "a funny physical tic which I could never understand. If he was thinking about something, or you were pressing him for some kind of an answer, he would flex and unflex his hands and you would see the muscles playing in the lower arm, and then he would do the same thing with his jaw muscles, so that you got this kind of muscle flexing thing going on all the time. . . . You didn't know whether that presaged some kind of a dreadful *strain*, or something. Still, I never heard Frank raise his voice to anybody. He could be cutting if he wanted to. And abrupt."

Outsiders found Wisner's staff meetings both quixotic at times and unpredictable, "not exactly overflowing the milk of human kindness," as Jack Blake remarked.[73] Until the end Frank would not hesitate to "saw you in half if you didn't perform," one subordinate remembers,[74] while another still shudders at the extent to which Wisner dressed down one chief of station in Rome before his assembled staff.[75] His pattern of assigning the same chore to as many as five subordinates and pressing them all produced more confusion than results, and kept him busy sorting among what reports he got. It remained a daily effort to preserve that aura of confidence, of control, of keeping his own counsel whatever the provocation while never discussing meaningful details of the business with anybody unless that person was immediately concerned. Wisner's working days started very often as early as eight and went straight through until eight or nine, when on many evenings he would ease himself into a dinner jacket he kept on hand in his office closet and bustle out directly for a party. Polly phoned sometimes to make sure he kept the schedule. Those State Department contacts especially remained vital to his position. "It was against nature for a man to work as hard as Frank did without something giving way," Joe Bryan says now.[76]

Under everything was deepening a very nearly obsessive sense that *he* had been selected to captain the global battle of Gog against Magog, his was the responsibility, his the sacrifice. Several of his best people, men he sent out, died abruptly on sensitive missions, apparently terminated by the KGB. He must evoke everything, consider everything, decide everything. "Even when I was there it was my hunch that some of the decisions he made were hastily taken," Tom Braden says. "In minutes. There was never any sense of delegation. He made every decision. Frank wasn't just a hard driver, he was a nervous driver, although I don't think he was much of an organizer. He spent interminable hours on what seemed to me insignificant details, endless time on telephones with newspaper men like Scotty Reston among others trying to keep something unimportant out of *The New York Times*."[77]

Stories made the rounds about confrontations with assistants he felt had botched assignments during which Wisner's inculcated self-possession entirely broke down. He railed; he leveled overwrought accusations; most ominously at moments he carried it far beyond the project, the subject at hand, the intent of the meeting, and drifted into charges and projections which left his auditors startled afterward, concerned that what they confronted wasn't just irrelevant but *irrational* by any reasonable analysis, leakage from some dimension in Frank Wisner's mentality nobody wanted to acknowledge. They watched his flushed jowls, his chinklike flashing eyes, the twig of blood vessels darkening as it forked up around the massiveness of his temples. There were no answers to satisfy such intensity.

All this happened rarely, and mainly at the office. During off-hours Frank somehow juggled his prominence around several of the choicer floating Georgetown salons with ambitions as a serious weekend sportsman and farmer. "I grew up in a household that was regularly filled with Charlie Thayer, Chip Bohlen, Llewelyn Thompson . . . ," Wisner's oldest son observes. His beloved father's namesake and himself a top U.S. Foreign Service officer, young Frank in middle age can spook acquaintances by his uncanny likenesses to his father a long generation earlier: also husky/chunky, an identical smooth baldness, the need to chainsmoke to relieve certain pressures, a weakness for formal, graven speech which skirts the sanctimonious. "Mother and father entertained a great deal," he muses now, astounded—like his siblings—at the remarkable *density* of the lives of their elders. "In those days it was a different Washington, it was a Washington in which the press and Congress and the Executive Branch all sat down and talked. Generally over dinner. A great deal was done at dinner. We were packed off, we weren't part of it."[78]

The blast and heat Senator Joseph McCarthy was putting on the Executive Branch just then had started to reach Wisner by the early fifties. Several of the Soviet specialists whose vision of internal process in Russia was frustrating to the Neanderthals in Congress were central to Wisner's social circle. George Kennan had returned abruptly from his short stint as ambassador to the Soviet Union non grata in either capital. The Right resented Bohlen, and took it out on Charles Thayer, his brother-in-law, against whom a vicious whispering campaign proceeded, based partly on allegations of sexual improprieties, to which his faithfulness to Carmel Offie over the years was counted as contributory evidence.[79]

A number of leaders in the Rumanian emigration had managed to attach themselves to Wisner. He entertained for the dethroned King Michael in Washington, and Rica Georgescu and his children—several of whom Wisner intervened to pressure the Rumanians to let out—[80] became regulars around the household. Other Rumanians "pressed on Frank all the time," Larry Houston recollects. " 'Omigod, here they come again,' " Houston remembers Frank groaning, searching for a back door.[81] In time it would become apparent that Princess Tanda Bragadiru, Frank's great good friend throughout the Bughouse mission, was in constant touch with the Communist regime's diplomatic representation in Paris, where she had resettled after 1945; her relationship with Wisner prompted widespread inquiries by FBI agents and military counterintelligence probers hoping to touch bottom as regarded the "Bucharest Incident."[82]

Within the Agency itself the implacable security director, Colonel Sheffield Edwards, entertained doubts about certain of Wisner's private contacts. One report homes in on the Wisners' "close social" friendship with the Alsop brothers. In 1953 Frank conceded that "Mrs. Wisner is very active socially and feels that she has every right to continue these friendships so that as a result the Wisners do entertain and see the Alsop brothers quite frequently." He admitted to frequent calls from Mr. Joseph Alsop "at the office. These calls are innocuous but they are embarrassing to Mr. Wisner."[83]

"Frank Wisner spent a great deal of time with people like Joe Alsop," remarks another member of the Wisner crowd, the prominent Time, Inc., journalist Charles J. V. Murphy. "There was a group, I've forgotten what it was called, they used to meet on Sunday evenings. . . . They used to go from one house to the other—people from the State Department, various people, mostly social people, and they would play games. A great deal of drinking. On Sunday night, always the worst of all nights to drink, with a hard week ahead of you.

"Frank loved the social life. Frank loved to sing, two or three of them would get together around the piano."[84] The Alsop brothers were usually there—Stewart, Joe, occasionally John—and sometimes George Kennan would turn up, and Tommy Thompson, and Kay and Phil Graham, even once in a great while Jock and Betsy Whitney.

Keyed up, excited by the bantering, Wisner could not bear to have the evening end. "Ah, just look around," Elizabeth Graham remembers a beaming Wisner exclaiming. "Have you ever seen so many beautiful women in one room in your life?"[85] Stimulus fed on stimulus. It would get late, and others would leave, Robert Amory says, "and Frank would say, 'Come on, it's too good, we've got to continue this conversation.' And so you'd have one more drink that you didn't need to have, and kick the can around a while longer, and maybe you'd get home Monday morning at two or two-thirty. It was exhausting."[86]

It was also claustral in ways nobody seemed to recognize. Arthur Schlesinger had maintained his OSS associations, and sometimes on a weekend when he happened to find himself in Washington he'd stop by. "Everybody knew everybody else, of course," he says. "All old personal friends. Bohlen, the Alsops, Dick Bissell. You couldn't help feeling the institutional dynamic at work at those times—they knew best, they decided who was to know what. There really wasn't any sense of accountability. I thought the whole thing was modeled on the British system. . . ."[87]

This was the top, whatever came out of conversation in one or another of these charming Washington town houses, stepped off the antique stones of P Street or O Street or tucked away behind Georgetown on Connecticut Avenue or above a Terrace. Littered with heirloom furniture, a clutter of billet-doux scrounged from all around the world, wherever American power projected itself. Bechsteins and Tibetan funeral tapestries, Moroccan valets and subliterate Colombian kitchen wenches, Iranian scrolls under glass and Hellenistic half-busts in porphyry. Between the foyer umbrella stand and the midwinter lushness of giant ferns in the conservatory the pheremones of command and control coming off these ambassadors and Undersecretaries were potent, pervasive, *irresistible* when crisis was up. If anybody in Washington, it was the Wisners of the period who managed to collect the densest concentration of what Frank Lindsay termed the "old boy network of political-military people involved in

World War II, many from the foreign service, people who think the same way and conclude, in effect: how can we each of us go about selling this thing to our superiors?[88] By this measure, the rumor that Frank Wisner had now become the fourth most influential personality around the government wasn't farfetched. Near enough the Potomac, power seems to replenish daily energy as convincingly as sleep. Contemporaries found Wisner "still gay, almost boyishly charming, cool yet coiled, a low hurdler from Mississippi constrained by a vest."[89]

Another side survived: this Frank Wisner's children felt, if intermittently, in perhaps its purest form. Young Frank remembers fragmentary weekends, especially at the farm. The Locust Hill farm was three hours north along the Maryland shore near Galena. "Often if he got there late Saturday afternoon he would be gone again early Sunday. He kept calling in. Even there he would work terribly hard. He was still physically very strong, and he liked to stay well exercised. As little boys my brother Ellis and I would work with him—chopping thistles, cutting wood, planting trees."[90] A photograph of Wisner and one of the boys catches Wisner in front of the barn, tossing spillover up onto the tailgate of a flatbed truck heaped high with silage. His hands clutch a great bunched wad of corn silk; beneath a shapeless, beanie-like cap his full face appears relaxed for once: gratified.

The Wisner daughter Wendy (Elizabeth), born in 1947, is struck in retrospect that both her parents were making a statement in using the farm the way they did: "My father would not allow us to join the Chevy Chase Country Club. He said it developed a 'chit' mentality—you know, you get a hamburger and you sign a chit. We ended up on the farm every summer and at all our holidays. My best buddy was the kid of the guy who worked for us there. Really, it was bare feet and horses and manure *all-my-childhood.* Not tennis and Fishers' Island."[91]

Whenever possible the Wisners carted personal friends up for the weekends and holidays, often the John Grahams or the more presentable among the operators, or Tracy and Janet Barnes. A regular duck-hunting buddy, Harry Sears, owned the next spread. Automobiles came and went, and frequently Wisner himself cooked. "From his time in the South he loved certain kinds of foods," Ellis says, "okra and all that. And one of my clearest images is him workin' in his garden. And he worked like hell in that garden, although mother might say not always to greatest effect. I can remember him on those hot days, sweating like hell. We had a paddle tennis court, and he didn't mind playing that, but he wasn't particularly good. I never saw him play golf. . . .

"So dad used to cook up crab gumbos. That was the big deal, whenever you would do that, and of course mother would say he made a total mess of the kitchen. I remember one day getting in a big basket of blue crabs, and getting the basket open. And of course, you know, those guys can move like hell across your arm. . . .

"I think if there's a time when, you know, there can be an air in the evening or something, and I have my memories of dad, it's often cookin' out of doors, summertime. He did swordfish, stuff like that. Having to baste the damn stuff all the time. How you can use an Italian Wishbone kind of dressing before you barbecue it? That's one of the things that sticks. The farm was the other major thing in his life. . . . It was part of the building of his character."[92]

As Washington speeded up, and Wisner got sucked steadily closer to the axle of the centrifuge, the farm at Galena offered traction, purchase, a way of distancing himself. A place to retain some hold on his origins, enrich the soil, design windbreaks, conserve, and reinvigorate. "My background?" he told one appreciative Virginia gentleman of Colonial ancestry. "Joe, I come from so deep in the country I had to get up extra early all the time I was a youngster to sweep the coon farts out of the kitchen."[93]

So Maryland could refresh for the moment *and* authenticate everybody's bearings. Young Frank was old enough to appreciate the artfulness it took for his father to remain articulate and friendly and very funny at times yet firm, determined to "push his children forward to the edges of their talents. . . . He set extremely high standards of what constituted correct conduct and honor, the old-fashioned sense of goodness and decency."[94]

Sometimes they let him down. Wendy was well aware of their father's disappointment that neither of the older boys took competitive sports seriously, and even at fifty he could easily beat either one in a footrace over the flat. He could lash out, she acknowledges, but mostly "he was the peacemaker when my mother and I fought." Especially on those long weekend car rides headed toward the Eastern Shore, Wendy reminisces, her father was a dependable fount of goofy jokes, of comic/exotic menus stuffed with giggle-provoking rhymes like nice and mice, coatamundi and salimundi. These alternated with "fabulous, mysterious ghost stories," or passages of David Copperfield read aloud.

She felt an urgency sometimes in his need to pass on what was best about himself, and especially to her and the last-born, Graham.

"He was absolutely fierce about honor," she says, and calls up one conversation he sat her down for. "He felt so deeply about it. I must have been maybe twelve at the time. He said: 'You know that story about George Washington and the cherry tree? In my book George Washington doesn't score for telling the truth. The truth is ground 0, the truth is what you do after telling the truth, that's what gives you the plus points.' "

A courageous and reflective woman, Wendy has had time to ponder the implications. Such an uncompromising ethic. "I balance the person who said that," she remarks slowly, "off against the person whose life was clouded with so many necessary not-truths. If you keep secrets, you've got to be lying along the way, you don't tell everybody everything, you know.

"I see a real conflict there, two different people living side by side inside the same head."[95]

17

THE SCRAMBLING KNIGHTS TEMPLAR

With Dwight Eisenhower's election victory in November 1952 the intelligence kaleidoscope rotated. Beedle Smith moved over—whether up or down was hard to ascertain, but he was not happy—to Undersecretary of State. Allen Dulles moved up to Director of Central Intelligence.

This wasn't by any means the foregone conclusion it appeared. Smith himself had at one phase or another dangled the CIA directorship before William Jackson and Gordon Gray, and while the Eisenhower cabinet posts were under discussion made it a point to sit down with the President-elect and air his "reservations about Allen's administrative capacity." He preferred Lyman Kirkpatrick. It appears that Smith committed himself to Dulles when Allen accepted the Deputy Directorship; Allen seems to have anticipated that Beedle was quite capable of sandbagging him, and preempted Smith by making sure that Foster—already designated as Secretary of State—locked Eisenhower in ahead of time.[1] As late as January 12 there was evidently some question, because Allen told David Bruce he wasn't "personally keen about the job," since it was likely to consume the rest of his life and cut him off from the "varied occupations which interest him."[2]

* * *

This was a transition, Frank Wisner's widow emphasizes, beset with anxiety for Frank. "At that point," Mrs. Fritchey says, "you may remember that General Donovan came back in and made a great pitch. There was a great deal of talk in the newspapers that he wanted again to be made director. Donovan was known to feel that Frank was too young to be in charge of the operations side of the house, and Frank turned from having liked General Donovan enormously to being rather unhappy with him."[3]

Wisner had been subjected for years to a series of battering, encroaching memos from Donovan to Smith which reverberated through Wisner's efforts. Always a punishing infighter, Donovan concentrated his attentions on precisely the undertaking which meant the most to Wisner, and which Frank fully realized always carried the most potential to veer straight off its track and into the newspapers to wreck his career—rollback in Eastern Europe. Wild Bill had moved on his own to stake out whatever assets looked useful to him, of which a number were indispensable to Wisner's own dreams of softening up the Soviet Bloc. Now, suddenly, Donovan seemed determined to ram through his personal liberation movement, and trusted that the CIA would contribute all it could.

One letter Donovan directed at Smith before Beedle moved down from Governor's Island leaves no doubt as to the old hero's omnivorousness. "Dear Bedell:," he starts right out. "In the matter of the projection into Russia proper in accordance with our talk, I have done the following." The following included a talk "with McCloy who appreciates its necessity and will help in his area in all respects, including housing, screening of applicants and assisting in collection of intelligence and establishment of freedom stations." Donovan had already "arranged with Lovestone for his particular native helpers" for intelligence collection, broadcasting, and "direction of émigrés." Dewitt Poole of the Free Europe Committee had agreed to "use of his transmitter in broadcasting into the Soviet area." Merle Fainsod of Harvard will provide a dozen academics to debrief defectors. With everything thus preprocessed, Donovan informs Beedle, "It will be necessary to find an effective, understanding man in your organization to tie in the different American elements engaged in this enterprise." Donovan is especially disquieted by rumors that the secret intelligence and subversive operations are operating on their own, since separating the two could "mess up your agency before you step in to take charge."[4]

In succeeding months Donovan regaled Smith with complaints about the defector program in Germany, about the underutilization of the remnants of the Vlasov army (ex-OSS sidekicks Serge Oblensky and W. Stafford Reid were pushing their own "brief plan for the penetration of the USSR by the use of a nucleus-force of some 45,000 former anti-Bolshevik Russian veterans who are available at once for organization and training into guerrilla units under joint U.S. and Russian leadership").[5] Donovan alerted Beedle to a manifesto prepared for presentation to Andrei Vishinsky in behalf of "500 Soviet exiles." To assure coverage (and keep the pressure on) "Winchell has been alerted." Donovan wants "indirect support," and to guarantee this "Frank Wisner has already been informed by Bert Jolis of the individuals concerned with this project."[6]

So month after month the phantom of OSS-past reappeared to breathe down Wisner's neck, second-guess his intentions, jeopardize his emerging purposes. Strategic leaks to columnist Walter Winchell became particularly maddening. By 1951 Allen Dulles was intervening where he could to damp Bill down and draw him off. Fielding Donovan's latest memos on "the organization of the groups abroad," Dulles praises "the plan as an excellent one," and claims to being "glad you are lending a hand." He closes with regrets about an injury to Wild Bill's arm: "I understand though, from mutual friends, that the newspaper account of your participation in a gun duel was exaggerated."[7]

Dulles's timeworn instinct to deal with a personal problem as a conciliator, not a puncher, was appreciated around the raw young CIA. He'd salved Donovan's ego, and he had kept him out. When Dulles had first come in and trumped Frank to emerge as the initial Director at Plans Wisner had been "sad," Polly acknowledges, even "bitterly disappointed.[8] For some months following the appointment Wisner had subjected Dulles to the same treatment he had accorded Hillenkoetter: he simply couldn't scratch together the time to attend very many staff meetings of the Clandestine Services, and so he rarely showed up or sent along a deputy.[9]

Such insouciance was possible for the moment because Smith was sitting on Dulles too, one bystander noticed, "with a hard ass." "Allen," Beedle countered to Dulles's suggestion of an administrative change at one meeting, "you don't know how to run *any*thing. What's the biggest thing you've ever run?"[10] "Allen isn't a *bad* administrator," Smith told one associate. "It's just that he's entirely *innocent* of administration."[11] Tom Braden can recall an errand that took him across to the bank of senior offices in the rat-ridden K Building. Without warning the shriveled, leathery figure of the Beedle popped into the corridor and bawled, toward the door of the adjoining suite:

"Dulles, God damn you! Get in here!"[12] Smith grabbed one bumbling Wall Street banker Allen brought down to tell him that he was probably the stupidest man he had ever met.

"Yessir," the assistant said.

"And in fact," Smith continued, "I've often thought of myself with my hands around your neck."[13]

"My God, if he is that terrifying now," one early subordinate murmured, "imagine what he must have been at full weight!"[14] It seemed a long way from the sedate, acquisitive hush of Sullivan and Cromwell.

Under all this flak Dulles cultivated his own perspectives. Leonard Mosley quotes Allen as waving off the possibility that Wisner might somehow object to being bumped down a level with a nonchalant: "Oh, he won't mind. We're friends. He's worked under me before."[15] In fact Wisner was undeniably miffed, Tom Braden saw, so "Allen attempted to be nice to Frank, but there was nevertheless a wariness about this young and—in Allen's mind—by reputation somewhat irresponsible man." There had been mistakes too substantial to brush aside, along with any number of secondary scorchers charring up the early records. Braden cites such gratituitous brainstorms as sending a couple of operatives disguised as hard hats to Sixty-Fourth and Madison to airhammer a tremendous hole into the pavement at the peak of the workaday traffic to find out precisely how the Manhattan authorities would react.[16] OSO careerists watched. "What next?" Jack Blake remembers thinking. "Can you trust them out there alone?"[17]

Like Smith, Dulles angled for some control by interposing his own people. He convinced Smith to appoint the socially prominent Robert Thayer as Senior Representative to France, setting off a row with the far more experienced OPC chief in Paris, Larry de Neuville, and with de Neuville's ouster sacrificing what little reliable access the Agency retained to the Deuxieme Bureau. To make quite sure nothing escaped his notice pertaining to the all-important Eastern European projections, Allen installed as senior vice president of Radio Free Europe one of Tom Dewey's advisers on ethnic politics, the Russian émigré who represented Donovan with the refugee governments in London and later filled in at Sullivan and Cromwell, Bernard Yarrow.[18]

Wisner's harum-scarum approach to staffing kept Allen off balance. Tom Braden was around the day Dulles worked up several questions about the Italian situation, and sent for the head of the OPC desk for Italy. "And a scruffy guy he was," Braden says. "He looked like the type of a guy that would knife you in the back in an alley, and had done it a number of times. Allen took an instant dislike to his mannerisms, his language. For all I know he was a hellova good operator, but he didn't speak English, he spoke high-school English, and this did not endear him to a Princeton-educated diplomat, which Allen was."[19] Quietly, but with a will, Dulles set about the gentrification of the CIA. "The social side was very important to Allen," Walter Pforzheimer observes, "and occasionally it warped his judgment."[20]

One priceless asset Dulles cornered soon after he set up at the Agency was a compounding measure of solicitous—avid—support from James J. Angleton. Angleton often had felt somewhat rebuffed by the brusque General Willard Wyman while Wyman ran operations at the OSO, and Kirkpatrick, while acknowledging Angleton's technical brilliance as well as his talent for talking people around, remained wary even then of Angleton's penchant for building up "an empire within the CIA which was untouchable," quite likely to bring down "damages" in the end "of a very high order."[21] So Angleton lost little time in bonding his own prospects to the romantic, accessible-seeming Dulles, and, another contemporary comments, wound up his Beria. Dick Bissell credits Angleton with supplying the nudge it took to guarantee that Wisner got the DDP plum when Dulles stepped up to Deputy Director.[22] Wisner hadn't yet shaken off his wartime distaste for the counterintelligence mentality, but Angleton saw beyond that. Frank Wisner was solid on dogma. They both were utterly convinced, Robert Amory maintains, that "every coincidence was KGB-inspired, and that a Communist heart beat in every Socialist."[23]

With Allen's implicit connivance Angleton proceeded to cast over the heretofore amorphous young Agency a tightening pall of apprehension, an awareness that Dulles's interests were looked after, widely, everywhere. One prominent official supposedly murmured in bed to his wife a few words bearing on Beedle Smith's distaste for both Dulles brothers; the next morning Allen called him in and required him to explain himself. "You'd better watch out," Dulles suggested, cheerfully. "Jimmy's got his eye on you."[24] Another senior man made reference over a casual country weekend with outsiders to a verbal backhander Smith dealt Dulles a few days previously. "That Monday morning when I walked into the office," the aide recounts, "Dulles said, 'What's this about your going around characterizing my relationship with Beedle?' And my heart absolutely sank. I always blamed that on Angleton. He taught me a lesson, planted a bug in that country house. Angleton did a lot of that, he was forever coming into Allen's office with stories about what somebody said to somebody else at dinner last night." With this the sobriquet "No-knock Angleton" began to attach itself to the starved-looking counter-intelligence virtuoso. Colleagues attempted to chuckle. It *was* amusing, but "Jesus Christ," as one of them remarked, "that was a lot of power."

Along with providing cover for the ascendant Dulles, Angleton persevered in piecing together *below* the conventional country-desk and analytical levels, an intelligence complex subject to him alone. Material he could make available—or, as Bill Colby later complained, choose not to—to the Director exclusively. Already prepared to arrogate to himself and the few he trusted all but supernal powers—"It is inconceivable," Angleton would blurt to a closed-door panel of the Church Committee, "that a secret intelligence arm of the Government has to comply with all the overt orders of the Government"—James Angleton arranged for an unauthorized and completely illegal mail-intercept program to ferret out "foreign involvement" in American affairs.[25]

This did not inhibit Angleton from steaming open (or overseeing Sheffield Edwards's hardnosed minions in steaming open) the international correspondence of the AFL in order to find out who *really* wound up with the several million dollars a year passed along through Lovestone and Irving Brown. Satisfied concerning the money, he proceeded to solidify a close, mutually respectful association with Jay Lovestone himself, and there were many undisclosed tradeoffs. This was the sort of muscular utilization of intelligence resources which impressed Allen Dulles. Tom Braden was actually dispensing the currency those start-up years, but apparently it suited both old-timers to keep Braden chugging in the dark.

Confident of Jim's loyalty, Dulles accorded Angleton a great deal of leeway in maintaining and deepening his well-worked contacts in Italy, from the papal secretariat to functionaries in Communist chief Togliatti's apparat. He remained on tap to the regular Agency personnel in the Rome station, or not, as circumstances warranted. Dulles recognized right away that none of the Arabists in Kermit Roosevelt's Near East Division were temperamentally right for dealing with the gunslingers founding Israel. Angleton's decade of sympathetic association with the Haganah veterans, from Ben Gurion and Sharatt to Teddy Kolek, left him the favorite to supervise the "Israeli Account." His years of coddling the Israelis would provide Angleton much deep-seated satisfaction, along with recurrent stomach pains. Angleton welcomed solemnly each enlargement of responsibility; even at that time, Kim Roosevelt remarks, Angleton remained "intensely secretive, and I don't think anyone else knew an awful lot about what he was doing, including Allen Dulles."[26]

It would remain a puzzle how Angleton was able to extrapolate from a mid-level staff function his all but transcendental influence. What outsiders couldn't factor in was the compelling quality of Jim Angleton's presence, the dutiful, devoted, *authentic* mannerisms he'd evolved to convey the urgency of the crisis, the sacrifices which he and his men were prepared to continue to make to seal the ramparts of the West. Who presumed to rebut, watching Jim wind one long pinstriped shank ever tighter around the other, tap out one more Virginia Slim, attempt one last time not merely in words but more, really, by way of that knitted, knotted, weaving, bobbing, wincing, stalking *lexicon* of body language—who undertook to challenge that? Angleton's small, sculpted head—each hair combed back, wet, to expose a central part of Edwardian integrity—craned forward: Angleton's mocha eyes shone, and as his lips parted, without warning a grin would irradiate that famously hollow face. A boon, utterly unexpected, to complement the fillip of true warmth that flickered and burnished Angleton's genuine midwestern inflections.

Once Allen took over, a measure of serenity appeared to settle upon the Agency. Dulles's eight-year directorship would later rouse nostalgia as perhaps the apex of the CIA's performance in the world, its "classic period." There was in fact some effort to sort things out, to recompute objectives and plan beyond the ever-looming crisis. Not many months before he left, Frank Lindsay was deputized by Wisner to convene a "Murder Board," to review "a lot of these operations which had been started up on short notice and panic, and go through them. We eliminated at least half of them."

Going beyond the operation-by-operation calculus of propaganda placements and bribes and useless leases and balloons in oversupply, Lindsay found himself disturbed by "rollback" projections for Central and Eastern Europe. Frank Lindsay had already gone to the mat with zealots from the Pentagon over requests for low-lying armies in the "denied areas" prepared to revolt "if we needed them."

It would be important, Lindsay was told, that we retain the capacity to "turn it off if we don't want it." "You turn it off just once," he responded, "and that will be the end of it. You don't play with people this way that are risking their necks."[27]

"A lot of senior OSO people," observes Tom Parrott, originally the deputy head of OPC's Soviet Union Division, "found it difficult to believe that the OPC was under a tremendous compulsion from the

Pentagon to have things like this in place—and they even had a date—by July 1, 1952. That was the date they projected for the outbreak of war. . . . I remember one time when some eager colonels came over from the Joint Staff. They had a special section for paramilitary warfare, it was called the Brown team, or the Rainbow team or something. Anyway—remember, this was already late 1950—they laid a requirement on us to have in place by the first of July of '52 people to sabotage every airfield in the Soviet Union. And I'm talking now about . . . about maybe like *fifty*. And Frank Lindsay, who was the chief of the Eastern European thing at the time—I was there in a staff capacity, as the overall operations man—Lindsay enthusiastically accepted that requirement. . . .

"You know, they were talking about . . . about mostly little airfields, the airfields in Russia at that time were dirt strips. So finally I said, well now, wait a minute, let's hold the phone here, will you tell us how you—you want us to sabotage every airfield. Will you tell us how you sabotage *one* airfield?

"And—there was a *deep* silence. These guys said, well, gee, uh, I guess we'll have to get back to you on that one. So that was the last we ever heard of that one."[28]

Thus Lindsay had lost some skin around the helter-skelter bureaucracy listening to the action types. The standing of covert around State and Defense was not improved by 1953, as both the WIN fiasco and apprehensions about the Albanian subversion continued to bubble through the floorboards. As he was picking up to separate from the Agency in the spring of 1953, Frank Lindsay was able to persuade Dulles to fund what Dick Bissell terms an "internal, no-holds-barred study of techniques, procedures that could be used to roll back the Communists in Europe." There was a project group created, and Lindsay came down when needed from his new position with the Ford Foundation in New York to chair a committee comprised of three of the younger, abler operators along with Bissell in a suite of offices set aside in one of the Agency's many temporary buildings, from where they "ranged around," Bissell says, "ragging our brains and other people's for ideas. The conclusions, I think, were essentially negative: There wasn't any collection of gimmicks you could use."

The Lindsay team wrote its report. Wisner took it in, Lindsay remembers, and kept his true response to himself. But Dulles was shocked. "Frank, you can't say these things," the normally blasé incoming Director burst out on looking over the findings. "We spent the whole of a Saturday going through the report that I'd written," Lindsay says, "sort of arguing over every word. I thought he was going to have a heart attack. I think I compromised, and agreed to water down here and there what I had said." The implications were vital: "Until Allen came in, no one had been that interested in this sort of thing." Even in its amended version, Lindsay discovered, his paper promptly "sort of disappeared."

Closer to Dulles's liking was the contingency planning underway in the paramilitary staff of the DDP just then. "The mission of the Agency," Bissell discovered, "was to identify stay-behind or potential stay-behind groups and train some of their members in techniques of guerrilla warfare, notably in communication, looking to the day when additional areas would be occupied by the Soviets and it would be possible to try to create behind Soviet lines the sort of underground that existed in France. . . . It was still believed that you could make preparations for stay-behind groups, for communicating with them for arms drops, or infiltration, this sort of thing. There was supposed to be a country plan written up for every Soviet bloc nation." Overall, Bissell says, "By the time I was briefed in, all this seemed to me the most unpromising activity I've never seen in government, almost ridiculous."[29]

❏

What stirred Dulles up, of course, was the extent to which "liberation," "rollback," had served as themes which he and his brother had energetically pushed on Eisenhower's campaign in 1952, and now felt honor bound to take up seriously. It raised nobody's spirits that WIN had barely been revealed—and by its perpetrators—as a flatfooted deception. To professional eyes, their adventures in Albania looked progressively more unpromising. When McCargar bowed out early in 1950 over the imposition of Hasan Dosti as chairman of the Free Albania Committee the OPC replaced him with a tough-minded regular army officer with a history in the Balkans, most recently in Bulgaria.

Like Lindsay and Bissell, Colonel Gratian Yatsevich went in at action levels subject to the concurrence of Averell Harriman; Yatsevich had served as a military attaché to the U.S. embassy in Moscow while Harriman was ambassador. Of recent Polish extraction, cosmopolitan, Harvard educated, with pert Baltic features and the instincts of a counterpuncher, the colonel had tried his luck before the war as a gold miner in Serbia. Throughout Yatsevich's first year on the project the Balli Kombetar leadership inside the Free Albania

Committee continued to lose its steam, and more and more the mountain fighters and palace bravos around King Zog came up with volunteers for Company 4000 near Waechterhof. Both drops and landings ran badly through 1951.

To many the explanation broke when Guy Burgess and Donald Maclean bolted for Moscow in May 1951. The disheveled Burgess had been holed up for much of his stint in Washington with Harold ("Kim") Philby. Within weeks of their spectacular flight Bill Harvey hashed together a 5-page memorandum which traced Philby's recent career and contacts, and asserted that Philby had to be a Soviet agent.[30] Beedle Smith immediately shipped off the damning Harvey material to "C," Stewart Menzies, in London, accompanied by a typically uncluttered cover letter: "Fire Philby or we break off the intelligence relationship."[31]

This provided a thought-provoking interlude for everybody involved with Albania. Like most Americans, Yatsevich found Philby "likeable and interesting, except for his high alcohol consumption." Gratian would count himself "fortunate that Philby had been whisked away that summer, just before he was to have accepted an invitation to join me on a holiday in Maine. . . . I always maintained a certain level of reserve with him, although I personally was not aware of the extent to which Philby was suspect until later, it just didn't sink into my head how much he might have damaged things."[32]

Yatsevich was perhaps lulled by the consideration that even after Kim got back to London, and a discreet investigation began, little improved in Albania. More men got caught, the few who escaped the machine guns and emplaced mortars around the target areas were soon served up at public trials and newspaper propaganda by the Tirana regime. As 1952 ended the Balli Kombetar leadership as well as the British were inclined to spare their wards another tumble through the meat grinder; what had started out as purportedly a "joint," or, until early 1952, a "coordinated" effort now landed by default on the Americans. King Zog visited America, and he and Gratian Yatsevich agreed to carry the fight with monarchists primarily. Members of the Royal Guard would serve under the experienced guerrilla tactician Hamit Matjani, who sapped and evaded the Italians and the Germans as well as the Communists.[33]

After that tactical operations started to take hold, or seemed to. The trials stopped; over OPC receivers in Greece messages started coming through in the designated codes. Three Sigurimi turncoats came out for debriefing and preparation for resistance projects. Bases went in among sympathizers in the Mati; their radio man, Tahir

Prenci, requested support ordnance; gold sovereigns and machine guns and transmitters and warm woolen clothes floated down for months into the pockets of anti-Communism from which the insurgency was intended to spread. By spring of 1953 the messages stressed general insubordination among the army and police, "final preparations" preliminary to a nationwide takeover. The moment had arrived for Hamit Matjani himself—who in the past had always entered Albania overland by secure routes known exclusively to himself and a few trusted followers—to parachute in. The OPC pilots inserted him and his lieutenants by prearrangement into Saint Gjergji, near Elbasan, on May Day, 1953.

In Washington optimism returned, although occasionally the details nagged. Radio teams in Greece kept noticing that the "fist," the key patterning established by their cipher man in the mountains, Tahir Prenci, had undergone an unexplained alteration. They attempted to inquire. The unlucky Prenci had fallen and broken his arm, according to what came back. Privately, the Agency's head of station in Greece, Al Ulmer, would concede that this venture had probably gone bad.[34]

The WIN hoax rankled. Worried, Gratian Yatsevich stopped by in Alexandria to hash through security problems with Zog and his entourage before Matjani went in. Yatsevich was again reminded, he recalls, of the "curious quirks in the Albanian personality. Zog once referred to somebody as being terribly reliable. And then when someone pointed out to him that that man had betrayed Zog to the Italians during the war he said, well, yes, but they gave him 20,000 Napoleons for that. . . ."[35]

Their battlefield would remain a political quagmire, Yatsevich could see that. With Angleton's help he and his Italian aides picked certain of the weaker plotters out of the Free Albania Committee in Rome and kept Joe Leib at arms length. Summer came, then autumn, and although the flow of heartening coded messages went back and forth, nothing in any way resembling an insurrection appeared to be materializing inside Albania.

Alongside the Reflecting Pool insiders from Paul Nitze and Robert Joyce to Sam Harpern had concluded that the thing was busted. Wisner shrugged them off. "It's a human weakness, a reluctance to give up on something that might be all right, to do something that might be ruthless in sacrificing somebody who might be a little bit uncertain," Colonel Yatsevich says.[36] And yet it came as a relief on New Year's Eve 1954, when Tirana Radio announced that Matjani and his followers were rotting in custody. The Sigurimi, backed up by

Soviet countersubversion experts, had concocted the uprising which charged up Wisner's spirits so. There followed a resounding show trial, a round of gruesome public executions, a nationwide dragnet operation. The purge left Hoxha more solidly in control of Albania than before, and delighted to crow in print at how successfully "our famous radio game brought about the ignominious failure of the plans of the foreign enemy. . . .[37]

Both Wisner and Dulles had "felt that all the available information was insufficient to make a firm decision to stop," Yatsevich relates. "There was enough wishful thinking around, perhaps, not to attribute sufficient weight to what was alarming." Wisner personally was "manifesting signs of stress." There was a recurrent irritability, and by that point he clearly "drank more than was good for him. He held it well, but you got physical symptoms—puffy features, that kind of thing. He smoked a great deal, and that is always a bad combination. . . . The indicators are rather subtle, when a chap feels rather hard pushed, especially with the hours he kept in the office and the kind of hours he kept outside the office. . . ."

Allen's involvement was dependable all along, but he was able, typically, to browse the margins, to overhang this high-risk project without venturing too close. "He had a kind of grandfatherly interest in things," Gratian says, which "reflected itself in telephone calls and brief meetings at his office. Even at his house. He was not cognizant of the Albanian operation in great detail, but every now and then he'd pick up on some little item or individual or organization that seemed to intrigue him. If you suffered a setback he would ask questions about that, or if you brought in a new personality he hadn't heard about before." Before long it had become Dulles's practice to bypass intermediary administrative levels, to reach down and deal directly with the operators themselves, "run things out of his hip pocket sometimes," Colonel Yatsevich says. "Or try to." With subordinates this engendered "rather a satisfying feeling, and made you feel that you were doing something important."[38]

This propensity of Dulles's to grope without notice into delicate ongoing operations inevitably told on Wisner. Frank had been greatly relieved when Dulles came in as Director in 1953 instead of Wild Bill Donovan, but even with that, his widow concedes, Wisner's satisfaction with Allen as a boss was "on-and-off." At that point a potentially lucrative business offer came in, but "Frank was so plainly fascinated by this whole business, and he just didn't want to go back to New York." One reason Wisner had shuddered at the prospect of Donovan's return was his perception of the general as a "publicity seeker." Now, it appeared shortly, "Allen, for whatever reasons, competition with his brother perhaps, was making everything much more public," Mrs. Fritchey remarks. "He went around, and made speeches all the time, and Frank felt deeply that the Agency and the whole operation should be quiet, small, non-public."[39]

Theirs became, Polly admits, something of a "love-hate relationship." Dulles soon exerted his own manner of indulgent geniality, a benign cunning Wisner remained at a loss effectively either to accept fully or stave off. Dulles's neo-Edwardian paternalism was so compelling that most of the emerging "barons" who looked after the branches and divisions and directorates and frequently—and openly—detested one another gradually slipped into venerating Dulles. Robert Amory, for example, the outspoken Harvard Law School professor who entered the Agency to replace Loftus Becker as head of the Intelligence Directorate in 1952, made no secret of his uneasiness about Jim Angleton and his methods while continuing to cherish Allen as "the member of his generation who meant the most to me, excepting only my own father."[40] Dulles was the sun now; month by month, he exerted his drag even on Wisner's loyal lieutenants. Before long top-level staff meetings turned into a jousting among the barons, a gut-deep struggle to see which one among these scrambling Knights Templar could best gratify their legendary chief.

Richard Bissell had known Wisner socially for years in Washington, and admired his charm and intelligence, while allowing that Frank "was not the most systematic thinker I've ever known." Bissell entered the Agency to fill in on the operations side full-time in 1954, and was quickly struck by what he labels Wisner's "strong sense of the believed enmity of the opposition. Let me shorten it—he was quite a suspicious person. Now, this is probably a goddamned good quality in an intelligence officer. But I thought Frank carried it too far; it came out for the most part as a suspicion of others in the Agency and in the intelligence community."[41] The problem became especially poignant for Frank, as month by month Dulles registered his fascination with the irrefutably brilliant Bissell.

Another problem for Wisner was the amusing and well-born Robert Amory, who caught Dulles's eye while teaching his kids to sail on Long Island Sound before the war. An old-family card-carrier in the Knickerbocker-Brook Club tradition, Amory's punchy, fearless commentary tended to cut through enough to sway Allen sometimes and even to denigrate by implication much of the superheated crypto-Crusader rhetoric in which both Wisner and Angleton often indulged. Amory scoffed outright when Wisner would attempt to electrify a meeting with announcements like: "We've just received word of the murder of one of our key agents in Austria and the kidnapping of another one in Singapore *both within twelve minutes!* That's the KGB sending back a message!" It annoyed Wisner whenever he and some top-level visitor were forced to wait as much as an hour in Dulles's outer offices while the director and Amory chuckled away on an interoffice line over what Frank regarded as unproductive gossip. At staff meetings it very often pleased Allen to throw out a subject, a project, like so much hamburger for the hounds, then watch his competing directorate heads scramble and dive in competition around the world until one came up with the results Dulles wanted.

"Right after Stalin died," Amory would recall, "Allen convened a meeting to try and anticipate who his successor was likely to be. General Cabell, the Agency's overall Deputy Director, was there, and Frank brought in George Kennan, who was back from the Moscow embassy, and Chip Bohlen, who would be replacing him. Both State Department regulars felt that Molotov was the likely choice; he had been the most loyal to and trusted by Stalin. I had been briefed, and my people all felt that Georgi Malenkov, who was a sleeper, would be the man. Within twenty-four hours Moscow radio announced Malenkov's ascendency. Frank was really peeved, he felt that my academicians were basically playing games, while his operatives should have come up with the scoop."

It continued to irk Wisner, to provoke what Amory calls his "petty-aggressive" side, as time after time Amory and his analysts of the "intelligence culture" lucked into answers first. When Washington discovered that Dick White would be moving across from chief of MI5 to chief of MI6, Allen put word out that he expected his people to find out on their own who would replace White at MI5. All stations were alerted. Amory simply arranged to dine with the head of the British Mission, Sir William Elliot, and after a "very mild Scotch or so" ventured, "Bill, just how is the new chief of MI5 or MI6 selected these days?" Elliot launched a disquisition—the time-worn procedures, the way the cabinet secretary was accountable for putting such a thing together—"and then he said, perfectly casually, 'And that's the way it's been with Roger Hollis.' "

There was a staff meeting on the subject the next morning at CIA. Allen went around the table soliciting opinions from Wisner, Helms, Larry Houston. "Have you got anything, Bob?" he asked Amory. Amory named the new director of MI5.

"Wisner almost fell over backward," Amory maintains, "and then he turned on Helms and told him, 'Christ, you just let Amory wipe our noses in shit!' "[42]

* * *

It was 1956 by then, of course, and Frank had been up and down a good many times. One complication all along had been the fact that the preponderance of his senior colleagues—as well as luminaries at State and Defense in a position to bail Wisner out or drive through initiatives he cared about—were doctrinally committed Democrats. Once Eisenhower took office in 1953 Truman's establishment "Wise Men"—Harriman, Bohlen, and Kennan especially—exerted very little carryover influence. At the new President's insistence Bohlen went out to direct the Moscow embassy, but the newly installed Secretary of State, Allen's edgy brother Foster, declined to be photographed with his ambassador and bemoaned Bohlen's intention of flying to Moscow a week or so ahead of his family, mercilessly advising Chip that such an action could open him up to "veiled charges of homosexuality."[43]

Such was the hysteria of the moment. A precisely orchestrated whispering campaign cost Bohlen's brother-in-law—and Wisner's close friend—Charlie Thayer his State Department berth. At Foster's request Wisner smoothed the "Charlie situation"[44] over with Bohlen. Another senior Department expert, the China specialist John Paton Davies, got dragged before board after board in an effort to trump up sufficient grounds to let him go and propitiate the rampaging Republican Right; exasperated, Foster simply fired him. Working closely with Wisner as a principal idea man on the Policy and Planning Staff, Davies had recommended hiring qualified anti-Soviet but pro-Mao fellow travelers to fabricate black propaganda, "The Tawney Pippet project,"[45] to exacerbate the inherent Sino-Soviet split. This proposal itself died; activists from the OPC's Psychological-Warfare Staff, who resented *any* intrusion, leaked word to investigators from the McCarthy Committee that it was Davies's intention to load up the government's payroll with unrepentant Commies.[46]

"As far as most of us were concerned," Richard Bissell emphasizes, "McCarthy was the domestic enemy." Wisner concurred in this, and demonstrated enough character to shelter and defend Charles Thayer when the fiercest howls arose. Angleton was especially irked, in that McCarthy's generally sloppy work lumped together traitors and fools.[47] Allen Dulles despised McCarthy; liberals took note approvingly of Dulles's willingness to refuse, politely (but firmly and publicly, openly risking his post) when Tail Gunner Joe demanded that the CIA dump Dean Acheson's son-in-law William Bundy for contributing to a defense fund for Alger Hiss years before. Under equivalent pressures, Foster continued to offer up political virgins to the dyspeptic Right.[48]

Nevertheless, gamesters that they were, the opportunity to rid themselves of assorted repulsive office-mates and insufficiently zealous summer soldiers by feeding doctored personnel files whole to the undiscriminating Wisconsin troglodyte tempted several around the Agency. Insiders credited Lyle Munson with slipping through the black hand on Thayer and Offie as well as testifying outright against Davies, etc.[49] Despite the passage of time Colonel John ("Frenchy") Grombach had continued to stymie the attempts by Lyman Kirkpatrick and others to integrate his venerable network, The Pond, into the established circuitry of the CIA. Grombach became "quite close" to Senator McCarthy when he was running wildest, and passed McCarthy's subcommittee investigators whatever paperwork looked damaging in hopes of undermining the damnable Agency. This thickened the file with which J. Edgar Hoover's agents were already cramming the subcommittee's maw.

Pushed, Dulles dredged up a Pond veteran still close enough to Grombach to elicit his confidence, and organized a double game. Allen arranged for his intermediary to kick back copies of everything McCarthy was looking at; then Dulles brought Angleton in, who produced the typewriter on which a lot of the more compromising material was written up; with Ray Rocca's assistance the CI forgers introduced into the flow of documents going up to the Senate such quantities of misleading and diverting sludge as to throw the McCarthyite investigators completely off track. Before long the Senator himself lost interest, and turned his siege guns against the U.S. Army.

18

THE COLOSSUS OF THE NORTH

It remained the overriding fact that Allen Dulles had become CIA Director by dint of Foster's influence. At sixty he regularly betrayed his bone-deep subservience to Foster, the way his voice dropped even over the telephone when Foster needed something, his resigned silence whenever Foster overruled his recommendations. Foster's agenda continued uppermost.

On March 5, 1953, Josef Stalin was inconsiderate enough to die on Foster. Anti-Stalinism had energized the incoming Secretary of State. In *Life* just before the elections, Foster trained his fire on the pusillanimous containment policy pursued by the Truman administration, a recipe for sacrifice and expenditure ". . . not . . . in order to be able to live *without* this peril—but to be able to live *with* it, presumably forever," as "gigantic expenditures unbalance our budget and require taxes so heavy that they discourage incentive" while at the same time "this concentration on military matters . . . transfers from the civilian to the military decisions which profoundly affect our domestic life and our foreign relations."

Meanwhile, the Republican leadership "wants and expects liberation to occur" in Eastern Europe, and proposes "task forces" to implement a "freedom program" which, while not calling for "a series of bloody uprisings and reprisals," was intended to "put heavy new burdens on the jailers" and induce "separation from Moscow."[1]

Such talk was humbug, Democratic speech-makers came back, particularly rollback in the East for nickels and dimes. The upcoming leadership had something in mind. It expected to confront the larger challenges with "brinkmanship," atomic weaponry—cheaper than conventional arms, "more bang for the buck"—while reducing and dissolving the Soviet (and hopefully the Chinese) hegemonies through inexpensive applications of subversive technique. What statesmanship couldn't manage the Agency had better: Allen liked to allude to the house that Beedle rebuilt as the State Department for Unfriendly Nations.

By 1953 and 1954 the Polish and—more and more—the Albanian efforts tasted sour against the memory; other ventures seemed promising. To break the logjam over Korea and get the peace talks moving, Eisenhower called for a National Intelligence Estimate to specify effective choices should the war continue. The Agency quickly drafted a six-part options study, led off by massive nuclear bombardment of Manchuria and scaled down level by level. The paper was distributed among the Western intelligence centers, and officers in the field made sure a copy was leaked to the Indian ambassador to Peking, Panikkar, confident that it would find its way to Chou En-lai. "Never were intelligence and disinformation more beautifully blended," notes one of the study's authors, who credits the presentation with producing the armistice.[2]

Eastern Europe remained too hard; suddenly, the summer of 1953, there arrived a sprinkle of success. In Persia a weepy semi-invalid with a dropsical nose named Dr. Mohammed Mossadegh had become the National Front's premier. Mossadegh whipped through the Iranian parliament, the Majlis, a 1951 bill which nationalized Iran's oil fields, including the preponderant holdings of the Anglo-Iranian Oil Company. This move wiped out a fifty-year-old concession negotiated by the then Anglo-Persian stock company for oil rights in nearly one-half million square miles of Iranian territory in return for change and 16 percent of the company's net profits. At Winston Churchill's instigation, the British government itself in 1913 bought 51 percent of Anglo-Persian to assure the Admiralty of fuel for its warships.[3]

The 1951 decree shook even the Labor government, and with the return of the Conservatives under Churchill the British brought down a worldwide boycott of Iranian oil, complete with cruiser patrols off the Abadan refinery. For two years the intransigent Iranians refused to come to terms. There was an oil glut, and the outraged

English saw no reason to cave in and concede the Iranians the sort of 50–50 split Aramco extended its Arabs.

American sympathies were unpredictable. Harry Truman's Attorney General was investigating the Stateside oil majors with an eye to breaking them up on antitrust grounds, while across town Acheson and his State Department tended to coddle the oil boys as "for all practical purposes, instruments of our foreign policy. . . ."[4]

By 1951 the relations between England and Iran had long been drama-laden. The British without ado had plucked up and dumped into exile in 1941 the coarse, tough, self-made army sergeant who grabbed off the Peacock Throne, Reza Shah, for coddling Nazi advisors. They installed his son, the callow Mohammad Pahlavi.

Even then the United States was something of a factor. From 1942 to 1948 a capable ex-New Jersey cop named Colonel H. Norman Schwarzkopf, U.S. Army, reorganized the Imperial Iranian Gendarmerie and set up a secret police instrumentality, SAVAK, to backstop the stripling Shah and suppress the Iranian Communist Party, the Tudeh. American aid programs, pushing war surplus weapons, filled in as England scaled back her military positions throughout the vital Middle East.[5]

United States economic scouts quickly set about reconnoitering this unique British oil monopoly. In April of 1949 the Shah brought over from the United States a small delegation of engineering and economic experts, "Overseas Consultants," among whom the legal spokesman was Allen W. Dulles. The one-time chief of the State Department's Near East desk had remained professionally aware of developments in the region through contact with the London J. Henry Schroder merchant-banking managers. Schroder looked after the lead holdings of the Tiarks family, among which Anglo-Iranian stood near the top. Now, poking through feudal debris, Dulles and his cohorts recommended to the Shah that he upgrade his economic infrastructure according to the "reasoned requirements" of the Iranian economy, ignoring the "self-interests of any foreign company" as well as "uninformed political or public clamor."[6]

The nationalization of Iran's oil in 1951 tinctured crisis with opportunity. By 1952 British nerves were wearing thin, Mossedegh wouldn't budge, and Sir John Cochran, "a very senior man in their Intelligence who is in charge of the operation for British interests," as Wisner's Middle-Eastern satrap Kermit Roosevelt later wrote, had approached Roosevelt with an offer of access to "their principal Iranian friends" if he would do whatever was necessary to reverse the situation.[7] It was a prime specimen of "the kind of thing the Brits are inclined to say," carps one seasoned Iranian hand: " 'We have the brains and know-how, you have the lolly, let's put the two together.' "[8]

T. R.'s grandson, Kermit ("Kim") Roosevelt started out teaching government to undergraduates at Harvard, and he has retained into later life the mild, reasoning persona of a superannuated section man. Before he got back into intelligence work for Wisner in 1950, Roosevelt had taught humanities at Cal Tech, joined Ralph Bunche in founding the Coordinator of Intelligence Office (at the suggestion of his cousin, Joe Alsop), and uncovered his crypto-diplomatic potential in Cairo with the OSS under State Department cover. Demobilized, Roosevelt composed the official War Report of the OSS, then roamed the Middle East for *The Saturday Evening Post.*

Kim Roosevelt's quiet courage and uncanny feel for situations across the Arab world had distinguished him well before Iran became a problem. One early Roosevelt assignment had been to dry-clean Egypt's sybaritic King Farouk, another uneven boy monarch the British took sharply in hand during World War II. Miles Copeland has documented Roosevelt's efforts to tidy up palace intrigues once Farouk's grasp faltered.[9] Roosevelt himself still chuckles remembering one frantic chase around Cairo with Mustapha and Ali Amin to find and install in time the capable monarchist Ali Maher as premier early in 1952. Almost a decade before, Kermit finagled an off-the-books OSS grant for the Amin brothers to buy up the dominant Cairo daily, *Al-Akhbar.*[10]

With Farouk increasingly hopeless, Roosevelt supported the Amin brothers and Mohammed Heykel behind Colonel Gamal Abdel Nasser and his takeover-minded Society of Free Officers. With that the Acheson State Department rubberstamped the fateful coup that installed Nasser's front man, Colonel Naguib, as president of the United Arab Republic.[11]

The Americans followed up with an aid program calculated to engineer a dependency. Allen Dulles shipped $3 million along to Nasser, which the emerging strong man was adroit enough to slough off into public works.[12] For a number of months the political nutcutter in the office adjacent to Gamal Nasser was a CIA career man.[13] To retrain the mildewed Egyptian army, several hundred ex-Wehrmacht specialists reached Egypt; in addition fifty or so ex-SS intelligence technicians manned the delegation controlled by Otto Skorzeny to shape up Nasser's security service, the Mukhabarat.

"And at the request of Allen Dulles and the CIA," Reinhard

Gehlen wrote afterward, "we at Pullach did our best to inject life and expertise into the Egyptian secret service, supplying them with the former SS officers I have mentioned."[14] Included were the notorious Goebbels smear artist and Eichmann collaborator Franz Buensch, Hermann Lauterbacher, Hitler's chief of bodyguards Leopold Gleim, and Joachim Daemling, who structured the Egyptian apparatus after the RSHA.[15] For over a decade Skorzeny stoked up the increasingly meglomaniacal Nasser, putting together extremely proftable arms deals through Hjalmar Schacht's Duesseldorf bank, often with East Bloc weaponry. American participants seemed surprised at objections by the displaced British to such an overpowering influx of defunctive Nazis.[16]

"For a long time I acted as liaison on Nasser's behalf with the British," Kermit Roosevelt currently observes, "but that went out of practice. Later on we came to the conclusion that it was not a smart thing to be training the Egyptian secret service."[17]

When this finally stopped, after the Suez crisis, Colonel Nasser loomed large and troublesome indeed. America and her clients had made him all but impregnable.

When John Cochran (a.k.a. George Clutton) first accosted Roosevelt at the end of 1952 in hopes the Yanks might relieve the stalemate in Iran, Kermit offered little reassurance. The essence of Cochran's proposal, a power play ruthlessly engineered to prop up the Shah while bumping out Mossadegh, would never get much of a hearing in Washington so long as the deadlocked Truman administration limped through its lame-duck winter weeks. All during this transition period the bitterly anti-Communist U.S. ambassador to Iran, Loy Henderson, continued to bombard Washington with word that Mossadegh was rejiggering the Majlis, that he was ruling largely by intimidation and phony referenda, that he was increasingly the creature of the Communist Tudeh and looked to Moscow for aid and commerce.[18]

Henderson understood too quickly. Mossadegh hinted in every direction, but throughout the worst of the crisis the unpredictable old landowner in the tear-stained pink pajamas intrigued solely to recover Iran for the Iranians, and "refused," as Harry Rositzke has written, "to legalize the Tudeh Party or to accept its cooperation."[19] The weak point Mossadegh decried in his campaign to take back the oil fields was the sickly and indecisive Shah, and early in 1953 Mossadegh primed his agitators in the streets to demand the abdication of the monarch.

The Shah prepared to flee, then—taking heart from demonstrations—hung on, luggage packed. The young monarch "may pull out at the last minute, he is an unaccountable character, but the sister has agreed to go," Allen told his brother on July 24.[20] At a July meeting of senior personalities in the State Department Kermit Roosevelt presented his revised version of the increasingly hackneyed British scheme to stiffen the unreliable Shah and dispense with Mossadegh, Operation Ajax. Roosevelt was already convinced that both the people and—all important—the Schwarzkopf-trained gendarmerie along with the core of the army would dig in behind the Shah.

The trick was lining up the right people. The intermediaries the British preferred were a pair of brothers named Rashidian. Roosevelt had talked with these men, but he discerned better prospects for bringing on results through another couple, "Naran and Cilly," both journalists, who approached Roosevelt's Teheran chief of station and demanded Roosevelt personally. Kermit heard them out, established their veracity through polygraph tests, and conceived of a plan built around an attempt to eucre the Shah into driving the crisis to a head, then back him up with a mass uprising of mobs from the bazaar.[22]

Roosevelt pitched his proposal at a June 25 meeting at the State Department in front of the Dulles brothers, a bluff, probing Undersecretary Beedle Smith, Doc Matthews, the recently inaugurated Policy and Planning Staff Director Robert Bowie, Loy Henderson, Engine Charlie Wilson, Henry Byroade, and the ranking Foreign Service professional from State, Robert Murphy, Deputy Undersecretary for Political Affairs. The idea went through, but everybody except Allen seemed ominously noncommittal.[22]

The Shah remained uncertain; British Foreign Secretary Anthony Eden was rumored widely to dislike the proposal. Schwarzkopf, flying into Teheran to drop off several million dollars at the U.S. Embassy for Roosevelt to disperse harbored limited hope once Mossadegh responded to Tudeh charges that the ruler listened only to "brainless agents of international reaction" by calling for a referendum to depose the king. The Shah fled unexpectantly to his summer palace on the Caspian, where an intermediary from Roosevelt finally worked him around into signing a decree dismissing Mossadegh in favor of General Fazollah Zahedi, an aging Nazi sympathizer the British had locked up through much of the war against Hitler. At this news Mossadegh laid claim to all power, the Shah darted off for Rome, and riots swept Teheran.[23]

Roosevelt's crisis was peaking. Having driven in furtively days before from Baghdad, he ensconced himself behind the walled garden of the Agency's new Senior Representative in the area, the wire service veteran Bill Herman. Herman's cover in the embassy left him in perfect position to coordinate the campaign of official pressure on the increasingly unnerved old Prime Minister with Roosevelt's carefully phased covert program of mayhem in the streets.

Curled beneath a blanket in the back seat of an unmarked automobile, Roosevelt swung by to pick up perhaps $100,000[24] at the American Embassy and dispensed it among his designated street leaders. Meanwhile, Loy Henderson cornered Mossadegh and threatened to evacuate all United States citizens—an act which unquestionably would precipitate the curtailment of U.S. aid to Iran ($23.4 million for fiscal 1953) at a time when oil revenues had effectively dried up. After that, conceivably, intervention. Mossadegh telephoned out orders which permitted the police to restrain his extremist sympathizers. This left the avenues of Teheran wide open, and on cue an exultant melee led by a couple of hundred well-paid, strutting weight lifters flanked by a consignment of friendly tanks along with bevies of eager souvenir vendors surged toward Mossadegh's residence. A two-hour battle broke out; the loyalists prevailed. The premier had already decamped.[25]

Allen Dulles himself had flown into Geneva to track the countercoup and monitor Roosevelt's moves by radio. Once serious rioting started Undersecretary Smith sent word through via the British circuits in Cyprus to scrub the entire maneuver.[26] (". . . I felt that the British should be allowed to make some sort of meaningful contribution to Ajax," Roosevelt later volunteered.)[27] Success overtook Beedle's TWIX. Days afterward, stopping over in London, Roosevelt savored a congratulatory brandy with Winston Churchill.

By then the headlines had died out. A geopolitical reckoning followed. In August of 1954 the Iranians agreed to market their oil entirely through a consortium put together under the eye of the State Department's Herbert Hoover, Jr. Anglo-Iranian got 40 percent, the five big U.S. corporations pooled 40 percent, and 14 percent went to Shell, with 6 to Compagnie Française des Petroles. According to a "participants agreement" kept secret from the Iranians, the amount each member of the consortium lifted was to be limited by a complicated quota agreement which kept down production—and payments to the government—as long as oil enough was available cheap elsewhere. Iran's oil became captive to the vicissitudes of Mideast oil politics, a lever the petroleum cartel could depend on to keep the sheikhs in line.[28]

* * *

Heartened, pressure from their counterparts at Aramco seem to have tempted higher-ups in the Agency to sponsor a pro-Saudi infiltration attempt to grab the Buraimi Oasis, a coveted green stopover shared by the British protectorates of Oman and Abu Dhabi. England sent in Omani troops, and subsequently the whole mess wound up in court in Geneva.[29] "As far as I'm concerned it never happened," Roosevelt grumps now, and also consigns to the trash basket of bad ideas an attempted coup in Syria, where the OPC had already engineered the Husni Za'im coup of 1949, propping up another headstrong reformer who lasted just long enough (5½ months) to take an insulting tone to his U.S. preceptors before a replacement revolving-door colonel came through to brush him straightaway into the local French cemetery.[30]

❏

On September 4, 1953, before an easel decked up with logistical charts and garrison locations, Roosevelt conducted a White House briefing which recapitulated Operation Ajax. From Eisenhower down, he noticed, he held his audience, and one onlooker seemed "almost alarmingly enthusiastic. John Foster Dulles was leaning back in his chair. Despite his posture, he was anything but sleepy. His eyes were gleaming; he seemed to be purring like a giant cat." Soon afterward, Kermit would record, "I was offered command of a Guatemalan undertaking already in preparation."[31]

Roosevelt reviewed the thinking so far. "I told Allen," Roosevelt says now, "that this will only work if the people, or at least the army, want the same thing you do. I wasn't convinced that the same conditions existed in Guatemala. I didn't think the Guatemalan people, the Guatemalan farmers, wanted what Foster Dulles wanted for them."

We had our will of Guatemala in 1954, Kermit Roosevelt concedes, but by his lights "it wasn't really accomplished by clandestine means."[32] Kermit remains a historian, and retains the generalist's awareness that there are considerations that transcend results, a feeling for ultimate national interests. In Iran a demogogue, an aberration, was surreptitiously and professionally bumped out of the flow of history. Money changed hands, the shadow of larger powers fell across Teheran—events recovered their momentum, almost in the British manner.

Our intervention in Guatemala bespoke colder purposes. The

Eisenhower administration planners manifestly intended to throttle off economically, then destabilize, finally overrun a legitimate Central American government. What Allen and his brother obviously had in mind was reminiscent of Reinhard Heydrich and his pack of overeducated weasels gnawing open Czechoslovakia and Poland. The whole scheme reeked of Nazi methodology. "I looked into it," Kermit Roosevelt says, "and I decided that it didn't add up."

Commentators on the left have tended to prejudge the U.S. intervention in Guatemala along predictable Marxist guidelines.[33] By this reading, powerful figures close to the all-seeing "Colossus of the North" were displeased with the drift of affairs since 1944 in Guatemala, when reform-minded army officers ousted the caudillo Jorge Ubico Castaneda, an obsessive who despised the unscrubbed Maya rabble and had his initials stamped into every government bullet so malcontents "would carry his personal emblem into eternity." In 1936 Ubico consented to a ninety-nine-year lease with the Boston-based United Fruit Company, already directed by the agile Sam ("The Banana Man") Zemurray. Zemurray hired Sullivan and Cromwell to button up an understanding which left United Fruit ("La Frutera") the proprietor of excellent plantation land, mostly on the coasts, which exceeded 50 percent of the holdings of all other Nicaraguan landowners combined. It handed out over half the wages across the sweltering republic. In return, La Frutera could depend on negligible taxes and minimal export duties. Sullivan and Cromwell's managing partner, John Foster Dulles, drew up this landmark sweetheart arrangement.[34]

The Dulles brothers were especially attuned to affairs in Guatamala owing to the persistent involvement of the J. Henry Schroder Banking Corporation in the development of the area. Also in 1936, Foster guided a power play which left United Fruit in control of the International Railways of Central America (IRCA), the owner of most of the existing trackage. Foster brought in, to finance the takeover, the Schroder Banking Corporation, where he—then Allen—sat in as general counsel and board members. The president of the Schroder bank hung on as a member of the IRCA board through 1954. IRCA owned outright the nation's only harbor on the Atlantic, Puerto Barrios, from where Company freighters ("The Great White Fleet") plied the banana trade.[35]

A revolution in 1944 produced elections a year later which installed a plump, otherworldly professor of philosophy named Dr. Juan José Arevalo Bermejo. Arevalo's elevation worked out because two of his supporters, Major Francisco Arana and Captain Jacobo Arbenz

Guzman, brought down a bloodbath on superior officers at Fort Matamoros and handed out small arms to the discontented cadet corps. The incoming president defined his creed as "spiritual socialism." Along with a universal franchise (except for illiterate women) and broad personal freedoms, a form of social security was enacted; then, in 1947, a controversial "Labor Code" went into the books to protect the plantation workers. Available land was redistributed, at first the sizable tracts confiscated from German owners during World War II.

Francisco Arana was expected to inherit the presidency in 1950, but on an inspection tour one day he was allegedly shot to pieces by the chauffeur (and later secretary) of Jacobo Arbenz. This simplified the presidential campaign of 1950: Arbenz lined up younger officers along with respected labor and peasant leaders and prevailed over a Ubico loyalist. With more than 65 percent of the tally, Arbenz became, in November 1950, the second democratically elected president in Guatemalan history.

Arbenz was thirty-seven, quick, fair-complected, difficult of approach, high-strung, with a sharply etched Scott-Fitzgeraldian profile. The child of an unstable Swiss pharmacist and a ladino woman, Arbenz had married the vivacious daughter of a wealthy Salvadoran coffee grower, who stimulated her inward husband with fantasies of remedial social experiment. Several of Señora Arbenz's intimates were already celebrated Latin-American Communists. Arevalo had actively supported such regionwide restructuring efforts as the Caribbean Legion, the movement to throw out rightist dictatorships which brought on true democracy in Costa Rica.

Arbenz pledged "to convert Guatemala from a backward country with a predominantly feudal economy into a modern capitalist state." He meant to construct a second port on the Atlantic coast, cut through a highway to break the IRCA transportation monopoly, and compete with the endemic foreign ownership until control of production and distribution gravitated into Guatemalan hands. Arbenz inaugurated a hydroelectric plan to offset the hegemony of the American and Foreign Power Company, a Foster Dulles client since the 1920s.[36] In June of 1952 he squeezed through the legislature his agricultural reform bill, which expropriated the uncultivated segment of the latifundi-size plantations and repaid their owners with 3 percent, twenty-five-year bonds based on the evaluation of the properties for tax purposes. Since United Fruit had connived to force down the assessment of its properties to an insignificant fraction of their obvious worth, this turn of events electrified the management in Boston, which regarded the nefarious Decree 900—and correctly—as tantamount to confiscation.

Zemurray at United Fruit reacted by bankrolling one of the great full-court presses in public relations annals. He had already cranked up the peppy, Napoleonic Edward Bernays to whip the more moderate U.S. media into a standing froth, with selected delegations of *New York Times* and *Herald Tribune* nabobs as high as Arthur Hays Sulzberger junketed through to appreciate the well-policed, squared-off company towns. Massachusetts politicians from Henry Cabot Lodge ("the Senator from United Fruit") to John McCormack kept up a drumroll in Congress. In 1952 Zemurray instructed his corporation counsel, the lawyer/lobbyist Thomas ("Tommy the Cork") Corcoran to pump through whatever political grease seemed fitting to straighten this thing out. To penetrate the State Department, Zemurray laid on Truman's recent Assistant Secretary of State for Latin America, Spruille Braden, who roughed up the incoming Eisenhower publicly in a speech at Dartmouth for standing by while Guatemalan Communists feasted. Meanwhile—very quietly—Zemurray retained the McCarthyite John Clements Associates, with orders to churn up the police-blotter internationalists at *The American Mercury*.

Signatures on the agricultural reform act weren't dry long before the OPC was ready to wade ashore. Beedle Smith always warmed to the engaging Tommy the Cork, and wasn't above prospecting for something with United Fruit after he departed government. Smith conferred with Harry Truman directly, who authorized Operation Fortune, a scheme to send along a boatload of munitions in a United Fruit hold to Anastasio Somoza of Nicaragua, with which the dictator promised to "clean up Guatemala for you in no time." Presidents Trujillo of the Dominican Republic and Jiminez of Venezuela chipped in, Wisner's Latin American Division Chief J. C. King coordinated the shipment with Corcoran, and the entire consignment of "agricultural machinery" was already on the high seas in packing crates when Undersecretary of State David Bruce spotted references to the project.[37]

Something of a social friend, Bruce was increasingly leery of Wisner's off-the-shelf approach to nation-tampering. Once operational specifics about Operation Fortune reached his desk, David spread them out before Secretary of State Acheson, who hurried to Truman in time to call the shipment back. "Mssrs. Wisner and Col. King from CIA met with Mssrs. Miller, Matthews, Mann, Washington and myself to deal with a Latin American project that had been the subject of considerable study by us," Bruce's journal entry for October 1952 reads. "It was agreed it would not be undertaken."[38]

Then Eisenhower took office, and Smith became Undersecretary of State. The subject was reopened, immediately. This time around King arranged for OPC go-betweens to approach unhappy officers in the Guatemalan army and smuggle in small arms plus $64,000 in cash from the United Fruit Company; on March 29, 1953, two hundred men attacked the regional capital of Salama and held it briefly before Arbenz's soldiers arrived and flattened the rebellion. The involvement of the United Fruit Company came out in trial records, but there was no official reference to the CIA.

Weeks after the Salama fizzle the sitting Assistant Secretary of State for Inter-American Affairs, John Moors Cabot, dropped by in Guatemala City to interview President Arbenz in hopes the reformer might consider some form of "just compensation" for the 400,000 acres of Fruit Company property his government had already expropriated, roughly one-seventh of all the arable land in Guatemala. Like the Lodges, the Cabot family was seriously invested in United Fruit, and John Moors's brother, Thomas, had recently given up the presidency of the giant banana importer. The Assistant Secretary remarked afterward on Arbenz's "pale, cold-lipped look of the idealogue" and his disinterest in "my suggestions. . . . He had obviously sold out to the Communists and that was that."[39]

On his side, Arbenz eyed with concern the unpredictable government of the North as he devised strategy to repossess the nation's assets from the Fruit Company, now heckled quite openly among his followers as El Pulpo, the Octopus. His senior officers, so far, obviously supported his efforts, but the president was more than aware that most of them identified with the white, rich landowning class; many had been trained in the United States and so were involved day-to-day with the sizable U.S. military mission in place in Guatemala. Since 1948 the United States had imposed an arms boycott on Guatemala, based on a technical infraction of the Rio Pact.

Arbenz's officers nevertheless approved the nationalist side of the president's policies, but there were murmurs whenever Marxists eased in at subcabinet levels. Periodically, Communist agitators goaded hungry farmers into overrunning unused plantation scrubland. The abrasive Marxist organizer José Manuel Fortuny was able to insert himself, for a time, into the general secretaryship of Arbenz's personal power base, the Revolutionary Action Party; another avowed Communist labor leader, Victor Gutiérrez, had brokered his coalition into the Communist-directed World Federation of Trade Unions, visited Moscow and the East Bloc, and become a consultive resource to Jacobo Arbenz. Meanwhile, State Department cables of the time reflect the arrivals and departures of well-known Guatemalan Marxists from Cuba and Mexico. Raymond Leddy, ex-FBI and SSU, was now the U.S. Department of State's watchdog for Central American affairs. Leddy descried in Guatemala a version of Mao's "Yennan Way," taking power in coalition with middle-class politicians and army officers before squeezing them out.

Horror stories reached Washington. Howard Hunt passed along atrocity reports from a delegation of anti-Communist students who visited Guatemala City. Arbenz's loyalists promptly herded them together, Hunt reported, wired up their testicles, and power-hosed their mouths and rectums.[40] Throughout the CIA, remembers the sitting DDI, Robert Amory, indignation built at "all the vile tortures carried out under Arbenz," and there was a tape passed among the offices, "a small thing" purporting to convey "the shrieks and howls" of victims of the regime. There was much citing of Churchill's exhortation to strangle the cobra of Communism in its egg.

Such explicitness was helpful in overcoming certain . . . qualms around the Agency. "The necessity for doing it got all fogged up with the idea that Bobby Cutler and United Fruit and [Whiting] Willauer were *insisting* on it," Amory reflects. "That it was sort of an American capitalism thing to squench out Communists and expropriation down there." But Allen was actively promoting more "sharp" projects to balance off their disappointments in the East, and Amory would later term the liberal retort that Arbenz was merely a "peaceful agrarian reformer" a version of "reconstituted history."[41]

It would prove tempting later on to write up the Dulles brothers as social-register repo artists, enforcers for the Fruit Company. Pride played a part certainly—since Panama in 1903 Sullivan and Cromwell stood high among Wall Streeters as a full-service provider.

Undoubtedly the expropriations did it. "We saw the Fruit Company as a source of information, a check, rather than a contributor," one operator maintains. But once the incursion date got closer, Fruit Company officials were reportedly consternated and protested that perhaps they *could* do business with Arbenz after all.[42] By then it was already too late.

Frank Wisner could anticipate the line accountability on this one, but Allen Dulles himself nursed hunches he intended to play. By early 1953 his fellow Free Europe Committee board members Adolf

Berle and C. D. Jackson were talking up a variety of approaches to ridding the hemisphere of Arbenz; proposals bounced for months around sessions of the new government's International Information Activities Committee, chaired now by William H. Jackson but sparked by C. D. Jackson. In April Frank Wisner showed up to discuss the replacement of the U.S. ambassadors to Honduras and Guatemala with insiders before the flak started landing. The Flying Tiger pioneer Whiting Willauer went in at Tegucigalpa. Pistol-packin' John Puerifoy would get the Guatemala City boiler room.

Allen had already identified the fellow to ram this through on the ground: a strapping, self-willed knockabout colonel named Albert Haney, just then the Agency's station chief in Seoul. Haney's sidekick, William ("Rip") Robertson, was fond of escorting guerrilla parties in and out of North Korea with or without an okay from Washington. Wisner "disliked and distrusted" the high-handed Colonel Haney, who established his jump-off headquarters at the semi-deserted naval air base at Opa-Locka, not far outside Miami.[43] When Wisner's rigid Western Hemisphere Division chief J. C. King (a Johnson and Johnson retiree who preferred the podgy FBI-style approach when reordering Latino governments) proposed that Haney seek out Tommy Corcoran and commandeer that warehouse full of weapons left over from Operation Fortune, Haney fluffed King off, nastily. "If you think you can run this whole operation without United Fruit, you're crazy!"[44] King huffed back, and from then on the exchanges between Haney and King's staffers turned into a high-speed log roll.

The decision to go with the Agency on this came out of an August 1953 meeting; Eisenhower had already designated a committee of trusted senior bureaucrats to sign off on major covert projects. Beedle Smith and C. D. Jackson and Defense Secretary Wilson sat in to pass on Allen Dulles's overall proposal, although Robert Cutler (currently Assistant to the President for National Security Affairs) pointedly avoided the get-together. Cutler's position as board chairman of the Old Colony Trust in Boston had left him as automatic board chairman at United Fruit.[45]

Haney's projections fascinated Allen. While looking to Wisner and Dulles for "strategic decisions," Haney kept back "broad authority over CIA station chiefs in Central America" as well as a "free tactical hand. . . ." Broadly, the master plan Haney drafted called for a progressively more intense blanketing of Guatemala with layer upon layer of propaganda harassment and diplomatic hectoring throughout the spring of 1954. Before the rainy season set in in July, a "liberation army" of disaffected Guatemalan exiles would invade beneath a panoply of radio and leaflet support, heavy jamming and disinformation capabilities, backed up with enough reliable air support to disrupt the capital and keep panic building. Meanwhile, intermediaries must soften up susceptible figures in the clergy, skeptics among the army staff—anybody likely to turn on Arbenz once real pressure mounted.

Haney pegged the operation at $4.5 million; it wouldn't be many weeks before he was striding up and down the hallways of his two-story administration building at Opa-Locka pointing out to uniformed project officers where banks of telexes would go, where decoding equipment cables had better be run so shifts of security personnel—something over a hundred were already swarming the empty post, rotating the guard—could watchdog the classified materials. He maintained a forty-foot chart, updated in each category, overhanging his operations room.

Meanwhile J. C. King was badgering Wisner, stirring up Frank's own uneasiness that everything about Haney's projections was much too grandiose, too many people involved, too likely to leak, certainly in the wrong places. Why not swap political redress for a mouth-watering aid program pointed at the Guatemalan military? Let *them* bump Arbenz. Was anybody really ripe for "another Korean war right at our doorstep?" Better advised to "kill 'em with kindness," King urged Wisner.

"J. C., you've had four years to try that approach," Wisner argued back, but he was manifestly torn. King couldn't produce results, that much was evident; whatever spunk was left old J. C. reserved for intra-Agency dustups.

Not that Frank Wisner was prepared to live or die with Project PB/SUCCESS, as Haney's grand projection was tagged by then. Let Allen himself decide. But Allen wasn't foolish, and brought the entire matter up over cocktails with Foster in Georgetown.

He returned elated. "Colonel," he demanded of Haney, "there's one question I want to ask you. Do you really think you can succeed?"

"Sir, with your help, we can win."

Allen's leonine head lifted, he released that booming, gratified laugh, and clapped Haney powerfully on both shoulders. "Then go to it, my boy. You've got the green light." King stalked from the room.[46]

A laying-on of hands this public would make it harder and harder for Wisner to rein Haney in. "I think Frank Wisner had a hellova time controlling a number of people," Colonel Holcomb says. Wisner had pulled Holcomb back fast from Rome once PB/Success started and provided him a planning and monitoring staff to oversee sizable "hot" operations, a team which mounted quickly to more than thirty low-key paramilitary specialists. To assure Holcomb the clout he needed with Guatemala, Wisner appointed Holcomb Deputy Chief of the Western Hemisphere Division. Holcomb visited Opa-Locka and confronted Haney. "What Teddy Roosevelt did in Panama will pale by comparison with what you're planning to do in Guatemala," Holcomb told the commander. "You'll start a civil war and have the blood of thousands on your hands." Nothing made a dent. "We had our Oliver North kind of out-of-control type," Holcomb mused years afterward. "A bird named Haney."[47]

In hopes of slipping a bridle onto Haney, Wisner sent down an old friend he'd just taken on as Special Assistant for Paramilitary and Psychological Operations, C. Tracy Barnes, another Carter, Ledyard trainee.[48] Equanimity bespoke Barnes's pedigree: Groton, Yale, Harvard Law, *two* Croix de Guerre while jumping with the Jedburghs before rounding out Dulles's staff in Bern—Barnes smoothed people down, he and his perceptive wife, Janet, an Aldrich, were familiars among opinion makers in Washington that season.

Tracy came to town in 1950 to help out Archie Alexander at Defense, moved up as Deputy Director at the Psychological Strategy Board; in time the Eisenhower people sorted out the Strategy Board's functions between the NSC's Operations Coordinating Board and the United States Information Agency at State. Barnes required another office in town, someplace fashionable and supergrade. Wisner took him in.[49] That spring of 1954 the guard was changing; Barnes's mentor at Groton and Yale, Richard Bissell, grew weary of mooning around the Ford Foundation and returned to Washington as Allen Dulles's special assistant.

If Barnes ruffled anything at Opa-Locka the evidence escapes history. His lovely hair center-parted, Tracy remained "the soul of vagueness" around a thunderpit of government dominated by tense, contentious ball-squeezers at work invoicing Uzi shipments and phased bribes.[50] Insiders would shrug off rumors that Tracy Barnes's cousin, Michael Straight, appears to have confided in him directly—and early in the game—that he'd been running errands for several years for Moscow; Tracy neglected to bring this sensitive matter up around CIA. The day the newcomer David Atlee Phillips challenged the stoutly liberal Barnes as to the Agency's mandate to topple a freely elected government, Barnes circumnavigated the question; Phillips "detected in his face a flicker of concern, the reaction of a sensitive man."[51]

Richard Helms, still distrustful of these overblown "action projects," pointedly left the thrice-weekly Director's meetings before Guatemala came under discussion. Tracy Barnes sat on in the company of Wisner and Allen to read aloud his notes after another week in Opa-Locka. There wasn't customarily much: Kermit Roosevelt later decided that although Tracy was an agreeable fellow, neither then nor afterward had he betrayed "a shred of tradecraft."[52]

So Barnes flew in and out, although Haney scarcely noticed. Toward midspring the pressure started building. By prearrangement with the Agency, public figures from George Meany to Cardinal Spellman took out after Arbenz in public, respectively demanding that he purge Guatemala's unions of Communists and evoking a "pastoral letter" urging the populace to "rise as a single man against this enemy of God and country." In Caracas in March at an Organization of American States meeting John Foster Dulles strong-armed through a resolution specifying that "the domination or control of the political institutions of any American state by the international communist movement . . . would constitute a threat" to all the Americas, to be met with "appropriate action. . . ." Guatemalan Foreign Minister Toriello immediately attacked the resolution as a "pretext for intervening in our internal affairs.[53]

By April this onsetting barrage was starting to unnerve Arbenz. To test the atmospherics—a favorite Wisner term—Haney sent in the German-born Henry Heckscher, an operative of reputation around the Berlin station. David Phillips was scheduled to join Heckscher and run a notebook for propaganda broadcasts; Phillips would later write of how impressed he was when Heckscher sat stolidly on the edge of the adjacent hotel bed the night before their foray into Guatemala City hacking laundry marks out of his underwear with a razor blade.[54]

Heckscher surfaced in Guatemala City in the guise of a coffee buyer from Central Europe; he made his way from officer to officer, as cuddly and alert as Peter Lorre sizing up the consensus around the casbah, a semicomic figure in dark shades and Panama hat. Between smirks and hints Heckscher recurred to very large overseas bank accounts, to senior positions waiting in a reconstituted government. But Arbenz's palace guard was surprisingly resistant, and Heckscher was fortunate to recruit for Haney one officer on the President's planning staff. This man Haney sustained in place, and over many months picked up a reliable flow of important tactical information, culminating in mid-April with word that a long-awaited transaction in Prague had now been authorized.[55] Arbenz expected a boatload of Czech arms.

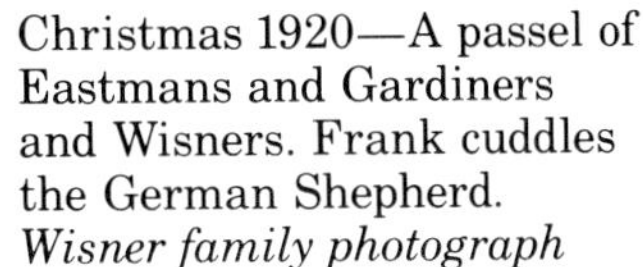

Christmas 1920—A passel of Eastmans and Gardiners and Wisners. Frank cuddles the German Shepherd. *Wisner family photograph*

Frank Wisner *(left),* in town to save Rumania (1944). *Wisner family photograph*

Frank Wisner, The Sporting Life I (1944). *Wisner family photograph*

Frank Wisner, The Sporting Life II (1944). *Wisner family photograph*

A soiree in Bucharest, 1944, Tanda Bragadiru in center. *Wisner family photograph*

Frank Wisner—OSS SI chief in Wiesbaden (1945). *Wisner family photograph*

Occupation duty—Wiesbaden 1945, Richard Helms on right. *Wisner family photograph*

'p on the farm—Ellis *(left),* Frank Wisner. *Wisner family photograph*

:earranging Asia—Frank Wisner third from right. *Wisner family photograph*

General Walter Bedell Smith, 1945. *Library of Congress*

A restive Allen Dulles chats up Mrs. Dwight Morrow, 1941. *AP/Wide World Photos*

Richard Bissell contemplates the Brandenburg Tor. *Richard Bissell*

James J. Angleton *(left)* presents David Ben Gurion an award from Allen W. Dulles. Mudd Library—*CIA Collection*

General Reinhard Gehlen, in full honors. *Yale University Collection*

James MacCargar, specialist in the stabilizing and destabilizing of eastern Europe, reflects on life's vindications. *Author photograph*

General Lucian Truscott, on point.
Library of Congress

Allen Dulles of CIA *(left)*, Robert Murphy of State *(right)*, doubleteam Sen. Theodore Green *(center)*, 1958.
Library of Congress

John Foster Dulles (counseled by Irene Dunne), damps down another crisis at the United Nations, 1958. *Library of Congress*

The End of the Affair—John F. Kennedy, Allen Dulles, John McCone. *Bettmann Archive*

As this sunk in, all hesitations about doing in a duly elected democratic president evaporated beside the Reflecting Pool. The East was rampant! Robert Amory still remembers how overwhelmingly the project went critical overnight, how all at once the "big argument made by Wisner and Stuart Hedden was the massive arms shipment from Czechoslovakia."[56] A wildness was up, especially disquieting at State. Allen himself was apprehensive that this venture too might lose its legs to the diplomats, and cautioned his ally Raymond Leddy against permitting the thing to get "interagencied" to death.[57]

It was to forestall such bureaucratic flank attacks that Wisner had found himself a tough-talking, take-no-prisoners hard case with backing in the Department named John E. ("Jack") Peurifoy to stage-manage the Guatemala City embassy. Orphaned as a child in South Carolina, Peurifoy had struggled upward from stock clerk and elevator operator jobs and on through the bureaucracy at State, making points en route by sneaking the classified security files on one of his sponsors, Alger Hiss, to McCarthyite Senator Karl Mundt while half-heartedly defending Hiss before an ambivalent Foster Dulles.[58] His big breakthrough came with his appointment as ambassador to Greece, where he hammered together a regime of colonels and stamped out embers behind the sputtering civil war.[59]

Dean Acheson somehow liked the bustling, braying Peurifoy; by 1953, as a career Democrat, his prospects were obviously narrowing once Foster moved in to restructure the Department. Here was a career man who knew how to appreciate a showy job. If everything went wrong, Peurifoy could take the dousing. "I picked him off the beach," Wisner explained with a grin to well-tailored friends, who wanted to hear exactly where he located an ambassador who paraded around the compound of the embassy in a jump suit, shoulder holsters, and a green Borsalino with a feather. Peurifoy kept the cables moving to Wisner and Beedle Smith directly, avoiding too much exchange of information either with the less-than-enthusiastic Assistant Secretary for Inter-American Affairs, John Moors Cabot, or the man who replaced him in March, Texas lawyer Henry Holland, Peurifoy's nominal boss.

Holland was reflexively opposed: he liked neither the scale, the publicness, "or the obvious risk of igniting a civil war." "Forget those stupid ideas and let us get on with our work,"[60] Smith growled back, but Holland would persist. He became a problem.

Most providential of freighters, the *Alfhem* was spotted in mid-April by a birdwatcher for the CIA taking on a shipment of weapons at the port of Stettin, in Poland, and then picked up intermittently as it bypassed Dakar and plowed the West Indies seas before it reappeared on May 13 at Puerto Barrios. Its arrival provoked massive consternation around the Agency, in that the DDI had been charged with tracking the freighter so that it could be intercepted before it made port and disgorged its cargo. After Dakar the entire U.S. electronic surveillance community had lost sight of the vessel. One participant remembers the officer in charge, Gates Lloyd, turning up in panic to announce that the *Alfhem* was already in Guatemala, unloading. "Gates was really crestfallen," the man recalls, "and Wisner just sat there, shaking his head. Then I said, 'Look, this is the best thing that could have happened. Now you've got an excuse for the operation, because here is a Communist power which is feeding arms in, they're *there*. And that's our excuse, in case anything goes wrong.' "[61]

The Agency was already collaborating with Somoza in planting cases of rifles with Soviet markings along the Nicaraguan coast. Now, after the *Alfhem* berthed, Allen Dulles convened the Intelligence Advisory Committee and presented the argument that Arbenz had arms enough already to roll down Central America and grab off the Panama Canal, 800 miles south. This won him additional discretionary funds with which to equip the swarthy, leather-jacketed rebel leader Haney picked to carry the land war to Guatemala City, Col. Carlos Castillo Armas. A quirky, self-dramatizing mestizo who rarely appeared without the butt of a .45 bulging above the placket of his chinos, Armas was already canvassing for freedom fighters among the mercado debris of Tegucigalpa.

Haney's understudy, Rip Robertson, took in a demolition team to blow the railroad trestle just as the arms convoy passed over en route to the capital. An untimely torrent soaked his detonators; all ten boxcars passed. Once Arbenz's armament officers began to inspect the shipment, however, they found that everything was virtually useless, a junkyard of cast-off, obsolete, antitank guns and mobilized artillery useless in the jungle, the entire array mismatched.[62]

The targeting of Guatemala intensified. Foster leaked to newsmen his fears that all these Communist arms foreshadowed the invasion of Honduras. The U.S. Information Agency planted hundreds of articles abroad, came up with thousands of anti-Arbenz cartoons and posters. Subject to a nudge from Tommy the Cork via Beedle, Allen replaced J. C. King's unhappy station chief in Guatemala in early June with a "local figure" with commercial contacts around town, John Doherty.

On his own authority Haney flew down a C-47 loaded with bazookas and grenade launchers, infuriating officials in both the State

Department and the CIA, J. C. King especially. When the appalled Wisner jerked Haney back to Washington, the colonel affected a detached "who me?" approach, while Allen intervened in that lofty, maddening way and compared his field commander with Admiral Nimitz, who contrary to instructions once tore into the Japanese fleet.

Nerved up, Wisner strained to immerse himself in planning details, to make sure *his* responsibilities were discharged down to the last jot. "He was a relentless memorandum writer," Cleve Cram acknowledges. "And he put in everything, every speck of dust."[63] As PB/Success eased toward invasion day the meetings became incessant, and contending with nitpickers from the regular military abraded Wisner's self-possession.

Colonel Philip Corso, the Operations Coordinating Board's delegate to the Policy Group already working on Guatemala, kept raking Wisner over once reports began circulating. "I found out that the CIA had sent Castillo Armas some German rifles, but didn't send them any ammunition," Corso says. "A man named Carlos was waiting in Guatemala City with all the files on all the secret police in Guatemala. He waited ten days, and nobody from CIA showed up. And then I was in a policy meeting one day. Frank Wisner was there. And the conversation began. Castillo Armas had one Piper Cub, and Wisner wasn't sure whether we should give him new tires or retreads. So I leaned over near C. D. Jackson, and said: 'C. D., why don't you call this discussion off, and we'll take up a collection and send him some new tires.' Can you imagine, with all that money they had? I think they were trying to stop it. We won, but the CIA operation should have lost."[64]

Days after the *Alfhem* arrived, John Foster Dulles proclaimed a "mutual defense treaty" with Honduras, and fifty tons of small arms went out in Air Force Globemasters for distribution to the Armas insurgents. Several U.S. submarines and three B-36 intercontinental bombers turned up amidst fanfare in the regional press, and on May 24 President Eisenhower told Congressmen that he had now ordered the Navy to stop and search all "suspicious foreign-flag vessels" off the Guatemalan coast. Henry Holland protested. The Department's legal brief suggested no justification for boarding neutral carriers, and even Robert Murphy warned Foster that "Our present action should give stir to the bones of Admiral von Tirpitz," and leave the Good Neighbor Policy sunk without a trace.[65]

Under attack across Latin America, Holland kept his objections rolling straight through the invasion itself. One professional blocking in a lot of the paramilitary detail recalls "a very embarrassing evening at Wisner's. Henry was a straight shooter, and Frank had got some fellow in the Agency to do a cartoon book of Holland doing everything he could to frustrate the Guatemala operation. I guess it was pretty clever, but I found it a little mean, because Henry was only doing what he thought was his duty. He kept *his* sense of proportion. One day I walked into his office at the Department. He looked up and said, 'I smell sulfur.'

"I said—I knew he represented the petroleum boys back home—'I smell oil.' " And we both laughed."[66]

Wisner caught it from every direction. David Atlee Phillips shared the prevailing opinion of Wisner as "alternately charming and . . . 'iron-assed,' " and impatient with the encroaching bureaucracy and its inevitable delays. Beyond that, Phillips sensed, having Allen Dulles reach in and rearrange things whenever he got an inspiration was galling. Phillips had already identified the real "danger that his personality couldn't accept the fact."[67]

It didn't let up. On June 15 Eisenhower staged a breakfast meeting devoted to Project PB/SUCCESS and informed the Dulles brothers, the Joint Chiefs, and a smattering of advisers that there was one outcome permissible: "When you commit the flag, you commit it to win."[68]

This made it harder to contemplate how little was usable on the ground. Since early May Phillips's "Voice of Liberation" transmitters—in Nicaragua initially, and then from Honduras and the Dominican Republic—kept ratcheting up the war of nerves, alternating entertainment and bulletins on the preparations of Castillo Armas to free his countrymen from a Leninist dictator about to disband his traditional military and arm only peasants and his "peoples' militia." After months of provocation no more than a few hundred dupes straggled over into Honduras. When one of the pilots in Arbenz's air force did defect, Phillips and his native assistants filled him with Scotch and baited him into a hypothetical ramble during which the drunken aviator haphazardly implored his fellow aviators to desert with their aircraft to Armas and the rebels. Phillips taped these maunderings, and spliced the usable sections for periodic rebroadcast. Alarmed, Arbenz grounded the few light trainers which constituted his air arm.

As the invasion date approached Phillips orchestrated a *Funkspiel* among his outstations that played up airdrops to fictitious rebel camps throughout the jungle and promised a nativist regime devoted to "Work, Bread and Country." At Wisner's instigation Allen Dulles arranged for the transfer of Sydney Gruson of *The New York Times,* whose stories from Guatemala kept stressing that it was *nationalism* primarily that motivated the Guatemalan leadership.

On invasion day, June 18, the troupe that rumbled over the border in a line of old trucks was perhaps 600 half-trained volunteers scraped together out of bars and alleys around Central America, luckless soldiers of fortune and dispirited aging exiles. Castillo Armas himself first reviewed this hodge-podge a week before the long-expected border crossing. "The Liberator," as he called himself, struck Americans as a swart, delicately boned, rather dreamy soldier whose solitary political assets remained "that good Indian look about him," in Howard Hunt's words, and almost a snakelike stamina and confidence in his destiny.[69] A postgraduate training tour at Fort Leavenworth, Kansas, had widened Armas's acquaintanceship inside what he referred to with appreciation as "the Government of the North."

Decked out on border-crossing day in all his characteristic scuzzy flair—leather flight jacket, checked shirt, the barrel of his inevitable .45 nestled alongside his groin—Colonel Haney's corps commander directed his lead car, a banged-up station wagon, perhaps six miles inside the frontier and parked and waited for victory. Native announcers over the "Voice of Liberation" were proclaiming the onset of a nationwide rebellion. But there were still few substantial defections. So Armas and his battalion bivouacked quietly and avoided all contact with the Guatemalan Army. Prospects for an effective ground campaign were guttering. A few days afterward several desultory attempts to seize Zapaca and Puerto Barrios fell back before Arbenz's American-trained cadres.

Simultaneously, pilots in Colonel Haney's air force (pulled together by Whitey Willauer and led by a skywriter named Jerry DeLarm) dropped hand grenades over Puerto Barrios which damaged several fuel tanks while another American ran out of gas attempting to strafe Coban and crashed in Mexico. Two follow-up aircraft got shot up so badly by ground fire that they were lucky to get back, and unflyable once down. This eliminated the Agency's tactical air capacity for the time being.

"Guatemala was a mess and Wisner knew it," reminisces Frank Holcomb, working hard to monitor the collapsing strike forces. He recalls the pandemonium at L Building once the battle communiqués started rolling in. "My problem with Wisner was that he didn't do enough. Haney should have been fired but Tracy protected him. And

Frank protected Tracy. Militarily, our little columns didn't at all accomplish what they were supposed to, we didn't defeat or impede the Guatemalan army. They didn't collapse, they remained loyal."[70] By June 20 enough of this fiasco was leaking to permit Wisner's friend Scotty Reston to refer to Allen Dulles in the *Times* as the type of adventurous administrator who might very well "start a revolution against the Communists in Guatemala."[71] The lid was lifting.

Haney was now screaming for replacement fighter-bombers; with Henry Holland dug in to block any escalation of hostilities it took an audience with Eisenhower to break two P-51s loose. "When I saw Henry walking into your office with three large law books under his arm, I knew that he had lost his case already," Allen assured the President. But these were nervous hours, not improved at all by a misbegotten Haney effort to bomb a Honduras airstrip and pin it on Arbenz. Every front was collapsing—an outraged Anastasio Somoza dismissed Armas as "poor timber. . . . a little prick"—while during the international exchanges the U.S. ambassador to the United Nations, Henry Cabot Lodge, struggled to keep the British and French from voting with Guatemala to send in a Security Council team of inspectors rather than wash the whole matter out to the Organization of American States, where Foster could strong-arm the outcome.[72]

The fighter-bombers were some help: They kept at Zapaca and helped the Armas irregulars hold Chiquimula. Eisenhower backed them up with sweeps by American-piloted bombers based at the Managua airport.[73] Their pretense of U.S. noninvolvement was now so tattered that Frank Wisner and Colonel Holcomb both threatened to resign if more overt U.S. military force was brought into play.

By then what *really* had started to make a difference was the chaos the "Voice of Liberation" imposed on the bewildered capital, "snuggling up" on the standard local frequencies to mourn tremendous losses among the Arbenz troops, to suggest that whole lakes had now been poisoned and entire divisions were defecting. Phillips's native speakers were already mimicking the area commanders, faking traffic among advancing hordes, "spoofing" established military signals to relay word of overwhelming victories, exultant body counts, simultaneously calling down raids by squadrons of imaginary support aircraft. All this they coordinated with amplifiers and jamming devices arrayed on the roof of the U.S. embassy in Guatemala City. Tapes of a tumultuous air assault boomed across the increasingly paralyzed capital at night, timed to scheduled passes by the two overworked fighter-bombers as sortie by sortie they sent up the nearby airport oil reserves or laid down smoke bombs that left the barracks choking. These "sulfatos" (laxatives) were depleting the population.

Even before the campaign started a number of Arbenz's senior staff officers (pushed relentlessly by Jack Peurifoy) had visited the president to recommend a purge of Communists and labor agitators. Arbenz brushed the delegation off, reminding them that he was himself a landowner and suggesting that Communism was, "like strychnine, beneficial in small doses." But as the noise level rose, and Communists like Gutiérrez started agitating for "commando brigades" to repel the invaders, army leaders were starting to grumble that Arbenz himself had better resign or risk a front-line armistice with the Armas forces. To still the transmitters at the U.S. embassy Arbenz ordered the power station shut; the blackout produced more panic; at this point David Phillips authorized "a final big lie,"[74] the announcement that two massive columns were converging on the agitated capital.

Desperate, drinking heavily, on June 25 Arbenz ordered the distribution of weapons to the "peoples' organizations and the political parties." To Arbenz's conservative officer caste, the gringos were substantiated: the president was now in bed with the devil. The Yankees were pulverizing everything; Rip Robertson had authorized one of his rampaging pilots to drop a bomb down the smokestack of a bypassing British cargo carrier. His top officers pressing him, the sagging Arbenz conceded to the formation of a transitional junta if that alone might preserve the accomplishments of the revolution. Army Chief of Staff Colonel Carlos Enrique Díaz went in to negotiate an end to this asphyxiation fantasy with the jubilant Peurifoy. Peurifoy, fanning off Díaz's jeremiads about buzzards pecking up bombing victims along the packed clay boulevards of Zacapa, disclaimed all talk of U.S. involvement in this revolutionary mayhem, then indicated that if "Díaz assumed power and ousted communists," he would "strongly recommend that U.S. attempt to bring about cease-fire. . . ."[75]

The word that Arbenz was resigning splashed into Opa-Locka like water across a very groggy boxer. "We thought we'd lost," David Phillips admitted afterward. "We were so surprised by his departure."[76] Less than two dozen of Arbenz's troops had died, for all the weeks of guerrilla theater, and literally a handful of Armas's followers. Washington echoed Phillips's relief. "Wisner was so glad when it was over," Frank Holcomb remembers. "He wrote a memo, which was basically translated into a cable to the State Department. The operative part went something like this: 'It is time for the doctors to move out and for the nurses to take over.' He was very happy to be rid of this thing, the nightmare was over. It had been troublesome throughout the OPC, a lot of animosities with the Opa-Locka crowd, with Tracy and Haney. . . ."[77]

For several vivid weeks the head nurse around Guatemala City was the indomitable American ambassador. "In my opinion the Guatemalan thing was effectively decided by the two ambassadors, Jack Peurifoy and Whitey Willauer," Holcomb says. "Without Peurifoy in there pounding on the table I don't think Arbenz would have been overthrown."[78] Cable traffic makes clear that during his exploratory talks with Díaz, Peurifoy seemed to go along with the Chief of Staff's proviso that "after massacres his air force caused" Armas must never be invited into the ruling coalition.

But Peurifoy was no man to underplay his hand. That summer the bodies slammed in every direction, and egos were crushed underfoot. When Díaz proved recalcitrant at one point Peurifoy called in a Jerry DeLarm air strike on the Fort Matamoros parade field. By July 8 Armas was in as President, the Labor Code was already forgotten, and worker organizers by the dozens had started to disappear without a forwarding address from United Fruit banana plantations.

Allen Dulles was utterly delighted, needless to say, and arranged for a slide show for the grateful Eisenhower. The evening that preceded the briefing he assembled the operative figures for iced tea around a table in the garden of his house on Wisconsin Avenue. David Phillips would remember how perfect Allen seemed for the role, all compliments and conviviality, his rimless spectacles twinkling in the dusk as he gestured with his pipe or patted his boardroom moustaches. Colonel Haney had been asked to prepare a rundown for the President, and Allen sat expressionless while Haney reviewed his material. "Al," Dulles said when Haney was finally done, "I've never heard such crap."[79] The Director asked Phillips to work with Haney to get together a presentation that made some sense. The thing was behind them, Eisenhower and his brother would certainly be satisfied, and it was past time to dispose of a fanatic like Haney.

Foster Dulles *was* pleased, although there were loose ends that nagged the Secretary. Armas reinstituted discipline—he brought back José Linares, Ubico's "enforcer," who specialized in electric baths for suspects and especially prized a contracting steel skullcap intended to "pry loose secrets and crush improper thoughts."[80] Armas changed the law to accord with Foster Dulles's conviction, as the

Secretary wired Armas at the end of July, that "Communists should be considered [a] class additional to common criminals not entitled [to] asylum." Pressing hard through Peurifoy, Foster demanded that Communists with no other criminal history be "convicted of having been covert Moscow agents." They must not escape to "recirculate" in the international political bloodstream. But asylum was a tradition in Central America, and Armas ultimately let hundreds—including the ruminative young Che Guevara—get out on safe conduct permits. Before Arbenz took off for Mexico, Armas arranged to have him strip-searched at the airport—mouth pursed, all martyr, a medallion of matted belly hair exploding dramatically against his flared-open shirt front before hundreds of the incoming President's contemptuous followers.

United Fruit soon recovered its properties, but that proved less of a triumph than anybody in Boston expected. Five days after Arbenz resigned, the U.S. Department of Justice instituted action against the Fruit Company on antitrust grounds. Tom Corcoran blamed Foster, and fumed that the whole thing was engineered to demonstrate that the pious Secretary of State now intended to scourge himself of all commercial taint while excoriating Godless Communism.[81] United Fruit deteriorated steadily. Politically, Guatemala became a hellhole.

Both Iran and Guatemala stacked up as cut-rate victories. With Eisenhower pushing budget concerns, the enthusiasm ran high for letting Allen continue these things. But inside the Agency, people saw this wobble all the way. Even "clandestinity" wasn't holding up. One senior Agency man who followed the action insists that halfway through the fighting a number of U.S. Navy gunboats were required to shell the Guatemalan regulars, who without them threatened to butcher Armas's amateurs.[82] What with the naval blockade and the repeated Agency bombing runs out of Managua, what we were really mounting here was low-intensity war. Under these circumstances, "plausible deniability" was all Washington hoped for; this wasn't in any way the genuine secrecy Helms preferred, and Lyman Kirkpatrick muttered about risks to men and reputation dependent on the judgment of "the likes of Tracy Barnes."[83] Allen personally favored selected leaks; he remained, after all, the virtuoso of the calculated indiscretion.

The United States prevailed for underlying reasons. A long-standing U.S. military mission catered to ruling-class anxieties. Jack Peurifoy turned up the gas under the Guatemalan military until so much paranoia about the left bubbled over that the hapless Arbenz effectively cooked himself. "Moscow-directed" Communism was never a decisive element. "We followed Arbenz afterwards," a CIA official allows. "He was his own person, he was not a Soviet agent. He didn't go to the Soviet Union and become a colonel in the KGB. Afterward he died horribly, of drugs and alcohol. Nobody came to help him."[84]

19

THE DOTING UNCLE

Iran and Guatemala sufficed to frame out Allen Dulles's reputation as the Cold War's spymaster, "the man who could overturn governments with a snap of his fingers," as Eisenhower historian Stephen Ambrose twitted the legend, "foil the KGB with the back of his hand, uncover secrets no matter where or how deeply hidden."[1] Dulles tinted the backdrops in during talk-show appearances and badinage with reporters. He worked Washington's cocktail-party circuits, booming away, a tremendous, vivacious social catch and salesman nonpareil. J. Edgar Hoover proved that fame brings job security.

Eisenhower needed outside opinions. Early in 1954 a task force under General Mark Clark launched into an overall appraisal of the intelligence community as part of the Hoover Commission's study of the executive branch. To retain confidentiality, the President commissioned a separate, classified report on the DDP by a special committee chaired by Lieutenant General James H. Doolittle, the daredevil who firebombed Tokyo during World War II. Doolittle was something of a pal of Wisner, and along with the other three Pooh-Bahs on his committee he welcomed this conflict with an "implacable enemy" toward whom "acceptable norms of human conduct do not apply." Alongside traditional modes of espionage and counterespionage he promoted the capacity to "subvert, sabotage and destroy our enemies by more clever, more sophisticated, and more effective methods than those used against us," backed up by efforts to win the American people over to "this fundamentally repugnant philosophy."[2]

Doolittle's complaints, in private, centered on Dulles himself, whose "unique knowledge of his subject" and devotion were evident. Dulles's weakness, according to Stephen Ambrose's paraphrase, was "in organization and the relatively poor quality of men he had around him." The juxtaposition of Allen and Foster Doolittle termed "unfortunate," and in Allen personally the hard-boiled aviator remarked traces of an "emotionalism" he sensed was "far worse than it appeared on the surface."

Obviously taken aback, Eisenhower defended his DCI, testifying to his steadiness as stage manager of "one of the most peculiar types of operation any government can have, and it probably takes a strange kind of genius to run it."[3] Meanwhile, the results of the more inclusive Clark Task Force study were in. It "found an excessive emphasis on covert action over intelligence analysis and in particular criticized the quality and quantity of the Agency's intelligence on the Soviet Union."[4]

What Eisenhower was hearing reverberated with the professional military man's impatience, as one later specified, with "intelligence dilettantes. They didn't want to go into the family business, so they went into the world. Everybody was plugged in with everybody else. From OSS days on General Strong was opposed to these people, General Truscott was against this, Beedle Smith quite obviously, Omar Bradley for certain. The OPC was an accident of birth, a place for Wisner to go play games. It was a sandbox. These people just get in your way if you've got a real operation to run. They considered themselves the shock troops of the Cold War. What these guys didn't realize was that the war was over. You change the world one piece at a time."

For all Allen's slide shows, Dwight Eisenhower was well aware that Guatemala had degenerated during its final weeks into a diplomatic and military bailout. Between the President and the wily CIA Director the contest was on, punctuated by repeated attempts by the White House to supervise and—whenever possible—disentangle Dulles from the many operations with which he loved to tinker. The cunning and personable Dulles calculatedly ignored and misunderstood and wherever possible reinterpreted his exasperated President's intentions. "I'm not going to be able to change Allen," Ike finally conceded. "I'd rather have Allen as my chief intelligence officer with his limitations than anyone else I know."[5]

The fall of Dien Bien Phu by early May of 1954 had already

helped suck the Agency into Indochina. As Foster saw matters, Anthony Eden had ratted out on an implicit commitment to back the French, too late to rouse American public opinion and consigning the West to mount a diplomatic delaying action against Ho Chi Minh. CIA staff support of Ed Landsdale's 1953 campaign against the Huks in the Philippines, which produced the clean-broom regime of Ramon Magsaysay, looked more and more like a prototype for Asia.[6] With Bao Dai vegetating in European spas, it took very little to install as premier Ngo Dinh Diem, a semiscrutable Roman Catholic whose immediate family resembled the road-company cast of *Terry and the Pirates*. Diem had been premier during an earlier incarnation under the Japanese.[7] Communists were overrunning Laos.

Asia was developing fast from the Agency's point of view.

Allen Dulles rounded out 1954 busily restaffing the Agency. In 1954 Beedle Smith finally gave up on a fifth star and took his overdue retirement. Dulles betrayed few regrets. Throughout Iran and Guatemala his former boss's attentiveness had provided an unwelcome strain—dissatisfaction pouching and crimping the little man's mouth, those black eyes constant enough to score glass. In October Smith wrote Allen at the "old shop." "You have been wonderful to work with," the Beedle acknowledged, "and best of all you have always forgiven me when I yelled and snapped and tried your patience."[8] Smith accepted the vice chairmanship of the American Machine and Foundry Company and joined the board of United Fruit.

The guard now underwent a thoroughgoing internal shift. With Frank Lindsay out, both Wisner and Dulles felt freer to experiment with rollback possibilities. The raffish Tom Braden gave up his place in the Agency to his deputy, Cord Meyer, who took over the important International Organizations Division. Once an idealistic founder of the United World Federalists, Meyer had hardened quickly into a "bright but rebarbative man," as Stewart Alsop wrote, "with a certain genius for making enemies. . . ." Meyer subscribed to the Angletonian vision of the all-encroaching Soviet diabolism. "Jim sucked Cord Meyer in, in my view," Braden rasps. "Cord became not only a great admirer, but also a believer."

Angleton more than anybody took courage from Allen Dulles's ascension. At the Director's fiat the counterintelligence specialists were upgraded in 1954 to coequals inside the DDP with the espionage and covert bosses, an elite staff proliferating into the hundreds before Dulles stepped down. "What you had in actuality was a marriage that went across the board," says one senior CI mandarin. "On the one hand we were supposed to be a shield for the Agency, but in a way we were the most exposed. We inherited a lot of odds and ends other people didn't have the guts to continue, as well as anything that involved real brainpower. . . ."[9] Resentment was widespread—though muffled at first—as Angleton and his internal-affairs people spread out across the Agency. "We never had a successful Soviet operation that Angleton and his crowd didn't cast some doubt on," complained John Maury, chief of the Soviet Union Division at the time. "In house it was all right to raise doubts, but Jim and a few of his close colleagues allowed his suspicions to be widely known around the Hill."[10]

Angleton's obsession with nurturing his friends started people referring to him, quite openly, as "Mother." "When Cord Meyer's ex-wife Mary was murdered while exercising on the path next to the Potomac canal," one bystander alleges, "Angleton had already let himself into her house with a key he kept to the place even before the cops turned up. I think he was after papers he knew she kept in her bedroom which had to do with her affair with John Kennedy."

But where should justifiable doubts end and paranoia begin? "Angleton would sidle up," Tom Braden still remembers, "and out of the blue he'd hit you with something like: 'Last week the Polish military attaché stayed an extra night in Peking. Does that have any significance for you, Braden?' "[11] Others appreciated this supervailing presence, especially after those patchy start-up years around the OPC. It forced responsible people to examine their own work. The WIN humiliation rankled, and although even acolytes of Angleton's acknowledged that they too lacked the capacity to "unscrew the inscrutable," CI's new legitimacy as resident devil's advocate and operational security screen could hedge everybody's exposure.

"Our view of the counterintelligence staff ranged from comical to one of horror," confesses a veteran of the era. Angleton claimed to commune with foreign sources nobody else ever identified; at efforts to pin him down he scratched around so much dust his challengers exited, coughing. How could anybody contend with—unless one accepted purely, baldly, on faith—certain of the conclusions Jim and his troops adduced after years of pouring over scraps of administrative paperwork from a dozen governments, a mélange of recently cut travel orders and ancient yearbook bios and cryptonyms off the VENONA transcriptions, random phrases of conversation scribbled on a cocktail napkin. Was Tito Khrushchev's stalking horse? Could Averell Harriman actually be a Soviet agent? Intuitions played a lead role—he wasn't, Angleton confessed willingly enough, a "linear thinker."

Side moves were incessant. After a murderously long working day the shadowy insomniac was likely to slip across the bridge to Arlington and his restive wife, Cicely. While calmer men slept he hovered through the off-duty hours above his prize-winning orchids, soldered bits of hammered gold into jewelry for friends. Society hostesses thrilled halfway into the salad course as he husked out references—no details, of course, but Kee-rihst, the implications!—of unreported fracases in aboriginal corners of the planet on which Western survival would depend before the week was out. Angleton's mystique bloomed unceasingly, verdant as any lady's slipper.

No administrator, Angleton brought back Ray Rocca, a confidant since X-2 days, from Italy in 1953 to preside over the all-important "research" efforts of his accumulating staff. A sensitive, dedicated linguist, skittish as a faun, Rocca labored to insinuate rationality. By then even Wisner seemed to be coming around. "Frank grew in the job," a CI senior observes. "I found him a better and better friend as time went on. He came around to recognizing one of the basic elements that X-2 had stood for—that every covert action manager has to be perfectly willing to organize and enforce operational security."

Already cast as Merlin in Allen Dulles's refulgent Camelot, Angleton took his holy screed after 1962 from the meglomaniacal Anatoli Golitsin, a KGB defector who burst in on both the British and Americans overflowing hints and clues bearing on hundreds of Soviet penetrations into the Western services along with blueprints for a worldwide Soviet disinformation campaign and word that both the apparent Yugoslav and Chinese breaks with the Kremlin were hoaxes. Angleton adopted the defector—"He built his whole position on Golitsin," argues one Soviet Bloc chief—in part because the erratic Russian's revelations squared perfectly with everything Angleton feared.[12] A pragmatic, even companionable fellow off the job, Angleton stiffened at the very contemplation of "the nature of the threat," as the catch phrase went. Wisner shared Angleton's demons, along with his presumption that *anything* went which undermined and vitiated the vast, dark congeries of advancing Communist evil.

Inevitably they combined forces. Information Angleton's men were processing, much of it brought out of Eastern Europe through refugee Jewish networks, accorded with the grumblings Wisner's OPC case officers heard from the Ukrainians and Byelorussians and Balts and Ustases and Iron Guard and Arrow Cross soreheads they'd sustained, generally through Gehlen, for almost a decade. A mesmerizing Yugoslav ex-diplomat was still retailing royalist fantasies around the salons of Georgetown, and Frank and Jim both surprised their subordinates by taking quite seriously such tales of rebellion in the making.[13] Meanwhile, detachments of "Special Forces" hung in at Bad Tolz and along the Tegernsee; promising officer material reached Fort Bragg, and there were reportedly top-secret units as remote as the Pacific trust territories. Once "rollback" started they'd have their troops on the line.

Within the Directorate itself Wisner compartmented off his Munich-based liberation teams from the more sedate OSO professionals who managed the Eastern desks day-to-day. But broad intentions leaked. In 1952 Peter Sichel came back to Washington to sit in as chief of operations for Eastern Europe. He was quickly tangling with Wisner over the proliferation of OSS retreads clogging up the division, many obviously incompetent and kept on the payroll largely because of their romantic attachment to the business. "One day you're going to wake up and you're going to throw them out," Sichel told Frank, "and they will have missed the boat and have a terrible life. At first Frank was very aggressive about it, but he understood. He just had a very short fuse. But he was an enormously generous person, he took people seriously, and he would talk to people who had things on their minds and *listen* to them. He was a very moral guy, there were a lot of layers to Frank. It's just that he was an enormously tense human being in the office because everything was important. There were a lot of crises created that were not crises."[14]

By 1955 nobody in Sichel's chair could miss the patterns taking shape. "The Agency that is collecting intelligence should not get involved in dirty games," he insisted to Allen just before his last assignment, to Hong Kong. "We got all sorts of rightist groups in Germany to set up resistance groups in case the Russians attacked, et cetera. It never works when you become the client and the provider of intelligence at the same time. Your intelligence gets slanted."[15]

Sichel was alluding here to a scandal which broke over the German stations the winter of 1953–1954. The free spirit who fabricated this debacle was a tubby blond ex-Austrian labor organizer who spooked as Henry C. Sutton. A "walking dictionary of German and Austrian political activity," he reminded Sichel of "a nondrinking Bill Harvey. He had the same kind of brain, the same capacity to absorb an enormous amount of detail. Yet at the same time we all realized that Sutton had no practical sense.

"But then the OPC turned up and recruited him into political action."[16] In the Frankfurt area, "Sutton went at the job with his usual energy and competence,"[17] the veteran Tom Polgar says. "He was the powerhouse, he could outtalk, outbull everybody else at any conference,"[18] Truscott's key advisor Peter Jessup adds. Truscott was increasingly watchful: Wisner had a weakness for these self-styled wheeler-dealers, and recently had passed along $100,000 to the semi-retired Polish flying ace Boleslav ("Mike") Gladych, who promised to steal into the DDR and bring out the new MIG. But Boleslav got waylaid by dozens of girls and wound up out of cash in a suite at the Vier Jahrezeiten in Munich.

During this period the Communists were heavily into youth-dominated front organizations. Henry Sutton's pièce de résistance, the sprawling Bunddeutsche Jugend, "became the vehicle to counter this effort," Polgar submits. "And among other things they drew up a secret list of leftist politicians who had to be eliminated the day the Russians attacked. So they wouldn't survive to form a, you know, a Quisling-type government.

"The trouble was that their definition of what was a leftist politician to be eliminated included practically all the leaders of the Social Democratic Party." Polgar, a Hungarian by birth, can't suppress a hollow, ironic laugh. "And when this came to the attention of the public, the shit, as the saying goes, hit the fan. It was my unenviable role to accompany General Truscott to the office of the Minister-President of Hesse, who was a Social Democrat, and explain that this whole thing was sort of the unauthorized activity of a couple of careless junior officers." Projects across the board got leveled, and Henry Sutton, shrugging, wound up buried alive in Washington, once more a clerk.

"Sutton was not a Nazi," insists another Agency stalwart, "but certainly by 1953 the Bunddeutsche Jugend was predominantly Nazi in nature. Ex-Nazis were the only ones Sutton felt we could rely on in case the Russians came in. With Sutton as their main brain they stashed radios in a number of places, along with weapons and money. . . . It was still possible in those days to suppress the majority of the details, but there were a few flaps in the German press, with question marks raised." In Washington additional controls went on.

Throughout the many desks an awareness was spreading that liberationists at the top of the OPC were not only preparing for rebellion in the East but slanting their analytic conclusions to justify the action programs underway. Efforts by Tracy Barnes were especially confusing, mushing together propaganda and covert initiatives. All timetables were speeded up. "These Wall Street lawyers the OPC had were suddenly sort of in there sending propaganda to places in Czechoslovakia without exactly knowing where it was on the map," remembers Howard Roman, who managed a progression of Bloc desks.[19]

By then Khrushchev's gestures to decouple Moscow politically to some extent from the satellite governments had Washington vertiginous. Roman recalls being "called to meetings where Frank Wisner would hold forth, very much the high priest of political intelligence and psychological warfare. I remember talks to the branch chiefs when Gomulka and all that was happening. On how all the nationalist Communist movements were something Washington must absolutely learn to exploit, on how we must look at who the people were in each particular country who would fall in that category and what to do to create divisiveness among them. This was all high-priest kind of stuff to us, it was way over the heads of a lot of our guys. And it was highly impractical."

When two Titoist defectors appeared from one of the Bloc countries and Wisner dispatched a couple of "high-speed psychological warriors" to Holland to squeeze up other names the OPC might recruit, Roman's boss, John Baker, told his confused staffers that "for all we knew these fellows were sent out by Paderewski, and we didn't really need to do anything like that." Wisner was evidently spoiling for a repeat of WIN.

The discrepancy between what Wisner and his friends at State and the Pentagon were bent on game-planning and what was out there amounted to "a joke," Howard acknowledges. "From time to time somebody would come over from the Pentagon and talk to us. There was a map up there. I remember when Mike Hoffa came with his green flags showing what was what on the other side of the border—where the escape and evasion routes were, where the radio operators would broadcast from. . . .

"This was flimsy stuff. Maybe somebody had said once, 'Yeah, I could help you guys sometime.' Every once in a while somebody who was a fairly fancy type did get out, and he gets debriefed. Then you got some little guy who seemed to be willing to risk his life and go through the barbed wire and hope that his ex-girlfriend in some town will put him up for the night . . . One night he climbs three flights of stairs to where the former head cashier of the bank sits, in hopes he'll know what's happening to the finances of the Communists and he can persuade the guy to work for the Americans.

"Or maybe you'd send in a cross-border operator who was supposed to contact a fellow he knew who worked in the aircraft factory, and our guy happened to bump into another fellow who had a house in the country. He brought that back, and we'd say, ah, great, we'll fill that in for an escape and evasion route, that's where an aviator can hide. . . . Or a radio operator. Farms usually had big manure heaps, which was of course where they would stick the transmitters. . . ."

D.C. was awash with refugees who purported to speak for vast, combustible undergrounds. "The real fun," Roman says, "which you could waste your life on, was trying to keep the peace among the contending exile party chiefs. The OPC people tended to believe what these guys told them. . . . Exploiting Free Europe Committee contacts and longstanding business associations, a number of upscale ex-dignitaries contrived to "make themselves popular at fairly high levels," Roman says, "particularly with the Dulleses. They would get shunted off to some fancy-pants assistant, who would take them to the Metropolitan Club, where they would hand out a *hell* of a lot of crap."

CI paperwork especially was replete with reports of resistance groups coalescing throughout the Balkans picked up by Angleton's listening posts. The top administrators heard what they wanted to hear, and in the battle over policy "there was a hell of a lot of shystering," Roman could see. His bosses craved action. "I'm only intimating here," Howard says, "and there *were* sources, but even Angleton was not above having sources that were not all that . . . reliable, you know. He had so many. . . ."

By then the Agency's Technical Assistance Division was providing the CI branch with ten to fifteen sets of counterfeit documents a year for agents headed into the Soviet Union itself.[20] Angleton was already pushing for his own liaison man in London.[21] Colonels around the G-2 headquarters in the Pentagon bitched constantly about having to squeeze out Angleton's informants, lying low like wood ticks among the clerks and secretaries.[22]

There remained a contempt for verification sometimes which put off those supergrade outsiders, Beedle Smith's Senior Representatives; they survived, if weakened, under the indulgent Allen. In both the Far East and later in London Admiral Oberresch clashed openly and often savagely with Wisner. Lieutenant General Lucian Truscott—now protecting a heart condition—couldn't contain his disgust at the sheer self-*delusionary* atmosphere Wisner seemed to encourage.

"Early in Truscott's time in Germany Wisner came over," Peter Jessup recollects, "and I think Helms and a couple of the other higher-ups. To Munich, on a trip. And they had to talk to General Handy in Frankfurt, and then they went on to Stuttgart where the Eighth Army was. . . .

"And at the end of the day Wisner drafted a cable. For the general to sign, since he was the Senior Representative. They were all staying in one of the Nazi Ministers' palazzos, Ley, I think it was, the Labor Minister's. They all had drinks, it was about six o'clock in the afternoon, and they submitted this tour d'horizon cable to send back eyes-only to Dulles. And Truscott sipped on his drink. And then he said, 'Well, the first paragraph is untrue, the second paragraph, well, that's a lie. . . .' He went through the cable, shredding it. And they were absolutely boggle-eyed. They thought they had some old fogy there. He just said that the cable was a lot of crap, and he wanted it redone."[23]

Over on the analysis side, Ray Cline was beginning to hear about "a series of programs intended to recruit Soviet and Eastern European Communists" with a nationalist orientation, although "it was not altogether clear whether they were to serve as espionage agents or for covert action purposes." Arms caches were smuggled in and buried, lists of potential insurgents initialed as they passed among selected offices. All this accorded nicely with a "whole system of war planning," Cline discovered, "it was a kind of calculation of assets that might be created behind the Iron Curtain if a World War III-type of war were to break out. Military intelligence people at the time were obsessed with the doctrine that there was a strong probability that war would break out two years hence. Always two years hence. Whether Frank and Jim, who were very close, believed that, I don't know, but they were very happy to have the military say this, because it gave them a role. It made it possible for them to do the clandestine and covert things that made the Agency operational. I think they were thinking of peacetime operations, but they didn't mind exaggerating their wartime potential."

Taking over as station chief in Germany in 1966, Cline came upon a trove of "papers, plans, a map of clandestine assets that could have been activated behind the Iron Curtain in a military emergency. These resources had long before evaporated." Afterward, Cline relates, Angleton liked to muse that there had been a "big potential for something happening there, but, Jim, being Jim, he would never tell you what it was."[24]

Allen Dulles personally never seems to have been troubled long by the dangers of compiling assault logistics based on the reminiscences of ex-Count X or premier-in-retirement Y over cocktails at his club. The agents sent over to scout the battleground itself, as Howard Roman describes them, were not especially reassuring—"usually people with criminal problems: embezzlers, men who had trouble with their wives, mental cases. . . ."[25] Who else was willing to scale those triple barbed-wire fences, with alarm sirens wailing away and machine-gun bullets jerking open the plowed strips between the watchtowers, while hungry dogs yowled and scampered and sniffed along the margins of the concertina wire.

That wasn't Allen's level. "When we had problems Dulles wasn't there, it wasn't his baby," Roman contends. "That stuff didn't interest him very much, you know. We'd end up seeing General Cabell, the Deputy Director. Allen Dulles was the man who gave you good advice—somebody would give him a glimpse of the Red Sox–Red Cap proposal for resistance in Hungary, for example, and his reaction was, sure, give 'em a free hand. Give 'em a gold star for drawing up something like this. Allen Dulles was first of all a man who had very little knowledge of counterespionage. When Allen was head of SI in Bern, he hadn't cared for X-2 at all." Most of the preparations for destabilizing the Bloc countries thus depended on agents nobody took the trouble to vet. Allen applauded the big picture, projections of the sort that emerged over cognac with cherished informants like the Archduke Otto, pretender to Austro-Hungary.[26]

Frank Wisner was similarly inclined to cut to the expansive formulation, and manifested an upper-class impatience with too much follow-up once decisions were in. He preferred the drafting phases. "Wiz always prepared his projects with the greatest eye for detail," John Bross says, "and made sure to ask for twice as much of everything he needed to give them a chance."[27] Colleagues remember Wisner avidly pouring over an operational draft, breaking off to harangue somebody on the telephone, then snapping back immediately, picking up the subject precisely where he had left off, frequently in midphrase. He alone on the operational side had access to policy-making levels of the government. One aide recalls how eloquently his boss could deal at State Department conferences on almost any subject "even when he didn't know damn-all about it. He would study a workup of the particulars on the way over in the car, and by the time he got there he seemed as knowledgeable as anybody in the room."

As the fifties deepened the eyes Wisner felt more and more burning holes in his back were those of Lyman Kirkpatrick. Lyman still couldn't forget how polio had cost him control of operations, and resented in particular "the fact that nobody from Washington had the courage to come and tell me that this had been done. . . ."[28] Once he had returned, Dulles offered him the post Stuart Hedden vacated,

Inspector General. Lyman found that "Mr. Dulles . . . didn't intend to require all of the units to submit to inspections," especially on the operational side, and "we settled in to what became a fairly intensive jurisdictional struggle."[29] He now characterizes the entire covert palette as pretty much a matter of "who's manipulating whom. That's why controls are so important. It's done through money, the development of friendships, of mutuality of interests. You get people so much in your debt, under your control, that they can't break off or betray you. . . ."[30]

There was a morbidity about such a vision which repelled romantics like Wisner and Dulles. In time a glimpse of Kirkpatrick's wheelchair bouncing down a corridor, his ruddy, implacable countenance—this produced complicated feelings in the emergent leadership. "Wisner hated him," Dick Bissell says flatly. "Allen ended up hating him. Kirkpatrick is a funny person. He is very bright, well informed, articulate, but he would knife anybody in the back for not much more than twenty-five cents worth of advantage."[31]

Bissell seems a gentle soul, quite old and cherubic now, and the fact that he would relieve himself of such a scorcher a quarter of a century after the Bay of Pigs suggests the intensity of emotions around the expanding Agency. What Allen made sure of while Kirkpatrick was convalescing was that he wouldn't have to operate too close to this protégé of Beedle's now that real resources were arriving to contest the Soviets. Helms didn't appreciate paramilitary, but he was invaluable for keeping the paperwork straight so that the operators might disport. "Helms is a professional," Kirkpatrick sums it up. "He's been in this work a long, long time. He's a meticulous administrator, which in those days was especially appreciated by the staff. I myself admired Richard Helms greatly for his stolidity."[32]

❏

What Dulles was organizing toward, quite clearly, was the recovery of the East. The Church Committees said as much by emphasizing that the "CIA station in West Berlin was the center of CIA operations against Eastern Europe, and the German Branch of the European Division was the Agency's largest single country component." Meanwhile, "In the period 1952 to 1963 the Agency acquired most of its clandestine information through liaison arrangements with foreign governments."[33] Except for the fading assets of the SIS, almost everything Washington saw bearing on East Germany, and much of the

Soviet detail, came through from Pullach. By then an estimated 80 percent of the CIA's overall budget went into covert undertakings. Espionage acquired secondhand helped keep the totals manageable.

Dulles endorsed these dependencies; nothing shook his dedication to the "good Germans" who made his wartime reputation. In 1950, just before taking on the CIA full time, Dulles endeavored to pull strings in behalf of General Alexander von Falkenhausen, an old-school Junker whose contempt for Hitler hadn't inhibited him from executing hostages in Belgium throughout the war and ordering the deportation to death camps of 25,000 Jews.[34]

Allen wrote Erika Canaris—she had reproved him for suggesting in *The German Underground* that her martyred husband was of Greek descent—and now that Agency funds were available, Dulles and Reinhard Gehlen resettled the admiral's widow on a pension in Spain. Old chums from Bern had no trouble finding Dulles. By 1950 the hulking Hans Bernd Gisevius had lurched into Washington, where Tom Braden and his wife looked after him for some months as a favor to Dulles. Already something of a hardship case, Gisevius would stultify Allen with long stories about his efforts in the interests of the Lutheran Synod. Nevertheless, Dulles retained "a great fondness for him," Braden says, and throughout this period "Allen was feeding him money, I know that Allen was signing chits for $5,000 at a time for Gisevius."[35]

Another regular was Gaevernitz, who pressed the association throughout the remainder of Dulles's life and included himself as a kind of collaborator in the production of Dulles's last book, *The Secret Surrender*. Gaevernitz luck—and judgment—in business associations had not improved noticeably over the years. He struggled with investments in Peru. Roman recalls that Gaevernitz had committed the preponderance of his funds to cargo in an eccentrically designed refrigerator ship. The freighter proved top-heavy in a storm and disappeared at sea with all hands.

Dulles kept contacts up with lifelong pleaders for the German officer caste like his prewar informant Colonel Truman Smith. Long after Dulles became head of the Agency, Smith continued to pass along the apprehensions of such General Staff alumni as Franz Halder and Hans Speidel. Speidel, Rommel's Chief of Staff, impressed on Dulles through Smith his perception that Pierre Mendès-France was surrounded by "fellow travelers," and chivied Dulles for everything from favorable reviews for his books to support for the reviving German Army.[36] "Following our interesting dinner with General Speidel," Dulles reported to Truman Smith in November of 1955, "I had a chance to entertain him and bring him in touch with some of the civilian side of the government:—Gordon Gray, Assistant Secretary of Defense who is handling foreign matters in the Defense Establishment, Bob Murphy and one or two others, including several people from my shop. . . ."[37] By 1957 Speidel was commander of all NATO Forces in Western Europe.

Inevitably, Dulles relied on tested commercial associations to mask the Agency's widening fund transfers. The J. Henry Schroder Banking Corporation and the Schroder Trust functioned as prime depositories for CIA monies throughout the fifties and sixties, long after the New York branch had formally been reabsorbed by the London-based J. Henry Schroder and Company, Limited.[38] Like the Kaplan Foundation and half a dozen others which ultimately served as conduits between the accumulating fronts and the proliferation of committees and congresses and institutes and societies which augmented Wisner's Wurlitzer, the banking nexus depended on how many layers of concealment an operation might require.[39] Schroder dealt with sensitive cases, although "There were certainly no biases in that matter," Richard Helms concludes. "Hell, the Agency sloshed money all over the world."[40]

Another *retour du personnage* from those heroic days and nights at Herrengasse 23 would be the eternally winning Fritz Molden. "He was one guy who built an empire on CIA money," declares a retired official in a position to monitor the process. "He became a newspaper publisher in Vienna. In time he got very, very big on CIA subsidies, and then he went bust. That really was one of the most spectacular CIA careers. I suppose this to some extent taints Dulles, because Fritz was, after all, Allen's son-in-law for a time."

Molden enjoyed a brief marriage to Allen's oldest daughter, Joan. Never really a family man, Dulles found his children a source of bafflement and frustration. Most anguishing was Allen, Junior. During the Korean war, his father had personally nixed the young Princeton honor student's appointment through the Agency to a safe quasi-diplomatic outpost. "There will be no special treatment for my son,"[41] Allen declared, and months later the boy went in with the U.S. marines at Inchon and took a severe head wound. He left the hospital morose, limp, and antagonistic toward his father and his oppressive Uncle Foster. In 1955 Allen referred in a letter to an operation his son had recently undergone to implant a metal plate "where the skull had been torn away. This went well, and I think will have a good psychological effect as he has always worried somewhat about the 'hole in his head.' It is almost too much to hope, however, that it would have any real bearing on the mental or physical problems."[42] Young Allen would languish for years in an expensive Swiss sanitarium, lashing out whenever his father looked in. He reportedly remained in the clinic until word came through that Allen, Senior, had indeed passed on.[43]

❑

For all his sermonizing, it really wasn't Foster so much as Allen who carried the Cold War can between 1945 and Korea. His meager, solemn mouth twisted throughout the Truman decade with bipartisan political pieties, Foster had come tardily to his outrage over containment. By 1953 he'd worked up a high, permanent lather. Even the militant Beedle Smith could see that Foster was starting to bypass healthy reality. "Dulles is still dreaming his fancy about reactivating the civil war in China," Smith noted at the time.[44]

Democrats who once sat with him on international commissions and conferences with the Soviets derided his eleventh-hour breakthrough during the 1952 campaign into a "fire-breathing warmonger who would obliterate Europe with hydrogen bombs in order to free Poland and so gain votes in Hamtramck."[45] English leaders were also contemptuous of Foster's Elmer Gantry hobgoblinizations. Even before his nomination Anthony Eden attempted to talk Eisenhower out of letting Foster lead the State Department. Churchill loathed the very prospect of confronting Foster's white, looming face, and referred to him snidely as "Dullith." On hearing that Allen would be running the CIA, Winston groaned and responded: "They tell me that there is another Dullith. Is that possible?[46]

This reception augured poorly for the Grand Alliance, but undoubtedly it invited the historical abrazzo between Konrad Adenauer and Foster. Apart from their common Christian-authoritarian philosophical matrix, ponderousness and doomsday rhetoric went down better at Bonn than anyplace inside Whitehall. They shared a dedication to Germany as an outpost of the Christian West, and with or without the restless, unpredictable Prussians. This had been brewing since Foster was a bright young aide at Versailles and Adenauer a prominent Rhenish separatist. The crisis that very nearly obliterated the European Defense Community in 1954 agonized both leaders; unity must be cemented, as Townsend Hoopes reprises Foster's thinking, "while Germany was still dependent and militarily weak, and while Adenauer was still in control. Adenauer fully shared this view, fearing (or professing to fear) that, left to their own devices, the West Germany people would gravitate inevitably toward unification on Communist terms."[47] And beneath all this, as Joyce and Gabriel Kolko have written, United States planners intended "to integrate Germany in order to control it in future years. . . . To protect the West against Germany rather than Russia was the ultimate basis of this calculus, which Dulles retained until his death."[48] The end of the Austrian occupation in 1955 threatened to provide a seductive model for a reunited Germany. The Soviets were pushing. Foster preferred armed truce.

He managed his counterattack largely from the air, approaching or departing conferences; perhaps he traveled constantly because he was never really at home in Washington. Around Foggy Bottom his mission-oak personality and heart-stopping sour breath kept most careerists treading at a distance. Eisenhower on taking office had hedged Foster in with three diplomats he knew well: Smith, Douglas MacArthur II, and the seemingly jointless and eternally complaisant Robert Murphy. All three betrayed a throttled look as Foster's grip tightened, and remained as accommodating as feasible while edging toward retirement. Foster did permit a modicum of guff from the new Policy and Planning head Robert Bowie and the Department's legal adviser, Herman Pfleger, a tough-minded attorney from San Francisco. At senior administrative levels Foster installed—rarely bothering to check them out until they were underfoot—a collection of clunkers. Of these the most unfortunate choices were reportedly the Undersecretary of State for Administration, Donald Lourie (lately the president of the Quaker Oats Company), and two erratic newspapermen, Carl McCardle and Scott McLeod. McLeod, it developed, regarded himself primarily as a commissar for Senator Joe McCarthy.[49] "Dulles' people," the disheartened Dean Acheson wrote one former assistant, "seem to me like Cossacks quartered in a grand city hall, burning the paneling to cook with."[50]

To deal with Central and Eastern Europe, Foster relied on Herbert Hoover, Jr. Hoover's conservatism remained paramount, and he stood in as the enforcing presence should others consider wavering. Expertise sold off, sharply. "There really was only one man at State who understood Eastern Europe, Jake Beam," a contemporary maintains, "and he was powerless under Herbert Hoover, Jr."[51] It suited Foster better not so much to lead the State Department as preside over its occupation.

❏

At ground level, Allen Dulles had been nudging toward some sort of traditionalist alignment in Europe for decades. He identified the main players early. From Berlin in August 1945 he circulated the name of Dr. Hans Globke (who drew up the enabling legal commentary on the anti-Semitic Nuremburg Laws in 1935) for consideration as a provisional minister of the interior.[52] Once Adenauer rose, Globke emerged as his administrative chief, state secretary, and crossruffed trusted staffers in his own secretariat with appropriate representatives of Reinhard Gehlen's Org. In November of 1953 the half-fledged German government would embarrass Allen by attempting to route diplomatic sticking points through him, bypassing State's James Conant.[53] "Gehlen was considered a window through which American influence could be exerted on the development of the Federal Republic," John Bross comments.[54] Favors went both ways. While Pullach was technically a U.S. subsidiary, a lot of staff time there went into screening the Zone for troublemakers—that is, non-Communist political activists disinclined to fall in alongside Adenauer's Christian Democrats.[55]

In 1951 the Allied High Commission, succumbing to the wishes of its British and French members, imposed on Adenauer's administration at the Palais Schaumberg a Federal Internal Security Office (the Bundesamt Fuer Verfassungsschutz—BFV) headed by a naive lawyer with small experience in the field but an undisputed anti-Nazi record, Otto John. When John referred publicly to one of the activist groups of Eastern refugees as a "potential camouflage organization for illegal political activity," Adenauer sent over Globke to dress him down. Gehlen's sleuths stayed close to John. In June of 1954 Otto John visited the United States, where Allen Dulles provided lunch one day before lobbying John for help in pulling together the European Defense Community with or without the French. The sort of armed forces John had in mind for Germany was based on a grass-roots militia, nothing like the mini-Wehrmacht Hans Spiedel and his friends trumped up. A month later John bobbed up unexpectedly in East Berlin—drugged and Shanghaied, he would later maintain. This opened the way for Gehlen and his apparat to entrench themselves uncontested as the official information service for the Federal Republic, the Bundesnachrichtendienst (BND), in April of 1956.[56]

What Gehlen already meant to the Agency was plain once careers started somersaulting through the windshield after Allen collided with one of the most redoubtable personalities the military could field just then, Major General Arthur Trudeau. Very much a soldier's soldier, Trudeau trained his amphibious engineers into devastating across-the-beach units which excelled in action from Iwo Jima to Anzio. As the Cold War sharpened, Trudeau had taken command of the First Constabulary Brigade, which policed the U.S. Zone in Germany; even then his intelligence staffers had started to drag in evidence that CIA sources were routinely being scooped. Each time the military turned up a prospect with lines into Pullach a rash of agents defected, entire nets closed down amidst widespread arrests in the DDR.[57]

In November of 1953, back from a hitch in Korea, Arthur Trudeau became the U.S. Army's top intelligence officer, head of G-2. The restoration of sovereignty to the Republic of Germany had now been finalized for 1954, and Trudeau was increasingly concerned at the prospect that all NATO documents would soon be automatically available for review by Gehlen's senior analysts. "My operatives in the U.S. and Europe were keenly concerned because of the growing number of losses through the Gehlen establishment of operatives in Eastern Europe," the general recalls. Trudeau made it a point to hint strongly that it was time for the Germans to appoint an army attaché, somebody of equivalent rank, with whom he might pursue this pesky security question.

"One day in the spring of 1955," Trudeau says, "the German ambassador, who I believe was still Hans Krechler, called me in my G-2 offices at the Pentagon and asked me to come over. He had a visitor who would be glad to see me." The ambassador led Trudeau into the garden of the embassy, where Chancellor Adenauer awaited him.

Trudeau had brought along a packet of more than thirty 3×5 file cards on Gehlen employees he was convinced were reporting to the Eastern services. "Despite my amazement," Trudeau says, "I felt compelled to present the situation as I saw it. I used the figure that more than thirty of Gehlen's operatives had been identified in the last eighteen months. Adenauer asked several questions, and at the end of the conversation he requested the cards. Somewhat taken aback, I could do nothing but turn them over to him."

Scarcely a week afterward the new Army Chief of Staff, Maxwell Taylor, called Trudeau in and informed him that he had been directed by the Secretary of Defense, Charles Wilson, to terminate Trudeau's appointment as chief of Army intelligence and move him out of the country. The letter that precipitated this career-shattering reversal "not only had the vigorous support of Allen Dulles," the general insists, "but also, I understand, of his brother, the Secretary of State."[58] Allen needed Gehlen badly, which meant his people *couldn't* be subjected this way to boat-rocking from ham-handed military.

"Some of the military intelligence officers in Germany were making allegations, they were reporting allegations," James Critchfield says now, not without a palpable weariness. "Now, what Trudeau should have done, he should have taken these cases up at the intelligence community level. But instead he took Adenauer down the garden path, literally. He fished these three-by-five cards out of his pocket and began to read some of them to Adenauer. When the old fox came back, he called Globke in, and he turned the cards over to Globke. Globke made two inquiries, I think of Henry Pleasants and somebody else up there at the time. And then they sent them down to me. We did not discuss them with Gehlen. I had my staff—I had an excellent counterintelligence staff in Germany, and we had developed very detailed files—and I gave them these allegations, these cases, and within twenty-four hours we had information on them. I wrote a long telex to headquarters. And Allen Dulles took it, after he cut the top off of it, and the bottom, and handed it to the Deputy Secretary of Defense."

Everything reached the President's desk, Critchfield remembers, "and the next thing I heard he'd fired Trudeau. . . . We didn't find the allegations impressive."[59]

Impressive or otherwise, it ultimately was fully demonstrated in the courts of the Bundesrepublik that even as these cables flew back and forth, and for six more years, Gehlen's own counterintelligence chief and liaison to NATO Heinz Felfe continued to photocopy card files, doctor evidence, pass EDC current intelligence wrap-ups to the East German clearing house at Karlshorst, feed disinformation back through, monitor radio intercepts.[60] "I will tell you that we had decided that there was a penetration of the organization," Critchfield divulges now. "We were getting close," Critchfield maintains, but then the BND itself moved in on Felfe—along with his accomplices Hans Clemens and Erwin Tiebel—in November 1961. Jim Critchfield will hint with great delicacy that Felfe himself was used up at that point, and thrown to the investigators by the Soviets to protect a deeper, more strategic contact.

Felfe's arrest was expertly timed; it broke into headlines around the world a matter of weeks after Allen Dulles resigned from the Agency. From Allen's standpoint, a well-conceived liaison arrangement was every bit as productive as outright technical ownership. Gehlen followed Adenauer's lead by initiating closer exchanges with the French services than the Americans liked, and waving the English off.[61]

One biographer asserts that Dulles rounded their long proprietary association off by presenting the colorless Spartan an Agency draft for DM 250,000, and urged the general to go buy something livable for himself, something in the mountains, perhaps. Confused, Gehlen seems to have stared at Dulles unbelievingly for a moment, clicked his heels, and acquired a two-storied timbered chalet on the Starnbergersee.[62] Gehlen himself would subsequently pronounce Dulles "both fatherly and boisterous, and he would become a close personal friend of mine."[63] There really weren't many. In September 1968, when bad publicity and a nasty run of political cave-ins had forced the flange-eared master of the Org into uneasy retirement, he ventured a nostalgic trip to Washington. Both the failing Allen Dulles and current CIA Director Richard Helms entertained elegantly—if selectively—for their single-minded brother in espionage.[64]

It may yet develop that Allen Dulles's greatest contribution to the fledgling Agency was the unexampled range of his associations, his knack for engendering even in a cuttlefish like Reinhard Gehlen a kind of personal loyalty which transcended payoffs and beggared nationalism. "Allen Dulles had no real friends, but he certainly had a million warm acquaintances," comments one close observer.[65] Dulles understood the internal mechanics of a big bureaucracy: a tip by way of the CIA's Paris station revealed the identity of the Soviet illegal Colonel Abel, whom Allen served up cheerfully for the greater glory of J. Edgar Hoover and the FBI.[66] For all his commitment to the Adenauer regime, Allen saw no reason to prevent one senior political-action man, Seymour Bolten, from developing a close personal association with Willi Brandt, the Social Democratic heir apparent.[67] The Socialists in Germany would eventually become a prime CIA asset, a matchless conduit for money and information.

Senior Agency people were astonished at who turned up at receptions or filled out the table at those choice little stag dinners Allen hosted when he traveled: in effect the shadow governments across much of the planet. Characteristically, Dulles cared very little about keeping his whereabouts under cover. He relished without apology the long black chauffeured automobiles, the secret messages perking out of the scrambler-printer. Jim McCargar can still call up the lividity that darkened Bernard Yarrow's face when McCargar alluded to a Dulles stopover on the Niarchos yacht off Deauville. "How did you know that?" Yarrow snapped.

"How? Bernie, it's in the bloody *Paris Herald Tribune*. Look at the social notes."[68]

Like any doting uncle, Dulles expected total consideration from his universe of hand-picked nephews. A delegation from one station was scheduled to meet Dulles's plane during one of his regular inspection trips around the world. Through some sort of time-zone mix-up somebody got the time wrong; the Director waited, fuming, until his head of station finally pulled up alongside the plane in the anticipated car. Allen climbed out, dusted off his tweeds, then demanded a taxi to conduct him in solitary wrath to his hotel in the capital.

Wherever he turned up Dulles winkled the foot soldiers out. "He could really strike a note, build the morale of the station up," one says. "He was always complimentary, and what he had to say stuck. 'The NKVD have it all over us in every way except one,' he told me one time. 'The target will come to us. It's terribly important that we are always prepared for defectors.' "[69] Another cherishes his recollection of coming in from the field unexpectedly. His division chief told him to stop by the Director's office. "He had his feet on his desk," the operative says, "and he was finishing up a conversation on the White House phone. He reached out to sneak a look at a piece of paper that must have had my curriculum vitae on it, and then he jumps up, and grabs my hand, and says, 'Nick! Where have you been?' What a con artist. But you have to love him for that."

What braced the troops could elevate the blood pressure of managers struggling with the operations. Breaking in as Dulles's new special assistant the summer of 1954, Richard Bissell soon found that Allen "administered like JFK, he skipped many echelons below himself and went directly to whomever was closest to whatever he wanted to find out. When I protested at one point he was very direct: 'I will talk to anybody and give orders to anybody I want to in this Agency!' "[70] A *reclama* was permissible, of course, but very few applied. "Allen Dulles was not a Bill Casey, thank God," observes one veteran operator, "but he loved the adventure of it, the glamour, the travel, the sliding around. There was nothing Allen preferred to sitting round talking to a defector for hours on end. He was very active in the ladies department still. Suppose he did flit a bit from one operation to the next? People argue about how much he understood of the game. He felt he had established a certain reputation. When Dick Helms was being harassed about something Allen had done he said: 'You don't understand. Mr. Dulles was a figure of such magnitude on our horizon that we didn't question Mr. Dulles.' "

What all this pedals lightly, of course, was Allen's propensity to barge into projects whether he had much of a feel or not. "At the headquarters suite Allen had a group of people sitting around in his outer offices who simply screened everything for him," Howard Roman says. "They brought his attention to whatever they thought he ought to look at. Walter Elder, Jack Earman, his secretary Helen Allen. He never felt that it was necessary for him to do certain things, to understand certain things. He liked to be surrounded by capable people, people he trusted, who could tell him very quickly what the answer to any question was."[71]

Which redoubled Frank Wisner's obligation to impart some reality to whatever Allen liked the idea of, puffing at his pipe. "The pressures on Frank from Dulles and the State Department were very considerable," Richard Helms concludes, measuring each word. "Allen Dulles was an activist. Sometimes he would push when Wisner would feel that we did not have the right assets, that matters should be approached differently." Allen exerted the torque, and once he insisted on something there wasn't much disagreement after that.[72]

20

THE BLOOD OF MARTYRS

Perhaps the surest testimony that Stalin was really gone occurred a few months after he expired in June of 1953, when laborers in East Berlin rioted. The CIA base chief there, Henry Heckscher, cabled Washington for permission to hand out pistols and Sten guns to the rioters, already pelting the advancing Soviet tanks with rubble and cobblestones. John Bross was running the Eastern European Division at the time, and when the request came in he got to Wisner, who was away. " 'Give support,' Frank answered, 'and offer asylum. But don't issue guns.' With twenty-two Russian divisions in East Germany it was the same as murder."

"Allen Dulles's views on this were a little ambivalent," Bross notes. "Wisner agreed with me when we sent the cable out. But people around the administration were upset, and felt something different could have been done—they never said exactly what. People like C. D. Jackson, who held that the blood of martyrs fertilizes the tree of liberty. . . . Allen really never forgave me for the fact that we had not taken a more aggressive position at the time of the outbreak in 1953."

At that stage, Bross insists, Wisner recognized well enough that large-scale armed resistance in Eastern Europe was impossible. The operative question was whether some system of partisan guerrillas might somehow be slipped into place so that, in case the Red Army actually did move, insurgents could harass the main units, blow bridges, slow down the advancing Soviets to make them vulnerable to bombing strikes. "Frank's personal attitude as to whether even that was possible was 'I doubt it. But we have a mission to try to find out.' "

Between Albania and WIN it was becoming obvious to Bross, among others, that "the Soviets had the place taped. They had their own national resistance organizations. If you wanted to join one, you joined theirs." Most of the pressure to locate these potential supporting elements was coming from diehards in the military like Colonel McDowall, who remained confidant that "there *must* be latent resistance organizations in the Ukraine and elsewhere," Bross maintains, and whose pitch was, " 'if you fellows can't do this, stand aside. We'll do it.' "[1]

But little by little, as Allen dug in, breaking loose the captive nations acquired a fresh legitimacy. A man as sensitive to even the unspoken thoughts of superiors as Wisner soon grasped that more was expected now. What success they'd had could fuel this primary mission. For almost a year a joint CIA/SIS team had contrived to tap the landlines between the Red Army's Berlin headquarters and the Soviet Air Force message center at Karlshorst. G-2 sources insist that the project came into being under Army auspices, inspired in the first place when an East German communications engineer whose kids had gotten a military assist into the Western Zone passed along a schematic for the revamped Soviet cable system. The cover sheds had orginally been designed as quartermaster warehouses; when Bill Harvey moved to town as station chief he worked on Dulles to enlist his brother to let the Berlin base take over the prestigious enterprise. After that the proliferation of Agency managers in overcoats with briefcases began to arouse Russian suspicions.[2]

To approach the cable juncture, engineers chipped a 1,476-foot air-conditioned tunnel into East Berlin twenty feet underground, carting out the dirt at night inside a vast warehouse disguised by then as a radar station. The entire project was quickly referred to as "Harvey's Hole." The incomparable bug-eyed gumshoe had arrived to oversee Berlin in 1954, and now expected unimaginable feedback from this "technical avenue of approach to the intelligence problem," as Harvey phrased it in unadulterated FBI bureaucratese.[3]

In bristling midcareer, Bill Harvey had not toned down much rubbing shoulders with gentlemen. He still relished ready tail and unlimited booze (not in that order necessarily) and acknowledged the canons of civilized dress when the occasion called for it by toting his pearl-handled revolvers in matching holsters aflop against the sweat stains beneath his cavernous armpits. He'd dumped his Indiana-born wife, Libby, amidst a hail of flying drink glasses and sailing card tables. Harvey remained a blunt instrument. But given a hard, grubby job he had a way of jostling things along.

Harvey's Hole did produce a snowstorm of raw undifferentiated information—tons, flown back as tapes to Washington and transcribed with machinery which bypassed the Russian coding mechanisms by picking off the echo effect. Mostly this was Soviet order-of-battle material, the preponderance of which Gehlen and regular G-2 analysis could confirm. What the Agency ultimately got for its up to $30 million was publicity, priceless publicity, the kind that paved Allen's way to friction-free appearances before Congress. Dulles presented Harvey the Distinguished Intelligence Medal, muttering out of earshot that, win or lose, he regarded "that fellow Harvey" as a "conspiratorial cop."[4] The Soviet commanders allegedly stumbled on the tap after eleven months and eleven days while repairing a cable—other versions insist that an inexplicable thaw along the Schoenfelder Chaussee tipped the Communists off; Agency technicians were already too blasé and comfort-loving to keep the air conditioning on in the chilly midseasons, so that a telltale stripe melted away along the artery at street level. Later on, it became a question as to whether the KGB hadn't known all along about the tap, kept abreast by their agent George Blake, who sat in to take notes as the SIS recording secretary.[5]

In April of 1956, when word of the tunnel hit the newspapers, participants scrambled for cover. Robert Amory had stopped by to look in on Tracy Barnes when warnings of the disclosure broke, and he still laughs over their 180-kilometer-per-hour screecher up the Autobahn from Frankfurt to Bonn to break the news to U.S. Ambassador James Conant. But Conant already knew. "Conant greeted us," Amory says, "with 'Well, fellows, looks like you got your hands caught in the cookie jar. Tell me all about it.' "[6] The Free World laughed, and applauded. They had the momentum now, the Agency was nicely shaken down, and better than anything else, destructive vibrations were rippling through the captive East. It wouldn't be that long now.

So month by month it looked as if 1956 might be their big year, the year they truly connected. The initial foreshocks hit with the widely anticipated keynote address by Nikita Khrushchev at the Twentieth

Congress of the Soviet Communist Party the third week into February. By then the coarse, bouncy First Secretary was ebulliently in charge in Moscow, jazzed up to welcome the post-Stalin epoch of "peaceful coexistence" with both the West and the satellites. Understandings rather than intimidation would guide the Kremlin's treatment of the postcolonial "countries of southeastern Europe which in the past used to supply raw materials and manpower reserves to Germany . . . ," and even the renegade Tito was waved on to continue his experiment with "unique forms of economic management and organization of the state apparatus. . . ."

What juiced up salivary glands around the Agency was word that within hours of the February 25 convocation of the Congress, First Secretary Khrushchev went into a fervent, detailed rant itemizing the excursions and brutalities of the late Josef Stalin. The despot had overlooked all warnings of the Nazi invasion in 1941, then panicked and locked himself away while the Panzer armies closed on Moscow. In vast bogus purges before and after the Great Patriotic War, pioneering Bolsheviks were tortured and executed, while "the cadre of leaders who had gained military experience in Spain and the Far East was almost completely liquidated." In his utter "mania for greatness" the Soviet dictator had "completely lost consciousness of reality; he demonstrated his suspicion and haughtiness not only in relation to individuals in the USSR but in relation to whole parties and nations."[7]

Enough ripples had broken the international surface by the end of February to suggest that the Twentieth Congress presaged a major shift. "More than anything else in the world," Amory says, "Allen wanted the full text."[8] It had been axiomatic to Dulles's thinking all along that neither Stalin nor his heirs intended relinquishing their choke-hold on the Bloc countries, and that in fact there wasn't much profit in encouraging the evolution of semiautonomous—but still Communist—societies. Furthermore, "Allen Dulles felt that spontaneous uprisings were unlikely in any case," Bissell says, "and that even if they came about they were likely to prove unproductive, if only because they provided very little opportunity for intelligence."[9] What was really desirable was takeovers *we* planned, with political outcomes we could control.

This made it priority one to locate a transcription of the speech, in time to game-plan its impact and determine what countermeasures might open the situation up. Dulles made his wishes plain, and there erupted another scramble between the DDI and the DDP to bring home a transcript first. Amory personally marched U.S. Ambassador to Belgrade James Riddleberger over to the Yugoslav embassy, and "We had Tito on the brink, but he finally yielded to his KGB minister."

Meanwhile, several other versions of the speech came in. Gehlen claimed to have acquired the earliest transcript for the BND, but the most complete renditions seems to have been acquired through Angleton's mechanisms,[10] primarily by way of an Israeli plant in Poland. To mask its origin a Foreign Service linguist, Bill Barker, translated all 20,000 words into Russian, after which an English-language version came down for collating and authenticating.

To backstop themselves, Wisner sent for Ray Cline, a square-set, good-natured, intellectually fearless historian who at the time directed the Chino-Soviet section of the Office of Current Intelligence. In 1950 Cline and Jack Maury had contributed to Project Jigsaw, which challenged the central postulates of NSC-68 by bringing into question any Kremlin master plan for global domination.[11] Turning to an analyst in the midst of the privileged deliberations of the DDP came hard for Wisner, Cline realized: overall, "There was not a great deal of intercourse between the two areas, mainly because of DDP clannishness and fierce tradecraft indoctrination in security." While presenting textual evidence that there was plenty to substantiate Khrushchev's authorship of the document, Cline found himself arguing against both Wisner and Angleton's preference for leaking this material piecemeal, "feeding selected bits of the text to specific audiences on which they wanted to have an impact. They kept saying they wanted to 'exploit' the speech rather than simply let everybody read it."[12]

As Angleton remarked afterward, the best imaginable use for Nikita's mea culpa was months—years—off, when they'd had time to "organize and update" their "vast preparations for refurbishing operational groups" secretly training in West Germany under "a born leader, a Yugoslav, whose schooling was in the Hapsburg military academy." Only after these client armies of Poles and Hungarians and Rumanians were "up to snuff," Angleton had argued, should teasers excerpted from the Khrushchev statement be doled out to the captive populations as incitement to revolution, a means of discrediting the entire Bolshevik leadership and provoking a wide-scale political chaos into which to feed the paramilitaries the Agency was shaping up.[13]

Not long after certifying the precious document, Cline dropped into the Director's office to polish up an address with Dulles. Allen asked Cline to spell out his reasons for releasing the Khrushchev speech as they had it. Dulles heard him out, Cline would write, then announced, "By golly, I am going to make a policy decision!" He immediately informed Wisner (who took it well), cleared the release with his brother, then sent the unexpurgated text over to *The New York Times*, which printed the bulk of it on June 5.

Angleton disparaged Cline's input. "He wasn't a party to the discussions on the clandestine side," Angleton would declare later. "The decision to publish the Khrushchev speech was made by Eisenhower, Allen Dulles, and John Foster Dulles. They decided its significance should take precedence over political action. . . ."[14]

❑

As if to exemplify the dangers of permitting "Socialism with a human face" to sedate the captive populations, Poland with one clunk bounced off the Stalinist bandwagon and out of propaganda reach. Worker riots at Poznan in June of 1956 brought on a summer of intra-Party turmoil in Warsaw, culminating in early October in the resuscitation of Wladyslaw Gomulka, an unimpeachable Communist and a thorough Pole. Many years in prison had in no way softened Gomulka or induced him to confess to heresies—there was a story going around that the Soviets intended to test their latest atomic icebreaker on Comrade Wladyslaw. But once the crisis at Poznan dragged on, the Party leadership reelected Gomulka to membership in the Central Committee and abruptly fired a Russian officer, Marshal Rokossovsky, as Defense Minister and Army chief. Gomulka was promptly slated to step in as First Secretary.[15]

Within days a Tupolev 104 from Moscow set down outside Warsaw, and disgorged a glowering Nikita Khrushchev and several of the custodial Politboro porkbellies along with a phalanx of Red Army brass. Soviet tank divisions were already clanking out of their motor pools to occupy the major cities, Khrushchev blustered, because the reorganization in Poland had gone too far.

In short order Khrushchev attempted to force his way into a meeting of the Polish Central Committee and demanded Gomulka's ouster. His pallid hollow face as empty of expression as a soup bone with eyes, Gomulka came back with his own terms: "Unless the troops are called off at once, we will walk out of here and there will be no negotiations. We will not talk while cannons are pointed at Warsaw. Unless the troop movements are halted this instant, I,

Wladyslaw Gomulka, will go on the Polish radio and tell the people what had happened here."[16]

Khrushchev backed down. The principles of the Twentieth Congress had turned like artillery on Moscow.

❑

Everybody across the Agency was up on tiptoes once Gomulka brought off his bluff. Frank Wisner seemed particularly stirred. There was a ferocity about Wisner that season, something apocalyptic behind many of his utterances. The judicious Larry Houston, a familiar of Wisner's since law school, was starting to walk away from meetings "wondering if his mind was working at some higher level that I was not understanding." One day Wisner called Houston in, and launched into a long discussion of something in the propaganda field, and then he told Houston to go pursue the matter with Gordon Gray, who had moved around to Assistant Secretary of Defense for National Security.

Houston approached Gray, and attempted to represent Wisner's proposal. He discovered himself foundering. "I'm really quite puzzled as to what Frank wanted me to come in for," Houston finally confessed to Gray.

Gray paused. Frank Wisner and Gordon Gray had been close since prep school, and Frank and Polly had introduced Gordon to his second wife in 1953 after he became a widower. "I think Frank," Gray said slowly, "is in real trouble."[17]

What made people reluctant to harp on Frank's behavior was the fact that just as he really started to seem aberrant much of the time, overhectic, he reverted to—he smoothed out. Counterparts at State and the Pentagon still found him sharp, snappy, inventive when somebody needed something from the Agency, impatient with bureaucratic evasions. Like Allen he remained a bear on the European issues.

He'd started to gripe to underlings about too many assignments from everywhere and nowhere. They were unwieldy already, too big, too public, and it got harder every month to keep the operational mix manageable. "Jesus, will you look at all those damned things we set up for a year, a year and half," he muttered to an associate, flipping through status reports, "and most of them are still on our backs." Especially in the Far East, the panic to bottle up China inaugurated by gung-ho military imports like Dick Stilwell and Pat Johnson now left the Agency overbuilt, responsible for everything from a smattering of Hilton hotels to schools for Chinese dependents. Asia made Wisner uneasy; he was not enthusiastic when Allen agreed to sponsor the semiautonomous psy-war hot-dogging of Colonel Edward Lansdale in Vietnam. Frank brought Al Ulmer back from Greece to break in Tracy Barnes and learn the Far East. Through whatever happened Barnes somehow kept himself, Ulmer marvels, "innocent of tradecraft," though he had capacity as an administrator, and between them they managed to cut 5,000 indigenous agents in Asia from the rolls and sell Subic Bay back to the Navy.[18]

But Allen was pushing for bigger projects, naturally—more power, wider recognition—and so the project load mounted. Frank worked a six-day week, often more, and you could tell it was Saturday when nobody wore a necktie. But even in shirtsleeves an incidental exchange could turn into a pounding once Frank had hung up on some unforeseen detail. For all his steadfast visionary glitter Wisner could ramble badly, and too often there was no discernible agenda. Newcomers like David Phillips tended to write him off as "something of a fireworks type. He lacked both oars in the water at times."[19]

He scrutinized everybody now, frequently brooding and suspicious. Nobody cared to interrupt Frank, and only Dick Helms had assurance enough to break into one of those interminable anecdotes of Wisner's and lead him back to whatever was at hand. He was easily slighted. Not long before Hungary erupted Charlie Saltzman came back into the State Department, and wangled a bed at the Wisners' through perhaps the hottest summer he could remember in Washington. Polly and the children were up at the farm. "One night Frank and I went to dinner at Joe Alsop's," Saltzman recalls, "and afterward we went back to the pantry to have a glass of milk each. He told me something Allen Dulles had done that hurt his feelings. I remember thinking, this is very peculiar, this isn't like Frank Wisner to bother about that, much less tell me. I'm convinced it was an indication of accumulated fatigue."[20] Dulles's September 1956 fitness report concludes an appreciative rendition of Wisner's strengths with the observation that "his principal weakness is an oversensitiveness to criticism."[21]

Wisner was feeling bypassed, overtaken by new approaches. The day before Thanksgiving in 1954, Eisenhower empowered Dulles to look into the development of some kind of high-altitude reconnaissance aircraft to overfly the denied areas. Allen dumped the assignment within hours on Special Assistant Richard Bissell, whose ingenuity in bringing the Europeans under control by means of footnotes to the Marshall Plan was still the envy of bureaucratic Washington.

Sequestered in a downtown office with a project staff which never went beyond eight subordinates, Bissell directed the syncopated evolution at the top-secret Lockheed "skunk works" in California of the unlikely craft Ray Cline has described as "more like a kite built around a camera than an airplane."[22] This aeronautical curiosity in effect crashed every time it landed, tipping sideways until reinforced skids on its wingtips scraped it along to a halt. Edwin Land of Polaroid had perfected a camera array for the U-2 alleged to produce pictures from 80,000 feet of such unimagined resolution that photo interpreters at the DDI could make out truck models in a Moscow parking lot. Bissell and his assistants brought in a prototype within months, at $3 million below the original cost estimate. "Kelly Johnson of Lockheed had promised me that if I'd give him the quotes and specs on what I wanted he'd set a price ten percent below what he would offer the Pentagon," Bissell says.[23] Anticipating Soviet countertechnology, Bissell was quickly set to work contracting out the first photoreconnaissance satellite, which he had operational by 1961.

The U-2 promised to rescue American intelligence from its dependence on scraps from the British, on exchanges with Gehlen's questionable hierophants (much smugger and far more critical of the Amis since passing under Adenauer's auspices). With 1,200 photointerpretation specialists set up in the DDI before the fifties ended, verifiable answers—and, accordingly, augmented power in the community—moved necessarily to the K Building. Administrators were growing skeptical about Wisner's stagnating empire of weapons depots around the Soviet perimeters, his notoriously funky labor battalions and papermills and wrangling exile committees. A lot was out there, Jack Blake remembers well, "to arm those Hottentots if anything ever happened. I don't think anybody ever thought through the transport requirements. On a cost-effective basis, I doubt if you could ever get ten cents on the dollar out of any of it."[24]

So influence was eroding. Dulles turned to Bissell increasingly—their technocrat, their genius, whose pale eyes and chunky retroussé nose gave him the aspect so often of an impatient child, one writhing with speculation and subject to momentary tantrums when anything endangered his timetables.[25] Frank Wisner hung on as Dulles's acknowledged heir apparent, but Bissell was getting such spectacular results. Expectations had to shift. "I was not always sure Allen and Frank's relationship was of the closest," Polly Fritchey admits reflectively. "Dickie Bissell got on far better with Allen than Frank ever did. Far better."[26]

❑

Two days after Poland rebuffed Khrushchev, on October 23, Hungary too went insurrectionist. Pressure had been building for years on Hungary's Stalinist First Secretary Matyas Rakosi, whose repressions and purges had alienated a majority even of homegrown Communists. Rakosi's regime bottomed out during the show trials of 1949, when much of the leadership of his government was marched through confessions on counts that ran from war crimes to plotting to overthrow the Socialist order. Rakosi's prize catch was Laszlo Rajk, the forty-year-old Minister of Foreign Affairs, a magnetic lifelong Communist whose bona fides included heroism with the Rakosi battalion during the Spanish Civil War. As Interior Minister in 1947 Rajk had directed Hungary's Security Service, the AVH, in the purging of the postwar coalition government.

The Rajk trial centered on the state's claim that, as early as 1944, Rajk and his fellow traitors threw in with the capitalists in Switzerland and utilized their help and money to get themselves back to Budapest, into "the territories liberated by the Soviet troops," to spy, undertake sabotage actions, and infiltrate the Hungarian Communist Party. The American the Hungarian prosecutors harped on was Allen W. Dulles. Dulles's primary conquest was Tibor Szonyi, spokesman for the Communist delegation in Switzerland throughout the war and afterward the Party's personnel chief at headquarters in Budapest. In November of 1944, the broken Szonyi testified, "Dulles explained to me at length his political conception for the period after the war and told me that the Communist Parties would obviously become government parties in a whole series of Eastern European countries which would be liberated by Soviet troops. So support for an American orientation and the American collaboration policy should be carried on first of all within the Communist Party." Dulles then "showed me, as a means of terrorizing me, the receipt I had signed on a previous occasion for Noel H. Field" when Field had passed along a financial handout from the OSS. Arrangements were soon made to stay in touch under pseudonyms. An envoy from the Titoist faction, Misa Lompar, would deal with travel needs and supply a back channel for future intelligence delivery.

In his statement, Laszlo Rajk also admitted to having received marching orders from Noel Field. "I would," Rajk testified, "working in the Party and according to the instructions received from the Americans, disorganize and dissolve the Party and possibly even get the Party leadership into my hands." Meanwhile, he should employ Szonyi "to place rightwing, nationalist, chauvinist and anti-Soviet elements in various positions throughout the Communist Party." At home in Budapest, Rajk claimed, he got his "explicit instructions" from Martin Himmler, whom he could reach through Lieutenant Colonel Kovacs of the United States Military Mission.[27]

Like many Stalinist offerings there were indeed verifiables somewhere at the bottom of all these overcooked allegations, richly smothered in paranoia. The OSS had, through Field, subsidized and even relocated a number of Communist functionaries trapped in Western Europe by the eruption of war. Despite his tantalizing name, Martin Himmler was a Hungarian Jewish coal miner who escaped Hitler and advised Al Ulmer from his OSS-SSU days in Vienna on psy-war techniques. After the Russian occupation Himmler nursed contacts throughout the coalition government in Budapest up to the Minister-President, Zoltan Tildy, whom he advised to go slow, play along with Moscow, avoid a Kremlin-directed coup.[28]

By 1949 the brutal Stalinist Rakosi dominated Hungary, and every demonstrable contact with the West was retroactively traitorous. Anybody who trafficked with Noel Field after 1939 might be presumed to have succumbed to contamination by Dulles. Political ricochets nailed hundreds of unlucky functionaries. The chief of the Communist Party in Czechoslovakia, Rudolf Slansky, took down a mob, and casualties in East Germany included Gerhart Eisler, broadcasting overseer Leo Bauer, and Paul Merker, Walter Ulbricht's top rival.[29] Rolling devastation lasted years. One journalist has concluded that Allen Dulles provoked this rockslide ("Operation Splinter Factor") by conniving with Lt. Colonel Josef Swiatlo, a disgruntled senior investigator in the Polish security service: Swiatlo was purportedly under instruction to remain in place and distort enough documents and plough up enough suspicions to incite Stalin to decimate an entire upcoming generation of promising Communist functionaries, a heavy majority Jews.[30]

With the Soviet gerontocracy now bent on cannibalizing its young in public, pressure built on Wisner and the others to raise to an action status the would-be governments-in-exile emerging under the sponsorship of the Free Europe Committee. Factions inside the emigrations were now contesting bitterly for control. Among the Rumanians, for example, the tilting for leadership was soon between the transplanted industrialist Malaxa (a legal client by 1951 of Adolf Berle) and the unquenchable Max Ausnit, Frank Wisner's erstwhile host at so many sumptuous soirees while Bucharest was changing universes.[31]

Hungary was especially touchy, with mobs of inflamed dignitaries speechifying for the meatier positions. Dissatisfaction in Budapest looked made to order to prominent exiles and their ingenuous American sponsors. In 1950, Frank Lindsay called in James McCargar, who'd worked Budapest under cover while the Communists collapsed the government in 1947, and asked him to intervene wherever he could to piece together an effective Free Hungary Committee.

After months of hand holding and soft soap behind locked doors at New York's St. Regis, McCargar brought in as de-facto Minister of Defense the conservative Smallholder Tibor Eckhardt, a Grombach mainstay, whose credentials in Washington went back to undisclosed wartime liaison duties.[32] They'd build on him; then, abruptly, McCargar found out that Carmel Offie had heard about the appointment, and summoned Eckhardt, and let him know the arrangement was off. Furthermore, any discussions he might have pursued with McCargar were "completely unauthorized."[33]

Amour propre aside, McCargar was jarred badly by reports that Offie, on CIC recommendations, intended to replace Eckhardt with General Andras Zako. Like the regrettable Dosti, Zako was a stock figure out of the militantly Fascist right, one of the whip hands behind the violence-hungry anti-Semitic Arrow Cross movement who helped direct the notorious Horthy intelligence service and escaped the Soviet dragnet to resurface in Pullach as one of Gehlen's "senior assistants" in the Hungarian department.[34] The general had again become quite visible early in the fifties as the organizer of the Fraternal Society of Hungarian Fighters, which supervised a blatantly pro-Fascist array of exile centers and military training camps in several of the Western bastions. To identify the committee in a public way with Zako's reactionary armies was guaranteed to frighten off whatever middle-class idealists were left in either the exile community or the motherland as well as identify the United States with efforts to reimpose the discredited protofeudal politics of the Horthy years.[35]

All this was urgent, boiling inside McCargar as he rushed by what Stewart Alsop describes as the OPC's "scrabby old hideouts, with the plaster peeling and stopped-up toilets,"[36] and plunged through to confront Frank Wisner. The L Building literally creaked underfoot, a hodgepodge of intersecting corridors of ratty molasses-brown congoleum jammed in between rickety plywood partitions that looked quite likely to wallow in place were anybody to stumble into one. Wisner's private office wasn't much of an improvement: a worn leather couch, some sort of coffee table, and backed against the window the usual big, battered federal-issue desk, behind which Frank Wisner was frowning over paperwork.

"Carmel Offie has cut the ground out from under me," McCargar remembers blurting. This could get nasty, he realized suddenly—Offie's desk was through the door to Wisner's left. "If this goes on I don't see how I can continue here."

Wisner raised his head. His baldness had advanced to the extent that back across his crown he retained at best a suggestion of closely clippered hair, a stippling, to dot his powerful cranium. With his compact features and tightly fitted ears and something of a fullness coming into his jawline his head looked sunken into his shirt collar: clean-cut yet almost torpedo-like, reminiscent somehow of Herblock's drawing of the atomic bomb. He obviously didn't care for this much abruptness just then. Wisner's mouth was set, and absent the expectation of humor which normally wreathed his lips in McCargar's presence.

McCargar struggled to explain himself. Tibor Eckhardt knew Hungary, but he also understood the democratic system. He'd had considerable experience with the American military. He was a familiar personality, somebody all the elements from Hungary would understand. Zako—Jesus, for all practical purposes, Zako was a Nazi. Or something pretty close. Should this man speak for an organization backed by the United States? McCargar found it difficult to believe they would be so stupid as to try and raise any kind of levee among these people with the idea of sending them into combat. And security-wise? In Hungary the Arrow Cross veterans had *flocked* to the Communists once the clamps went on.

Then—taking the leap: "I feel that Carmel Offie is using this organization for his personal aggrandizement."

Whatever affability Wisner started with had blanked out. He sat there working loose the big bunched muscles of his forearms, and suppressed emotion had started the hinges of his jaws jerking.

What he could not say was draining the color from his face. This thing went far beyond Zako. The Joint Chiefs wanted results, and this plainly meant that they were going to have to hold their noses, and gamble, and back whatever militants with followings of their own came forward and touched their caps. Once there was momentum enough it might conceivably be that Zako's troops jumped in there and made the difference alongside their own brigades. These people were experienced. You employed the available—the OPC had also recently agreed to take Bandera and his crowd off the hands of the British, provided cash and support facilities for raids into southern Russia. They depended on Offie to look after their contacts with the Right, that everybody knew, but the fact remained that dealing through individuals whose politics might make one's flesh crawl was pretty much the business they found themselves in.

Not that Wisner articulated this, not in those words. Once he had collected himself he simply replied, "not harshly but very firmly," as McCargar recalls, " 'What makes you think I'm going to let Offie use this organization for his personal aggrandizement?' "

"This was the kind of question there isn't any answer to," McCargar knew. Above Frank Wisner's skull and across the drive the Reflecting Pool shimmered. "I think I said, 'He already is,' " McCargar recalls. But he was winding down. "I tried to phrase it in such a way that I wasn't saying that Wisner was being an ass."

So McCargar left. He reactivated his commission in the foreign service, and Wisner stepped in and helped McCargar find something of interest in Paris. Just before he left, Carmel Offie—all broad, fixed smiles—invited McCargar to lunch. The conversation was lively, and lunch turned into dinner and after dinner Carmel hosted McCargar and his wife to the circus.

"What's more," McCargar laughs, "he arranged for me to lease at a high rent one of Bullitt's apartments, on the Rue de Pon Thieu, when I got there so I'd have a place to stay. Whether Offie was attempting to make amends, or whether he was lulling me to eventually slaughter me I don't know.

"I do know that I got in trouble with my boss in Paris, who essentially was under Offie's thumb. We got into an awful row, and of course if you do that in the foreign service you've had it. I knew that when Offie came to town he was seeing my boss, although he would deny it." McCargar's work was mainly with the Eastern European exile community in Paris—always a challenge—and once he had given up his State Department career a place was found for him in Paris in a branch operation of the Free Europe Committee.

As events worked out, it was the same squat, ham-faced Lieutenant Colonel Swiatlo whom speculation would identify as Dulles's agent provocateur in Poland who perhaps as much as any individual in fact helped break loose the anti-Communist tide that swamped Eastern Europe in 1956. On December 5, 1953, Swiatlo ditched his superior officer during a shopping expedition in an East Berlin department store and defected to the West. Notorious as the torture-master of the Polish secret police's Department Ten, Swiatlo was, as he explained in a press conference, "in a position to learn all the facts concerning the falsification of history, the falsification of biographical background of the leaders, and the innermost secrets concerning the political and private lives of top officials." He had been uniquely placed to follow the long series of "political trials . . . organized under Soviet supervision and for the interests of Soviet imperialism. . . ."[37]

Over Radio Free Europe, month after month, Swiatlo beamed into the East Bloc a smorgasbord of niceties about the apparatus he had served, every tidbit of corruption down to the identities of office snitches. The disgust which overwhelmed Poland soon sharpened into the clear realization that such a scapegoat as Noel Field was little more or less than an idealistic goon, nothing like the notorious "superagent" lured back to Budapest and sentenced to solitary confinement for having traduced a generation of rising Comintern princelings.[38]

By established Communist ritual, resurrection is every bit as cumbrous and bureaucratic a process as damnation. Eyes crazed, hair gone white, Noel Field and his wife, Herta, were hauled without ceremony out of their dungeon lockups and permitted to finish out their days in a suburb outside Budapest. The hanged, rehabilitated corpse of Laszlo Rajk underwent a solemn second interment before whatever officialdom survived.

The ostentatiously penitent Rakosi replaced himself with his detested stooge Erno Geroe, who proposed assorted half-measures. The grumble level rose. By October 22 the Radio Free Europe coverage of Gomulka's successful defiance of Khrushchev was galvanizing Budapest, and throngs of workers, students, and intellectuals had started to chant for Imre Nagy's return, the withdrawal of Soviet troops, and open national elections. Within one day a mob approaching 300,000 was advancing on the parliament building. A pair of welders fanned up a frenzy of pleasure in the crowd by taking an acetylene torch to the monumental bronze statue of Stalin, slicing it off at the knees and leaving the colossal boots to rise like hollow trunks on the abandoned pedestal. Meanwhile, demonstrators and workers and soldiers waded into the machine gun emplacements of the secret police, the AVH. Soldiers mutinied. Disaffection was spreading. Civilian police opened up the frontier with Austria.[39]

By October 24 Soviet armored units started to close on Budapest. Early the same morning Allen Dulles woke up his division chiefs to alert them that "all hell" was breaking loose in Hungary. The Soviets hadn't thought to sever the teletype lines west. Allen told his brother that "the Hungarian National Committee have been hard at work and have a lot of ideas," and he was "afraid they might jump the gun—by going to the UN via the Latinos."[40] The blood of martyrs. . . .

A few months earlier the initial U-2 mission started clicking away above Moscow and Leningrad and wobbled to a stop to fierce official applause from halfway around the world. Frank Wisner had authorized a stepped-up campaign of "saturation broadcasting" on Radio Free Europe to get the most out of the Twentieth Congress disclosures.[41] Additional thousands of giant semidiaphanous hydrogen balloons started trailing their cartons of propaganda leaflets East to spew the captive societies with updated versions of Operation Prospero, along with Operation Focus and Operation Veto. Veto concentrated on Hungary, and called for the regime to confront the "Twelve Demands of the National Opposition Movement."[42] These demands were formulated, of course, by refugee political savants holed up inside the multiwinged two-story blockhouselike headquarters of RFE alongside Munich's Englischer Garten. Including its New York directorate, staff levels at Radio Free Europe now approached 1,500, and much ideological latitude was encouraged in the 500 or so native specialists.

The face-off in Warsaw had obviously called for finesse from Agency instruments, and RFE announcers were careful to warn the Poles not to push too hard. But at the same time, as hour by hour the crisis with Gomulka built, Cord Meyer's Munich editorialists gave "full news coverage to internal developments and cross-reported into Hungary in depth on the Polish drama, which undoubtedly raised hopes for liberalizing changes." Once the Hungarian revolt erupted and spread, fourteen low-power provincial radio stations inside Hungary appealed to RFE in Munich to "replay their revolutionary demands on its powerful transmitters so that the whole country could be informed of the speed and depth of the revolt."[43] Allen bucked Meyer along to Robert Murphy at State, who supplied the go-ahead.

Everybody wanted the Red Army out, the dissolution of the secret police, free elections, and Hungary's withdrawal from the Warsaw Pact. There has been informed speculation that sizable Red Sox–Red Cap advance parties fanned out inside Hungary as soon as the borders opened to coordinate the political agenda.[44] Simultaneously, the head of news for Radio Free Europe, Allan Michie, sent eight staffers over to telephone out tactical color. "Politically, all this was very dangerous stuff," one player emphasizes now. "All the Russians had to do was pick up eight RFE types and they would have a great case for how the Fascist imperialists were about to take over the country. Then they could justify a Russian invasion." Somebody went after Michie at five in the morning in Vienna and told him to get his reporters back. "I don't care how mad you are," Michie heard, "you get your goddamn people out as fast as you can or we are all going to be in trouble." Five made it home, but Soviet roadblocks cut off three in Gyor, and it took major off-stage negotiation to recover them by November 11.[45]

At that stage the Russians could afford the gesture. The last five days of October, what began as reformist demonstrations blossomed like a refinery fire. All up and down the west of Hungary, where Red Army garrisons were spotty, the Hungarian military fell in with the freedom fighters, handing out Russian weapons while mobs from the revolutionary and workers' councils took over local government and ran off Communist technical advisers. Revolutionaries seized the radio stations and rounded up and shot a number of functionaries of the secret police, the detested AVH. Geroe and Rakosi both were already on their way to the Soviet Union.

Obviously stunned, the Soviet area commanders saw no alternative to playing for time. It seemed for some days that what these aroused Magyars wanted most was the return of the moderate Communist Imre Nagy, whom Khrushchev had helped install in 1953 as part of his destalinization program and Rakosi had forced out in 1955. On October 24 the Politboro in Budapest had summoned Nagy to Party headquarters and reappointed him—some say at gunpoint—premier. He was instructed to invite the Soviets to reoccupy Budapest to calm the streets. The unpredictable Janos Kadar would back him up as first secretary. A conciliatory old functionary of the Bela Kun era and something of a coffee-house theoretician, "Uncle Imre" managed to talk himself free of what amounted to office arrest, set up in the parliament building, and bargained toward a kind of cease-fire predicated on the withdrawal of the Soviet forces from Budapest. Then, day by day, as the week progressed, he made a series of radio announcements authorizing the formation of alternate political parties with the prospect of free elections and a coalition government.[46]

Endeavoring to keep up, Washington pulsed with great hopes and greater apprehension. The weekend after Hungary boiled over, Al

Ulmer and Allen Dulles had driven up to Wisner's farm on the Eastern Shore to sort out the possibilities. Allen especially was walking a precarious line. "Allen Dulles was a pretty smart guy," says Jacob Beam, the Department's ranking expert on Eastern Europe that year of uprisings, and participant in all the top-level meetings. "He had to be controlled." Beam's air of reminiscence from the stratosphere permits no challenge. "We had a strong Secretary of State, John Foster, and he wouldn't let Allen get out in front. In one or two meetings he openly reprimanded his brother. Allen was a very active man, very shrewd. He was full of ideas, he wanted to stir up more trouble than was absolutely necessary. Particularly on information, propaganda, things like that. Sending up balloons, etc. He liked gadgets. It wasn't serious, it wasn't important.

"John Foster's ideas ran along those lines, rollback," Ambassador Beam muses. "But then he put a stop to it, he pulled back very, very hard. After Khrushchev's speech, when Poland threatened. They were having riots. John Foster didn't want uprisings in Hungary, but Allen Dulles did. I know that some of his people did, working at the lower levels. They made suggestions over the radio about getting guns, going out on the streets. . . .

"It was certainly not our policy to involve ourselves in that. There was a meeting—it went up pretty high, this meeting. Some of the military, and maybe Allen. There were some voices in the State Department that we should hold military maneuvers. And then we figured the damned thing out: to hold maneuvers, and try to get across Austria, to Hungary. . . . It would break up a state treaty with Austria, and we'd just lose Austria. Which I think was very sound."[47]

Reality had overtaken Foster. As early as 1952, when Foster had pledged in speech after speech that the United States would "use every means" to liberate the captive nations, Eisenhower had called in to remind him to be sure and insert the adjective "peaceful" between "every" and "means."[48] Once Hungary went up, the President cut off all proposals of direct military involvement with reminders that Hungary was politically landlocked, "as inaccessible to us as Tibet."[49]

At Locust Hill farm that fateful, frustrating weekend the exchanges went back and forth, various contingencies came up, but there was very little anybody could really imagine to save the situation. "Wisner was still looking for daring solutions," Ulmer says. "He was wrought, but not overwrought. We all knew direct intervention was not feasible."[50] Foster wouldn't permit intervention. Wherever Foster was concerned Allen would remain subservient, awed even.

Allen was still hesitant to ask the State Department for cover assignments for overseas case officers, most of whom were fortunate to secure respectable housekeeping slots.[51]

The day after Dulles, Ulmer, and Wisner convened in Maryland the Israelis attacked Egypt. Their surprise attack highlighted the Eisenhower administration's propensity for misread intelligence and fatuous judgment calls at both the policy level at State and on the Clandestine Services end at the CIA. Foster Dulles professed himself particularly contemptuous of Nasser, preferring for some months to believe that General Naguib was in fact the leader in Egypt despite continual nip-ups by Kermit Roosevelt. Nasser's prominence among the nonaligned leaders at Bandung in 1955 especially irked Foster, who had no use for godless "neutralism." Throughout State supercilious officers referred to the gathering as "the Dark-Town Strutters' Ball."[52]

Foster waffled now whenever the United States commitment to construct the Aswan Dam came under review, and after the Nasser government bought arms from Russia, Dulles canceled the project. Nasser exercised his option to nationalize the Suez canal.[53]

Accredited thinkers at State favored the English attitude, which Robert Amory encapsulates as, "Well, let us admit, gentlemen, that first and foremost the wogs are a dog's breakfast." The Egyptians weren't bluffing. Meanwhile, "The top dogs in the State Department—Herman Pfleger, Herbert Hoover, Jr., John Foster Dulles—were saying such stupid things as, 'The Russians could never build the Aswan Dam, they couldn't even afford a shipment of MIG 21s, etc.' "[54]

Toward the end of October Kermit Roosevelt could see that some manner of attack on Egypt was coming, soon. "I remember going to a U.N. Security Council meeting," Roosevelt says, "and talking to John Foster Dulles. While I was there I told him this thing was about to happen, and that I was opposed. He ignored me, he just stood there and stared out the window. Finally he said, 'Is that all, Kim?'

"I said, 'Yes, sir.'

"And he said, 'Thank you very much.' "[55]

Nobody else made headway. Ulmer remembers an exchange with a counterpart in the SIS, John Lockhart, who strained "to let us know, if obliquely" what was already afoot. " 'I'm going to have to go get into my uniform' " he told Ulmer. " 'We can't let Suez go, you realize it's the lifeline of our Empire.' "[56]

Over on the analysis side "a lot of stuff was smoking visibly,"

Robert Amory saw. Military attachés were returning to Tel Aviv, and even Amory's local jeep driver, a game enough fellow "blind in one eye and a double amputee had been called to the colors. I went right down to see Allen, and I said, 'You know as well as I do, Allen, that it's a general mobilization when you grab a military attaché and a crippled jeep driver to add to your motor pool.' "

Dulles summoned Angleton. "Look what Bob has brought in," he told Jim.

"Doesn't mean a thing," Angleton said. "I've just spent all night with our friends in the Israeli embassy."

Amory blew up. "This is where the buck stops," he rounded on the Director. "You either believe me or you believe this coopted Israeli agent!"

"From then on," Amory saw, "all Angleton wanted to do was to blot my copy book."

That was Friday morning. On Saturday Amory was reviewing a speech with Dulles in which he predicted a "peaceful outcome" to the tension in the Middle East. "I said 'A lot of us believe war will break out early Sunday or Monday morning.' "

" 'That's not what the Watch Committee said.' "

Amory left, quite steamed. When the invasion struck Monday Eisenhower rushed back to Washington on the *Columbine* and called in the principals of the National Security Council. "What's up?" Ike asked Allen.

"Well," the Agency's Director offered, as mollifying as ever, "We believe that this thing is a bluff. If the Israelis are going to do anything rough they're going to do it against Jordan."

"The next word we get," Amory says, "the Israelis are on the Suez Canal. I can only conclude that Angleton got to Allen at home on Sunday morning and worked him over."[57]

An awareness that blunder after blunder had marked the administration's long slog into the Middle East only sharpened widespread dismay, which quickly became fury, as it became evident that the Israeli blitzkrieg initiated a combined assault. Most of the White House rancor was concentrated on the British. The uprisings in Hungary, as they themselves would later concede, "provided assurance to the conspirators that they could proceed to chew up and spit out Nasserism with no more Russian reaction than huffing and puffing."[58] "It is nothing less than tragic," Foster managed—ashen, days before his first operation for stomach cancer—"that at this very time, when we are on the point of winning an immense and long-hoped-for victory over Soviet colonialism in Eastern Europe, we should be forced to choose between following in the footsteps of Anglo-French colonialism in Asia and Africa, or splitting our course away from their course."[59]

Wisner felt personally betrayed; shocked, as his daughter stresses, "that people he had worked with for years, sat across the table from so many times, had acted this way."[60] As the emergency worsened Wisner and John Baker stopped over in London, then went on to Paris to pull together Wisner's overseas section leaders in hopes that out of a strategy session might come some approach to stabilizing Budapest. But at the same time "Intelligence reports reaching Washington showed that the Soviet Army was assembling a large force, gathering troops from Rumania and all over the Ukraine and moving them toward the Hungarian frontier."[61]

Soundings by his European staffers looked ominous to Wisner. Jim McCargar was presiding in Paris over a subsidiary of the Free Europe Committee called the Free Europe Citizens' Service, a kind of welfare clearing house for refugees. When the revolution hit, the academic who rapped out policy guidelines for the Radios in Munich, Bill Griffith, contacted McCargar and urged him to fly over a professional acquaintance from the pre-Communist Coalition, deposed Prime Minister Ferenc Nagy, to tap resurfacing colleagues. McCargar rushed the Peasant Party veteran to Vienna and kept him on the telephone to Budapest. Before the week was out Nagy reached Zoltan Tildy, his president from the 1947 government. Euphoria was still universal, but Tildy could tell the jaws were closing. "Speak for us in the West," he implored Nagy.[62]

The overwrought Imre Nagy had lost all feel for political realities, he was manifestly overreaching. His revived, libertarian Hungary would henceforth stand as a "neutral" between East and West, he announced at 2 P.M. on November 1; it would renounce its membership in the Warsaw Pact. Barely a week earlier Marshal Zhukov had instructed the Poles himself on that point: "Comrade Gomulka, I don't give a [expletive deleted] what you do with your agricultural cooperatives or your factories, but if you tamper with your Warsaw Pact obligations I march, Comrade Gomulka, I MARCH."[63] Nagy understood this. Meanwhile, unlike Cardinal Wyszynski in Poland, the inept Cardinal Mindszenty denied the shaky regime the support of the Church and got on the radio to call for the legalization of a Hungarian Christian People's Party and a traditional political order.[64]

The Friday and Saturday before Wisner reached Paris the United Nations Security Council took up a plea from Nagy for independence and protection. The Soviets were regrouping. At the Paris embassy Wisner commandeered a conference room and presided over a session with McCargar, Bill Griffith, William Durkee (Cord Meyer's representative), the executive director of the Congress for Cultural Freedom, a Balt named Michael Josselson, and the Agency's inside man for Hungarian affairs, Karl Kalassay. Wisner himself appeared composed enough, but he was desperate for meaningful advice so that the deadlocked Agency might move with Foster pinning Allen down. After hours of discussion McCargar put together a long cable to the CIA Director to go out over Wisner's name which energetically recommended that the United States government exert every effort to swing support behind the government of Imre Nagy, which duplicated the coalition the Soviets subverted in 1947—namely, a mixture of Smallholders, Social Democrats, Communists, and leaders from the Peasants Party. There should be no encouragement to separate from the Warsaw Pact.

"I subsequently called Bernard Yarrow in New York," McCargar says. "I knew that he had access to Allen. I told him that there was only one way out of this. Which was to do a vigorous job at the United Nations. That they didn't do. I think Herman Pfleger sunk that, he talked Lodge out of making a great effort."

Perhaps nothing could have carried. As midnight approached on November 3, a party of NKVD directed by General Serov personally had pushed into the room in which the designated Hungarian Defense Minister, General Pal Maleter, and his aides were negotiating pullback with the Russians, cut the telephone lines, and taken the insurgents prisoner. The next day Janos Kadar and three other principals of the Nagy government deserted to the Soviets.[65]

At 5:20 A.M. on Sunday, November 4, Imre Nagy appeared at the station on Radio Budapest to announce that Soviet forces were already moving against the capital. A week of savage, grinding warfare broke out, with massed Soviet armor flattening out the barricades while leather-jacketed teenage "yobos" in waves threw themselves against the treads to touch off sticks of industrial dynamite. Replacement tanks roared by their predecessors' flaming, gutted shells above the Danube bridgeheads. Red Army units pounded house to house, sometimes room to room to flush out resistance in the factories and working class districts, called bombers in to knock out radio stations, manned dragnets for participants in the spreading general strike, and bundled them off in trucks and freight cars for deportation to Russia.

* * *

Wisner arrived in Frankfurt to reports of suicidal melee. He had arranged to lay over Tuesday night with Janet and Tracy Barnes to listen to the Stateside election returns and get some rest before pushing on to Vienna, where the Austrian authorities were already contending with hordes of frenzied Hungarian refugees.

"My husband thought Wiz was almost manic when he was there for that election," Janet observes. Since Wisner couldn't sleep she stayed up with him to hear the U.S. precincts come in. "Both Tracy and I thought that he was wound up overtight, like a clock. That he couldn't stop ticking, he couldn't stop thinking, whether it was about the Hungarians, whether it was about Suez, whether it was about the United States. That he was going around in these very tight, agitated circles. It was very hard to discuss it with him because he never stopped talking, that was one of the main problems. I think the combination of Suez and Hungary was too much for him. He was overwrought, I always thought this was part of his disease."[66]

On November 8 Budapest fell. Wisner was in Vienna, caught up in the enveloping bucket-brigade atmosphere. Vienna was the hot spot; paramilitary junkies from William Donovan to Vice President Nixon were back and forth, hitching rides to the border in hay trucks, wheeling in and out of the overworked embassy. Bill Hood was on an errand in Europe; Wisner brought *him* out, along with John Baker and anybody else he could impress into service. His mood was extremely high, which made it hard to respond sometimes, break through. "We were all working around the clock, the same as anybody would who was concerned with the political affairs in Eastern Europe," Hood says.[67] A good part of what ultimately numbered 190,000 escapees were flooding into Austria, the first rush near Hegyashalom as long as the Soviet flanking units hadn't cut off the customs post, and after that through forests or sidestepping along a slimy log above a canal or fording the verges of the quagmire off the Neusiedler See.[68] Wisner himself slept—what little he slept—at the embassy as a guest of the Llewelyn Thompsons. He seemed in command of himself to Hood—beautifully dressed, as always, and abounding political enthusiasms.

Across the frontier the wholesale slaughter crested. Molotov cocktails crashed down on tanks, which answered by razing entire avenues of masonry with concerted cannon fire. Manifestoes bounced in and out by way of the superpowerful Radio Free Europe transmitters. Demands ran from the "rejection of the Soviet loan offer" to membership in the "Danubian Federation proposed by Kossuth." As the fighting sharpened a Hungarian RFE editor in Munich, "Colonel

Bell," later identified as the journalist Ladislas Farago, demanded sabotage of rail and telephone lines and "implied that foreign assistance would be forthcoming if the resistance fighters succeeded in establishing a 'central military command.' "[69]

The Agency's own after-action report to the White House admits to "evidence of attempts by RFE to provide tactical advice to the patriots as to the course the rebellion should take and the individuals best qualified to lead it."[70] Meyer himself will concede that the "Hungarian exiles reported the debates in the U.N. Security Council as if the international organization could provide real protection to Hungary's fragile and newly declared neutrality."[71] It was, remarks Andor Klay, a State Department desk man through much of the crisis, in part the way "certain phrases take on different connotations in Hungarian ears. They listened, and thought it all meant that the Americans would arrive."[72]

The Hungarians expected this, they expected help. "Frank had gone out to the border," Bissell says, "and he had seen the Hungarians attempting to flee into Austria. People had been killed by the Russians as he stood there, in his sight. It was a profound emotional shock."[73] For Wisner, confronting this slaughter by machine-gun fire, it was the midwinter boxcars in Bucharest all over again, the Stalinist monster foraging upon the innocent. From a nearby Vienna hotel underlings of General Zako, Carmel Offie's checkered contribution as Free Hungary's military spokesman, were shipping over bulletins which Radio Liberty broadcast, proposing a border meeting with the insurgents and assuring the rebels that "the Western world's material aid is on its way to you."[74]

In Washington the cables from Wisner were incessant. We must do something. At least let the labor battalions fight. The culls that Gehlen and RFE were reported to be arming and pushing back over hadn't amounted to anything. Only troops could save the situation. How important *was* Austrian sovereignty? "He felt the U.S. Army could have gone in," Bissell says flatly.[75] Our word was involved. These people *must* be saved!

Wisner went to Greece next, and it was there that he appears to have eaten the plateful of raw clams that brought on hepatitis. By election day Eisenhower's intransigence had forced a cease-fire on the British-French-Israeli "police action"—too late to refocus on Hungary or save the Nagy experiment. Even the business-oriented West German Free Democrats were lambasting Radio Free Europe for loosing "the bloodbath which has occurred in Hungary"[76]—a signal to Foster that rollback was yesterday's slogan. Still at Walter Reed,

Foster Dulles in slippers received British ambassador Selwyn Lloyd with, "Well, once you started, why didn't you go through with it and get Nasser down?"

"Foster, why didn't you give us a wink?"

"Oh!" exclaimed the recuperating Presbyterian, "I couldn't do anything like that!"[77] Dwight Eisenhower's straitened notion of international morality left nobody squirm room. Robert Amory had compiled a comparative study of U.S. and Russian stockpiles of fusion warheads. He concluded that a "surgical nuclear strike" limited to Lvov and several of the passes could destroy Soviet resupply. On that basis he drafted a one-page ultimatum for the President, which he sent over with Allen Dulles, "calling for a halt to all further Soviet reinforcement of its forces in Hungary on pain of our taking military measures at our disposal, etc."[78] This got little hearing. The President sat in on exchanges with the Soviets through much of World War II, and took most seriously their determination to control the historic invasion routes. Pushed hard enough, Eisenhower felt, the Russians might well "resort to extreme measures," even "start a world war."[79] In Budapest our embassy gave long-term asylum to Cardinal Mindszenty but flushed back into the streets authentic democrats like Bela Kovacs. Kovacs could be obtuse at times, and at the zenith of the rebellion had cautioned his followers that "No one must dream of going back to the world of counts, bankers and capitalists; that world is definitely over."[80]

From Vienna Wisner made himself felt, "urging everybody up and down the line to move," Andor Klay says. Puffy, sallow, his narrow eyes all but lost in his swollen face, Frank Wisner was barreling through his days and nights fueled up with far too many gulped highballs but very little rest. Checking teletype dispatches, jumping out of staff cars to wade to the front of observer teams as they filed into refugee pens—in Austria he'd seemed solid. By Greece the starch was out, leaving only the intensity. One Athens operations man never forgot the afternoon Frank marched back and forth, "dictating a number of cables on what had to be done all over the world. I'm telling you, I sat there listening to him dictating telegrams that did not make *any* goddamn sense. . . . This wasn't Frank Wisner, who was a tremendous guy. Frank was not well at this point."

He reached Rome frustrated and exhausted. Under Foster's tutelage, Allen Dulles was reacting to Wisner's demands, Leonard Mosley has written, by asking how anything could be "done about the Russians, even if they suppress the revolt, when our own allies are guilty of exactly similar acts of aggression."[81] The sophistry behind reasoning like that made everything unpalatable. The DDP's Italian operations chief, Bill Colby, assessed Frank as "near a nervous breakdown." Wisner and his lieutenants, "especially those on the covert action side, were fully prepared with arms, communications stocks and air resupply, to come to the aid of the freedom fighters. This was exactly the end for which the Agency's paramilitary capacity was designed." But Eisenhower's unyielding veto "established, once and for all, that the United States, while firmly committed to the containment of the Soviets within their existing sphere of influence, was not going to attempt to liberate any of the areas within the sphere, even if the provocation was as dramatic as that in the Hungarian situation."[82]

Rollback was a bust. But rollback was the primary mission of the OPC, its excuse for being. Was that now over? And where would this leave Wisner?

Back home in Washington, his liver infection incubating, friends found Frank Wisner excitable, overtalkative sometimes, but more keyed up and hyperactive from November's stresses than . . . than *sick*, exactly. Tom Powers memorializes John Baker's attempt to report on the trip to the assembled DDP, with Wisner himself interrupting every few minutes with irrelevancies, such as a "long, detailed, thoroughly scatological story which involved some Russians, a confusion between the men's room and the women's room, and a great deal of toilet paper."[83] He was embellishing this somewhat amusing anecdote at conferences and over the telephone for nearly a month while the hepatitis took hold.

By then even Foster would concede to intimates that "liberation" had been a misbegotten concept, and obviously a political mistake. Suspicious of Wisner anyhow—"there was this gang down in Georgetown, I mean the Thayers, the Bohlens, the Thompsons, the Wisners, who used to meet and enjoy themselves criticizing Foster, it was just a little indoor sport they had"—Foster's adoring sister Eleanor resented especially Frank's outspoken conviction of betrayal. "Frank Wisner came out to my house, and sat on my terrace and drank my liquor and told me my brother was a no-good so-and-so!" she snaps when Wisner comes up.[84]

Paul Nitze invited Frank Wisner to his farm shortly after he returned to town. Despite his lifelong Republicanism, Nitze had been dumped from Foster's State Department because of his Acheson ties, part of the "no more Bohlens" campaign by Senator Knowland and others of the Republican hard Right. Small, rich, tough-minded, and extremely leathery, Nitze had brushed off Senator McCarthy's attacks on himself as a "Wall Street operator" and continued to question what seemed to him a weakness for ill-conceived adventures by the covert people, a willingness to lose themselves in projects that simply couldn't work. Bred to investment banking, Paul Nitze retained a natural horror of frittering away capital.

In company now with bystanders like Harriman, Kennan, Lovett, and David Bruce, Nitze observed with mounting distaste as the self-righteous Secretary of State careened along the brink of war, preached of "massive retaliation," mortgaged our foreign-policy future to paper alliances with virtually any tyrant available to grab our handouts. "I always hated Foster Dulles,"[85] Nitze admits cheerfully, and although Allen was more agreeable personally, Foster was the one who put the plays up on the board.

Wisner's appeal to old-guard policymakers, Democrats especially, accounted for his career. Contemporaries recognized his capacity to joke and think and tease and argue at the strategic level. "In the end, Allen's position depended on Foster's," Al Ulmer notes. "But Frank had support, Allen recognized that Frank was now a star in his own right."[86] By 1957, the trouble was that most of Wisner's regular sponsors, his real friends, were extraneous to the governing process, powerhouses like Nitze, or Kennan, or the Thompsons, or Charlie Thayer, who in fact saw Wisner often and jibbed him mightily. Everything about Frank's upbringing, his breeding, his definition of honor, now made it necessary for him not only to defend but to believe in, to respect, the men and policies into which he continued to pour his uneven energies.

"Frank had a hard time during that period," remembers Charles Murphy, who was often around. "Most of the men around Frank detested Foster Dulles. They made fun of Eisenhower. They sat around Frank's table, and it was a strain for him listening to the criticism and ridicule of the men for whom he worked, it must have been destructive of his spirit. People like George Kennan were beginning to modify their views toward Russia, toward our intentions, and Frank was proposing most of these operations, they had to come from Frank's own shop. He himself took the contest with the Soviets very seriously. He admired Foster Dulles. Foster Dulles had called for the rollback. There was no question of Foster Dulles's attitude toward the Soviet Union."[87]

Then Hungary went critical. Foster waited, and watched, and reviewed his options while up to thirty thousand Hungarians were butchered. And then Foster cleared his throat and reneged. No reputations were risked over catastrophe in Budapest. Some felt that all along the Dulles brothers had intended the Red Sox–Red Cap programs as a "tease," as one commentator has written, "to sucker the Soviets into acting more repressively and brutally in the satellite countries in order to secure propaganda victories for the West."[88] Several of the thinkers on the policy level at State under John Foster Dulles were known to prefer the most obnoxious authoritarianism possible. Where was the profit in a rash of Titos? Why make Communism liveable under Imre Nagy? Let Hungary go.

"That broke his heart," Paul Nitze saw, sitting alongside his pool with Wisner and absorbing his grievances. "He faulted Cabot Lodge for the way he'd handled it at the United Nations. Frank was just deeply disappointed. It was while he was there sitting at our swimming pool, and I was talking to him, that I became persuaded that he had crossed the border of rationality. He was so mad at some fella who was the president of the New York Times company, he'd begun to believe that *The New York Times* and all the people connected with it were traitors to the United States. At this stage it was clear that he'd lost his connection to reality."[89]

21

THE LAST TRUE BLOW-OFF

Hungary and Suez both had broken over the Eisenhower administration without warning, Press Secretary James Hagerty observed to the media. The President himself found out about each of these disasters "through press reports," and each was a "complete surprise." In this manner Ike hinted at his displeasure with Allen, who responded by divulging that "we had the Suez operation perfectly taped," while Hungary had been anticipated for months in Agency appreciations worked down to considerable detail.[1] Neither allegation holds up, but Dulles routinely warded off this sort of brickbat by flooding the White House with paper on the basis of which almost any eventuality seemed feasible in retrospect. Allen himself demanded one-page summaries, at most. But he kept Eisenhower inundated, partly as a fallback. Had the Oval Office been neglecting the voluminous packets of raw intelligence product the Agency sent over virtually every day?

With Foster still massively ensconced Allen remained secure. But Eisenhower was irked. That slew of undifferentiated and frequently contradictory cable material along with a mealy-mouthed daily briefing report provided very little direction. The President wanted "maps . . . red arrows . . . headline summaries. . . .[2] At upper level policy meetings, where responsibility got handed around, Allen would frequently hold back, "in his usual fashion," as Kermit Roosevelt noted, "gruffly noncommital.[3] As Eisenhower understood the arrangement, the Agency had been brought into being to coordinate information collection from around the world. Now they were flabbergasted by everything that happened, while most of Allen's attention—along with a preponderance of the Agency's budget—went into those high-risk, low-percentage "operations" the Director kept fiddling with.[4]

Eisenhower was already suspicious that under Allen's lax administration not only was the CIA often striking out largely on its own, but worse, beyond that, *inside* those dilapidated tempos which flanked the Reflecting Pool each of its semi-autonomous directorates was putting along, looking out for itself, subject largely to internal drives and geopolitical preoccupations unrelated to the others. Along with the military-industrial complex, Eisenhower could already discern the potential rogue elephant. He authorized administrative changes.

On the President's instructions, in March of 1955 the National Security Council instituted the 5412 Committee, mandated by NSC 5412/1 and referred to much of the time as the Special Group. It would be chaired by Gordon Gray, who had moved on from attempting to pin down OPC activities at the Psychological Strategy Board and its 1953 successor, the Operations Coordinating Board, to Assistant Secretary of Defense and Director of the Office of Defense Mobilization, and now took on enlarged responsibilities as National Security Assistant. Meetings of the 5412 Committee normally included Gray, one of the senior figures from the Defense Department, the complaisant Robert Murphy sitting in for Foster, and Allen, who limned in what he regarded as the larger or potentially troublesome operations out of the thousands of worldwide undertakings the Agency was routinely sponsoring. Gordon Gray himself would carry up the Special Group recommendations to Eisenhower, who gave the final nod.[5]

There had been mutterings in Congress that the legislators too should get some chance to follow in reasonable detail the activities of this swelling secret Agency, with its reputed unvouchered billion-dollar budget. Allen Dulles remained quite scrupulous about appearing once or twice a year before the Appropriations Committee of the Senate and House. He enjoyed the bumpkin adulation, and met with a straight face such queries as, "The Commies still giving us a hard time, Allen?" To something more specific, Senator Styles Bridges confided after one session, "He said it was too dangerous for Congress to take up." Allen remained assiduous in cultivating Clarence Cannon, whose House Appropriations Committee signed off on all Agency funds.

Most Congressmen still skirted these mysteries of the deep, like a delegation of nuns tiptoing by the Vatican's legended pornography collection. "The difficulty with asking questions and obtaining information," decided Massachusetts's cold-water Yankee Leverett Saltonstall, "is that we might obtain information which I personally would rather not have. . . ." Both the Doolittle Commission and Beedle Smith—who knew Allen—had promoted the formation of a joint Congressional "watchdog" committee. But Dulles wasn't receptive, and in his urbane, pneumatic way he continued to put out word that most of the shortfalls for which the Agency was blamed in the press resulted from the inertia of higher-ups, who God knows got bushels of the finished intelligence they asked for but ignored its implications. Lamentably, Allen drawled, "Often we know a bit more about what is going on in the world than we are credited with, and we realize a little advertisement might improve our public relations."[6]

When Roger Hilsman went in as Director of the Bureau of Intelligence and Research at State in 1961 he discovered that Allen had arranged things so as to submit each covert proposal to the intragovernmental committee most likely to give the go-ahead. He himself chaired the U.S. Intelligence Board, and he had installed his sister Eleanor as the senior independent member at Intelligence and Research to assure compliance there. "In many situations the institutions he was dealing with didn't know what one another were doing," Hilsman found. "He played the system in very sophisticated ways."[7]

Eisenhower disliked the drift Allen's Agency kept taking. To backstop himself on intelligence matters overall and rough-cut meaningful alterations at the CIA, the chief executive moved at the beginning of 1956 to create the President's Board of Consultants on Foreign Intelligence Activites (PBCFIA), which a chastened Jack Kennedy would reauthorize after the Bay of Pigs as the President's Foreign Intelligence Advisory Board (PFIAB, Piff-ee-ab). As cochairmen of the Eisenhower board James Killian of MIT and General John E. Hull went in, backed up by leaders in the industrial and technological communities, several generals (including Jimmy Doolittle and Omar Bradley) and admirals, Joseph P. Kennedy, David Bruce, Robert Lovett, and assorted secondary dignitaries of relentless and predictable orthodoxy.[8]

After months of study, the board recommended that Allen Dulles detach himself from day-to-day activities at the Agency and concentrate on his other role as the Director of Central Intelligence—that is, as advisor to the President, whose primary mission would be to assess and coordinate the torrent of information coming in from all the intelligence-gathering offices of the government, from the FBI to the Atomic Energy Commission. Dulles received this advice with a particularly nimble buck and wing, and countered with his own proposal to remedy this defect in his leadership so "apparent to all who knew and worked for him," in the Church Committee's words, by bringing aboard General Lucian Truscott as his "deputy for community affairs."[9] Eisenhower wanted the whole thing set up "the other way around" he proclaimed at a meeting on January 17, 1957, but Allen wasn't listening.[10]

More heat and light both rose out of the sparks thrown off by a panel report on covert operations entrusted to Robert Lovett and David Bruce by the PBCFIA board chairmen. Second only to Donovan throughout the OSS years, David Bruce had somehow retained a relaxed probity which all but invalidated him for invisible-government involvement. It had been Bruce's intervention that flummoxed the Truman-era move on Arbenz, and now this perusal of all the garbage strewn behind the CIA after four years of Allen's management left Bruce quite alarmed. "He approached it from the standpoint of 'what right have we to go barging around into other countries buying newspapers and handing money to opposition parties or supporting a candidate for this, that or the other office,' " Lovett testified later. "He felt this was an outrageous interference with friendly countries."

As one of Frank Wisner's original backers at the State Department, Robert Lovett also recoiled at what he and his fellow Achesonians had wrought. Bruce's panel report was wide-ranging and unsparing. It decried "the increased mingling in the internal affairs of other nations of bright, highly graded young men who must be doing something all the time to justify their reason for being." This messianic white-shoe cabal of the "busy, monied and privileged" was out there ringing up " 'successes'—no charge is made for 'failures'—and the whole business is very much simpler than collecting covert intelligence on the USSR through the usual CIA methods! . . ." Approval of "almost any action" is "pro forma," at "informal lunch meetings" of the Operations Coordinating Board. Consequently, "no one, other than those in the CIA immediately concerned with their day-to-day operation, has any detailed knowledge of what is going on." All this inevitably contorted our foreign policies and is "responsible in a great measure for stirring up the turmoil and raising the doubts about us that exist in many countries of the world today. . . . Where will we be tomorrow?"

The PBCFIA board itself picked up these themes and berated the "extremely informal and somewhat exclusive methods" the clandestine people favored, "operating for the most part on an anonymous and free-wheeling basis in highly critical areas . . . sometimes in direct conflict with the normal operations being carried out by the Department of State," whose officers were often aware of "little or nothing" of Agency machinations. The resulting snarl-ups were "almost unbelievable."[11]

Official Washington boggled, fellow clubmen who without a demurrer had accepted Dulles's assurances that he was grooming up a "league of gentlemen" over on the covert side. The PBCFIA report to the President landed on his desk on December 20, 1956. By then the capital was churning with rumors that one reason the Hungarian uprising had collapsed into such a hash was that certain of the clandestine types had irresponsibly goaded the revolutionaries into taking on the Soviets. The word came down that Lucian Truscott had now been deputized by Ike to pull that whole mess apart for the President.

In Truscott Dulles seemed to assume that he had hit on a deputy Dwight Eisenhower would know from years of combat who at the same time would sympathize with his own unremitting efforts to gentrify the intelligence community. Tintype handsome, the general married a Virginia Randolph of the Thomas Jefferson branch and built a following as one of the outstanding polo players in the American military. Even under combat conditions Truscott had insisted on flowers and Oriental cuisine in his tent.[12]

Dulles misread the general. Truscott reconnoitered the checkpoints of incipient rollback, its landscape of impacted refugee compounds and labor battalion barracks and émigré institutes and deadlocked conference centers. In Hungary's wake, Truscott opened matters up by debriefing the salient personalities among the torrent of freedom fighters both State and Immigration were processing through Camp Kilmer. Truscott concluded that the Red Sox–Red Cap organizers the services inserted into Hungary as agents provocateurs had consistently, programmatically overpromised Western support.

Little or nothing showed up indicative of the long-promised "stay-behind" arrangements—systems for intelligence transfer, safe houses, escape and evasion chains, couriers. What Wisner had come up with continued to rely primarily on papermills, the penetrated Gehlen staffs, endless retreaded Nazis, who depended on outdated information and obsolete methodology. Under Carmel Offie's ministrations the Free Europe Committee had encumbered itself with reactionary émigré leadership irrevelant to—generally repugnant to—authentic protesters around Eastern Europe.

Over nearly a decade, both politically and militarily, they'd concocted a botch. "In Truscott's opinion," William Corson sums up, "the results of this information were devastating. They indicated a failure on the CIA's part to recognize the differences between insurrectional violence, mass uprisings, and revolutionary action in the mid-twentieth century." Planning along these lines "could not possibly succeed in any country in which the military and security forces were under the state's control."[13]

Eisenhower looked over Truscott's conclusions, and sent them along to the Joint Chiefs. They'd better dismantle rollback. By then the operators were agitating to give it one last shot in Czechoslovakia, where the mysterious Dr. Slani had taken several OPC holdovers in hand and convinced them that he was in control of a far-flung Slovak underground.[14] But the President was immovable. Shrugging away the might-have-been, Allen Dulles passed down orders to disestablish.

Allen bypassed Tracy Barnes in Frankfurt and delegated the scut work to the heavy-duty William Harvey at the Berlin base: the responsibility for closing down the refugee reception centers in Berlin and Bavaria, for terminating subsidies, for checking off training weapons as they were trucked back and dunked in cosomoline by American armorers. Harvey's old-time FBI sidekick and State Department wheel man Raymond Leddy doubled up with an Army Counterintelligence Corps veteran from the control group which continued to manage the posts, Arnold Silver. Except for the Radios and a handful of well-tried émigré collaborators like the mottled NTS apparat, involvement with the refugees was skeletonized. Most of the long-time American wards and agent-handlers were deliberately "scattered" to preclude future blowbacks.[15] By 1958, as Angleton would comment regretfully, "the units were disbanded . . . causing great disillusion and bitterness among the members."[16]

❑

The spinout after Hungary helped break down another pioneer advocate of liberation, the unquenchable William Donovan. Wild Bill was in and out as a consultant to the Agency as early as the Beedle Smith reorganization. In May of 1953 Donovan accepted for a year and a summer an appointment as ambassador to Thailand, where a U.S.

military mission was already headed to shore up defenses against the threat of Chinese and North Vietnamese expansion. He was also entrusted with the delicate business of disarming and crating up for return to Taiwan the irregulars Dick Stilwell had installed along the Burma frontier to harass South China. The majority still preferred to concentrate on the heroin trade.[17]

With disappointment and rejection Donovan had inexorably gravitated into the company of grumblers and confrontationalists. Like his ideological allies C. D. Jackson and the reflexively conspiratorial Jay Lovestone, Donovan continued to spy out opportunities to bluff the Soviets back behind their original borders.

Within the Administration itself a never-say-die contingent sloughed off the Truscott report and continued to pound the table for rollback. On C. D. Jackson's staff at the Operations Coordinating Board, responsibility for salvaging the guard battalions fell now to the hotspur Colonel Philip Corso—who until 1955 had liaised closely with Nelson Rockefeller, for some months Eisenhower's Special Assistant for Cold War Strategy. Rockefeller's Open Skies Policy had functioned in large part as an eleventh-hour smoke screen to suffocate the promising disarmament talks of the period. Now Corso plowed vigorously into the planning stages of a proposal to reactivate the fifty surviving garrisons of Eastern European paramilitaries hanging on in Germany, each running to fifty or sixty carbuncular veterans. Corso's working group projected a training nucleus of division strength, liberation's shock troops, rechristened the Volunteer Freedom Corps.

Another round wouldn't sell. One day both Foster and the Secretary of Defense, Wilson, after passing around the outlines of the proposal, summoned Jackson and explained that Konrad Adenauer had bristled at even a reference to such a naked provocation on German soil. Corso claims the Chancellor was misrepresented, that freedom's last chance was laid to rest as a result of "lies by our liberal darlings, Kennan and Bohlen."[18]

Donovan had become fractious. He berated Foster as "churchy" and politically unscrupulous, and Allen as overly timid. Some of his symptoms suggested the onset of strokiness. His financial situation worsened, although he waved off Allen's offer of handouts from the CIA. Dulles tracked his moves. "In view of the number of complaints which General Donovan has asked me to look into in the past," Larry Houston wrote Allen after a comparatively quiet New York lunch with the old terror in March of 1955, "this was a pleasant change."[19]

In November of 1956 Bill Donovan hurried to Vienna as the

chairman of the President's Hungarian refugees' relief program, Anthony Cave Brown relates, and "was to be found night after night on the Austro-Hungarian frontier, physically helping refugees coming through the great frozen bulrush swamps as Soviet tanks clanked in the darkness and flares arched across the night sky."[20] Hungary provided Donovan's last campaign. A few months later a team of specialists at the Mayo clinic established that Wild Bill's right cortex was shrinking; his family must look for consequences of arteriosclerotic atrophy of the brain. He sank into reveries. Eisenhower rushed up the National Security Medal, Winston Churchill wrote reassuringly, but Donovan had finally been cornered by the extinction he'd faced down so many times. The shrewd old warrior was laid to rest in Arlington Cemetery in February of 1959 beneath a flurry of trumpets, virtually to the end the wily and insatiate war lover who all but single-handed introduced "special means" to American policymaking.

❑

Co-workers tend to date from the Hungarian uprising Frank Wisner's progressive breakdown, the episodes of uncontrollable logorrhea and exaggerated expressions of anguish shot through with paranoidal railings. This was, people felt, by way of a side effect from the ravages of the hepatitis he'd picked up abroad.

Responding to a request from his attendants at Georgetown Hospital, Drs. Smadel and Brick, Wisner strained to compose his own account. The memorandum does suffer from a telltale discursiveness, a need to transform even this routine questionnaire into an opportunity for public service. He includes a preamble. Along with a rendition of the "causes and circumstances leading up to the attack," he intends to venture "a description of the main phenomena" with an eye to "assisting in research in the field. . . . Also, an effort will be made to draw as clearly as possible certain distinctions between manifestation of the attack which I sustained (insofar as they were observable to me) and those which others have had with which I am familiar, with a view to pointing up the rather unusual character of my particular attack which appears to have been of exceptional virulence and to have come on very suddenly and which further appears to have run the course of the main phases of the disease rather more quickly than is normally the case in the lower grade infections which carry along for weeks and weeks before coming to a head, or becoming identifiable."

The thing came over him on Sunday afternoon, December 16, at about 4:15. Driving up to park his car in Georgetown after a weekend of duck hunting on the farm "I received the first chill." While barnstorming the European stations he had undergone an "irritation or infection similar to laryngitis" for six or seven days, and earlier the same afternoon he'd noticed "a small flush of fever." But upon emerging from his automobile, "the chill struck with such force that it was practically impossible to get myself into the house. . . . This particular bug may be somewhat different or distinguishable from other Hepatitis bugs around about, but in any case he walked straight up to me and hit me right on the end of the nose without any preliminaries whatsoever."

Wisner's fever was already approaching 102 degrees, and during the following forty-eight hours he underwent "a series of recurrent cycles consisting of first chills, then heavy fevers and then pervasive sweats." By early in the week his temperature hit 106, and he found himself "partially be-fogged in my mind and not in a position to make clear judgements or discriminating decisions."[21]

Tests indicated that Wisner was suffering from viral infectious hepatitis, which he was relieved to hear was both less punishing and less drawn-out than the amoebic form. Either manifestation was likely to tax the system to the breaking point, with bouts of nausea and listlessness bringing on a conviction of utter, irreversible incapacity, and leading into prolonged depression. At one point his doctor seems to have subjected Frank to extremely heavy dosages of cortisone, an experimental therapy at the time which was later discovered to augment and intensify latent emotional instability. Wisner was still feverish one day when his doctor looked in on him to find that he had transformed his hospital room into an office. Several secretaries from the Agency were taking dictation while Frank marched up and down on his bed in his hospital johnny dictating.[22]

By early in January Wisner was stable enough to write up this astonishing episode, but he was still quite weak. Resting much of the time at home, he found himself reduced willy-nilly to something of a bystander while Helms, and to an increasing extent Bissell, looked after the managerial side of the DDP while Frank came around. "When dad got hepatitis we were all *very scared*," Wendy, who was ten, remembers.[23] Wisner himself remained keyed up. Ambitions within the Clandestine Services were far too naked and express for him to lie low long, especially with conditions in Indonesia already generating the prospect of a full-scale line operation within a matter of months. They needed something substantial, another Guatemala, to recover their esprit and influence after muddling through Hungary.

❑

Eisenhower's repudiation of paramilitary follow-up in Eastern Europe amounted to a slap at Wisner. Upset visibly about Hungary, back on his feet by the spring of 1957 but uneven and low at times as he struggled for vitality enough to plow through the days against the exactions of his depleted liver, Wisner concentrated with everything he could muster on meeting the emergency he'd thought he sensed in the making in Indonesia.

Action breeds recovery. Ray Cline has written that the Indonesia project was "the only major paramilitary undertaking I know of where covert action enthusiasts in the CIA took the initiative."[24] Wisner had evidently determined that Indonesia was starting to go bad even before Hungary imploded, and commented to Al Ulmer, just moving in as chief of the Far East Division in early autumn of 1956, "I think it's time we held Sukarno's feet to the fire."[25] All through his recuperation Wisner seems to have plinked away at Ulmer to get his FE-5 station (Malasia and Indonesia) cracking, and over that winter Djakarta operations officer Joseph Smith records the station's anxiety that they had already passed the "deadline for producing a plan for Wisner."

Smith himself soon acknowledged that he was responding to an unstated directive to send back *justification* for moving in on Sukarno, not evidence: "In many instances, we made the action programs up ourselves after we had collected enough intelligence to make them appear required by the circumstances." Once rebellion was brewing, "we began to feed the State and Defense departments intelligence that no one could deny was a useful contribution to understanding Indonesia. When they had read enough alarming reports, we planned to spring the suggestion we should support the colonels' plan to reduce Sukarno's power."[26]

Their first, most critical sell was John Foster Dulles. Foster was increasingly rigid, extremely hard to influence from below. But he was more affronted every day by the upsurge of whippersnapper nationalism sweeping the postcolonial world.[27]

A million dollars U.S. got converted to rupiahs to prop up the

Moslem-oriented Masjumi party and give Sukarno competition. In the 1955 elections which followed, the indigenous Socialists very nearly disappeared, and much of their traditional support wound up behind the Indonesia Communists. With that the politically boneless President Sukarno segued into a new format he labeled "guided democracy," a kind of cabinet directorate through which the avuncular "Bungkarno" and his cronies would make the patriotic choices. Meanwhile, regular officers of the Indonesian military continued their training in the United States while the United States' Economic Cooperation Administration tuned up the police: a retired colonel from Angleton's staff looked after the reorientation process and scraped out intelligence particulars.[28]

Sukarno was another bozo it made Foster uncomfortable to think about. Of indeterminate parentage, the swarthy Javanese spellbinder had built his reputation plotting against Dutch rule. After the Japanese invasion Sukarno played along with the occupiers, and he and the Nationalist Party he had founded in 1927 in effect inherited political dominance. They confiscated the Dutch plantations and mines and oil wells throughout the 3,000-island sweep and imposed a top-heavy civil bureaucracy which printed money night and day to compensate its supporters.

A compact, bald demogogue approaching his middle fifties, by Foster's lights Sukarno's personal life approximated his economic discipline. The President's golden stare and rounded, melted-look features had always magnetized women, and there was a steady buzz up and down the islands each time he moved one favorite or another in or out of the palace. The Secretary was even more put off by the way the Communists' 6-million-vote tally in the 1955 elections seemed to predispose Sukarno to lean toward leftist labor groups. Here was Arbenz in a *pitju*. Furthermore, the squalid little rabble-rouser from Java had minced around as host of the Bandung conference early in 1955, where he and his supporting banshees helped legitimize the Red Chinese and capered to the pipes of neutralism.

Given Foster Dulles's mood, Wisner's increasingly shrill reports got a receptive reading at State. The other shoe dropped in April of 1957. A cable reached Washington indicating an approach to the Agency by Lt. Col. Achmad Hussein, the Indonesian Army topkick in central Sumatra. Lieutenant Colonel Hussein made it clear that he and his colleagues felt supplies were in short supply, the out islands were overtaxed, the leftward drift continued. "Guided democracy" approximated dictatorship. The colonels had set up certain bank accounts in Singapore, and they would welcome assistance.

In April of 1957 President Voroshilov of the Soviet Union settled in as President Sukarno's houseguest, after which Sukarno dreamed up the supervailing "national council" which henceforth would represent all segments of the population. This implied Communist participation. During the autumn of 1957 Wisner presented the DCI a "simple voucher" which entitled him to draw up to $10 million for the Indonesian operation. Allen Dulles signed, reportedly, "with a little flourish."[29] Vice President Richard Nixon was especially supportive.

Apprehensive officials, led by the U.S. ambassador in Djakarta, John Allison, were dropped from the planning loop. Ulmer's predecessor, Desmond Fitzgerald, who knew the region, remained chary all along. Another critic was Admiral Arleigh Burke, the chief of naval operations, whose submarines were essential for "over-the-beach" landings of supplies, men, and guns.[30]

As usual the analytic side of the house saw little in advance that bore on the upcoming Archipelago project, alternatively referred to as Operation Haik. But "after hours and over lunch" the DDI, Robert Amory, picked up the outlines of involvement and concluded that "that was a bad scene, basically. Because while Sukarno was a bad guy, a bad actor, the officers who were leading the revolt were worse, sort of like the French generals in Algeria." Their movement was based largely in Sumatra and Celebes Island, from where they had issued their Charter of Common Struggle, the acronym for which, PEMESTA, now signified their movement.

An inveterate "purple suiter," Amory had kept up his reserve commission and stayed in touch with the training side of the Pentagon. "Some of the best officers they had ever developed at the Fort Leavenworth Command and Staff school were Indonesians. The Chief of Staff of the Indonesian Army was a highly thought-of soldier, trained at Fort Norfolk, and he had under him extremely competent engineers, and amphibious commanders. . . . Most of the rebel recruits were almost on a level with the Sioux, and the guys Sukarno was going to send were like General Sheridan. I said, 'You're going to get a bloody nose,' and I would repeat this in many staff meetings. It was such opera bouffe stuff, like talk of our airmen bombing the place into submission."[31]

But Foster hated Sukarno. All through the turn of the winter he stewed, while Wisner held out for a "stalling period" to give himself time to soften the government in Djakarta up through psy-war methodology. Along with the familiar radio saturation and an Asia-wide recruitment of mercenaries, Wisner and Al Ulmer kept everybody busy thinking up novel methods for discrediting Bungkarno personally. They claimed the Communists were behind a fluky grenade attack on Sukarno. They leaked to friendly publications a succession of sightings of the raunchy President in company with a blond, professional-looking Soviet stewardess.

To reinforce the notion that Sukarno was being led by his oversized susceptibilities into Russian control, officials around the Far East Division decided on a documentary. After screening a wide selection of grainy blue movies available in the Los Angeles underground (where they had hoped to scavenge among enough squat, tawny Chicanos to surface a body double for Sukarno) they commissioned the Agency's Technical Services Division to devise a pullover latex head mask incorporating the President's gleaming features. Between sharply focused angle shots of the purported world leader gamboling with his infidel temptress, the cameraman was under instruction to pan in on Sukarno's mahogany pate, something he took great pains to conceal from his electorate with the traditional Moslem headgear during speeches and photo sessions.

The film got wide underground distribution in the islands, where experts subsequently concluded it served to deepen Bungkarno's popularity.[32] That winter contractual arms shipments started arriving from the Soviet Union. A bomber-length airstrip was going in north of Sumatra. Foster wrung his hands. "Today we have substantial assets with which to deal," he complained to Allen as November 1957 ended. "We will, however, have only half those assets six months from now."[33] The British were balky about trans-shipping over Singapore. Foster pressed for a formal declaration by the rebels, some grounds for diplomatic recognition.

January was over before Allen's fourteen-page appraisal of the PEMESTA rebellion reached Foster's desk. Allen fueled and stoked Foster's lust for intervention. The insurrectionaries could count on one, at least, of the major political parties, the CIA analysis insisted, presumably the Masjumi. They could easily defend their out islands, and stir up trouble on Java with guerrilla warfare. Only this last statement, the analysis concluded, could possibly be open to challenge, and then only after a lot more Soviet weapons arrived.

Wisner's "stalling period" ended on February 15, when Howard Jones went in at Djakarta to replace Allison. Frank Wisner himself turned up several times that spring over the course of a month-long Western Pacific junket. He sat in on strategy meetings at the Agency base at Singapore, just across the Straits of Malacoa from northern Sumatra. Wisner wasn't really . . . functional, his bosses agreed, and Al Ulmer took over Project Archipelago day to day, including serious policy applications. The head of intelligence at State, Hugh Cummings, now pinned his political hopes on Mohammed Hatta, Sukarno's rebellious Vice Premier.

Wisner was kept busy that spring "sort of smoothing over the British, from whom we needed exceptional favors," Ulmer recollects. He bounced from Taiwan and the Phillipines to Indochina; on part of the junket he doubled up with the future SIS director Maurice Oldfield, to whom he confided his uneasiness about U.S. dabbling in Vietnam and Laos.[34]

With Jakarta passing across Foster's sights, a regionwide complex of training and support facilities was falling into place under General Cabell's command. Supply officers reactivated abandoned Filipino runways and warehouses of backup equipment in Okinawa and the Philippines; training companies now rotated cadre for tens of thousands of insurgents, while hundreds of pilots and crews, many Nationalist Chinese, stood ready to climb aboard fifteen B-26s from the Agency's own Civil Air Transport (CAT) tactical air arm, each modified with a nose assembly for eight 50-caliber machine guns. A pair of U.S. Navy destroyers swung ominously at anchor off Singapore harbor.[35]

That same February 15 on which Howard Jones took over the Jakarta embassy the PEMESTA colonels proclaimed themselves a rebel government. As Robert Amory predicted, the well-trained brass on Sukarno's General Staff struck quickly and effectively. Directed by the independent-minded Colonel Abdul Haris Nasution, the Indonesian military cleared out its rebel officers, brought up a warship to pound their fortress in Sumatra, Padang, and bombed and strafed out of existence the radio stations at Padang and the rebellion's capital, Bukittinggi.

A few days later Foster Dulles underlined at a press conference that the rebellion was an internal matter, no arms must be provided to either side, the Indonesians should settle their dispute "without intrusion from without." Meanwhile, according to State Department logs, the Secretary was digging at his advice-torn brother, assuring him "he has the feeling we can't play too safely here and we have to take some risk because it looks to him it is the best chance we have. Allen is glad to hear it."[36]

By mid-March government troops were already ashore in Sumatra, backed up by strategic airdrops. Padang fell in April. The Secretary registered surprise; his brother assured him that reverses of this sort were not entirely unexpected: "We have to be careful not to get too far out on a limb," Allen cautioned now. Fearful of "too many white faces," the Director authorized a single radio team to report out on the beleaguered rebels, and only toward the end agreed to ship in three. When Foster prodded hard for consensus on recognizing the insurrectionary government, Allen staved him off with advice to wait another week.[37] On May 4 Bukittinggi fell, and what was left of PEMESTA set up on Celebes.

The B-26s flew mission after mission; they bombed a number of government-held targets along with a British tanker. Coyly, Sukarno publicly recurred to the involvement of U.S. and Chinese "adventurers," an opening for Eisenhower to quip at a press conference that "every rebellion that I have ever heard of has its soldiers of fortune."[38] But on May 18 one of the CIA's prime pilots, Allen Lawrence Pope, looked out to find the wing of his B-26 afire while he was laying down a stick of bombs upon a crowd of churchgoers in provincial Ambon. He bailed out. Assured that the pilot was checked over for personal effects before flying the mission, Wisner and his colleagues brushed off all imputation of involvement with Pope. But Pope was savvy, he knew that stateless pilots got shot upon capture, and so he included in his flight gear his recent transfer orders, and a PX card for Clark Air Force Base in Manila—enough documents to confirm his official status, and save his ass.[39]

What died that Sunday noon was plausible deniability. Pope went on display at a press conference in Djakarta. Foster Dulles summoned Al Ulmer and honked out a resonant little Ike-style speech about never committing the flag unless you were willing to forge through unto victory, and so forth. But on the ground the Sumatrans wouldn't fight, they ran for their lives at the shadow of their own supply planes—explanations befouled the committee rooms. The operation was busted.[40]

To placate the smirking Sukarno and spirit Pope away from the press before he blabbed his cold, mercenary heart out, Eisenhower quickly authorized the transfer of 37,000 tons of rice and repealed his embargo on $1 million worth of military equipment for Djakarta while Nasution was cleaning out whatever diehards had survived. Sukarno welcomed this hush money, and kept the enormity of the Indonesian fiasco from puffing out into headlines and humiliating the Republican administration.[41]

A follow-up study by the President's Board of Consultants on Foreign Intelligence tracked down the culprit behind this caper and deposited its pelt on history's doorstep: "The Indonesian operation was at no time considered formally by the Operations Coordinating Board's Special Group as contemplated by the provisions of NSC 5412. It came before that group only in catch as catch can fashion and as action progressed. On different occasions it was considered by the President, by the National Security Council, and by assorted ad hoc groups for various purposes. There was no proper estimate of aims nor proper prior planning on the part of anyone, and in its active phases the operation was directed, not by the DCI, but personally by the Secretary of State, who, ten thousand miles away from the scene of operation, undertook to make practically all decisions down to and including even tactical military decisions." The consequence overall, the document specifies, "was greatly to strengthen the position of the Communist Party in Indonesia."[42]

❑

Even at headline levels, 1958 was largely a holding operation; the fatigues of swimming against six years of postcolonial tides were accumulating all up and down thc weary Eisenhower government. Before the autumn expired a severe inflammation of the intestine signaled the return of the stomach cancer that week by week now debilitated John Foster Dulles, who struggled with impressive courage throughout the Berlin crisis of the succeeding winter but resigned in April 1959. He died in late May.

With Foster losing ground, support for cut-rate sapping operations was harder to find every month. Increasingly, the President was making sure his staff secretary General Andrew Goodpaster was standing at his elbow whenever Allen came in to pitch for additional covert. Goodpaster was increasingly skeptical. He was already characterizing the flow of background information on Vietnam from the Agency as "inadequate, poor, terrible," and cautioned Eisenhower in 1960 that the CIA's espousal of a paramilitary experiment with Cuban exiles "would build up a momentum of its own, which would be hard to stop."[43]

For Wisner the summer of 1958 turned into a slog. What chance would anything have, between the Dulles brothers? After Hungary opened up Allen had argued where he could find an opening, but Foster had shut them down. When the Indonesian rebels faltered Foster seemed to want to follow the situation in, but Allen got cold feet. The heavyweights reeled around, and Wisner got mashed.

What served Allen best, it very often seemed, was his notoriously short attention span. That and his vanity. He remained an actor, Mr. Chips doing intelligence. He took such obvious, boyish pleasure in all the "side" the position provided—the limousine pickups, the secret inks, the world-girdling inspection tours, punctuated by dead-of-night takeoffs the moment he climbed aboard bundled into his custom-made jumpsuit. Now he was preoccupied with the overlays for the seven-story monument to civilian intelligence going up at Langley, Virginia. This was to institutionalize his work, to provide for Allen's Foggy Bottom.

It inflamed Wisner even to think about turning this most privileged and discreet of governmental functions into a gargantuan public bureaucracy. " 'Well, it's important that we get the message across, what we're trying to do,' Allen used to tell Frank," Polly Fritchey remembers. "Frank had to feel that it was a mistake to have made the Agency so public in a city so small. He very much objected to the size of the new building, the increase in personnel. He wanted it to remain quiet, small, downtown. . . . And there was Allen—I don't know, for whatever reason, maybe it was competition with his brother, out there making *speeches* all the time. . . ."[44]

Every time Allen came by the house, Wendy still recalls, "you got that feeling that everybody was a little on edge. I think my father was a little bit in awe of Allen Dulles."[45] Wisner was increasingly upset. Strung up, and worse. "One afternoon when Allen was away somebody put a call through to me from Lewis Strauss," Robert Amory says. " 'Bob, I can't tell you how troubled I am about somebody in your organization,' " Strauss opened right up. " 'A friend of mine, who has a cattle farm on the Eastern Shore, just called me. He said he'd just gotten a call from Frank Wisner—this on a working day—and Wisner had announced that he had decided to expand his entire operation, and offered to buy his herd. I know that Frank and Polly have both got family money, but it is definitely not of the scale you throw around buying up 500 Black Angus and Herefords.' My friend felt that what he was listening to came straight out of some sort of manic episode."[46]

Everyone near Wisner worried. The inactive recuperative stretch after his hospitalization for hepatitis had caused his weight to jump, he looked increasingly dumpy. "For the first time, at that stage, I noticed that whenever he disagreed with you his voice had a tendency to rise, he would become excited, even quite shrill," Charles Murphy comments.[47] His jowls inflated, folds thickened the corners of his intent eyes, and under sustained attack a kind of frozen grimace sometimes seemed to contort his mouth into a defensive rictus, as if to show that enough was left to sustain him no matter how they piled it on.

Always an idea-a-minute man, many of Wisner's latest inspirations seemed frightening. Frank Lindsay had attended a get-together in Yugoslavia to commemorate the fifteenth anniversary of the rescue of Tito and his staff from the Nazi ambush at Bosnia. When Lindsay got back Wisner invited him to an evening party at the Wisner house on P Street. The group was no more than five or six, Lindsay recalls, and he was soon only too aware that his host was on a kind of emotional high, railing out in "tremendous bursts of talking energy, many of which did not make sense. This was enough different from the Wisner I'd known a few years earlier to really startle me."

In light of the new Khrushchev rapprochement to Yugoslavia several Soviet staff officers had attended the ceremonies, a detail which fascinated Wisner. "By God," he broke out suddenly to Lindsay. "Get me the uniform of a Russian general. I'll appear before Tito and send a shock into him!" He seemed utterly serious. The evening broke up on rather a muted note, Frank Lindsay and the others trailing down the front steps both puzzled and apprehensive.[48]

The swings of urgency and obsession grew wider and wider. He became a wanderer at night, he could not sleep, he refused all medication and dismissed any suggestion of doctors, limiting himself to an occasional consultation with Alan Walker, a nose and throat specialist and one-time schoolmate. Wisner's elegantly tuned Southerner's ear for the chivalric was undependable now, the stories he launched into could sometimes be off-putting, pointlessly clinical and on occasion quite labored and aimlessly crude. Days emptied into nights of runaway overemotionalized nattering; confusion affected his gait, he tottered noticeably. By September 1958 representatives of the government were talking privately with Polly, and it was agreed all around that Frank would be better off under institutional auspices.[49]

The place they arrived at was Sheppard Pratt, the psychiatric annex of Johns Hopkins in Baltimore. Everybody hoped that Baltimore, while accessible, was remote enough to discourage casual dropping by from pals in the Agency, everybody primed with the shop-talk allusions that tended to leave Wisner speeding again. Treatment was largely rest, with sessions of therapy and discussion once he had begun to recover his equilibrium. Little by little, as winter came on, the years of stress and anger and frustration and resentments began to work to the surface. By then Richard Bissell had replaced Wisner as Deputy Director–Plans. "I think my husband was crushed when Allen made Bissell the head of the DDP and not

Dick Helms," Polly says, but even at that, mulling the whole thing over, Frank uncovered deeper explanations for what had gone wrong. Wisner's son Ellis remembers the ferocity with which, during one visit, his father "let out a blast at Dick Helms, rightly or wrongly I don't know."[50]

He took his demons on, frequently confusing his doctors. ". . . I talked to his psychiatrists," Paul Nitze reminisces, "and told 'em that I didn't think all these businesses about his having trouble with his wife or some sexual problem in his youth—all that was nonsense. The thing that had broken his spirit had to do with the *work* he was doing. . . ."[51] Toward spring, once Frank Wisner was clearly coming back into possession of himself, he started to spend much of his available time sculpting. He had always been fascinated by the work of the Greeks, Wendy knew, and one day she found him completing a "beautiful, headless male figure."

Wisner spent the summer largely resting at the farm. Allen protected his seniority by appointing him Special Assistant to the DCI at his earlier $20,000 annual salary level and cast about to find something prestigious enough to occupy this uneven retainer. "Against many people's advice he was taken back," Lyman Kirkpatrick observes, ever cut-and-dried. "I said it was unfair to him."[52] The post Allen hit upon was station chief in London.

The mission in London was something of a quasi-diplomatic operation, its day-to-day responsibilities involving the heavy flow of information between the CIA and MI5 and MI6. For obvious political reasons the British were not to be penetrated or subverted in the accustomed manner. Wisner had returned to service in September 1949 visibly shaky—"diffident" is the word his deputy in London, Carleton Swift, comes up with first to describe Frank's attitude settling in around the London embassy. Swift was a Far East specialist with OSO credentials and wartime experience in the Pacific. His failure to "predict or control the 1958 coup d'etat in Iraq" had recently set his own career back, Swift acknowledges, and that, coupled with his expertise as a "professional plumber on espionage operations" recommended him to Wisner just then, in that "I didn't present any threat to him."[53]

"He relied heavily on me," Swift says. "After a year of shrinkerage you tend to come out a little unsure of yourself." Swift supervised the transfer of the station to the new embassy on Grosvenor Square, wrote the Thursday cables to Washington, dealt with "5" and "6." There was a lot of back and forth with the British Joint Intelligence Board, especially concerning Soviet intentions toward Berlin. By that point a great deal of hard strategic detail was coming out of the U-2 overflights. Many estimates were shared, and British pilots started flying some of the U-2s. English experts contributed to the interpretation of signal data coming back from the big intercept station in northern Iran, by then the major source of data on Soviet weaponry.

What Frank brought personally to the exchanges in London as bit by bit he acclimated himself was access to the ambassadorial level of society and public affairs. By winter his gift for drawing in and interesting people of cultivation and accomplishment, his returning exuberance, were turning the dinner parties he and Polly mounted into calendar events of London's social season. The U.S. Ambassador, Jock Whitney, had been a friend for years. "They ran a pretty high-level salon," Swift volunteers, "and anybody who made a trite comment wasn't welcome. Every party featured a serious talk about international affairs." Martha Gellhorn dropped by, along with Arthur Koestler and Oxford's (and the SIS's) Balkan expert Richard Deakin and Dick White, the incumbent "C." Both of the brothers Alsop were in and out. "From what I heard they must have decided that everybody in Burke's Peerage was going to pass through their drawing room," sniffs one colleague. Several blamed Polly. She herself in fact was doing what she could just then to keep Frank coming home early. One summer they rented a cottage in Scotland on one of the Balfour estates, where Frank and the boys went grouse shooting together.

Wisner himself seemed solider all the time. For all his puncture-proof aplomb Allen tended to return the undisguised British discomfiture with himself and Foster with an uncharacteristic aloofness. A lifetime of contacts had confirmed his childhood anticolonialist bias; concern that the SIS remained slovenly about security would stir him to lash out every once in a while at "that bunch of pansies" at Broadway, although he would make a point of treating his injured British colleagues with tact and solicitousness after Suez.

Wisner allowed more easily for cultural differences. He downplayed American annoyances at the pigheadedness of the English at suggestions that they get busy and vet or flutter their people, stop mincing around and bring the Philby situation to a head. At Dulles's urging, Wisner got close enough to Roger Hollis to break loose "a really valuable body of evidence about Philby," Cleve Cram says, "which filled in a lot of the chinks and helped overcome the horrified reaction around the Agency when we were given to understand that MI6 was running him still."[54] Back on his toes, Wisner kept the senior Britishers amiable, and they were pleased to come by and sample his whiskey. Everybody enjoyed him personally, one top official acknowledges, "but of course they kept Wisner at something of a distance because they recognized that he was unstable."[55]

Wisner found himself regretting certain of the Agency's touchier operations from across an ocean. The blowback was nasty in 1960 when Allen decided to double-cross British intelligence by recruiting his own agents in Singapore just before it passed from British protection into the Malaysian Federation.[56]The CIA was already stuffing ballot boxes and provoking local rebellions with Soviet backing to force its right-wing strong man, General Phoumi Nosavan, into power in somnolent Laos.[57]

In May 1960, weeks before the Eisenhower-Khrushchev summit, CIA misestimates of the range and maneuverability of improved SAM missiles contributed to the downing of a U-2 over Soviet territory. After years of Agency assurances to the White House that "self-destroying mechanisms" were built in to obliterate both the aircraft and its pilot in case of interception, most of the plane along with miles of exposed film and all of Francis Gary Powers turned up in Soviet hands at a press conference. Like Allen Pope, Powers had intended to survive, whatever the dislocations registered at the imminent summit meeting in Paris.[58]

Largely uncontaminated by tradecraft, Bissell—and Allen—were stumbling even before the Bay of Pigs. Once action against Cuba had started to come on line Frank Wisner's senior operations man, Colonel Frank Holcomb, was automatically "brought in to be a member of the board. I got so mad that I said that I would not have my feet on American soil when that operation came off. I had other things to do in Europe, and so I left the country. So I was sitting in London with Frank Wisner when we started getting the news. I'd briefed him: *This is hopeless*. Crazy operation. And so we just sort of sat there and gloomed."[59]

The apparatus Frank Wisner had invented was caterwauling toward catastrophe.

❑

The Bay of Pigs would constitute the last true blow-off of classical-era covert, something like the Fourth-of-July finale when all the whistlers and rockets and chrysanthemums of streaming light arc through the blackness above the stiffening onlookers. Every mistake went up. When everything came down the men around JFK stood gawking at a kind of giant East–West road accident, while scavengers from the media hopped back and forth in the mess to peck the entrails into view.

Until the Cuban disaster the *management* of whatever publicity emerged from the larger operations had undoubtedly constituted Allen's most meaningful accomplishment. When something worked out, like Iran or Guatemala, at least an oblique reference was likely to peek through before long in the big, laudatory, richly photographed, semiauthorized montage articles about the Director which appeared regularly in *Time* or *U.S News and World Report* or *The Saturday Evening Post.* When something caved in, from Albania through Indonesia, the conspiracy of silence held, although there had been one scratchy moment when the *Chicago Daily News* ran a dispatch about the airdrops to PEMESTA.[60] Even the U-2 downing reflected a kind of banked glamour on the Agency. They finally picked one off, the subtext ran, but boy have we ever been running a drill on the Russkies.

The Bay of Pigs was something else entirely. Enough of the Agency's intentions and modus operandi had leaked long before the brigade stumbled ashore to give the working press a handle on the story. It wouldn't be many weeks before the slapdash planning, the unrealistic assumptions, the faulty intelligence, the evasions and misrepresentations and outright lies which greased the interface between the Agency and the Kennedy administration would spread like an oil slick across the surface of the news and toxify Allen's directorship.

John Kennedy's first blunder had been to credit a legend. "I know that outfit," his father the ambassador and board member of PBCFIA volunteered as the debacle settled, "and I wouldn't pay them a hundred dollars a week. It's a lucky thing they were found out early."[61] Either Joe hadn't presented his advice, or Jack hadn't listened.

Kennedy's youth, his Catholicism, and something of the ideological freebooter about his style had made it vital to reassure the power elite. What he wound up with was essentially bipartisan, an assortment of Cold-War centrists from Clarence Dillon's son Douglas and McGeorge Bundy (Republicans) to Dean Rusk and Averell Harriman (Democrats). The best-known liberal-intellectual in the group was manifestly Chester Bowles.

The fact was, on inauguration day most of the counselors and advisers to the new President regarded the Agency as sympathetic ground. Unlike his politically born-again brother, Allen Dulles knew a Socialist from a Bolshevik. Most of the leadership of the CIA was enlightened, preponderantly Democratic, with emerging senior managers like Tracy Barnes and Dickie Bissell quite dedicated social reformers. Bissell was a particular favorite of Chester Bowles, who had sailed with the young economist for decades and given him his start in government during the Roosevelt years when Bowles ran the Office of Price Stabilization. Bissell fought Bowles's interagency battles for him. Once Bowles got in as Undersecretary of State he angled hard for Bissell as Deputy Undersecretary for Political Affairs. Kennedy personally scotched the appointment, divulging that Bissell was slated to "take Allen Dulles's job. . . ."[62]

The Kennedy administration's tendency to perceive the CIA as an enclave of survivors from the Acheson dispensation helped lull the new men, who treated it as quite competently run, effective, and realistic about projections. The roll of confrontational rhetoric with which the young President announced his tenure accorded with the combative spirit abroad just then; the Agency discreetly trumpeted itself as permanently at war so that the rest of the nation might enjoy itself. Just then the threat of the season was Fidel Castro. Many agreed that perhaps the first thing the freshly inaugurated President could do for his country was relieve her of a Communist outpost ninety miles off Florida.

It would become clear in time that neither of the U.S. Presidents involved came in that willingly. Eisenhower would subsequently maintain that, with respect to Cuba, "there was no tactical or operational plan discussed," while he was in, although an evolving "program" came up from time to time.[63] As much as anybody the insecure Vice President kept jostling the project along. A pro-forma encounter on Capitol Hill during the spring of 1959 had convinced Nixon that behind the nonstop harangues, the yearning onyx eyes, Fidel's avid mixture of evasion and bluff meant that he was already an instrument of the Kremlin. Shortly Castro and his claque in Havana were expropriating U.S. refineries for refusing to process Russian crude. They followed up quickly by taking over American-owned pharmaceutical plants, and cane fields, and any other assets they liked the looks of down to the Mafia's crap tables.

Even then any *planning* against Castro moved at a watchful pace. Latino specialist Jake Esterline and other Agency covert draftsmen were the first to work something up in one of those dumpy, roach-ridden offices in the K Building.

The short answer seemed inevitable, time-tested: assassination. Responding to a nod from Allen Dulles, Bissell was already reviving a wide-ranging "executive-action" program which targeted unwelcome leaders around the world from General Kassem in Iraq to Trujillo in the Dominican Republic. The Agency's Science Adviser, Sidney Gottlieb, had concocted a standard-issue biological poison kit, complete with rubber gloves, with which to dispense with the unruly Patrice Lumumba in Leopoldville. Castro seemed comparatively accessible. Initial attempts to polish off Castro were delegated to security head Sheffield Edwards, who worked through Howard Hughes's legman Robert Maheu to hire the Mafia organizer John Roselli.[64]

Eight CIA attempts to murder Castro would be documented quite fully over the five upcoming years until Lyndon Johnson finally axed the project; it ran on inertia after Dulles stepped down. Before long the headsman who supplanted Sheffield was the irreplaceable William Harvey, hauled back from Germany to put together a "special group." Harvey was a closer, useful, for all his limitations in chic. He'd become a pyramid of flab, frank enough to characterize himself as a reliable consumer of three martinis at lunch—"two doubles and a single."[65]

Harvey stayed with Roselli, and set the fee for the hit at $150,000. Roselli picked up a botulin-based liquid for transfer to Cuba, but as another mafioso of the period would ultimately concede, it and similar potions from the Technical Services laboratories "had been simply flushed down the drain." "There's not much likelihood that this is going any place," Harvey growled in the end to Roselli, who remained a social friend.[66]

Something incomparably more complex and precarious was already on train to unseat Castro and went forward simultaneously. At a National Security Council meeting on March 17, 1960, Ike gave his assent to a program which envisaged the formation of a government in exile, propaganda, and some kind of coherent action and information net inside the island itself.[67] A week after that Richard Bissell mounted with characteristic fluency a full if sketchy projection of the thinking so far. Convened in Dulles's office, the meeting included Allen himself, Deputy Director General Charles Cabell, Tracy Barnes, Dick Helms, and David Phillips. Phillips later would write that throughout Bissell's explanations Helms "listened carefully, often inspecting his carefully manicured fingernails."[68] Colonel J. C. King, the Western Hemisphere chief, was again omitted from the all-important briefing list.

Bissell brought to Plans his Yankee-tinkerer's exactitude of mind, showing up at moments in displays of fussiness, fecklessness, an abrupt way of lunging stoop-shouldered through doors or unexpectedly throwing aside the paper clips he was impatiently straightening and bellowing at an aide who simply wasn't getting some very simple point. Bissell became a link between Allen Dulles and JFK.

Richard Helms edged wide. Perhaps it was resentment—even the stoic Helms hadn't been able completely to hide his disappointment when Bissell became DDP. Stiff-backed, utterly professional, mouth like a string, his straight hair barbered to the nines behind that high widow's peak, it was like standing there, for Helms, and watching the crowd from the office clustered beside the curbstone to cram sizable chunks of a freshly dismembered corpse into a leaky suitcase at rush hour. As operations chief, technically, Helms let down enough, on picking up on certain of the Cuban details, to gasp out: "harebrained!"[69] He exerted what influence he could—as inobtrusively as he could—to keep his best people out of this Dieppe in the making.[70]

"It's a sad thing," Lyman Kirkpatrick would later observe, "this business of trying to run a special operation like that as a sort of barnacle on the side of a ship. If you're going to run the operation, you should actually put the best assets in your Agency in it. It didn't have the best assets."[71] Conspicuous among the malassigned was Gerry Droller ("Frank Bender"), a heavily accented German immigrant borrowed from the Swiss desk, whose popinjay exploits among the Cuban émigré factions helped confuse and infuriate the leaders of the chaotic *Frente* Washington was attempting to weave into a presentable government-in-exile; Droller liked to impress on his high-strung clients, through puffs of cigar smoke, that he personally "carried the counterrevolution around in his checkbook."[72] Unhappy with Droller's obtuseness, kingmaker E. Howard Hunt ("Eduardo") turned up on schedule to pass cash around in support of his own choice for brigade leader, Manuel Artime, a malleable turncoat psychiatrist as flashy and now almost as right-inclined as E. Howard himself. Simultaneously, even the embittered J. C. King was lobbying hard in the corridors against discredited Batista discards.

Allen Dulles had intimated to nominee John Kennedy that some manner of infiltration and propaganda offensive against Castro was already afoot. Shortly after the election Allen Dulles and Richard Bissell slipped down to Joe Kennedy's Palm Beach hacienda to update the President-elect. Bissell records the finesse with which his courtly boss, hobbling ever so slightly beside the youthful, attentive Kennedy along a hedge of bougainvillea, chuckled reassuringly, hinted of the wonders it now had become routine for himself and his people to produce, and thus through slow, mesmerizing salesmanship soon got the inexperienced leader intrigued and committed.[73]

Muffled warnings weren't heeded. As early as January 28, 1961, when JFK at a National Security Council meeting instructed the Joint Chiefs to review—but not to involve themselves in—the Agency's Cuban planning, the professionals the Chiefs sent over to headquarters at Quarters Eye were " 'surprised and shocked,' " Peter Wyden quotes General David Gray as noting, "to get nothing more than 'a verbal rundown.' Apparently the Agency men had never assembled their ideas in one place. The team from the Joint Chiefs 'had to pull it out of them.' They spent one afternoon at it, sitting around a conference table, scribbling furiously into stenographers' notebooks." Home in the Pentagon they pooled their notes and wrote a twenty-five-page plan.[74]

On March 11, 1961, Kennedy arranged a meeting for a carefully selected assortment of advisors in the Cabinet Room. By then the planners had settled pretty definitely on some sort of landing along the Cuban coast, most probably near Trinidad. Volunteers for the brigade, now over a thousand, lounged scrubby and bug-infested in Guatemala, its count of AWOLs increasing until President Ydigoras obliged the Agency by restocking the brothels to smooth down the restive, prickly troops. Although the CIA's tidy little air arm of B-26s had done the caudillo a good turn in November by bombing into submission a local military rebellion, these many restless men and now a rash of worldwide publicity was not really . . . comfortable to the dictator, steadily less so, while disbanding the brigade at this point would present a "disposal problem," as Allen Dulles himself put it to the President at a top-level meeting on March 11, since "we can't have them wandering around the country telling everyone what they have been doing."[75]

A disposal problem! Whatever the political outcome, the Agency couldn't miss. Our little brown surrogates would turn Cuba over, or they'd be slaughtered on the beaches. The important thing was "plausible deniability." Kennedy himself defined the dilemma as largely of balancing: ". . . The smaller the political risk," in Arthur Schlesinger's paraphrase, "the greater the military risk, and visa versa." To this end, Kennedy sent the CIA planners away to find a landing site more conducive to a "quiet" night landing, and three days later they returned with their maps and the recommendation of Cochinos Bay, the Bay of Pigs, about 100 miles to the west of Trinidad in the Zapata section.[76]

Closed in by swamps and bogs, Castro already had plans to utilize the area for large-scale alligator breeding. There was some hope, off and on, that if the mission should abort the survivors of the brigade could "melt into the surrounding mountains." Overflights of the shallows suggested prevalent dark forms, just below the surface. Those must be seaweed, the photo interpreters decided; only when the jagged coral formations were in fact tearing the bottoms out of several waves of landing craft was every doubt settled.

The strategic purpose remained: get people ashore. News of the landing would rouse the population against the dictator, Dulles and Bissell hoped, and provide a "presence" on the island on which to base some sort of "Two-Cubas" policy and diplomatic recognition. Then troops and supplies could follow them in quite openly until Havana itself fell.

Of all his mistakes that spring, sitting still while all these overnight changes were imposed still rankles old Dick Bissell most: "Everybody in the world who could read a newspaper knew that it was perfectly obvious that the U.S. was involved." Bissell squeezes his long elbows together, half warding the memory off. "We should have quit making operational sacrifices to keep a fig leaf that had blown away anyway. Around that table, with a lot of bright, tough people, nobody stood up. And I'm the one who should have stood up. . . ."[77]

The Bay of Pigs had catastrophically overloaded the system. Even the wary Helms tiptoed across the chalkline to suggest to Bissell that, with reports and harbingers of the Agency's most jealously concealed provisional plans breaking out in everything from *The Nation* to the Guatemala City *La Hora,* mightn't it be prudent to assign more than a token presence of Angleton's now close to 300-member counterintelligence staff to screen the babble of furious Cuban politicians inflaming Miami just then? Bissell didn't think so.[78]

Roger Hilsman later emphasized that Robert Amory, the CIA's own intelligence and analysis chief, was "also kept in the dark," which "meant that the President was denied the judgment of CIA's own estimators. . . ."[79] Amory had, it developed, come upon the contours of the operation and hinted to Dulles—they'd needed his photoanalysis people, after all, to read the overflight results—but Dulles brushed him off, so Amory allegedly muttered "Screw 'em!" to himself and went home and played five sets of tennis. He relinquished his duty officer's post to the Agency's Deputy Director, Major General Charles P. Cabell.[80]

This produced a fateful snafu. Although allowed to sit in, Cabell resented his own exclusion from much of the high-level planning and discussion all through the Dulles regime. While Amory played tennis and Dulles conspicuously conducted business as usual in San Juan, Puerto Rico, Cabell intercepted the request coming through from the beachhead to authorize the famous "second strike" against the remains of Castro's ramshackle air force, and bucked the decision along to Secretary of State Dean Rusk.

Bland as a water torture, Rusk had been imploring Kennedy to keep the diplomatic "noise level" low; now, handed *his* chance, Rusk prevailed on Kennedy to cancel the action. This left Castro's remaining jet trainers and B-26s in place to send to the cove's bottom the Cuban brigade's communications ship and cut off resupply efforts.

Throughout the Agency's war the spectrum of involvement would run from the frantically conspiring to the drowsily aware to the suspicious to the blissfully uninformed. Tom Powers alludes to symptoms of a kind of low-grade palace revolt within the Plans directorate at the "branch chief and staff level" once the details floated up, and passes along scuttlebutt of an initiative, pressed by Tracy Barnes, to get the pessimistic Helms sidetracked, reassigned abroad, which Lyman Kirkpatrick scotched.[81]

Kirkpatrick contended with misgivings too, and requested of Dulles the chance to let a couple of his inspectors in. Dulles fluffed him off. That could undercut everything.

One inhibition might well be termed the old-school reassurance factor. Even high-minded, wordy Undersecretary of State Chester Bowles, who tumbled very late, felt obliged to hold his objections in at dress-rehearsal briefings. Again the British model—one soldiered along ignorant where peers were involved. One victim was Ambassador to the United Nations Adlai Stevenson. Nagged by a belated awareness that somebody had better get Stevenson involved if only to forestall another siege of Adlai whimpering his flatfooted way along the reception lines, Kennedy authorized a team from the White House and the CIA to proceed to Manhattan and fill Stevenson in.

Less than a week before the landings were penciled in, Arthur Schlesinger arrived late at the U.S. Mission on Saturday, April 8, and found that the Agency's dapper specialist in fur-smoothing, Tracy Barnes, had already presented to his old friend Stevenson a sanitized scenario which ascribed the fireworks anticipated to rising forces inside Cuba, abetted by "some outside participation." This would not entail, definitely would not, "any American participation," Barnes was quite sincere about reassuring the Ambassador. Stevenson was particularly skittish, since a United Nations debate on Cuban charges of aggressive U.S. intentions was scheduled to open simultaneously with the landings. "But our briefing," as Arthur Schlesinger later wrote, "which was probably unduly vague, left Stevenson with the impression that no action would take place during the UN discussion of the Cuban item."[82]

Again, Barnes exemplified his navigational instincts by averting his own eyes. It is a testimony to Tracy Barnes's charm that he was able to keep even Arthur a little at sea while chloroforming the U.N. ambassador. Stevenson wound up waving high a photograph of one of the Agency's doctored B-26s landing in Miami after purportedly fleeing the dictator. Betrayed, Adlai would muddle along through mounting depression, still flying his reputation with all its accumulating bullet holes.

"The integrity and credibility of Adlai Stevenson," Kennedy had assured Schlesinger, "constitute one of our great national assets."[83] People at the top of the Agency knew that as well, and relished its expenditure. The West was aflame, Communism was entrenching itself ninety miles off our coastline, and Dulles and his followers felt sure no sacrifice would loom very large if this thing played at all.

The CIA's own intelligence wrap-up was discredited and avoided. Castro had rounded up and jailed the 100,000 or so identifiable dissidents on whom any internal support depended. The population which survived, maintained the head of the Agency's own Board of National Estimate, Sherman Kent, could not "portend any serious threat" to the regime. Very few seemed cognizant at all that the sine qua non which made success conceivable in Iran and Guatemala—a conservative, indigenous officer caste in place, working closely with an all-seeing U.S. military mission—had long since been scourged by Castro and the wised-up Che Guevara.

When, on Sunday, April 17, the final go had been pried out of Kennedy and waves of the Agency's pathetic flotilla moved out over the horizon and beyond the protective shadow of the U.S. Navy to scramble the brigade ashore, a rabble of 1,400 or so half-trained and politically contesting irregulars against Castro's 200,000-man military, there weren't many doubts even among the staunchest action enthusiasts about what to expect. Even Dulles was privately without hope. For all his sophistication, a long lifetime's inability to discriminate between romance and fact had tracked Allen down finally, and caught him square.

The disposal problem shifted. Within days it came to include the leadership of the Agency.

22

HOME FROM THE EMPIRE

"If this were the British government," the shaken President told Bissell in May, "I would resign, and you, being a senior civil servant, would remain. But it isn't. In our government, you and Allen have to go. . . ."[1] The summer of 1961 provided a decent interval; Lyman Kirkpatrick burrowed in to compile his notorious Inspector General's report on what exactly led up to the Bay of Pigs. It remains tightly classified, but certainly the thrust comes through in a lecture Kirkpatrick gave years later at the Naval War College.

"There is no other place to put the blame," he would conclude flatly, "than on the agency mounting the operation. There was a totally erroneous estimate of the quality of Castro's fighting forces, a lack of realism in evaluating the potential resistance, and therefore as a corollary, a lack of realism in estimating the number of forces required to do the job. There was a lack of knowledge about Castro's control in Cuba, even though the British and French intelligence reports were available on the subject.

"Organizationally, a large part of CIA was excluded from the operation. The present Director of the Central Intelligence Agency, Richard Helms, who was then Chief of Operations for CIA, was not involved in the operation. . . . In like manner, the bulk of the military expertise of the Pentagon was excluded because knowledge of the operation was handled on such a close basis within the Joint Staff."

In fact, "the operators running the operation were assessing and evaluating the intelligence, not the intelligence directorate. . . . Much of the intelligence came from the Cuban resistance, which was not always an objective intelligence source."

At policy levels only Chester Bowles, "who had inadvertently heard about the operation," in the end opposed it, while Roger Hilsman, the senior intelligence official at State, was refused a briefing.[2]

Apologists for Allen Dulles insist that Kirkpatrick's report went much further. They claim he loaded the arguments to home in on Bissell's stewardship, to knock him out once and for all as DDP or, eventually, Director. Bissell himself was particularly exercised at the charge that an "adverse selection" mechanism came into play to make sure the better people would survive this collective suicide leap, which Kirkpatrick concluded followed from the insane operating principles Frank Wisner bequeathed the Agency. Several assert that Kirkpatrick himself rushed over a ribbon copy of his scarifying study and pushed it on Allen Dulles's replacement, the brilliant California industrialist John McCone, while he was alighting from an open car with Dulles and JFK to accept nomination as the Agency's new boss in September.

Kirkpatrick became the scapegoat, especially after he tacked on the title of Executive Director of the CIA and promoted the retirement of a number of his chief detractors. But Kirkpatrick hadn't felled the lion. Allen's reassurances to Eisenhower and Kennedy that his operators could finish Castro had seemed so unequivocal even he couldn't waltz away. "I'll never forget the arrival of McCone," Kirkpatrick says. "He was a tough, no-nonsense Irishman, very decisive, and he didn't have a high regard for Allen. They conversed, but there was a lack of warmth."[3] A UPI photo survives of Kennedy, Dulles, and McCone leaving the Naval War College grounds in the back of an open convertible. Both Kennedy and McCone peer forward, while Allen, squeezed in between them, appears to be scanning the skies, perhaps for eleventh-hour redemption. His Teddy-Roosevelt mustache and seven-button Edwardian vest give him a dated look, overnight an arthritic wowser attempting to breast the Space Age.

❑

As public events broke, Wisner couldn't have *chosen* a better time to stay out of Washington than before and just after the Bay of Pigs. The convulsion that capsized the careers of Allen Dulles and Richard Bissell drove Frank Wisner's name into contention again. By 1962 the Wall Street policy architects and Cold War intellectuals who tagged Frank originally to fend off the KGB—Kennan, Harriman, Bohlen, Lovett et al.—were back on top as the Kennedy administration reached out for tempered, proven statesmen. Several moved up automatically from second- to first-rank administrative status. David Bruce replaced Jock Whitney at the Court of St. James, and he and others were reporting back that Frank Wisner was himself again—as capable and ebullient as ever, working full time.

Himself again, Wisner simply couldn't turn down a collaborating role in an early 1962 SIS attempt to depose the left-leaning Prime Minister in British Guiana, Cheddi Jagan. A self-governing crown colony, British Guiana's native government had abruptly imposed heavy taxes and invited in Soviet oil technologists, who discovered a major field. White capital fled. With that, the Western services responded. On February 16 ("Black Friday"), street demonstrations blew up into a general strike, violence and arson spread in Georgetown, and eighty were hurt. Five died. Jagan's grip was loosened. "Frank never did anything even 100 percent," one participant in the operation volunteers. "He did everything 250 percent. He decided he had a sacred mission, and of course he worked himself into a frenzy."[4]

In June of 1962 Frank and Polly put in for home leave to attend their eldest son's graduation from Princeton. "A lot of his pals were up in the White House," Carleton Swift relates. "He was back for about a week. As I gather it, I don't think he went to bed that whole week. He'd gone back to the seat of power, of policy-making for the whole world, and he spent every night up, talking with them, discussing what ought to be done. Frank and his Scottish doctor and the rest of us felt that he was now all right, that the repair was fine. But the veneer was a little bit thin. When the opportunity came to get back, and feel that he and his friends had the baton of world power in their knapsacks he . . . he went manic. It was too much stress."

Just before the Wisners were scheduled to return to London, Secretary of State Dean Rusk asked Frank to join a delegation attending a conference in Geneva. Carleton Swift and Polly went out to Heathrow to await his plane from Switzerland. "We were within sight of the steps leading down from the plane," Carleton remembers, "and we saw Frank walking down the steps, and I remember Polly saying: 'Ohhhh!' And she saw him, you know, weaving just a tiny bit, and walking in a way that she was familiar with, which was an indication that he was in a manic state. I remember her exclamation of fear, disappointment, anxiety at seeing that he was showing characteristics of his earlier problems."[5]

"Several people had already called to tell me that Frank was on quite a high," Polly will acknowledge.[6] Watching her overwrought husband struggle down from the plane confirmed everything she feared. Nobody said very much. Frank went back to work, but it was quickly apparent that he was out of control. "Propaganda continued to be his main interest," Swift says. "Some issue was up, and we were in some trouble, and he got on the telephone to one of the cabinet ministers. And just spent half an hour berating him for what the British were doing or not doing. . . .

"It was like the time before he went off to Sheppard Pratt—nobody around him wanted to speak up and say: Oh, Frank, you've overstepped a bit. We rolled with it. His doctors were in, and they said he ought to stay home a bit more. We went back to this thing of bringing the cables over to his house. I'd get his views. I could temper him a little."

Before long Wisner was spending the whole time at home. "I'd go around to see him and sort of pretend that he was the boss. And I sort of took the responsibility—with Polly's knowledge—to tone down his positions as they went home. . . . I communicated this to Helms, and Helms sent over one of the doctors, and we padded him down. . . ." Helms was still covering for Frank as much as he was able, and McCone was reportedly outraged when he himself first got an inkling of Frank's condition from a remark of Polly's over lunch. McCone was particularly concerned, one aide saw, "that British psychiatrists had gotten their hands on Wisner. There was no reflection of Frank's illness or absence in the official communications."

"We all watched him like a hawk," Polly sighs. Determined to contain this sensitive situation as closely as possible, practitioners selected by the Agency attempted to deal with Wisner at home. He underwent a course of increasingly intense shock treatments. After weeks of shattering therapy his handlers concluded that he was stabilized enough to travel. Wisner was returned without incident to the security of Washington.

Nobody doubted that Frank was utterly played out; even then the habits of paternalism Allen Dulles had ingrained in the Agency were such that Wisner was signed to a consultancy contract and pulled in regularly once enough of his memory had returned to leave him largely on his own again. "John McCone arranged to recruit Wisner as his own special assistant to take advantage of Frank's close ties to *The Washington Post* and the Alsop brothers," Charles Murphy submits.[7] But this was primarily to get him through his initial summer in the United States, and Wisner was self-aware enough to recognize as that ended that he was not going to be involved in things, that he did not have meaningful access any more. He removed himself formally from the active rolls at the end of August, when he was awarded the Distinguished Intelligence Medal. He rented a tiny law and business office at 1210 Eighteenth Street, N.W., with a friend, Sam Spencer, and began to dabble in what was available as a civilian.

Its rewards were mixed. His shifts of mood could make him demanding, irascible; close friends stood by. John Graham was particularly loyal, and helped with his portfolio as well as the financial management of the Laurel oil properties he was soon attempting to promote. Ellis calls to mind such exploratory enterprises as "The Great Lakeshore Dehydrating and Processing Company—one of dad's business fiascos."[8] By now a familiar, blocky figure toward afternoon at the F Street and Metropolitan clubs, Wisner joined the Advisory Council of the Johns Hopkins School of Advanced International Studies and became a trustee of the Conservation Foundation. Frank Lindsay had moved on; now president of the Itek Corporation, he took Wisner in as a consultant in 1964.[9] Wisner collected Greek artifacts, arranged bridge games, bustled around the acreage at Galena to patch up the blinds and toss corn around to attract enough ducks to assure good shooting for cohorts from the Agency who could be enticed up for a nostalgic weekend.

Premature semiretirement wasn't nearly enough; Wisner's tendency to brood about his uncompleted mission and an increasing prickliness whenever leaked Agency operations attracted media attacks now made him seek out editorial opportunities for "grinding certain special axes," as he himself specified. Even now, in print, his weakness for pomposities was veined with unpredictable insights, with flashes of insider experience and a sly defense of his own uneven performance. In an intra-Agency review of Allen Dulles's *The Craft of Intelligence* in 1963, amidst the lumbering, paragraph-long sentences, Wisner protests that "Though the high-flying Mata Haris of today may with their glass eyes be able to discern the most minute of man-made molehills . . . these are not and will never become any substitute for the older and less 'exotic' measures which are essential to the discovery and frustration of subversive intent."[10] As for the Soviet operative Eugene Ivanov, whose involvement with Christine Keeler destroyed the ministerial career of John Profumo, ". . . it was just *lagniappe* that on the earlier occasion Jack met Christine by chance encounter at the pool. . . ." Ivanov was "the beneficiary of the most extraordinary series of failures of coordination on the part of British authorities concerned, the security services having been well aware of his significance and the game that he was playing with the wretched Dr. Ward as his tool nearly two years before the final explosion."[11]

Following up the obligatory salute to Allen as "one of the leading and most revered experts in the field," Wisner surmises that "the author himself might be willing to acknowledge the existence of an unbalance in favor of intelligence tradecraft . . . some larger measure of recognition for the contribution of the researchers and analysts would be in order." Warning of prisoner exchanges, Wisner alludes to a mid-twenties trade in Moscow which impacted even "the highly reputable German diplomat, Gustav Hilger. . . ." Why so much indignation now? Clandestine political warfare, Wisner sums up, "involves relatively few casualties," and he can find "no rationality in the fact that people, certainly including Americans, will cheer the spectacle of massed military forces exterminating one another . . . by the millions," while deploring "as somehow unnatural and immoral the kind of activity on our part which can contribute so much to forestalling the necessity for armed conflict." By then the Kennedy administration planners were concluding that covert was largely a mirage, and made this plain around the Agency by stripping out its budget.

Quarrels from the past and decomposing buried doubts squeezed to the top of Frank Wisner's disordered brain. His years of accommodating his Wall Street seniors by helping prop up the recrudescent Right in Germany seems to have stirred in him a kind of compensatory revulsion at the prospect that Martin Bormann had indeed escaped Berlin, a notion Wisner evidently encountered in a novel called *The Year of the Rat*."[12] "He was on a thing about this," Wendy remembers, "that we should pool our sources and resources and get Bormann. He talked about the 'mysterious and sinister figure of Martin Bormann.' He wrote millions of letters. If there really was a CIA connection to Bormann in South America, who knows if he wasn't feeling terrible about it? If he's starting to yell and scream about these Nazis, who in the CIA is starting to get worried about it? Was he hallucinating?"[13]

Bats raged around Frank, streaming in from every quarter. By the spring of 1965 he was in hectic correspondence with Mr. and Mrs. Gilbert Highet (Helen McInnes) over the possibility that a roguish Charlie Murphy may be baiting them all with a bogus volume purporting to anticipate the story line of *A Venetian Affair,* confident that Wisner would rise like a trout to such a guileful show of literary bait.[14] He dispatched a grim letter to John McCone after drawing out an NBC producer embarked on a documentary on the CIA at a dinner party and concluding that a one-sided exposé by David Brinkley and John Chancellor lurked in the offing. He composed and disseminated a seventeen-page jeremiad in the form of a confidential memorandum to underpin his one-man "campaign" against Morris West's novel *The Ambassador,* which he interpreted angrily as a major threat to the State Department.[15]

"He'd become too high again, too loquacious," Polly could see. "Everything was overexaggerated. There would be a modicum of truth, but he would make it into a terrific fantasy."[16] Another stint of hospitalization dragged into another summer.

"Mr. Wisner recently lunched with Mr. Helms," a CIA memorandum for the record of September 22, 1965, records. "At this time, he explained to Mr. Helms that the pressure of his personal business and the advice of his physician made it impossible for him to devote any time to the Agency. He said that he had his contract for renewal but had not returned it and would not return it but wished Mr. Helms to know the reason why. —asked me to be sure that we closed that contract out and that we would not communicate with Mr. Wisner."[17]

That autumn Frank's passages of logorrhea ran down for the first time into episodes of depression, the sure knowledge that this was life from here on out. He had been instrumental in October in getting together a party to rent an estate in Spain guaranteed to be heavy with partridge. A couple of CIA officers returning from Europe got requests through channels to bring back shotguns Frank was having repaired abroad.[18] Stories made the rounds in Washington that Frank was stockpiling revolvers at Locust Hill.

As his embarkation date approached Wisner collapsed again. "He was obviously in no condition to go to Europe," Polly realized, and Wisner attempted to sell his place on the shooting party headed for Spain to Joe Bryan's brother Lamont and decided to spend the last weekend of October on the Galena farm. Before they drove up on October 29 Polly telephoned the caretaker and asked him to make sure there was nothing unusual—no hand guns—lying around the place. Just before the weekend Janet Barnes and a couple of other friends stopped by the P Street house for lunch. "I asked Polly if it was all right to go say hello to Frank," Janet recalls. A year of intermittent hospitalization had put a good deal of weight on Wisner, his cheeks had ballooned and there was a dullness to his eyes that alarmed Janet: "I saw this really sad, sad face, and you knew that he was worried and discouraged. Depressed, and there was nothing anybody could do to help him."[19]

The talking jag had finally ended. John Graham had spoken to Wisner just before he started for the farm, Charles Murphy maintains, and claimed that "Frank went off in the best of moods. Perhaps he was misleading John, although he obviously wasn't thinking clearly by the time he arrived up there. It was an untidy way to do it, blow his brains out at the top of the stairs in his own house."[20]

Mrs. Wisner had been occupying herself below, and heard the explosion of the 20-gauge shotgun. The charge had torn through the right temple and desecrated the plasterwork. Her husband was dead before the ambulance could reach the farm.

Frank died at fifty-six. The obituaries were guarded, but even in the early releases there was a ceremonial fervor to the comments, as if from onlookers standing on a shore watching a Viking funeral barge blazing out at sea. *The New York Times* was told that Wisner "had been despondent ever since a hernia operation last spring. . . ."[21] *The Washington Post,* borrowing language from Angleton, pegged Wisner as "one of a half dozen of the most important men in Washington during his CIA career," who rose "to meet the long, prepared challenge of the vast Stalinist intelligence and subversion net. . . ." He had been "deeply American above all."[22] A floral display designed around the number "7" signified that Frank had indeed been tapped at UVA as one of his generation's secret leaders. As the eulogies concluded there rose the strains of "Unfurl the Banner," followed by the patient drive toward Arlington Cemetery.

❑

Carmel Offie blamed Polly. "I don't think Frank ever got laid properly after he left Bucharest," Carmel brayed to one listener, while on another he conferred the explanation that all those years of hectic oversocializing by the Wisners were traceable to Mrs. Wisner's avidity to blot out girlhood setbacks in Westchester owing to a Jewish forebear. Polly's aunt had married the quiet, scholarly Joseph Seligman. Bouncing around the private sector, Carmel had not lost his aptitude for saucing up gossip or adding tang to scraps of insider detail.

He was as high-handed as ever. Very much like Wisner, Carmel Offie was propelled into the Cold War directorate by a cordon of State Department Eastern-Europe specialists. Many of the same personalities—Charlie Thayer, the Bohlens, the ever-glamorous Robert and Jane Joyce, George Kennan, Robert Murphy—who consistently boosted Frank remained devoted to Offie; in almost every case the association was surprisingly deep-rooted. In 1946 Kennan had referred to Carmel in a War College wrap-up as "a man who wore on his sleeves his faults and his virtues," which George termed "mutually complementary." He testified to Offie's "unbounded energy, enthusiasm, a highly sociable nature and a great loyalty and helpfulness with respect to those who take a personal interest in him."[23] As always with Kennan, suggestions of the grittier realities had a way of chalking through the lines.

Offie had moved adroitly during the later forties to shore up a power base of his own inside the OPC. "Here was a poor Italian boy out to be in on the action," Polly Fritchey remembers. "Chip told Frank that he'd be interesting to work with. But before long he was starting to bring in people Frank didn't know, friends of Bill Bullitt." Nobody inquired too closely: Offie was so serviceable at a time when even the amenities came hard. "You called him up and he knew where everything was," Polly stresses. "We had four children at that point, and we needed a cook. He produced one, immediately." On rainy days, Ellis Wisner remembers, he and his brothers went over to the Offie house to watch home movies of Charlie Chaplin and Felix the Cat.

This made it harder when the time came to force Offie out. "The story I heard was that he made a pass at an Air Force colonel, who filed a report," Mrs. Fritchey maintains.[24] The fact was, Carmel's perch at Wisner's elbow seems first to have wobbled disastrously with very little warning on April 25, 1950. Challenged on the floor of the Senate by the head of the Senate Foreign Relations Subcommittee, Millard Tydings, to substantiate his charges of "subversive activities by certain Federal Government employees," Senator Joseph R. McCarthy recurred angrily to a State Department veteran who "has now been assigned to the Central Intelligence Agency." McCarthy's prey, "who was a homosexual . . . spent his time hanging around the men's room in Lafayette Park."[25]

Such publicity was intolerable. That same session, McCarthy sidekick Sen. Kenneth Wherry announced that he was "privileged to say—and I am now going to say it—that within the last thirty minutes I have been informed by the head of a Government agency that the man against whom the Senator from Wisconsin (McCarthy) made a charge on the Senate floor this afternoon, has finally resigned. . . ."[26]

Others greased the slide. It made such intimates of the Wisners as the courtly Virginian Joe Bryan uneasy to watch an oily, self-aggrandizing promoter like Offie fast-talking the overworked Frank Wisner. Bryan regretted, as Ulmer would phrase it, the extent to which Offie chivied Frank into being "more and more elastic in his ethics as concerned the Eastern European troops,"[27] the unmistakable yearly slippage as assorted Nazi "experts" bobbed up in Washington under the Paperclip exclusion or hundred-man exemption. Bryan wasn't particularly surprised when Averell Harriman brought up the time he returned to his office unexpectedly one night and startled Carmel Offie rummaging among his records.[28]

A raw file was compiling fast at FBI headquarters, where the homophobic J. Edgar Hoover was personally incensed that a "degenerate" of Offie's ilk remained a government employee. An extended memorandum of March 4, 1950, had advised the Bureau Director of "an anonymous letter making certain allegations against Charles W. Thayer of the State Department, which letter indicates that one Carmel Offie, if contacted, could furnish further derogatory information concerning Thayer."[29]

By July of 1950 Hoover had authorized an intermittent—and at times intensive—surveillance which would drag out for decades. Its rubric was "Espionage." Teams of special agents shadowed Carmel Offie through well-established gay haunts like Mickey's Grill and David's Bar; they submitted a file entry each time some youngster in uniform rebuffed Offie; they logged strangers entering and leaving Offie's residence at 3105 Woodley Road, N.W.; they trailed an unidentified visitor who left carrying a manila envelope which "appeared to contain three cylindrical objects about the size of Ediphone records."[30]

Hoover's people were on hand as Offie took up office space off Dupont Circle (1346 Connecticut Avenue, N.W.) and arranged for a consultancy slot with the law firm of Cummings, Stanley, Truitt and Cross. Cummings was Homer Cummings, FDR's first Attorney General, while Max Truitt was a son-in-law of Alben Barkley. Douglas MacArthur II, another son-in-law of the Vice President's and installed in the upper reaches at State after the Eisenhower restructuring, had been a proponent of Carmel's since their Paris years together.

Offie's employer of record after he was forced out at OPC was the

American Federation of Labor. Jay Lovestone in America—and Irving Brown in Europe—remained invaluable distributors of OPC funds. Recordkeeping was perfunctory. As director of the International Labor Information Service, Offie remained in position to nursemaid Wisner's Eastern European interests, especially the labor battalions. By 1951 watchdogs for the Bureau were beginning to conclude that "Offie may be employed in a covert capacity or on a special project by the Army." Hoover personally never bought the political conversion of ex-Communist Lovestone; he endorsed the recommendation of his case officer S. J. Tracy that the Bureau pursue an "independent investigation with a view to eliminating him [Offie] from his present employment in the A.F.of L."[31]

"I believe it will be worthwhile to render every possible assistance in this situation for the reason that in his present position Offie is dangerous to the security of the country," the Director wrote. A week later, informed by Interior's legal experts that false statements on an application were an insufficient basis for court action, Hoover scrawled on the bottom of the Assistant Attorney General's conclusions: "Can we establish the at least covert government employment? It is outrageous for such a character to escape prosecution on such a technicality."[32]

Everything fell in place, to Hoover's matchless eye, but there was nothing could be done. "The usual 'brush-off' all around," J. Edgar wrote after one summation.[33] To start with, where was this pint-sized Iago with a mid-level government salary getting all the money he continued to scatter around Washington? He'd bought the Woodley Road house for $34,000 a few months after returning to the United States, and from then on Offie had continued to pick up one expensive property after another in Northwest D.C., along with a sizable farm near Markham, Virginia. Shortly after Dwight Eisenhower became President, Beedle Smith attempted to placate Hoover with the explanation that the $10,000 of seed money with which Offie had begun his real estate maneuverings in the United States came from a payoff he'd collected for taking the fall in Paris when several of the senior people had almost gotten caught abusing their pouch access. ". . . Back in the early days," Hoover advised his top staff, "when the intrigue was going on with Ambassadors Joseph Grew, Bullitt, 'and another very close gentleman whose former wife is a Newmont Mining Company lady' (General Lucius Clay is on the Board of Directors), something came up within the Department itself about the unauthorized use of pouch privileges. . . . Carmel Offie took all the blame for it. As a result, he was either given or allowed to buy at a very favorable option price some stock in the Newmont holdings in North Africa, which gave a fabulous payoff, which money Offie shrewdly invested in Georgetown real estate so that now he is semi-independent."[34]

Another explanation going around built on the rumor that at one stage William Bullitt presented Carmel with $30,000. But years before that Offie's scrounging and percentage playing had begun to tip the balances. He had a house in Georgetown as early as 1942, where Bullitt—unsure of his own future, and suffering from the erosion of trust capital—put up when convenient. "Bill said that Offie had sponged off him for many years," Henry Wallace wrote in his diary, "and now he was sponging off Offie."[35]

Eisenhower was still President-elect when another shadow darkened Carmel's thickening dossier. A few months earlier, barnstorming Italy with Irving Brown, Offie had several times switched into his big-dealer mode to impress local industrialists. He bruited about the totals the United States intended to spend in each allotted category pursuant to the Off Shore Procurement Program, a Buy-European initiative under the direction of its Senior Representative in Europe, the multipurpose William Draper.[36]

This information was precious to interested businessmen, something worth paying for. The details were classified, supposedly unavailable to Offie, and although he ran through his entire repertoire of long, wet, recriminatory glances and outraged assertions that he personally "acted as a sort of liaison man between AF of L and MSA, headed by Averell Harriman," Defense Secretary Robert Lovett was steamed. It appeared that Offie was in cahoots with Lovett's special assistant, A. E. Van Cleve, whom Defense Department investigators were after for "alleged influence deals with a Belgian munitions combine" in return for undisclosed payoffs.[37]

Even Eisenhower saw evidence that Offie was a dubious piece of work. He was flagrantly corrupt; the conviction was spreading that Hoover might well be right about this mid-level drifter: Offie was in all probability a serious security risk. "He understood something about the Communist world, how they operate. I don't know whether Carmel Offie was a double agent or whether he was not," Paul Nitze breaks out apropos of something else. "He didn't scare anybody because everybody knew he was a pansy."[38]

Time was past overdue to separate Offie permanently from sensitive government involvement. Some deal would have to be struck. Offie knew too much, his associations ran high as well as deep. "Maybe Carmel Offie had a hand in this somewhere," Angleton himself would murmer occasionally when something profound and meticulously planned out there inexplicably fell apart.[39]

Among John Foster Dulles's telephone notes a tantalizing fragment dated March 24, 1954, deals with the last-minute tradeoffs it took to secure the nomination of Chip Bohlen as U.S. ambassador to the Soviet Union. "Sen. Taft brought up the report about the first Moscow mission, Offie's confession, etc. and said that for Bohlen's own future this ought to be cleared up. The Secretary said that he would call the Attorney General, and unless he called Sen. Taft right back he should go ahead on this theory."[40]

So Offie was finished, severed, although he wasn't down. "Frank hated to let him go," Mrs. Fritchey remarks. Not very long before Carmel had given a luncheon party for Bullitt and Mrs. Chennault, and Wisner had promised to attend. "We waited for Frank," Polly says, "but he never made it, he was very absent-minded sometimes. Offie was furious beyond all reason. When Offie was finally out he turned on Frank so badly. He was really awful to him." One day without a word Offie appeared at the Wisner residence, confronted the cook he had procured for Frank and Polly, and ordered him to resign, that moment. "I walked into the kitchen and the cook was gone." Polly smiles, if bleakly. "I must say, I was as cross as two sticks at the time."[41]

Thwarted, Hoover dogged Offie's footsteps. Bureau files contain a clip dealing with the return of Douglas MacArthur II from a Paris posting: he and his wife spent several nights in Washington as guests of Offie, who entertained them in Bill Bullitt's big house on Kalorama Road.[42] Via a Congressional Committee, Hoover made sure Offie did not get another government job to which he aspired. Glancing over Offie's paperwork, Hoover scribbled, "It seems to be an inherent part of a pervert's malaise to be also a pathological liar." Over the succeeding years Hoover's people staked out Offie in hopes of catching him involved in malfeasances from gun running to operating a white slavery ring at his Markham farm. One special agent complained that those dark Bureau sedans were hard to conceal at the crossroads of open country lanes.[43] As late as 1969 Bureau investigators were able to nose up leads linking Offie to the bribery-conspiracy and election fraud charges and misallocation of Office of Economic Opportunity funds which ruined Sen. Daniel Brewster of Maryland, a cohort of Offie's since they conspired to finish Sumner Welles.[44] Several reckless driving convictions caught Hoover's attention, and it was duly noted that Offie didn't scruple to invite skilled workmen from the AF of L unions out for the weekend in return for help with his remodeling projects.

But there was never quite enough to justify major prosecution, especially keeping in mind the shitstorm Carmel was guaranteed to mount. Within the Agency itself, James Angleton observed shortly before he died, nobody had even recommended vetting Offie. "I don't know whether anybody ever questioned his loyalty. He was known to be a very tough infighter. Being a bachelor, he was all over the place, so to speak. He liked intrigue. With that vast ring of friends, sources and so on, I don't think anything could have happened in Georgetown or any other place that wouldn't have come to his attention. After all, he'd been in the Department, he knew some very prominent people, ambassadors and so on."[45] Besides, Angleton and Lovestone were long since joined at the hip.

Offie had moved on from public servant to principal in a couple of New-York import-export operations he founded, the American Arka Corporation and Global Enterprises, Incorporated.[46] Robert Murphy had finally left the State Department in 1959 to serve with Corning Glass, and he made office space for Offie as an "industrial consultant."

His wiry surviving hair protected by a raked businessman's fedora, Carmel Offie looked more every year like a semiretired Cuban ponce. He collected good porcelain.[47] Wary ex-colleagues who ran into him once in a while at State Department weddings and funerals confronted with a start that lip-heavy grin, more gums than teeth, the unique composite of the unscrupulous, the dazzling, the truckling, and the unabashedly sentimental which fueled Carmel's rise. At some diplomatic event his companions might range from Mrs. George Meany to Margaret Biddle. Hector Prudhomme remembers weekending with his family on Offie's farm when unexpectedly a limousine swung into the courtyard. It contained their host, a deteriorated William Bullitt, and Alice Roosevelt Longworth. Observing that the farmhouse itself was occupied, the three aloof dignitaries never left the automobile, picknicking behind the chauffeur before driving off.[48]

Most of Offie's business seemed to be concentrated in France, Germany, and Italy. In 1963, soon after the Agency's expensive and fitful effort to destabilize Cuba through sabotage and assassination fell apart, Richard Helms parked William Harvey as station chief in Rome to keep him as far away as possible from a smouldering Robert Kennedy. According to Harvey's deputy, Mark Wyatt, Carmel Offie's regular visits to Rome provided a severe test for Harvey's faltering control of himself. Harvey had been slipped the complete, clear-text file on Offie by friends in the FBI, and he was completely convinced by what he saw that Offie had functioned all along as a Soviet plant inside the Agency who more than anybody else had managed to disbalance and undermine any prospects for recovering Eastern Europe. By this late date Bill Harvey was pounding back the martinis throughout his three-hour lunches more relentlessly than ever; his characteristic muzzy truculence and gruff, froggy delivery were very poorly suited on the brightest of afternoons for dealing with the subtle anteroom politics of the Italian services.

Harvey went onto red alert whenever Offie hit town. Carmel made it a practice to put up at the U.S. Embassy, the Villa Taverna, where the ambassador and his wife, Mr. and Mrs. G. Frederick Reinhardt (another of those well-placed old Moscow hands Offie collected), were delighted to entertain their outrageous but compelling colleague. Before long reports were coming across Harvey's desk of solitary evening forays by Offie, whole nights of chicken-hawking behind the Vatican in recognizable embassy cars. Harvey's obscene roars were audible a couple of offices down the hall.[49]

Almost a decade afterward Carmel Offie was pressing still, still giving off great wet sparks and striving toward some obscure but powerful fulfillment when fate cut him off. In Europe to line up a consulting contract with Hughes Aircraft, one Sunday in 1972 his British European Airways jet crashed on takeoff at Heathrow, killing thirty-four Americans aboard. Douglas MacArthur II stood waiting, increasingly worried, for hours at the Brussels airport.[50]

Like so many others, Offie's obituary writer remained in something of a quandary over how to characterize his complex, evasive subject. He was "a dapper diplomat with a tiny black moustache," the writer ventured finally, "with a reputation for efficient operation behind the scenes. . . ."[51]

❑

Offie's world, perhaps appropriately, ended with a bang. Bullitt's petered out. Driven forth by Roosevelt after the contretemps over Welles, Bullitt fiddled and steamed in his largely honorific post at the Navy Department until his outspoken advocacy of Admiral King's "Japan first" ideas cooked him with Marshall. He leaked military secrets, most conspicuously to Offie. In July of 1953 he abruptly announced his candidacy for mayor of Philadelphia, where he was bombarded with charges ranging from Communist sympathies to elitism along with an ungovernable plutocratic outlook. He listed as his address in town the snobbish Rittenhouse Club. Bullitt lost by 64,000 votes.[52]

At this point William Bullitt attempted to join the American military, failed, and wangled a post as a field-grade officer on the staff of the high-handed General Jean de Lattre de Tassigny with de Gaulle's forces. Early in 1945 a vehicle accident during the battle for Alsace left Bullitt with a splintered vertebra. It, along with a form of chronic lymphatic leukemia, kept Bullitt in increasing misery for the next twenty years, and between "the sensation of having the bottom of my spine become a bowl of pebbles" and a pattern of enlarged lymph nodes and spleen and repeated skin cancers, a lot of what energy survived in Bullitt was lost in propping up his flagging health.

He still had vitality enough to remain a hot-spot of political controversy. A trip to Asia in July 1947 left him a tremendous Chiang supporter. A *Washington Post* exchange with Walter Lippmann—something of an intimate of Bullitt's when the two agreed—points up the ambassador's terminal bitterness and ferocity. Lippmann's published opinion that right-wing bids to the government to allocate $450 million a year for three years and send in U.S. advisers to backstop the Kuomintang could only bring on protracted "diplomatic boondoggling" outraged Bullitt. He wrote the *Post* disparaging the series of articles "someone using the same name, Walter Lippmann, published in your paper. . . . If this Mr. Walter Lippmann really exists, and is not a chameleon pantologist, he should be more careful—otherwise he will cease to be even the matrons' mentor."[53]

By then a mainstay of the China lobby, Bullitt became a Republican and rose to suggestions that he might well become the Undersecretary of State in the Dewey administration. He played a significant role in brokering Bao Dai into power in Saigon in 1949, and so helped deepen U.S. involvement in the region.

After years of tortured and inconclusive exchanges with Sigmund Freud's heirs, Bullitt brought out the book-length case study he and Freud had mushed together of Woodrow Wilson. The book's psychoanalytical theses—that Wilson's struggle to idolize the overbearing father he secretly hated ultimately feminized his personality, and kept him seeking an "affectionate relationship with a younger and physically smaller man"—offended his peers even in December 1966. Rebutting this approach in *Look* (which had published excerpts), Allen Dulles objected to the "deep note of bitterness" the manuscript betrayed, the portrayal of Wilson as "an ugly, unhealthy, 'intense'

Presbyterian, with a neurotic constitution and little interest in the amenities of life." Bill Bullitt was fickle, Dulles charged, while Wilson was "inspiring."

Bullitt himself was dying. He succumbed in February 1967. Attending by his bedside in the American Hospital in Neuilly were his daughter Anne, his brother, his close cousin Dr. Orville Horwitz, and, inevitably, Carmel Offie.

❑

Frank Wisner's abrupt suicide caught Allen at about the midpoint of his enforced retirement. With both at leisure there had been time for extended lunches, for afternoons of bridge. Resorting to a pun, in one note Wisner chided Dulles about picking up so quickly the niceties of the "Burlinggame," a variety their mutual friend Ella seems to have taught them both.[54] But Allen was not what he had been, and after one session Polly discovered Frank perhaps a bit dejected that Allen seemed to be losing his subtlety and sharpness.

After JFK was shot Lyndon Johnson tapped Dulles to serve on the Warren Commission and attempt to sort out the circumstances of the assassination. As historians would comment, most noteworthy of all was the way Allen blanked out whenever the discussion touched Castro. Some hint just then of the Agency's program to liquidate the Cuban might well have forced the expansion of the inquiry, encouraged doubts that Oswald—and Oswald alone—had perpetrated this abomination. All of the bureaucracies involved were guilty of administrative slovenliness at a minimum, and pushed the panel members hard to certify the lone killer thesis. When the English don H. R. Trevor-Roper presumed in the London *Times* to point up the sluggishness and illogic behind the Warren Commission Report, Wisner took it on himself to try and whip up a campaign to refute the purported meretriciousness of the piece by Trevor-Roper.[55]

Allen shrugged it off. More markedly each season he found himself lapsing into the lineaments of the habituated Washington clubman, content to fill his days with fussing over editorial chores and correspondence required by the final two books he put his name to—*The Craft of Intelligence* and *The Secret Surrender*—reminiscing, arranging reunions, and holding court whenever somebody from the Great Game stopped by to buck him up. At home a bent figure in unpressed tweeds who lived in bedroom slippers to ease his gout attacks, he continued to maintain his accustomed sumptuary standards—his wines in particular were always the choicest obtainable, while his Guatemalan cook, Natalia Birdsong, was so well regarded around the District that Allen had to stay alert that nobody stole her. Between relaxing summer visits to Henderson Harbor and long, luxurious layovers during the raw months with wealthy friends like the Charles Wrightsmans in Palm Beach, Allen presented himself as ever when the company mattered—spruce, tanned, vigorous.[56]

But he was slipping. "People think I'm very rich," he confided to a friend. "But I'm not." Individuals close to the household will divulge that he and Clover "spent money very foolishly, carelessly. They each had private secretaries full time, to keep their checkbooks and deal with minor things. There were a number of maids." The handsome retirement house off Q Street with its elaborate square of flanking gardens was rented at great expense. Distinguished still but starting to falter a bit with age, Clover continued to go through capital with almost a self-destructive indifference. "They never saved anything," one confidant of Allen's saw. "It worried him. His children were very expensive, and that worried him."

Those last years Clover struggled against the inroads of Parkinson's disease. If anything, this heightened the otherworldly cast of her personality, her instinct to escape the pedestrian—if not indeed sordid—realm where Allen remained involved and concern herself with the I Ching and Saint Teresa of Avila. Much of the income which supported their fashionable tastes came out of Clover's trusts, built up several generations earlier out of iron mill proceeds and bank holdings in Baltimore. "She didn't let money trouble her," Garner Ranney noticed. Ranney was a highly refined State Department retiree who came down several days a week to help Allen out with sorting his papers and getting his library together. Garner found himself admiring Clover's feeling for detail, the "air of charming cosiness" she bestowed in passing. Agency types regarded Clover as a puzzle—"she was the sort—she was interested mainly in impractical things," one points out. "Prison reform, things like that."

"She had periods of nervous exhaustion from living with Allen," Ranney comments. "But you could see she was doing what she could. Those last years they obviously were very devoted to each other. I always thought Clover was very discreet. I know she did find it difficult to do things like play the hostess at dinner parties where most of the guests—whom she already knew—were there under assumed names. It took a great deal of concentration on her part to keep the pseudonyms straight."

Fortified by el-dopa, she "rose above her Parkinson's," Ranney recollects. "I remember one day she had a luncheon party at the F-Street Club for the Auchinclosses, and when she and I went into the hallway there she suddenly had to catch hold of the newel post. She put her head down and tried to stand there, for fear of fainting away. But in a moment she recollected herself, and walked into the sitting room, and you wouldn't have thought anything was wrong."[57]

Her husband as well had started to show his years. His hands were becoming progressively more misshapen from arthritis. He underwent the first of a series of mild strokes in a taxicab on his way home from an Agency reunion dinner in a club off Lafayette Square. Until he felt better this was a problem for the household, since nobody was trusted with power of attorney. He remained stimulating company, a practiced host, and an extraordinary raconteur, but year by year he began to lose a lot of the assurance and bluffness which caused people to liken Allen to some ruddy, retired senior administrator out of the pages of Kipling, home from the Empire but alert at any moment to defend its prerogatives. When Harry Truman deplored in the press the nasty turn the CIA had taken, Allen wrote him directly, defensive yet unmistakably crestfallen. He became an elder in the Presbyterian church, and began to characterize public events according to whether Foster would have approved or might not have cared for something.

The strokes kept coming, and regretfully he gave up the tennis and swimming he'd depended on to stay in shape. He lost peripheral vision. There was a kidney stone. Allen retained Howard Roman to draft the books he kept puttering with, so Howard was in and out all through the rest of Allen's life. "You'd spend the day with Allen," Howard says, "and it was a slow, laborious process. He'd lost a great deal of his ability to concentrate, he couldn't remember things. He'd mislay things, and then he'd keep attempting to find them long after somebody else would have given up."[58]

On Christmas morning of 1969 a call from Jim Angleton alerted Howard to a crisis at the Dulles's. Allen himself had never made it down to mingle with the family and the handful of close friends who traditionally stopped by on Christmas eve. When Clover and the girls finally got a moment they found that one of his "sinking spells," aggravated by grippe, had taken an irreversible turn. The crumpled old gallant was stretched out and incoherent in one of the bedrooms upstairs, hair matted with perspiration against his waxen temples and the avuncular fell of his moustaches glistening and wet.

Flu was becoming pneumonia. Sometime in the early morning, long after a team of stretcher-bearers from the Georgetown

University Hospital had come for Allen, Clover Dulles had straggled home after registering her husband and let herself back into the deserted premises at 2723 Q Street and repaired to her bedroom suite and started to draw for herself a deep, hot bath. Befuddled with fatigue and worry, she left the taps open and trailed out confusedly to bed. When she woke up a wide expanse of the family quarters of the mansion was flooded, and all through the elegant public areas below, in room beyond room, several tons of ceiling plaster were darkening and saturated. In several places plaster was starting to bulge and drip.

"I was the only person who had access to the place, and knew the servants, and I guess I was sort of the clean-up man in a lot of ways besides literary ones," Roman says, and so when Clover reached Angleton, Jim contacted Howard. Insurance adjusters were prowling when Roman arrived. Whatever the repairs cost, whoever paid for them, Clover kept emphasizing, "Under no circumstances must you say anything about this to my husband."[59]

Dulles never found out. He died on December 30; his death at seventy-five marked indelibly the passing from the center of influence in Washington of the generation which recognized its mission at Versailles and felt its way into power once Franklin Roosevelt faltered. By 1969 Allen's star was largely obscured. President Nixon had meetings to attend and dispatched Spiro Agnew to represent the executive branch at the funeral along with "a large wreath of red and white carnations."[60] "It was a tremendous funeral," Ranney found, "with the streets closed off to traffic. Tout le monde was there, the church was packed to the doors. I will always remember Clover Dulles's face as she came down the aisle afterward. She looked absolutely . . . frozen, as if she'd been turned to stone. It was like looking at Niobe or something. . . . It was a wonderful effect.

"The Agency people took over the house, and put in all the telephone lines. The house was *awash* with these workmen and technicians and people from the Agency taking messages. Flowers from attic to cellar, orchids by the dozen. I think the hurly-burly and *world*liness of it all was very hard on her at that time."[61]

Redoing those Q-Street ceilings was worse even than Clover feared. As for American intelligence? Many revere Allen's legacy—his raffish charm, the civility and devotion on which his co-workers could depend. Yet they too almost without exception will concede that between Dulles's taste for action and his propensity to indulge his favorites he . . . he warped the mechanisms, and often enough irreversibly. Under Wisner and Dulles the CIA overflowed worse than Clover's bathtub. It leaked through between the laws, and helped rot out many societies it touched. Its example provided justification to William Casey and Ollie North; it exchanged the ripoff of the moment for confidence in America's political decency.

Taking over Beedle Smith's integrated, top-down intelligence bureaucracy, Allen Dulles and Frank Wisner couldn't really help imbuing their crusade with Wall Street's ethos. A fever for longshot deals and overnight profit-taking overstimulated the swelling secret enterprise, an ominous new language quickly evolved in which "assets" meant people, dupes, and "executive action" meant murder. Cliques thwarted sensible oversight. To lock in their coup of the week they catered to just about any "local champion, willy-nilly," as Thomas Powers notes. "Thus a policy carelessly developed and casually adopted in Washington will be implemented on the local scene by rootless, alien, and presumably unknown CIA officers who are free to walk away from the wreckage."[62] Too often secrecy guaranteed impunity, and impunity, irresponsibility.

After everything, nevertheless—they were what we had. The Bear seems moth-eaten these days, the satellites are available for picking up the tab. Socialism itself sells poorly. It's easy to forget how, seventy years earlier, this century's monstering history opened abruptly along a fault line which transected Versailles, and left an entire generation gasping above the abyss. If Allen seemed unscrupulous finally, or Wisner increasingly befuddled with rage—well, they knew what terrified them. Something *was* out there.

ACKNOWLEDGMENTS

Ten years of work on this project have left me in the debt of a wide array of individuals and institutions. I have to start with the many intelligence professionals generous enough to share their reminiscences. Of these the proponderance are identified through source notes, normally in dated interviews. Others, although consenting to help, requested anonymity; their contributions I've buried in the text.

Several contributors deserve particular appreciation. Wendy Hazard, the daughter of Frank Wisner, turned over a mass of documents bearing on her father's performance in Rumania squeezed out of the Washington apparat. I benefited several times from talks with the iconoclastic writer and lawyer John Loftus, who provided me a number of extremely useful documents from his own extraordinary gleanings. At various turns Eleanor Dulles, Frank Lindsay, Chris Simpson, and Arthur Schlesinger, Jr. came through with official paper of substantial value. The CIA veterans who oversee the use of the Allen Dulles papers at Princeton remained stubborn about their mandate, but reasonable in the end. Richard Harris Smith and Peter Grose were very kind about letting me see and excerpt segments from their research into the life of Allen Dulles. I appreciate the cooperation of Nancy Lisagore and Frank Lipsius, Joe Goulden's leads, and the advice and archival access provided by Charles Higham.

Much time and energy went into the perusal of library collections.

Most vital in general has certainly been the wealth of paperwork in the National Archives. Essential to this projection have been the wonderful OSS and German holdings of the Military History Section, presided over by the ineffable John Taylor, and the State Department archives in Suitland, Maryland, where John Baker has assisted me greatly in narrowing the field. I am in addition most indebted to the talented staff people of Princeton (Mudd Library, pace Ben Primer) and Yale (Sterling Library), Harvard (Widener), the law library of Harvard University, the Franklin D. Roosevelt Library at Hyde Park, New York, the New York Public Library, the Virginia Historical Society in Richmond, the George C. Marshall Library in Lexington, Virginia, the Doheny Library at the University of Southern California, the Libraries of the University of New Hampshire (Durham) and the Franklin Pierce Law Library (Concord, N.H.), and of course the Library of Congress. Beyond that, year in and year out, the patient and skillful personnel at Dartmouth (Baker Library) and especially at the State Library of New Hampshire in Concord have seen this endless project through.

Here, perhaps more than with anything I've ever done, the highs were very high but the setbacks at times seemed irreversible. Friends, many of them writers, pitched in to read manuscript and pass along suggestions. My appreciations in particular here to Charles Gaines, the late Tom Gerber, Robie Macauley, Joe McGinniss, Thomas Powers, Walter Robinson, Arthur Schlesinger, Jr., Daniel Schorr, and the late, irreplaceable Peter Sylvester. Many years of membership in the New England Chapter of the Association of Former Intelligence Officers provided durable friendships and surprising insights, for which I am particularly grateful to Mike Speers.

Any work which draws its material from as many historical levels as this does necessarily requires a major commitment of the imagination to compose, and an almost equal leap to see through the publication process. A lot of the thrust behind the appearance of this book came from my agent, David Black, whose associates Janice Gordon and Lev Fruchter remained indispensable. At Scribner's the spark plug throughout has been my unfailingly supportive editor, Ned Chase, whose fascination with the period obviously at least equals my own. I remain appreciative every day of the skillful detailing provided by Hamilton Cain and the meticulous legal vetting by James Rittinger of Satterlee, Stephens, Burke, and Burke. Patricia McEldon has directed many months of copyreading with amazing flexibility and patience, while Sarah Van Tuyl coordinated early publicity. Throughout, the benign overview of Barbara Grossman has unmistakably proved beneficial.

Sandy Burrows, Susan Latham, and Richard Whitman helped out with typing and research chores. Inevitably, the preponderance of the heavy clerical lifting fell to my assistant, Janet Byfield, and my wife, Ellen. Both hung on patiently through publishing weather from every direction; for all their steadfastness, special thanks.

Notes

A Note on Sources

Establishing the scholarly sources of the far-flung array of facts and opinions on which this sort of book is based is not an uncomplicated affair. Over most of a decade I've talked to a great many participants in our intelligence history—almost everybody I approached, well over a hundred—and managed almost always to tape their comments and reminiscences. Many have spoken freely, without reservation; others had no problem with helping out but specified that at least a part of their observations remain uncited, or at least unattributed; another group—relatively few, surprisingly—demanded that they be neither quoted nor even mentioned. In each case, I have tried to comply.

Accordingly, here and there throughout this manuscript, statements and/or anecdotes pop up which remain unattributed in the note system. In such situations I've cross-checked until I was satisfied with accuracy and relevance, then put it in. Whenever something seemed aribtrary to me, or appeared to involve the revelation of information potentially damaging to American interests or dangerous or compromising to the individuals involved—the names of agents, personal details which blacken a reputation or a memory—I've left it locked up in notes and tapes, unavailable for the moment. This book is history, but it is by no means *ancient* history.

Apart from interviews and secondary sources, this work draws comprehensively on a far-flung documentary base. I've attempted wherever possible to conform to standard academic practice and identify the library in which I discovered important material, the collection which contained it, such specifics as dates and author and recipient wherever relevant, down to the box, etc., wherever these are available. A number of the people I've stayed in touch with, many themselves writers, were themselves digging into a related body of history, and have been kind enough to make available useful documents. On occasion the archival details of this paperwork have not come through, although the authenticity of the material is beyond question and in most situations the origin of the source can readily be reconstructed.

Attribution is sometimes harder when dealing with the thousands of pages of raw information I've received by way of the Freedom of Information Act from the U.S. Government departments and agencies—the FBI and the CIA and State Department principally, although the General Accounting Office and a variety of other subdivisions of the government have also contributed. This sort of productive if unpredictable rough catch comes through after a generalized ransacking of long-neglected files (attended all too often by the wholesale sanitizing of purportedly sensitive material with some kind of government-issue broad-tipped felt marker flowing oceans of India ink). The semicomprehensible result gets reproduced—sometimes years too late—and shipped to the despairing applicant. In many cases the category, repository, and indeed the original bureaucratic intention which justified the collection of much I have now acquired can only be adduced.

CHAPTER ONE

1. William Donovan personal files, private memoir of 1947 conversation with Allen Dulles, Carlisle Barracks Archive, Carlisle, Pennsylvania, Switzerland section, Folder 82, Box 120B. Successive running quotes from same source.

2. Leonard Mosley, *Dulles,* p. 131.

3. Allen Dulles papers, Mudd Library, Princeton University, self-edited article on exploits in Switzerland, accompanies Medal of Merit Citation, 1946, Box 19.

4. John Maynard Keynes, *The Economic Consequences of the Peace*, p. 42.

5. Stephen Bonsal, *Unfinished Business*, p. 47.

6. This material largely from Leonard Mosley's family biography, *Dulles*, pp. 35–38 et al. Mosley is not always a reliable source, but this material squares with primary documents.

7. Treatment of House from many sources, perhaps the most useful having been Robert Ferrell's solid *Woodrow Wilson and World War I.*

8. Rhodri Jeffreys-Jones, *American Espionage*, p. 44.

9. William Corson, *The Armies of Ignorance*, p. 57 et al.

10. Lawrence Gelfand, *The Inquiry*, p. 41.

11. Joseph Grew, *Turbulent Era*, vol. I, p. 379.

12. Charles Mee, *The End of Order*, p. 78.

13. Gelfand, op. cit., p. 29.

14. *Current Biography*, 1940. Published annually by H. W. Wilson, N.Y. Citations are alphabetized.

15. Charles Seymour, *Letters from the Paris Peace Conference*, pp. 61, 62, 75.

16. Jeffreys-Jones, op. cit.

17. Drawn from Seymour, op. cit., pp. 106, 129.

18. Exchange February 3, 12, 1919, Allen Dulles to Walter Davis. Walter Davis Archive (Record Group 469), Yale University Library.

19. Interview with Eleanor Dulles, June 9, 1988.

20. Mosley, op. cit., p. 13.

21. Ibid, p. 39.

22. Gelfand, op. cit., p. 107.

23. Jeffreys-Jones, op. cit., pp. 74, 94, 95.

24. M. P. Edwards and Kenneth Dunne, *A Study of a Master Spy*, pp. 9, 10.

25. Jeffreys-Jones, op. cit., p. 82.

26. Edwards and Dunne, op. cit., p. 14.

27. So far the best biography of John Foster Dulles is Ronald Preussen's *John Foster Dulles—The Road to Power*, from which much detail has been extracted. An acerbic—and useful—version is Townsend Hoopes's *The Devil and John Foster Dulles.*

28. Hoopes, op. cit., p. 26. Foster's wily moves soon caught the eye of founding partner William Nelson Cromwell, whose clients included J. P. Morgan and E. H. Harriman and who was himself acknowledged as the attorney who "taught the robber barons how to rob." Cromwell had retained John Foster to help expedite the formation of the New Panama Canal Company (Nancy Lisagor and Frank Lipsius, *A Law Unto Itself*, pp. 31, 34, 35, 61).

29. Preussen, op. cit., p. 27. Lisagor and Lipsius (op. cit., p. 66) note that Foster's original commission, as a captain, was with military intelligence, on assignment to the War Trade Board.

30. Hoopes, op. cit., pp. 29, 40.

31. Gelfand, op. cit., p. 177; Preussen, op. cit., p. 30.

32. John R. Beal, *John Foster Dulles*, p. 67.

33. Preussen, op. cit., p. 53.

34. Mee, op. cit., p. 193.

35. Mee, op. cit., p. 222.

36. Mosley, op. cit., p. 60.

37. W. B. Fowler, *British-American Relations 1917–1918*, p. 196.

38. Gelfand, op. cit., p. 173.

39. Bonsal, op. cit., p. 93.

40. Mee, op. cit., p. 194.

41. Grew, op. cit., pp. 375, 377.

42. Seymour, op. cit., p. 122.

43. Best overall treatment of Bullitt so far is Will Brownell and Richard Billings's *So Close to Greatness*. There is also excellent material in Orville Bullitt's well-edited collection of his brother's letters, *For the President*.

44. Fowler, op. cit., p. 183.

45. Orville Bullitt, op. cit., p. xi.

46. Mee, op. cit., pp. 15–18. Another helpful version appears in Justin Kaplan's fine biography of Lincoln Steffens.

47. Janet Flanner, profile of William Bullitt. *The New Yorker*, December 17, 1938.

48. Perhaps the fullest detail of this episode is available in Beatrice Farnsworth's *William C. Bullitt and the Soviet Union*.

CHAPTER TWO

Donovan's life has been quite fully documented in several full-scale biographies. The treatments by Corey Ford and Richard Dunlop stay close to Donovan's personal life, while Anthony Cave Brown's indispensable book, *The Last Hero*, moves out into detailed treatments of the major OSS operations.

1. Dunlop, op. cit., p. 125.

2. Brown, op. cit., p. 75.

3. Ford, op. cit., p. 16.

4. Dunlop, op. cit., p. 29.

5. Brown, op. cit., p. 29.

6. Dunlop, op. cit., p. 43.

7. Ibid., p. 80.

8. Ibid., pp. 80, 81.

9. Brown, op. cit., pp. 76, 77.

10. Ibid., p. 87.

11. Dunlop, op. cit., p. 153.

12. Brown, op. cit., p. 114.

13. Brownell and Billings, op. cit., p. 31.

14. Associate of Ernesta Bullitt.

15. Turns up in such exchanges as Bullitt to Colonel House, May 20, 1918, William Bullitt Collection, Microform # HM5, Yale University Library.

16. Brownell and Billings, op. cit., p. 105.

17. Ibid.

18. Bullitt to Walter Lippmann, January 21, 1920, William Bullitt Collection, Microform # HM5, Yale University Library.

19. *Current Biography*, 1940.

20. Brownell and Billings, op. cit., p. 267.

21. Orville Bullitt, op. cit., p. 402.

22. Ibid., p. 66.

23. Orville Bullitt, op. cit., p. 69.

24. Ibid., p. 116.
25. Ibid., p. 84.
26. Ted Morgan, *F.D.R.*, p. 679.
27. George Kennan, *Memoirs 1925–1950*, p. 61.
28. Brownell and Billings, op. cit., p. 175.
29. Frederick Propas, *Diplomatic History*, Summer 1984, vol. 7, no. 3, pp. 209 ff.
30. Kennan, op. cit., p. 59.
31. Daniel Yergin, *Shattered Peace*, pp. 21, 33.
32. Isaacson and Thomas, *The Wise Men*, p. 150.
33. Kennan, op. cit., p. 11.
34. Ibid., p. 119.
35. Isaacson and Thomas, op. cit., p. 149.
36. Ibid., p. 166.
37. Brownell and Billings, p. 185.
38. Ibid., p. 219. Colonel Philip R. Faymonville was already a controversial member of the Moscow delegation. War Department scuttlebutt would have it that Faymonville was a career-long Communist sympathizer whose services to the Kremlin went back to helping the Red Army crush Admiral Kolchak. This made it especially painful for the senior military when Faymonville caught Eleanor Roosevelt's eye. Despite reports that Faymonville was a close personal friend of Beria, Faymonville became the military attaché to the White House. According to such military intelligence experts as Colonel Robert Crowley, George Marshall was so incensed that he denied Faymonville cryptographic clearance (interview with Robert Crowley, June 6, 1989).
39. Kennan, op. cit., p. 80.
40. Isaacson and Thomas, op. cit., p. 163.
41. Bohlen, *Witness to History*, p. 73.
42. Ibid., p. 17.
43. Isaacson and Thomas, op. cit., p. 163.
44. Brownell and Billings, op. cit., p. 149.
45. Interview with Douglas MacArthur II, August 30, 1988; Selective Service documents, March 9, 1944 (G. Howland Shaw, F.O.I.A.).
46. Interview with Hector Prudhomme, December 6, 1986.
47. Orville Bullitt, op. cit., p. 99.
48. Ibid., p. 170.
49. Ibid., p. 135. Bullitt's tendency to turn his personal assistants into diversions went back some years. Lincoln Steffens, part of Bullitt's mission to Lenin in 1919, observes that the envoy "had brought along his secretary Lynch, apparently to play with. On trains and boats they skylarked, wrestling and tumbling like a couple of bear cubs all along the Arctic Circle" (*The Autobiography of Lincoln Steffens*, p. 791.) This relationship put off Loy Henderson, according to Robert Crowley, who appreciated Offie's thoroughness about "emptying the ashtrays and Hoovering up the flat" while regarding him as a "dubious security risk, though somewhat down the list as Henderson sized up the embassy" (Robert Crowley interview, June 6, 1989).
50. Bullitt to U.S. State Department, Offie efficiency report, May 11, 1935 (F.O.I.A.).
51. Orville Bullitt, op. cit., p. 182.

CHAPTER THREE

1. William Dodd, *Ambassador Dodd's, Diary*, p. 233.

2. Martha Dodd, *Through Embassy Eyes*, pp. 178, 179.

3. William Dodd, op. cit., p. 433. According to Anthony Sutton, the Schacht family in New York worked for Equitable Trust, a Morgan financial creature; "throughout his life Hjalmar retained these Wall Street connections" (Anthony Sutton, *Wall Street and the Rise of Hitler*, p. 17).

4. Ibid., p. 304.

5. Hoopes, op. cit., p. 47.

6. Preussen, op. cit., p. 60. Preussen's meticulously researched book is by far the most balanced treatment of Foster Dulles's career as an international lawyer. In Paris during the treaty negotiations Dulles resumed his association with Richard Merton, whose Metallgesellschaft combine would become an important constituent of I. G. Farben. Dulles's close association with the allies and constituents of the Farben cartel would last through the rest of his life. (Lisagor and Lipsius, op. cit., p. 81).

7. Ibid., pp. 62, 63.

8. Ibid., p. 75. Not coincidentally, between 1924 and 1931 Sullivan and Cromwell, largely under Foster Dulles's direction, handed $1.15 billion dollars in lending to Europe, the largest single component to Germany. Foster shrugged off efforts by such State Department administrators as Leland Harrison to oversee loans to armament producers like Krupp, still being watched—with reason—for violations of the Versailles requirements. When the Department persisted, Foster "wasted no time in neutralizing the Department" by recruiting into Sullivan and Cromwell official supervisors of the Dawes Plan mandated loans such as Robert E. Olds (Lisagor and Lipsius, op. cit., pp. 91, 92). Dulles himself bought none of these risky bonds (ibid., p. 95).

9. John F. Dulles, "Our Foreign Loan Policy." *Foreign Affairs*, October 1926.

10. *Prevent World War III*, March–April 1949.

11. *Current Biography*, 1942.

12. Ferdinand Eberstadt papers, Ferdinand Eberstadt to James Forrestal, November 24, 1927, Box 60, Mudd Library, Princeton University.

13. *Prevent World War III*, March–April 1949.

14. Ibid.

15 *J.F.D. Oral Histories*, John Foster Dulles to George C. Sharp (Mudd Library, Princeton University). Nancy Lisagor and Frank Lipsius have winkled out in fascinating detail the cross-association of Foster Dulles with the private investment bank of Monnet and George Murnane, in which Foster himself invested $25,000. The firm arranged for a major loan—$285 million dollars—to the conservative Bruening government. When Hitler moved in, Dulles and Murnane helped Bruening escape from Germany, while longstanding Dulles confederate Hjalmar Schacht made sure the Bruening interest payments continued coming through long after Hitler repudiated Germany's other foreign debts (op. cit., pp. 111–124).

16. Preussen, op. cit., p. 118.

17. From R. Harris Smith research papers, to be deposited at the Hoover Institution of Stanford University and intended for use in the upcoming biog-

raphy of Allen Welsh Dulles, *Gentleman Spy*, by Peter Grose and R. Harris Smith. This source will be cited in these notes as R. Harris Smith manuscript henceforth.

18. Propas, op. cit.

19. Nye, Vandenberg Hearings. U.S. Senate Hearings before Munitions Committee 73rd Congress, Part 9, December 4, 5, 1934, p. 2254.

20. Allen Dulles, "Diplomacy Not a Poor Man's Job." *Literary Digest*, October 16, 1926. It may not be entirely coincidental that during this period, in 1927, the State Department gave up its role, assumed during the Inquiry period, as coordinator of foreign intelligence and counterintelligence. Once this office, dubbed U-I, lapsed, coordination of intelligence under civilian auspices would await the Coordinator of Intelligence in 1941 (see *The CIA and American Democracy*, by Rhodri Jeffreys-Jones, p. 13, etc.). It then devolved upon such natural intelligence coordinators as Bill Bullitt and the information nets of international lawyers and bankers to fill the breach.

21. Interview with Walter Pforzheimer, May 11, 1982.

22. Mosley, op. cit., p. 74. Mosley's omnibus biography of the Dulles family has proved most useful in providing suggestive personal detail. Lisagor and Lipsius turned up a letter from Allen to Clover from Paris, in which Allen himself refers to an evening with " 'Gregorie', . . . an attractive (but not beautiful) Irish-French female whom I took to Scheherazade where we stayed until the early hours as usual—somewhat to the annoyance of her husband. . . ." (op. cit., p. 130).

23. Smith mss., op. cit. Lisagor and Lipsius discovered that Allen Dulles kept busy detailing the boilerplate on ninety-four foreign securities through 1931, and functioned as "his brother's eyes and ears around the world, a role that earned him the nickname 'the little minister' " (op. cit., pp. 129, 135).

24. *In Fact*, February 1, 8, 1943, and August 15, 1949.

25. Mosley, op. cit., pp. 77, 78.

26. John Foster Dulles papers, Allen Dulles to John Foster Dulles, May 13, 1932 Mudd Library, Princeton University.

27. John Foster Dulles papers, ibid., November 14, 1932.

28. John Foster Dulles papers, ibid., Allen Dulles to John Foster Dulles, May 18, 1932.

29. Smith mss., op. cit.

30. John Foster Dulles papers, op. cit., John Foster Dulles to Hjlmar Schacht, October 12, 1933. Box 12.

31. Allen W. Dulles, "The Protection of American Foreign Bondholders." *Foreign Affairs*, April 1932.

32. Mosley, op. cit., p. 92.

33. Preussen, op. cit., p. 131.

34. Anonymous family source.

35. Brown, op. cit., pp. 119–121.

36. Dunlop, op. cit., p. 172.

37. Ibid., p. 151.

38. Ibid., pp. 190–191. Joseph Persico notes in *Piercing the Reich* that "Donovan clients included Standard Oil of New Jersey, large New York banks, and leading international companies." However indirectly, this made Wild Bill the spokesman for the primary Farben affiliate in North America. Preponderant blocks of securities were exchanged between Standard and Far-

ben, while Standard's president served on the board of "American I.G." In turn Standard Oil retained two top Nazi industrialists, key members of the "Friendship Circle of Heinrich Himmler," as directors of its German subsidiary, Karl Lindemann and Emil Helffrich. Lindemann remained a close contact of the Dulles brothers (Charles Higham, *Trading with the Enemy*, p. 20, et al.; Josiah DuBois, *The Devil's Chemists*, p. 24).

39. Brown, *"C,"* pp. 123–124.
40. Brown, *The Last Hero*, pp. 128–129.
41. Dunlop, op. cit., p. 123.
42. Brown, op. cit., pp. 142–143.
43. Ibid., pp. 132–133.

CHAPTER FOUR

1. Orville Bullitt, op. cit., p. 123.
2. Ibid., p. 126.
3. Brownell and Billings, op. cit., p. 209.
4. Orville Bullitt, op. cit., p. 233.
5. Ibid., p. 237.
6. Brownell and Billings, op. cit., p. 191.
7. Janet Flanner, *The New Yorker,* December 17, 1938.
8. Robert Murphy, *A Diplomat Among Warriors*, p. 31.
9. Orville Bullitt, op. cit., p. 145.
10. Ibid., pp. 300–301.
11. Propas, op. cit.
12. Charles Bohlen, *Witness to History*, p. 43.
13. Interview with Douglas MacArthur II, August 30, 1988.
14. Interview with Jacob Beam, June 11, 1987.
15. *Current Biography*, 1940.
16. Murphy, op. cit., p. 35.
17. Orville Bullitt, op. cit., p. 404.
18. Ibid., pp. 171–172.
19. Brownell and Billings, op. cit., photo section.
20. Orville Bullitt, op. cit., p. 241.
21. Brownell and Billings, op. cit., p. 205.
22. Orville Bullitt, op. cit., p. 453.
23. Brownell and Billings, op. cit., p. 234.
24. Orville Bullitt, op. cit., p. 273.
25. Bohlen, op. cit., p. 83.
26. FBI office memorandum, July 22, 1953, A. H. Belmont to D. M. Ladd (F.O.I.A.), also William Bullitt to U.S. State Department (G. Howard Shaw, October 13, 1939, F.O.I.A.). This involvement of Offie with Joseph Kennedy's operation is particularly interesting when compared with the strange case of Tyler Kent. Kent, a well-educated, multilingual code clerk who served in Moscow during the Bullitt-Offie incumbency would reappear in London to transmit classified documents for Joseph P. Kennedy. Kent was apprehended after having stolen many classified messages, which he turned over to Anna Wycoff, the Duchess of Windsor's dressmaker and a fanatic White Russian émigré, who in turn sent them along to German intelligence.

Years afterward the SIS reportedly determined that Kent had been entrapped in Moscow and functioned as a Soviet agent (see Charles Higham, *The Duchess of Windsor*, and the Tyler Kent entry in G. J. A. O'Toole's *The Encyclopedia of American Intelligence and Espionage*.)

27. Brownell and Billings, op. cit., p. 204.

28. Interview with Douglas MacArthur II, August 30, 1988.

29. Orville Bullitt, op. cit., p. 219.

30. Carmel Offie to Missy LeHand, November 9, 1936, PPF4151, October 4, 1939, OF796A (of 800), FDR Library.

31. Brownell and Billings, op. cit., p. 211.

32. FDR to Carmel Offie, op. cit., November 9, 1936 (FDR Library).

33. Brownell and Billings, op. cit., p. 254.

34. *Diary of Harold Ickes*, vol. III, p. 344.

35. Carmel Offie obituary, *Washington Post*, June 20, 1972.

36. Orville Bullitt, op. cit., p. 466.

37. Brownell and Billings, op. cit., p. 262.

38. Interview with Douglas MacArthur II, op. cit.

39. Preussen, op. cit., p. 124.

40. Joseph Borkin, *The Crime and Punishment of I. G. Farben*, pp. 166–170.

41. Ibid., p. 43.

42. Ibid., p. 177.

43. Preussen, op. cit., pp. 127–130. Allied, whose board Foster Dulles challenged to force it into line with worldwide Farben policies, ultimately submitted to Dulles's guidance, retained Sullivan and Cromwell, and accepted George Murnane as a director (Lisagor and Lipsius, op. cit., pp. 124, 125). As attorney for the Robert Bosch Company, Foster continued to press Bosch patents which impeded American efforts to produce vital diesel-fuel injection motors for the military (ibid., pp. 124, 148).

44. Howard Ambruster, *Treason's Peace*, p. 84.

45. Charles Higham, *Trading with the Enemy*, p. 133.

46. Ibid, pp. 36, 39.

47. David C. Martin, *All Honorable Men*, p. 67.

48. Charles Higham, op. cit., pp. 138–141.

49. See John Foster Dulles, "Should Economic Sanctions Be Applied In International Disputes," *Annals of the American Academy*, July 1932.

50. John Foster Dulles papers, John Foster Dulles to William Castle, November 8, 1940, Box 19, Mudd Library, Princeton University.

51. John Foster Dulles papers, John Foster Dulles to Henry Leech, September 30, 1937, Box 16, Mudd Library, Princeton University.

52. John Foster Dulles, "The Road to Peace." *The Atlantic Monthly*, October 1935.

53. John Foster Dulles, *War, Peace, and Change*, p. 58.

54. Rhodri Jeffreys-Jones, *American Espionage*, pp. 57, 62.

55. OSS postwar interview with Albert, Foster Adams, R.G. 238, entry 52D. Albert and Westrick handled the legal end of a great many of the "reparations loans" through which Wall Street relieved the German economy of its Versailles-dictated burden. They were particularly active troubleshooting the J. Henry Schroder flotations. As he took on responsibility for ITT's enterprises throughout the Third Reich, Westrick seems to have performed

impressively. In *Wall Street and the Rise of Hitler*, Anthony Sutton recurs to a 1933 meeting between Hitler and ITT's Sosthenes Behn and Wall Street's indispensable Henry Mann, helping Behn out for the moment (p. 79). As late as May 1939, Westrick wrote Behn directly after accompanying ITT executive A. G. P. Sanders and a senior executive of the Siemans Company on a scouting trip to freshly prostrated Czechoslovakia. After reconnoitering Czech telegraphy and electrical installations, Westrick judged the plant "considerably better than the one in Vienna," and awaited further instructions from "dear Colonel Behn." Sanders would reappear as part of an Allied investigation team immediately after the war; he played an important role in reconstructing postwar Germany under its prewar industrial leadership (Sutton, pp. 66, etc.).

56. The author ran into versions of this story many times, with perhaps the most credible in Hoopes's *The Devil and John Foster Dulles*, p. 47. Perhaps it's worth noting that ITT properties, including the Folke-Wullff fighter-bomber factories, emerged unscathed from World War II (Sutton, p. 63). John Grombach points out that throughout 1939 and 1940 ITT had access to the diplomatic pouches of both German and English diplomatic services for "top secret business information" (Grombach, *The Great Liquidator*, p. 112). In *The Nazis Go Underground* (p. 118), Curt Reiss points out that German industrialists of the Nazi era paid far lower taxes than their Western counterparts, treatment also accorded the ITT affiliates and a big inducement to Behn and others to compound their investments in the Third Reich.

57. Mosley, op. cit., p. 89. Allen Dulles had been introduced to Hitler personally in 1933 by Fritz Thyssen, and although he referred privately to "those mad people in control of Germany," Allen continued to promote Nazi purposes on a daily basis. Sullivan and Cromwell led the effort to push through securities refunding efforts which would have tied the interest of major American investors to the solvency of the Nazi government. As late as 1938 and 1939 Allen was endeavoring to help the Germans buy out the American Potash and Chemical Corporation to reconsolidate their cartel (Lisagor and Lipsius, op. cit., pp. 137–139).

58. R. Harris Smith, op. cit.

59. Allen Dulles and Hamilton Fish Armstrong, "Legislating Peace." *Foreign Affairs*, October 8, 1938.

60. *The New York Times*, January 31, 1969.

61. R. Harris Smith, op. cit. State Department archives at Suitland, Maryland, R.G. 84, Safe Haven Name files, Economic Security Control Division, 1942–1949 Subject Files, activities of E. D. V. Wight, Jr., suggest the pattern of much of this, especially May and June 1945 and background materials. Anthony Sutton (op. cit., p. 154) points out that the director of J. Henry Schroder in New York, Victor Emanuel, was a prominent financier of the Nazi party and a member of the Himmler circle of friends.

62. Allen Dulles papers, Allen Dulles's client lists, Sullivan and Cromwell, Box 14, Mudd Library, Princeton University.

63. Kilgore Committee hearings (Kilgore Subcommittee on War Mobilization, U.S. Senate, June 1945); high points in *In Fact*, August 15, 1949, with citations from Hearings on Scientific and Technical Mobilization, Military Affairs Committee, U.S. Senate (cartel practices, pp. 2074, 2075), September 1944.

64. This complicated cross-ruffing of interests is developed quite fully by Charles Higham in *Trading with the Enemy*, p. 22 and afterward, and extended beyond that by James and Suzanne Pool, *Who Financed Hitler*, p. 311, etc.

65. R. Harris Smith, op. cit.

66. Ibid.

67. Ibid.

68. According to James and Suzanne Pool, who cite Putzi Hanfstaengl, Smith was already touting Hitler on as a U.S. assistant military attaché in Munich as early as November 1922 (Pool and Pool, op. cit., p. 47).

69. Ladislas Farago, *The Game of the Foxes*, p. 556.

70. Ibid., p. 509; Higham, op. cit., pp. 93–99. By then Foster Dulles was under direct attack even within his own law firm. Lisagor and Lipsius reprint as an appendix a memorandum from Foster's old friend and partner Eustace Seligman in which Seligman charges "your position now is that the Allies's position is in no respect morally superior to Germany's, and in fact you even go further and apparently take the view that Germany's position is morally superior to that of the Allies." The memo was dated October 25, 1939, while the Wehrmacht was in the process of razing Poland (Lisagor and Lipsius, op. cit., p. 339).

71. Allen Dulles papers, John Foster Dulles version, August 20, 1940, Box 15, Mudd Library, Princeton University. E. H. Cookridge ascribes to Westrick, the "commercial counselor" in New York in 1940, organization of "a number of daring landing operations for spies and saboteurs on the East Coast" (*Gehlen*, p. 243).

CHAPTER FIVE

The best overall sources on the founding of the office of the Coordinator of Information and the OSS continue to be Thomas Troy's *Donovan and the CIA*, which has stood for some years as the CIA's favored version of events, and R. Harris Smith's *OSS*. On British involvement, the books *Room 3606* and *Secret Intelligence Agent*, by H. Montgomery Hyde, are the most reliable. Much of William Stevenson's *A Man Called Intrepid* has been discounted by scholars, although the book certainly has its moments.

1. Brown, op. cit., p. 148.

2. Anthony Read and David Fisher, *Colonel Z*, p. 32.

3. Nigel West, *M16*, pp. 54–55.

4. Mooney was a joiner; Charles Higham has followed his operations in several books, and has him not only building tanks for Hitler in 1938 but conspiring with Emil Puhl of the Reichsbank and Joseph P. Kennedy to bail Hitler out in 1939. Perhaps the real point here is that a number of the moguls on Dansey's list saw a lot of potential in Hitler while remaining well aware that he might indeed get carried away. Puhl, too, Hjalmar Schacht's most talented protégé, worked hard to maintain his connections outside Germany all through the war and cashed several chits with Allen Dulles well before the dust settled (Higham, *The Duchess of Windsor*, p. 310).

5. Nigel West, op. cit., pp. 70–71. See also worthwhile detail in *Her Majesty's Secret Service*, by Christopher Andrews, p. 358.

6. H. M. Hyde, op. cit., p. 249.

7. Brown, *Bodyguard of Lies*, p. 5.

8. Dunlop, op. cit., p. 209.

9. Stevenson, op. cit., p. 128.

10. Brown, *The Last Hero*, p. 151.

11. Ibid., p. 156.

12. Bradley Smith, *The Shadow Warriors*, p. 52.

13. Hyde, *Room 3606*, pp. 227–228.

14. Troy, op. cit., p. 57.

15. H. M. Hyde, *Secret Intelligence Agent*, p. 253.

16. Brown, op. cit., p. 174.

17. Dunlop, op. cit., p. 276.

18. Bradley Smith, op. cit., p. 63.

19. Brown, op. cit., p. 194. New Deal bureaucrats like Berle were increasingly suspicious that Donovan—like Allen Dulles after him—regarded collection and analysis as primarily a "cover" for secret operations. Both men would push covert hard in the postwar period (see Jeffreys-Jones, *The CIA and American Democracy*, pp. 16 ff.).

20. Dunlop, op. cit., p. 196.

21. Ibid., p. 319.

22. Brown, op. cit., p. 172.

23. Bradley Smith, op. cit., p. 209.

24. Troy, op. cit., p. 205.

25. Ibid, p. 106.

26. The well-liked Ellis, it would grudgingly be conceded in years to come, had functioned at some point as at least a Nazi, and possibly a Soviet, agent. Furthermore, according to the controversial G-2 spymaster John V. ("Frenchy") Grombach, Solborg too was a Soviet plant (*The Great Liquidator*, pp. 120–121). Solborg played an important if confusing role in North Africa prior to Operation Torch. Chapman Pincher would hound into public Ellis's many problems (*Their Trade Is Treachery*, p. 198).

27. R. Harris Smith, op. cit., p. 41.

28. Troy, op. cit., p. 141.

29. Ibid., p. 202.

30. Brown, op. cit., p. 170.

31. Troy, op. cit., p. 150.

CHAPTER SIX

1. Ted Morgan, *F.D.R.*, p. 675.

2. State Department career man who coordinated with Allen Dulles and prefers anonymity.

3. Mosley, op. cit., pp. 107–108.

4. Allen Dulles and Hamilton Fish Armstrong, *Can America Stay Neutral?*, p. 154. Carroll Quigley, in his monumental *Tragedy and Hope*, tags the Council on Foreign Relations as in essence "a front for J. P. Morgan and Company in association with the very small American Round Table Group."

He associates many of the academics in The Inquiry—James Shotwell, Charles Seymour, and Isaiah Bowman—and suggests support from the presiding Wall Street personalities of the period, from Hall Cravath to John McCloy, and includes "the Dulles brothers" (p. 952).

5. Mosley, op. cit., p. 104. The Agency's own biographical sketch of Allen Dulles alludes to one "special mission to Bolivia in 1941 for the U.S. Government to de-Germanize the Bolivian airlines."

6. Ibid., p. 114.

7. Donald Downes, *The Scarlet Thread*, p. 63.

8. David Bruce, COI Files, R.G. 226, entry 108, Washington Station, February 26, 1942. This record group is available through the National Archives, Room 13W (Military History).

9. Interview with Jacob Beam, June 11, 1987.

10. According to the Pools, Bruening was also known as the I.G. Chancellor because he was receiving such heavy subsidies from the Farben Trust (James and Suzanne Pool, op. cit., p. 88). Zu Putlitz speculates as to why Bruening had exploited his chancellorship to push "German equality and rearmament" and backed Treviranus in demanding the return of Danzig, both established Nazi planks (*The Putlitz Dossier*, Wolfgang zu Putlitz, p. 43). The Pools note that Treviranus led the Reichstag deputies who supported the Young Plan, and so endeared himself to the U.S. investment banking community (p. 224). By 1944 Treviranus was already inveighing against refugees who pressed to punish top Nazis as "stooges of the late Comintern," and urging Wall Streeters to keep Germany's war industries intact (Reiss, *The Nazis Go Underground*, p. 179).

11. Downes, op. cit., p. 72.

12. R. Harris Smith, op. cit., p. 209.

13. Stephen Ambrose, *Ike's Spies*, p. 174.

14. Mosley, op. cit., p. 125.

15. Becket, *The Dictionary of Espionage*, p. 162.

16. R. Harris Smith, op. cit., p. 209.

17. R.G. 226, entry 159, Phenix to Hugh Wilson, August 19, 1942.

18. Allen Dulles papers, Allen Dulles biographical sketch, Box 19, Mudd Library, Princeton University.

19. Mosley, op. cit., p. 132.

20. Anthony Read and David Fisher, *Operation Lucy*, p. 112.

21. R. Harris Smith mss., op. cit.

22. Persico, op. cit., pp. 54–55.

23. Mosley, op. cit., p. 133.

24. Mary Bancroft, *Autobiography of a Spy*, p. 289.

25. West, op. cit., p. 223.

26. Bancroft, op. cit., p. 130.

27. Interview with Howard Roman, November 25, 1987.

28. Bradley Smith, op. cit., p. 391.

29. Allen Dulles himself validates much of the Kolbe material in *Great True Spy Stories*, p. 19, by certifying the piece by Edward Morgan. A postwar interview of Kolbe by Dewitt Poole produces more detail (State Department Interview, September 29, 1945, National Archives [Microcopy M679]), while Mosley comes up with his version. Dulles later provided Donovan such details as his manipulation of Dr. Sauerbruch (Carlisle Barracks records, Allen Dul-

les file, Folder 82, Box 120b). OSS and CIA stalwart Peter Sichel (interview of June 4, 1987) who handled the moody Kolbe after the war, testifies to his dedication to the West.

30. Anthony Read and David Fisher, *Colonel Z*, p. 312.

31. Brown, op. cit., p. 279.

32. Kim Philby, *My Silent War*, p. 107.

33. Brown, op. cit., pp. 278–283. The suspicion that Allen Dulles was naive and suggestible was spreading in Washington. Colonel John V. Grombach, who ran The Pond, the Army's counterpart organization to the OSS, later wrote that "the Abwehr considered Allen Dulles . . . a dupe." Grombach notes Dulles's availability to Noel Field, Wilhelm Hoettl, and subsequently Otto John (*The Great Liquidator*, p. 119).

34. Ibid., p. 284.

35. Brown, op. cit., p. 286.

36. This material has been distilled out of Gaevernitz's folder in the Safe Haven name files, op. cit. The documents detailing Gaevernitz's background ran in series from April 25, 1945, through November 18, 1946.

37. Safe Haven name files, op. cit., Gaevernitz to Allen Dulles, October 22, 1945.

38. Safe Haven name files, op. cit., Legge to Gaevernitz, October 22, 1945.

39. Safe Haven name files, op. cit., October 4, 1945.

40. Allen Dulles papers, W. E. Ulrich to Allen Dulles, February 28, 1953, Box 55, Mudd Library, Princeton University.

41. Allen Dulles papers, Bruening to Allen Dulles, May 28, 1946, Box 20, Mudd Library, Princeton University.

42. West, op. cit., p. 223.

43. Allen Dulles papers, Allen Dulles to Marcus Wallenberg, February 5, 1946, Box 27, Mudd Library, Princeton University.

44. Allen Dulles papers, Allen Dulles to Reid Dennis, April 22, 1947, Box 29, Mudd Library, Princeton University.

45. *Prevent World War III*, Summer 1945, Number 46. Martin, op. cit., pp. 105–106.

46. Mosley, op. cit., p. 138.

47. Josef Garlinski, *The Swiss Corridor*, p. 126.

48. Farago, op. cit., p. 439.

49. Allen Dulles papers, Allen Dulles, roundup of activities in Bern, p. 20, July 18, 1946 (with H. Truman citation), Box 19, Mudd Library, Princeton University.

50. Heinz Hoehne, *Canaris*, p. 485. According to Jochen von Lang's important book on Martin Bormann, it was Dulles's inept code security which cost Langbehn his life. When Gestapo chief Heinrich Mueller picked up the transcripts relating to Langbehn's activities he routed them around Himmler, directly to Fuehrer headquarters. On the spot, Himmler sent Langbehn to his death to shut him up (von Lang, p. 290). Also see captured German records, National Archives, R.G. 242, SS records T125, roll 80, #259961, Langbehn to Wolff, October 19, 1941.

51. Allen Dulles papers, Allen Dulles to Pringsheim, January 2, 1946, Mudd Library, Princeton University.

52. Ambrose, op. cit., p. 92.

53. The Dulles-Hohenlohe exchanges appear quite fully in such works as

A Study of a Master Spy, by Edwards and Dunne. Archival SS documents in the National Archives, R.G. 81 VIB3106, April 30, 1943, substantiate much of this. The important elements come into view in Heinz Hoehne's major books *Canaris* (p. 485) and *Order of the Death's Head* (p. 520), which he sources directly from the Hohenlohe papers and SD reports of Bezimenski.

54. Edwards and Dunne, op. cit., p. 33.

55. Ibid., p. 31.

56. Garlinski, op. cit., p. 129.

57. Hoehne, *Canaris*, pp. 45–46.

58. Allen Dulles papers, Allen Dulles to William Piel, Jr., May 12, 1965, Box 142, Mudd Library, Princeton University.

CHAPTER SEVEN

1. Brown, op. cit., p. 510.
2. Ibid., p. 509.
3. Troy, op. cit., p. 206.
4. Brown, op. cit., p. 206.
5. Bradley Smith, op. cit., p. 102.
6. Ibid., p. 173.
7. Kermit Roosevelt, *The Overseas Targets*: *War Report of the OSS*, vol. II, page 5.
8. Brown, op. cit., pp. 300–302.
9. Bradley Smith, op. cit., p. 173.
10. Kermit Roosevelt, op. cit., p. 5.
11. William Corson, *The Armies of Ignorance*, p. 204.
12. Kim Philby, *My Silent War*, p. 190.
13. Ibid., p. 90.
14. Garlinski, op. cit., pp. 125–128.
15. R.G. 242, National Archives, Schellenberg interrogation by SIS, final report on the case of Walter Friedrich Schellenberg, September 30, 1946.
16. Zu Putlitz, op. cit., p. 183.
17. Garlinski, op. cit., p. 127.
18. Best overall biographical treatment of Field is *Red Pawn*, by Flora Lewis.
19. Bradley Smith, op. cit., p. 213.
20. Wilhelm Hoettl, *The Secret Front*, pp. 193–195.
21. Brown, op. cit., p. 382.
22. Ibid., p. 386; see also Donovan papers, Allen Dulles to Donovan, Folder 82, Box 120B, Carlisle Barracks.
23. Interview with Arthur Goldberg, November 24, 1986.
24. Allen Dulles papers, Hoettl interview material from raw files, *Time* magazine, February 19, 1966, Box 151, Mudd Library, Princeton University.
25. Hewel had long been close to Hitler and shared his confinement at Landsberg Prison (Gustav Hilger, *The Incomparable Allies*, p. 295).
26. Allen Dulles papers, Allen Dulles to Florimond Duke, October 22, 1965, Box 151, Mudd Library, Princeton University.

27. Allen Dulles papers, Lawrence Houston to Florimond Duke, October 29, 1965, Box 142, Mudd Library, Princeton University.

28. Hoettl, op. cit., pp. 165–166.

29. National Archives, R.G. 334, Records of Interservice Agencies, OSS memo for General John Deane, August 20, 1943, from William Donovan.

30. Many sources, including Robert Lamphere and Thomas Shachtman's *The FBI-KGB War*, p. 38.

31. Brown, op. cit., p. 390.

32. Ibid., p. 400.

33. R. Harris Smith, op. cit., p. 150.

34. John Ranelagh, *The Agency*, p. 79.

35. R. Harris Smith, op. cit., p. 150.

36. Interview with Frank Lindsay, July 17, 1987.

37. R.G. 226, entry 108, OSS cable traffic from Bern, Caserta of September 27, 1944, number 342, and October 2, 1944, number 683.

CHAPTER EIGHT

1. Allen Dulles, *Germany's Underground*, Forward XII.

2. Stefan Lorant, *Sieg Heil*, p. 323.

3. *Prevent World War III*, Winter, 1964–1965.

4. Allen Dulles, op. cit., p. 30.

5. Peter Black, *Ernst Kaltenbrunner*, p. 163.

6. Allen Dulles, op. cit., p. 4.

7. Heinz Hoehne, *The Order of the Death's Head*, p. 356.

8. Konrad Heiden, *Der Fuehrer*, p. 371.

9. Allen Dulles, op. cit. p. 170.

10. R.G. 226, entry 134, Box 169, Bern, August 14, 1944.

11. R.G. 84, Records of the Foreign Service Posts of the Department of State, Bern Legation, Economic Section, March 9, 1946. R.G. 84 is available at the National Record Storage Center at Suitland, Maryland, a National Archives depository.

12. Final report on the case of Walter Friedrich Schellenberg, op. cit.

13. U.S. Senate, Kilgore Committee Hearings, op. cit., November 25, 1945, pp. 30, 31.

14. R.G. 226, entry 108, Bern station, Headquarters and Headquarters, February 5, 1945.

15. R. Harris Smith, op. cit., p. 209.

16. National Archives, R.G. 84, Office of the U.S. Political Advisor for Germany, Berlin, 1944–1949 (in future, POLAD, Berlin, etc.), Top Secret Records of the Political Advisor, Robert Murphy, 1944–1949, Box 1, Robert Murphy to H. Freeman Matthews, February 11, 1945.

17. R.G. 226, entry 108, Bern station, Dulles to Donovan, January 22, 1945.

18. R.G. 226, entry 108, Bern station, February 27, 1945, April 4, 7, 16, 18, 25, 1945.

19. Wilhelm Hoettl, *Argosy*, November 1953.

20. Wilhelm Hoettl, *The Secret Front*, pp. 284–285.

21. Ibid., p. 287.

22. Black, op. cit., p. 224.
23. R.G. 226, entry 108, Bern station, January 20, 1945.
24. Allen Dulles papers, Allen Dulles to Rodney Minott, Box 114, January 21, 1963, Mudd Library, Princeton University.
25. Kenneth Strong, *Men of Intelligence*, p. 124.
26. Allen Dulles, *The Secret Surrender*, p. 60.
27. Hoehne, op. cit., p. 56.
28. Tom Bower, *Blind Eye to Murder*, p. 403.
29. Hoehne, op. cit., p. 526.
30. Bradley Smith and Elena Agarossi, *Operation Sunrise*, p. 70.
31. National Archives, Microcopy M679, Dewitt Poole State Department interrogation of Schellenberg, September 26, 1945.
32. Allen Dulles, op. cit., p. 119.
33. R.G. 84, Switzerland, Bern Legation Economic Section, Safe Haven name files, 1942–1949 (hereafter Safe Haven), Haniel to M. Bach, U.S. Legation, May 15, 1948.
34. Forrest Davis, "The Secret History of a Surrender." *The Saturday Evening Post*, September 22, 29, 1945.
35. R. Harris Smith, op. cit., p. 116.
36. Max Waibel, *Kapitulation in Norditalien*, p. 43.
37. Allen Dulles, op. cit., p. 103.
38. Ibid., p. 93.
39. Allen Dulles papers, Gaevernitz to Edwin Sibert, March 10, 1944, Mudd Library, Princeton University.
40. Bradley and Agarossi, op. cit., p. 29.
41. Allen Dulles, op. cit., p. 103.
42. Edwards and Dunn, op. cit., p. 29.
43. Waibel, op. cit., p. 74.
44. Smith and Agarossi, op. cit., p. 96.
45. Allen Dulles, op. cit. p. 129.
46. Schellenberg interrogation, op. cit.
47. Ibid.
48. Smith and Agarossi, op. cit., p. 123.
49. R. Harris Smith, op. cit., p. 144.
50. Ibid., pp. 117, 231.
51. Forrest Davis, op. cit., September 29, 1945.
52. Waibel, op. cit., p. 102.
53. Waibel, op. cit., p. 103. See also Black, op. cit., p. 242.
54. Smith and Agarossi, op, cit., p. 135.
55. Waibel, op. cit., p. 116.
56. Smith and Agarossi, op. cit., p. 141.
57. Ibid., p. 144.
58. William Donovan files, Carlisle Barracks, Allen Dulles folder 82, Box 120 B.
59. Allen Dulles, op. cit., p. 197.
60. Forrest Davis, op. cit., September 29, 1945.
61. Smith and Agarossi, op. cit., p. 146.
62. Interview with Howard Roman, November 25, 1987.
63. Robert Wistrich, *Who's Who in Nazi Germany*, Karl Wolff entry.
64. *Time*, October 9, 1964, p. 32.

65. R.G. 84, POLAD, Berlin, Top Secret Cables to the State Department, 1945–1949, Box 1, Robert Murphy to Secretary of State, August 11, 1947.

66. Allen Dulles papers, James Riddleberger to Gaevernitz, January 23, 1948. Box 35, Mudd Library, Princeton University.

67. Smith and Agarossi, op. cit., p. 190.

68. Mosley, op. cit., p. 480. A few years afterward Allen Dulles thanked Robert Murphy for keeping him informed on the "Karl Wolff case. Since the facts regarding his part in the German capitulation in Italy were brought to the attention of the court and taken into account, as against the earlier background of long association with Himmler, it seems to me that reasonable justice has been done" (R.G. 84, POLAD, Berlin, Classified Records of POLAD, 1945–1949, Box 8).

69. Robert Conot, *Justice at Nuernburg*, p. 287.

70. Allen Dulles, op. cit., p. 253.

71. Wistrich, op. cit., Wolff entry.

72. *Time*, October 9, 1964, p. 32.

CHAPTER NINE

1. Dunlop, op. cit., p. 453.

2. Decades afterward such researchers as William Corson and Susan and Joseph Trento (*Widows*, pp. 8–11) would unearth the history of such a Dulles underling in Bern as James Kronthal. They depict Kronthal as a homosexual entrapped by the Gestapo and subsequently the NKVD, and allude to Kronthal's "guilty knowledge associated with the activities of John Foster Dulles." Kronthal was the first CIA Station Chief at Bern, in 1947. His is the sort of tree up which Army intelligence veterans like Frenchy Grombach became especially fond of barking.

3. Bradley Smith, op. cit., p. 190.

4. R.G. 226, entry 134, Box 169, Bern station, August 7, 1944.

5. R.G. 226, entry 108, Bern station, January 13, 1944.

6. Charles De Gaulle, *The Complete War Memoirs of Charles DeGaulle*, p. 630.

7. Allen Dulles papers, Allen Dulles to Larry Collins, January 30, 1964, Box 123, Mudd Library, Princeton University.

8. Bradley Smith, op. cit., p. 212. See also Morgenthau papers, E. J. Putzell to Henry Morgenthau, January 22, 1945, Box 812, Roosevelt Library, Hyde Park, N.Y.

9. Brown, op. cit., p. 422.

10. Dunlop, op. cit., p. 466.

11. Persico, op. cit., pp. 167, 168.

12. Dunlop. op. cit., p. 454.

13. R. Harris Smith, op. cit., p. 128.

14. Interview with Arthur Goldberg, November 24, 1986.

15. Flora Lewis, op. cit., p. 186; also Stewart Steven, *Operation Splinter Factor*, pp. 85, 86.

16. Persico, op. cit., p. 232.

17. See Heinz Hoehne and Hermann Zolling, *The General Was a Spy*, pp. 56, 57, etc.

18. Mosley, op. cit., p. 224.
19. Charles Mee, *Meeting at Potsdam*, p. 18.
20. George Kennan, *Memoirs*, vol. I, pp. 237, 267.
21. Kennan, *From Prague After Munich*, p. 86.
22. Ibid., p. 103.
23. Kennan, *Memoirs 1925–1950,* p. 176.
24. Ibid., p. 198.
25. Isaacson and Thomas, op. cit., p. 177.
26. Mee, op. cit., p. 272.
27. R.G. 226, entry 125, Box 11, Bern station, April 27, 1945.
28. R.G. 84, entry 108, Bern station, March 21, 1945, Dulles to Donovan.
29. National Archives, OSS, Bern station, R.G. 238, entry 52D, Bern station. Dulles himself was obviously of continuing help to ITT. In *The Alliance*, by Richard J. Barnet, the author refers to an ITT history which registers appreciation for having "helped to arrange I.T.T.'s return to Europe by the American Army. . . ." Meanwhile, Sosthenese Behn personally sent a messenger by jeep to pick up Westrick and his wartime records and whisk them over to Paris. Colonel G. P. Sanders, Westrick's erstwhile companion in Prague, arranged momentarily to get all necessary clearances for Westrick as an employee of the U.S. Bombing Survey (R.G. 84, Safe Haven name files, Behn to Dunn, August 15, 1945). See also *Prevent World War III*, December 1946–January 1947, May–June 1948.
30. Allen Dulles papers, Blake to Gaevernitz, April 1, 1947, Box 30, Mudd Library, Princeton University.
31. Allen Dulles papers, Allen Dulles to Patterson, April 18, 1947, Box 30, Mudd Library, Princeton University.
32. The material validating this exposé of Gaevernitz's activities is derived largely from his file in R.G. 84, Safe Haven name files, 1942–1949. Most of it was dug up by the U.S. Treasury attachés at the Bern Legation, Harry Conover and Carl Hapke, during the summer and fall of 1945.
33. The above is substantiated by R.G. 226, entry 88, Box 152, October 19, 1945, Bern, Bastedo to Allen Dulles; includes brief of Harrison report. See also *Prevent World War III*, December 1946–January 1947.
34. Another trove well worth exploring is the E. V. D. Wight file in R.G. 84, Safe Haven name files, 1942–1949. Treasury suspicions of Wight and Dulles are specified in a series of letters to and from Maurice W. Altaffer from Conover and Hapke as well as Daniel Reagan, the commercial attaché, and J. Klahr Huddle, largely in the summer and autumn of 1945. The U.S. Minister to Switzerland, Leland Harrison, was kept up to speed on all of this.
35. R.G. 226, entry 190, Box 12, Joyce to McGruder, November 13, 1945.
36. Bradley Smith, op. cit., pp. 356, 357.
37. Hoettl soon picked up a job with U.S. Army Counterintelligence in Austria, then did a stint, along with other SD specialists on the East such as Heinz Jost and Franz Six, in the Gehlen "Org" (Andre Brissaud, *The Nazi Secret Service*, p. 212, etc.).
38. Allen Dulles papers, R.E.L. to Allen Dulles, July 23, 1953, Box 56, Mudd Library, Princeton University.
39. Interview with Garner Ranney, June 9, 1988.
40. Bancroft, op. cit., p. 242.

41. Ibid., p. 244.

42. See Martin, op. cit., p. 25; also *Prevent World War III*, December 1946–January 1947.

43. Martin, op. cit., p. 52.

44. Morgan, op. cit., p. 677 ff.

45. Higham, op. cit., p. 86.

46. Bullitt to FDR, July 1, 1941 (FDR Library).

47. Bullitt to FDR, June 18, 1942 (FDR Library).

48. James Grafton Rogers, *Wartime Washington*, p. 91.

49. Higham, op. cit., p. 87.

50. Interview with Jacob Beam, June 11, 1987.

51. Interview with James McCargar, December 7, 1986.

52. Ibid.

53. Interview with General Richard Stilwell, April 29, 1987.

54. Interview with Hector Prudhomme, December 6, 1986.

55. Interview with General Richard Stilwell, op. cit.

CHAPTER TEN

1. Mosley, op. cit., p. 225.

2. Allen Dulles papers, Allen Dulles forward to Per Jacobsson's report on the surrender negotiations with the Japanese in July and August 1945, Box 142, Mudd Library, Princeton University.

3. Martin, op. cit., pp. 105, 106.

4. R.G. 84, Safe Haven name files, 1942–1949, Haniel, May 15, 1948. See also R.G. 659, U.S. Department of State decimal files, 1945–1949, 501, 850; in addition, National Archives, R.G. 242, N.S.D.A.P. records, January 18, 1950.

5. R.G. 84, Safe Haven name file, Haniel, Bern, July 11, 1950.

6. *Prevent World War III*, May–June 1948.

7. Allen Dulles papers, Albert to Allen Dulles, December 10, 1946, Box 23, Mudd Library, Princeton University.

8. Cables available in R.G. 226, entry 88, Box 151, August 11–October 11, 1945.

9. Blessing's wartime history can be pieced out from references in Karl Richter's *Die Deutsche Widerstandsbewegung*; see also file entries in National Archives S.S. Records for Fritz Kranefuss (R.G. 242, T-175, Captured German Records), such as guest list December 12, 1943 (microfilm); see also William Manchester, *The Arms of Krupp*, p. 804, etc.

10. See Hoehne and Zolling, op. cit., p. 177, etc. There have been repeated attempts to whitewash Globke's Nazi record; perhaps the most complete treatment is to be found in *The New Germany and the Old Nazis*, by T. H. Tetens. Along with his responsibility for the drafting of the Nuremberg laws, Globke advised and ran the Office of Jewish Affairs during the holocaust and seems to have been directly implicated in the liquidation of 20,000 Macedonian Jews (pp. 38, 39).

11. Flora Lewis, op. cit., p. 185.

12. R. Harris Smith, op. cit., p. 237; Mosley, op. cit., p. 226.

13. Interview with Arthur Schlesinger, June 30, 1982, October 9, 1986.

14. Mosley, op. cit., p. 223.
15. Troy, op. cit., p. 382.
16. R. Harris Smith mss. on Allen Dulles.
17. Mosley, op. cit., p. 225.
18. For detailed treatment of Helms's career see Thomas Powers, *The Man Who Kept the Secrets*.
19. Interview with Peter Sichel, June 4, 1987.
20. R.G. 226, entry 88, Box 151, October 30, 1945.
21. Interview with Peter Sichel, op. cit.
22. R.G. 226, entry 88, Box 152, November 15, 1945.
23. E. H. Cookridge, *Gehlen*, p. 92. This version of Gehlen's heresy is supported by Schellenberg's SIS debriefing (op. cit., p. 186). Schellenberg adds that Gehlen in March of 1945 espoused a last-ditch movement "on the lines of the Polish resistance," to be commanded by Heinrich Himmler.
24. Hoehne and Zolling, op. cit., p. 34. This is a reliable source, with a deep research base.
25. Cookridge, op. cit., pp. 16–20.
26. Ibid., pp. 48, 49.
27. Hoehne, *Canaris*, p. 465.
28. Cookridge, op. cit., p. 57.
29. Hoehne and Zolling, op. cit., pp. 39–44.
30. Cookridge, op. cit., p. 121.
31. Ibid., p. 128; also Hoehne and Zolling, op. cit., p. 61.
32. R. Harris Smith mss.
33. Thomas Powers, op. cit., p. 24.
34. Cookridge, op. cit., p. 135.
35. The last days of the OSS are best chronicled in Troy, op. cit., pp. 218, 230.
36. Ibid., p. 252.
37. Ibid., p. 256.
38. Dunlop, op. cit., p. 468.
39. Interview with Sir Douglas Dodds-Parker, June 30, 1986.
40. Bradley Smith, op. cit., pp. 406, 407.
41. Ibid., p. 407.

CHAPTER ELEVEN

1. Charles Mee, *The Marshall Plan*, p. 17.
2. Joyce and Gabriel Kolko, *The Limits of Power*, p. 58.
3. Troy, op. cit., p. 311. Grombach was particularly outraged at McCormack, a would-be officer with "an adopted name" whom G-2 concluded was getting his assignments through "high-level, pro-Soviet supporters" (John V. Grombach, *The Great Liquidator*, pp. 108, 124.)
4. Ibid., p. 315.
5. R.G. 84, POLAD, Berlin, Classified Records, Department of State cable, E.O.C. 1040, Moscow, Harriman to Byrnes, April 6, 1945. Even conservative historians have admitted that some understanding existed which would leave Eastern Europe a Soviet sphere of influence; see Daniel Yergin, *Shattered Peace*, p. 59.

6. Charles Mee, *Meeting at Potsdam*, pp. 305–306.

7. R. Harris Smith mss., op. cit. As early as autumn of 1946, Allen Dulles was involved (along with Hoyt Vandenberg and William Donovan) as a "Technical Advisor of the Joint Research and Development Board," which had been authorized to give the new CIG some direction. Dulles also functioned in a consultant's role during the Vandenberg and Hillenkoetter directorships. Meanwhile, Donovan had publicly attacked the CIG in *Life* for September 30, 1946 (Darling, op. cit., chap. 4, p. 108); he liked to call the CIG a "committee of secretaries." The more mollifying Dulles was already in demand before Congress to testify on the possibilities of intelligence as a civilian career (Darling, op. cit., chap. 5, p. 24, chap. 6, p. 3). Lisagor and Lipsius suggest that Allen had taken a six-month leave from Sullivan and Cromwell, "to recruit former Nazi spies for a new American anti-Soviet spying unit that would be incorporated into the Central Intelligence Agency" (Lisagor and Lipsius, op. cit., p. 157). In *General Reinhard Gehlen*, by Mary Ellen Reese, the author asserts that Colonel John Deane, Jr., on Vandenberg's suggestion, arranged in the fall of 1946 to "sell the Gehlen Organization to former Army Intelligence officer William Jackson and the OSS's Allen Dulles" (p. 90). Allen Dulles's input was everywhere as the bureaucracy put CIA legislation into order. He pushed for the anticipated Agency to take over the evaluative functions of State, and urged before the House Expenditure Committee the recruitment of American businessmen, professors, and so forth. The Agency should be civilian-run, he insisted, with loosely defined functions (Jeffreys-Jones, *The CIA and American Democracy*, pp. 39, 43).

8. "Dewitt Poole," *Current Biography*, 1950.

9. *The New York Times*, Sunday, January 20, 1946.

10. Allen Dulles papers, Poole to Allen Dulles, February 8, 1946, Box 23, Mudd Library, Princeton University.

11. Allen Dulles papers, Bell to Allen Dulles, January 28, 1946, February 9, 1946, Box 23, Mudd Library, Princeton University.

12. Allen Dulles papers, Bell to Allen Dulles, February 16, 1946, Box 23, Mudd Library, Princeton University.

13. Allen Dulles papers, Allen Dulles to Bell, February 18, 1946, Box 23, Mudd Library, Princeton University.

14. *The New York Times*, January 20, 1946.

15. Allen Dulles, "Good-Bye Berlin." *Colliers*, May 11, 1946.

16. Preussen, op. cit., pp. 273, 293.

17. R. Harris Smith mss., op. cit.

18. Joseph Alsop, *The New York Herald Tribune*, September 6, 1946.

19. Like the John F. Carter ("J. Franklin") organization which Roosevelt authorized to run espionage independent of the OSS, "The Pond" leadership regarded Donovan's people both as dilettantes and dupes of the British (Troy, op. cit., p. 275, etc.; see also the Arthur Darling CIA study of its first three years, National Archives, R.G. 263, chap. 1, pp. 43, 44, etc.).

20. See House Hearings on H.R. 2319, preparatory to the completion of the National Security Act, June 27, 1947, Grombach testimony. Out of these exchanges came much of the shape of the imminent CIA. Allen Dulles testified in favor of an unorthodox warfare function for the envisaged Agency. Beyond that, he proposed both a collection and evaluation function for the Agency (Darling, op. cit., Summary, p. 96, etc.). Witnesses from the regular military, such as Brigadier General H. Kroner, opposed vigorously all opera-

tional capacities for the CIA. As early as November 1945, precocious cold warriors such as Robert Lovett had been promoting Dulles as a possible first civilian Director of Central Intelligence (Darling, op. cit., chap. 7, p. 3).

21. Interview with William Quinn, June 8, 1987.

22. *Time*, February 24, 1975.

23. Brown, op. cit., p. 284.

24. Ibid., p. 286.

25. R. Harris Smith mss., op. cit.; also Arthur Goldberg interview, November 24, 1986.

26. Corson, op. cit., p. 288. There is a very full treatment of this period in Robin Winks, *Cloak and Gown*.

27. Interview with James Angleton, October 27, 1982.

28. R. Harris Smith, op. cit., p. 163.

29. Corson, op. cit., p. 288.

30. This tidbit from Al Ulmer interview, June 7, 1988.

31. See David Martin, *Wilderness of Mirrors*, pp. 17–21; also Charles J. V. Murphy, *Time*, February 24, 1975, and interview, August 3, 1987.

32. High-level source prefers anonymity. As for the activities of Paterni and others, see Robin Winks, op. cit., pp. 341, 363. Another interesting workup of Angleton's career is the undergraduate thesis of Ted Mosle, at Yale, "Where Differences of Long Standing Begin (1987)," which focuses on the slow-burning conflict between William Colby and James Angleton. Also see author's piece, *Dragons Have to Be Killed,* in September 1985 *Washingtonian*, p. 158.

33. CIC subdetachment Salzburg, Austria, April 11, 1950. Records of CIC units are available in R.G. 407 (Suitland), Adjutant General's Office, 1917 forward. Applies to subsequent CIC citations.

34. CIC subdetachment Rome, June 23, 1947 (case number 5080). Also see CIC 230 Detachment U.S.F.A. Austria, August 21, 1946.

35. See Wilhelm Hoettl, *The Secret Front*, p. 123.

36. Magnus Linklater, Isabel Hilton, and Neal Ascherson quote Pavelic as defining "a good Ustase" as "one who can use his knife to cut a child from the womb of its mother" (*The Nazi Legacy*, p. 187). Estimates of the Ustase slaughter of Serbs and others has run into the millions, but current figures suggest several hundred thousand victims. The human eyes statistic comes from Michael Bar-Zohar, *The Avengers*, p. 126.

37. For details on the Pope's advocacy of the Ustase atrocities, see Branko Bokun, *A Spy in the Vatican*, p. 10. The quote is from Vatican Secretariat of State, Document Number 116898/SA, March 27, 1946.

38. CIC Records, Zone 1, September 12, 1946. Also see CIC subdetachment Salzburg, December 11, 1947.

39. CIC subdetachment Rome, September 12, 1947, case number 5650-A. In *The Israeli Secret Service*, by Richard Deacon, the author identifies Pavelic as Adolf Eichmann's contact and protector in Argentina. Pavelic lost his influence with the Argentinian secret police when the Frondizi regime came into power, which cut Eichmann adrift and opened the way for the Israeli abduction (p. 111).

40. CIC subdetachment Rome, June 23, 1947, case number 5080.

41. R.G. 226, entry 88, Box 638, SSU official dispatch, February 21, 1946, IN33127.

42. Interview with General William Quinn, June 8, 1987.

43. Ranelagh, op. cit., p. 102, etc.

44. Corson, op. cit., p. 278; Kirkpatrick, *The Real CIA*, p. 107. In *The CIA and American Democracy* (pp. 34–36), Jeffreys-Jones points up Souers's importance as a grey eminence to Truman. He compounded many of the principles on which the ultimate CIA would rest, including direct accountability to the NIA and freedom to perform, in the famous phrase, "such other functions and duties related to intelligence as NIA may from time to time direct." Through this unperceived crack in the dyke an ocean of upcoming operations would pour over the years.

45. See Troy, op. cit., p. 363; see also Darling, op. cit., chap. 2, p. 59, passim.

46. On October 17, 1946, Edwin Sibert came back to Washington as Assistant Director for Operations inside the CIG. His close personal relationships with both Gehlen and Dulles riveted future connections down (Darling, op. cit., chap. 4, p. 40).

47. Interview with William Quinn, op. cit.

48. R. Harris Smith, op. cit., p. 364.

49. Ambrose, op. cit., p. 165.

50. Interview with Henry Hyde, November 8, 1985.

51. Corson, op. cit., p. 286.

52. Many sources such as Martin, op. cit.; Powers, op. cit.; Nigel West, *MI5*.

53. Lamphere, op. cit., p. 167. Harvey's FBI records obtained through F.O.I.A. bear this out.

54. Lamphere, op. cit., p. 40.

55. The Director of Special Operations during this period was Colonel Donald Galloway. Ambitous and activist, he whetted Angleton's taste for large-scale covert adventures (Darling, op. cit., chap. 4, p. 40); see also Martin, op. cit., p. 38.

56. Lamphere, op. cit., pp. 84, etc.

57. The FBI's post-resignation (August 22, 1947) efficiency report on William Harvey, along with many examples of his tendency to jump the gun and ignore legal controls, suggests that Harvey was increasingly depressive and sloppy about follow-up. There was special reference to the fact that, after having been tipped off by captured German documents that Klaus Fuchs was solidly under Russian control, Harvey kept this information out of the Bureau's counterespionage index: "It was felt the principle responsibility for the failure to more promptly have had that material put in the Bureau's files was that of former Supervisor William Harvey." Experts have suggested that Fuchs's treachery moved up the development of the Soviet atomic bomb by several years.

CHAPTER TWELVE

1. Office of the Assistant Secretary of War, Stephen Penrose to Colonel Galloway, August 21, 1946. Many of the papers on which this treatment of Wisner's early life and military service are based came through subsequent F.O.I.A. requests to the CIA and FBI. Accordingly, although they are usually

dated and the source indicated, record groups and precise location in the files are often unavailable.

2. OSS Interviewer's Report, March 16, 1945.

3. Most of this material on the early history of the Wisner family came from extended interviews with Frank's widow, Mary (Polly), now Mrs. Clayton Fritchey (May 24, 1985, October 13, 1987, etc.) and three of his children, Frank, Jr., Ellis, and Wendy Hazard (May 22, 1985, June 5, 1985, June 9, 1987, and August 17, 1987, respectively).

4. 1948 application for federal employment.

5. Source prefers anonymity.

6. Interview with Mrs. John Graham, July 28, 1987.

7. See note 5.

8. Frank G. Wisner personal history statement, October 9, 1943 (F.O.I.A.).

9. See note 5.

10. OSS Memo, McBaine to Whitney Shepardson, March 1, 1943 (F.O.I.A.).

11. OSS Memo, McBaine to David Bruce, October 19, 1942 (F.O.I.A.).

12. 1948 application for federal employment, Frank G. Wisner (F.O.I.A.).

13. Frank G. Wisner to Chief SIOSS, March 27, 1945 (F.O.I.A.).

14. William Donovan memo to Joint Chiefs, April 1944 (F.O.I.A.).

15. For Dogwood details see Brown, op. cit., p. 358 et alia, and Nigel West, *MI6,* p. 226.

16. Interview with Frank Lindsay, June 6, 1985.

17. Persico, op. cit., p. 57.

18. West, op. cit., p. 226.

19. Al Ulmer, then in Istanbul himself, remembers the beating McFarland's SI officer, a scrupulous lawyer named John Wickham, had taken when X-2 reports suggested "several known Axis agents" among Dogwood's informants (F.O.I.A., X-2 Reports 3–31, August 1944). "Packy fired Wickham. Nobody would tell us what the sources of the information were, and we just did not want to put our chop on it. Packy, of course, was behind it. It was all he had" (interview with Al Ulmer, April 27, 1987).

20. Interview with Lawrence Houston, October 4, 1987.

21. Wisner to Dolbeare, September 28, 1943 (F.O.I.A.).

22. SI Report for August 1, 1944 (F.O.I.A.).

23. Wisner to Toulmin, August 26, 1944 (F.O.I.A.).

24. Department of State, H. Freeman Matthews to Leland Harrison, May 14, 1945 (F.O.I.A.).

25. Lt. General Ira Eaker to Hap Arnold, September, 1944 (F.O.I.A.).

26. Follow-up report by Russell Dorr, October 2, 1944 (F.O.I.A.).

27. Legion of Merit Recommendation for Frank G. Wisner, February 4, 1945 (F.O.I.A.).

28. One excellent source on Rumania during this period is Robert Lee Wolff, *The Balkans in Our Time.*

29. Robert Bishop and E. S. Crayfield, *Russia Astride the Balkans*, p. 198.

30. Nicholas Nagy-Talavera, *the Green Shirts and the Others*, p. 326. Hoettl, op. cit., is good on the SD involvement in these atrocities.

31. Otto von Bolschwing to Charles Dodd, Office of Special Investigations, December 22, 1970; also see Nagy-Talavera, op. cit., p. 325.

32. Henry Roberts, *Rumania*, p. 265.

33. OSS Washington Report UB1369, September 2, 1944. Most of Wisner's dispatches and reports are now available at the National Archives, usually as a part of R.G. 226, many in entry 162.

34. Bishop and Crayfield, op. cit., p. 94.

35. Ibid.

36. See OSS Donovan to Deane, U.S. Military Mission, Moscow, September 20, 1944, OSS Wisner to Caserta, Number 3824, September 23, 1944 (F.O.I.A.).

37. Roberts, op. cit., p. 259.

38. Bradley Smith, op. cit., p. 351.

39. OSS Wisner cable, September 26, 1944, number 21164 (F.O.I.A.).

40. OSS, Donovan to Wisner, October 2, 1944, number 19284 (F.O.I.A.).

41. Beverly Bowie, *Operation Bughouse.* R. Harris Smith claims that Bowie was the first OSS man to arrive in Bucharest, and successors found him "already a regular guest at meetings of the Romanian Cabinet" (Smith, *OSS*, p. 30).

42. OSS Caserta to Director, October 3, 1944, W21762 (F.O.I.A.).

43. OSS Wisner cable, October 17, 1944 (F.O.I.A.).

44. State Department Moscow, October 27, 1944, also, OSS 41667 (F.O.I.A.).

45. OSS Caserta to Director, October 9, 1944, number 21999.

46. One of Donovan's earliest if most independent-minded sources in Rumania, Ausnit bucked the trend of Wisner's reports by professing "no regard whatsoever for the current [Monarchist] government due to their anti-Soviet sentiments and feels that vacillation and refusal to recognize the inevitable has jeopardized the Rumanian position" (Caserta to Director, October 4, 1944, number 21890, F.O.I.A.). Ausnit remained a skeptic and moved into the Soviet era as an organizer of a SOVROM for the timber industry (Bishop and Crayfield, op. cit., p. 203). Ausnit and his brother Edgar were masters of Balkan politics, having alternately connived and fought with their industrialist counterpart Nicolae Malaxa long before the war. According to Charles Higham (*American Swastika*, p. 207), the Ausnits financially backed the Iron Guard, became a threat to the Antonescu regime (ibid., p. 223), and by 1941 were feasibly in cahoots with Donovan, reportedly in Sofia when the Guard revolted (ibid., p. 227). Otto von Bolschwing thus functioned as an early U.S. intelligence asset, if this stands up. The Ausnits and Malaxa, still feuding and collaborating, all wound up in New York by the later forties to madden the Agency functionaries attempting to make something out of the Committee for a Free Europe (see chap. 14).

47. Bishop and Crayfield, op. cit., p. 101.

48. Ibid., p. 107.

49. OSS Wisner to Joyce, Maddox, November 3, 1944, number 24604 (F.O.I.A.).

50. Wolff, op. cit., p. 279.

51. Bishop and Crayfield, op. cit., p. 106.

52. OSS Maddox to Wisner, November 3, 1944, number 42248 (F.O.I.A.).

53. OSS Caserta to SI, November 27, 1944, IN26730 (F.O.I.A.).

54. OSS, Buxton to F.D.R., December 27, 1944 (F.O.I.A.).

55. OSS, November 30, 1944, Number 4375 (F.O.I.A.).

56. See Headquarters OSS, William Kerry to Donovan, January 22, 1945 (F.O.I.A.).

57. OSS, Caserta to Director, January 10, 1945 (F.O.I.A.).

58. OSS, Schuyler memo, Wisner to Joyce, Maddox, Bailey, January 18, 1945 (F.O.I.A.).

59. OSS, Wisner field report, March 27, 1945 (F.O.I.A.).

60. Nagy-Talavera, op. cit., p. 338.

61. Bishop and Crayfield, op. cit., p. 123; see also undated OSS document.

62. Interview with Mrs. Clayton Fritchey, May 24, 1985.

63. Paul Johnson, *Modern Times*. p. 435.

64. Bishop and Crayfield, op. cit., p. 106. The Sigurantza claimed two hundred active agents in Russia, and a matchless file on Soviet operations (Brown, op. cit., pp. 681, etc.).

65. Bishop and Crayfield, op. cit., p. 108.

66. OSS, Wisner to Donovan, March 30, 1945 (F.O.I.A.).

67. OSS, GB-2653, November 17, 1944 (F.O.I.A.).

68. Wolff, op. cit., pp. 278–283.

69. OSS, Caserta Report 6244, March 3, 1945 (F.O.I.A.).

70. OSS, William Donovan to F.D.R., March 13, 1945 (F.O.I.A.).

71. Roberts, op. cit., p. 265.

72. OSS interview form, February 9, 1945 (F.O.I.A.).

73. Exchange in OSS Summary by Maddox, February 27, 1945 (F.O.I.A.).

74. OSS, Wisner to Magruder, Shepardson, March 14, 1945 (F.O.I.A.).

75. OSS, John Hughes to Shepardson, March 2, 1945 (F.O.I.A.).

76. OSS, January 22, 1945 (F.O.I.A.).

77. See Recommendation of Oak Leaf Cluster to Legion of Merit, March 29, 1946 (F.O.I.A.).

78. Interview with Peter Sichel, June 4, 1987.

79. See note 77.

80. SSU, Shepardson to Sgt. Cady, January 22, 1946 (F.O.I.A.).

81. Undated, Legion of Merit Citation (F.O.I.A.).

82. R. Harris Smith mss.

CHAPTER THIRTEEN

1. R. Harris Smith mss., op. cit.

2. Interview with Peter Sichel, June 4, 1987.

3. Interview with Mrs. Clayton Fritchey, October 13, 1987.

4. Corson, op. cit., p. 307.

5. Interview with Charles Saltzman, November 5, 1985.

6. Allen Dulles papers, Wisner to Dulles, October 1, 1947, Mudd Library, Princeton University.

7. Attachment A 1947 State Department job description (F.O.I.A. submission).

8. See Select Committee to Study Governmental Operations with respect to Intelligence (Church Committee 1976, Report, Book IV, p. 7).

9. John Loftus, *The Belarus Secret*, p. 90.

10. SWNCC Document 304/6 November 28, 1947. Like State, Army, Navy, Air Force Coordinating Committee (SANACC 395), the predecessor State, War, Navy Coordinating Committee documents are available on microfilm and identifiable by date, author, and recipient (Scholarly Resources of Wilmington, Delaware, 1978).

11. See note 7.

12. Yergin, op. cit., p. 319.

13. James Forrestal, *The Forrestal Diaries*, pp. 50, 127.

14. James Martin, op. cit., p. 229.

15. The Ferguson Commission report on Decartelization, April 15, 1949.

16. There is a substantial body of left-wing documentation of the overnight recovery of Nazi industrialists. Much of the best surfaced in *Prevent World War III* between 1947 and 1951. James Martin's *All Honorable Men* and Tom Bower's *Blind Eye to Murder* developed this material fully. Students of Nazi industrialization were particularly incensed when Nazi coat-holders like Robert Pferdmenges went in to preside over the German Economic Council and Hermann Abs, who scavenged Eastern Europe for the Deutsche Bank, stepped up to deputy head of the Reconstruction Loan Corporation to select Marshall Plan beneficiaries. Prominent retired saboteur and Ford Motor envoy Geheimrat Heinrich Albert became a trustee for the resuscitated Krupp. BIS chairman Thomas McKittrick turned into the chief financial adviser to the Economic Cooperation Administration, administrator to the Marshall Plan. And so forth.

17. Yergin, op. cit., pp. 348, 349.

18. R.G. 84, POLAD, Berlin, State Department, 1944–1949, Classified Records, Lewis Douglas to Charles Saltzman, June 2, 1948. Number 5377.

19. Yergin, op. cit., p. 369.

20. Cookridge, op. cit., p. 203.

21. Interview with Charles Saltzman, op. cit.

22. Interview with Paul Nitze, April 30, 1987.

23. Kennan, op. cit., p. 328; Kolko, op. cit., p. 364.

24. Interview with Paul Nitze, op. cit.

25. Kolko, op. cit., pp. 148, 348.

26. *Foreign Affairs*, letters section, April 1978.

27. Ranelagh, op. cit., p. 115; Ray S. Cline, *The CIA Under Reagan, Bush, and Casey*, p. 122.

28. Corson, op. cit., p. 296; interview with Lawrence Houston, op. cit. Hillenkoetter's disinclination to descend to covert payoffs prompted Forrestal to turn Allen loose among the Morris chairs of the Century Association with a tin cup (see R. Harris Smith mss.). As Christopher Simpson notes, CIA hesitations dictated that "much of this campaign was handled on an ad hoc basis out of the offices of Allen and John Foster Dulles at the Sullivan and Cromwell law firm in New York" (Simpson, op. cit., p. 90).

29. Winks, op. cit., pp. 384–386.

30. Christopher Simpson, *Blowback*, p. 91.

31. Kolko, op. cit., p. 438.

32. Winks, op. cit., p. 386.

33. Edward Mark, "The Question of Containment." *Foreign Affairs*, January 1978. See also Trevor Barnes, "The Secret Cold War." *Historical Journal*, 1981, vol. 24, no. 2, pp. 402, 413.

34. See SANACC 395 memo, November 8, 1948, to Kennan, Davies.

35. George Kennan, *Memoirs 1950–1963*, pp. 96, 97.

36. Simpson, op. cit., p. 99.

37. SANACC 395.

38. SANACC 395, Lovett memo, May 27, 1948.

39. The SANACC exchanges suggest the political trepidation. Department Counselor Chip Bohlen refers to Lovett's proposal to inform selected Congressmen against the day "the inevitable undesirable alien" tripped off alarm bells on Capitol Hill, although "some leading members of Congress might rather resent being cut in on something over which they had no decision or control but which they would be expected to defend. . . ." (SANACC 395, Bohlen to Saltzman, July 3, 1948).

40. SANACC correspondence, April 26, 1948.

41. State Department Decimal File, Wisner, June 25, 1948. Number 033-1140/6 2548. Available at National Archives, Diplomatic Branch (Rm. 6E-3).

42. Broad references, see Powers, op. cit., p. 31, etc.

43. Ranelagh, op. cit., p. 135.

44. Interview with John Bross, May 23, 1985.

45. Corson, op. cit., p. 308. Obviously, Frank Wisner—and Allen Dulles soon after him—were looking for an uptown, Ivy-League senior staff. A train of Grotonians—Richard Bissell, Tracy Barnes, John Bross, Billy Bundy, and Kermit and Archie Roosevelt—moved into senior staff posts on the operational side. They expected compensation appropriate to their pedigrees. Jeffreys-Jones, in *The CIA and American Democracy*, notes that a quarter of the CIA's "top people appear to have obtained at least one degree from Harvard" (p. 71). In *CIA Life*, Tom Gilligan notes that "by the late 1950s the agency had given up on the idea of hiring by referral from the Ivy League, although it was still the preferred source of the Junior Office Training (JOT) program," its future leadership (p. 14).

46. Steward Alsop, *The Center*, pp. 228, 229.

47. Dunlop, op. cit., p. 488.

48. Cave Brown, op. cit., pp. 780, 795.

49. See the journals of David Bruce (unpublished), Virginia Historical Society, Richmond, April 4, 5, 1952.

50. Dunlop, op, cit., p. 494.

51. Forrestal papers, Donovan to Forrestal, August 14, 1947, Mudd Library, Princeton University.

52. William Stevenson, *Intrepid's Last Case*, p. 153.

53. Dunlop, op. cit. p. 488.

54. Preussen, op. cit., pp. 316–320.

55. R. Harris Smith mss., op. cit.

56. Ibid.

57. Ibid. Lisagor and Lipsius (op. cit., p. 163) assert that Allen took a leave of absence during the Italian elections and handed out $20 million of the CIA's funds to assure the outcome.

58. R. Harris Smith mss., op. cit.

59. Corson. op. cit., p. 325; Kirkpatrick, op. cit., p. 146.

60. Isaacson and Thomas, op. cit., p. 440.

61. Interview with Jacob Beam, op. cit.

62. Interview with James MacCargar, op. cit.

63. R. Harris Smith mss., op. cit.

64. See Wolff, op. cit., p. 289.

65. R. Harris Smith mss., op. cit.; the deliberations of the so-called Dulles Committee would become a subject of particularly heated disagreement

within the Agency itself. According to CIA historian Ludwell Montague, "It appeared to [William] Jackson that Dulles had no plan to conduct a systematic survey, that he was interested only in writing out his personal prescription for the proper organization of clandestine operations" (Ludwell Lee Montague, *General Walter Bedell Smith: As Director of Central Intelligence, October 1950–February 1953*, DCI Series, Both available on order from CIA archives. Smith, vol. I, p. 87). Jackson convinced Forrestal to permit Robert Blum to draft the body of the report, while Jackson himself wrote the survey. It was Dulles's contention that "there was nothing the matter with CIA that the recruitment of more competent personnel would not correct" (Montague, op. cit., vol. I, p. 88). Dulles focused his attack on the DCI, Admiral Hillenkoetter, especially for the purported security lapse in Bogota; Hillenkoetter reacted by referring to "rumors in the fall of 1948 that one member of the survey Group (Dulles) would be named DCI when Mr. Dewey took office as President" (Montague, op. cit., vol. I, p. 93). Arthur Darling's treatment of the pre-Smith period brought down a similar reading, which later caused Dulles to mandate "restriced access to the history" (Arthur B. Darling, *The Central Intelligence Agency: An Investment of Government*, R.G. 263, chap. 1, note).

66. R. Harris Smith mss., op. cit. Lisagor and Lipsius maintain that Allen was extended the offer, and turned it down to avoid embarrassing Foster (op. cit., p. 133).

67. Isaacson and Thomas, op. cit., pp. 392, 409. After Forrestal went down, his replacement, Louis Johnson, showed no interest in the activist CIA Allen continued to promote (Darling, summary, p. 183, etc.)

68. R. Harris Smith mss., op. cit.

69. Kolko, op. cit., p. 430.

70. Ibid., p. 381.

71. Ibid., p. 381.

72. Peter Wyden, *The Bay of Pigs*, p. 13. Bissell worked closely on foreign aid problems with Averell Harriman and became the central organizer of the Economic Cooperation Administration.

73. Interview with Richard Bissell, May 3, 1983, December 5, 1986.

74. Interview with Frank Lindsay, June 6, 1985.

75. Church Committee, op. cit., Book IV, pp. 31, 32.

76. Jeffreys-Jones, op. cit., p. 156.

77. Ronald Radosh, *American Labor and United States Foreign Policy*, p. 307.

78. R. Harris Smith mss., op. cit.

79. Ibid.

80. Radosh, op. cit., pp. 308, 309.

81. Val R. Lorwin, *The French Labor Movement*, p. 110. For example, Brown funneled important money through the New York Jewish Labor Committee to make a factor out of the Force Ouvrière, which took a position to the left of the Communist Party and drew off enough Unionists to undermine working-class solidarity (see Kolko, op. cit., p. 346; Radosh, op. cit., pp. 319, 320, 323, etc.).

82. R. Harris Smith mss., op. cit.

83. Interview with James Angleton, March 1, 1987.

84. Interview with Jacob Beam, op. cit.

85. Radosh, op. cit., p. 334.

86. Interview with James Angleton, op. cit.

87. Thomas W. Braden, "I'm Glad the CIA Is Immoral." *The Saturday Evening Post*, May 20, 1967.

88. Mosley, op. cit., p. 243. Hillenkoetter continued to believe that the "noise" covert psychological operations generated directed unwanted attention to clandestine information gathering, and regretted any related CIA responsibilities. "Furthermore, from his experience in wartime France, he believed that guerrilla tactics and resistance movements, yielded inadequate returns" (Darling, op. cit., summary, p. 128).

CHAPTER FOURTEEN

1. Interview with Frank Lindsay, November 3, 1986. At several points the author attempted to communicate directly with George Kennan to help ascertain the details of his involvement with the OPC. This correspondence had many turnings, and Professor Kennan, after seemingly making himself available, fell back to protestations of outrage and bad health once the author had itemized—at Professor Kennan's request—the specifics into which he hoped to inquire. On November 19, 1985, Professor Kennan wrote from the Institute for Advanced Study, at Princeton, that he was not informed of the operations of OPC even in the matters on which he had given guidance, much less in cases where he had not given it. He recalled only one instance of discussing these matters personally with Mr. Wisner, and that by telephone, and one social meeting with Wisner after leaving government and retiring to teach at Princeton. Nevertheless, George Kennan was to remain a close social friend and regular houseguest of Mrs. Fritchey. The declassified Policy and Planning Staff and State Department documents of the period are perhaps a more useful source on the collaboration between Kennan and Wisner, often by way of Robert Joyce and Carmel Offie.

2. John Prados, *The President's Secret Wars*, p. 33.

3. Interview with Ray Cline, October 14, 1987.

4. Interview with Frank Lindsay, op. cit.

5. Interview with Jack Blake, November 24, 1987.

6. Church Committee, op. cit., vol. IV; Ambrose, op. cit., p. 297.

7. Interview with John Lawrence, June 19, 1988.

8. Interview with James McCargar, November 23, 1987.

9. Interview with Colonel John R. Deane, July 18, 1988. Colonel Deane is the son of the general who helped coordinate the Joint Chiefs of Staff during the Second World War and wound up military liaison in Moscow. The colonel ran the compound at Oberursel where Gehlen found his postwar feet, then returned to Washington and key staff positions.

10. R.G. 59; encomiums came in from every direction, and are available in the State Department decimal file 1945–1949 (State Department Headquarter European Command, Huebner to Robert Murphy, August 20, 1948).

11. Ibid., State Department telegram 2554, May 13, 1948.

12. Ibid., State Department, Murphy to Huebner, August 19, 1948.

13. See Carmel Offie, Selective Service System Request for Occupational Classification, March 7, 1944, State Department decimal files. Biddle's claim

on Offie would entice them both into the currency transactions which finished Offie's diplomatic career and produced Cochran's devastating report (Cochran memo, Paris, December 6, 1947, State Department Archives, F.O.I.A).

14. R.G. 84, POLAD, Berlin, Classified Records, Murphy to Matthews, April 17, 1945.

15. R.G. 59, State Department decimal files 1944–1949, Kirk to Holmes, number 1192, May 7, 1945; also August 3–5, 1945.

16. Cyrus Sulzberger, *A Long Row of Candles*, pp. 346, 347.

17. Brownell and Billings, op. cit., p. 288.

18. R.G. 84, POLAD, Frankfort, Top Secret Records, 1948–1949, Box 1, POLAD to Chief of Staff, July 16, 1946.

19. Ibid., Offie to Thompson, April 14, 1948.

20. Ibid., Thompson to Offie, April 30, 1948.

21. Ibid., Offie to Thompson, May 27, 1948.

22. Interview with Harry Rositzke, October 8, 1987.

23. R.G. 84, POLAD, Berlin, Top Secret General Records, 1944–1949, Box 4, Airgram, U.S. Legation in Budapest, April 10, 1948; Parsons Amvat to Page, July 7, 1948.

24. R.G. 84, POLAD, Frankfurt, Top Secret Records, 1948–1949, Box 1, Barbour to Offie, May 12, 1948.

25. Ibid., Offie to James Dunn, April 15, 1948.

26. CIC Report Region VI, 90 CIC Detachment, May 7, 1948 (see chap. 11, note 33).

27. R.G. 84, POLAD, Frankfurt, Top Secret Records, 1948–1949, Box 1, Offie to Beam, May 13, 1948.

28. Loftus, op. cit., p. 41. Christopher Simpson has also delved into Hilger's history, and credits him with such incidental contributions as lending a hand to SS specialists rounding up Italian Jews (Simpson, op. cit., p. 113).

29. R.G. 84, POLAD, Frankfurt, Top Secret Records, 1948–1949, Box 1, Kennan to Offie, April 10, 1948. Offie's records in Frankfurt testify to his urgency in re Hilger as well as the touchiness of some of the favors he had in mind. Concerned about Hilger's "rather low . . . morale" he pushed hard by sending Bohlen "a copy of Hilger's squibs for our intelligence authorities," especially Kennan (March 19, 1948). Offie launched a full-scale campaign through Murphy and others to secure "certain blocked funds" for Hilger (see Offie to Murphy, November 22, 1948). Even Lovett bridled at Offie's insistence that "Hilger and family should arrive in this country with assumed names" (State Department cable, September 28, 1948).

30. Simpson, op. ct., pp. 115, 116. In time Hilger and Alfred G. Meyer wrote a book, *The Incompatible Allies*, which dealt with German-Soviet relations between the Wars. He credits "the drive of Mr. George F. Kennan" for securing "the generous grant" required to complete the work. Hilger's collaborator took pains in the preface to single out Carl Friedrich of Harvard and, inevitably, Carmel Offie for their attentive reading of the manuscript (preface pp. viii, ix).

31. Simpson, op. cit., pp. 86, 87. Herwarth had gotten through the war directing anti-Partisan units in Yugoslavia and filling in as senior political officer attaché to the Vlasov Army.

32. R.G. 84, POLAD, Frankfurt, Top Secret General Records, 1948–1949, Box 1, Davies to Offie, March 8, 1948, number 1742.

33. Ibid., Offie to Davies, May 13, 1948.

34. Ibid., Offie to Davies, May 19, 1948.

35. Simpson, op. cit., p. 120. Simpson develops the particulars in Poppe's case, including his extended residency at the Holocaust Planning Center at Wannsee under Franz Six. In 1948 Poppe was shuttled undercover to the United States.

36. R.G. 84, POLAD, Berlin, Classified Records, Internal Route Slip, Offie, attention Colonel Schow, July 15, 1948.

37. R.G. 84, POLAD, Frankfurt, Top Secret Records, Box 1, Headquarter European Command, Offie to Robert Murphy, March 6, 1948.

38. R.G. 59, State Department Decimal files, Offie to Kennan, May 5, 1948.

39. State Department Report (F.O.I.A.).

40. Interview with Mrs. Clayton Fritchey, October 13, 1987. A confidential memo from Hector Prudhomme to Robert Murphy suggests that Wisner was already plugging Offie in during visits to Germany while both worked for State; Prudhomme mentions one encounter in Offie's salon in July 1948 (see R.G. 84, POLAD, Berlin, 1944–1949, Classified General Records, Box 10, Prudhomme to Murphy, February 8, 1948).

41. Interview with Ed Applewhite, June 5, 1988.

42. Interview with Lloyd George Wiggins, November 13, 1988.

43. Interviews with John Bross, Lawrence Houston, op. cit.

44. Allen Dulles papers, Wisner to Dulles, December 30, 1947, Box 32, Mudd Library, Princeton University.

45. Allen Dulles papers, Wisner to Dulles, March 10, 1948, Box 37, Mudd Library, Princeton University.

46. See Allen Dulles papers, Coudenhove-Kalergi to William Donovan, November 24, 1949, Box 38, Mudd Library, Princeton University.

47. Prados, op. cit., p. 55.

48. See Cookridge, op. cit., pp. 205, 376.

49. R.G. 59, Policy and Planning Staff Records, 1947–1953 NND 760154, Box 33, Marshall Library. Allen had reached the stage where, as his correspondence suggests, he was gloomily inclined to regard his intelligence career as part of his past, and was actively involving himself in Manhattan's clubland existence while angling for fresh decorations. By then he boasted the Medal for Merit (1946); Medal of Freedom (1946); Officer of the French Legion of Honor (1947); Order of S.S. Maurizio e Lazzaro, Italy (1946); Belgian Cross of Officer of Order of Leopold (1948).

50. J. C. Grew, lead article. *The American Foreign Service Journal*, September 1949.

51. Interview with Lawrence Houston, op. cit.

52. R. Harris Smith mss., op. cit.

53. Loftus, op. cit., p. 107.

54. Simpson, op. cit., p. 126.

55. Cord Meyer, *Facing Reality*, p. 110.

56. James McCargar, op. cit.

57. Loftus, op. cit., p. 107. In *The CIA and American Democracy*, Jeffreys-Jones makes the telling point that Smith and Dulles both took pains to keep the administrations of Radio Free Europe and Radio Liberty separate, partly to control their outspoken backers more easily. Dulles and Wisner were "apprehensive" about their "strength and independence" (p. 84).

58. R.G. 59, Policy and Planning Records, 1947–1953, NND 76154, Kennan to Wisner, January 6, 1949, Box 33, Marshall Library.

59. Frederick Propas, "Creating a Hard Line Toward Russia." *Diplomatic History*, Summer 1984, p. 209.

60. Cookridge, op. cit., p. 205.

61. See "C. D. Jackson," *Current Biography*, 1951.

62. Cookridge, op. cit., p. 376.

CHAPTER FIFTEEN

1. Richard Deacon, *A History of the British Secret Service*, p. 340.

2. So far, the best and most comprehensive treatment of the Albanian incursion is Nicholas Bethell's *The Great Betrayal*. Certain of Lord Bethell's conclusions—e.g., that Kim Philby's involvement alone was the main source of Albanian access to tactical details of the operation—have been challenged by other experts. But Bethell's overall rendition certainly holds up. Unless otherwise noted, quotes and details here are from Bethell.

3. Stevenson, *Intrepid's Last Case*, p. 282.

4. Christopher Andrews, *Her Majesty's Secret Service*, p. 488.

5. Interview with Frank Lindsay, June 6, 1985.

6. *The New York Times*, Ralph Blumenthal, June 20, 1982.

7. Interview with James McCargar, November 24, 1986.

8. Interview with Lindsay, op. cit.; also, Bethell, p. 119.

9. Michael Burke, *Outrageous Good Fortune*, p. 142 on. Burke's volume has been sanitized here to an extent that no living detail can survive upon its surface. But the atmospherics are interesting.

10. Kim Philby, *My Silent War*, pp. 193, 194.

11. Powers, op. cit., p. 61.

12. See Hoehne and Zolling, op. cit., p. 66, etc. Liebel seems to have demanded that Gehlen turn over the identities of his many agents to his CIC handlers. He refused—Waldman supported him in this—and then and later Gehlen was able to fend off American attempts to assess his sources, probably an important reason for Gehlen's turning into a colossal security disaster by the later fifties (Reese, op. cit., pp. 97, 178).

13. Apparently a carton full of currency which Baun normally kept under his bed spilled during a Jeep accident in the Taunus, enough for Hilger to allege confusion if not corruption. The best of this Gehlen-Hilger material comes from interviews with Eric Waldman, July 17, 1988, and Colonel John Deane (retired), July 18, 1988.

14. Interview with James Critchfield, July 9, 1988. Gehlen himself concedes his black market involvement (Gehlen, *The Service*, p. 140). According to Mary Ellen Reese (op. cit., p. 106), Eleanor Dulles, who had gotten to know Critchfield in Austria, recommended to her brothers that the CIA find something for him.

15. Pleasants's range in Bonn is suggested by the following entry in David Bruce's diary (op. cit.): June 30, 1959. "Indeed, through Henry Pleasants, another 124 bottles of Mosel today from the Schaumburger Hof." A few months later Bruce was sending along red wine to Adenauer "through Globke" (October 29, 1959).

16. Hoehne and Zolling, op. cit., p. 117. Mary Ellen Reese passes along a KGB defector report to the effect that Stefan Bandera was murdered in 1959 "by the man with whom he was having supper. His dinner companion, it happened, had been Heinz Danko Herre, for years Gehlen's friend and closest associate" (op. cit., p. 157).

17. Strong clues as to Jay Lovestone's grip on American intelligence comes through in David Bruce's journals. Bruce regularly recurs to top-level meetings with Lovestone in conjunction with powerhouses like Averell Harriman (December 10, 13, 1949), and finds himself caught in the middle of a turf battle between Irving Brown and Walter Reuther over U.S. Government support and access to the French unions (September 25, November 2, 1951). Meanwhile, Jim Angleton and Frank Wisner are in and out of the Paris Embassy regularly.

18. Interview with James McCargar, op. cit.

19. See Ludwell Montague, monograph, op. cit., vol. III, pp. 173–174. Sibert squirmed loose and went back on military duty on June 4, 1948.

20. See Darling, op. cit., chap. V, p. 48.

21. Policy and Planning were well aware of the dubiousness of many of these bootleg immigrants. In one memo, Robert Joyce attempted to lean on State's Southern European Division for special entrée, since "my friends state that they would prefer not to approach the visa division direct" (Blumenthal, op. cit.).

22. Interview with Marc Truitt, December 14, 1985; see also Blumenthal, op. cit.).

23. Although not identified directly, Deva receives full and unmistakable treatment in the Tipton Report issued by the Comptroller General of the United States, General Accounting Office, June 28, 1985, which profiles certain of the more controversial new Americans brought in under the Agency's auspices. The report quotes the U.S. intelligence officer who debriefed Deva as having concluded, despite "voluminous files of adverse information," that Deva was a "person of uncompromising personal honor," a pure patriot, and an outstanding "operational contact and source of information." Deva ultimately died peacefully in Palo Alto.

24. Philby, op. cit., pp. 195–196.

25. Prados, op. cit., p. 46.

26. Interview with Al Ulmer, April 27, 1987. As OPC station chief in Greece at the time, Ulmer was running the main insertion effort.

27. Interview with James McCargar, November 23, 1987.

28. Interview with Joe Bryan, October 11, 1987.

29. Orville Bullitt, op. cit., p. 80; *Current Biography* 1950; Darling, op. cit., chap. VI, p. 1.

30. See Church Committee, op. cit., Report, Book IV, pp. 36, 37, April 23, 1976. See also Darling, op. cit., chap. VI, p. 92.

31. Philby, op. cit., p. 190.

32. Interview with Gen. Richard Stilwell, op. cit.

33. Interview with Charles Murphy, August 3, 1987.

34. Bethell, op. cit., p. 99.

35. Interview with Al Ulmer, op. cit.

36. Interview with Richard Helms, June 6, 1988.

37. See Loftus, op. cit., pp. 75 ff.

38. Also see note 41, chap. 13.

39. Interview with Tom Parrott, June 9, 1988.

40. Loftus, op. cit., p. 74.

41. R.G. 84, POLAD, Berlin, Classified Records, Lovett to Murphy, Riddleberger, number 10885, September 29, 1948.

42. Ibid., OMGUS memo, Murphy from Riddleberger, October 12, 1948.

43. Cookridge, op. cit., p. 242.

44. Loftus, op. cit., p. 36. Until Gehlen grabbed Six, one of the Org's primary sponsors in the Ruhrlade, Mannesmann, found Six a cover as head of an industrial group (see *Prevent World War II*, Summer 1953, no. 42, p. 33, and Brissand, op. cit., p. 212). Perhaps the best-documented presentation of the sweetheart arrangements between Gehlen and the Slavonic Nazis appears in the recently published history of the CIC, *America's Secret Army*, by Ian Sayer and Douglas Botting (chap. 12). The connivance by Wisner and Lucius Clay is underlined (p. 342) along with the OUN's extensive assassination program.

45. Cookridge, op. cit., pp. 241, 242.

46. Loftus, op. cit., p. 81.

47. The best treatment of the NTS turns up in a State Department paper done by the external research staff, Office of Intelligence Research Series 3, number 76, December 10, 1951. As gentrification set in Kuchel wound up running the White Ruthenian Institute of Arts and Sciences in Brooklyn, while his fellow homicide technician Stanislaw Stankievich went in as Chairman of Russian Research in Munich (Loftus, op. cit., pp. 106, 107).

48. Philby, op. cit., p. 192. While Gehlen reportedly warned the Americans off Bandera, he had no scruples himself about mining the OUN for information (see Gehlen, *The Service*, in which he calls Bandera "one of our men," p. 241). Meanwhile the U.S. Army's CIC had recruited Bandera immediately after the war. Although they did break off direct contact early, they evidently protected him for several years. (Sayer and Botting, op. cit., p. 355).

49. Philby, op. cit., p. 202.

50. Cookridge, op. cit., p. 154. Tetens (op. cit., p. 178) observes that by the end of the fifties, "the Bureau Gehlen is staffed with 4,000 former SS officers and SD (security) agents."

51. Von Bolschwing confided his hopes and fears to Charles Dodd of the U.S. Office of Special Investigations (op. cit., chapter 12, note 31) on December 22, 1970.

52. Ernest Volkman, in *Warriors of the Night*, credits von Bolschwing, under the spur of U.S. Army Intelligence, with having attempted a coup, in Romania, using his outdated Iron Guard contacts. He links this with the 1947 fiasco which largely destroyed the anti-Soviet underground there.

53. Cookridge, op. cit., pp. 158, 218, 351; Hoehne and Zolling, op. cit., p. 88.

54. Waldman insists that he blocked Bandera's access to the Org, and turned down Schellenberg's feelers.

55. See Tom Bower, *The Butcher of Lyon*, pp. 128, 146. As Sayer and Botting observe, Augsburg helped murder thousands of Jews in Eastern Europe under Eichmann, before collaborating with Barbie (op. cit., p. 332). In *American Swastika*, Charles Higham (pp. xv ff.) ties Barbie's activities closely to the early Gehlen undertakings.

56. See Hoehne and Zolling, op. cit., pp. 161, 165; Cookridge, op. cit., pp. 325–326.

57. Tom Powers, op. cit., p. 41.

58. David Bruce diaries, op. cit., September 22, 1949.

59. Harry Rositzke, *The CIA's Secret Operations*, pp. 168–171.

60. Interviews with Cleve Cram, June 7, 1988, and Howard Roman, November 25, 1987.

61. Frank Lindsay remembers arguments with MacDowell, who wanted to drop covert commando teams "into Eastern Europe to operate pretty much on their own." Lindsay stressed working with local resistance, developing intelligence sources, etc. (Frank Lindsay interview, November 3, 1986).

62. This transcription of the radio broadcast which ended the WIN operation is from the files of William Donovan, Donovan collection, Carlisle Barracks, Pennsylvania (Box 8A-2).

CHAPTER SIXTEEN

1. Stevenson, op. cit., p. 153.

2. Ranelagh, op. cit., pp. 188, 189.

3. Hoehne and Zolling, op. cit., p. 277.

4. Corson, op. cit., p. 319.

5. Source prefers anonymity. Kenneth Strong, British Chief of Allied Intelligence under Eisenhower, remembers Smith remarking at war's end that while he would remain "a personal friend," the United States regarded Russia as "the country of the future," and his official cooperation would be with them. Shortly, Smith was busy sneaking Gehlen into America behind Ike's back (Kenneth Strong, *Intelligence at the Top*, p. 298).

6. Walter Bedell Smith, *My Three Years in Moscow*, pp. 14, 316, 331.

7. Interview with Lawrence Houston, October 4, 1985.

8. Mosley, op. cit., p. 490.

9. Yergin, op. cit., p. 207.

10. Ibid., pp. 401, 402.

11. Kolko, op. cit., pp. 507, 508; Hoopes, op. cit., p. 194.

12. Interview with Paul Nitze, op. cit.

13. Originally, like Lovett and Forrestal, Kennan had been a supporter of the movement to install Allen Dulles as the head of the operations-oriented "small project" State intended to pursue (Darling, op. cit., chap. VII, p. 36). With time Kennan would become apprehensive at the thought of turning over "responsibility for political warfare" to so independent-minded a crowd as the Agency showed signs of becoming (Darling, op. cit., chap. VIII, pp. 54, 55). As to Kennan's shift in priorities see Isaacson and Thomas, op. cit., p. 481. During the Truman years Kennan served as one of the "Princeton Consultants," who met four times a year to hash over the analytical product of CIA's Office of National Estimates. After Eisenhower came in, Kennan, disgusted by the railroading of John Paton Davies, Jr., gave up all CIA affiliation (Jeffreys-Jones, *The CIA and American Democracy*, pp. 67, 76).

14. Kennan, *Memoirs 1925–1950*, p. 119.

15. See David Bruce journals, op. cit., September 24, October 8, 1951.

16. R.G. 218, Section 23, Box 147, Joint Chiefs of Staff, Stevens to Wisner, July 5, 1951.

17. Trevor Barnes, "The Second Cold War," Part 2. *The Historical Journal*, 1982, vol. 25, no. 3.

18. Kennan, op. cit., p. 184.

19. George Kennan, "Morality and Foreign Policy." *Foreign Affairs*, Winter 1985–1986, pp. 213–215.

20. Interview with Mrs. Clayton Fritchey, October 13, 1987.

21. Smith's feelings about these Wall-Street managers he was bringing in comes through very plainly in Ludwell Montague's official write-up of the Smith directorship. "Smith never felt the same confidence in Allen Dulles and Frank Wisner that he did in William Jackson. During 1951 he had Jackson 'survey' (investigate) the offices under Dulles's supervision. With reason, he came to suspect that Dulles and Wisner were actually pursuing a policy contrary to his own. In exasperation, he visited upon them more violent manifestations of his wrath than he did upon anyone else" (Montague, op. cit., vol. II, p. 85). Montague further observes that Dulles often "rubbed him [Smith] the wrong way," and that Smith "lacked confidence in Dulles' self-restraint. . . . Smith feared that Dulles' enthusiasm for covert operations would eventually lead him into some ill-conceived and dangerous adventure" (Montague, op. cit., vol. V, p. 113). Accordingly, "Bedell Smith, who had never before been a covert operator, spent almost all his time with his Deputies discussing covert operations" (Montague, op. cit., vol. II, p. 95).

22. Cline was moving around at senior staff levels in the Agency, having come over from State to head the Central Reports Staff (Darling, op. cit., chap. III). During this period Cline was Chief of the Global Survey Group in the Office of Reports and Estimates (Darling, op. cit., chap. VIII, p. 45). Ludwell Montague was forming his own opinions. Kirkpatrick, for example, he judged "a highly ambitious young man" (he was thirty-five in 1951). As executive assistant, and later as ADSO, he was always "playing his own game (not OSO's). His constant object was to outflank Frank Wisner, as ADDP and later as DDP" (Montague, op. cit., vol. IV, p. 61). For Kirkpatrick's version, see Kirkpatrick, *The Real CIA*, p. 94.

23. Interview with Jack Blake, November 24, 1987. Montague makes the point throughout his chronicle that Bedell Smith resisted the idea of *merging* the OSO and OPC (vol. II, p. 83, etc.), obviously concerned that the operators would swallow the spies, and intended the Office of Deputy Director for Plans to serve as a "substitute for the integration at OSO and OPC, not a step in that direction" (vol. IV, p. 58). He also resisted the attempts of Dulles, Wisner and Company to evade control by State and Defense, even in wartime (vol. II, p. 54). Nevertheless, Smith too resented the refusal of the Joint Chiefs to share its papers and estimates with CIA (vol. V, p. 36).

24. Kirkpatrick, op. cit., pp. 90, 91.

25. Church Committee Hearings, op. cit., Book IV, pp. 33–36.

26. McNarney had authored a critique of the Dulles report for the Joint Chiefs, and so was familiar with the details of intelligence reorganization during the Forrestal era (Darling, op. cit., chap. IX, pp. 2 ff.). This gloss, like the Dulles report itself, was largely drafted by Robert Blum. Hillenkoetter would conclude that "they had all been misled by a clever clerk, Robert Blum" (Montague, op. cit., vol. II, p. 2).

27. Interview with Gen. Richard Stilwell, op. cit.

28. Interview with Paul Nitze, op. cit.

29. Victor Marchetti and John D. Marks, *The CIA and the Cult of Intelligence*, pp. 115, 116.

30. Church Committee Hearings, op. cit., Book IV, p. 32.

31. Ibid., p. 31.

32. Interview with Harry Rositzke, October 8, 1987.

33. Interview with James McCargar, November 24, 1986.

34. William Colby, *Honorable Men*, p. 115.

35. Interview with W. Mark Wyatt, October 13, 1987.

36. Ibid.

37. Gehlen's involvement in Egypt is interesting because so many of his splashier confederates resurface as Agency contract players. For example, Otto Skorzeny was recruited, evidently at Allen Dulles's request by way of Hjalmar Schacht, to arm and train Nasser's security people (see chap. 18). At his Madrid headquarters Skorzeny was still running the remnants of both the SPINNE network to exfiltrate wanted Nazis from Europe and the increasingly vocal ODESSA lobby, which spoke up with notable success for the political claims of retired senior SS. The notorious Alfred Naujocks, Heydrich's senior button man, helped Skorzeny out for a while (many sources, including Cookridge, op. cit., p. 253).

38. Colby, op. cit., p. 132.

39. Interview with Lyman Kirkpatrick, October 5, 1985. Tom Parrott points up Offie's rather public propensities when he reminisces about having met Carmel during the war, when Offie attempted, unsuccessfully, to slough off a couple of like-minded young majors of whom he had tired on Parrott's section. Parrott blocked the transfers, and "he was furious with me. So that was the end of that, and I never thought of it again until I found him sitting outside of Wisner's office, giving me the beady eye" (interview with Tom Parrott, June 9, 1988).

40. Interview with James McCargar, op. cit.

41. Interview with Lawrence Mitchell, April 27, 1987.

42. Interview with Tom Braden, October 6, 1986.

43. Braden, op. cit.

44. Interview with Tom Braden, op. cit.

45. Interview with Frank Holcomb, November 23, 1987.

46. Beedle Smith had been very close to the formation of wartime Intelligence, and had in fact talked Donovan into giving up his black propaganda division so that the OSS might survive (Bradley Smith, op. cit., pp. 118, 119).

47. At this stage Dulles was coordinating with H. Freeman Matthews at State while Wisner continued to deal with Robert Joyce, by now himself reporting to Matthews. Jealous of State's continuing influence with Wisner, Smith instructed Wisner "not to accept any summons to the State Department," but Wisner wasn't likely to alienate his longtime supporters in the Department (Montague, op. cit., vol. V, pp. 14, 15; see also Prados, op. cit., pp. 86, 87).

48. Interview with Howard Roman, op. cit.

49. Prados, op. cit., p. 82.

50. Interview with Chet Hanson, April 28, 1988.

51. Interview with Lawrence Houston, op. cit.

52. Ibid. For all his ferocity with underlings, Beedle never lost his staff officer's instinct for conceding what the political situation required to superiors. At the worst of the McCarthy blitz he told one Congressional Committee that undoubtedly "there are Communists in my organization," although none had turned up yet. Furthermore, with Smith's help, Agency officials were feeding documents in quantity to the insatiate Wisconsin senator. Richard Nixon reportedly negotiated a backstairs compromise (Jeffreys-Jones, *The CIA and American Democracy*, pp. 66, 74, 75).

53. Interview with Richard Stilwell, op. cit. Montague recurs to this image (vol. II, pp. 86, 90) and suggests that Wisner's way of presenting himself as "unduly slow and vague in his responses" was a technique through which Smith priorities such as pushing guerrilla operations off onto the Joint Chiefs was "discreetly opposed and eventually frustrated by Allen Dulles and Frank Wisner" (vol. IV, p. 35).

54. See Penny Lernoux, *In Banks We Trust*, p. 67.

55. Interview with Richard Stilwell, op. cit.

56. Interview with John Bross, May 23, 1985.

57. Interview with Gratian Yatsevich, January 15, 1988.

58. Interview with Mrs. Clayton Fritchey, May 24, 1985.

59. Ranelagh, op. cit., p. 198.

60. Interview with Al Ulmer, April 27, 1987.

61. Interview with Robert Amory, October 9, 1985.

62. Interview with Kenneth Giniger, June 5, 1987. Montague also mentions a "notable animosity in the personal relationship between Hedden and Wisner" (Montague, op. cit., vol. II, p. 120).

63. Barnes, op. cit., p. 667.

64. Giniger cites in particular Fritz Molden who built—and lost—a publishing empire in Vienna.

65. Interview with Lyman Kirkpatrick, May 11, 1982.

66. Ranelagh, op. cit., pp. 200, 201.

67. Interview with Howard Roman, op. cit.

68. Interview with Ed Applewhite, op. cit.

69. Interview with Richard Helms, October 8, 1985.

70. Interview with Mrs. Clayton Fritchey, op. cit.

71. Thomas Powers, op. cit., p. 49.

72. Interview with James McCargar, November 23, 1987.

73. Interview with Jack Blake, November 24, 1987.

74. Interview with Cleve Cram, June 7, 1988.

75. Interview with Roger Hollingshead, May 19, 1988.

76. Interview with Joe Bryan, op. cit.

77. Interview with Tom Braden, op. cit.

78. Interview with Frank Wisner, Jr., op. cit.

79. Thayer's inclinations in many departments remain hard to establish for sure; his friends insist that women were his entire game, and frequently his undoing. At one point, according to Frank Lindsay (interview, November 3. 1986), Thayer involved himself with the daughter of the Italian ambassador to the Quisling government in Croatia, Petrucci. Evidently Offie was instrumental in spiriting Petrucci out of Yugoslavia ahead of Tito's Partisans. Later on, in Austria, Thayer seems to have had a child with his Russian secretary, to whom he was married briefly.

80. Wolff, op. cit., p. 473.
81. Interview with Lawrence Houston, October 4, 1985.
82. See undated F.O.I.A. FBI file memo; Rumanian contacts in Paris.
83. CIA memo Sheffield Edwards, September 2, 1953 (F.O.I.A.).
84. Interview with Charles Murphy, op. cit.
85. Interview with Elizabeth Graham, op. cit.
86. Interview with Robert Amory, October 29, 1982.
87. Interview with Arthur Schlesinger, Jr., June 30, 1982. David Bruce's diaries throughout the fifties are replete with mention of dances, dinners, and drinking bouts at the Wisners' (see entries January 17, December 5, 7, 1953). On April 4, 1957, Bruce notes a long session of eating "the black stuff" (caviar) with Frank and the Phillip Grahams.
88. Interview with Frank Lindsay, op. cit.
89. Braden, op. cit.
90. Interview with Frank Wisner, Jr., op. cit.
91. Interview with Wendy Hazard, June 6, 1985.
92. Interview with Ellis Wisner, June 9, 1987.
93. Interview with Joe Bryan, op. cit.
94. Interview with Frank Wisner, Jr., op. cit.
95. Interview with Wendy Hazard, op. cit.

CHAPTER SEVENTEEN

1. Hoopes, op. cit., pp. 145, 146. Lucian Truscott and William Donovan himself also supposedly came into consideration.
2. David Bruce Journals, op. cit., January 2, 1953.
3. Interview with Mrs. Clayton Fritchey, October 13, 1987.
4. Donovan Archives, Carlisle Barracks, Donovan to Smith, September 21, 1950, Box 1A, Folder 7. Well afterward Donovan kept pounding away at Agency officials, as indicated by his exchange of March 21, 1957, with Lawrence Houston over admitting Vladko Macek of the Croation Peasant Party and his effort—prodded by Jay Lovestone—to bring Peter Stankovic into the United States.
5. Ibid., W. Stafford Reid to Donovan, January 29, 1951.
6. Ibid., memo, Donovan to Smith, November 3, 1950.
7. Ibid., Allen Dulles to Donovan, June 16, 1951.
8. Interview with Mrs. Clayton Fritchey, op. cit.
9. Interview with James McCargar, November 23, 1987.
10. Interview with Lyman Kirkpatrick, May 11, 1982.
11. Interview with Walter Elder, June 8, 1988.
12. Interview with Tom Braden, op. cit.
13. Interview with Walter Pforzheimer, May 14, 1982.
14. Lyman Kirkpatrick, *The U.S. Intelligence Community*, p. 33.
15. Mosley, op. cit., p. 273.
16. Interview with Tom Braden, op. cit.
17. Interview with Jack Blake, November 24, 1987.
18. Interview with Tom Braden, op. cit.
19. Ibid.
20. Interview with Walter Pforzheimer, op. cit.

21. Interview with Lyman Kirkpatrick, op. cit.

22. Interview with Richard Bissell, December 5, 1986.

23. Interview with Robert Amory, October 9, 1985.

24. Seymour Hersh, *The New York Times Magazine*, June 25, 1978.

25. Ibid. This sense that Angleton compartmented heavily even inside his CIA shop is seconded strongly by John Hadden, who oversaw the Israeli desk (interview with John Hadden, November 30, 1988).

26. Interview with Kermit Roosevelt, October 28, 1982.

27. Interview with Frank Lindsay, June 6, 1985.

28. Interview with Tom Parrott, June 9, 1988.

29. Interview with Richard Bissell, op. cit.

30. As matters developed, Angleton had been tipped off by Teddy Kollek years before as to Philby's final loyalties (interview with Kermit Roosevelt, op. cit.). Angleton resisted the idea, although he would later insist to the author, among others, that he had played disinformation back to Moscow through Philby.

31. Ranelagh, op. cit., p. 153.

32. Interview with Gratian Yatsevich, January 15, 1988.

33. See Bethell, op. cit., pp. 182–198.

34. Interview with Al Ulmer, op. cit.

35. Interview with Gratian Yatsevich, op. cit.

36. Ibid.

37. Bethell, op. cit., p. 198.

38. Interview with Gratian Yatsevich, op. cit.

39. Interview with Mrs. Clayton Fritchey, May 24, 1985, October 13, 1987. Interestingly enough, one of Dulles's primary complaints about Hillenkoetter had been that he was not careful enough about protecting the Agency.

40. Interview with Robert Amory, October 29, 1982. Amory had prepared for his role as DDI by succeeding M.I.T.'s Max Millikan as Assistant Director of the Agency's Research Branch (Montague, op. cit., vol. III, p. 95).

41. Interview with Richard Bissell, May 3, 1983.

42. Interview with Robert Amory, op. cit.

43. Hoopes, op. cit., p. 160.

44. See Department of State Telephone Summaries, Herder, Reel #1, number 939, March 21, 1953 (Yale University Library).

45. Simpson, op. cit., p. 239. Foster was particularly touchy at the prospect of right-wing charges of masking a certain measure of Establishment liberalism, and several times changed his mind publicly about whether he had or had not had hired Alger Hiss as president of the Carnegie Endowment (Lisagor and Lipsius, op. cit., p. 200).

46. Interview with Frank Lindsay, op. cit.

47. Interview with Ray Rocca, October 14, 1987.

48. Interview with Robert Amory, op. cit.; Powers, op. cit., p. 63.

49. Also see Simpson, op. cit., p. 237, etc.

CHAPTER EIGHTEEN

1. Hoopes, op. cit., pp. 126, 127.

2. Interview with Robert Amory, October 29, 1982.

3. Anthony Sampson's *The Seven Sisters* is a good source for the background of the crisis.

4. Ibid., p. 124.

5. Ambrose, op. cit., p. 193.

6. R. Harris Smith mss., op. cit. Smith further notes that in November 1950, Allen arranged a "red carpet reception" in New York for the Shah. He and other informed friends had concluded that certain economic opportunities ought to flow from our military patronage, presumably at British expense.

7. Kermit Roosevelt, *Countercoup*, p. 15.

8. Interview with Gratian Yatsevich, op. cit. For many of the happiest years of the U.S. association with Iran, Yatsevich was the CIA station chief in Teheran.

9. Miles Copeland, *The Game of Nations*, p. 63.

10. Interview with Kermit Roosevelt, op. cit.

11. Ibid. Richard Bissell emphasizes that for several years after he joined the Agency, managing Nasser was at the very top of the CIA list of operational priorities (interview with Richard Bissell, May 3, 1983).

12. Miles Copeland, *Without Cloak or Dagger*, p. 63.

13. See *The New York Times*, April 26, 1966.

14. Reinhard Gehlen, *The Service*, p. 260.

15. See Cookridge, op. cit., pp. 353, 354; also Bar-Zohar, *The Avengers*, p. 146.

16. In *Skorzeny*, by Glen Infield, the author traces the details of Skorzeny's thirteen-year relationship with Nasser. As an agent for recovering German industrial clients from Krupp to Messerschmitt, Skorzeny utilized his banking connections widely. He was Hjalmar Schacht's nephew by marriage (Infield, op. cit., pp. 169, 189, 190). In Bonn Skorzeny exerted a lot of clout as organizer of the ODESSA lobby of one-time SS officers, and captured as a spokesman Allen Dulles's intimate Eugen Gerstenmaier, the Christian Democratic Speaker of the Bundestag. A few years earlier a goon squad headed by Skorzeny had very nearly machine-gunned Gerstenmaier just after the July 20, 1944, attempt on Hitler's life (see Charles Wighton, *Adenauer*, p. 287, etc., and Allen Dulles, *Germany's Underground*, pp. 116, 117, 194).

17. Interview with Kermit Roosevelt, op. cit.

18. Ambrose, op. cit., pp. 197–199.

19. Rositzke, op. cit., p. 188.

20. State Department, Herder Telephone Summaries, John Foster Dulles, number 939, Reel #1, July 24, 1953, Yale University Library.

21. Interview with Kermit Roosevelt, op. cit.

22. Roosevelt, op. cit., pp. 1 ff.

23. Ambrose, op. cit., p. 204.

24. This figure, considerably lower than the usual estimates, came from Roosevelt himself (interview, op. cit.).

25. Ambrose, op. cit., pp. 199–209.

26. Corson, op. cit., p. 353.

27. Roosevelt, op. cit., p. 22.

28. Sampson, op. cit., pp. 130–133. Once Mossadeq was out, Sullivan and Cromwell helped negotiate the redivision of Iran's reserves which cut the American Sisters in. To compensate old client British Petroleum, Sullivan and Cromwell helped it onto the North Slope of Alaska, arranged a takeover

of Standard Oil of Ohio, and protected it from antitrust legislation in American courts (Lisagor and Lipsius, op. cit., p. 210).

29. Mosley, op. cit., pp. 348, 349.

30. See Copeland, *The Game of Nations*, pp. 50, 54.

31. Roosevelt, op. cit., p. 209.

32. Interview with Kermit Roosevelt, op. cit. Kim was increasingly restless in any case. Robert Amory maintains (interview, October 29, 1982) that Allen called Kermit in once Nasser became troublesome, and instructed him to get the dictator out. "Kim was absolutely terrified at the thought of going out there and arranging for the overthrow of Nasser with the support of the Egyptian army," Amory said. "He knew something of their torture methods, he just wouldn't do it." A botched attempt to line up the Syrian military against the leftist Ba'ath leadership further sullied Kim's reputation as "Mr. Political Action." He moved out and became a Gulf Oil executive, then a private consultant.

33. Two books seem to cover this incident most completely: *The CIA in Guatemala*, by Richard H. Immerman, and *Bitter Fruit*, by Stephen Schlesinger and Stephen Kinzer. Background details are largely derived from these two sources. The Fruit Company side is available in the book by Thomas McCann and Henry Scammell, *An American Company*.

34. Immerman, op. cit., pp. 71, 124.

35. Schlesinger and Kinzer, op. cit., p. 70.

36. Preussen, op. cit., p. 64.

37. Schlesinger and Kinzer, op. cit., p. 102.

38. David Bruce Journals, op. cit., October 8, 1952.

39. Schlesinger and Kinzer, op. cit., p. 103.

40. E. Howard Hunt, *Under Cover*, p. 183.

41. Interview with Robert Amory, October 29, 1982.

42. Corson, op. cit., p. 357.

43. Powers, op. cit., p. 86.

44. Schlesinger and Kinzer, op. cit., p. 110.

45. Months later, looking over the after-action reports, the prudent Cutler pointed up the "considerable hazard in depending on such strays" as Haney picked, and particularly in "allowing the indigenous force to select its own leaders" (Corson, op. cit., p. 358).

46. Schlesinger and Kinzer, op. cit., p. 112.

47. Interview with Frank Holcomb, November 23, 1987.

48. Church Committee, op. cit., Report IV, pp. 43, 58.

49. Immerman, op. cit., p. 111; interview with Janet Barnes Lawrence, November 8, 1985.

50. See Wyden, op. cit., pp. 38, 39.

51. David Atlee Phillips, *The Night Watch*, p. 34.

52. Interview with Kermit Roosevelt, op. cit.

53. Schlesinger and Kinzer, op. cit., p. 142.

54. Phillips, op. cit., p. 37.

55. See E. Howard Hunt, op. cit., pp. 99, 100.

56. Interview with Robert Amory, op. cit.

57. Corson, op. cit., p. 357.

58. Preussen, op. cit., pp. 370, 371.

59. Ibid.; Schlesinger and Kinzer, op. cit., pp. 132 ff.

60. Ibid., p. 145.
61. Interview with Frank Holcomb, op. cit.
62. Ibid.
63. Interview with Cleve Cram, op. cit.
64. Interview with Philip Corso, June 30, 1988.
65. Schlesinger and Kinzer, op. cit., p. 161.
66. Interview with Frank Holcomb, op. cit.
67. Interview with David Atlee Phillips, June 14, 1985.
68. Schlesinger and Kinzer, op. cit., p. 170.
69. Ibid., p. 122.
70. Interview with Frank Holcomb, op. cit.
71. Schlesinger and Kinzer, op. cit., p. 23.
72. Ibid., pp. 175–178.
73. Stephen E. Ambrose, *Eisenhower the President*, vol. II, p. 195.
74. Phillips, op. cit., p. 48.
75. Schlesinger and Kinzer, op. cit., p. 196.
76. Ibid., p. 204.
77. Interview with Frank Holcomb, op. cit.
78. Ibid.
79. Schlesinger and Kinzer, op. cit., p. 217.
80. Immerman, op. cit., p. 199.
81. Schlesinger and Kinzer, op. cit., pp. 220, 221.
82. Interview with Kermit Roosevelt, op. cit.
83. Interview with Lyman Kirkpatrick, October 5, 1985.
84. Interview with Frank Holcomb, op. cit.

CHAPTER NINETEEN

1. Ambrose, *Ike's Spies*, p. 244.
2. Church Committee Report, op. cit., chap. IV, p. 54.
3. Ambrose, *Eisenhower*, vol. II, pp. 226, 227.
4. Church Committee Report, op. cit., chap. IV, pp. 54, 55.
5. Ibid., p. 62.
6. Eleanor Dulles article in *The Forensic Quarterly*, vol. 43, August 1969.
7. Kolko, op. cit.
8. Allen Dulles papers, Beedle Smith to Dulles, October 4, 1954, Box 64, Mudd Library, Princeton University.
9. Interview with Ray Rocca, op. cit.
10. Interview with John Maury, February 10, 1982.
11. Interview with Tom Braden, op. cit.
12. Interview with John Maury, op. cit.; see David Martin, op. cit., p. 109.
13. Interview with James Critchfield, op. cit.
14. Interview with Peter Sichel, July 24, 1988.
15. Ibid.
16. Interview with Peter Sichel, July 24, 1988.
17. Interview with Tom Polgar, July 23, 1988.
18. Interview with Peter Jessup, July 23, 1988. Sutton's centerpiece, the Bund Deutscher Jugend, soon numbered 22,000 would-be saboteurs and assassination specialists. According to Tetens (op. cit., p. 76), not only the CIA

but also the Bonn government and several major West German businesses were supplying weapons, money, and training facilities to this Freikorps-like assembly of ex-Wehrmacht and SS officers. By this point, it's worthwhile to remember that the CIA's own station in Germany counted an overblown 1,700 people, America's purported infrastructure for rollback (Gilligan, op. cit., p. 211).

19. Interview with Harry Roman, November 25, 1987.

20. Interview with Colonel Trapper Drum, June 18, 1988.

21. Interview with Cleve Cram, op. cit.

22. Interview with Colonel Earle Larette, June 18, 1988.

23. Interview with Peter Jessup, op. cit.

24. Interview with Ray Cline, October 14, 1987.

25. Interview with Howard Roman, op. cit.

26. See David Bruce Journal, op. cit., November 15, 1949.

27. Interview with John Bross, May 11, 1985.

28. Kirkpatrick, op. cit., p. 128.

29. Ibid., p. 130.

30. Interview with Lyman Kirkpatrick, May 11, 1982.

31. Interview with Richard Bissell, December 6, 1986.

32. Interview with Lyman Kirkpatrick, op. cit.

33. Church Committee Report, op. cit., chap. IV, p. 49. Arthur Schlesinger, Jr., in *Robert Kennedy and His Times* (p. 456), quotes the Bruce-Lovett report as ascribing "more than 80 percent" of the CIA budget to clandestine operations.

34. See the exchange of letters between John McCloy and Allen Dulles at Princeton. McCloy is responding to a plea from Allen to intervene when Falkenhausen was about to stand trial in Belgium. McCloy did what he could "indirectly and informally" and got Robert Murphy, then U.S. ambassador to Belgium, to exert some drag on the situation. Falkenhausen drew a twelve-year sentence but was out of jail after three weeks (McCloy to Allen Dulles, March 16, 1950, Box 45, Mudd Library, Princeton University). Dulles had already approached McCloy concerning Ewald Loeser, a Krupp manager and important Crown Jewel.

35. Interview with Tom Braden, op. cit.

36. Allen Dulles papers, Truman Smith to Allen Dulles, September 23, 1954, Box 64, Mudd Library, Princeton University.

37. Allen Dulles papers, Allen Dulles to Truman Smith, November 25, 1955, Box 68, Mudd Library, Princeton University.

38. Corson, op. cit., pp. 469–471.

39. *Newsweek*, March 6, 1967.

40. Interview with Richard Helms, June 6, 1988.

41. Interview with Al Ulmer, April 27, 1987.

42. Allen Dulles papers, Allen Dulles to Truman Smith, November 25, 1955, Box 68, Mudd Library, Princeton University.

43. Mosley, op. cit., pp. 480, 485.

44. Hoopes, op. cit., p. 172.

45. Ibid., p. 132.

46. Ambrose, op. cit., p. 221.

47. Hoopes, op. cit., p. 246. Foster understood the quid pro quo between politics and economics. To the end he opposed the breakup of the Farben

complex and backed Everett Dirksen's efforts to surrender property confiscated by the Alien Property Custodian to prewar owners. When the Stinnes coal assets came up for auction, Foster helped rig the situation so that the Deutsche Bank, under Hermann Abs, picked up these vast holdings at well below market value (see Lisagor and Lipsius, op. cit., p. 209).

48. Kolko, op. cit., p. 702.

49. Hoopes is probably the best and toughest on Dulles as Secretary of State (see pp. 145, 158).

50. Isaacson and Thomas, op. cit., p. 563.

51. Interview with James McCargar, November 23, 1987.

52. See OSS-SSU documents, R.G. 226, Entry 88, Box 151, OSS cables, Allen Dulles to Lea, Hughes.

53. State Department cable summaries, Herder Group Number 939, John Foster Dulles, Reel #1, November 13, 1953, Yale University Library.

54. Interview with John Bross, June 6, 1988.

55. Hoehne and Zolling, pp. 178, 179, 191.

56. See Otto John, *Twice Through the Lines*, pp. 223, 226, etc. Especially on the American military intelligence side, a consensus would emerge that John had been a Communist plant all along. The British were less convinced, remembering that John had advised them in proceedings against Field Marshal von Manstein, Gehlen's original patron.

57. Interview with Colonel Earle Larette, op. cit.

58. Interview with Lieutenant General Arthur Trudeau, June 5, 1988.

59. Interview with James Critchfield, op. cit.

60. Hoehne and Zolling, op. cit. pp. 233, 235. Mary Ellen Reese has talked to a number of the successive CIA liaison appointees to Gehlen's Organization, and, sympathetic as she remains to them as individuals, notes their "lack of sophistication . . . (they could not even speak the language), and of professionalism in the field of intelligence." Several discount Gehlen's reports ("Die Uebersicht"), and maintain that Gehlen never even had a successful penetration of the East Bloc (op. cit., pp. 175, 183). Reese herself mentions one successful Gehlen source, Elli Barczatis" (ibid., p. 210). It is perhaps of interest that one counterintelligence specialist who stayed close to the Gehlen operation from the start, and became increasingly dubious, Clare Edward Petty, would ultimately be driven from the Agency by Angleton, Allen's security alter ego, on what are now perceived as the flimsiest of grounds (Reese, ibid., pp. 145, 212). (See David Martin, *Wilderness of Mirrors*, et al.).

61. Interview with James Critchfield, op. cit.

62. Cookridge, op. cit., p. 308.

63. Gehlen, op. cit., p. 196.

64. Allen Dulles papers, Allen Dulles to Charles J. V. Murphy, September 9, 1968, Box 167, Mudd Library, Princeton University.

65. Interview with Tom Braden, op. cit.

66. Cookridge, op. cit., p. 308.

67. Interview with John Bross, June 6, 1988.

68. Interview with James McCargar, op. cit.

69. Interview with Mark Wyatt, op. cit.

70. Interview with Richard Bissell, op. cit.

71. Interview with Howard Roman, op. cit.

72. Interview with Richard Helms, October 8, 1985.

CHAPTER TWENTY

1. Interview with John Bross, May 23, 1984. According to John Prados (op. cit., p. 120), McDowall was not alone. When Eisenhower himself attempted to push his one-time Army colleagues in behind the formation of an Eastern European unit, several resisted the idea. " 'Fellows,' Ike reportedly responded, 'tell me this. Just how high does a fellow have to go in this outfit before he can call the shots?' "

2. Interview with Colonel Earle Larette, op. cit. Jeffreys-Jones, in *The CIA and American Democracy*, claims the tunnel idea came out of Gehlen's shop (p. 105).

3. For the best treatment of the Tunnel Project see David Martin, op. cit., pp. 72–90.

4. Ibid., p. 67.

5. Ibid., p. 100.

6. Interview with Robert Amory, October 9, 1985.

7. See Walter Lefeber and Arthur Schlesinger, *Dynamics of World Power: A Documentary History of U.S. Foreign Policy*, vol.II, pp. 541, 548; *The New York Times*, June 5, 1956.

8. Interview with Robert Amory, October 9, 1985.

9. Interview with Richard Bissell, May 3, 1983.

10. See Stewart Steven, *The Spymasters of Israel*, p. 96.

11. Barnes, op. cit., pp. 651, 655.

12. Ray Cline, op. cit., pp. 186, 187.

13. David Binder article, *The New York Times*, November 30, 1976.

14. Interview with James Angleton, op. cit. Cline regards this incident as evidence that both Angleton and Wisner tended to overstate the importance of psychological resistance to the Soviets: "And I think it did tend a little bit in both cases to lead to a kind of admiration and idealization of the KGB model" (interview with Ray Cline, October 14, 1987).

15. See Stewart Steven, *Operation Splinter-Factor*, p. 158.

16. Ibid., p. 213.

17. Interview with Lawrence Houston, October 4, 1985.

18. Interview with Al Ulmer, April 8, 1988.

19. Interview with David Atlee Phillips, June 14, 1985.

20. Interview with Charles Saltzman, op. cit.

21. F.O.I.A., Fitness Report.

22. Cline, op. cit., pp. 179, 180.

23. Interview with Richard Bissell, May 3, 1983.

24. Interview with Jack Blake, November 24, 1987.

25. See Peter Wyden, op. cit., p. 10.

26. Interview with Mrs. Clayton Fritchey, May 24, 1985.

27. Allen Dulles papers, file transcript Rajk trial, Box 40, Mudd Library, Princeton University.

28. Interview with Al Ulmer, April 27, 1987.

29. *The New York Times*, September 2, 1950.

30. Stewart Steven, op. cit.

31. In time a considerable crowd of the less savory Eastern Europeans the OPC had brought in began to break the surface of the media. Howard Blum has nosed up several of the worst in his expose *Wanted! The Search*

for Nazis in America. Many of these new Americans traced back to the White Russian fanatics around General Wrangel who influenced Alfred Rosenberg, the Nazi theoretician (see *Who Financed Hitler?* by James and Suzanne Pool, pp. 55–59, etc.) Blum picks up Alexis Wrangel, the general's son, and traces his involvement with the Tolstoy Foundation (p. 69). Another favorite of Blum's is Bishop Valerian Trifa, last mentioned here while climbing into Baron Otto von Bolschwing's car to escape the Antonescu purge of the Iron Guard. Financed in the United States by Nicolae Malaxa (at that point a business partner of Otto Skorzeny), Trifa supposedly functioned as an OPC asset for the disruption of Romania. Sullivan and Cromwell represented Malaxa. Another beauty we imported was Andrija Artukovic, the Ustase Interior Minister and Eichmann apprentice during the Pavelic era.

32. Simpson, op. cit., p. 235.

33. Interview with James McCargar, November 23, 1987.

34. Cookridge, op. cit., p. 304.

35. See Bill Lomax, *Hungary 1956*, p. 129.

36. Stewart Alsop, *The Center*, p. 250.

37. Flora Lewis, op. cit., p. 239.

38. See *The New York Times*, September 2, 1950.

39. See Cord Meyer, *Facing Reality*, pp. 123–127.

40. State Department, John Foster Dulles, telephone summaries, Herder Series #939, Reel #5, October 25, 1956, Yale University Library.

41. Prados, op. cit., p. 123.

42. Allan Michie, *Voices Through the Iron Curtain*, pp. 138–158.

43. Meyer, op. cit., p. 128.

44. Corson, op. cit., p. 371. East German publications soon after the uprising went into detail. *Die Leipziger Volkszeitung*, for example, referred to a "Hungarian department" under the command of "a certain Colonel Kollenyi"; its "armed emigrants" joined a "league of Hungarian fighters under General Emil Justzi," which coordinated with U.S. Army counterintelligence "assault battalions." These "went over the border to Hungary after 23 October." Meanwhile, the "Free Europe" committee "collected numerous former members of the Hungarian SS . . . and on 25 and 26 October sent them in Red Cross vehicles across the Hungarian border," etc. "Colonel Bell"—Ladislas Farago—is cited as the "leader of the general staff" of this operation, and Lajos Somogyvari and four others from Radio Free Europe infiltrated to Cyoer "to lead the uprising there. . . ." Excerpts from this article appear in translation in an information summary distributed by the 66th CIC Group, Heidelberg, U.S. Army, and are classified as from a "usually reliable" source and "probably true" (from files of Charles Higham, *American Swastika*, Box 5, University of Southern California, Cinema-Television Library and Archives, Doheny Library).

45. Michie, op., cit., pp. 229, 230.

46. Substantial rumors were already making the rounds projecting a provisional government under former Minister-President Zoltan Tildy, and including the venerated Anna Kelthy and Bella Kovacs, the free-thinking leader of the outlawed Freedholders' Party (see "Hungary" in the *Encyclopedia Britannica*, 1957; also Kolko, op. cit., p. 215).

47. Interview with Jacob Beam, op. cit.

48. Ambrose, *Ike's Spies*, p. 236.

49. Prados, op. cit., p. 124. James Critchfield, op. cit., remembers "the Eastern European ops energetically pitching plans to Foster when Suez erupted."

50. Interview with Al Ulmer, April 27, 1987.

51. Interview with Howard Roman, November 25, 1987.

52. See Hoopes, op. cit., p. 350, etc.

53. Foster Dulles's habit of losing himself in lawyerly ingenuities supposedly prompted Churchill to characterize him as "the only bull I know who carries his own China cabinet around with him."

54. Interview with Robert Amory, October 9, 1982.

55. Interview with Kermit Roosevelt, op. cit.

56. Interview with Al Ulmer, April 27, 1988.

57. Interview with Robert Amory, op. cit. At the peak of the crisis, Sullivan and Cromwell primo Arthur Dean was functioning as intermediary among Foster Dulles, the oil companies, and Israel to keep both information and oil moving (Lisagor and Lipsius, op. cit., p. 210).

58. From Robert Amory address to Literary Society of Washington. D.C., March 15, 1975: "Hungary '56," pp. 14, 15. Ralph McGehee in *Deadly Deceits* refers to a CIA coup in Syria which was attempted—and failed—the same day Israeli troops invaded Egypt. There was obviously concern that Eisenhower's moral indignation might sound a lot less convincing if that got out (p. 28).

59. Hoopes, op., cit., p. 377.

60. Interview with Wendy Hazard, August 19, 1987.

61. Amory speech, op. cit., p. 20.

62. Interview with James McCargar, November 23, 1987.

63. Amory speech, op. cit., p. 20.

64. Michie, op. cit., p. 256. As the Kolkos remark, to the Hungarian "Prince-Primate" a proper status quo meant "the Hapsburg throne, the great estates, the privilege and the oppression." Meanwhile, inside the Hungarian Church, Jesuits were arguing for the feasibility of a Christian society within the Marxist state, while Mindszenty's Bench of Bishops agitated for confrontation (Kolko, op. cit., p. 213). See also Lomax, op. cit., pp. 133–137. There is a masterly treatment of the background of the Hungarian situation in James McCargar's classic, *A Short Course in the Secret War*, written under the nom de plume Christopher Felix.

65. Robert Amory speech, op. cit., p. 29.

66. Interview with Janet Barnes Lawrence, op. cit.

67. Interview with William Hood, October 10, 1987.

68. Michie, op. cit., p. 219.

69. See Cookridge, op. cit., p. 304; Michie, pp. 226, 258.

70. Prados, op. cit., p. 126.

71. Meyer, op. cit., pp. 129, 130.

72. Interview with Andor Klay, October 12, 1987.

73. Interview with Richard Bissell, May 3, 1983.

74. Lomax, op. cit., p. 129; Robert T. Holt, *Radio Free Europe*, pp. 198, 199.

75. Interview with Richard Bissell, op. cit. Stephen Ambrose (op. cit., p. 238) has written that "The CIA sent Red-Sox/Red-Cap groups in Budapest into action to join the Freedom Fighters and to help organize them."

76. Michie, op. cit., p. 251.
77. Hoopes, op. cit., p. 381.
78. Robert Amory speech, op. cit., p. 22.
79. Ambrose, *Eisenhower*, vol. II, p. 356.
80. Lomax, op. cit., p. 74.
81. Mosley, op. cit., p. 420.
82. Colby, op. cit., pp. 134, 135.
83. Powers, op. cit., p. 75.
84. Interview with Eleanor Dulles, op. cit.
85. Interview with Paul Nitze, op. cit.
86. Interview with Al Ulmer, April 8, 1988.
87. Interview with Charles J. V. Murphy, op. cit.
88. Ranelagh, op. cit., p. 307.
89. Interview with Paul Nitze, op. cit.

CHAPTER TWENTY-ONE

1. Warren Unna, "Who Watches the Watchman?" *Harper's Magazine*, April 1958.
2. Ibid.
3. Kermit Roosevelt, op. cit., p. 120.
4. Arthur Schlesinger, op. cit., p. 456.
5. Ambrose, *Ike's Spies*, pp. 240, 241; also see Gray obituary, *The New York Times*, November 27, 1982; also see Barnes, op. cit., p. 668. Jeffreys-Jones remarks that Gordon Gray sometimes complained that the special group was not kept informed fully by Allen Dulles, and threatened initiatives of its own (*The CIA and American Democracy,* p. 96).
6. Unna, op. cit.
7. Interview with Roger Hilsman, May 31, 1987.
8. See Ambrose, op. cit., pp. 242, 243; Corson, op. cit., pp. 372, 373.
9. Church Committee Report, op. cit., vol. IV, pp. 60–62.
10. Ambrose, *Eisenhower*, vol. II, p. 395.
11. Arthur Schlesinger, op. cit., pp. 455, 456.
12. *Current Biography,* 1945.
13. Corson, op, cit., p. 371.
14. Interview with Howard Roman, November 25, 1987.
15. Interview with William Corson, March 25, 1988; interview with Ray Cline, October 14, 1987. The distinction between CIA and CIC units was sometimes more bureacratic than meaningful since many of the carryover OPC elements operated under CIC cover.
16. David Binder, *The New York Times*, November 30, 1976.
17. Dunlop, op. cit., pp. 501, 502.
18. Interview with Philip Corso, op. cit.
19. Allen Dulles papers, Houston to Dulles, March 10, 1955, Box 66, Mudd Library, Princeton University.
20. Brown, op. cit., p. 830.
21. Wisner description illness, F.O.I.A., January 4, 1957 (CIA release).
22. Interview with Walter Elder, June 8, 1988.
23. Interview with Wendy Hazard, June 6, 1985.

24. Cline, op, cit., p. 205.

25. Joseph Smith, *Portrait of a Cold Warrior*, p. 197.

26. Ibid., p. 220.

27. Nasser especially annoyed Foster Dulles, in view of American largesse. "If that Colonel of yours pushes us too far," Allen Dulles told Miles Copeland, "we will break him in half" (Powers, op. cit., p. 85).

28. Smith, op. cit., pp. 213, 214.

29. Prados, op. cit., p. 134.

30. L. Fletcher Prouty, *The Secret Team*, p. 327.

31. Interview with Robert Amory, October 29, 1982.

32. Joseph Smith, op. cit., p. 232.

33. Prados, op. cit., p. 136.

34. Interview with Al Ulmer, April 27, 1988; Mrs. Clayton Fritchey, May 24, 1985.

35. See Prouty, op. cit., pp. 323, 324.

36. Prados, op. cit., pp. 139, 140.

37. Ibid., p. 141.

38. Ibid., p. 143.

39. Prouty, op. cit., pp. 325, 326.

40. Interview with Al Ulmer, April 27, 1988.

41. Marchetti and Marks, op. cit., p. 299; in *Deadly Deceits*, Ralph McGehee, who worked Southeast Asia for the Agency for some years, directly implicates the CIA in the revolt of 1965 which ruined Sukarno and the Indonesian Communist Party.

42. From detailed notes of P.F.I.A.B. summation in 1958, J. P. Coyne to Robert F. Kennedy, May 12, 1961.

43. Ambrose, *Ike's Spies*, pp. 262, 303.

44. Interview with Mrs. Clayton Fritchey, May 24, 1985.

45. Interview with Wendy Hazard, June 6, 1985.

46. Interview with Robert Amory, October 9, 1985.

47. Interview with Charles J. V. Murphy, op. cit.

48. Interview with Frank Lindsay, June 6, 1985.

49. Interview with Mrs. Clayton Fritchey, June 9, 1987, April 19, 1988.

50. Interview with Ellis Wisner, June 9, 1987.

51. Interview with Paul Nitze, op. cit.

52. Interview with Lyman Kirkpatrick, May 11, 1982.

53. Interview with Carlton Swift, April 17, 1988.

54. Interview with Cleve Cram, op. cit.

55. Interview with Al Ulmer, April 27, 1987.

56. An Agency recruiter sent down from Tokyo blew out a hotel electrical circuit with his heavy-duty polygraph equipment. The ensuing police raid landed both case officer and agent in jail and required a written apology from Dean Rusk to extract Allen's intelligence officer (*The New York Times*, April 25, 1966).

57. Ibid.

58. Ambrose, op. cit., p. 285.

59. Interview with Frank Holcomb, November 23, 1987.

60. Prados, op. cit., p. 142.

61. Arthur Schlesinger, op. cit., p. 456.

62. Wyden, op. cit., p. 96. Another excellent, solid source is Haynes Johnson's *The Bay of Pigs*.

63. Wyden, op. cit., p. 24 (footnote).
64. Powers, op. cit., pp. 146, 147.
65. Ibid., p. 137.
66. Jimmy ("The Weasel") Fratiano, *The Last Mafioso*, p. 238.
67. Wyden, op. cit., p. 25.
68. Phillips, op. cit., p. 130.
69. Wyden, op. cit., p. 34.
70. Interview with Al Ulmer, April 27, 1987.
71. Interview with Lyman Kirkpatrick, op. cit.
72. Arthur Schlesinger, *A Thousand Days*, p. 230.
73. Interview with Richard Bissell, May 3, 1983.
74. Wyden, op. cit., pp. 88, 89.
75. Schlesinger, op. cit., p. 242.
76. Ibid., p. 243.
77. Interview with Richard Bissell, op. cit.
78. Arthur Schlesinger, op. cit., p. 235; Powers, op. cit., p. 109.
79. Roger Hilsman, *To Move a Nation*, p. 31.
80. Wyden, op. cit., pp. 190–199; interview with Robert Amory, October 29, 1982.
81. Powers, op. cit., p. 109.
82. Arthur Schlesinger, op. cit., p. 271; also interview with Arthur Schlesinger, June 30, 1982; also see Wyden, op. cit., p. 157.
83. Arthur Schlesinger, op. cit., p. 271.

CHAPTER TWENTY-TWO

1.Wyden, op. cit., p. 311.
2. Lyman Kirkpatrick, "Paramilitary Case Study: The Bay of Pigs." *War College Review*, November–December 1972, pp. 39, 40.
3. Interview with Lyman Kirkpatrick, op. cit.
4. Interview with Walter Elder, op. cit.; see also *Encyclopedia Britannica Yearbook*, 1963, British Guiana, p. 223.
5. Carlton Swift, op. cit.
6. Interview with Mrs. Clayton Fritchey, April 13, 1988.
7. Interview with Charles J. V. Murphy, op. cit.
8. Interview with Ellis Wisner, op. cit.
9. Material from F.O.I.A. releases via CIA; Frank Wisner obituary, *The Washington Post*, October 31, 1965.
10. This material, obtained via F.O.I.A., had even the title of the publication removed before it was made available. Probably *Studies in Intelligence*.
11. According to Archie Roosevelt in *For Lust of Knowing*, JFK was reputed to have had a go at Christine Keeler in July of 1962, a source of concern to John McCone. As London station chief, Wisner was presumably responsible for keeping track of this episode, and he must have been familiar with the principals of the Profumo Affair.
12. Mladin Zaubica, *The Year of the Rat*.
13. Interview with Wendy Hazard, June 6, 1985.
14. See Arthur Krock Papers, Frank Wisner to Gilbert Highet, April 19, 1964, Box 61, Mudd Library, Princeton University.

15. Allen Dulles Papers, Frank Wisner to John McCone, March 4, 1965 (copy to Allen Dulles), Box 139, Mudd Library, Princeton University.
16. Interview with Mrs. Clayton Fritchey, May 24, 1985.
17. F.O.I.A. disclosure from Wisner file.
18. Interview with William Hood, October 10, 1987.
19. Interview with Janet Barnes Lawrence, op. cit.
20. Interview with Charles J. V. Murphy, October 10, 1987.
21. Obituary, *The New York Times*, October 30, 1965.
22. Obituary, *The Washington Post*, October 31, 1965.
23. The F.O.I.A. State Department Report, Fall Term 1946.
24. Interview with Mrs. Clayton Fritchey, October 13, 1987.
25. Congressional Record, April 25, 1950.
26. Frenchy Grombach, who is believed to have slipped McCarthy most of his ammunition here, was now under suspicion himself for having received unauthorized payoffs from the Dutch electrical giant Philips. According to Christopher Simpson (*Blowback,* pp. 235, 236), one of Grombach's key assets was former SS General Karl Wolff.
27. Interview with Al Ulmer, April 8, 1988.
28. Interview with Joe Bryan, op. cit.
29. F.O.I.A., F.B.I. memo, March 4, 1950.
30. F.O.I.A., F.B.I. Field Report, August 2, 1950; F.B.I. office memo from Guy Hottel, July 21, 1950.
31. F.O.I.A., F.B.I. records, Tracey to Hoover, June 13, 1951.
32. F.O.I.A., F.B.I. records, James McInerny to J. Edgar Hoover, June 21, 1951.
33. F.O.I.A., F.B.I. records, Belmont to Keay, August 7, 1950.
34. F.O.I.A., F.B.I. records, memo Tolson to Ladd, February 5, 1953.
35. Brownell and Billings, op. cit., p. 286.
36. F.O.I.A., F.B.I. report, December 10, 1952; see also Secretary of Defense, Memo for General Olmsted from Thomas Murray, October 6, 1954; see also *The Washington Times-Herald*, November 11, 1952.
37. F.O.I.A., F.B.I. reports, W. A. Branigan to A. H. Belmont, November 21, 1952.
38. Interview with Paul Nitze, op. cit.
39. Interview with Cleve Cram, op. cit.
40. State Department, Herder Series, Telephone Summaries, number 939, Reel #1, March 24, 1954.
41. Interview with Mrs. Clayton Fritchey, October 13, 1987.
42. *The Washington Star*, December 8, 1952, February 27, 1953.
43. The F.B.I. memos fly thickest during 1954 (February 24, March 6, 18, 31, etc.).
44. F.O.I.A., F.B.I. reports, U.S. Department of Justice, U.S. Attorney Baltimore Report, October 24, 1969, file 58-398.
45. Interview with James Angleton, March 1, 1987.
46. Offie Obituary, *The Washington Post*, June 22, 1972.
47. Interview with Mrs. Llewelyn Thompson, June 9, 1987.
48. Interview with Hector Prudhomme, op. cit.
49. Interview with Mark Wyatt, op. cit.
50. Interview with Douglas MacArthur II, op. cit.
51. Offie obituary, *The Washington Post*, June 22, 1972.

52. See last section Brownell and Billings, op. cit.

53. *The Washington Post*, December 15, 1947.

54. Allen Dulles Papers, Wisner to Dulles, February 3, 1964, Box 137, Mudd Library, Princeton University.

55. Allen Dulles Papers, Wisner to Dulles, Box 137, December 30, 1964, Mudd Library, Princeton University.

56. Interview with Howard Roman, November 25, 1987. As with Foster, Allen often enjoyed the hospitality of Clarence Dillon, including the use of his country homes; Dillon's generosity helped establish the specialized library system at Princeton where so many of the Cold-War archons ultimately deposited their papers.

57. Interview with Garner Ranney, June 9, 1988.

58. Interview with Howard Roman, op. cit.

59. Interview with Howard Roman, July 30, 1988.

60. *The New York Times*, February 2, 1969.

61. Interview with Garner Ranney, op. cit.

62. Thomas Powers, op. cit., pp. ix, x.

Bibliography

Accoce, Pierre, and Pierre Quet. *A Man Called Lucy*. New York: Berkley, 1968.

Alexander, Charles C. *Holding the Line: The Eisenhower Era, 1952–1961*. Bloomington: Indiana Univ. Press. 1975.

Allen, Peter. *The Windsor Secret*. New York: Stein & Day., 1984.

Alsop, Stewart. *The Center*. New York: Harper & Row/Hodder & Stoughton, 1968.

Alsop, Stewart, and Thomas Braden. *Sub Rosa*. New York: Reynal & Hitchcock, 1946.

Ambrose, Stephen E. *Ike's Spies*. New York: Doubleday, 1981.

———. *Eisenhower the President*. New York: Simon & Schuster, 1983, 1984.

Ambruster, Howard Watson. *Treason's Peace*. New York: The Beechhurst Press, 1947.

Andrews, Christopher. *Her Majesty's Secret Service*. New York: Elisabeth Sifton Books/Viking, 1985.

Bancroft, Mary. *Autobiography of a Spy*. New York: Morrow, 1983.

Barnet, Richard J. *The Alliance*. New York: Simon & Schuster, 1983.

Barron, John. *The KGB Today*. New York: Berkley, 1983.

Bar-Zohar, Michael. *The Avengers*. New York: Hawthorne, 1967.

———. *Spies in the Promised Land*. Boston, Houghton Mifflin, 1972.

Beal, John R. *John Foster Dulles*. New York: Harper, 1957.

Becket, Henry S. A. *The Dictionary of Espionage*. New York: Stein & Day, 1986.

Bethell, Nicholas. *The Last Secret*. New York: Basic Books, 1974.

———. *The Great Betrayal*. New York: Hodder & Stoughton, 1984.

Bidwell, Bruce W. *History of the Military Intelligence Division, Department of the Army General Staff: 1775–1941*. Washington, D.C.: Univ. Publications of America, 1986.

Bishop, Robert, and E. S. Crayfield. *Russia Astride the Balkans*. New York: Robert McBride, 1948.

Black, Peter R. *Ernst Kaltenbrunner*. Princeton: Princeton Univ. Press. 1984.

Blum, Howard. *Wanted!* New York: Quadrangle, 1977.

Blum, John Morton. *The Morgenthau Diaries: The Years of War, 1941–1945*. Boston: Houghton Mifflin, 1967.

Bohlen, Charles E. *Witness to History 1929–1969*. New York: Norton, 1973.

Bokun, Branko. *A Spy in the Vatican*. New York: Praeger, 1973.

Bonsal, Stephen. *Unfinished Business*. New York: Doubleday, Doran, 1944.

Borkin, Joseph. *The Crime and Punishment of I. G. Farben*. New York: Free Press/Macmillan, 1978.

Bower, Tom. *Blind Eye to Murder*. London/Toronto: Granada 1983.

———. *The Butcher of Lyon*. London: Michael Joseph, 1984.

———. *The Paperclip Conspiracy*. Boston: Little, Brown, 1987.

Bowie, Beverly. *Operation Bughouse*. New York: Dodd, Mead, 1947.

Brissaud, Andre. *The Nazi Secret Service*. New York: Norton, 1974.

Brown, Anthony Cave. *The Last Hero*. New York: Times Books, 1982.

———. *Bodyguard of Lies*. New York: Harper & Row, 1975.

———. *"C"*. New York: Macmillan, 1987.

Brownell, Will, and Richard N. Billings. *So Close to Greatness*. New York: Macmillan, 1987.

Bullitt, Orville H. *For the President*. Boston: Houghton Mifflin, 1972.

Bullitt, William C. *The Great Globe Itself*. New York: Scribner's, 1946.

Burke, Michael. *Outrageous Good Fortune*. Boston/Toronto: Little, Brown, 1984.

Childs, J. Rives. *Let the Credit Go*. New York: Giniger, 1983.

Christy. Jim. *The Price of Power*. New York: Doubleday, 1984.

Cianfarra, Camille M. *The Vatican and the War*. New York: American Book-Stratford Press, 1944.

Cline, Ray S. *The CIA under Reagan, Bush and Casey*. Washington, D.C.: Acropolis Books, 1981.

Coffin, William Sloane, Jr. *Once to Every Man*. New York: Atheneum, 1977.

Colby, William. *Honorable Men*. New York: Simon & Schuster, 1978.

Colvin, Ian. *Chief of Intelligence*. London: Victor Gollancz, 1951.

Conot, Robert. *Justice at Nuremburg*. New York: Harper & Row. 1983.

Cookridge, E. H. *Gehlen*. New York: Random House, 1972.

Copeland, Miles. *The Game of Nations*. New York: Simon & Schuster, 1969.

———. *Without Cloak or Dagger*. New York: Simon & Schuster, 1974.

Corson, William R. *The Armies of Ignorance*. New York: Dail Press/James Wade Books, 1977.

Corson, William R., Susan B. Trento, and J. Joseph. *Widows*. New York: Crown, 1989.

Deacon, Richard. *The Israeli Secret Service*. New York: Taplinger, 1980.

———. *A History of the British Secret Service*. London/Toronto: Panther Books/Granada, 1980.

De Gaulle, Charles. *The Complete War Memoirs of Charles De Gaulle*. New York: Da Capo, 1967.

Demaris, Ovid. *The Last Mafioso*. Toronto/New York: Bantam, 1981.

Dodd, Martha. *Through Embassy Eyes*. New York: Harcourt, Brace, 1939.

Dodd, William E., and Martha Dodd. *Ambassador Dodd's Diary (1933–1938)*. New York: Harcourt, Brace, 1941.

Downes, Donald. *The Scarlet Thread*. New York: British Book Centre, 1953.

DuBois, Josiah E., Jr. *The Devil's Chemists*. Boston: Beacon Press, 1952.

Dulles, Allen, *The Craft of Intelligence*. New York: Harper & Row, 1963.
———. *Germany's Underground*. New York: Macmillan, 1947.
———. *Great True Spy Stories*. New Jersey: Castle, 1968.
———. *The Secret Surrender*. New York: Harper & Row, 1966.
Dulles, Allen, and Hamilton Fish Armstrong. *Can America Stay Neutral?* New York: Harper, 1939.
Dulles, Eleanor Lansing. *The Bank for International Settlements at Work*. New York: Macmillan, 1932.
———. *John Foster Dulles: The Last Year*. New York: Harcourt, Brace, 1963.
Dulles, John Foster. *War, Peace and Change*. New York: Harper, 1939.
Dunlop, Richard. *Donovan*. New York: Rand, McNally, 1982.
Edwards, M. P., and Kenneth, Dunne. *A Study of a Master Spy*. London: Housmans Publishers/Dalton House, 1961.
Emerson, Steven. *Secret Warriors*. New York: Putnam, 1988.
Farago, Ladislas. *The Game of the Foxes*. New York: Bantam, 1971.
———. *Aftermath*. New York: Simon & Schuster, 1974.
Farnsworth, Beatrice. *William C. Bullitt and the Soviet Union*. Bloomington: Indiana Univ. Press, 1967.
Felix, Christopher. *A Short Course in the Secret War*. New York: Dutton, 1963.
Ferrell, Robert. *Woodrow Wilson and World War I*. New York: Harper & Row, 1985.
Finder, Joseph. *Red Carpet*. New York: Holt, Rinehart & Winston, 1983.
Fischer-Galati, Stephen. *The New Rumania*. Cambridge: MIT Press, 1967.
Foot, M. R. D. *SOE in France*. London: Her Majesty's Stationary Office, 1966.
———. *SOE 1940–46*. London: B.B.C., 1984.
Ford, Corey. *Donovan of OSS*. Boston: Little, Brown, 1970.
Forrestal, James. *The Forrestal Diaries*. New York: Viking, 1951.
Fowler, W. B. *British–American Relations 1917–1918*. Princeton: Princeton Univ. Press, 1969.
Fratiano, Jimmy. *The Last Mafioso*. New York: Bantam, 1981.
Funk, Arthur Layton. *Charles de Gaulle*. Univ. of Oklahoma Press, 1959.
———. *The Politics of Torch*. Univ. of Kansas Press, 1974.
Garlinski, Jozef. *The Swiss Corridor*. London/Toronto: J. M. Dent, 1981.
Gehlen, Reinhard. *The Service*. New York: World, 1972.
Gelfand, Lawrence E. *The Inquiry*. New Haven: Yale Univ. Press, 1963.
Gilligan, Tom. *CIA Life*. Guilford, Conn.: Foreign Intelligence Press, 1991.
Gisevius, Hans Bernd. *To the Bitter End*. London: Jonathan Cape, 1948.
Grew, Joseph C. *Turbulent Era*. Boston: Houghton Mifflin, 1952.
Grombach, John V. *The Great Liquidator*. New York, Doubleday, 1980.
Hagen, Louis. *The Secret War for Germany*. New York: Stein & Day, 1969.
Heiden, Konrad. *Der Fuehrer*. Boston: Houghton Mifflin, 1944.
Higham, Charles. *American Swastika*. New York: Doubleday, 1985.
———. *The Duchess of Windsor*. New York: McGraw-Hill, 1988.
———. *Trading with the Enemy*. New York: Delacorte, 1983.
Hilger, Gustav, and Alfred G. Meyer. *The Incompatible Allies*. New York: Macmillan, 1953.
Hilsman, Roger. *To Move a Nation*. New York: Doubleday, 1967.
Hoehne, Heinz. *Canaris*. New York: Doubleday, 1979.
———. *The Order of the Death's Head*. London: Secker & Warburg, 1980.

Hoehne, Heinz, and Hermann Zolling. *The General Was a Spy*. New York: Coward, McCann & Geoghegan, 1972.
Hoettl, Wilhelm. *Hitler's Paper Weapon*. London: Rupert Hart-Davis, 1955.
———. *The Secret Front*. New York: Praeger, 1954.
Holt, Robert T. *Radio Free Europe*. Minneapolis: Univ. of Minnesota Press, 1958.
Hoopes, Townsend. *The Devil and John Foster Dulles*. Boston: Little, Brown, 1973.
Hunt, E. Howard. *The Gaza Intercept*. New York: Stein & Day, 1981.
———. *Give Us This Day*. New York: Arlington House, 1973.
———. *Under Cover*. New York: Berkley, 1974.
Hyde, H. Montgomery. *Secret Intelligence Agent*. New York: St. Martin's Press, 1982.
———. *Room 3603*. New York: Farrar, Straus, 1963.
Ickes, Harold L. *The Secret Diary of Harold L. Ickes*, New York: Simon & Schuster, 1953.
Immerman, Richard H. *The CIA in Guatemala*. Univ. of Texas Press, 1982.
Infield, Glenn. *Skorzeny*. New York: Military Heritage Press/Marboro Book Co., 1981.
Isaacson, Walter, and Evan Thomas. *The Wise Men*. New York: Simon & Schuster, 1986.
Irving, David. *Goering*. New York: Avon, 1989.
Jeffreys-Jones, Rhodri. *American Espionage*. New York: Free Press/Macmillan, 1977.
———. *The CIA and American Democracy*. New Haven/London: Yale Univ. Press, 1989.
John, Otto. *Twice Through the Lines*. New York: Harper & Row, 1972.
Johnson, Haynes. *The Bay of Pigs*. New York: Norton, 1964.
Johnson, Paul. *Modern Times*. New York: Harper & Row, 1983.
Jones, John Price, and Paul Merrick Hollister. *The German Secret Service in America*. Boston: Small, Maynard, 1918.
Kaplan, Justin. *Lincoln Steffans*. New York: Simon & Schuster, 1974.
Kahn, David. *Hitler's Spies*. New York: Macmillan, 1978.
Kennan, George F. *From Prague after Munich*. Princeton: Princeton Univ. Press, 1968.
———. *Memoirs 1925–1950*. Boston: Little, Brown, 1967.
———. *Memoirs 1950–1963*. Boston: Little, Brown, 1972.
Keynes, John Maynard. *The Economic Consequences of the Peace*. New York: Harcourt, Brace & Howe, 1920.
Kimball, Warren. *Swords or Ploughshares?* Philadelphia: Lippincott, 1976.
Kirkpatrick, Lyman B., Jr. *The Real CIA*. New York: Macmillan, 1986.
———. *The U.S. Intelligence Community*. New York: Hill & Wang, 1973.
Kolko, Joyce, and Gabriel Kolko. *The Limits of Power*. New York: Harper & Row, 1972.
Lamphere, Robert, and Thomas Shachtman. *The FBI–KGB War*. New York: Random House, 1986.
Lang, Jochen von. *The Secretary*. Ohio Univ. Press, 1981.
Langguth, A. J. *Hidden Terrors*. New York: Pantheon, 1978.
Latham, Aaron. *Orchids for Mother*. Boston/Toronto: Little, Brown, 1977.
Lernoux, Penny. *In Banks We Trust*. New York: Anchor/Doubleday, 1984.

Lewis, Flora, *Red Pawn*. New York: Doubleday & Co., 1965.

Linklater, Magnus, Isabel Hilton, and Neal Ascherson. *The Nazi Legacy*. New York: Holt, Rinehart & Winston, 1984.

Lisagor, Nancy, and Frank Lipsius. *A Law Unto Itself*. New York: Paragon House, 1989.

Loftus, John. *The Belarus Secret*. New York: Knopf, 1982.

Lomax, Bill. *Hungary 1956*. New York: St. Martin's Press, 1976.

Lorant, Stefan. *Sieg Heil*. New York: Norton, 1974.

Lorwin, Lewis L. *The International Labor Movement*. New York: Harper, 1953.

Lorwin, Val R. *The French Labor Movement*. Cambridge: Harvard Univ. Press, 1954.

Macmillan, Harold. *The Blast of War*. New York: Harper & Row, 1968.

———. *Riding the Storm*. New York: Harper & Row, 1971.

Marchetti, Victor, and John D. Marks. *The CIA and the Cult of Intelligence*. New York: Knopf, 1974.

Manchester, William. *The Arms of Krupp*. Boston/Toronto: Little, Brown, 1968.

Martin, David C. *Wilderness of Mirrors*. New York: Harper & Row. 1980.

Martin, James Stewart. *All Honorable Men*. Boston: Little, Brown, 1950.

Masterman, J. C. *The Double Cross System*. New York: Ballantine, 1972.

May, Ernest R. *Knowing One's Enemies*. Princeton: Princeton Univ. Press, 1984.

McCann, Thomas, and Henry Scammell. *An American Company*. New York: Crown, 1976.

McGehee, Ralph. *Deadly Deceits*. New York: Sheridan Square, 1983.

Mee, Charles L., Jr. *The End of Order*. New York: Dutton, 1980.

———. *The Marshall Plan*. New York: Simon & Schuster, 1984.

———. *Meeting at Potsdam*. New York: M. Evans, 1975.

Meyer, Cord. *Facing Reality*. New York: Harper & Row, 1980.

Michie, Allan A. *Voices Through the Iron Curtain*. New York: Dodd, Mead, 1963.

Monnet, Jean. *Memoirs*. New York: Doubleday, 1978.

Morgan, Ted. *FDR*. New York: Simon & Schuster, 1985.

Mosle, Ted, and Robin Winks. "Where Differences of Long Standing Begin." (Undergraduate thesis, Yale Univ., Davenport House, 1987).

Mosley, Leonard. *Dulles*. New York: Dial, 1978.

Murphy, Robert. *Diplomat Among Warriors*. New York: Doubleday, 1964.

Nagy-Talavera, Nicholas M. *The Green Shirts and the Others*. Stanford, Calif.: Stanford Univ., Hoover Institution Press, 1970.

Nutting, Anthony. *Nasser*. New York: Dutton, 1972.

O'Toole, G. J. A. *The Encyclopedia of American Intelligence and Espionage*. New York: Facts on File, 1988.

Page, Bruce, David Leith, and Phillip Knightley. *The Philby Conspiracy*. New York: Ballantine, 1981.

Pash, Boris. *The Alsos Mission*. New York: Charter, 1969.

Persico, Joseph E. *Piercing the Reich*. New York: Viking, 1979.

Philby, Kim. *My Silent War*. New York: Grove Press, 1968.

Phillips, David Atlee. *The Night Watch*. New York: Atheneum, 1977.

Pincher, Chapman. *Their Trade Is Treachery*. New York: Bantam, 1982.

Pool, James, and Suzanne Pool. *Who Financed Hitler*? New York: Dial, 1978.
Powers, Thomas. *The Man Who Kept the Secrets*. New York: Knopf, 1979.
Prados, John. *The President's Secret Wars*. New York: Morrow, 1986.
Prouty, L. Fletcher. *The Secret Team*. Englewood Cliffs, N.J.: Prentice Hall, 1973.
Pruessen, Ronald W. *John Foster Dulles—The Road to Power*. New York: Free Press/Macmillan, 1982.
Putlitz, Wolfgang Zu. *The Putlitz Dossier*. London: Allan Wingate, 1957.
Quigley, Carroll. *Tragedy and Hope*. New York: Macmillan, 1966.
Radosh, Ronald. *American Labor and United States Foreign Policy*. New York: Random House, 1969.
Ranelagh, John. *The Agency*. New York: Simon & Schuster, 1986.
Read, Anthony, and David Fisher. *Colonel Z*. New York: Viking, 1985.
———. *Operation Lucy*. New York: Coward, McCann & Geoghegan, 1980.
Reese, Mary Ellen. *General Reinhard Gehlen*. Fairfax, Va: George Mason Univ. Press, 1990.
Reiss, Curt. *The Nazis Go Underground*. New York: Doubleday, Doran, 1944.
Reitlinger, Gerald. *The SS: Alibi of a Nation (1922–1945)*. Englewood Cliffs, N.J.: Prentice Hall, 1981.
Ritter, Gerhard. *Carl Goerdeler und Die Deutsche Widerstandsbewegung*. Stuttgart: Deutsche Verlags-Anstalt, 1955.
Roberts, Henry L. *Rumania*. New York: Archon Books, 1969.
Rogers, James Grafton. *Wartime Washington: The Secret OSS Journal of James Grafton Rogers*. (Frederick, Md.: Univ. Publications of America, 1987.
Roosevelt, Archie. *For Lust of Knowing*. Boston: Little, Brown, 1988.
Roosevelt, Elliott. *As He Saw It*. New York: Duell Sloan & Pearce, 1946.
Roosevelt, Kermit. *Countercoup*. New York: McGraw-Hill, 1981.
———. *The Overseas Targets*, Vol. 2., New York: Walker & Co., 1976.
Root, Waverly. *The Secret History of the War*. New York: Scribners, 1945.
Rositzke, Harry. *The CIA's Secret Operations*. New York: Reader's Digest Press, 1977.
Rowan, Richard Wilmer. *Secret Service*. New York: Hawthorn, 1967.
Sampson, Anthony. *The Seven Sisters*. New York: Viking, 1975.
———. *The Sovereign State of ITT*. New York: Stein & Day, 1973.
Sayer, Ian, and Douglas Botting. *America's Secret Army*. New York: Franklin Watts, 1989.
Sayers, Michael, and Albert E. Kahn. *The Great Conspiracy*. Boston: Little, Brown 1946.
Schlesinger, Arthur, Jr.: *Robert Kennedy and His Times*. Boston: Houghton Mifflin, 1978.
———. *A Thousand Days*. Boston: Houghton Mifflin, 1965.
———. (ed.). *The Dynamics of World Power*. New York: Chelsea House, 1973.
Schlesinger, Stephen, and Stephen Kinzer. *Bitter Fruit*. New York: Doubleday, 1982.
Schloss, Henry H. *The Bank for International Settlements*. Amsterdam: North Holland Publishing, 1958.
Seldes, George. *Even the Gods Can't Change History*. New York: Lyle Stuart, 1976.
———. *Facts and Fascism*. New York: In Fact, Inc., 1943.

———. *Iron, Blood and Profits*. New York: Harper, 1934.

———. *Never Tire of Protesting*. New York: Lyle Stuart, 1968.

Seymour, Charles. *Letters from the Paris Peace Conference*. New Haven: Yale Univ. Press, 1965.

Shirer, William L. *The Collapse of the Third Republic*. New York: Simon & Schuster, 1969.

Simpson, Christopher. *Blowback*. New York: Weidenfeld & Nicolson, 1988.

Smith, Bradley F. *The Shadow Warriors*. New York: Basic Books, 1983.

Smith, Bradley F., and Elena Agarossi. *Operation Sunrise*. New York: Basic Books, 1979.

Smith, Joseph B. *Portrait of a Cold Warrior*. New York: Ballantine, 1976.

Smith, Richard Harris. *OSS*. Univ. of California Press, 1972.

Smith, Walter Bedell. *My Three Years in Moscow*. Philadelphia: Lippincott, 1949.

Steffens, Lincoln. *The Autobiography of Lincoln Steffens*. New York: Harcourt, Brace, 1931.

Steven, Stewart. *Operation Splinter-Factor*. Philadelphia: Lippincott, 1974.

———. *The Spymasters of Israel*. New York: Macmillan, 1980.

Stevenson, William. *A Man Called Intrepid*. New York/London: Harcourt Brace Jovanovich, 1976.

———. *Intrepid's Last Case*. New York: Villard Books/Random House, 1983.

Stimson, Henry L. *On Active Service in Peace and War*. New York: Harper, 1947.

Strong, Kenneth. *Intelligence at the Top*. New York: Doubleday, 1969.

———. *Men of Intelligence*. London: Giniger Books/Cassell, 1970.

Sulzberger, Cyrus. *A Long Row of Candles*. New York: Macmillan, 1969.

Sutton, Anthony. *Wall Street and the Rise of Hitler*. Seal Beach, Calif.: '76 Press, 1976.

Tauber, Kurt P. *Beyond Eagle and Swastika*. Middletown, Conn.: Wesleyan Univ. Press, 1967.

Taylor, Edmund. *Awakening from History*. Boston: Gambit, 1969.

Tetens, T. H. *The New Germany and the Old Nazis*. New York: Random House, 1961.

Thayer, Charles W. *Bears in the Caviar*. Philadelphia: Lippincott Co., 1951.

———. *Diplomat*. New York: Harper, 1959.

Troy, Thomas. *Donovan and the CIA*. Frederick, Md.: Univ. Publications of America, 1981.

Turner, Henry Ashby, Jr. *German Big Business and the Rise of Hitler*. New York: Oxford Univ. Press, 1985.

Volkman, Ernest. *Warriors of the Night*. New York: Morrow, 1985.

Waibel, Max. *1945—Kapitulation in Norditalien*. Frankfurt: Helbing & Lichtehahn, 1987.

Wedemeyer, Albert C. *Wedemeyer Reports!* New York: Henry Holt, 1958.

West, Nigel. *The Circus*. New York: Stein & Day, 1983.

———. *The Friends*. London: Weidenfeld & Nicolson, 1988.

———. *MI5*. New York: Stein & Day, 1981.

———. *MI6*. New York: Random House, 1983.

Whiting, Charles. *Gehlen: Germany's Master Spy*. New York: Ballantine, 1972.

Wighton, Charles. *Adenauer*. New York: Coward-McCann, 1963.

Wighton, Charles, and Guenter Peis. *Hitler's Spies and Saboteurs.* New York: Henry Holt, 1958.

Winks, Robin. *Cloak and Gown.* New York: Morrow, 1987.

Winterbotham, F. W. *The Nazi Connection.* New York: Harper & Row, 1978.

Wistrich, Robert. *Who's Who in Nazi Germany.* New York: Bonanza Books, 1982.

Wofford, Harris. *Of Kennedys and Kings.* New York: Farrar, Straus & Giroux, 1980.

Wolff, Robert Lee. *The Balkans in Our Time.* Cambridge, Mass.: Harvard Univ. Press, 1956.

Wright, Peter. *Spycatcher.* New York: Viking Penguin, 1987.

Wyden, Peter. *The Bay of Pigs.* New York: Simon & Schuster, 1979.

Yergin, Daniel. *Shattered Peace.* Boston: Houghton Mifflin, 1977.

Zarubica, Mladin. *The Year of the Rat.* New York: Harcourt, Brace, 1964.

Index

Acheson, Dean, 172, 175, 218–19, 221, 256–57, 262, 285, 330–31, 338, 345, 370, 427
Adenauer, Konrad, 157, 218, 251, 369–74, 411
Albania, covert operations in, 6, 244, 261–66, 269–74, 296, 319–23
Albert, Heinrich, 71–72, 156–57
Alexander, Archibald, 287–88, 343
Allison, John, 416–17
Alsop, John, 184, 307–8, 424, 438
Alsop, Joseph, 176, 184, 307–8, 384, 424, 438
Alsop, Stewart, 184, 228–29, 307–8, 388–89, 424, 438
Ambrose, Stephen, 355–56
American Federation of Labor (AFL), 238–39, 317; Offie and, 444, 447
Amory, Robert, 301–2, 308, 324–25, 421; Bay of Pigs operation and, 431; Guatemalan intervention and, 340, 345; Hungarian insurrection and, 401; Indonesia project and, 416, 418; Khrushchev's Twentieth Congress address and, 380–81; Suez crisis and, 395–96; and tapping Soviet military communications in East Berlin, 379
Anders, Wladtslaw, 279–80
Angell, James, 48, 221
Angleton, James Jesus, 108, 254, 324, 357–59, 452–53; Albanian incursion and, 272–73, 322; background of, 178–83; Bay of Pigs operation and, 431; CIA reorganization and, 292; and creation of Israel, 181; Dulles and, 179, 316–18, 357, 359; Gehlen affair and, 269; Italian Communist Party and, 223, 231–32, 293; Khrushchev's Twentieth Congress address and, 381–82; McCarthy and, 326–27; Offie and, 445–47; OPC and, 239–40; OSO joined by, 188; SIS and, 180; Soviet agents of, 363; Suez crisis and, 396; Ustase and, 183; Wisner and, 359–60, 364, 441
Angleton, J. H. "Hugh," 180–81
Antonescu, Ion, 115, 196–201
Arana, Franciso, 336–37
Arbenz Guzman, Jacobo, Guatemalan intervention and, 336–37, 339–42, 344, 346, 348–54
Arevalo Bermejo, José, 336–37
Arkel, Gerhard van, 148, 158
Armstrong, Hamilton Fish, 75, 90, 258
Ausnit, Max, 115, 204–5, 207, 388
Austria, 19, 22–23, 94; after German defeat, 124; end of Allied occupation of, 370; Hungarian refugees in, 399

Badoglio, Pietro, 55, 118, 180
Baker, John, 362–63, 397, 399
Bancroft, Mary, 95, 101, 148–49
Bank for International Settlements (BIS), 143, 155, 157, 160
Barnes, C. Tracy, 95, 287–88, 361, 379, 384, 399, 410, 426–28; Bay of Pigs operation and, 432; Guatemalan intervention and, 343–44, 349–50, 352–53

Barnes, Janet, 343, 399, 440–41
"Basis for a Permanent U.S. Foreign Intelligence Service, The" (Donovan), 165–66
Bauer, Leo, 109, 139, 387
Baun, Hermann, 162–64, 233, 267
Bay of Pigs operation, 1, 6, 366, 425–26, 428–36
Beam, Jacob, 61, 91, 152, 247, 370
Becker, Loftus, 164, 301, 324
Belarus Secret, The (Loftus), 274
Bell, Laird, 46, 149, 175, 257
Benes, Eduard, 22, 60, 210
Berle, Adolf, 26, 85, 106, 115, 257; Guatemalan intervention and, 340–41
Berlin, Bast: labor riots in, 377; tapping Soviet military communications in, 378–79
Berlin, West, Soviet blockade of, 219–20, 234, 239, 252
Bernays, Edward, 26, 338
Berry, Burton, 205–6, 221
Bessenyey, Baron George, 111, 146
Biddle, Anthony Drexel, 64–65, 245–46
Bissell, Richard, 304–5, 308, 316, 343, 366, 413, 422–23, 426–27; Bay of Pigs operation and, 425, 428–29, 431, 434–36; on Dulles, 375; Dulles's relationship with, 384–86; Hungarian insurrection and, 400; Khrushchev's Twentieth Congress address and, 380; McCarthy and, 326; OPC and, 236; rollback programs and, 319–20; on Wisner, 324
Blake, Jack, 289, 305, 315, 385
Blum, Leon, 59–60, 67
Blum, Paul, 128, 179
Bogdan, Norbert A., 149–50
Bohlen, Charles "Chip," 39, 61, 221, 251, 306–8, 325–26; Offie and, 252; Soviet mission of, 41–42
Bolschwing, Baron Otto Albrecht Alfred von, 200, 277–78
Bonsal, Stephen, 16, 28
Bormann, Martin, 126, 131, 439
Bosch, Robert, 78–79, 100
Bowie, Beverlie, 202–3
Bowie, Robert, 333, 370
Bowles, Chester, 426–27, 432–33
Braden, Spruille, 186, 338
Braden, Tom, 296, 306, 314–17, 357, 367
Bradley, Omar, 140, 189, 280, 287–88, 356
Bragadiru, Princess Tanda, 201, 204, 307
Brandt, Willi, 139, 374
Brewster, Owen, 151–52
Britain, Battle of, 80–82
Bross, John, 228, 301, 365, 371, 377–78
Brown, Anthony Cave, 56, 87, 97, 412
Brown, Irving, 139, 238–40, 255, 317; Offie and, 295–97, 444–45
Bruce, David K. E., 7, 49, 56, 138, 140, 312, 436; COI and, 91–92, 194; Guatemalan intervention and, 338–39; Kolbe's intelligence and, 96; PBCFIA and, 407
Bruening, Heinrich, 48, 52, 91, 99
Bryan, Joe, 272, 305, 440, 443
Bughouse, Operation, 197
Bulgaria, 114–15
Bullitt, Anne, 37, 450
Bullitt, Ernesta Drinker, 19, 36
Bullitt, William C., 4, 6, 15, 18–20, 30, 35–39, 448–50; anti-Soviet polemics of, 41; conflict between House and, 37; conflict between Welles and, 150–52, 448; death of, 450; egotism of, 45; French mission of, 58–68; and German occupation of France, 66–67; German-U.S. relations and, 59; Lippmann's relationship with, 449; marriages of, 36–37; Offie and, 42–44, 62–66, 150–51, 245–46, 253–54, 442, 444–48, 450; and overtures to Soviets, 28–29; Paris Peace Conference and, 19–20; Roosevelt attracted to, 37–38; Roosevelt's break with, 68; Soviet-German non-aggression pact and, 61; Soviet mission of, 29, 38–39, 41–44, 58; Versailles Treaty and, 29; Wilson's break with, 35–36
Bundy, William, 90, 236, 326
Burke, Michael, 266, 269
Buxton, Ned, 85, 105, 107, 205
Byrnes, James F., 174, 176, 228

Cabell, Charles P., 325, 418, 428, 431
Cabot, John Moors, 339, 345
Canaris, Wilhelm Franz, 56, 79, 92, 99–102, 111, 162
Cannon, Clarence, 406–7
Casey, William, 138, 165, 375, 454
Castillo Armas, Carlos, 346–53
Castro, Fidel, 450; Bay of Pigs operation and, 430–35; CIA assassination plots against, 427–28
Central Intelligence Agency (CIA): assassination of Castro plotted by, 427–28; Bay of Pigs operation and, 426, 429–34; Board of National Estimates of, 289; central directorates of, 288; classic period of, 318; creation of, 172, 176–78, 183–88, 217; Current Intelligence Office of, 289; documentaries on, 440; Dulles's appointment to, 312, 314–20, 323–25, 328; Dulles's contributions to, 374–76, 454; Dulles's resignation from, 373; East Berlin riots and, 377; Egyptian secret service and, 331–32; funding of, 407; fund transfers of, 368; Gehlen's liaison with, 277; gentri-

Central Intelligence Agency (*continued*) fication of, 316; Guatemalan intervention and, 341–49, 352–54; Hungarian insurrection and, 392, 398–400, 410; Indonesia project of, 6, 414–20; intensity of emotions around, 366; interest in history of, 2; International Organizations Division of, 357; Italian Communist Party and, 223; Korean War and, 329; liaison between AFL and, 239; mandate of, 272; OPC and, *see* Office of Policy Coordination; OSO and *see* Office of Special Operations; palace revolt in, 432; PBCFIA on, 407–9; political orientation of staff of, 426–27; proprietaries of, 299–300; Psychological Strategy Board (PSB) of, 297–98, 343; reorganizations of, 233–34, 288–92, 304–5, 357–59; rollback programs and, 319–20, 366–67; SIS conflicts with, 425; Smith's appointment to, 282–83, 287; Special Procedures Group of, 223; and tapping Soviet military communications in East Berlin, 378–79; Technical Assistance Division of, 363; Truman's dissatisfaction with, 282; vicissitudes of, 2; WIN and, 281; Wisner's contributions to, 454; Wisner's promotion in, 303–4, 316; Wisner's resignation from, 438, 440

Central Intelligence Group (CIG), 185–87

Chiang Kai-shek, 300, 449

Chicago Daily News, 175, 426

Church Committee, 272, 274, 290–91, 317, 366, 408

Churchill, Winston, 29, 34, 78–82, 340, 369, 412; German surrender negotiations and, 130–31; Greek civil war and, 209; Iranian crisis and, 329–30, 334; Kolbe's intelligence and, 98; and OSS-SIS cooperation, 107; Smith and, 283; Stephenson's U.S. mission and, 79–80, 84; and U.S. aid to Britain, 82; Yugoslavia and, 113

Clark, Mark, 355–56

Clay, Lucius, 213, 217, 221, 226, 233, 239, 241, 269; Dulles and, 155, 160; German surrender and, 134; Murphy and, 149, 152–55; Nazi war criminals and, 275; OSS criticized by, 160; and reviving German economy, 218

Cline, Ray, 165, 385; Communist defector recruitment and, 364; Indonesia project and, 414; Khrushchev's Twentieth Congress address and, 381–82; OPC and, 242

Cochran, H. Merle, 64, 245–46

Cochran, Sir John, 330, 332

Colby, William, 292, 294, 317, 402

Conant, James, 301, 371, 379

Congress, U.S.: Albanian incursion and, 269; 5412 Committee and, 406; Guatemalan intervention and, 347; Italian Communist Party and, 223; and reviving German economy, 218; and tapping Soviet military communications in East Berlin, 379; Versailles Treaty and, 29

Congress for Cultural Freedom, 302

Corcoran, Thomas "Tommy the Cork," 299; Guatemalan intervention and, 338, 341, 346, 353

Corso, Philip, 347, 411

Corson, William, 187, 216, 410

Council on Foreign Relations, 50–51, 90, 175, 216

Craft of Intelligence, The (Dulles), 438–39, 450

Czechoslovakia, 60; German invasion of, 75; independence for, 22–23; Wisner's request for assignment in, 210–11

Dalton, Hugh, 81, 83

Dansey, Edward Majoribanks "Uncle Claude," 17, 78–79, 96

Davies, John Paton, 221, 226, 295, 326–27; Offie and, 251–52

Deane, John R,, 107, 114, 130, 244, 267

Defense Department, U.S., 286, 318–19; Bay of Pigs operation and, 430, 435; CIA reorganization and, 290; Communist defector recruitment and, 362; Indonesia project and, 414; OPC and, 228, 237, 242

de Gaulle, Charles, 125, 137, 151, 449

Dewey, Thomas, 46, 90, 230, 255, 315, 449

Díaz, Carlos Enrique, 351–52

Dien Bien Phu, fall of, 356–57

Dodd, William, 59; Schacht and, 45–46

Doering, Otto, 85, 105

Dolbeare, Frederick, 18, 75, 196, 257

Dollmann, Bugen, 128, 134

Donovan, Ruth Rumsey, 33–34, 54–55, 57

Donovan, William J. "Wild Bill," 3–5, 7, 31–35, 49, 54–58, 107, 157, 179, 227, 282, 399, 410–12; Balkan operations and, 196–97, 202, 204, 206, 209, 211; British mission of, 80–82, 86, 88; Central and Eastern European mission of, 34; childhood of, 32; COI and, 3, 14, 84–92, 194; and creation of CIA, 176–77, 184; criticisms of, 216; death of, 412; on Dulles's lack of administrative skills, 141; and Dulles's reassignment to Switzerland, 11–15; early fact-finding missions of, 55–57; education of, 32; and end of

OSS, 136; German peace imitiatives and, 104–5; German surrender and, 132, 136–38; Helms and, 160; Hitler's acquaintance with, 55; Hitler's rise to power and, 56–57; Hungarian operations and, 111; Kolbe's intelligence and, 97; law background of, 3, 32, 34–35, 54–56, 171; managerial style of, 85, 87, 106; Nazi Redoubts and, 123; NIA and, 186; and peace negotiations with Axis satellites, 114–16; and peacetime role of OSS, 165–67; Poland and, 203; postwar career of, 229–30; private life of, 57; in recruiting Germans to collapse Nazi Reich, 138, 140; rollback projects and, 411; and Russian civil war in Siberia, 4, 31–32; on Salazar, 142; social contacts of, 55–56; Stephenson's relationship with, 77, 79; Thai mission of, 410–11; and U.S. aid to Britain, 82, 90; WIN and, 281; Wisner and, 313–14, 323–24
Doolittle, James H., 355–56, 407
Dosti, Hasan, 262, 270, 320
Douglass, Kingman, 185, 289
Draper, William H., Jr., 149, 217–19, 226–28, 445
Duke, Florimond du Sossoit, 111–13
Dulles, Allen Welch, 1, 5–7, 150, 230–34, 244, 255–57, 269, 299, 302–3, 329–31, 363–64, 424–25, 449–54; Albanian incursion and, 265, 323; ambitions of, 148; Angleton and, 179, 316–18, 357, 359; on arms trafficking and disarmament, 49–50, 52; and attempts on Castro's life, 427–28; Balkan operations and, 196; Bay of Pigs operation and, 425, 428–33, 433; in brush with Lenin, 22; Bullitt and, 449–50; childhood of, 20–21; CIA appointment of, 312, 314–20, 323–25, 328; and CIA depositories for fund transfers, 368; CIA restructuring and, 233–34, 288–90, 357–59; Clay and, 155, 160; COI and, 14, 89–98; on concessions to Axis powers, 75–76; and corruption in OSS, 159–60; in creating Austrian federation, 23; criticisms of, 232–33, 356, 411; Czech independence and, 23; death of, 453; diplomatic credits maintained by, 52; dirty tricks and, 360; Donovan and, 89–90, 314; East Berlin riots and, 377; education of, 4, 14, 21, 50; Egyptian secret service and, 331–32; Eisenhower's relationship with, 405–6; and end of OSS, 136; 5412 Committee and, 406; Foreign Service background of, 14, 19, 21; Foster's relationship with, 51–53, 93, 403; Gehlen and, 164, 374; on German debt, 53; German defeat and, 122–24; German dissidents and, 95–104, 119–21; German mission of, 141, 211–12; German peace initiatives and, 102–4, 108–9; German surrender and, 125, 127–38, 158; Good Germans defended by, 156, 173, 175; Guatemalan intervention and, 335–36, 340–42, 346–50, 352–56; Helms and, 160-61; heritage of, 14–16, 19; high-altitude reconnaissance aircraft and, 384–85; on Hitler, 52–53, 72–73, 75, 90; Hoettl's revelations about, 148; Hungarian insurrection and, 392, 394–95, 398, 401, 404; Hungarian operations and, 110–13; illnesses of, 452–53; Indonesia project and, 416–19; on intelligence, 22; Iranian crisis and, 333–35; Italian Commumist Party and, 232; Japanese surrender and, 155; Kennedy and, 428–29; Khrushchev's Twentieth Congress address and, 380–82; Kirkpatrick and, 365–66; law background of, 3, 14, 50–52, 171, 173; legacy of, 374–76, 453–54; McCarthy and, 326–27; managerial style of, 92, 141, 375–76; in missions to occupied Europe, 5; National Committee for Free Europe and, 257–59, 265; Nazi Redoubts and, 123–25; Nazi sympathizers supported by, 156–57; obituary of, 73; offhandedness of, 27; OPC and, 236–37; Operation Torch and, 12; and OSS-SIS cooperation, 108–10; Pan-Danubian Federation proposed by, 182; Paris Peace Conference and, 19–20, 26–27; PBCFIA on, 407–8; and peace negotiations with Axis satellites, 114–18; peacetime intelligence career sought by, 215; and peacetime role of OSS, 167; and permanent division of Germany, 174–75; Philby on, 284; and plots against Hitler, 119; popularity of, 26–27; private life of, 51–52, 148–49, 368–69; pro-Communist informants of, 109–10; in professional dealings with Nazis, 53–54, 70–77, 89–90, 100, 144–47; public relations skills of, 6; Rajk trial and, 386–87; and rebuilding West Germany, 143, 145, 218; in recruiting Germans to collapse Nazi Reich, 138–40; reputation of, 355; and restructuring national intelligence, 189; retirement of, 450–52; rollback programs

Dulles, Allen Welch (*continued*) and, 319, 366–68, 410; Safe Haven investigations and, 145–46; Smith and, 314–16, 357; on Soviets, 25–26, 175; Suez crisis and, 396; Swiatlo and, 390–91; Swiss missions of, 11–16, 21–23, 93–101; and tapping Soviet military communications in East Berlin, 378–79; and Trudeau's allegations against Gehlen, 372–73; Truscott and, 409; and U.S. influence over development of Germany, 371; and verifying intelligence, 364–65; Vienna mission of, 20–21; Warren Commission and, 450; Wisner and, 194, 196, 211, 213, 215–16, 314–15, 323–24, 376, 384–86, 403, 420–23, 437–39, 450, 454; Wolff's war crimes and, 135; womanizing of, 14, 27, 92, 95; Yugoslavia and, 113, 116–18
Dulles, Clover, 51, 53, 92–93, 148–49, 179, 451–54
Dulles, Eleanor, 46, 402, 407
Dulles, Janet Avery, 24–25
Dulles, Joan, 140, 368
Dulles, John Foster, 4–7, 14, 30, 46–50, 148–49, 173, 230–32, 286, 320, 345, 356, 363, 368–69, 405, 424, 452; Allen's DCI appointment and, 328; Allen's relationship with, 51–53, 93, 403; Berlin mission of, 27; childhood of, 21; comparisons between Allen and, 95; criticisms of, 232, 402–3, 411; death of, 420; Donovan written off by, 89–90; education of, 24; on German debt, 53; German mission of, 46–49; German policy of, 369–70; Guatemalan intervention and, 335–37, 340, 342, 344, 346–48, 350, 352–53; heritage of, 15–16; on Hitler, 46, 53, 70–73, 75; Hungarian insurrection and, 394–95, 398, 401, 403–4; Indonesia project and, 414–20; Iranian crisis and, 333, 335; isolationism of, 57; Khrushchev's Twentieth Congress address and, 382; Kolbe's intelligence and, 97; Latin American missions of, 24, 47; law background of, 24, 46; McCarthy and, 326; Paris Peace Conference and, 25–26; in professional dealings with Nazis, 53–54, 68–73, 75–77, 90, 143–44; rancor at British expressed by, 396–97; and rebuilding West Germany, 143; respect garnered by, 26; rollback programs and, 328-29; on Soviet threat, 176; Suez crisis and, 395, 401

Earman, John, 226, 376
Eberstadt, Ferdinand, 4, 48, 172
Eckhardt, Tibor, 388–89
Eden, Anthony, 209, 333, 357, 369
Edwards, Sheffield, 254, 307, 428
Eggen, Wilhelm, 108, 121, 125
Egypt: Israeli invasion of, 395–96, 400–401; secret service of, 331–32
Eisenhower, Dwight D., 1, 5, 118, 150, 164–65, 256–57, 269, 312, 326, 412, 420, 433, 444–45; A.W. Dulles's relationship with, 405–6; Bay of Pigs operation and, 428; Clark Task Force and, 355–56; criticisms of, 403; 5412 Committee and, 406; Guatemalan intervention and, 336, 339, 341, 347–48, 350, 352–53, 356; high-altitude reconnaissance aircraft and, 384; Hungarian insurrection and, 394, 401–2, 409–10, 414; Indonesia project and, 419; J.F. Dulles and, 369–70; Khrushchev's summits with, 425; Khrushchev's Twentieth Congress address and, 382; Korean War and, 329; National Committee for Free Europe and, 257; Nazi Redoubts and, 125; Offie and, 445; PBCFIA and, 407–9; and permanent division of Germany, 174; presidential campaign of, 320; rollback projects and, 410; Smith and, 283; Suez crisis and, 396, 400–401
Ethiopia, Italian invasion of, 55

Farben, I. G., 68–70
Federal Bureau of Investigation (FBI), 7, 76, 80, 115; and creation of CIA, 184–88; Offie investigated by, 443–48
Field, Noel H., 95, 109–10, 138–40, 158, 386–87, 391
5412 Committee, 406
Fitzgerald, Desmond, 300, 303, 416
Foreign Affairs, 47, 51, 53, 75, 218
Forgan, James Russell, 127, 140
Forrestal, James V., 4, 48, 149, 202, 226, 230, 238, 287; anti-Soviet polemics of, 218; and creation of CIA, 172, 176–78; decline of, 234–35; Dulles's relationship with, 232–34; Italian Communist Party and, 222–23, 231–32; Nazi war criminals and, 275; OSO and, 224; in professional dealings with Nazis, 70
France: Bullitt's mission to, 58–68; Communist Party in, 230, 238–39, 296; German invasion of, 66–68; and German invasion of Poland, 63; German relations with, 59; German surrender and, 137; Guatemalan intervention and, 350; Indochinese defeat of, 357; Vichy, 12–13, 15

Franco, Francisco, 57, 68, 70
Frasheri, Midhat, 262–63, 265, 270
Free Trade Union Committee (FTUC), 238–39, 295
Freud, Sigmund, 37, 62, 449–50
Fritchey, Mary Wisner "Polly," 190, 193–94, 208, 216, 253, 287–88, 301, 305–7, 313–14, 324, 384–86, 421–24, 436–37, 440–41, 446, 450

Gaevernitz, Gero von Schulze, 98–99, 102, 140–41, 157, 213, 367; anti-Soviet German POWs sought by, 159; and Dulles's German mission, 141; German surrender negotiations and, 126, 128–29, 132, 134–35; Safe Haven investigation of, 144–46
Gehlen, Reinhard, 6, 147, 157, 226, 233, 250, 266–69, 277–78, 367, 385; Dulles's friendship with, 374; Egyptian secret service and, 331–32; Hungarian insurrection and, 400, 409; Italian intelligence and, 294; Khrushchev's Twentieth Congress address and, 381; National Committee for Free Europe and, 259; Nazi war criminals and, 275–76; OSO and, 266-68; Soviet intelligence records of, 161–65, 186; and tapping Soviet military communications in East Berlin, 379; Trudeau's allegations against, 372–73; and U.S. influence over development of Germany, 371
Germany, Federal Republic of (West), 285, 371; Dulles's policy on, 369–70; Hungarian insurrection and, 400; rebuilding of, 143–45, 218; restoration of sovereignty of, 372; Wolff's war crimes and, 135
Germany, Imperial: Paris Peace Conference and, 18, 27; surrender of, 27
Germany, Nazi, 45; anti-Semitism in, 120; COI and, 91–95; Czech operations of, 210–11; Czechoslovakia invaded by, 75; debt of, 100; dissidents in, 119–21; Dulleses' professional dealings with, 53–54, 68–77, 89–90, 100, 143–47; and Dulles's transit through Vichy France, 12–13; France invaded by, 66–68; French relations with, 59; Kennan's ambivalence toward, 141–42; Kolbe's intelligence on, 96–97; Operation Torch and, 12; peace initiatives from, 102–5, 108–9; Poland invaded by, 57, 61, 63; rearmament of, 56–57, 79; Redoubts of, 123–25; reparations from, 142–43; rescuing war criminals of, 274–76; Rumanian alliance with, 200–201; Rumanian operations of, 197–99, 202, 205, 207; Soviet non-aggression pact with, 61, 64; Soviet peace negotiations with, 114; Soviet Union invaded by, 82, 151, 200; surrender of, 122–38, 158; U.S. relations with, 59; Yugoslavia invaded by, 82
Germany, Occupied: denazification of, 174; Dulles's mission in, 141, 211–12; ferreting out Communist sympathizers in, 158; holding down economy of, 174–76; infiltrating Soviet Zone of, 139; Marshall Plan money for, 235; Offie in, 247–52; permanent division of, 174–75; reviving economy of, 218–19; trade unionism in, 239; Wisner's posting in, 211–15
Germany, Weimar Republic of: anti-Semitism in, 53; debt of, 47–49, 53; Dulles's economic missions to, 46–49; Nazi overthrow of, 56; restrictions on arms trafficking to, 50, 52
Germany's Underground (Dulles), 119, 173, 367
Gisevius, Hans Bernd, 95, 99–102, 109–10, 121, 157, 367
Glaser, Erika, 157–58
Globke, Hans, 157, 371, 373
Goerdeler, Carl, 78–79, 100–101, 119–20
Goering, Hermann, 46, 58, 119; and Battle of Britain, 81; German-U.S. relations and, 59
Goldberg, Arthur, 139, 158; COI and, 91; Hungarian operations and, 111–13
Gomulka, Wladyslaw, 362, 392, 397; Khrushchev defied by, 382–83, 386, 391
Gottlieb, Sidney, 427–28
Graham, Elizabeth, 193, 308
Graham, John, 227, 438, 441
Gray, Gordon, 227, 287–88, 312, 368, 383; 5412 Committee and, 406; psychological warfare and, 297–98
Great Britain: and creating U.S. civilian intelligence organization, 83, 85; Donovan's mission to, 80–82, 86, 88; Dulles's criticisms of, 396–97; and German invasion of Poland, 63; Guatemalan intervention and, 350–51; Iranian crisis and, 329–30, 332–34; and rise of Communism in Soviet Union, 29–30; on Rumania, 202; and Russian civil war in Siberia, 31; Suez crisis and, 395; U.S. aid to, 79–83, 90, 171; U.S. Indonesia project and, 417–18

Greece: civil war in, 209, 261–62; Soviet expansionism and, 176; U.S. Albanian incursion and, 265
Green, Ed, 242–43
Green, William, 238, 257
Grew, Joseph C., 18, 28, 257–58, 444
Griffith, William E., 259, 397–98
Grombach, John V. "Frenchy," 86, 177, 185–86, 327
Groza, Petru, 176, 205, 209, 234
Guatemalan intervention, 6, 335–56
Gurfein, Murray, 91, 115, 194
Gutiérrez, Victor, 339–40, 351
Gysling, General Consul, 131, 133

Halder, Franz, 162, 367
Haney, Albert, Guatemalan intervention and, 341–44, 346–47, 349–50, 352
Haniel, Alfred, 100, 156
Hapke, Karl, 145–46
Harding, Warren G., 34–35, 69
Harriman, Averell, 131, 141–42, 172, 202, 216, 236, 304–5, 320, 326, 426, 443, 445
Harrison, Leland, 18, 145–47
Harvey, William King, 187–88, 321, 410, 428; Offie and, 447–48; and tapping Soviet military communications in East Berlin, 378–79
Hedden, Stuart, 302, 345, 365–66
Heinrich, Antoine, 146–47
Helms, Richard, 160–61, 212, 325, 363, 366, 368, 384, 413, 423, 447; Albanian incursion and, 273–74; background of, 160; Bay of Pigs operation and, 428–29, 431–32, 434; and corruption in OSS, 160; on Dulles, 375–76; Gehlen and, 268, 374; Guatemalan intervention and, 344, 353; OSO and, 186; Wisner and, 211, 303–4, 437, 440
Henderson, Loy, 39, 42, 332–34
Herter, Christian, 15, 20, 49, 218, 236
Herwarth von Bittenfeld, Hans "Johnny," 42, 61, 251
Hesse, Kurt, 248, 361
Heydrich, Reinhard, 103, 112, 120, 124, 163
Hilger, Gustav, 42, 61, 162, 250–51, 267, 274–76, 439
Hillenkoetter, Roscoe, 39, 64, 67, 217, 223, 226–28, 234, 238, 256; Albanian incursion and, 272; Gehlen affair and, 268; OPC and, 240, 242; psychological warfare and, 298; Truman's dissatisfaction with, 282; Wisner and, 314
Hilsman, Roger, 407, 431, 435
Himmler, Heinrich, 73, 96, 102, 123, 157, 163, 276; German surrender and, 130–31, 137; Wolff and, 126, 129, 135
Hiss, Alger, 188, 326, 345
Hitler, Adolf, 5, 27, 62, 151, 173, 175, 277, 287; anti-Semitism of, 72–73, 75; A.W. Dulles on, 52–53, 72–73, 75, 90; British invasion planned by, 81; death of, 133; Donovan and, 55, 79; Gehlen and, 163; on German debt, 48–49; German surrender and, 127, 131; Hungary and, 111–12; J.F. Dulles on, 46, 53, 70–73, 75; Kennan's ambivalence toward, 142; Offie and, 154; plots against, 100–103, 110, 114, 119–21; propaganda war and, 80; Redoubt plan and, 124–25; rise to power of, 56–57, 65, 74; Rumania and, 200–201, 207; rumored illness of, 123; Schacht and, 45–46, 49; Soviet–German nonaggression pact and, 61; Wolff and, 126, 129, 131, 135; Yugoslavia and, 113, 116
Hoettl, Wilhelm, 111–13, 117, 124, 147–48
Hohenlohe–Langenburg, Prince Max Egon zu, 102–4, 112
Holcomb, Frank, 296–97; Bay of Pigs operation and, 425; Guatemalan intervention and, 342–43, 349–52
Holland, Henry, 345–48, 350
Hoover, Herbert, 26, 35, 54, 218
Hoover, Herbert, Jr., 334, 370, 395
Hoover, J. Edgar, 35, 76, 88, 106, 150, 238, 355, 374; and creation of CIA, 184–87; McCarthy and, 327; Offie investigated by, 443–44, 446–47
Hora, La, 431
Horstenau, Glore von, 113, 116–17
Horthy, Nicholas, 28, 110–11
House, Edward, 4, 16–20, 28–29, 37
Houston, Larry, 196, 223, 255, 307, 325, 383, 411; Smith and, 283-84, 299
Hoxha, Enver, 261–62, 264–65, 271
Hungary: extermination of Jews in, 112; government-in-exile of, 388–90, 400; independence for, 22–23; insurrection in, 386, 391–95, 397–404, 409–10, 412, 414; OSS operations in, 110–14; rise of Communism in, 26–28
Hunt, E. Howard "Eduardo," 340, 349, 429
Husmann, Max, 127, 131, 134
Hyde, Henry, 129–30, 137, 187

Indonesia: CIA project in, 6, 414–20
In Fact, 232
Inquiry, The, 4, 17, 22, 28
Iran: covert intervention in, 6, 332–35; oil fields nationalized by, 329–30, 332–34; Soviet expansionism and, 176
Israel: Angleton and, 317; creation of, 181; Egypt invaded by, 395–96, 400–401

Italy, 292–94; Angleton's posting in, 178–83; Communist Party in, 221–24, 231–32, 238, 240, 292–93; Croatian refugees in, 182–83; Ethiopia invaded by, 55; labor activities in, 297; surrender of German forces in, 125–36
It's Not Done (Bullitt), 36

Jackson, C. D., 259, 341, 347, 377, 411
Jackson, William Harding, 189, 233, 256, 297, 303, 312, 341; CIA appointment of, 287–88
Jacobsson, Per, 143, 155
Jagan, Cheddi, attempt to depose, 436
Japan, surrender of, 155
Jebb, Gladwyn, 261–62, 264
Jessup, Peter, 361, 363
Johnson, Kilburn "Pat," 303, 383–84
Johnson, Lyndon, 428, 450
Journal de Geneve, 93
Joyce, Robert, 118, 147, 151, 189; Albanian incursion and, 262, 264, 271, 273, 322; CIA reorganization and, 290; Offie and, 252; OPC and, 241; Poland and, 203; Rumania and, 206

Kadar, Janos, 393, 398
Kaltenbrunner, Ernst, 124, 131, 133
Kapitulation in Norditalien (Waibel), 132
Kelley, Robert Francis, 39–41, 49, 60–61, 259
Kennan, Annelise Soerensen, 40, 141–42
Kennan, George F., 5–6, 103, 162, 241, 267, 286, 307–8, 325–26, 403; ambivalence toward Nazis of, 141–42; Bullitt's Soviet mission and, 38–39, 41–42; CIA reorganization and, 291; education of, 40; Italian Communist Party and, 222, 224; Kelley's influence on, 39–41; and Lend-Lease to Soviet Union, 141; National Committee for Free Europe and, 257, 259; Offie and, 245, 250–52, 442; Policy and Planning Staff of, 220–21; on Soviet Union, 40–41, 142, 224–26, 285–86
Kennedy, John F., 63–64, 358, 375; assassination of, 450; Bay of Pigs operation and, 1, 425–26, 428–35; on CIA, 426–27; on clandestine political warfare, 439
Kennedy, Joseph P., Jr., 63–64
Kennedy, Joseph P., Sr., 60, 63–65, 80, 407
Kent, Sherman, 164, 289, 433
Kesselring, Albert, 129–30
Keynes, John Maynard, 15–16, 26
KGB, 278, 306; Nitze on, 222; OPC and, 243; Philby used by, 274; and tapping Soviet military communications in East Berlin, 379; Ukrainian revolt and, 249
Khrushchev, Nikita, 362, 394; Eisenhower's summits with, 425; Gomulka's defiance of, 382–83, 386, 391; Hungarian insurrection and, 393; Twentieth Congress address of, 379–82; Yugoslavian rapprochement of, 422
King, J. C., 428–29; Guatemalan intervention and, 338–39, 341–42, 346–47
Kirkpatrick, Lyman, 237, 288, 295, 303, 312, 316, 327, 365–66, 423; Bay of Pigs operation and, 429, 432, 434–35; Guatemalan intervention and, 353
Klay, Andor, 400–401
Knox, Franklin, 57, 67, 77
Kolbe, Fritz, 95–98, 111, 157, 164
Kolchak, Aleksandr V., 26, 31–32
Korean War, 299–300, 329
Kovacs, Bela, 387, 401
Krizari (Crusaders), 183
Krock, Arthur, 4, 26, 234
Kun, Bela, 26, 28–29
Kupi, Abas, 262, 265
Kushel, Franz, 275–76

Langbehn, Carl, 102, 126
Langer, William, 86, 289
Lansdale, Edward, 357, 384
Lansing, Robert, 14–16; A.W. Dulles's Foreign Service career and, 21; on Czech and Hungarian independence, 22–23; J.F. Dulles's Latin American mission and, 24; Paris Peace Conference and, 16, 18–20, 25; rivalry between House and, 16, 18–19; State Department under, 16–18
Leddy, Raymond, 187, 340, 345, 410
Legge, Barnwell R., 99, 146
LeHand, Marguerite "Missy," 37–39, 66
Lend-Lease, 82–83, 141, 171
Lenin, 31, 173–74; Bullitt's Soviet mission and, 29; Dulles's brush with, 22; power seized by, 27–29, 40
Leverkuehn, Paul, 56, 195
Lieb, Joseph, 273, 322
Life, 176, 328
Lindbergh, Charles, 57, 71, 76
Lindsay, Frank, 116–18, 195, 225, 299, 303, 308–9, 357, 422, 438; Albanian incursion and, 264, 273; CIA reorganization and, 291; Hungarian government-in-exile and, 388; Murder Board of, 318–19; OPC and, 236–37, 242; rollback programs and, 319–20
Lippmann, Walter, 4, 37, 230, 449; Paris Peace Conference and, 15, 17, 26

"Lithuania and Poland, the Last Barrier between Germany and the Bolsheviks" (Dulles), 23
Litvinov, Maxim, 41, 58
Lloyd George, David, 29, 34
Lodge, Henry Cabot, 338, 350, 404
Loftus, John, 250, 274, 276
London, Wisner's mission to, 423–25, 436–37
London *Times*, 450
Look, 449
Lovestone, Jay, 139, 238–40, 255, 269, 302, 313, 317, 411; Offie and, 295–96, 444, 447
Lovett, Robert, 143, 185, 217, 227; Nazi war criminals and, 275; Offie and, 445; PBCFIA and, 407–8
Luce, Henry, 3, 257

MacArthur, Douglas, 33–34, 299
MacArthur, Douglas, II, 61, 370; Bullitt's French mission and, 64–65; and German occupation of France, 67–68; Offie and, 443, 446, 448
McCargar, James, 244, 292, 295, 305, 374; Albanian incursion and, 264, 266, 269–70, 273, 320; Hungarian government-in-exile and, 388–90; Hungarian insurrection and, 397–98
McCarthy, Joseph R., 285, 307, 326–27, 370, 403; Offie attacked by, 442–43
McCloy, John, 143, 155, 172, 266, 275, 301, 313
McCone, John, 294, 440; Bay of Pigs operation and, 435; Wisner's illness and, 437–38
McCormack, Alfred, 172, 185
McCormick, Vanc , 20, 25–26
McDowell, Robert, 116, 226, 237, 279, 378
MacFarland, Lanning "Packy," 111, 195–96
MacLeish, Archibald, 85, 180
McWilliams, Carey, 1–2
Maddox, William, 165, 205, 210
Magruder, John, 105–6, 164, 172, 177, 187, 206, 211, 216, 290
Malaysian Federation, 425
Mann, Henry, 74, 144, 147
Mannicatide, Theodore, 208–9
Mao Tse-tung, 43, 300
Margarete I, Operation, 112
Marshall, George, 167, 219–20, 224, 233, 448; OPC and, 228; Wisner and, 226–27
Marshall Plan, 221, 238, 251, 255, 291; OPC and, 235–36
Masaryk, Thomas, 22–23, 220
Masson, Roger, 122, 108
Matthews, H. Freeman "Doc," 64, 122–23, 246, 333
Maury, John, 358, 381
Meany, George, 238–39, 344
Mee, Charles, 18, 141
Mendès-France, Pierre, 367
Menzies, Stewart, 56, 84, 321
Merker, Paul, 109, 387
Messner, Franz Josef "Cassia," 94, 196
Meyer, Cord, 357–58, 392, 400
Michael, King of Rumania, 197, 199, 201–2, 209, 211, 227, 307
Military Security Act, 286
Miller, Gerry, 244, 297, 303
Mindszenty, Cardinal, 249, 401
Mohammad Reza Shah Pahlavi, 330, 332–33
Molden, Fritz, 94, 140, 368
Molotov, Vyacheslav, 64, 250, 325; German surrender negotiations and, 130–31; on Rumania, 201; Soviet expansionism and, 172–73; on war reparations, 171
Monat, Der, 302
Monnet, Jean, 15, 26, 49, 62, 231
Montini, Giovanni, 293–94
Moore, R. Walton "Judge," 37, 43–44, 62, 151
Mossadegh, Mohammed: Iran's oil fields nationalized by, 329–30, 332–34; overthrow of, 332–35
Murphy, Charles J. V., 307, 403, 421, 438, 440–41
Murphy, James, 85, 105, 208; on Angleton, 180; and OSS-SIS cooperation, 106
Murphy, Robert, 95, 139, 213, 226, 368, 370; Bullitt's French mission and, 59–60, 64; career successes of, 149–50, 152; Clay and, 149, 152–55; 5412 Committee and, 406; German defeat and, 122–23, 134; and German occupation of France, 67; Guatemalan intervention and, 347; Hungarian insurrection and, 392; Iranian crisis and, 333; Nazi war criminals and, 275; Offie and, 150, 152–54, 245–47, 250, 252–53, 447; Safe Haven investigations and, 145–46; Yugoslav negotiations and, 118
Mussolini, Benito, 52, 66, 180, 222; Donovan on, 55; Dulles on, 71; and surrender of German forces in Italy, 128

Naguib, Bey, 331, 395
Nagy, Imre, 391, 393, 397–98
Nasser, Gamal Abdel, 331–32, 395
Nasution, Abdul Haris, 418–19
Nation, 1–2, 431
National Committee for Free Europe, 5, 257–60, 313, 340–41, 363; Albanian incursion and, 265; governments-in-exile sponsored by, 387; Hungarian insurrection and, 409–10; mission of, 257–58; teeth and claws of, 259
National Intelligence Authority (NIA), 185–86

National Security Act, 5, 177, 217
National Security Council (NSC), 7, 177, 217; anti-Communist offensives and, 226–27; Bay of Pigs operation and, 428–30; creation of, 172; 5412 Committee and, 406; Indonesia project and, 420; Italian Communist Party and, 223; Operations Coordinating Board of, 343; OSO and, 224; Suez crisis and, 396
Neues Deutschland, 139–40
New York Times, 4, 73, 177, 234, 306, 338, 349–50, 382, 404, 441
Nitze, Paul, 149, 220–22; Albanian incursion and, 322; CIA reorganization and, 290–91; conflict between Dulles and, 402–3; Offie and, 445; on Soviet Union, 285–87; on Wisner's breakdown, 423
Nixon, Richard, 399, 416, 427, 453
North, Oliver, 186, 343, 454
Nosavan, Phoumi, 425

O'Brian, John, Lord, 17, 31–32
Office of Naval Intelligence (ONI), 233; CIG and, 186–87; and creation of CIA, 184–85
Office of Policy Coordination (OPC), 226–29, 235–37, 239–45, 260, 286, 318–19, 335, 352–56, 360–63; action programs justified by, 361–64; administration of, 243–45; Albanian incursion and, 263–64, 269–74, 296, 320–22; CIA restructuring and, 288–92; Communist defector recruitment and, 362–63; Guatemalan intervention and, 338–39; integration of OSO with, 303–5; in Italy, 292–93; Korean War and, 299–300; National Committee for Free Europe and, 257–60; Offie and, 245, 252–55, 295–97; origins of, 5; and overseeing overseas action sectors, 298; Psychological-Warfare Staff of, 326; Smith and, 284, 301, 303; staffing of, 242–43, 255, 315–16; WIN and, 279
Office of Research and Evaluation (ORE), 185
Office of Special Operation; (OSO), 185–88, 223–24, 228–29, 235, 237, 239–40, 242, 318–19; Albanian incursion and, 272; CIA reorganization and, 291–92; Gehlen affair and, 266–68; integration of OPC with, 303–5; in Italy, 292–93; and overseeing overseas action sectors, 298; Smith on, 284; Soviet Division of, 249; WIN and, 279
Office of Strategic Services (OSS), 7; Angleton's background in, 178–81; Balkan operations and, 196–205; case for peacetime use of, 165–67; corruption in, 159–60; and creation of CIA, 184; Donovan's managerial style and, 106; Dulles's Swiss mission and, 11, 14; end of, 136, 167, 171, 213; German surrender and, 123, 127–29, 132–33, 136, 158; humiliations of, 179; Hungarian operations of, 110–14; Kolbe's intelligence and, 96–97; mission of, 105–6; OPC compared to, 228; origins of, 5; and peace negotiations with Axis satellites, 114–18; Planning Group of, 11; public relations campaign of, 167; in recruiting Germans to collapse Nazi Reich, 138–40; Secret Intelligence (SI) branch of, 195; SIS cooperation with, 106–10; size of, 105; Strategic Services Unit (SSU) of, 172, 176–78, 180, 182–85; Swiss office of, 93–101; Wisner's career in, 194–214; X-2 branch of, 107–8, 178, 180, 194–95, 198, 206, 208
Office of the Coordinator of Information (COI), 3, 5, 14, 84–95, 179; creation of, 194, 331; Donovan's management of, 85, 87; Dulles's joining of, 89–91; Dulles's managerial style and, 92–93; Dulles's staffing of, 91; size of, 105
Offie, Carmel, 5–6, 245–55, 307, 327, 441–48; Albanian incursion and, 266, 269–71; Bullitt and, 42–44, 62–66, 150–51, 245–46, 253–54, 442, 444–48, 450; bureaucratic nerve of, 152–54; death of, 448; FBI investigation of, 443–48; Foreign Service background of, 42–43; Gehlen affair and, 266–67, 269; German defeat and, 123; and German occupation of France, 67; Hungarian government-in-exile and, 388–90, 400; Hungarian insurrection and, 409–10; Kennedys and, 63–65; McCarthy's attacks on, 442–43; Murphy and, 150, 152–54, 245–47, 250, 252–53, 447; National Committee for Free Europe and, 259; in Occupied Germany, 247–52; OPC and, 245, 252–55, 295–97; Poland and, 63, 203; resignation of, 245–46, 252; Rumania and, 206; social nerve of, 153; Soviet defectors and, 251; Wisner and, 245, 252–53, 255, 295–96, 441–44, 446
Operation Bughouse (Bowie), 202–3 Organization of American States, 344, 350
Oswald, Lee Harvey, 450

Paderewski, Ignace, 22
Papen, Franz von, 71–72
Paperclip, Operation, 165
Parilli, Baron Luigi, 127–28

Paris Herald Tribune, 374
Paris Peace Conference, 15–20, 25–28
Parri, Ferrucio, 128, 130–31, 179, 222
Parrott, Tom, 318–19
Pash, Boris, 165, 226, 243
Patterson, Eleanor "Cissy," 36–37, 151
Patterson, Robert, 144, 177, 218
Paul VI, Pope, 293–94
Pavelic, Ante, 182–83
PB/SUCCESS, Project, 342–43, 347–48
Penrose, Stephen, 189, 216
Petain, Henri-Philippe, 13, 67, 109
Pfleger, Herman, 370, 395, 398
Pforzheimer, Walter, 50, 316
Phenix, Spencer, 91, 93
Philby, Harold "Kim," 97, 188, 424; Albanian incursion and, 264, 266, 270–72, 274; on Angleton, 180; anti-Soviet malcontents and, 276–77; Harvey's memo on, 321; and OSS–SIS cooperation, 108; on Smith, 284
Phillips, David Atlee, 384, 428; Guatemalan intervention and, 343–44, 348–52
Phillips, Wallace Banta, 87–88
Pilsudski, Joseph, 34, 58
Pius XII, Pope, 128, 134, 179, 182
Plattenberg, Countess Elizabeth von, 195
Pleasants, Henry, 268, 373
Poland: evacuating Polish intelligence agents from, 203; German invasion of, 57, 61, 63; insurrection in, 6, 382–83, 386, 391; Swiatlo's operation in, 390–91; WIN and, 279–80
Polgar, Tom, 360–61
Polignac, Marquis and Marquise de, 62
Polk, George, 230
Pond, The, 177, 185–86, 327
Poole, DeWitt Clinton, 4, 38, 40, 97–98, 137–38, 173–75, 259, 313
Pope, Allen Lawrence, 419, 425
Powers, Francis Gary, 425
Powers, Thomas, 266, 304–5, 402, 432, 454
Prenci, Tahir, 321–22
President's Board of Consultants on Foreign Intelligence Activities (PBCFIA), 407–9, 419–20
Prevent World War III, 232
Protestant, 232
Prudhomme, Hector, 43, 153–54, 447
Puerifoy, John E. "Jack," 341, 345, 351–54

Quinn, William, 177–78, 239; Angleton and, 178, 181; and creation of CIA, 183–87; OSO and, 186–88

Radio Free Europe (RFE), 6, 258–59, 269; Hungarian insurrection and, 392–93, 399–400
Radio Liberty, 6, 259
Rado, Emmy, 95, 141, 158
Rajk, Laszlo, 110, 391; trial of, 386–87
Rakosi, Matyas, 386–87, 391, 393
Ranney, Garner, 451–53
Reader's Digest, 102
"Recovery of Germany, The" (Angell), 48
Reinhardt, G. Frederick, 151, 241, 448
Renaud, Paul, 59, 63, 67
Reston, Scotty, 306, 350
Reza Shah Pahlavi, 330
Ribbentrop, Joachim von, 61, 64, 74, 91, 95, 112, 162, 250; German peace negotiations and, 127; Kolbe's intelligence and, 97
Richards, Atherton, 85, 105 Riddleberger, James, 134, 174, 275, 381
Robertson, William "Rip," 341, 346, 351
Rocca, Ray, 327, 359
Rockefeller, Nelson, 84, 88, 411
Rogers, James Grafton, 88, 105, 137–38
Roman, Howard, 298, 367, 452–53; Communist defector recruitment and, 362–63; on Dulles, 364–65, 375–76
Roosevelt, Eleanor, 37–38, 89, 91
Roosevelt, Franklin D., 3–5, 45, 55, 57–58, 75, 173, 192, 218, 448, 453; Bullitt attractive to, 37–38; Bullitt's break with, 68; Bullitt's French mission and, 59–63, 66; Bullitt's Soviet mission and, 39, 41, 43, 58; and Bullitt-Welles conflict, 150–52; COI and, 3, 84–85, 88–89, 93; death of, 131, 166; Donovan's relationship with, 106–7; and German occupation of France, 67–68; German peace initiatives and, 105; German surrender negotiations and, 130–31; German-U.S. relations and, 59; Greek civil war and, 209; Hitler's rise to power and, 57; OSS investigation authorized by, 159; and OSS-SIS cooperation, 107; and peace negotiations with Axis satellites, 115; and permanent division of Germany, 174; and Soviet Balkan takeover, 197, 205, 209, 211; Soviet-German non-aggression pact and, 61; and U.S. aid to Britain, 79–80, 82–83, 90; Vichy France and, 12
Roosevelt, Kermit "Kim," 56, 303, 317–18, 330–35, 406; Egyptian operation and, 331–32; Guatemalan intervention and, 335, 344; Iranian crisis and, 332–35; Suez crisis and, 395
Roselli, John, 428
Rositzke, Harry, 186, 249, 291, 332

Royall, Kenneth, 219, 280
Rumania: anti-Semitism in, 200; German alliance with, 200–201; government-in-exile of, 387–88; history of, 199–200; intelligence on Soviet Union boot-legged out of, 208–9; Nazi intelligence discovered in, 198–99, 202; OSS operations in, 114; Soviet enslavement of ethnic Germans in, 207; Soviet plundering of, 205; U.S. postwar intelligence in, 233–34; Wisner's operations in, 189, 196–211
Rusk, Dean, 426, 431–32, 436

Salazar, Antonio, 142
Saltzman, Charles, 216–17, 219–20, 227, 244, 252, 258, 384
Saturday Evening Post, 167, 295, 331, 426
Scattolini, Virgilio, 179, 223
Schacht, Hyalmar Horace Greeley, 27, 74, 90, 99–100, 135, 143; Dodd and, 45–46; Egypt and, 332; German debt and, 48–49, 53, 100; German–U.S. relations and, 59
Schellenberg, Walter, 111, 121–23; surrender negotiations and, 102–4, 108, 125–27, 130
Schlesinger, Arthur, Jr., 308; Bay of Pigs operation and, 430, 432–33; in recruiting Germans to collapse Nazi Reich, 139; on Wisner, 158–59, 211–12
Schow, Robert, 267, 269
Schroder, J. Henry, 73–75, 89–90, 100, 143, 146, 150, 330; and CIA depositories for fund transfers, 368; Guatemalan intervention and, 336
Schroeder, Baron Kurt von, 54, 60, 68, 72–74, 127, 150
Schuyler, Courtland van Rensselaer, 205–7, 227
Schwarzkopf, H. Norman, 330, 333
Secret Intelligence Service (SIS), 78–79, 180; Albanian operations and, 261–62, 265; CIA conflicts with, 425; COI collaboration with, 91, 94; German dissidents working for, 98, 100; German surrender negotiations and, 130; Jagan and, 436; OSS cooperation with, 106–10; rollback programs and, 366–67; and tapping Soviet military communications in East Berlin, 378–79; WIN and, 279
Secret Surrender, The (Dulles), 367, 450
Seymour, Charles, 19–20, 28
Shepardson, Whitney, 161, 197, 211
Sherwood, Robert, 84–85
Siberia, Russian civil war in, 4, 26, 31–32
Sibert, Edwin, 128, 134, 140, 213, 233, 248, 267, 269, 277; Gehlen and, 164–65
Sichel, Peter, 160; dirty tricks and, 360; on Wisner, 212–13, 215–16, 360
Sienko, S., 279–80
Sima, Horia, 200, 204
Six, Franz, 275
Skorzeny, Otto, 112, 135, 163, 331–32
Smith, Harold, 88, 106, 165, 167
Smith, R. Harris, 73, 235
Smith, Truman, 76, 367–68
Smith, Walter "Beedle," 5, 27, 282–85, 287–90, 329, 356, 363, 407, 410, 454; A.W. Dulles and, 314–16, 357; CIA appointment of, 282–83, 287; CIA restructuring and, 288–90, 304; Donovan and, 313–14; Gehlen and, 164; Guatemalan intervention and, 338, 345; Iranian crisis and, 333–34; J.F. Dulles and, 369–70; Korean War and, 300; Offie and, 295, 444–45; OPC and, 284, 301, 303; and overseeing overseas action sectors, 298–99; on Philby, 321; psychological warfare and, 297–98; retirement of, 357; testiness of, 299–302, 314–15; Wisner and, 284, 299, 301–2, 304, 314
Solborg, Robert M., 87, 103
Somoza, Anastasio, 338, 346, 350
Soviet Union, 4–5, 385; Angleton's agents in, 363; atomic bomb acquired by, 285; Austria as buffer between West and, 23; Balkan operations and, 196–98, 200–209, 211; Berlin blockaded by, 219–20, 234, 239, 252; Bohlen on, 41; Bullitt's mission to, 29, 38–39, 41–44, 58; and civil war in Siberia, 4, 26, 31–32; Communist seizure of power in, 27–30; Czech independence and, 23; defectors from, 251; Dulleses on, 25–26, 175–76; East Berlin riots and, 377; expansionism of, 172–76, 217, 219, 221–22, 255, 411; fusion warheads stockpiled by, 401; Gehlen's intelligence on, 161–65, 186; German defeat and, 122–23; German invasion of, 82, 151, 200; German non-aggression pact with, 61, 64; German peace initiatives and, 114; German surrender negotiations and, 129–32; Hungarian insurrection and, 392–93, 397–402, 404; Japanese surrender and, 155; Kennan on, 40–41, 142, 224–26, 285–86; Lend-Lease to, 141; Lenin's takeover in, 27–29, 40; militarization of policy toward, 286; Nitze on, 285–87; OPC and, 235; and OSS operations in Hungary,

Soviet Union (*continued*) 113; and peace negotiations with Axis satellites, 114–17; planning destabilization of, 224–27; plans to sabotage airfields of, 319; Poland and, 203; reparations and, 171, 174, 218; rollback programs and, 366; Suez crisis, 395; tapping East Berlin communications of, 378–79; Ukrainian revolt in, 248–49; U.S. Albanian incursion and, 266, 323; U.S. Indonesia project and, 416–17; U.S. recognition of, 38; Wisner on, 158–59; Wisner's collection of intelligence on, 208–9

Special Operations Executive (SOE), 81–83

Speidel, Hans, 367–68, 371

Stalin, Joseph, 155, 171, 238, 264, 286–87; brutalities of, 380; Bullitt's Soviet mission and, 38; death of, 325, 328, 377; German surrender and, 130, 137; Greek civil war and, 209; in peace negotiations with Germany, 114; and permanent division of Germany, 174; Poland and, 203; on Rumania, 207–8; Smith and, 283; Soviet expansionism and, 173, 176; Soviet–German non-aggression pact and, 61; on war reparations, 142–43; Yugoslavia and, 113

State-Army-Navy-Air Force Coordinating Committee (SANACC), 217, 224–26

State Department, U.S., 4–5, 7, 14, 21, 319; Albanian operations and, 262–65; A.W. Dulles's background in, 49–51; and A.W. Dulles's dealings with Nazi Germany, 89; A.W. Dulles's Swiss mission and, 21–22; Bay of Pigs operation and, 435; Berlin blockade and, 219; Bullitt's French mission and, 59–60, 64, 67; Bureau of Central European Information of, 19; CIA reorganization and, 290; and Clay's relationship with Murphy, 153–54; COI and, 92; Communist defector recruitment and, 362; Czech independence and, 23; end of Kelley's influence in, 60–61; German defeat and, 122–23; and German occupation of France, 67; Guatemalan intervention and, 340, 346–48, 351–52; Hungarian insurrection and, 394–95; Indonesia project and, 414–15, 418; Interim Research and Intelligence Service of, 172; Iranian crisis and, 333–34; J.F. Dulles's administration of, 369–70; J.F. Dulles's European missions and, 47; under Lansing, 16–18; Military Intelligence Division of, 17; Near East Division of, 49; OPC and, 228, 235, 241; Paris Peace Conference and, 18–20; and permanent division of Germany, 174; Policy and Planning Staff of, 220–21, 225, 228, 241, 248, 250, 286, 292, 326; on Rumania, 205–6; and Russian civil war in Siberia, 32; Safe Haven investigations and, 145; Suez crisis and, 395

Stauffenberg, Klaus Philip Schenk, Count von, 120, 207

Stephenson, William, 77–81, 229; background of, 77–78; COI and, 91; and creating U.S. civilian intelligence organization, 83–84, 87; Donovan's relationship with, 77, 79; intelligence on Nazi arms resurgence provided by, 79; and OSS-SIS cooperation, 107–8; and U.S. aid to Britain, 83

Stevenson, Adlai, 432–33

Stilwell, Richard, 153, 273, 290, 383–84, 411; Korean War and, 299–300

Stimson, Henry, 57, 67, 90, 155

Stinnes, Hugo, Jr., 98, 145

Strasser, Otto, 92, 250

Strong, George V., 86, 140, 159, 164, 166, 176–77, 356

Strong, Sir Kenneth, 92, 125

Strunck, Theodor, 99, 101

Suez crisis, 332, 395–96, 400–401, 405

Sukarno, Achmed, attempts at destabilizing, 414–20

Sutton, Henry C., 360–61

Swiatlo, Josef, 387, 390–91

Swift, Carleton, 423, 436–37

Switzerland, Dulles's missions to, 11–16, 21–23, 93–101

Szonyi, Tibor, 386–87

Szymanska, Halina, 100, 109

Thailand, Donovan's mission to, 410–11

Thayer, Charles W., 39, 224–26, 251, 306–7, 326–27, 443

Thompson, Llewellyn, 226, 306, 399; Albanian incursion and, 265; Offie and, 248–49, 252

Thyssen, Fritz, 48, 149

Tildy, Zoltan, 387, 397

Time, 426

Tito (Josip Broz), 113, 116–17, 152–53, 198, 251, 422; German surrender and, 133; Khrushchev and, 380–81; U.S. Albanian incursion and, 264–65, 272; Ustase opposition and, 183

Treasury Department, U.S., Safe Haven investigations of, 144–47

Treviranus, Gottfried, 79, 91–92

Trudeau, Arthur, 220, 371–73

Truman, Harry S., 5, 155, 164, 213, 228, 235, 242, 256, 330, 332, 452; CIA restructuring and, 234; con-

tainment policy of, 328, 369; Guatemalan intervention and, 338; and Lend-Lease to Soviet Union, 141; NIA directive of, 185–86; and peacetime role of OSS, 165–67; psychological warfare and, 297; reelection of, 219, 231; and reviving German economy, 218; Smith and, 282, 284; on war reparations, 142
Truscott, Lucian, 268, 298, 356, 361, 363–64, 408–10

Ukraine, Bandera Party of, 248–49, 275–77
Ulmer, Alfred, 273, 296, 322, 384, 387, 395, 403, 443; Hungarian insurrection and, 393–95; Indonesia project and, 414, 416–17 418–19
United Fruit Company, Guatemalan intervention and, 336–40, 352–53
United Nations: Bay of Pigs operation and, 432; Hungarian insurrection and, 397–98, 400, 404; and peace negotiations with Axis satellites, 114–15
Universal, 203–4
U.S. News and World Report, 426
Ustase, 182–83
"Utilization of Refugees from U.S.S.R. in U.S. National Interest (SANACC 395)," 224
U-2 affair, 425–26

Vandenberg, Arthur, 186, 231
Vandenberg, Hoyt, 134, 185–87, 224
vanden Heuvel, Frederick "Fanny," 78, 94–96, 100
Versailles Treaty, 4, 29–30, 71, 453
Vienna, Dulles's mission in, 20–21
Vietinghoff, Heinrich von, 129–30, 132–33
Vinogradov, General, 205, 207–8
Voice of America, 85, 224, 258

Waetjen, Edward von, 98–99, 101
Waibel, Max, 108, 127–28, 132–34
Waldman, Eric, 267, 269, 278
Wallace, Henry, 101, 445
Wallenberg, Marcus, 69–70, 100
"War, Peace, and Change" (Dulles), 71
War Department, U.S.: and permanent division of Germany, 174; Secret Intelligence Division of, 177; SSU and, 172, 176–78; Wisner's relationship with, 214–15
Warren Commission, 450
Washington Post, 438, 441, 449
Washington Times-Herald, 151, 166
Wedemeyer, Albert, 76, 141, 219, 226
Weizmann, Chaim, 26, 49
Welles, Sumner, 60–62, 88, 446; conflict between Bullitt and, 150–52, 448
Westrick, Gerhard, 71–72, 76, 83, 121, 144
White, Harry Dexter, 174, 188
Whitney, Jock, 287, 308, 424, 436
Wight, E. V. D., 99, 144, 146–47, 161
Wiley, John, 39, 138, 151
Willauer, Whiting, 340–41, 352
Wilson, Charles, 333, 341, 372, 411
Wilson, Hugh, 21–22, 75, 123, 139
Wilson, Woodrow, 4–6, 23, 31; Bullitt's break with, 35–36; death of, 30; Donovan's military career and, 33; Dulles and, 24; Freud's psychoanalytical study of, 37, 449–50; House and, 16–17; The Inquiry, 17; and overtures to Soviets, 28–29; Paris Peace Conference and, 16, 18, 25, 27–28; on rise of Communism, 27–28; Versailles Treaty and, 29
WIN (Wolnose i Niepodlenose), 279–81, 319–20, 358, 362
Wiseman, Sir William, 17, 27–28, 56
Wisner, Elizabeth, 190, 191
Wisner, Elizabeth "Wendy," 309–11, 423, 439
Wisner, Ellis, 309–10, 423, 438, 442
Wisner, Frank, Jr., 306–7, 309–10
Wisner, Frank Gardiner, 5–6, 159, 221, 286–88, 318, 323–26, 330–31, 355–57, 363–64; Albanian incursion and, 262–63, 266, 269, 271–73, 323; Amory and, 324–25; Angleton and, 359–60, 364, 441; anti-Communist malcontents recruited by, 274–77; anti-Communist offensives and, 226–27; anti-Soviet sense of mission of, 158–59; background of, 190–214; Bay of Pigs operation and, 425, 435–36; Berlin blockade and, 219–20; and CIA depositories for fund transfers, 368; CIA promotion of, 303–4, 316; CIA restructuring and, 234, 288–92, 304–5; on clandestine political warfare, 439; COI and, 194; Communist defector recruitnent and, 362; Czech posting requested by, 210–11; death of, 441, 450; dirty tricks and, 361; Donovan and, 313–14, 323–24; Dulles and, 194, 196, 211, 213, 215–16, 314–15, 323–24, 376, 384–86, 403, 420–23, 437–39, 450, 454; East Berlin riots and, 377; on Eastern European partisan guerrillas, 377–78; Gehlen and, 164, 269; German surrender and, 158; government job accepted by, 216–17; Gray and, 297–98; Guatemalan intervention and, 338, 340–52; Hungarian government-in-exile and, 389–90; Hungarian insurrection and, 392, 394–95, 397–404, 409, 414; illnesses of, 402, 404, 412–14, 423–24, 436–41; Indonesia project and, 414–19; Jackson and, 287–88; Jagan and, 436;

Wisner, Frank Gardiner (*continued*) Khrushchev's Twentieth Congress address and, 381–82; Kirkpatrick and, 365–66; Korean War and, 299; law background of, 3, 171, 189, 192–94, 215; London mission of, 423–25, 436–37; McCarthy and, 326; managerial style of, 305–6; National Committee for Free Europe and, 257, 259–60; in Occupied Germany, 211–15; Offie and, 245, 252–53, 255, 295–96, 441–44, 446; and old boy network of political–military people, 308–9; OPC and, 228–29, 235–37, 240–45, 252–55; operational decisions of, 365; and overseeing overseas action sectors, 298–99; peacetime intelligence career sought by, 214–16; physical changes in, 421–22, 441; private life of, 193–94, 306–11, 424; psychological warfare and, 298; resignation from CIA of, 438, 440; and restructuring national intelligence, 189; Rumanian operations of, 189, 196–211; semiretirement of, 438–40; Smith and, 284, 299, 301–2, 304, 314; uneasiness of, 383–85; Warren Commission and, 450; WIN and, 280
Wisner, Frank George, 190, 215
Wolff, Karl, 6, 124–35; background of, 125–27; German surrender negotiations and, 125–35; immunity granted to, 134–35; war crimes of, 135
Wyatt, W. Mark, 292, 294, 447–48

Yarrow, Bernard, 115, 315, 374, 398
Yatsevich, Gratian, 270, 301, 320–23
Year of the Rat, The (Zaubica), 439
Yugoslavia: Angleton's operations in, 181; German invasion of, 82; German surrender and, 133; Khrushchev's rapprochement to, 422; peace initiatives from, 113, 116–18; Ustase revolutionaries in, 182–83

Zako, Andras, 388–90, 400
Zemurray, Sam "The Banana Man," 336, 338
Zhukov, Georgi, 211, 397
Zog, King of Albania, 262–63, 265, 321–22